A History of Brazil

A History of Brazil

Second Edition

E. Bradford Burns

Columbia University Press New York

Library of Congress Cataloging in Publication Data

Burns, E   Bradford.
 A history of Brazil.

  Bibliography: p.
  Includes index.
  1. Brazil—History. I. Title.
 F2521.B89 1980   981   79-27306
 ISBN 0-231-04748-7
 ISBN 0-231-04749-5 pbk.

Columbia University Press
New York   Guildford, Surrey

To the Memory of
Ambassador Mauricio Nabuco (1891–1979)
Whose Kindness, Friendship, and Help I Deeply Appreciate
and
Ao Povo Brasileiro
Pela Sua
Amabilidade, Hospitalidade E Cooperação

Contents

Acknowledgments

Looking back over the decade separating this revised edition of *A History of Brazil* from the first edition, I realize more than ever the academic debts I have accrued. My colleagues here and in Brazil always have been generous in sharing information, willing to discuss ideas, and above all patient in listening. I have learned much from them. I profited from their assessment of the first edition and incorporated many of their suggestions into this edition. I cannot salute by name all those who have contributed to my knowledge and better understanding of Brazil, since the list would be far too long. They will recognize their contributions and salutary effects on this revised edition.

My students also contributed significantly. I taught Brazilian history at Columbia University and continue to offer it at UCLA. The first time I taught the class, 1963–64, five students enrolled. Over the years, as interest in Brazil has grown, so has the size of the class. In 1978, over one hundred students appeared for the lectures on modern Brazil. Perceptive questions from students have helped me to sharpen my perspective. Our discussions form the basis for this text, and its outline reflects the direction the course has taken.

Doubtless the major advantage to being a specialist in Brazilian history is that one gets to travel to Brazil. Anyone who has been there understands the allure of that land and its people. Over the last two decades my research has taken me to Manaus, Belém, São Luís, Recife, Salvador, Rio de Janeiro, São Paulo, and Curitiba. My pleasures have taken me much farther afield in Brazil. The facility of access to Brazilian museums, libraries, and archives increased the pleasure of research and study. I extend my warmest thanks to those institutions as well as to the helpful Brazilian scholars who made my visits to their country such delightful and rewarding experiences.

For the information, facts, and interpretations in this book, I bear the full responsibility. The errors, too, must bear my imprint.

E. Bradford Burns

Hollywood Hills
January, 1980

List of Illustrations

Maps

Introduction

Brazil always excites the imagination of those who behold it. The intensity of the light, the brightness of the color, the richness of the vegetation, the vastness of the landscape, the beauty of the people combine to make a seductive sight few have been able to resist. The alternating simplicity and complexity of the land and its inhabitants further intrigue any who delve even shallowly beneath that alluring surface. The Portuguese who discovered, explored, and settled Brazil were not immune to the attractions of the land. In their more enthusiastic moods, they saw it as a terrestrial paradise. The first description of the newly discovered domain speaks of it as "so well favored that if it were rightly cultivated it would yield everything." A Jesuit father, dazzled by what he saw, wrote back to the metropolis in 1560, "If there is paradise here on earth, I would say it is in Brazil." A chronicler later in that century prophesied, "This land is capable of becoming a great empire." The Brazilians expressed equal confidence. In the first history of Brazil, written in 1627, Frei Vicente do Salvador confided, "This will be a great kingdom." The enthusiasm continued. In the history published by Sebastião da Rocha Pita in 1730, that Bahian rhapsodized, "Brazil is the earthly paradise regained." Within a century, one Brazilian poet, Francisco de São Carlos, had reversed the comparison. In his long poem *A Assunção*, he depicted Paradise in terms which made it sound strikingly similar to Brazil.

The attractions of Brazil did not go unnoticed by other Europeans. At various times, the French, Dutch, and English sought their fortunes in Brazil. Indeed, the British presence was a major economic reality of the nineteenth century.

While throughout much of the nineteenth and twentieth centuries Brazil attracted only limited and sporadic attention from the United States, the years since World War II witnessed a burgeoning interest and concern on the part of the North Americans. U.S. investments in Brazil during this century rose spectacularly. When it became evident by the late 1950s that Brazil would exercise a major international role not only in the Western Hemisphere but on a global scale as well, United States government leaders, military officials, scholars, and businessmen rushed to learn more about the South American giant. President John F. Kennedy reminded his listeners that one had only to glance at a world map to appreciate the geopolitical importance of Brazil. During the past fifteen years, an ever increasing volume of studies on Brazil in English has appeared, eloquent testimony to the "discovery" of Brazil and the importance ascribed to that nation. The list of books on Brazil in English which appeared in the "Suggestions for Additional Reading" of the 1970 edition of this history seems puny indeed when compared to the one in this second edition. Citizens of the United States have awakened to the significance of Brazil and in so doing have succumbed to its allure.

Brazil's history records the dramatic struggle for survival against natural elements, for independence from foreign domination, and for the creation of a viable national state. Most impressively it reveals the transference of European ideas and institutions to South America where, albeit challenged and influenced by the Indians and Africans, they tenaciously took root and flourished. They persevered and prevailed over the centuries, providing an astonishing continuity to the flow of Brazilian history. For anyone interested in the history of the nations of the New World, Brazil offers invaluable points of comparison, as well as significant contrasts, with Spanish America and Anglo-America. While the nations of the New World might not have a common history, they do share some common historical experiences. Europeans discovered the Americas during an exciting era of rapid commercial expansion. Throughout this hemisphere, they encountered and confronted Indians whose civilizations varied widely. Exploration, conquest, and settlement challenged the English, Spanish, and Portuguese and elicited different responses from them. They transplanted European institutions to the Western Hemisphere, and their adaptation and growth here took various courses. The Europeans hoped to solve their pressing labor problems by coercing the natives to work for them and, where that failed, by importing legions of African slaves. The metropolises all tried—once again with differing degrees of success—to impose mercantilism on their American domains. Within a span of less than half a century, colonies from New England to the Viceroyalty of the Plata revolted, threw off their European yoke, and entered the community of nations. The struggles to establish national states, to develop economically, and to assert their self-identity absorbed the energies of the newly independent peoples.

In the course of their growth, first the colonies and then the nations of the New World often responded quite differently to similar stimuli. The English in North America and the Spaniards in Argentina fought the Indians, while the Spaniards in Mexico incorporated them as an integral part of the colony. The Peruvians bitterly debated in the early nineteenth century the type of government they wanted; the Brazilians quietly coronated the resident Braganza prince as their emperor. The North Americans and Brazilians expanded westward, incorporating territory claimed by others; the Bolivians, Ecuadoreans, and Venezuelans ignored their hinterlands. The military played a predominant role in the first half-century of Peruvian independence, while during approximately the same years the military of Chile and Brazil exercised minimal influence.

Within the framework of hemispheric experiences, Brazil displayed some unique characteristics. For example, in the nineteenth century, its change from a colony to an independent empire, from a monarchy to a republic, and from a slaveholding society to a free society occurred essentially without violence, thus giving it an evolutionary character rare in the New World. Further, its ability to homogenize the three diverse racial elements into a single society on such an immense scale aroused the world's admiration. Although not free of racial tensions and inequities, Brazil perhaps serves as one of the best examples of extensive miscegenation and racial harmony. It would seem to have much to teach the rest of the world on the difficult topic of racial relations. Thanks to the varied racial contributions, Brazil boasts a unique civilization. Indeed, on that fascinating level alone, it merits study. Certainly Brazil provides many useful insights into the problems faced by a nation whose governments have been determined to "modernize," that is, to recreate their nation after the image of Western Europe or the United States.

The Visconde do Pôrto Alegre once remarked, "To know the biographies of all the outstanding men of a period is to know the history of those times." Much of Brazil's historiography reflects that view. A later nineteenth-century Brazilian historian, João Capistrano de Abreu, suggested an alternative approach to history:

In history we only point to the dominant figures, those who destroyed or constructed, leaving behind a trail of blood or a ray of light. We do not remember the shoulders which bore them, or the courage of the masses which gave them their strength, the collective mind which exalted their minds, the unknown hands which pointed out to them the ideal which only the most fortunate attained. And often the unknown man is the one whose cooperation was the most vital in bringing about the great event.

The unnamed too deserve their place in history. It was not only princes, prelates, and politicians who built Brazil but the anonymous *bandeirantes* who explored, conquered, and opened up vast tracts of the interior, the forgotten black slaves upon whose skill and muscle the growth of Brazil depended, and the persistent missionaries who infused European Church-centered civilization into the New World. Heroes appear as they must, but they serve to illustrate and to particularize broad trends of their times. Most often historians of Brazil have so emphasized the individual that the trends or their significances have been slighted. As a refreshing change, Capistrano de Abreu, whose *Capítulos de História Colonial* is the most perceptive history of colonial Brazil, prided himself on being able to write the history of Brazil without a single reference to Tirandentes, the overly eulogized precursor of independence. His works broadened the study of Brazilian history from its overreliance on the biographies of the great and on political events to pay at least equal attention to social, cultural, and economic movements. Indeed, Brazil is far too complex for its history to be treated as a political chronicle.

Among the many themes which constitute Brazilian history there are some which deserve particular attention if one is to grasp the significance of modern Brazil. One of the most dramatic is that of expansion and conquest. Capistrano de Abreu singled this theme out as the dominant one of the colonial period, but its importance extends to the early twentieth century as well. The Luso-Brazilians swept across the South American continent from the Atlantic coast to the foothills of the Andes. Missionaries, cattle herders, and gold prospectors made good the exaggerated claims of the explorers. The continuous fusion of European, African, and Amerindian populations into a homogeneous society is a second important theme. Thanks to the peaceful and thorough amalgamation of the three races in the tropics a unique civilization emerged and flourished. Brazil has had, and still has, its racial problems, yet of the many multiracial societies in the world Brazil enjoys the most harmony. A third theme is political evolution from colony to viceroyalty to kingdom to empire to republic. This process continues in the twentieth century in the drive to democratize Brazil, a goal more the ideal of selected intellectuals and the aspiration of the masses than a reality. Seemingly the period 1945–64 witnessed some effort and some success in the realization of that goal. But in the mid-1960s the effort at democratization was dashed against the rocks of economic realities. The fearful privileged classes and foreign interests pushed the military to seize the government and rule for their benefit. Frustrated for the time being, the urge for democratization promises to be a catalytic force of the future.

Urbanization got under way in the eighteenth century, spurred by the discovery of gold and increasing commerce. The opening decade of that century had not ended before the first urban-rural clash occurred. Antagonisms have not abated. In the last half of the nineteenth century the cities emerged as a major force, and thereafter they have shaped the course of Brazilian growth. Within the cities, both modernization and industrialization took place, becoming significant forces in the shaping of Brazilian history by the end of the nineteenth century, and accentuating the differences between the cities and the more traditionally oriented countryside. Nationalism, a force which can be considered seriously in the twentieth century, is also nurtured in an urban environment. Urbanization, modernization, industrialization, and nationalism mutually interact, and their combined strength accelerates the rate of change. By the end of the nineteenth century, dynamic new groups appeared in Brazilian society in sufficient numbers to play influential roles: industrialists, European immigrants, a middle class, and a proletariat. The middle class, coopted by and supportive of the economic, political, and social elites, exercised a major influence over events in the twentieth century.

As elsewhere in the underdeveloped world, a desire for change pervades contemporary Brazil. The masses now understand the difference between their afflictions and the affluence of the privileged few. Fully aware of that difference, they seek to diminish it by improving their own conditions. To do so means to challenge the past, those conservative, oligarchical, and paternalistic traditions, patterns, and institutions which have governed Brazil for so long. The challenge intensifies.

Bitterly opposed to each other are those who strive to maintain the old structures and those who struggle to destroy them. The changeless are pitted against the changing.

They provide the dialectic and drama of modern Brazil. In the opinion of the eminent contemporary Brazilian historian José Honório Rodrigues, "The struggle which is now taking place is not between liberals and conservatives, it is between progressive reformers and counter-reformers." He affirms that two principal characteristics of the Brazilian people are a desire for progress and an optimism about the future.

It takes a strong dose of faith and courage to be optimistic in the face of alarming conditions. As this text will point out, illiteracy has remained high, wages low, nutritional levels minimal, under- and unemployment endemic. The Physical Quality of Life Index based on an average of index ratings for life expectancy, infant mortality, and literacy in the mid-1970s gravely illustrates this human tragedy. Prepared by the Overseas Development Council for the nations of the world, the Index rated Brazil with a 68 out of a possible 100 points, far below Cuba's 86, Argentina's 84, and even Mexico's 75. In fact, Brazil ranked closer to Ecuador (68) and El Salvador (67). Of the major Latin American nations, Brazil stood at the bottom of the Physical Quality of Life Index, a sobering reality for a nation seeking world power status. That is the harsh reality of twentieth-century Brazil, and to dwell on it would be to present a gloomy picture of that nation. When the American visitor Herbert H. Smith surveyed Brazil at the opening of the last decade of the empire, he remarked, "If ten American travellers were asked to give their views of Brazil, we would hear ten different opinions, grading all the way from paradise to despair." Neither "paradise" nor "despair" should be emphasized to the exclusion of the other.

Despite many handicaps, growth in Brazil has been steady if perhaps slow and erratic. Brazil has maintained its unity in the face of every obstacle, emancipated its slaves without civil war, evolved from a monarchy to a republic without bloodshed, and laid the foundations for a modern and industrial society. The economy is no longer a simple extractive one. The illiteracy rate has fallen gradually. The nation has shown that it can exercise greater independence in its international relations. The population in general is becoming aware of those advancements, is proud of them, and is enticed by the mystique of a greater Brazil that will provide a fuller life for all. In the past centuries, Brazil has had more than enough prognosticators who foresaw a brilliant future for the country, often very unrealistically. It is not the task of the historian to dispense prognostications, but no historian who has followed Brazil's versatile adaptation and its bold resolution of some of its problems can fail to be affected by some of the Brazilians' own enthusiasm and optimism about the future of their country.

Chapter One

In the Beginning

The recorded history of Brazil began with the arrival of the Portuguese. The sudden discovery of unknown land in the West surprised the experienced sailors. What they saw impressed them. They puzzled over the Indian, unlike the African and Asian they already knew, and they marveled over the lush tropical coast. The land promised much, but the natives traded reluctantly. To exploit the potential wealth and to protect the extensive coastline from foreign interlopers, the Portuguese resolved to settle Brazil. They thus began their largest colonizing effort and in the process transferred Portuguese civilization to a South American environment.

The Land

On any global map, Brazil stands out. It is huge, the world's fifth largest nation. It dominates South America and the South Atlantic, and geopolitical realities confer on it a prominent international role. Occupying nearly half of South America, it stretches from the Atlantic in the east to the Andes in the west, from the Guiana Highland in the north to the Plata Basin in the south. Most of this territory lies in the tropics. In a certain sense this subcontinent of 3,200,000 square miles is an island surrounded by the Atlantic Ocean and the Amazon and Plata river networks, for those fluvial systems reach inland from the ocean like giant, clutching hands whose fingers come within a few miles of touching each other in the west of Brazil. (See Map 1, *Brazil and Neighboring Countries*, and Map 2, *Rivers of Brazil*.)

The Atlantic, bathing 4,600 miles of coastline, serves as the highway to the world carrying immigrants and merchants, capital and ideas to Brazil and bearing the products of the land away. The obvious importance of that vital connection has exerted a powerful influence on the formation of Brazil. For one thing, the Portuguese and their American descendants preferred to remain close to the sea. In the picturesque language of a seventeenth-century historian, "They cling crablike to the beaches." Unlike Hernando Cortés in Mexico, they never performed the symbolic act of burning their ships. To the contrary, their penetration of the interior, compared with that of the Spaniards in Mexico and Peru, was tardy and slow. In the past, as at the present, a majority of the population, as if mesmerized by the sea, concentrated within a relatively small coastal zone.

That coastal belt is narrow. North of the Amazon it confronts the Guiana Highland, gently rounded hills with stumps of eroded mountains. South of the Amazon it is pressed between the ocean and the Brazilian Highland. Between Salvador and Pôrto Alegre the shore is·bordered by a steep, wall-like escarpment, whose average elevation is 2,600 feet, although in certain places mountains rise to 7,000 and 8,000 feet and in rare instances exceed 9,000 feet. Some deep bays, such as Todos os Santos, Vitória, and Guanabara afford excellent harbors. A few rivers such as the Paraíba, Doce, Jequitinhonha, and Paraguaçu—all, incidentally, north of Cabo Frio—provide possible routes of penetration inland. South of Santa Catarina the coastal barrier gives way to lowlands. Much of the state of Rio Grande do Sul forms a part of the fertile pampas shared with Uruguay and Argentina. The seacoast plain is well watered, some areas averaging as high as 150 inches of rain a year. Tropical rainforests, with their

Map 1. Brazil and Neighboring Countries, Showing States and Territories of Brazil and Their Capitals.

monkeys, sloths, snakes, and infinite variety of birds and insects, once covered much of the plain. However, in the course of four and a half centuries man has eliminated large tracts of that rainforest with the resultant disappearance of the wildlife. It was along this luxuriant coastal plain that some Europeans during the early years of exploration believed they had located at long last the evasive earthly paradise. The learned Jesuit missionary Manuel da Nóbrega reported in the mid-sixteenth century on the pleasant climate, neither hot nor cold, on the ever green foliage, and on the abundance of nature which provided a large variety of fruits, fish, and animals. His descriptions perfectly fit those given of the terrestrial paradise by medieval scholars. To Nóbrega's way of thinking, the Creator had made of Brazil a showpiece. Foreigners and Brazilians alike agree. The varied geography provides an always dramatic scene for the historical drama.

Westward, beyond the plain and the escarpment, stretches an extensive and uneven plateau, roughly five-eighths of the national territory. Approximately 2,000 miles in length, the rolling tableland slopes gently from south to north as the course of the São Francisco River, famed for its union of the north and south, indicates. Low mountains characterize the west, particularly the southwest, of the plateau. Irregular rainfall condemns the northern portion to periodic droughts, with severe, often castigating effects on the hardy population. On other occasions, flash floods inundate the area. Scrub forest or *caatinga* dominates that landscape. Savannas characterize the vast plateau regions of Goiás and Mato Grosso. South of the frost line mixed forests of pine and broadleaf species and expanses of tall prairie grasses are typical.

Of the two extravagant river networks draining the interior, the Plata system is the less important. Only the upper reaches of the Paraná and Paraguay penetrate Brazilian territory, thereby linking Brazil with Paraguay, Argentina, and Uruguay. Historically they have served as important highways of commerce and routes of communication with the immense states of Goiás and Mato Grosso. By using the various branches of the Paraná and Paraguay, one can travel

Map 2. Rivers of Brazil with Amazon and La Plata Networks.

by water most of the distance from São Paulo to Cuiabá in the heart of Mato Grosso. In 1827, for example, the consul-general of Russia made that 2,000-mile journey in seven and one-half months. Despite difficulties, the water routes were in the long run quicker and more convenient than overland travel.

Unquestionably, the dominant river is the Amazon—referred to very aptly and descriptively in Portuguese as the "river-sea"—the largest river in volume in the world, with fourteen times the volume of the Mississippi. In places it is impossible to see from shore to shore and over a good part of its course it averages 100 feet in depth. Running eastward from its source 18,000 feet up in the Andes, it is joined from both the north and south as it rushes across the continent by more than 200 branches, some of them mighty confluents such as the Negro, Purús, Madeira, Tapajós, Xingú, and To-cantins. Together this majestic river and its tributaries provide 25,000 miles of navigable water. Small ocean-going vessels can navigate as far inland as Iquitos, Peru, some 2,300 miles from the sea, where the river is already 2,000 feet wide. This entire network of rivers furnished the means of penetrating both the north and far west of Brazil. The largest in the world, this river basin drains 3 million square miles and in Brazil covers approximately 36 percent of the national territory. In the far west the Amazon plain stretches to more than 800 miles in width, but as the river flows eastward both the Brazilian and Guiana Highlands close in so that the plain narrows to less than fifty miles, expanding again at the river's mouth which measures nearly 200 miles in width and 200 feet in depth. The magnitude of the river always has excited the imaginations of the men who traveled on it since Francisco de Orellana first discovered and descended it in his expedition of 1541–1542. William Lewis Herndon, who made a similar journey down the river a little over three centuries later, marveled, as many had before and would after: "The march of the great river in its silent grandeur was sublime, but in the untamed might of its turbid waters, as they cut away its bank and tore down the gigantic denizens of the forest it was awful. I was reminded of our Mississippi at its topmost flood."

Amazônia exhibits the world's largest tropical forest. Rainfall is abundant; humidity is high; but the temperature, with an average of 79° F., is not oppressive. Never does the thermometer soar to the highs registered on a summer day in Chicago, New York, or Washington. The warmth, humidity, and rainfall have created a lush botanical spectacle of unequaled variety on the globe. In places, the luxuriant selva offers as many as 3,000 different species per square mile. Animal life abounds as well. There are over fifty species of monkeys, an uncounted assortment of insects, and myriad birds and reptiles. Large animals, however, are rare. The tapir is the largest land mammal. In the rivers swim an impressive variety of species of fish. The estimates range from 500 to 2,000. Dense forests in many places surrender to grassy prairies, particularly notable in extension on the island of Marajó, between the Purús and Madeira rivers, and along the Branco River.

In order to better study this vast, diverse land, geographers have divided it into various more or less cohesive regions. Although the number of these regions depends on the criteria of classification each geographer employs, one of the most commonly used divisions, by the National Council of Statistics of the Brazilian Institute of Geography and Statistics, designates five regions: the North, which includes the Amazon Basin, the southern slopes of the Guiana Highland, and the northern slopes of the Brazil Highland; the Northeast, whose principal characteristic is the arid *sertão*, although a forest covers some of its coastlands and there are rich coastal sugarlands; the East, historically important because it contains the two old capitals of Salvador and Rio de Janeiro and economically important for its fertile land which produces more of the country's agricultural output than any other region; the South, the temperate zone from São Paulo to Rio Grande do Sul, essentially a region of high plateaus; and the Center West, the huge, underpopulated states of Mato Grosso and Goias, whose high plains support isolated mountain ranges.

From the first discoverers down to the present, the potential of this immense area has impressed all who have considered it. The epithet "land of the future" was fastened on

Map 3. Comparative Size of Brazil. The boundaries of Brazil easily encompass all the European countries.

Brazil early in its history and remains to taunt its inhabitants. The challenge of the land has been all the greater because of the relatively few humans who have inhabited it.

The Indian

Conservative estimates placed the number of Indians inhabiting Brazil at the opening of the sixteenth century at somewhere about a million, but more recent, revised estimates have raised that figure to approximately two and one-half million. Whichever estimate one favors, that vast area of South America was still strikingly underpopulated. In fact, large parts of it were uninhabited. The ancestors of the indigenous population probably migrated to the Western Hemisphere from Asia over 40,000 years ago. Most evidence seems to indicate that they crossed from one continent to the other at the Bering Strait, slowly moved southward, and dispersed through North and South America.

In the immensity of Brazil those few Indians fragmented into innumerable small tribes. For general purposes of classification, the Portuguese tended at first to divide the diverse tribes into two groups: the Tupí-Guaraní and those once called Tapuya. The Tupí predominated along the Amazon and in the coastal area from the Amazon to the Plata under a variety of tribal names: Tupinambás, Potiguaras, Tabajaras, Castés, and Carijos. They spoke a related language, later referred to by the Portuguese as the "língua geral," which gave a very superficial cohesion to them. Located more in the interior, although in some places found along the coast as well, were the Tapuyas. The best known of the many tribes were the Aymorés, Goytacazes, and Cariris. They spoke a mixture of languages which seemed to exhibit little or no apparent relationship. All the Indian groups shared a few physical characteristics in common. They tended to be short in stature, to be bronze in color, and to have straight, black hair. Beyond that their physiognomy varied considerably.

Modern anthropologists have abandoned the earlier classification of the Indians as Tupí or Tapuya. Although they emphasize the heterogeneity of the indigenous peoples, they suggest, for purposes of convenience and simplicity, another classification dividing the natives into two main groupings—Tropical Forest cultures, inhabitants of rainforest areas dependent primarily on agriculture and fishing, and Marginal cultures, inhabitants of the plains and arid plateaus dependent on hunting, fishing, and gathering.

Because of their predominance along the coast, the Tupí tribesmen—a major component of the Tropical Forest cultures—were the first natives the Europeans encountered and for a long span the only major Indian group with which the new arrivals maintained sustained contact. The Tupí, willingly or unwillingly, wittingly or unwittingly, facilitated the European adaptation to the new land, and this tribe appears to be the single most important native element contributing to the early formation of a Brazilian civilization. The anthropologist Charles Wagley concluded. "The Indian heritage of Brazil is, then, in the main a Tupí heritage."

The Tupí tribes tended to be very loosely organized, with populations estimated between four and eight hundred. Their small and temporary villages, often surrounded by a crude wooden stockade, were, when possible, located along a riverbank. The Indians lived communally in large thatched huts, approximately 250–300 feet long and 30–50 feet wide, in which they strung their hammocks in extended family or lineage groups of as many as one hundred persons. Patrilineal kinship was central to their societal organization. They usually practiced monogamy but polygamy was not unknown. Most of the tribes had at least a nominal chief, although some seemed to recognize a leader only in time of war and a few seemed to have no conception of a leader. There is evidence that some tribes had councils of warriors and/or groups of respected elders who met with the chief to advise him on important matters.

More often than not, the shaman or medicine man was the most important and powerful tribal figure. He communed with the spirits, proffered advice, and prescribed medicines. The religions abounded with good and evil spirits. Thunder, wind, rain, the sun, the moon—in short, nature—received their major attention. The Tupí demonstrated a dread of forest spirits who could bring sickness, misfortune, bad luck, and defeat in warfare. Because the spirits displayed a fondness for the night and prowled about under cover of darkness, the Tupí stayed close to his fireside after sundown. Part of their rich mythology is still very much alive in Brazilian folklore. Still told, for example, are the tales of Saci-perere, the one-legged Indian who creates mischief; Iracema, the captivating beauty with long green hair and a seductive voice who lures young warriors into the depths of the waters; and Uirapurú, the Amazonian bird that gives happiness in love. Less romantic aspects of tribal rites included ritual cannibalism. Prisoners taken in battle were pampered while being systematically fattened. Much later they were ceremonially clubbed to death, cooked, and eaten. How far cannibalism extended beyond ritualism is a moot question among anthropologists.

The tribes had frequent opportunities to capture prisoners because warfare was almost constant. For that reason, the sturdy warrior occupied a place of high esteem. The bow and arrow, spear, club, and blowgun were the most common weapons.

Warfare, however frequent it might have been, occupied only a part of the Tupí male's time. He also cleared away the forest to plant crops. Nearly every year during the dry season, the men cut down trees, bushes, and vines, waited until they had dried, and then burned them. The burning destroyed the thin humus and the soil was quickly exhausted. Hence it was necessary constantly to clear new land and eventually the village moved in order to be near virgin soil. In general, although not always exclusively, the women took charge of planting and harvesting crops and of collecting and preparing the food. Manioc was the principal cultivated crop. With a wide variety of uses, it served mainly as a flour. Maize, beans, yams, peppers, squash, sweet potatoes, tobacco, pineapples, and occasionally cotton were the other cultivated crops. Forest fruits were collected. The men hunted monkeys, tapirs, armadillos, and birds. They also fished, shooting the fish with arrows, trapping them with funnel-shaped baskets, or poisoning the water and collecting them. The self-sufficient tribes produced, gathered, and hunted food for themselves, not for trade. They attached scant importance to surpluses. The Tupí made ceramics, wove baskets, and developed loom weaving.

To the first Europeans who observed them, those Indians seemed to live an idyllic life. The tropics required little or no clothing. Generally nude, the Indians developed the art of body ornamentation and painted elaborate geometric designs on themselves. Into their noses, lips, and ears they inserted stone and wooden artifacts. Feathers from the colorful forest birds provided an additional decorative touch. Their gay nude appearance prompted the Europeans to think of them as innocent children of nature. The first chronicler of Brazil, Pero Vaz de Caminha, marveled to the king of Portugal, "Sire, the innocence of Adam himself was not greater than these people's." In the beginning, the Europeans overlooked the Indians' grim affinity for fighting and anthropophagy to emphasize their inclinations toward dance and song. The flute provided a lively accompaniment for their capering. On witnessing such a scene, Caminha reported, "They danced and footed it continuously with our people to the sound of one of our tambourines." Such observations affected European thought. On the basis of information on Brazil and its natives from the French colonist Durand de Villegaignon, who was in the Guanabara Bay region between 1555 and 1559, Montaigne wrote *Des Coches*. He advanced the theory of the natural goodness of men, a condition to which primitive men—in this case the Tupí—corresponded more closely than others. Repeated contacts with the Indians caused later chroniclers to tell quite a different tale in which the Indians emerged as villains, brutes who desperately needed the civilizing hand of Europe.

What the Europeans failed to appreciate was the harmony of the Indians with their environment and the high degree of their self-sufficiency. Indeed, the Indians' economic behavior contrasted sharply with the capitalistic motivations of their "discoverers." The Indians maintained a communal or reciprocal attitude toward production and consumption. The notion of private ownership hardly existed, and nature was to be revered, not exploited. Tribal status did not derive from material affluence, and economic considerations took second place to kinship, social dictates, religion, and community. The European never succeeded in comprehending the Indian values.

The cultures of the Brazilian Indians can in no way be compared to the remarkable civilizations of their contemporaries, the Aztecs of central Mexico, the Mayas of Yucatan and Guatemala, and the Incas of Peru. The Brazilian Indians possessed no well-established tribal organization; their agriculture was simple; they did not know how to use stone to build; they lacked any animal for transportation; they had no written means of communication. On the other hand, they had adapted well to their tropical environment, and they had much to teach the European invaders in the utilization of the land, its rivers, its forests, and their products.

The European

As the sixteenth century approached that European invader was not far off. Europe, on the eve of a commercial revolution, searched for new trade and new lands. Portugal led that quest.

A crossroads of many peoples—Iberians, Celts, Phoenicians, Greeks, Carthaginians, Romans, Visigoths, and Moslems—Portugal mingled many cultures. From that mixture, the first modern European nation emerged. To assert its independence, Portugal had to free itself both of Moslem control and Castilian claims. In 1139, Afonso Henriques of the house of Burgundy used for the first time the title "King of Portugal," a title officially recognized in 1179 by the pope, then arbiter of such matters. The struggle to expel the Moslems from Portugal lasted until 1250, when their remaining armies were driven from the Algarve region in the south. Neighboring Castile then conceded recognition of Portugal's claim to the Algarve and the national boundaries were delineated much as they remain today. The task of consolidating the state fell to King Denis, whose long reign, 1279–1325, marked the emergence of the truly modern national state. Desiring to create a stronger secular state, he challenged the Roman Catholic Church by curtailing its land holdings. His success encouraged the growth of the relatively weak State at the expense of the more powerful Church. Furthermore, he substituted Portuguese for Latin as the official language of government. He favored agriculture as the true source of wealth, founded Coimbra University, patronized the arts, established a navy, and signed a commercial treaty with England. A grave crisis threatened the independence of the nation when the last heir of the house of Burgundy died in 1383. Repudiating the claims to the throne put forth by the king of Castile, the Portuguese people crowned João of Aviz and made good their action by defeating Spain on the field of battle in 1385.

Under the leadership of the Aviz kings, Portugal became Europe's foremost sea power. Lusitania (as the Romans named that province of their empire perched on the westernmost tip of continental Europe) was well situated for its maritime role. Most of the sparse population, less than a million in the fifteenth century, inhabited the coastal area. They faced the great, gray, open sea and nearby Africa.

At that time European knowledge of the world beyond the continent was vague and contradictory. Educated men accepted the idea that the earth was a sphere. Norsemen had reached some unknown world beyond the seas. The travels of Marco Polo in Asia at the end of the thirteenth century had excited considerable speculation and interest. Knowledge of Africa was imperfect, limited to northern Africa only. Primitive navigational aids, frail ships, and fear of the unknown had kept men off the high seas and confined to European waters. In the Portugal of the Aviz monarchy, however, there developed an urge to expand into distant and either little-explored or totally unknown regions. By the end of the fourteenth century, the nation was at relative peace. The state had been consolidated; internal struggles had ended; foreign threats were not imminent. Thus Portugal could turn its attention outward and the Portuguese initiated their overseas expansion in heretical Africa, with the conquest in 1415 of strategic Ceuta, guardian of the opening to the Mediterranean.

In a society dominated by the Church, religious motives for expansion played at least a superficially important role. The Lusitanians hoped to defeat the enemies of their faith in Africa and to carry the word of God to that continent. They sought to circumvent Moorish domains in order to attack their enemy from the rear. They also wanted to make contact with a potential ally, the oft-mentioned Prester John, sovereign of a Christian kingdom somewhere in Africa. Commercial reasons for expansion were probably even more compelling. Direct trade with the fabled Orient via an all-water route would break the Italian commercial monopoly and bring cascades of riches to Portugal. Lisbon as the entrepot of Eastern pepper, cinnamon, ginger, nutmegs, cloves, tapestries, and porcelains created a vision of wealth alluring to people of all classes.

The first to understand fully that the ocean was not a barrier but a vast highway of commerce was Prince Henry (1394–1460), known as "the Navigator" to English writers although he was a confirmed landlubber. That provident prince, significant as the symbol of Portuguese expansion, surrounded himself with navigators, cosmographers, and maritime scholars at his residence on Sagres Peninsula, the harshly beautiful westernmost tip of Portugal. Listening to the expert advice of his day, he defined Portugal's policy of exploration: systematic voyages outward, each based on the intelligence collected from the former voyager and each traveling beyond its predecessor.

The improvements in geographic, astronomical, and navigational knowledge which characterized a century of accelerating sea-borne activity facilitated the task of the men of Sagres. Throughout the fifteenth century, improved, practical charts, the *portolani,* kept the sailors abreast of the latest maritime experience and were reasonably accurate in showing distances and coastal configurations. Through careful study, the heavens became a guide to the navigator out of sight of the land. Stars, particular the Pole Star, were observed in order to take latitude fixes. Later the experts learned to calculate latitude by observing the sun's zenith north or south of the equator at noon. For that, tables of the sun's declination were carefully worked out. Still with no means of finding longitude, the navigators continued to rely on dead reckoning, but with a firmer knowledge of latitude and the help of improved charts that calculation was made both easier and more accurate. The compass, in use since before 1300, continued to undergo refinements. The astrolabe, which permitted the navigator to take a fix on a celestial body, was cumbersome and tended to work far better ashore than aboard a rocking ship. Nonetheless, it was helpful for determining latitude. The invention of the quadrant in the fifteenth century faciliated taking sights, usually on the Pole Star, to enable the navigator to locate the ship's latitude. Though the inventors of neither the compass, nor the astrolabe, nor the quadrant, the Portuguese were the first Europeans to experiment with their use on the open seas. Their mastery of the science of ocean navigation made them tutors to the rest of maritime Europe in the fifteenth and sixteenth centuries. In a moment of great maritime triumph, the Portuguese launched the caravel, a ship which could tack, and thus sail against the wind. As a direct consequence of those improvements and with the encouragement of Prince Henry, the Lusitanians sailed farther and farther out to sea and away from their base. They reached the Madeira Islands by 1418 or 1420, the Azores between 1427 and 1432, Cape Bojador by 1434, and at the time of the death of the prince were sailing the Gulf of Guinea. Then three decades later, in 1488, Bartolomeu Dias rounded the Cape of Good Hope and pointed the way to a water route to India.

The Lusitanians were shaken momentarily in 1492 when Columbus reported—mistakenly—to João II that he had reached India by sailing west, sad news to a Portugal on the verge of reaching Asia by circumventing Africa. Both Spain and Portugal jealously guarded their sea lanes and each feared the incursion of the other. War threatened until diplomacy triumphed. At Tordesillas in 1494, representatives of the two monarchs agreed to divide the world. An imaginary line running pole to pole 370 leagues west of the Cape Verde Islands gave Portugal everything discovered for 180 degrees east and Spain everything for 180 degrees west. Then, within the half of the world reserved for Portugal, Vasco da Gama discovered the long-sought water route to India, as his protracted voyage in 1497–1499 joined East and West for the first time by sea. It was a profitable discovery. The cargo he brought back to Lisbon repaid sixty times over the original cost of the expedition, and the new lucrative trade promised to enrich the realm.

In the decades following the return of Vasco da Gama, Portuguese vessels appeared in the most distant ports. The Aviz kings abandoned the agricultural policies of the House of Burgundy and became merchants. Indeed, under Manuel I (1495–1521), the commercial interests of the kingdom became inextricably intertwined with national interests. Along the distant coasts of Africa and Asia, the Portuguese eagerly established their commercial—not colonial—empire. Trade attracted them rather than settlement. Lisbon and other Portuguese ports served as great warehouses through which the trade of three continents passed to the delight and profit of the Portuguese. They succeeded in setting up a global trading empire in the sixteenth century and reaped substantial rewards from the crown's maritime policies. Using sword and diplomacy, Afonso d'Albuquerque, Governor of India (1509–1515), consolidated Portugal's commercial claim in the East. The acquisition of Goa in 1510 broke the Moslem trade monopoly with India. Such were the deeds of those intrepid seamen that Pedro Nunes, Chief Cosmographer of the Realm, could boast, "The Portuguese discovered new islands, new lands, new seas, new people; and what is more, new sky and new stars." It was a glorious age for Portugal both abroad and at home. Historians such as João de Barros, Fernão Lopes de Castanheda, and Diogo do Couto recorded the valor of a nation. A popular dramatist, Gil Vicente, wrote with a witty pen of both commoner and king. Later, one of the great epic poets of all times, Luís de Camões, composed his poem *The Lusiads* to commemorate the heroic exploits of Vasco da Gama.

Within a short period of far less than a century, the Portuguese seaman landed on three distant continents bearing a cross in one hand and carrying a market basket in the other; when the native inhabitants challenged him, he readily substituted sword and lance for both. He represented a church-centered civilization in which both God and King commanded his loyalty. He was capable of the most sublime spiritual acts and of the crassest materialism. In all his tasks he demonstrated an almost fanatical fatalism: God had ordained and man acted out his role accordingly. But, in addition to his religious mission—as important as that might be—he was also the agent of a commercial empire in which trade and profit were the requisites for success. The long struggle against the Moslems and then against the sea had given him a set of dual characteristics. On the one hand, he had learned to act as an individual and to depend on himself, while, on the other hand, he submitted to hierarchy. He enjoyed commanding but was still capable of obeying. Still, neither personal discipline nor rigid regulation was his forte, for, above all else, he was an individual. Lack of organization characterized both him and the state. He possessed an exaggerated sense of dignity and considered himself a noble, particularly on his missions abroad. As a hearty, robust, adventurous, and resourceful knight errant with the whole world as his stage it was little wonder that he believed in his own privileged and special position and deprecated the menial tasks of common labor. In the most admirable fashion, he proved himself to be adaptable in both time and space. And nowhere was he more adaptable than in Brazil.

Discovery and Confrontation

Manuel I appointed Pedro Alvares Cabral to command the fleet being prepared to follow up the discovery made by Vasco da Gama. Amid colorful pageantry and with the kingdom's best wishes, 13 ships with 1,200 men sailed from the Tagus River on March 8, 1500. The voyage to India began routinely. Then, on the 20th of April, the sailors unexpectedly sighted weeds and reeds in the ocean and an occasional bird in the sky. Two days later at 17° south latitude land unexpectedly appeared in the west. Cautiously the fleet approached the coast. After landing to explore, the curious Cabral claimed the newly discovered island (or so he thought it) for his sovereign. Then he spent a week reconnoitering the coast. Before continuing on to Asia, Cabral dispatched news of his find to the king in a literate and highly descriptive letter written by the scribe Pero Vaz de Caminha. That letter is the official chronicle of the birth of Brazil. That was not the first name the new land bore, however. Cabral christened it *Ilha de Vera Cruz*, although it was also variously known as *Terra* or *Provincia de Santa Cruz*. But none of those names entered into popular usage. The merchants who were soon attracted to the plentiful stands of brazilwood, source of an excellent red dye, called it *Terra do Brasil*, and the name Brazil quickly gained popular acceptance. That name first appeared on a map in 1511 when Jeronimo Marini so identified the land mass of eastern South America on his globe.

The discovery of Brazil raised a series of historical questions which have never been definitively answered. First, there is the matter of priority of discovery. The French held that Jean Cousin had discovered it in 1488, but they failed to substantiate their claim with any documentary proof. The Spaniards claimed that Columbus probably had touched the northern coast of Brazil on his third voyage in 1498. They also affirmed that Vicente Yáñez Pinzón and Diego de Lepe on separate expeditions in 1500 had navigated along the northern coast too. Again the documentary proof is lacking. At any rate, Spain never pushed its claim because the newly discovered land fell within the Portuguese sphere as delineated by the Tordesillas Treaty. Cabral, therefore, has been accepted as the official discoverer of Brazil. Second, the belief has persisted among some historians that Portrugal already had discovered Brazil and until 1500 protected its discovery with secrecy, a useful weapon for a weak nation. Some vague hints and cryptic references to that effect can be found, but for the moment satisfactory documentary proof does not exist to substantiate such an historical hypothesis. A third historical question asks whether Cabral reached Brazil accidentally or intentionally. It is certain that he was far off his course, but the reason has never been known. Some hold that he purposely veered off course to investigate rumors of land to the west or to authenticate a previous discovery. What is known of his instructions do not call for him to sail so far westward. Others explain that still unknown navigational reasons caused him to sail a westerly course. Cabral had the best nautical gear of the period as well as the most talented navigators with him. It is difficult to believe that with that combination the fleet could have made so gross an error. Yet, the surprised tone pervading Caminha's chronicle seems to indicate an accidental discovery. There is much room for speculation about the causes of Cabral's westward course, but the result of his venture to the west soon became known throughout Europe. The first cartographic notification of Cabral's discovery was the Cantino chart finished no later than 1502.

Mild surprise characterized the reaction in Portugal to the new discovery. After nearly a century of discoveries the Lusitanians had become somewhat blasé; and then, in comparison with the dazzling treasures of Asia the simple peoples of the coast of South America were of peripheral interest. At first the Portuguese imagined that Brazil would be a convenient waystop for the India fleets, but winds, currents, and distances made that impossible. As a matter of fact, between 1500 and 1730 only about twenty ships, all broken off from the main India fleets by some extraordinary circumstance, took shelter in Brazilian ports. On the other hand, Brazil strategically provided excellent flank protection for the vital and profitable sea lane to the East. Brazil initially served as a sentinel.

Of the native reaction to the arrival of the bearded, white adventurer, no account exists. The Indians at first were shy—but not astonished. They maintained a certain distance between themselves and the strangers, reluctant at first to receive the *degredados* (those criminals exiled to serve their sentences) who were ordered to live among them to learn their languages. Later, an increasing number of degredados, deserters, and shipwrecked men found their way into Indian tribes where they apparently flourished. Some of them, such as Diogo Álvares, known as Caramurú, in Bahia, Antônio Rodrigues in São Vicente, and João Ramalho in Piratininga, became almost legendary figures. They sired an army of mestizo offspring, exerted a powerful influence over the Indians in their areas, and later helped the Portuguese establish their first colonies. They adapted perfectly—and it would seem happily—to their new surroundings. According to João Capistrano de Abreu, Brazil's foremost historian of the colonial period, each became "morally a mestizo."

Expeditions with the dual purpose of trade and exploration followed the discovery. Although the extent of those activities during the early years remains undetermined, it would appear that within a decade after discovery the coast had been at least cursorily explored and a few trading posts established to traffic in the lucrative brazilwood. During those first decades, dyewood was an easy export since it grew abundantly along the coast from Rio Grande do Norte to Rio de Janeiro. The Crown established a monopoly over its exploitation and eagerly sold its rights to merchants. Fernão de Noronha was the first to buy the contract, and in 1503 he dispatched ships to fetch the dyewood. The ship captains bartered with the Indians, exchanging trinkets for the brazilwood they cut. This trade was spurred by the welcome the new European textile industries accorded the red dye, and by the end of the sixteenth century about a hundred ships annually sailed from Brazil to Lisbon loaded with the wood. When the coastal stands were gradually exhausted it became necessary to search inland for it.

The handsome profits from the brazilwood trade not only enticed Lisbon merchants to pursue it but awoke the interest of foreigners as well. Indeed, Europe eagerly sought to establish overseas trade. As the era of commercial expansion got underway, other Europeans resented and challenged the Iberian claims to international trade monopolies. Increasing numbers of French ships explored the extensive Brazilian coastline in open challenge to Portuguese claims. Both Manuel I and his successor, João III (1521–1555), protested to the French court but with little result. To discourage the interlopers, those kings ordered a coastguard detachment under the command of Cristóvão Jacques to Brazil in 1516–1519 and again in 1526–1528. Those tiny fleets found it impossible to police effectively the 3,000-mile coastline with its innumerable coves, bays, and inlets. When diplomacy and coastal patrol failed to eliminate the French threat to Brazil and hence to the Asian sea lane it guarded, João decided upon a third method: to colonize. Colonization was a novel undertaking in the Portuguese commercial empire. Up until that time, with the notable exception of the Atlantic islands, the Portuguese preferred simply to establish trading posts. Nonetheless, the monarch sent Martim Afonso de Sousa with 5 ships, 400 crewmen and colonists, seeds, plants, and domestic animals to establish one or more colonies and in the process to destroy French trade and to explore the coast. After reconnoitering the coast from Pernambuco to the Plata, Martim Afonso founded the settlement of São Vicente in 1532 in the area near present-day Santos. A chapel, a small governmental headquarters, two tiny fortresses, and quarters for the men were built. Using the broad powers delegated to him by the king, the captain appointed municipal officers and distributed land. Wheat, grape vines, and sugar cane were planted; cattle were introduced; the first sugar mill was put into operation in 1533. On the plateau above São Vicente, those first colonists founded a second small settlement, Piratininga, the future São Paulo. When Martim Afonso de Sousa returned to Europe in March of 1533, he left behind the first permanent settlements in Portuguese America.

Martim Afonso also had established the pattern of land distribution to be followed thereafter. Because Brazil was vast and the colonists few he distributed the land with lavish generosity. In Portugal, quite to the contrary since 1375, the king sparingly parceled out the sesmarias, the traditional, individual land grants, so that no one person would receive more than he could effectively cultivate. Martim Afonso ignored such a precaution, a precedent followed thereafter in colonial Brazil. As one consequence, the good coastal land was quickly divided into immense sugar plantations and not many more decades elapsed before huge sesmarias for cattle ranches in the interior put much of the backlands under claim as well. Grants along the coast of twenty to fifty square miles of land were common, and in the interior they frequently encompassed areas ten to twenty times that size. Small property holdings were rare. Realizing that the gigantic estates created a type of semifeudalism in practice if not in name and that they kept much of the best land fallow and hence unproductive, the king belatedly tried to reverse the course. Repeatedly promulgated decrees—in 1695, single sesmarias were limited to 4 leagues by 1 league in size; in 1697, they were reduced to 3 by 1; in 1699, all land not under cultivation was to be expropriated, and so on throughout the eighteenth century—sought vainly to limit the size of the estates. One of the viceroys late in the eighteenth century, the Marquês de Lavradio, complained bitterly that those huge estates, poorly managed and often only partially cultivated, retarded the development of Brazil. He pointed to the unused fields held by their owners as symbols of prestige, while at the same time he noted that farmers petitioned him for land to till. Some of the captaincies had to import the food they were perfectly capable of producing themselves. Nonetheless, the latifundia which originated at the birth of the colony remained as a dominant characteristic of Brazil.

Establishment of the Colony

Brazil was a challenge to the Portuguese commercial empire. The Indians proved to be at best reluctant and unreliable traders. The French scoffed at Lusitanian claims of exclusivity. In order to keep Brazil and to carry on trade with it, the Portuguese government realized it would have to colonize on a much broader scale than that begun by Martim Afonso. Yet, the Crown, already overextended in Asia and Africa, had no resources to do so. In view of that, the king resolved to implement the donatary system successfully used in the Atlantic islands. Given enormous territory and broad powers, each donee was expected in return to colonize his own captaincy at private expense. Between 1534 and 1536, King João III divided Portuguese America into fifteen captaincies distributed among twelve donees. Each averaged fifty leagues in width and extended inland to the nebulous Tordesillas line. Those inalienable land grants transmitted by inheritance to the oldest son brought to the New World some of the residues of feudalism long on the wane on the Iberian peninsula. In effect, the donatary system interposed between the king and his subjects a hierarchy of landlords who enjoyed certain attributes of government: they could tax, impose law and justice, make appointments, and distribute the land in their captaincies in sesmarias. Like the medieval vassal required to render military service to his lord in return for his fief, the donees were expected to defend their captaincies from attack and thus to hold Brazil in the name of the king. Some characteristics of feudalism were undeniably present, although, of course, it was a long way from the classical feudalism of the Middle Ages. Those who would minimize the charge that the donatary system introduced feudalism into Brazil argue that the king, at least in theory, did fix, limit, and regulate the powers of each donee and that the captaincies were expected to engage in imperial trade rather than pursue the self-sufficient household economy of the medieval manor. In one sense surely, the donees were capitalists investing their money in the New World with the expectation of reaping handsome profits. Thus, despite vestigial feudal characteristics, the captaincies were supposed to be partially linked to the emerging capitalist system as well.

Few of the donees rose to the challenge confronting them. They were representatives of the minor nobility and middle class whose incomes from Asian ventures, governmental salaries, or landholdings proved inadequate for the expenses demanded. They had distinguished themselves as mariners or soldiers or bureaucrats. However, as a group, they lacked experience and ability as well as capital to execute their heavy responsibilities. Furthermore, they confronted a hostile, untamed—indeed, unknown—environment. Compounding the difficulties were the lack of discipline among the colonists, the Indian attacks, and French harassment. It is not surprising then, that a majority of the captaincies failed. Two of them, however, Pernambuco and São Vicente, did achieve prosperity. Pernambuco was by far the richest and most important of the sixteenth-century captaincies. The captaincy closest to Portugal, it offered extensive stands of brazilwood along the coast and excellent soil, the massapê, for sugar cane. The intelligent and aggressive donee, Duarte Coelho, took advantage of the presence of Vasco Lucena, a Portuguese who had lived for years among the local Indians and knew their language well, to avoid many of the wars with the native population with decimated other colonies. He understood the importance of commercial crops and ordered cotton, tobacco, and sugar cane planted at once. He proudly reported to the king, "We have extensive fields planted with sugar cane. The people here have all worked as hard as possible and I have given them all the aid possible and soon we will complete a very large and excellent sugar mill."[1] By mid-century, fifty mills were producing enough sugar to load annually forty to fifty ships for Europe. By 1580, Coelho's son was the richest man in Brazil and one of the wealthiest in the empire. In Pernambuco the operation of an agricultural colony for profit enjoyed its greatest success.

The São Vicente captaincy, initially established by Martim Afonso de Sousa, also flourished. There, too, sugar was the basis for prosperity. Families of Italian sugar growers from the Madeira Islands immigrated to that southern captaincy bringing much needed agricultural and technica' skills. By 1545 the colony possessed six sugar mills. Together Pernambuco and São Vicente implanted the sugar industry in Brazil. Likewise they accounted for much of the brazilwood trade. The first to cultivate the soil of the New World on a commercial basis, the two captaincies proved that profitable agricultural colonies could be established far from the moth-

1. Duarte Coelho to King, April 27, 1542, in José Antônio Gonsalves de Mello and Cleoner Xavier de Albuquerque (eds.), Cartas de Duarte Coelho a El Rei (Recife, 1967), p. 29.

erland and could provide a relatively constant source of wealth for crown, landowner, shipowner, and merchant, a novel concept for mid-sixteenth century Europe and one which did not go unobserved. Spurred first by the examples of rich mines in Spanish America and then by lucrative agricultural settlements in Portuguese America, Europe moved to change its far-flung trading routes into more complex overseas mining, agricultural, and commercial empires. Such a move resulted from and reinforced Europe's adoption of modern capitalism.

Clearly, however, those two prosperous captaincies were exceptions to a general trend all too evident in the rest of Brazil. The other captaincies were reduced in a short time to a sad spectacle, as their surviving colonists degenerated into a demoralized lot. Bickering and insubordinate, they engaged in smuggling and other criminal activities. Moreover, French interlopers continued to violate the coast with impunity. It was obvious that the captaincy system had failed to produce the expected results.

After studying the unhappy situation in his overseas domain, King João III concluded that a centralized administration was needed to coordinate further colonization, to provide effective protection, to unify the execution of justice, to collect taxes properly, and to prohibit French contraband trade. He thus intended to reduce the independence as well as the powers of the donees. In 1548, he bought back the captaincy of Bahia from the family to whom he had given it and made it a crown captaincy, seat of the new general government for Brazil. He appointed Tomé de Sousa, a loyal soldier who had served him well in Africa and India, as the first governor-general in charge of all civil and military administration. Named to assist him were a *provedor-mor*, a chief treasurer, and an *ouvidor-geral*, a chief justice. One thousand soldiers, government officials, carpenters, masons, artisans, and colonists accompanied the new governor-general to South America.

The fleet of six ships dropped anchor in the splendid Bay of Todos os Santos on March 29, 1549. Caramurú, the

white adventurer who had settled in Bahia, presented himself to offer assistance and to guarantee the cooperation of
the local Indians. The first task was to construct the new capital. Concurrently the new central government was given
form and substance. Scattered along the extensive coast
were approximately fifteen Portuguese settlements. Tomé de
Sousa dispatched the chief justice and the chief treasurer to
the various captaincies in an effort to eliminate abuses and to
regularize administration. He himself paid a prolonged visit
to the South. To accelerate economic development, he generously distributed sesmarias, imported cattle from the Cape
Verde Islands, and encouraged the construction of more
sugar mills. The Indians reluctantly provided the labor force
during the early decades of the colony. The governor-
general was particularly concerned with the regulation of
that labor force—an obvious source of wealth for the
colony—and with the welfare, particularly the Christian in-
doctrination, of the Indians. After all, the monarch had written specifically in his orders to Tomé de Sousa, "The principal reason motivating my decision to settle the land of
Brazil was in order that the people of that land might be con-
verted to our Holy Catholic Faith." To fulfill Portugal's obligations to those natives, Tomé de Sousa relied heavily on
the Jesuits.

Very significant for the formation of Brazil was the presence in the official party of 1549 of six Jesuits under the leadership of Manuel da Nóbrega. True, clerics had accompanied
all the expeditions to Portuguese America from the visit of
Cabral onward. The Franciscans were particularly evident in
those early decades. But, until 1549, the Church played a
minor role in Brazil. With some exceptions, the clergy attended more to the affairs of the Portuguese colonists than
to the Christianization of the Indians. The king desired to
propagate the Catholic faith in the New World and chose the
Jesuits to be his instruments. Only 128 Jesuits arrived between 1549 and 1598, but with exceptional zeal they left a
lasting imprint on the new land. They carried European
church-centered civilization to the Indians and nurtured it in

the tropics by establishing—and for two hundred years maintaining—most of the best educational facilities of the colony. In a very real sense they conquered Brazil spiritually. To be Portuguese was to be Roman Catholic. The two were intimately intertwined, although not quite so inextricably as in Spain, and consequently Church and State appeared as one. The populace embraced the Catholic faith unquestioningly, and, whether understanding its dogmas or not, defended it devotedly. The Luso-Brazilians were born, reared, married, and buried Catholics. The Church pervaded every aspect of their lives. The king defended the faith within his realm, in return for which the Pope conferred royal patronage upon the Crown, temporarily in 1515 and permanently in 1551. Holding power in all but purely spiritual matters, he collected the tithe and decided how it was to be spent, appointed (and at times recalled) the bishops, priests, and other officials, authorized the construction of new churches, determined the boundaries of the bishoprics, and—of great significance—approved and transmitted papal messages—or refused to. In 1576, the king conferred authority on the governor-general to make nominations for clerical positions in Brazil.

To the degree that Portuguese control expanded in the New World so did the Roman Catholic Church. The establishment of the general government of Brazil was followed in 1551 by the creation of the bishopric of Brazil. Previously Brazil had belonged to the diocese of Funchal in the Azores. Fittingly, the bishop resided in Salvador alongside the governor-general. In 1676, the archbishopric of Brazil was created with Salvador as the metropolitan see. Two new bishoprics, Rio de Janeiro and Pernambuco, were established at the same time. By the end of the eighteenth century, there were four others: Pará, Maranhão, São Paulo, and Mariana (Minas Gerais). Salvador remained throughout the colonial period—indeed, until 1907—the religious capital of Brazil. Its archibishop headed the Roman Catholic Church in Brazil, and the religious orders maintained their principal representatives there. The Church structure in Brazil with its well-defined hierarchy, its regular and secular clergy, its bishoprics and parishes, followed perfectly the European model. It is interesting to note that the African bishoprics of São Tomé and Angola also were suffragan to the archbishop of Bahia. The Church in Angola depended heavily on Brazil. Serafim Leite, distinguished historian of the Jesuits in Brazil, has affirmed, "The evangelization of Angola was in the hands of the Jesuits of Portuguese America." Actually the ecclesiastical traffic moved both ways. A few Jesuits crossed from Angola to Brazil, and some Portuguese born in Angola moved to Brazil to study in Jesuit colleges. A number of Brazilian Jesuits mastered African languages, a skill which most of those from Angola already had, so that they could catechize the newly arrived black slaves.

The Jesuits have already been singled out as the most important religious order contributing to the formation and development of Brazil, but they were by no means the only representatives of the regular clergy. The Franciscans had been the first to reach Brazil, and they too played an important role. The Capuchins, Benedictines, and Carmelites were all represented in Brazil before the end of the sixteenth century. The Crown hesitated to sanction the building of convents for nuns in Brazil, feeling that the smaller number of women in the colony should be encouraged to become wives and mothers rather than virginal recluses. Not until 1665 did the king grant permission for the establishment of such a convent, and authorization for a second did not come until seventy years later. By the mid-eighteenth century, half a dozen such convents could be found in the major coastal cities.

Of major importance for Brazil were the *irmandades*, voluntary associations of the faithful which became an integral part of colonial social life. They built handsome churches, merrily celebrated the feast days of patron saints, and dutifully maintained charitable institutions such as hospitals and orphanages. Indeed, works of charity, education, and social assistance compose some of the noblest chapters of the history of the Roman Catholic Church in Brazil.

The Church maintained as careful a vigil as possible over

its flock in Brazil. Nonetheless, some examples of moral corruption among the clergy provided bawdy gossip for colonial ears. Backsliders—especially Jewish converts, the New Christians—could expect to account for themselves before the Inquisition. As an institution it was never established in Brazil, but it operated there through the bishops and through three visitations: Visitor-General Heitor Furtado de Mendoça spent 1591–1595 in Bahia and Pernambuco, Visitor-General Marcos Teixeira called at Salvador in 1618, and to the surprise and apprehension of the citizens of Belém, Inquisitor Giraldo José de Abranches arrived in that northern city in 1763 and remained six years. Nonetheless, the hand of the Inquisition rested lightly on Brazil, where a liberal degree of toleration developed.

A major challenge to the Church was the conversion of the Indians. The Jesuits, under the skilled and dedicated leadership of Manuel da Nóbrega and José de Anchieta, rose to meet that challenge. They deemed it wisest to gather the nomadic natives into villages, the *aldeias*, where they could more easily be instructed, Christianized, and protected under the watchful eye of the Church. Some would add that the aldeia system facilitated the exploitation of Indian labor. The system permitted the maximum use of the few regular clergy in Brazil: usually one or two brothers administered each village and in that way supervised many Indians. Each aldeia centered on a church, built of course by the indigenous converts themselves. Around it were a school, living quarters, and warehouses. The ringing of church bells awoke the neophytes each day, summoning them to mass. Then, singing hymns along the way, they marched outside the village to cultivate the fields. The brothers taught reading, writing, and the mastering of useful trades to the young and able. Indian sculptors, painters, masons, carpenters, bakers, and locksmiths, among others, were soon practicing their trades. Many of the villages achieved a high degree of self-sufficiency, and most sold some of their products to outside markets. Although the brothers administered the missions through various Indians whom they appointed to office and invested with the customary symbols of that office, those churchmen in the final analysis rigidly controlled the lives of their charges. It was not a simple figure of speech when they spoke of the neophytes as "their children," for that was exactly how they regarded them. Under their guidance, the Indians contributed to the imperial economy, worshiped as Roman Catholics, dressed like Europeans, mastered European trades, and paid homage to the king in Lisbon. Thus, those touched by the aldeia system were brought by the determined hand of the missionaries within the pale of empire. Approving and encouraging the aldeia system, the first governor-general cooperated fully with the Jesuits. It is not surprising, therefore, that Nóbrega left this laudatory description of Tomé de Sousa: "I do not believe that this land would prosper so if there were any other governor. Of the many who came here none has the love for this land which he shows. The others only want to make a profit no matter what the cost of this land so that they can flee it."

The administration of the second governor-general, Duarte da Costa (1553–1557), was less edifying. A courtier without military service, he proved to be an irritable executive. An acrimonious quarrel with the first bishop of Brazil, Pero Fernandes Sardinha, who had arrived in 1552, shook the administration and established a pattern repeated occasionally thereafter. The righteous bishop criticized some of the activities of the governor-general's rather free-living son. Duarte da Costa naturally came to the defense of his offspring, and the fight was on. The tiny capital reverberated with threats and insults. In 1556, the king persuaded Sardinha to journey back to Europe, hoping thus to give the disputants time to reflect. Alas, his ship foundered along the coast of Rio Grande do Norte, and the Indians captured and devoured the good bishop. That quarrel—although not its outcome—was typical of others which beset the colony when forceful but tactless civil and religious authorities occupied the highest posts. The examples of such animosity were many, and one more suffices to make the point. At the end of the seventeenth century, the second bishop of Maranhão, Timóteo do Sacramento, quarreled with the municipal government of São Luís, the governor, and the chief justice, whom he excommunicated. The chief justice then ordered soldiers from the local garrison to surround and isolate the episcopal palace until the testy bishop was ready to come to terms. In truth the duties and responsibilities of civil and religious authorities frequently overlapped or were vaguely defined. Each was sensitive about his dignity and desirous of pushing his authority to the maximum. Such rivalries divided the basically weak colonial society and detracted from the harmony requisite for its growth. The disputes eventually would reach the ears of the king who would then intervene to restore tranquillity to his colony.

The cultured Mem de Sá, a noble and a soldier of long service to his sovereign, brought peace and a certain degree of prosperity to Brazil after his arrival in 1558. The Jesuit Nóbrega, among others, sang his praises, "As soon as Mem de Sá took the reins of government, he began to show his prudence, zeal, and virtue both in the good government of the Christians and the Indians by putting everything in order as Our Lord showed him." To increase the base of economic prosperity, he encouraged agriculture in general and sugar culture in particular. The number of sugar mills multiplied, particularly in the captaincies of São Vicente, Rio de Janeiro, Espírito Santo, Bahia, and Pernambuco, where the huge sugar plantation and its mill quickly became powerful agricultural, industrial, and social organizations. The labor shortage continued to harass the colony. The Indians had proved to be unsatisfactory plantation hands but at first they were the only readily available workers. The Portuguese tried three methods to incorporate the Indians as laborers into their agricultural system: first as slaves, second as a type of indigenous "peasantry" through detribalization and acculturation in the aldeias, and third as wage earners slowly integrated into the capitalist system. The controversy over Indian labor sparked acrimonious debates between the Jesuits and the planters. The vocal Jesuits—and the Church in general—regarded the enslavement of the Indians as contrary to the Christian intentions of the king, and intensified efforts to save them both physically and spiritually by gathering them into the villages. The planters loudly criticized that interference with their labor supply. Mem de Sá maintained close relations with the Jesuits and to the disappointment of the landowners approved the continuation of the village system. In the end, all the methods to incorporate the Indians failed. The Indians were reluctant to surrender their life style for the inexplicable work demanded by the Portuguese, work which had few if any rewards for them. The gap between the communal, self-sufficient Indians and the capitalistic Portuguese could not be bridged.

Internal concerns gave way to external threats. Governor Mem de Sá devoted much of his attention and resources to the perennial French threat. In 1555, Vice-Admiral Durand de Villegaignon founded France Antartique around Guanabara Bay, an area rich in brazilwood. One contemporary Portuguese Jesuit marveled, "The land is some of the best there is in Brazil." The French presence there isolated São Vicente from the rest of Brazil. Mem de Sá attacked the invaders on several occasions. On March 1, 1565, he established Rio de Janeiro as a base to fight against the stubborn French and after prolonged siege expelled them in 1567. After the defeat of the French, Rio de Janeiro grew rapidly in size and importance, partly because of its excellent harbor and partly because of the sugar industry which prospered on the fertile soil of the region. The Crown manifested its delight with the accomplishments of Mem de Sá's administration by retaining him as governor-general long after his four-year appointment expired. He stayed on until he died in office in 1572.

The last of the Aviz kings died eight years later, after which the Spanish monarchs ruled Spain and Portugal jointly for sixty years. By 1580, however, the patterns of colonial Brazil already had been well established. The trends which would characterize colonial Brazilian history were already under way and, if anything, would be strengthened during the "Babylonian captivity" of Spanish rule.

Chapter Two
The Colonial Experience

Brazil's colonial apprenticeship lasted more than three centuries, until 1808, when the royal family arrived in Rio de Janeiro. During much of that time the colony slumbered in quiet isolation. Yet, slowly—at times imperceptibly—changes occurred. It is easier in retrospect to observe those changes and to discern their part in building the foundations upon which the future nation would rest. Reviewed in the broadest possible terms, Brazil during those three centuries was characterized by social amalgamation, territorial expansion, economic dependency, and political fluctuation.

Social Amalgamation

The Portuguese adapted quickly to the new environment, whose geography and climate approximated those they had encountered in their extensive travels in other parts of the world during the fifteenth and early sixteenth centuries. The Portuguese evidenced a flexibility, both physical and psychological, which seemed to make them sufficiently malleable to learn from the conquered. In the case of Brazil, the blending of the Lusitanian and Amerindian cultures was facilitated by the favorable attitudes of both toward miscegenation.

The Portuguese monarchs customarily sent out on their global expeditions a combination of soldiers, adventurers, and petty criminals condemned to exile. Women were excluded. The Portuguese female was noticeably rare during the first century of Brazilian history. Her scarcity conferred a sexual license on the conquerors, already well acquainted with Moorish, African, and Asian women and, seemingly attracted to dark-skinned beauty. The Indian women submitted to the desires of the European males. Men like Caramurú attested to the Iberian sexual prowess by siring villages of miscegenated offspring. As a result, there appeared almost at once a "new race," the *mameluco* or *caboclo*, a blend of European and Indian well adapted physically and psychologically to the land. Drawing the essential from the diverse cultures of both parents, they accelerated the amalgamation of the two civilizations.

The Indians provided more than sexual gratification: they facilitated the Portuguese adjustment to the new land. They taught the invader the best methods of hunting and fishing, the value of the drugs the forests offered, the quickest way to clear the lands, and methods of cultivating the crops of the New World. They introduced him to new foods such as the manioc, soon the dietary staple of the Luso-Brazilians. The Lusitanians quickly adopted the light boats skillfully navigated by the Indians on the inland waters. The new arrivals copied the methods used by the Indians to build simple, serviceable structures. In time, Portuguese domestic architecture underwent some significant modifications in the tropics: the severity and exclusiveness of the Portuguese house gave way to the open, outwardly oriented Brazilian residence with its extensive veranda communicating with the world. Another concession to the tropics was the universal adoption of the Indian hammock. One early arrival noted his delight with the hammock in these words: "Would you believe that a man could sleep suspended in a net in the air like a bunch of hanging grapes? Here this is the common thing. I slept on a mattress but my doctor advised me to sleep in a net. I tried it, and I will never again be able to sleep in a bed, so comfortable is the rest one gets in the net."[1] Words from various Indian tongues, such as *hamaka* (hammock), *tobako* (tobacco), *manioca* (manioc), and *typyoca* (tapioca), slipped into the Portuguese vocabulary. In the seventeenth century, the Luso-Brazilians began to substitute Indian for Portuguese place-names in geographic nomenclature. A modern dictionary, *Pequeno Dicionário Brasileiro*, lists some 20,000 words of Indian origin. In truth, the European depended heavily on the Indian during the early decades of settlement in order to accommodate himself successfully to the novel conditions. Thomas Turner, an Englishman who lived in Brazil for two years at the end of the sixteenth century, summed up that dependence in his observation: "The Indian is a fish in the Sea, and a Foxe in the Woods, and without them a Christian is neither for pleasure or profit fit for life or living."[2]

The newly arrived Portuguese also depended on the Indians as the labor force in the growing colony. The Portuguese, for their part, revealed a reluctance to engage in common labor and a persistence in forcing others to do it for them. Under increasing pressure which soon resulted in enslavement, the Indians paddled canoes filled with Portuguese along the rivers; guided them through the interior; planted, tended, and harvested their sugar, tobacco, and cotton; and waited upon them in their homes. They were the instruments by which wealth was created in the new colony and as such indispensable to the European.

The Crown, eager to see the Indians brought within the pale of empire as Christianized subjects, proved loath to permit their enslavement. The papal grant authenticating Portuguese territorial claims had made it clear that the monarch must Christianize, civilize, and protect the Indians, a responsibility the kings took very seriously. At great expense, missionaries were dispatched to preach to the heathen, to con-

---

1. Letter of Padre Ruy Pereira, Sept. 15, 1560, from Bahia, in *Cartas Jesuíticas II, Cartas Avulsas* (Rio de Janeiro, 1931), p. 264.

2. Samuel Purchas, *Purchas His Pilgrimes* (London, 1625), IV, 1243.

vert them, and to induce them to live in villages under the guidance and protection of Church and Crown. As we have seen, the Jesuits were the most active of the religious groups fulfilling those obligations. They ardently defended the Indians and rigorously prodded the royal conscience. Setting the tone for future action, Manuel da Nóbrega, after his arrival in Bahia in 1549, pointed out that the Indians were as "blank paper upon which we can write at will." The missionaries had a formidable task before them. Not only did they have to master the Indian languages, win the Indians' confidence, and persuade them to embrace Catholicism, but they had to fight against the planters who feared the interference of the Church with their slave labor system. They had every cause for their fear. Alarmed by the mistreatment of the natives and their mounting death rate, the missionaries, particularly the Jesuits, spoke out against the practices of the colonists.

In their anger and concern, the Jesuits took the Indians' case directly to the king to whom they vividly reported the mistreatment and enslavement of his American subjects. The planters dispatched to the court their own representatives who emphasized the barbarian nature of the Indians, their indolence and refusal to work without coercion. Domingos Jorge Velho tersely summarized the planters' point of view to the Crown in 1694: "And if we subsequently use them for our tillage and husbandry, we do them no injustice; for this is done as much to support them and their children as to support us and ours. This is so different from enslaving them that it is rather doing them a priceless service, since we teach them to till, to sow, to reap, and to work for their keep—something which they did not know how to do before the whites taught them."[3] Unfortunately we do not have the Indian view, but their predilection to flee Portuguese colonization indicated they did not appreciate the "priceless service" the planters offered them. The debate over the role and place of the Indian within the empire, much like the one already under way in Spain, raged for several centuries.

3. Quoted in C. R. Boxer, *Race Relations in the Portuguese Colonial Empire 1415–1825* (Oxford, 1962), p. 95.

By and large the monarchs sympathized with the Jesuits' case. As early as 1511, King Manuel I had ruled that no one was to harm his Indian subjects upon pain of the same punishment as if he had injured a European. In his instructions to the first governor-general of Brazil, King João III called for tolerance, understanding, and forgiveness toward the Indians. Relations with them were above all else to be peaceful so they might more easily be Christianized. Permission was granted, however, to enslave any Indians who fought against the Portuguese, a provision which offered a gaping loophole for the colonists to obtain their native slaves. Predictably the colonists righteously swore that their Indian slaves had been taken in a "just war." The *Mesa da Consciência e Ordens* (the Board of Conscience and Orders), a religious council in Lisbon, handled, in theory at any rate, questions arising from the interpretation of these laws, and one of the thorniest questions before it was to determine which slaves were held justly and which unjustly. In a variety of different and at times contradictory decisions, the Mesa defined as "just" (i.e., justly held) slaves those Indians who sold themselves or their children into slavery for reasons of dire need, Indians who practiced cannibalism, Indians rescued from being sacrificed, and, of course, any Indians who fought against the Portuguese. The Mesa rigorously declared that peaceful Indians living in harmony with the Portuguese could not be enslaved. Theoretically any planters found guilty of unjustly holding Indians as slaves were liable to punishment.

The theological and judicial debate over the enslavement reached its first climax during the reign of the devoutly religious King Sebastião (1557–1578). In 1570, he prohibited the enslavement of any Indians except those taken prisoner in a just war. King Philip II in 1595 confirmed that decree and reduced the term of slavery for prisoners to ten years. In 1605 and again in 1609 King Philip III went even further. He declared that all Indians, whether Christian or heathen, were by nature free, could not be forced to work, and must be paid for their work when they volunteered it. Strong pressures from the planters, including riots in Brazil, induced him to modify his position in 1611 in order to permit once again the enslavement of war prisoners, a concession much abused. Repeated attempts were made to regulate the relations between the Europeans and the Indians. The conflicts between the Jesuits and the planters over such regulations on occasion became violent. The high death rate among the Indians exposed to European demands and diseases, their retreat into the interior, their amalgamation into the new Brazilian society through miscegenation, and the increasing importation of Africans to supply the growing labor needs of the colony did more to solve the complex question of Indian-European relations than did all the altruistic but impractical or ignored legislation of the Portuguese kings.

The final word on European-Indian relations came from the authoritative Sebastião José de Carvalho e Melo, better known by his title, the Marquês de Pombal, an enlightened but despotic ruler of the Portuguese empire in the name of José I from 1750 to 1777. That prime minister expelled the most tenacious protectors of the Indians, the Jesuits, in 1759, accusing them, among other things, of isolating the Indians and thereby inhibiting their incorporation into the empire. Pursuing the centuries-old desire to incorporate the Indians into the empire, he raised them to the rank of equality with all the king's other subjects. A new law guaranteed the personal freedom of each Indian who thereafter received a Portuguese surname and was required to speak Portuguese. Henceforth, each Indian village was to have a school where Portuguese was taught rather than the native language. To more quickly assimilate the Indians, Pombal decreed that any Portuguese who married an Indian would improve his (or her) chances of preferment and promotion. Under severe penalty, he forbade the use of any pejorative adjectives or nouns to describe a person's mixed Indo-Portuguese background. He hoped through that varied legislation to make the Indian an integral and active participant in Brazilian life. In at least one way he partially accomplished that goal. To the degree that Pombal broke down the Indians' isolation and made them a part of the empire, he integrated the North, where the majority of the remaining Indians could be found in the late eighteenth century, into the rest of the colony, an accomplishment which helped to insure the future unity of Brazil. Of course, practically speaking and whatever the intention of those laws, they simply facilitated the exploitation of the Indians. The planters realized soon enough that the Indian was not a satisfactory answer to the labor problem. At the same time, the rapid growth of the sugar industry sent the demand for workers soaring, thereby intensifying the labor shortage. The planters soon focused their attention on Africa as the most likely source for their labor. Blacks had been imported into Portugal at least since 1433, and by the mid-sixteenth century the Portuguese were well acquainted with the West African coast and its inhabitants. The blacks proved well adapted to the tasks required by the colonists. Furthermore, the troublesome reservations about using Indians as slaves rarely extended to the use of Africans. For those reasons a forced migration of millions of Africans began in the mid-sixteenth century and continued apace until 1850. It is believed that the first blacks directly imported from Africa arrived in Brazil in 1538. In that year, a ship of Jorge Lopes Bixorda, an experienced and well-known slave trader, unloaded its human cargo from Guinea. One Jesuit father wrote from Pernambuco in 1552, "There are in this captaincy a great number of slaves, both Indian and African." In 1585, out of a total population of 57,000 there were some 14,000 African slaves, a majority of whom were in Pernambuco. Thereafter a deluge of slaves poured out of Africa.

Once the traffic became well established the black cargo moved uninterruptedly across the Atlantic. Brazil sent its tobacco, sugar, manioc, beans, flour, spirits, cloth, and sweetmeats eastward in exchange for the slaves and to a lesser extent for palm oil, rice, ivory, gold, and the products of Asia. The trade between Angola and Brazil reached such proportions that the former became practically a dependency of the latter. The Portuguese historian Jaime Cortesão has affirmed, "Angola was during the seventeenth and eighteenth centuries a Portuguese province of Brazil." At one point in the mid-seventeenth century, 1658–1666, two successive governors of Angola, João Fernandes Vieira and André Vidal de

Negreiros, were Brazilians. By the close of the eighteenth century, the merchants of Rio de Janeiro alone were dispatching some twenty-four ships a year to that African colony. The direct trade route was not the only one followed. About half a-dozen European nations, principal among which were Portugal and the Netherlands, used a triangular route: European goods to Africa, African slaves to Brazil, Brazilian sugar to Europe. By whatever means they came, the number of Africans imported was staggering. A conservative estimate figured the number of blacks surviving the Atlantic crossing to Brazil over the span of three centuries at about 3.5 million. By centuries, the estimated numbers were: sixteenth, 100,000; seventeenth, 600,000; eighteenth, 1,300,000; nineteenth, 1,600,000. Thus the Portuguese imported into Brazil several times more blacks than the Indians they found there.

The African origins of Brazil's slaves were extremely varied. They came from Guinea, Dahomey, Nigeria, the Gold Coast, Cape Verde, São Tomé, Angola, the Congo, Mozambique, and many other parts of Africa. Precise origins are difficult to ascertain because of the mixing of the slaves in Brazil as well as miscegenation with whites and Indians, and because the government in 1890 ordered destroyed all official records relating to slavery. A study of Negro cultures surviving in Brazil enables anthropologists to identify three major African contributors to Brazilian society. The first are the Sudanese groups of which the Yoruba and Dahoman predominated. They originated in the African areas which later became Liberia, Nigeria, the Gold Coast, and Dahomey. Although scattered throughout Brazil, the Yorubas seemed to be concentrated principally in Bahia and the Dahomans in Bahia and Maranhão. The slave buyers considered these Sudanese blacks particularly desirable because they were tall, strong, brave, and intelligent and reputed to be hard-working and good-natured. The Mohammedanized Guinea-Sudanese groups composed the second classification of African contributors. Those Malé blacks of whom the Hausa were probably the best known were found mainly in Bahia. They followed the austere precepts of their religion. Some of them were literate in Arabic, and they possessed numerous skills, not the least appreciated of which were gold-mining techniques. Among slave-owners, they bore the reputation of being intelligent and industrious but somewhat sullen, resentful, and rebellious in captivity. The Bantu groups from Angola, the Congo, and Mozambique were the third contributors. They could be found principally in Rio de Janeiro and Minas Gerais, although once again individuals from these groups were dispersed throughout Portuguese America. Regarded as peaceful and easily domesticated, they knew how to work metals, weave, and make pottery. They tended livestock and farmed.

Blacks could be found in every part of the colony, but the greatest concentrations of them were in Maranhão, Pernambuco, Bahia, and Rio de Janeiro, where they worked at various agricultural tasks, and in Minas Gerais, where they mined gold and diamonds. With the exception, then, of Minas Gerais, the Africans exerted their greatest influence in the coastal areas and their presence and influence were less obvious as one moved farther and farther into the interior.

The black contribution to Brazilian evolution was great and varied. The African cook introduced into the Brazilian diet new staples such as red peppers, black beans, and okra and new culinary concoctions such as caruru or vatapá, and into the kitchen new utensils such as the wooden spoon and the mortar and pestle. The "mammy" who raised all the children of the planter related to them stories of an African origin and sang to them the songs of that continent. The children were intimately exposed to the pronunciation, habits, and ideas of the African, who in many respects formed them mentally. The lady of the mansion chose favored black women to be her companions, and they likewise amused her with tales and songs of Africa. The plantation house offered the logical place where African and European cultures met and mingled. Before too many decades had passed, African cultural traits were easily visible in the colony's dress, music, dance, and religion. On one level a syncretized Afro-Brazilian religion developed, known as Candomblé in Bahia, Xangó in Pernambuco, and Macumba in Rio de Janeiro. On another level, the blacks smoothed away some of the asperity of Roman Catholicism. They enlivened Church festivals, drawing them out into the street to commemorate the patron saint's day and adding folk plays and dances of a religious nature rooted in syncretism.

Doubtless the blacks' major contribution was their labor. Their strong muscles supported Brazilian civilization. They did much more than simply work in the fields. They brought with them or learned in the New World many skills essential for the growth of Brazil. They were the carpenters, painters, masons, jewelers, sculptors, locksmiths, tailors, cobblers, and bakers. They made technical contributions in metallurgy, mining, cattle-raising, and agriculture. In the judgment of Prince Johan Maurits, the famed viceroy of Dutch Brazil, "It is not possible to effect anything in Brazil without slaves . . . and they cannot be dispensed with upon any consideration whatsoever; if anyone feels that this is wrong, it is a futile scruple."[4]

The Africans helped to explore and conquer the interior as well as to defend Brazil from attack. In times of war, they were the soldiers who fought the hostile Indians or the foreign invaders. Black regiments under black leaders—notably the much-praised Henrique Dias—struggled against the Dutch in the seventeenth century. When the French sacked Rio de Janeiro in 1711, the governor of Minas Gerais rushed to the aid of the city with 1,500 horsemen and 6,000 armed blacks. They were an indispensable ingredient of colonial Brazil. In truth, the conquest, settlement, and development of Brazil were joint Afro-European ventures.

Few Europeans felt slavery was wrong. Portuguese law sanctioned it. The attorney-general of the state of Maranhão, Manuel Guedes Aranha, expressed a typical view in 1654, when he wrote, "It is a known fact that different men are fitted for different things: we [the whites] are meant to introduce religion among them [Indians and blacks]; and they to serve us, hunt for us, fish for us, work for us."[5] Such a

---

4. Quoted in C. R. Boxer, *The Dutch in Brazil, 1624–1654* (Oxford, 1957), p. 83.

5. Quoted in Gilberto Freyre, *The Mansions and the Shanties* (New York, 1963), p. xxi.

classic statement of racism constituted the core of European imperialism for centuries. Always solicitous of the welfare of the Indian and uncertain of the morality of his enslavement, the Roman Catholic Church accepted African slavery so long as the blacks were Christianized. However, a few voices— principally from the Jesuits—did eventually speak up in defense of the blacks. In the seventeenth century, the humane Padre Antônio Vieira on several occasions denounced brutal punishments and abuse of the black slaves. During one famed sermon, he cried emotionally,

O inhuman traffic in which the merchandise is men! Few masters, many slaves; masters richly dressed, slaves despised and naked; masters banqueting, slaves dying of hunger; masters swimming in gold and silver, slaves loaded down with irons; masters treating their slaves like brutes, slaves in fear and awe of their masters as if they were gods; masters present at a whipping, standing like statues of might and tyranny, slaves prostrated, their hands strapped behind their backs, like debased emblems of servitude.
Peradvventure these men are not our brothers?
Were these souls not redeemed with the blood of the same Christ? Are not these bodies born and do they not die like ours? Do they not breathe the same air? Does not the same sky cover them? Are they not warmed by the same sun?[6]

Vieira even went so far during some sermons as to question the institution of slavery itself. On one such occasion, he asked rhetorically "Can there be a greater want of understanding, or a greater error of judgment between men and men than for me to think that I must be your master because I was born farther away from the sun, and that you must be my slave because you were born nearer to it?" He must have startled many of his listeners with the remark, "An Ethiope if he be cleansed in the waters of the Congo is clean, but he is not white; but if cleansed in the water of baptism, he is both."
In the opening years of the eighteenth century, both André João Antonil and Jorge Benci wrote to urge better

6. Quoted in Donald Pierson, *Negroes in Brazil* (Chicago, 1942), p. 55.

treatment of the black slaves. For its part, the Crown promulgated edicts in 1688, 1698, and 1714 against the maltreatment of black slaves. They had no enduring effect. One unique exception to the general acceptance of African slavery in eighteenth-century Brazil was a singular book, *Ethiope Resgatado, Emphenhado, Sustentado, Corrigido, Instruido e Libertado* (The Ethiopian Ransomed, Indentured, Sustained, Corrected, Educated, and Liberated), published in 1758. Written by a secular priest, Manuel Ribeiro Rocha, the book condemned the excessive punishment of slaves in Brazil and enthusiastically adovcated the manumission of the African. In 1761, Pombal liberated all the slaves in Portugal, but slavery, the very sinew of the mercantile economy, continued in Brazil without any real protest except from the slaves themselves.

On occasion the slaves rebelled, killed their masters, and set fire to the plantations, both buildings and fields. More often, they simply disappeared into the trackless interior where they sometimes established small settlements known as *quilombos*. Of the many quilombos established in Portuguese America—and scholars still have not directed sufficient attention to this topic to allow even a calculated estimate of the size or number of the quilombos—the longest-lived and largest from this perspective seems to have been the famous Palmares in the interior of Alagoas. There, throughout most of the seventeenth century, a pseudo-African state with a population of approximately 20,000 flourished. Palmares is significant as the major attempt by the blacks in Brazil to organize a state with African traditions. To the Luso-Brazilians the quilombo posed a threat to established order because the blacks enticed other slaves to flee the plantations and join them. Furthermore, the lands Palmares occupied blocked westward agrarian expansion. Repeated campaigns against the stronghold failed. Between 1672 and 1694, Palmares withstood an average of one Portuguese expedition every fifteen months. Finally a combination of dissension within the quilombo and the royal government's use of ruthless and persistent Paulista *bandeirantes* destroyed it at the end of the seventeenth century. Throughout the colonial period—for that matter well into the national period—the threat of slave rebellion hung ominously in the air, causing the plantation owners and even the city dwellers endless uneasy hours. Rebellions, quilombos, and runaways were ample testimony to the fact that the few voices and the crown's edicts condemning harsh treatment of slaves were either not heard or not heeded. Indeed, in his description of Bahia, *Notícias Soteropolitanas e Brasílicas,* based on twelve years of residence there at the end of the eighteenth century, Luís dos Santos Vilhena repeated the condemnations of the abuses of slavery—overwork, sadistic punishments, underfeeding—which the Jesuits had catalogued nearly a century earlier.

The miscegenation characteristic of Portuguese-Indian relations also characterized Portuguese-African relations. Within their permissive slave society, the white men of the plantation houses took full advantage of the black women. As a consequence, a mulatto population appeared early and grew rapidly. The population of Salvador da Bahia, in the heart of rich sugar and tobacco country, in 1803 very well exemplified that miscegenation. In an estimated population of 100,000, approximately 30,000 were white, another 30,000 mulatto, and the remainder black. Of Brazil's approximately 3.5 million inhabitants in 1818, only slightly more than a million could be classified—very liberally—as white, a half million as mulatto, and about 2 million as black. With good reason, Vieira observed, "Brazil has the body of America and the soul of Africa."

Of the three groups contributing to the increasingly homogeneous nature of Brazilian society, only the Indians declined in number and hence in importance and influence during the colonial period. The European and African influx continued. Of course European immigration never approximated the numbers forcefully sent from Africa. In the late seventeenth century, the Lisbon government urged greater immigration of married Portuguese couples. In the extreme north and south, it succeeded in persuading families from the Azores to settle in appreciable numbers. The first Azoreans arrived in Para in 1673 and in Santa Catarina and

Rio Grande do Sul in 1747. Each head of a household received a small land grant as well as supplies and provisions, all gratis. The discovery of gold in the late seventeenth century lured greater numbers of Europeans to Brazil. Estimates indicate that the population of European stock increased tenfold during the eighteenth century. The three groups, Indian, European, and African, lived and mixed together with, all factors considered, a minimum of friction, although the brutality of the experience for the Indians and blacks should not be dismissed. In the process three continents fused sexually, socially, linguistically, and culturally to form a nation much more homogeneous than any other of comparable size. A hybrid civilization emerged and so did a new type of person, the Brazilian, the compounded product of extraordinary diverse elements. It would not be an exaggeration to affirm that this new "race" conquered the new land.

Territorial Expansion

One of the most dynamic aspects of Brazilian history has been continuous territorial expansion. The Luso-Brazilian sweep across the South American continent from the Atlantic to the Andes constituted one of the greatest epics of Brazilian history. Portugal responded defensively to foreign threats and interlopers in the New World by establishing tiny, isolated, agricultural nuclei along the coast. Olinda to the north, Salvador da Bahia in the center, and São Vicente to the south were the first settlements of strategic and commercial importance. Seaborne foreigners and the hostile Indians of the interior menaced those fragile settlements. The Crown's efforts to strengthen and to connect them meant that for many decades emphasis was put on coastal settlement to the neglect of inland expansion. At first the government even put legal restrictions on inland penetration. Governor-General Tomé de Sousa was ordered to prohibit expansion into the interior without special permission. The foundation of Rio de Janeiro in 1565 helped to unite Salvador with the South, just as the establishment of São Cristóvão de Rio Sergipe in 1589 helped to unite the colonial capital with the North. With the arrival of more colonists and the defeat of the defensive Indians, the area surrounding each of the settlements was conquered, settled, and incorporated into the agricultural economy of the colony.

From time to time some timid exploration filtered into the interior. Those *entradas* resulted from a curiosity to learn what the hinterland might offer and from a hope of discovering gold and other precious metals. Those expeditions also captured Indian slaves for the colonists. The entrada of Antônio Dias Adorno in 1574, for example, marched through the *sertão* (the backlands) of Bahia and entered what later would be called Minas Gerais. Those hearty explorers found no gold but returned with 7,000 Indian slaves to work the coastal plantations.

At first the colony expanded faster in the North in direct response to increasing European pressures on Portugal either to occupy the coast it claimed or to forfeit it to others. The union of the two Iberian crowns between 1580 and 1640 under the Spanish Philips eliminated the early rivalry between Spain and Portugal over the territory between São Vicente and the Rio de la Plata. Likewise in the South there was no brazilwood, a natural product much sought after by the French, English, and Dutch, who hovered along the northern coast because of its abundant stands of brazilwood, as well as its fertile land favorable to sugar culture. The presence of these Europeans motivated the Portuguese to expand in their direction. Engaged in such "defensive colonization," the Portuguese founded one settlement after the other, each north of the last one: Filipéia (present-day João Pessôa), 1585; Natal, 1599; Fortaleza, 1611; São Luís, 1614; and finally Belém, 1616, on the Amazon River.

The newly founded settlements of Sao Luís and Belém were isolated on the northern coast far from the Cape of São Roque, where the coast suddenly turns southward. It soon became apparent that because of winds and sea currents these settlers could communicate more readily with Lisbon than with Salvador. Accordingly, when the Crown appointed a judge for São Luís in 1619, it ruled that appeals should be made directly to Lisbon rather than to Salvador. Two years later, the king created the state of Maranhão (as contrasted with the state of Brazil) composed of Maranhão, Pará, Amazonas, and for a time parts of Ceará, and Piauí. The new state had a modest birth. Settlement consisted only of four forts, one in Ceará, others at São Luís, Belém, and the mouth of the Amazon, with minuscule villages at their side. For example, Belém in 1621 had only eighty inhabitants and fifty soldiers. The first governor, Francisco Coelho de Carvalho, generously distributed the land in sesmarias and created six hereditary captaincies with the hope that their donees would encourage immigration. Growth, however, was slow. The white population of the state numbered only 2,000 in 1700. In 1677 the bishopric of Maranhão was erected, suffragan to the archbishop of Lisbon. The seat of the government moved to Belém in 1737 because of the increasing importance of the Amazon River. The northern coast, for a long time neglected and then later only weakly held, tempted the expanding European powers.

The French were the most serious threat to Portugal's claims in the sixteenth and early seventeenth centuries. After their expulsion from Rio de Janeiro in 1567, they turned their attention to the North. From Paraíba to the Amazon they traded with the Indians whom they urged to oppose the Portuguese. In 1612, a French expedition under the command of Ravardière began to colonize Maranhão. The Portuguese reacted by sending expeditions against the French interlopers in 1614 and 1615. After their expulsion in 1615, they ceased to be a major threat to Portuguese hegemony in the New World. True, Jean-François du Clerc attacked Rio de Janeiro in 1710 and Duguay-Trouin captured and plundered that city the following year, but those were isolated attacks little related to colonization. France maintained its claims to Amapá, the territory between the Amazon and Oiapoque rivers, until 1900 when an impartial arbiter recognized the Brazilian claims as valid. The English made some annoying and costly raids on the coastal settlements in the late sixteenth century. Magnanimously James I bestowed some land grants in northern Brazil upon nobles of his court, but they made no serious effort to colonize. The final and major foreign threat came from the Dutch during the seventeenth century. The Dutch were quite familiar with Brazil. During some periods, Dutch bottoms carried over half of the trade between Brazil and Portugal. Before 1591, ships of any flag could trade in Brazilian ports so long as they were cleared from a Portuguese port first. Those ships carried away Brazilian products after paying the required taxes and duties and calling at Lisbon for clearance. Traditionally the Dutch and Portuguese had gotten along well together, but their amiable relationship ended when Philip of Spain ascended the Portuguese throne. The Dutch, fighting a protracted war for their independence from the Spanish Hapsburgs, were the sworn enemies of the Castilians. In the unification of the two kingdoms, Portugal inherited that quarrel. In 1585 and again in 1590, 1596, and 1599, Philip II ordered the seizure of all Dutch vessels in Portuguese ports and the imprisonment of their crews. The Dutch sought retaliation. They established a few trading posts along the lower Amazon in the early seventeenth century. However, the principal weapon of revenge was the Dutch West India Company, founded in 1621 to encourage colonization and commerce through conquest.

Lured by lucrative sugar exports and convinced that Portuguese America was the colony Philip held most weakly, the Dutch West India Company selected Brazil for its initial conquest. The Company's fleet first attacked Salvador, an excellent port well situated for future expansion, and carried it in 1624. The Luso-Brazilians expelled the Dutch the following year and repulsed two more attacks in 1627. The Company then shifted its attention from the political center of the colony to its economic center, Pernambuco. Its forces appeared off Recife in 1630. After capturing that port, they began a conquest which at its height extended from the São Francisco River northward into Maranhão.

The Calvinist soldier and intellectual Johan Maurits of Nassau-Siegen presided over the most fruitful years of Dutch occupation, 1637–1644. Captivated by Brazil, the viceroy put to work some forty-six scholars, scientists, and artists to study and to depict the land. He typified the Dutch curiosity about the tropics, a curiosity which the Iberians hitherto had lacked. Hence it was the Dutch who made the first—and for a long time the only—scientific study of the tropics. Albert Eckhout painted magnificent canvasses portraying the Dutch colony. Willem Piso studied tropical diseases and their remedies. Georg Marcgraf made collections of fauna, flora, and rocks. The Dutch maintained an aviary as well as zoological and botanical gardens. The first astronomical observatory and meteorological station were built in the New World in Recife.

Economic matters quite naturally commanded much of Maurits' attention as well. In an endeavor to avoid monoculture, he tried to make the colony self-supporting in foodstuffs. The company monopolized all trade in slaves, dyewoods, and munitions but permitted the inhabitants of the conquered colony to engage freely in all other trade. By reducing taxes and providing liberal credit terms to planters to rebuild ruined sugar mills and to buy slaves, the viceroy rehabilitated the sugar industry, which was well on its way to recovery from the ravages of fighting when he left. Those were splendid years for the Netherlands. Indeed, 1641 marked the apogee of Dutch power in the Atlantic, with fur trading posts on the Hudson River, fortresses in Guiana, the possession of Curacao and Aruba, the sugar colonies in Brazil and slave-trading posts in Africa. Understanding the importance of slavery to sugar, the Dutch seized part of Angola to insure a labor supply for their Brazilian plantations.

Shortly after the departure of Maurits the bitter guerrilla warfare raging for a decade and a half against the Dutch coalesced into an open campaign coordinated by Governor-General Antônio Telles da Silva from Salvador. Contacts between the leaders in Bahia and Pernambuco were made. André Vidal de Negreiros of Bahia met twice with João Fernandes Vieira, a wealthy mulatto planter who had collaborated with the Dutch until 1644, to promise that troops from Bahia would march overland to aid a rebellion in Pernambuco. Portuguese soldiers under Antônio Dias Cardoso, black and mulatto troops under Henrique Dias, and Indian levies under Felipe Camarão penetrated the hinterland of northeastern Brazil in early 1645, initiating their campaign to expel the foreign heretic.

New developments in Europe complicated the conduct of the war against the Dutch in Brazil. With popular support, the Braganzas seized the Portuguese Crown in 1640 and declared Portugal's independence of Spain. United by their mutual enmity toward Spain, Portugal and the Netherlands ceased hostilities toward each other in Europe. Portugal's determination to maintain its newly gained independence from Spain absorbed most of its attention and energy. The Brazilians, however, refused to come to terms with the Dutch and continued the struggle to expel them. *Mazombos* (whites born in Brazil), blacks, and Indians from all parts of the subcontinent joined ranks in the common campaign. Their victories at Guararapes in 1648 and 1649 proved their land superiority over the foreign invader. The Brazilians even carried their attacks to Angola. First, they sent munitions, guns, and supplies to the Portuguese besieged in the interior of Angola. Then, Salvador Correia de Sá e Benavides, bearing the imposing title "Governor of Rio de Janeiro and Captain-General of the Kingdom of Angola," sailed from Guanabara Bay with 2,000 men and recaptured Luanda from the Dutch, thus restoring Angola to the Crown. The "Restorer of Angola" thus reopened the intensive trade between the two South Atlantic colonies. By that time Dutch Brazil was clearly in the process of decay. Constant interprovincial bickering in the Netherlands resulted in poor leadership and irresolute policy within the Dutch West India Company. In turn, the Company neglected the colony and failed to pay the soldiers and sailors regularly. Their morale plummeted. By 1648 the Brazilians had reduced the Dutch to Recife and its immediate environment. However, as long as the Dutch controlled the sea, a stalemate resulted. At that point, Portugal reawakened to its need for Brazilian sugar, of which the Northeast was a primary producer, and took a more active interest in the colonial conflict. To break the impasse, Antônio Vieira suggested to the king that a Brazil Company be formed and given special privileges in the Luso-Brazilian trade, with the obligation that it build and equip a fleet of warships in Brazil. In 1649, the Brazil Company's first fleet sailed for the New World. The Dutch ships, undermanned, underprovisioned, and in lamentable condition, mutinied and returned home. Portugal for the first time took command of the seas. The outbreak of war between the Netherlands and England in 1652 sealed the fate of the Dutch in the South Atlantic. The Portuguese fleet blockaded Recife and completely isolated the demoralized Dutch garrison. The Dutch surrendered. By the terms of the capitulation of Taborda on January 26, 1654, they left Brazil, and the Luso-Brazilians triumphantly entered Recife several days later.

The consequences of the Dutch presence in Brazil, and of the long war, were many and significant. Historians agree that "the reconquest" awoke the first national sentiments among the varied and scattered inhabitants of the sprawling colony. The Brazilians, much more than the Portuguese, had fought the war and won the victory. They had defeated a major European maritime power, one in fact that had humbled Spain, once the occupier of Portugal. That achievement infused into the Brazilians a new pride which replaced their old feeling of inferiority before the Portuguese. Men of all regions, races, colors, and social positions had contributed in a united effort to the final victory, a feat that weakened former geographical, social, and color barriers. The protracted struggle had welded Brazil into an unprecedented psychological and social unity, so that its inhabitants thought of themselves, more than ever before, as Brazilians. The mercantile Dutch made Recife the first really bourgeois commercial center of Brazil. They found it a village of 150 houses and left it a bustling port with over 2,000 houses. They created an urban, commercial class in contrast to and eventually in conflict with the traditional rural class. The defeat of the Dutch marked the end of any major overt foreign threat to northern Brazil. Full attention turned from the northern coast to the southern and to the vast interior. The government in Lisbon was particularly concerned about the South; the Brazilians, with the interior.

By the mid-seventeenth century both the Spaniards and the Portuguese understood the importance of the Rio de la Plata network. Spain wanted to control it to prevent any penetration into the silver-mining regions of Upper Peru, while Portugal coveted it in order to open up and to protect the southern interior of Brazil. João Teixeira, a royal cosmographer, asserted in 1640 that Brazil's natural southern boundary was the Plata. A few years later, Salvador Correia de Sá e Benavides, member of the Overseas Council in Lisbon and a former governor of Rio de Janeiro, advocated the conquest of Buenos Aires as a base to control the river. Antônio Vieira echoed those sentiments, and the Paulistas at times seemed disposed to carry them out. In 1676, the pope gave the bishop of Rio de Janeiro jurisdiction over the area as far south as the Plata. The Portuguese colonization of the extreme South began in 1680 with the foundation of Colônia do Sacramento across the Plata estuary from Buenos Aires. The new settlement was far too isolated from the main body of Luso-Brazilian colonization to thrive, and the Spaniards immediately challenged it. The Luso-Brazilians established a supply base at Laguna in Santa Catarina in 1684 and a fortress at the southern end of Lagoa de Patos in Rio Grande do Sul in 1737. The triangle formed by Colônia, Laguna, and Rio Grande was the radiation point for expansion in the South. In 1739, the Crown created the captaincy of Santa Catarina and in 1760, the captaincy of Rio Grande do São Pedro, which it elevated to the rank of captaincy-general and renamed Rio Grande do Sul in 1807. The struggle to dominate the Plata turned out to be as prolonged as it was bitter. The area approximately encompassing contemporary Uruguay changed hands with bewildering frequency between 1680 and 1828, when the independent nation of Uruguay emerged, and no other area better symbolized the rivalry of the two Iberian monarchies for empire. That foreign rivalry intensified Portugal's attention to the South, just as it had in the North. Because of that challenge, Lisbon took a very active interest in the exploration, colonization, and fortification of the area. The settlement of the North and South through official encouragement contrasted markedly with the inland penetration from the center captaincies, characterized by spontaneity and the near absence of official impetus.

Westward expansion during the seventeenth and eighteenth centuries, in many ways a direct continuation of the adventurous spirit which had carried the Portuguese to the four corners of the world, accounts for the phenomenal territorial growth of Brazil. It was also the first Brazilian epic. The Portuguese empire had been coastal; Portuguese expansion, mercantile. The mazombos, mulattoes, and mestizos led the way into the interior. Brazilian inland expansion had its timid beginnings in the sixteenth century, became the marked characteristic of the last half of the seventeenth and first half of the eighteenth centuries and in certain phases lasted until the early twentieth century when Brazil acquired Acre, its westernmost state. That spectacular expansion resulted from the activities of hearty adventurers known as *bandeirantes*, a term derived from the Portuguese word for flag, *bandeira*. In medieval Portugal a bandeira signified a group of soldiers equal in size to a company and designated by a distinctive banner. The militia of São Paulo adopted the term and by extension it came to mean an expedition departing for the interior. Participants in such expeditions were called *bandeirantes*.

All three races contributed to the bandeirante expansion. *Mamelucos*, the offspring of Indians and Portuguese, composed the majority of the rank and leadership of the expedition, but blacks—in their status as either slaves or freedmen—participated too. Mulattoes on occasion led some bandeiras. The bandeirantes adapted perfectly to the land and were inured to the hardships of the interior. Europe meant nothing to them; the virgin land engulfing them meant everything. They disdainfully turned their backs on the coast and plunged into the interior to seek wealth and power. Indian slaves, runaway black slaves, precious metals, and land were the forms of wealth they pursued. By exploring new territory, opening new routes of communication, and claiming new regions for the Crown they hoped for the rewards of royal recognition and preferment. Clearly they paid homage to their distant king, but on the other hand they expressed little if any allegiance to Portugal. As a matter of fact, their pursuit of freedom from colonial bureaucracy was a further impetus to their movement into the interior. Wrote a crown judge to the governor of São Paulo in 1736, "These Paulistas only concern themselves with making new discoveries so as to live free from the judges. And when they see that these follow them, they continue to make other discoveries in remote regions where one cannot pursue them owing to the great distance."

The bandeirantes traversed those immense distances mainly by foot or canoe. Horseback was the exception. Rivers proved to be important routes into the sertão, and they became increasingly important in the eighteenth century. Where rivers did not exist, the bandeirante moved forward on foot. Barefooted, wearing simple, loose cotton trousers, sometimes with a cotton shirt and sometimes without, and with either a stocking cap or a broadbrimmed hat on his head, he carried a sword and pistols in his belt, a knife at his chest, a rifle slung over his shoulder and cartridge belts girded to his body. Many borrowed and mastered the bow and arrow of the Indians. Little wonder that this rugged and heavily armed explorer filled the Indians with terror and gave pause to his enemies.

The land challenged the bandeirantes. They traversed inhospitable mountains and forded turbulent rivers. Swamps and dense forests mocked their efforts. Arid stretches taught them to bless those numerous, troublesome streams they had so recently cursed. And everywhere they encountered hunger, their one certain traveling companion. Game was scarce and fruits, nuts, berries, and roots proved to be rare and coveted delicacies. The Indians possessed either meager rations or none at all. With great courage and no small amount of endurance the bandeirantes stoically met the challenge and triumphed.

The Paulistas, already separated from the coast by the Serra do Mar, were the most dedicated to the exploration of the interior, but they were not the only bandeirantes by any means. Salvador, Recife, São Luís, and Belém all served as staging points for daring marches into the unknown. Several examples will illustrate the fortitude of those bandeirantes. In 1637, Pedro Teixeira left Belém with 70 soldiers, a few priests, and 1,200 Indians and paddled up the Amazon, Solimões, and Napo rivers in 41 large canoes. Leaving their boats, they climbed the Andes to visit Quito. Returning, Teixeira took possession of the left bank of the Napo on August 16, 1639, in the name of Portugal. There he established Tabatinga, the farthest westward claim of Portugal in South America. In 1648, Antônio Raposo Tavares marched westward from São Paulo into Paraguay and northwestward to the foothills of the Andes and then descended the Madeira and Amazon rivers to arrive in Belém in 1651. In 1695, Francisco dos Santos with 4 soldiers and 20 Indians opened an overland route from São Luís to Salvador. Such feats were duplicated many times.

In the sixteenth and early seventeenth centuries a series of local communications networks centered on each major settlement: São Vicente, Rio de Janeiro, Bahia, Olinda, and later São Luís and Belém. Their only common contact was via the Atlantic Ocean. Bandeirante expansion invalidated the sea lanes as the only common unifier and established inland routes, some by river, others by land, still others by both river and land, to connect the newly established settlements with the older coastal population nuclei. Such lines of communication developed during the last half of the seventeenth century and multiplied during the eighteenth century until, converging one with the other, they connected all the major settlements. Transportation over those radiating routes of communication was by canoe if by river and by mule train if by land. The usual dugout canoe, 50 to 60 feet long, 5 to 6 feet wide, and 3 to 4 feet deep, carried about 12,000 pounds and a crew of eight who used short paddles and punting poles. The crews paddled by day and camped along the river banks at night. The mule trains, operating on regular schedules and charging fixed rates, consisted of 20 to 50 mules, each carrying approximately 250 pounds, and covered 20 to 25 miles a day. Where possible they halted at *ranchos*, establishments which quickly sprang up along the major routes to furnish provisions and shelter for both the mules and the *tropeiros,* that is, the drivers. The tropeiro was a distinctive Brazilian type. Rough and ready, he belonged to the same school as the bandeirante except that he also possessed a sense of business adventure and acumen. From the ports he distributed European merchandise throughout the interior; conversely he brought the products of the sertão to the coast for consumption or export. More than a mere merchant, he carried throughout Brazil ideas, expressions, news, and customs. In short, he was a significant agent of national unity. The navigators and their canoes played a similar role where the rivers made it possible. By the eighteenth century, fleets of canoes plied the inland waterways. The Tietê, flowing westward from the bandeirante capital, São Paulo, became one of the first and most important highways of travel to and trade with the far west of Goiás and Mato Grosso. The São Francisco, with its headwaters deep within Minas Gerais and its mouth between Sergipe and Alagoas, served as a vital link of communication between north and south. The Tocantins, Paranaíba, Paraguaçú, Jequitinhonha, Paraíba, and Paraná were but a few of the many rivers serving as routes of penetration into the interior and trade with that huge hinterland. The canoe fleets provided a cheap means of transportation. Since a small canoe usually carried the load of ten or eleven mules at about a third of the cost, canoe transportation was cheaper than mule transportation despite the more circuitous water routes. For example, to transport heavy merchandise from Rio de Janeiro or Salvador into Mato Grosso by way of the Madeira River was half the price of more direct overland transportation. Those vital transportation networks which linked the various regions of Brazil were the by-product of the bandeirantes' explorations.

The primary motivation of the bandeirante was economic. Like the Spanish conquistadores they marched into the sertão with the hope of finding riches. Here then, as elsewhere throughout the Western Hemisphere, the hope of discovering El Dorado enticed men into the unknown. The bandeirantes sought to capture Indians and sell them at a lucrative profit to the coastal planters or to use them on their own plantations. The Jesuit José de Anchieta reported tellingly in 1587, "The Portuguese go a thousand or more miles in search of Indians because they are so far from here [São Paulo], the land around here being depopulated." The colonial government eventually made use of the rugged bandeirantes in expeditions to pacify stubbornly hostile Indians or to recapture slaves grouped in quilombos. In 1671, for example, the Paulista Estévão Ribeiro Baião Parente at the governor-general's behest brought four hundred bandeirantes to the interior of Bahia to fight the pugnacious Indians of that region. They fought for two years in the "just war" and enslaved thousands of Indians. The governor-general rewarded them with generous sesmarias. Paulistas were also recruited in the final campaign against Palmares. The search for gold also impelled the bandeirantes. The first the bandeirantes from São Vicente and São Paulo pushed southward, attracted by minor discoveries of alluvial gold. The foundation of Paranaguá (1648), São Francisco do Sul (1658), Florianópolis (1678), and Curitiba (1693) resulted from that pursuit of gold. Other bandeirantes from São Paulo, Rio de Janeiro, and Salvador moved westward, converging in Minas Gerais, in their quest for gold and other precious metals and stones. Fernão Dias Pais of São Paulo conducted one of the most epic searches for wealth in Minas Gerais from 1674 until his death in 1681. He tramped across fabulous lodes of gold, but he failed to realize it. Searching without financial success, he did contribute significantly to the exploration of Minas Gerais. The continued quest for minerals drew the bandeirantes into Goiás, Mato Grosso, and Amazonia.

By the mid-seventeenth century, the bandeirantes were opening the Amazon to trade and settlement. In 1669, the Crown built Fort São José de Rio Negro at the point where the Rio Negro met the Solimões. That juncture became the first population center in the interior of the Amazon. Exploring the North were several other groups: official detachments of soldiers sent to expel Spanish interlopers; the *tropas de resgate,* those expeditions in search of Indian slaves; and the sertanistas, merchant adventurers seeking the wealth of the region. They sold cocoa, vanilla, spices, medicinal herbs, woods, fruits, nuts, and animal skins to

Belém, other settlements, and the metropolis. Also very active in the Amazon, as elsewhere in the interior, were the missionaries. Many of the missionaries were a kind of bandeirante in the sense that they too helped to explore, open up, and settle the interior. However, their motivations were quite different. They eagerly left the coastal settlements for the sertão in order to Christianize the Indians and to save them from the predatory slave-hunting bandeirantes. To the best that their limited numbers permitted, they persuaded the Indians to live within the protective confines of the church-oriented villages scattered throughout the interior from the Amazon to the Plata.

The consequences of the bandeirante expansion were enormous. Their explorations opened up the interior by pioneering routes of communication and transportation, supplying geographic information about huge areas which hitherto had remained blank on maps, and pacifying or decimating hostile Indians. In the wake of explorations a variety of economic activities began which infused new wealth into the Portuguese empire. Gold, diamonds, and cattle were the most conspicuous contributions of the interior to the economy. Finally settlements sprang up in the newly opened areas. Some settlements owed their origin to a crossroads, a rancho, or a watering place; some to a gold lode or a diamond discovery; others to a natural stopping spot or transfer point along the waterways; and still others to a mission village or agglomerations of a military nature.

Bandeirante activity was also a major contributor to Brazilian unity. From the seventeenth century onward, the Brazilians began to demonstrate a remarkable mobility, a mobility that over the centuries has strengthened national unity. In the interior men moved more freely from one region to another than they had among the population clusters of the coast, despite the availability of ocean transportation in the coastal areas. The waterways and paths eventually intertwined into a gossamer net binding the colony together. The long cattle drives, the mule trains, and the canoe fleets linked one region to another. The mines of Minas Gerais, Goiás, and Mato Grosso beckoned people from the entire length of the coast and mingled them together. Removed from the coast with its ties to Europe, the people who entered the sertão submerged themselves in the vastness of Brazil. They were forced to modify their European or pseudo-European ways to suit the terrain and the climate. They borrowed heavily from the Indians. What resulted was their transformation into Brazilians, and nowhere was the nascent Brazilian more easily identifiable than in the sertão. Remarkably similaı to the bandeirante was the Canadian *voyageur* of the same period. Those fur traders, many of mixed European and Indian ancestry, used the great Canadian river system to travel east to west, and those routes fostered future Canadian unity. Brazil too owes its territorial expansion to the bandeirante. The Treaty of Tordesillas had given the bulge of South America to Portugal. Portugal's "Babylonian captivity" had blurred the boundary lines between Spanish and Portugese America. For example, Philip IV of Spain granted much of the Amazon—which lay west of the Tordesillas line—in hereditary captaincies to two Portuguese nobles in 1637. Spain, preoccupied on the West coast of South America with the mines of Peru, failed to block the Luso-Brazilian expansion except in the Plata area, the back door to the mines. Too late the Spanish monarchs realized that by default they had forfeited half of South America to the Luso-Brazilians. In the mid-eighteenth century the situation on the Iberian peninsula—the Spanish monarch was married to a Portuguese princess and the heir to the Por- tuguese throne wed to a Spanish princess—favored a frank discussion of the South American boundaries based on realpolitik. The two crowns agreed to redraw their South American boundaries. The Treaty of Madrid of 1750 officially abandoned the Tordesillas line in favor of two principles: 1) *uti possidetis,* that is the ownership by occupation rather than by claim,[7] and 2) the recognition of natural boundaries, that

7. That occupation bestowed ownership was a concept already applied in other parts of the hemisphere. One reads with amusement the following resolution passed at a town meeting in Milford, Connecticut, in 1640:
   "Voted that the earth is the Lord's and the fulness thereof;
   voted, that the earth is given to the Saints;
   voted, that we are the Saints."
Quoted in George F. Willison, *Saints and Strangers* (New York, 1945), p. 392.

is the use of rivers, mountains, lakes, and other natural land-marks to mark the boundaries rather than using the always controversial astronomical fixes to do so. That was all very well, but then in violation of the principle of *uti possidetis* Spain got title to the Portuguese Colônia do Sacramento, which it regarded as a threat to its position in the Plata, and Portugal in turn received the Sete Povos das Missões, Spanish Jesuit mission settlements along the Eastern or left bank of the Uruguay River, which Portugal considered a threat to its control of Rio Grande do Sul. That authorized exchange of territories was the most unpopular aspect of the treaty. However, neither side surrendered those areas at that time.

The individual most responsible for the Portuguese success in the Treaty of Madrid was Alexandre de Gusmão, a Brazilian from Santos who had been educated at Coimbra University. He understood the importance of the principle of *uti possidetis* as the best means to gain legal recognition for bandeirante expansion, and he worked energetically for the incorpoation of that principle into the treaty. Thanks to his efforts, the formal territorial outline of Brazil took legal shape; the boundaries between Spanish and Portuguese America ever after kept the approximate contour given them by the Treaty of Madrid. Shortly after the signing of the treaty, the good feelings characteristic of Luso-Brazilian relations in 1750 gave way to renewed suspicions. Tensions mounted on the peninsula as well as in the Plata. Repeated difficulties in locating the frontiers meant that very few of them were actually marked. Most importantly, Pombal, who catapulted to power at that time, disliked the treaty. In 1761, the Treaty of El Pardo annulled it.

Several more turns of European diplomacy affected Brazil's boundaries in the ever-turbulent Plata. The Treaty of San Ildefonso in 1777 awarded both Colônia do Sacramento and Missões to Spain, leaving it in control of the Plata. As a repercussion of the Franco-Spanish war against Portugal in 1801, the Brazilians attacked the Spaniards in the Plata, captured Missões, and pushed the southern boundary to the Chui River where it remains today. The Treaty of Badajós, 1801, recognized that expansion.

Vigorous bandeirante activity had permitted Brazil to expand at will save in the Plata region where the two Iberian empires struggled jealously for control. The principle of *uti possidetis* injected into Portuguese diplomacy by a Brazilian provided the legal basis upon which Brazil based its boundaries thereafter. The Treaty of Madrid provided the primitive model for all future Portuguese and Brazilian claims. The lengthy frontiers enclosed an amazing variety of wealth which the Luso-Brazilians exploited almost indifferently during the colonial period.

Economic Dependency

"Brazil can sustain itself with its ports closed and without the aid of any other land," boasted Frei Vicente do Salvador in 1627 in his history of Brazil. The boast was not entirely idle. A map readily indicates why. The very size of the colony and the kaleidoscopic variety of its geography seem to insure a sufficiently diverse range of natural wealth to fulfill the boast.

Reverses in Asia caused the metropolis during the last half of the sixteenth century to focus its economic attention on a hitherto neglected Brazil. Thereafter, Portugal depended ever more heavily on Brazil to supply a variety of raw materials which were marketed profitably in Europe to the temporary relief of royal and commercial coffers. Brazilwood, sugar, tobacco, cotton, Amazonian drugs, gold, and diamonds were some of the most important natural products the young colony offered to the Old World. Agriculture was the principal source of wealth. Mining, although more glamorous and prized, was but an interlude and in comparison to agriculture a secondary producer of wealth. However, whether from the soil or subsoil, Brazil produced lavishly. During many years the products of Brazil constituted approximately two thirds of Portugal's export trade with foreign countries.

The abundance of economic possibilities may well have been more a curse than a blessing since it permitted, indeed encouraged, an economic dilettantism which handicapped orderly development. Despite a dazzling potential, the economy never diversified. It relied for its well-being on a single natural product whose sale abroad dictated the course of colonial prosperity. If the product sold well, the colony prospered; if not, stagnation and misery engulfed it. External demand decided the colonial well-being, a dependence exaggerated by stubborn reliance on one major export. The colony thereby abdicated authority over its own economic destiny. Nor did the Luso-Brazilians ever achieve any notable efficiency in the exploitation of any of those natural products with which a generous Nature endowed them. With haphazard, old-fashioned, and inefficient methods, they exploited one natural product until some other area of the world eager to share the profits outproduced and undersold the Brazilians through the employment of more efficient methods. Then the Brazilians, after some hesitation and considerable economic stress, turned to yet another natural product. Those economic cycles with their sharp alternation between prosperity and poverty began with brazilwood, continued through sugar, tobacco, cotton, cacao, and rubber, and can still be seen in the declining phase of the recent coffee cycle. From the beginning, extreme economic fluctuation has been a major characteristic of the Brazilian economy and a powerful influence on the course of Brazilian history.

The agricultural structure contributed to the preservation of those cycles. The huge plantations and ranches, owned by relatively few and often employing large numbers of slaves, sought to supply to the international market on as large a scale as possible the tropical product most in demand. Quick and large profits were the goal. Agriculture was thoroughly speculative. Those capitalistic pursuits were carried out within a semifeudal framework.

The large estate, the *fazenda* based on a generous sesmaria, could be considered as some remote vestige of the medieval manor. The estate owner, a true lord of the manor, was a patriarchal chief who ruled family, servants, slaves, and even neighbors—unless they were large estate owners like himself—with absolute authority. The great size of the estate, its isolation from royal officials, and the relative weakness of local bureaucrats all strengthened his power. Furthermore, the estate chaplain and local parish priest orbited around him like satellites, lending the prestige of the Catholic Church to augment his authority. From the shaded veranda of his house, because naturally the "big house" was the focal point of the estate's activity, the patriarch oversaw the land, listened to petitions, dispensed justice, and in general held court. Those large and often well-furnished houses sat in the midst of barns, stables, carriage houses, warehouses, workshops, and slaves' quarters. As far as possible the estate was self-contained. Carpenters, smithies, bakers, seamstresses, candlemakers, and a host of skilled and semi-skilled slaves satisfied nearly all the simple, local demands. Need for contact with the world beyond the estate's boundaries was minimal. A rough road led to the next estate and nearest village. Occasionally a tropeiro appeared to peddle his wares. More importantly the road served to carry away the estate's principal crop to the nearest port, which the patriarch and part of his family visited from time to time to purchase from the outside world a few luxury items for themselves. The rural economy consisted of much more than the patriarch, latifundia, slavery, and export crops. Yet, those features dominated, characterized Brazilian agriculture, and shaped much of the colony's social and economic life.

Although these patriarchal estates could be found in the sugar, tobacco, cotton, and, to a lesser extent, the cattle country, the sugar plantation as it developed along the coast from Pernambuco to São Paulo became the best known and perhaps most typical example of them. From the mid-sixteenth to mid-seventeenth centuries, Brazil supplied Europe with nearly all its sugar, a lucrative export encouraged by the Crown with tax exemptions, monopoly privileges, guarantees against court attachment of production facilities, and patents of nobility. Despite some obvious hardships—an untamed physical environment, hostile Indians, marauding European interlopers, high freight rates, and a chronic labor shortage—sugar quickly became the major crop. By 1600 sugar production exceeded 65 million pounds a year, a tenfold increase during the previous quarter century. By that time sugar yielded more profit to Portugal than all its exotic trade with India and the Europeans living in Brazil enjoyed a higher per capita income than their counterparts back home. Governor-General Diogo de Meneses did not exaggerate when he observed to the king in 1609 that sugar provided the real wealth of the empire. The number of mills multiplied rapidly: in 1550 there were 70 mills; in 1584, 115; in 1612, 179; in 1627, 230; and in 1711 their number had grown to 528.

The sugar industry was complex. The large sugar-plantation owner, the *senhor de engenho,* leased most of his land to small contractors, known as *lavradores,* for a portion of their crops. With his own slaves, the lavrador planted the cane (one planting sufficed for several years), cut it, and transported it by ox cart to the mill. The average lavrador produced 1,000 to 2,000 cartloads of cane a year. To do so, he needed 20 able-bodied slaves. The senhor de engenho possessed all the complex and expensive machinery to grind and process the cane. So large was the operation that his mill, turned by oxen, horses, or water, and all its adjacent buildings resembled a small village. He employed 15 to 20 Portuguese overseers and technicians and approximately 100 slaves. A mill of that size could expect to produce between 110 and 125 tons of sugar per year. The final product was divided between the senhor de engenho and the lavrador, the former receiving three fifths to two thirds and the latter one third to two fifths.

Between 1650 and 1715, increased competition from European colonies in the Caribbean caused Brazil's income from sugar to decline by two thirds. Shortly after their expulsion, the Dutch, assiduous students of every aspect of the sugar industry in Northeastern Brazil, established large-scale plantations in the Caribbean. Their efficient organization, use of new equipment, extensive financial resources, and favorable geographic position closer to the European markets meant that they could produce well and sell cheaply. France and England imitated the Dutch example in the Caribbean islands. The competition augured badly for Brazil's economy. Brazilian sugar lost most of its European markets. An increasing world supply of sugar lowered the price. By the last quarter of the seventeenth century Brazil's economy was in its doldrums. Despite the wide fluctuations in price and demand, however, sugar remained a major industry. Plunging to new lows in the 1760s and 1770s, the sugar industry revived later in the eighteenth century, when rebellion shook the Caribbean, particularly Haiti, and minimized Brazil's competition in the European market. The consequent rise in sugar prices rekindled Luso-Brazilian interest in the crop, and Brazilians began to look methodically and scientifically at its production and problems. José Joaquim da Cunha de Azeredo Coutinho, a fledgling economist who had studied canon law at Coimbra and had inherited the family sugar plantation near Rio de Janeiro, published a *Memória sôbre o Preço do Açúcar* (Memorial on the Price of Sugar) in 1791 which argued effectively against a proposed tax on sugar. José Caetano Gomes discussed the latest knowledge about sugar production in his *Memória sôbre a Cultura e Productos da Cana do Açúcar* (Memorial on the Cultivation and Products of Sugar Cane) in 1801. Sugar merited the attention: it made up approximately three-fifths of Brazil's exports during the colonial period.

After Caribbean competition had sent the Brazilian sugar economy into a tailspin and while the economic future looked most somber, the bandeirantes discovered gold in Minas Gerais. The cry of *gold,* in 1695, reverberated throughout the empire. People with visions of El Dorado dancing before them descended upon the mines from every direction. A chronicler of the period reported: "Every year great numbers of Portuguese and foreigners come in the fleets bound for the mines. From the cities, villages, inlets, and hinterland of Brazil there go whites, browns, blacks, and many Indians who are in the service of the Paulistas. The mixture is of every kind and condition of person: men and women, young and old, rich and poor, nobles and commoners, laymen, priests, and monks of all orders, many of whom have neither convent nor chapter in Brazil."[8]

8. João Antonio Andreoni (André João Antonil), *Cultura e Opulência do Brazil* (São Paulo, 1967), p. 264.

Rowdy, raucous lawlessness characterized the mining camps. Boom mining-towns sprang up overnight. From practically zero in 1695, the population of Minas Gerais (the General Mines) zoomed to 30,000 by 1709 and reached a half-million by the end of the century. The increase of population and importance of the southeastern interior prompted the government to create the captaincy of São Paulo and Minas Gerais in 1710. Minas Gerais became a separate captaincy in 1720. In the beginning most energy went into the search for gold. Little thought was given to agriculture, with the result that food was both scarce and expensive, particularly during the first decade of the rush when famine threatened in 1697–1698 and again in 1700–1701. When food was available it brought 25 to 50 times the price it commanded along the coast. It took many decades before the food supply assumed any aspect resembling normal.

For the task before them, the Luso-Brazilians possessed scant mining knowledge. They lagged far behind the Spaniards in mining techniques. The prospectors sought out the alluvial gold in riverbeds or secondarily they worked the riverbanks and shallow deposits in the neighboring hillsides. There was some subterranean mining, but it was not common. With the price of slaves rising, the miners had few excess funds to spend on mining equipment and would not have known how to use it had they been able to buy it. The government in Lisbon enacted a mining code in 1702 but failed to recruit and dispatch any mining experts to the interior of Brazil to bring a modicum of order and efficiency to the careless miners. The government was not so tardy about collecting the "royal fifth." A tax of 20 percent of the gold mined had to be paid to the Crown. The government erected a complicated bureaucratic apparatus to insure that the fifth was paid and to eliminate any smuggling, but no matter how elaborate the precautions they never succeeded in outwitting the crafty miners who made fine arts of smuggling and of dodging taxes.

The mania for gold propelled the bandeirantes farther west. In 1718 they discovered gold in Cuiabá, Mato Grosso, a seven months' river journey from São Paulo. The diggings were shallow there, and they were exhausted more rapidly than those in Minas Gerais, but that did not prevent a rush into Mato Grosso to exploit the new finds. By 1726, Cuiabá had burgeoned into a town of 7,000, of whom 2,600 were slaves. In 1725, Goiás witnessed the discovery of gold and the familiar pattern of rush and boom ensued. In recognition of the development of those western areas, the Crown created the captaincy of Goiás in 1744 and of Mato Grosso in 1748.

In the midst of such euphoria some prospectors found diamonds, first reported to Lisbon in 1729, in a section of Minas Gerais lacking in gold deposits. The government immediately isolated and thereafter rigorously regulated the diamond district, centered around Tijuco (Diamantina), to protect the small and easily satiated market. Later, other more limited finds were made in São Paulo, Bahia, and Goiás. In 1771, Pombal put the mines directly under the Crown's control in order to eliminate smuggling and maintain high prices. An estimate of the total production of diamonds during the century after their discovery places the figure in excess of three million carats. As in gold mining, smuggling abounded so that such an estimate must be given considerable latitude.

Mineral production increased yearly until 1760, the year of maximum output and the culmination of twenty years of intensive expansion. Throughout the eighteenth century approximately two million pounds of gold were produced legally, which meant that Brazil provided approximately 80 percent of the world's gold supply in that century. During the century mining absorbed the attention of both the population and the government. However, despite promise and appearance the mines never provided more than a façade of wealth. The gold and diamonds slipped through the fingers of the Brazilians and Portuguese into the hands of the northern Europeans, particularly the English, who sold manufactured goods to Portugal. In truth agriculture probably did more to develop Brazil. The average per capita income from the sugar industry, for example, was considerably higher than that from mining at a corresponding stage.

As was inevitable in the hectic boom of mining, disappointments and failures predominated. A few struck it rich and in the growing urban centers such as São João del-Rei, Sabará, Mariana, Tijuco, and Ouro Prêto, extraordinarily handsome civil and religious architecture testified to a measure of prosperity. Ouro Prêto, the capital of Minas Gerais, exemplified the flowering of rococo art in Brazil. Its thirteen churches, various government buildings, graceful fountains, and many two-storied houses, scattered picturesquely over the hills upon which the city rests, still recall the splendor of that city during its decades of greatest activity. In contrast with the rest of the captaincies in the eighteenth century, an essentially urban society characterized Minas Gerais. A small class of exalted governmental officials and successful miners and merchants dressed elegantly, furnished their residences with European luxuries, attended local theatres, and even read and discussed the latest French, English, and Portuguese books. None equaled the opulence of João Fernandes de Oliveira the younger, the millionarie diamond contractor who exercised the government's monopoly from 1759 to 1771. He lavished his wealth on his seductive mulatto mistress Xica da Silva, a former slave. Mansions, country houses, and European finery were not enough for her. He built a large lake to satisfy her whim to see a sailing ship and then constructed a model one. A crew of ten maneuvered it on the inland waters for the amusement and delight of all. It represented the giddy rich at their most gaudy moment.

The consequences of the discovery of gold and diamonds were tremendous, both for the colony and the metropolis. The discovery, coming at the precise moment when Portugal's economic situation was in decline, seemed, on the surface, to have saved the economy. Wealth poured into Lisbon to be misspent on extravagances. In reality, the gold simply paused briefly in Lisbon on its way to London and other European commercial centers. It has been observed with some sagacity and a little exaggeration that Brazilian gold mined by African slaves financed English industrialization. In 1703 Portugal had signed the Treaty of Methuen with England, agreeing to buy British manufactured goods in return for English importation of its wine and agricultural products. The balance of trade quickly tipped in England's favor and Brazilian gold paid the growing deficit. Freely spending Brazilian wealth, the Portuguese let the Industrial Revolution bypass them, and the influx of gold masked for some generations the unfortunate consequences of this position: economic stagnation, thwarted development, and dependence on the English. For Brazil, that situation meant double dependency. The South American colony was not only economically subservient to the mother country in true mercantilist fashion but, since Portugal exercised an ever diminishing degree of economic independence under expanding English domination, also found its destiny increasingly shaped in London rather than in Lisbon.

Throughout the Portuguese empire, the influx of gold drove prices up. The miners evidenced a willingness to pay almost anything for slaves, cattle, agricultural produce, and European products. The Portuguese in the metropolis were hardly more careful. Inflation menaced the imperial economy. In the long run, the gold enriched neither Portugal nor Brazil: to the contrary, it added to their impoverishment.

Gold also contributed to absolutism in eighteenth-century Portugal. Prior to that century the king, whether it pleased him or not, had to convene the Cortes (Parliament) in order to obtain money. When the Cortes adjourned in 1697, the monarchs did not summon it into session again until the Revolution of 1820 led to its convocation. The monarchs had no reason to request money since the royal fifth from the mines kept the exchequer properly filled. Gold thus contributed to despotism and prevented five generations of Luso-Brazilians from getting any legislative experience, however limited it might have been.

In Brazil, the discovery shifted the colony's population. Traditionally the inhabitants had clung to the coast, with the region between Bahia and Pernambuco being the most heavily populated. The discovery dislodged significant numbers of coastal dwellers who were enticed into the interior by dreams of wealth. The heady news of gold strikes also encouraged immigration from the motherland directly to the interior. Slaves were diverted from their usual coastal destinations to the gold fields. The resultant acute labor shortage along the coast aggravated the agricultural decline already well under way. In general, attention shifted from the Northeast to the Southeast and the transference of the colonial capital from Salvador to Rio de Janeiro in 1763 was dramatic proof of that change.

Mining served as an impetus to urbanization. New towns sprang up rapidly wherever gold was found. Commercial activities intensified in the Southeast with the resultant increase of the bourgeois class. More government officials arrived to oversee the minting, protection, and shipment of the gold and diamonds. Whereas in the seventeenth century only 4 cities and 37 towns were founded, the eighteenth century witnessed the creation of 3 cities and 118 towns.

The rising importance of gold exports significantly altered the carefully balanced relationship between the mazombos and the Portuguese by divesting the Brazilians of some of the local economic autonomy they had enjoyed, an ending of benign neglect if nothing else. As exemplified in the sugar economy, the mazombo planter elite oversaw the planting of the cane, production of sugar, and preparation of sugar exports, while the Portuguese merchants, maritime interests, and bureaucrats marketed it abroad, a harmonious division of labor profitable to both parties. Such harmony burst before the inundation of gold and diamonds. The crown believed those precious metals and stones to be too valuable to allow the continuation of the division between production and international marketing so well delineated in agriculture. Portuguese adventurers arrived in large numbers to search for gold; soldiers and bureaucrats invaded Brazil to protect the crown's interests and monopolies. In short, the Brazilian elite found itself shoved aside in the gold and diamond rushes. The Portuguese violated regional authority, local prerogatives, and economic interests, much to the disgust of the Brazilians. The collapse of the division of labor and greater intrusion of the Portuguese bureaucracy alienated many of the Brazilian elite and would contribute mightily to the causes leading to Brazil's independence.

After 1760, Brazil again began to stagnate economically. The exception was cotton, a native crop which the colony began to export at about that time. Maranhão was the first region to export it but soon Pernambuco, Bahia, and Rio de Janeiro were also growing it for sale abroad. Cotton production was simpler and required far less investment than sugar. By the end of the eighteenth century a typical cotton plantation employed 50 slaves and produced around 64,000 pounds of unseparated cotton a year. Production reached its peak during the early decades of the nineteenth century when the United States, because of President Jefferson's embargo policy and then because of war with Great Britain, failed to supply the European cotton market, opening a vacuum which Brazil eagerly filled. In those years, cotton accounted for a fifth to a quarter of Brazil's exports.

Tobacco was a third important crop, used widely for trade with Africa and, after the Dutch popularized its use, with Europe. In fact, the fine quality of the Brazilian leaf made it sought after even in distant Asia. Although its cultivation spread from Sergipe to São Paulo, Bahia was the center of tobacco production. The crop had a social as well as an economic significance: it could be grown profitably on small farms. No elaborate equipment was required, just a shed to cure the leaf, and few slaves were needed. Here then was a lucrative crop which the less substantial farmers could raise for export.

To a more limited extent, cacao, rice, and indigo were also produced for export. For home consumption, the farmers planted wheat, beans, potatoes, a variety of vegetables and fruits. Indigenous foods such as corn, the sweet potato, manioc, palmitos, the Brazilian banana, cajú, the pineapple, and myriad other domestic fruits were available in the marketplaces. They contributed some variety to the local diet but did not figure significantly in overseas commerce.

One other economic activity, cattle raising, exercised an influence over the growth of Brazil which far transcended the economic sphere. Martim Afonso de Sousa introduced cattle into Brazil between 1531 and 1533, and Tomé de Sousa brought more in 1549. They arrived regularly thereafter. In an approving letter dated 1557, Father Nóbrega noted, "At the end of July a ship arrived here from Portugal loaded with cattle." The earliest cattle centers were São Vicente, Bahia, and Pernambuco. Cattle ranches accounted to a large extent for the settlement of the lengthy coast between Bahia and Pernambuco during the last half of the sixteenth century.

In a certain sense, the cattle industry grew as a response to the needs of the sugar industry. In the third quarter of the sixteenth century, the sugar plantations and the cattle ranches occupied much the same territory. The meat provided an important source of food for the plantations with their relatively large numbers of workers. The oxen served as draft animals to haul firewood, so essential for the processing of sugar cane. More often than not they also turned the grinders in the sugar mills. They were equally indispensable to clear, plant, and harvest the fields. As cattle breeding expanded quickly in the second half of the sixteenth century, the Portuguese government moved to forbid it within ten leagues of the coast in order to protect the precious sugar lands and to reserve them exclusively for cane cultivation. That decision exiled the cattle industry into the interior, where it continued to flourish.

Cattle herds often followed close on the heels of the bandeirantes, moving thus ever farther into the sertão. There the *vaqueiro*, the sinewy cowboy of mixed Indian, African, and European blood, settled and held the frontier. At times he also contributed to its expansion. The vaqueiro was often the first line of defense against the hostile Indians. He battled bitterly and bravely, as his repression of the 1712–1713 Indian uprising in the Piauí cattle country amply illustrated. The vaqueiro either killed the Indians or drove them into the hinterland or, at times, incorporated them into the cattle frontier. Cattle herding was the one task in which the Indians participated with gusto, and they contributed skills and blood to the formation of the vaqueiro. A visitor to the interior of Maranhão described the vaqueiro dressed "in pants and shirt of rough cotton and eating and sleeping on a dried oxen hide spread on the ground," and characterized him as "hospitable, easy-going, and willing to help . . . with a rustic coarseness but sincere and full of good faith."

The constantly expanding cattle industry, notable for its insatiable need for large areas of land, radiated outward into the sertão from Pernambuco, Bahia, and São Vicente. Pernambuco was an exceptionally active nucleus of expansion. The industry penetrated the far South from Minas Gerais and São Paulo, crossing the southern valleys and plains into Paraná and Rio Grande do Sul. In the far South, a second type of cattleman appeared; this was the *gaúcho*, a combination of Spaniard, Portuguese, and Indian. Also an accomplished horseman, he spent long periods of time in the saddle, controlling the herds with his skillful use of the *lasso* and *bolas*. The gaúcho developed a fierce tradition of independence; personal freedom ranked highest among his characteristics. The words of one popular gaucho song declared:

> Who really a gaucho is,
> And a Riograndense as well,
> Loves above all else
> The warm sun of liberty.

In addition to expanding and settling vast stretches of the interior, the cattlemen contributed to colonial unification. The mobile nature of their product meant that they could walk it to market, and this they did on long cattle drives. With herds of 100 to 1,000 head, they ambled north, south, east, or west, wherever the market beckoned. Their long drives from Piauí or Maranhão to Pernambuco, Bahia, or Minas Gerais; from Rio Grande do Sul to São Paulo and Minas Gerais; from Minas Gerais to São Paulo, Rio de Janeiro, or Bahia—opened new communication routes and connected widely dispersed areas. The English merchant-traveler Henry Koster, using one such road when he penetrated inland from Recife in 1809 remarked, "The road we have travelled over is the highway from the sertão, by which the cattle descend from the estates upon the river Açu, and from the plains of this portion of the interior to the markets of Recife; therefore the continued passing of large droves of cattle has beat down the underwood, and made a broad sandy road."[9] Since Maranhão raised large herds of cattle which sold well in Brazil, the cattle industry served as an economic link important for the union of the states of Maranhão and Brazil. Along the most trampled routes, hamlets sprang up near watering holes, river-fording spots, or passes. An entire new business, cattle fattening, developed near the markets. Other businessmen bought and sold cattle. Obviously the industry was much more than regional in scope. Unlike sugar, mining, or other economic pursuits, it operated on a colony-wide basis, linking the sertão with the coast, the North with the South.

Furthermore, the cattle industry was a matrix enfolding the two principal economic activities of the colony: sugar and gold. The cattlemen acted as an economic link uniting two economically and geographically divergent regions. They circulated freely between the sugar and gold producers, selling to one or to the other or to both. The most obvious physical link between the regional economies of the Northeast and the Southeast, which is to say between sugar and gold, was the São Francisco River. It flows from south to north, from the goldfields to the sugar lands. It was also one of the centers of the cattle culture from which cattle moved north and south with equal ease. Gold mining with its heavy demands and enticing payments for food hastened the development of that valley. By the early eighteenth century, it was so well settled that a traveler easily passed along its entire 1,500-mile course by going from house to house, never over a day's journey apart. The chronicler André João Antonil spoke in 1711 of over 500 large ranches in the vicinity of the São Francisco. The demands of the miners also gave impetus to cattle and mule raising in the South. For generations those animals had sold at minimum prices. After 1695, prices rose spectacularly. Drives northward became regular events. During the eighteenth century at the fair of Sorocaba in São

9. Henry Koster, *Travels in Brazil* (Carbondale, Illinois, 1966), p. 28.

Paulo over 200,000 head of cattle from the South were sold biennially. The plodding feet of thousands of cattle and mules broke down the barriers between the far South and the rest of Brazil to facilitate its integration into the colony.

Cattle ranches varied in size. None, of course, were small, but some of them reached staggering proportions. The unmeasurable ranch of Diaz d'Avila by all accounts surpassed most European states in size. Begun in the late sixteenth century in northern Bahia, it centered on the São Francisco and extended endlessly into the sertão. The first step in the establishment of a ranch was to build a house for the rancher and corrals to break the cattle and keep them tame. Around the rancher's house, gardens were laid out and fields cultivated to provide food for the owner, his cowboys and his other workers. When necessary, the rancher ordered the land burned free of trees, bushes, or other growth to create pastures for the cattle. Not even the smallest ranch began with less than 200 or 300 head of cattle. The rancher strove to keep a herd of between 1,000 and 2,000 cattle. In addition, he needed horses to help round up the cattle and for the drives. A small ranch could get by with 25 or 30 horses, but a well-run ranch required between 50 and 60.

The ranches for the most part maintained the neofeudalistic atmosphere characteristic of the coastal plantations. The owners when at all prosperous had the power, prestige, and wealth to qualify for the ranks of the colonial aristocracy. Even more isolated from the centers of colonial government than their coastal plantation counterparts, they more often than not exercised complete authority over their subordinates. Still, in direct contrast to the coastal situation, the cattle industry could and often did provide some variance from the more rigid hierarchical system characteristic of the sugar industry. Some scholars choose to emphasize certain democratic features at work or latent in cattle raising. It would seem that often the ranch owners were closer to their workers, who were relatively few in number, and on occasion even worked right along with them, sharing the monotony of the long drive, the hazards of branding the cattle, or the diet of meat and milk (or maté in the south). Slavery was not a widespread institution in the cattlelands. As a means of payment to his vaqueiros, the rancher customarily shared the newborn calves with them. Every four or five years, the cowboys were entitled to take one out of every four newly born calves. In that way it was possible for the ambitious vaqueiro to start his own herd. Since the industry required little investment—no special equipment or machinery, no barns, no silos—some of the cowboys were able to move into the entrepreneurial class. Thus from one point of view a certain—if in practice limited—social and economic mobility was probably more evident in the cattle industry than in any other of the colony's economic activities.

The cattle industry was far more important in the long run than the short. It provided essential support for other economic sectors but contributed only slightly to colonial exports. No meat was exported. Hides were exported as wrapping for tobacco rolls or maté, or were shipped in separate consignments to shoe manufacturers in Europe. The total income from those exports was insignificant in comparison with the earnings of sugar, gold, cotton, and tobacco.

Despite wide fluctuations, the Brazilian economy grew and its trade expanded. Belém, São Luís, Recife, Bahia, and Rio de Janeiro—particularly the last three—were the principal ports through which passed increasing amounts of goods. Spanish influence in the 1580–1640 period restricted and regulated trade and brought an end to the more liberal commercial policies permitted by the Portuguese Crown under the Aviz kings. For example, to reinforce a 1591 decree, a law of March 18, 1606 restricted Brazilian trade to Portugal. Thereafter, most of European trade was funneled through Portuguese ports, although contraband trade was common. Direct trade with Africa flourished, and coastal trade thrived. The excellent port of Salvador illustrated the bustling colonial commerce. By the close of the eighteenth century, Salvador had well-plied routes to and from Europe and Africa and along the nearly 4,000-mile coast. An average of 50 ships a year crossed between Salvador and Oporto and Lisbon bringing European and Asian manufactured goods, wine, flour, codfish, butter, cheese, and salt to Brazil and carrying sugar, spirits, cotton, tobacco, coffee, woods, gums, balsams, and medicinal roots to the Old World. From Africa ships discharged slaves, wax, and gold dust in exchange for alcohol, tobacco, and coarse, printed textiles from Portugal. Small coastal trading vessels, averaging about 250 tons, filled the harbor. Salvador traded extensively with the south, particularly the Plata region, sending sugar, rum, earthenware, and European goods in exchange for silver, jerked beef, and hides. An Englishman who was witness to the Bahian trade in 1803 registered astonishment at the activity:

> The trade carried on in the immediate confines of the bay, of which a great part is inland, is astonishing. There are full eight-hundred launches and sumacks of different sizes, daily bringing their tribute of commerce to the capital: tobacco, cotton, and various drugs from Cachoeira; the greatest assortment of common earthenware from Iaguaripe; rum and whale-oil from Itaparica; timber from the province of Ilheus; farinha and salt fish from Porto Seguro; cotton and maise from the rivers Real and São Francisco; and sugar, firewood, and vegetables from all quarters. A degree of wealth, unknown in Europe, is thus put in circulation.[10]

Little wonder then that Portugal tried to monopolize colonial commerce.

Portugal proved to be tardy and relaxed in codifying its imperial mercantile policy, which took shape more by chance than by design. It hoped to obtain from Brazil a variety of products which could not be produced at home and to sell the surpluses to other European nations. The object, of course, was to maintain exports in excess of imports, the desired "commercial balance." In all ways, Brazil was expected to be a source of wealth to the metropolis. Royal officials looked upon the colony as a great "milch cow," which could be exploited for the benefit of the Crown, the metropolis, and—not least of all—the bureaucrats sent to the New World. As Governor Silva Gama of Rio Grande do Sul unabashedly expressed it, "Nothing interests me more than the

10. Thomas Lindley, *Narrative of a Voyage to Brazil* (London, 1805), p. 261.

fiscal matters of the Royal Treasury. To save on expenses as much as possible, diligently to collect all moneys owing to the Crown without undue harm to its subjects, and to devise new ways of increasing its revenue are the objects of my constant zeal."[11] The attitude of many officials remained much like that throughout the colonial period: they sought to enrich the metropolis through exploitation and taxation of the colony. Also, not a few of them sought to earn their fortunes during their tropical exile in order to return to Portugal and live well.

Portugal's mercantilist policies took a variety of forms over the centuries. One method, employed in an effort to monopolize all the Brazilian trade, was the convoy system. This provided for annual fleets, protected by men of war, to and from Brazil. The highly decentralized Portuguese trade patterns—so unlike those of its Iberian neighbor—and a shortage of both merchant ships and war ships reduced that effort to a few halfhearted attempts sporadically made over two-and-a-half centuries. In practice, foreigners blatantly conducted a profitable contraband trade with Brazil.

The economic companies, inspired by the Dutch and English India companies, fared little better than the convoy system. The Crown licensed four companies: *Companhia do Brasil* (founded in 1649, it was reformed in 1663 and put under government control until its abolition in 1721), *Companhia do Maranhão* (1678–1684), *Companhia Geral do Grão Pará e Maranhão* (1755–1778), and *Companhia de Pernambuco e Paraíba* (1759–1779). The first company played a decisive political-military role: its warships blockaded Recife in the early 1650s and thereby contributed to the final Luso-Brazilian victory over the Dutch. In general, however, the companies were unpopular with both the residents of Brazil and the Portuguese merchants. The Brazilians criticized them for abusing their monopolies and raising prices with impunity. The Portuguese merchants disapproved of the monopolies which eliminated them from much trade, and accused

11. Quoted in Caio Prado, *The Colonial Background of Modern Brazil* (Berkeley, California, 1967), p. 394.

the companies of charging outlandish freight rates. All sides bombarded the companies with charges of inefficiency. Historians have tended to be critical of the companies. It would seem that the government's good intentions, of using the monopolistic companies to accelerate the colony's economic development, went unrealized with the possible exception of the *Companhia Geral do Grão Pará e Maranhão*, one of Pombal's creations. The Companhia Geral brought both capital and labor to a region chronically short of both and significantly increased both rice and cotton production there.

The government made various attempts to control the economy. Monopolies flourished. Brazilwood, salt, tobacco, slaves, diamonds, to mention a few, felt at one time or another the hand of monopolistic bureaucracy. Taxes, many and varied, put special strains on the economy. There were taxes on agricultural, mineral, and pastoral products, known as the *dízimo*, or tithe, and the *quinto*, or fifth, levied on mineral resources. Until the middle of the seventeenth century, the major source of income for the Crown was the tithe on sugar. After the discovery of gold, the quinto became the single major contributor to the treasury. The Crown taxed both the internal and the external commerce of its colony. Customs houses in the principal ports collected the duty on overseas trade. Stations at the most important river crossings and along the most frequented roads exacted tolls and taxed internal trade. The *entradas,* duties on merchandise, slaves, and cattle entering Minas Gerais, were examples of a special type of tax exacted by the royal government. The Brazilians paid a series of excise taxes on locally produced and imported products, such as wines, tobacco, and salt, which could be classified as luxuries. There were also a variety of legal fees, quitrents on crown property, and "voluntary contributions" which further enriched the royal coffers. Indeed, the complete list of taxes, duties, and fees would be a long one. One foreign observer remarked in 1809 "Taxes are laid where they fall heavy upon the lower classes, and none are levied where they could well be borne."[12] The

12. Koster, *Travels in Brazil*, p. 20.

Crown did not always collect those taxes itself. Instead, it often used the Roman system of tax-farming and awarded a monopoly contract for a stipulated period, usually three years, in exchange for a fixed payment to the royal treasury.

Fearful that the colony might relax its efforts to produce the raw products most in demand in Europe, the royal officials kept a sharp eye peeled for unnecessary diversification of the economy. In the best mercantilistic manner, Brazil could produce nothing which Portugal already produced or could furnish. For example, in 1590 grape cultivation was forbidden because Portugal already produced a surplus of wines. With the exception of shipbuilding and sugar processing, the Crown disapproved of any manufacturing in Brazil. Fear that an incipient industry might develop to the detriment of Portugal's mercantilist goals called for a vexing variety of decrees, from that of 1578 forbidding the blacksmith Bartolomeu Fernandes of São Vicente to teach his profession, to that of 1785 prohibiting all manufacturing in Portuguese America. On the other hand, the Crown occasionally encouraged the production of new crops which would find a ready market in the metropolis or Europe. Though meeting with frequent frustrations, the Marques de Lavradio, viceroy from 1769–1779, diversified the economy slightly by promoting the production of indigo, rice, and wheat. Lack of imagination on the part of the Crown, the merchants (both in Portugal and America), and the local farmers probably did more to hinder economic diversification and growth than did stern mercantile decrees.

The Portuguese official who did most to codify and implement mercantilist policy was Pombal. He fully realized that Portugal's prosperity depended on the well-being of Brazil. A Brazil flourishing economically would provide a sound basis for Portugal's felicity. Under Physiocrat influence, he thought to survey scientifically the potential of Brazil as the basis for more exploitation. He hoped to strengthen, even diversify the economy.

The Brazilians did not docilely accept all the burdensome restrictions placed on them, and their protests reached Lisbon regularly. In particular, the municipal council chambers echoed with stormy debates, the results of which crossed the ocean as pleas or petitions to the monarch for one or another change. As the nineteenth century opened, educated *mazombos* like Azeredo Coutinho, João Rodrigues de Brito, and José da Silva Lisboa wrote eloquent appeals for a modification of the mercantilist policy. But the Brazilians also took action. A number of economic conflicts erupted into riot or rebellion which rent the otherwise tranquil air of the colony. The royal policies restricting or prohibiting Indian slavery occasioned violence in São Luís, Bahia, Rio de Janeiro, and São Paulo, where the colonists demonstrated in the streets and more than once threatened the Jesuits. In Maranhão, in 1684, Manuel Beckman, a wealthy landowner, led an armed revolt to protest against the detested *Companhia do Maranhão* and the government's Indian policy. After seizing control of the government of the state of Maranhão, he abolished the monopoly of the Company and expelled the Jesuits. The following year a new governor arrived who captured, tried, and hanged Beckman. Nonetheless, the Crown eventually did abolish the monopolistic Company.

Minas Gerais was a hotbed of disturbances in the eighteenth century. As the mining rush got under way, the Paulistas with their Indian slaves resented the arrival of the Portuguese or coastal prospectors with their African slaves. The Paulistas regarded the "foreigners" or "outsiders" as interlopers on their gold claims and derisively referred to all of them as *"emboabas."* Rivalry between the leaders of the two factions erupted in late 1708 into open warfare, which ended with the defeat of the Paulistas the following year. Trouble simmered in the mining region and in 1720 a popular rebellion against improved measures of taxation broke out under the leadership of Felipe dos Santos. The colonial government quickly repressed it. The mundane subject of delinquent taxes and rumors of attempts to collect them sparked some romantic poets of Minas Gerais, in alliance with a few planters, merchants, and clergymen, to plot in the name of independence. The plans came to naught in 1789 when the *Inconfidência,* as it has since been known in history, was exposed to the governor, who took swift action. The subsequent execution of the leader, Joaquim José da Silva Xavier, more picturesquely known by an epithet describing his profession as *Tirandentes*, or "the Toothpuller," created a martyr for Brazilian independence.

Meanwhile, in the Northeast, the rural aristocracy with its seat in Olinda felt challenged by the nearby growing commercial center of Recife, a bustling port of some eight thousand inhabitants by the opening of the eighteenth century. Most of the merchant class was Portuguese and more often than not those "mascates" (a pejorative term meaning "peddlers" which the Brazilians liberally employed) held the planters in debt. One contemporary anonymous writer complained, "They [the merchants] try only to get as much profit as possible in order to enrich themselves no matter what the cost to others, and they do not hesitate to extend credit one year to the planters so that the next they can demand all the income and profits of the sugar mills."[13] The planters consequently resented the power of the merchants, accusing them of seeking "to destroy all that is noble." They sought to redeem themselves through direct trade with English and Dutch ships, a commercial activity forbidden by Portuguese mercantilist policy and naturally opposed by the mascates. When the king elevated Recife to the rank of a city in 1710 and thus freed it from the political control of Olinda, the planters reacted by attacking and capturing the port. The following year the mascates rebelled against the forceful rule of the sugar aristocracy. A new governor dispatched from Lisbon to Pernambuco settled the War of the Mascates at the end of 1711 with a generous pardon for everyone. The sharp division between the Brazilian sugar aristocracy and the immigrant Portuguese commercial bourgeoisie lingered on for nearly two centuries to precipitate periodical rural-urban clashes. The mascates served as a constant catalyst. At first, they gave rise to or strengthened Brazilian nativism, and later Brazilian nationalism. Indeed, even as early as the 1710–1711

---

13. "Guerra civil ou sedições de Pernambuco," *Revista do Instituto Histórico e Geográfico Brasileiro*, 16 (1853), p. 7.

disturbance, some planters in their hostile reaction to the outsiders mentioned vaguely the possibility of creating some independent republic modeled on that of Venice.

Economic stagnation in the last third of the eighteenth century intensified the discontent already prevalent in Brazil. Exports declined. The gold fields had been exhausted and Portuguese technology was not sufficient to exploit the lodes which lay more deeply buried. Sugar sales were slow. Falling export revenues accompanied by a growing population meant that per capita income diminished. The only relief—temporary as it might have been—was provided by events far from Brazil over which it had neither control nor influence. The revolutionary war in the thirteen English colonies disrupted customary trade between Europe and North America, offering Brazil, particularly Maranhão, the opportunity to sell rice and cotton in European markets usually dominated by North America. The slave revolt in Haiti beginning in 1791 destroyed the source of much of Europe's sugar supply. The amount and value of Brazil's sugar exports grew proportionately. The temporary recovery and prosperity simply underlined the vulnerability of Brazil's economy. Brazil enjoyed another period of prosperity before lapsing back into decline and lethargy in its never-ending cycle of sharp economic fluctuations.

After reviewing colonial Brazil's economy, two major and depressing conclusions emerge. On the one hand, it fostered internal social inequity, while, on the other, it was a victim of external policies which implanted and nurtured dependency. The plantation economy required substantial wealth or access to capital. Thus, only a few could participate in it and benefit from it, that is the privileged with funds to invest. After receiving their sesmarias, they bought African slaves or recruited labor from the ranks of the poor and unskilled. They invested in sugar mills, warehouses, processing equipment, or whatever the plantation required to make it productive and profitable. The predominance of such a plantation economy accentuated the social, economic, and political differences between masters and slaves, patriarchs and laborers and perpetuated class distinctions to the extent of even having caste implications. Very few could aspire to upward mobility. The slaves or hired hands could hardly hope to become plantation owners, for even if they might acquire land the cost outlay for equipment was prohibitive. More likely the option of subsistence farming was open to them—manumitted blacks or free laborers—if they could escape the labor control mechanisms. Peasants and small farmers did exist; they certainly contributed to the local or regional economies; but they rarely crossed the lines which separated them from the planters who enjoyed wealth, preferment, and power. The great gap between the privileged few and the huge humble majority was a fact of life in colonial Brazil which transcended economics to have profound social and politiclal consequences as well.

Dependency meant that the Brazilian economic well-being, or lack of it, resulted from the consequences of decisions made far distant from South America, more often than not in Lisbon but increasingly in London as the Portuguese themselves became more dependent on the English. The dynamic sector of the Brazilian economy was exports and subject to the fluctuations of European markets over which the Brazilians exercised no control. The emphasis on a single export increased Brazil's economic vulnerability and multiplied the effects of capricious demand and/or of successful competition. The structures and dynamics of the Portuguese empire worked to the economic detriment of Brazil by imposing insidious patterns of economic dependency. The cycle of economic flunctuations was but one obvious symptom of that dependency.

Political Evolution

Brazil constituted only one portion, albeit an immense one, of the global Portuguese empire. For three centuries, the New World colony evolved within that larger framework in which the various components interacted. Portuguese America inherited many practices perfected elsewhere in the empire and likewise it contributed to the development of other parts of the empire; in particular it was closely associated with Angola. As early as the end of the sixteenth century, Brazil was emerging as Portugal's most valuable overseas possession. The mounting sugar profits and the subsequent discovery of gold confirmed its primary position. Still, until the royal house of Braganza moved its court from Lisbon to Rio de Janeiro in 1807, Brazil was governed by no special laws or institutions which would have distinguished it as a separate, distinct, or privileged entity within the larger empire.

Reviewing colonial Brazil's political evolution—its process of continuous advance from a simple to a complex state—over the course of three centuries, two general characteristics stand out. First, governmental control over Brazil grew stronger throughout the period, even though that process might have been erratic at times. By 1807, the king, his viceroy, and his governors exercised more power more effectively than at any time previously. Secondly, the political status of Brazil slowly improved throughout the course of three centuries. A central government under a governor-general, the personal representative of the king, began to exercise a modicum of authority in 1549 to bring some order and justice to the unhappy and generally ineffective rule of the donees in the captaincies. In 1646, the monarch elevated Brazil to the status of a principality, and thereafter the heir to the throne was known as the Prince of Brazil. After 1720, all the chiefs of government of Brazil bore the title of "Viceroy." Although no document exists to show the exact date of its elevation, Brazil was in effect a viceroyalty thereafter. Finally, Prince-Regent João raised Brazil to the status of a kingdom in 1815, thus, at least in theory, putting it on an equal footing with Portugal.

The concept of government prevalent during the centuries when Portugal possessed Brazil differed markedly from that of our own time. An astute student of the Brazilian past, Caio Prado, referred to the Portuguese government as "an undivided whole." By this, he meant that few of the subtleties of political science with which we must reckon today had yet come into being. There was neither division of power, nor any distinction between branches of government. Church and State were practically one. All power rested in the hands of the monarch, who was the state. He made, executed, and judged the laws. On the one hand, he formulated the general concepts which governed the empire, and on the other he decreed a staggering array of minutely detailed laws such as those which set the price of meat in a marketplace in India or those which ordered the type of clothing Brazilian Indians should wear. He protected and governed the Church within his vast domains. Indeed, he ruled by divine right. The one overpowering constant, then, in imperial government was the monarch. The houses of Burgundy and Aviz centralized and strengthened royal power at the expense of the nobility and the Church. The Braganzas, heirs to that trend and witness to the example set by the neighboring Hapsburgs, who had ruled Portugal for sixty years, exercised their jurisdiction and prerogatives as the supreme heads of the empire. Clearly the king was the unquestioned authority from which all power emanated. He spoke the final word.

To rule a vast and dispersed empire, however, required administrative assistance, and over the centuries a number of governmental organs emerged to fill that need. For a long time those bodies handled metropolitan and overseas matters in much the same way and without distinguishing between the two. The Portuguese law codes were the *Ordenações Afonsinas*, 1486–1514; the *Ordenações Manuelinas*, 1514–1603; and the *Código Filipino* of 1603, in full use in Brazil until 1823, and in partial use until 1917, when the Brazilian Civil Code was enacted. Though frequently amended and supplemented, they uniformly governed the entire empire regardless of their applicability or lack of it. The monarch viewed sophistically—or, one might argue, naively—the unity of the Portuguese empire. Scattered and varied it might be but uniformity persisted. To an impressive degree, the same officials moved uninhibitedly from one continent to another, thereby contributing to the unity, uniformity, and universality of the empire. The examples of those mobile administrators are many. The career of Antônio de Albuqerque Coelho de Carvalho was not exceptional. He was governor of Maranhão, 1690–1701; governor of Rio de Janeiro, São Paulo, and Minas Gerais, 1709–1713; and governor of Angola, 1722–1725. Naturally as the empire expanded some administrative specialization had to develop; only then did home and ultramarine affairs occasionally fall to bureaus treating specifically one or the other. Still, the Crown never authorized a special body to handle Brazilian matters exclusively. Only in some tax and Indian matters did the South American colony ever receive the individual attention its wealth and importance merited. Local administrators did become adept, however, in adapting the general imperial codes and fiats to suit the local scene. They had to. The third governor-general, Mem de Sá, remarked to the king, "This land ought not and cannot be ruled by the laws and customs of Portugal; if Your Highness was not quick to pardon it would be difficult to colonize Brazil."[14] Such extralegal liberties were tolerated because of the great distance separating king and colony and, not infrequently, because of absolute necessity.

For about two centuries, colonial and, therefore, Brazilian affairs were handled through a royal secretary or a secretary of state who, after 1736, bore the title of "Minister of Navy and Overseas." Men of this rank, selected because of loyal and often meritorious service, enjoyed unqualified royal confidence. They had direct access to the king's ear and were, of course, responsible only to him. They were assisted, in turn, by a variety of administrative organs which in the practice of the age excercised a mélange of consultative, executive, judicial, and fiscal functions. One of the most important of those bodies was the Overseas Council (*Conselho Ultramarino*) created by João IV in 1642. It was the evolutionary result of considerable experience, numbering among its distinguished predecessors the India Board (*Casa da India*) and the Council for India and Overseas Conquests (*Conselho da India e Conquistas Ultramarinas*). The latter,

14. "Carta a el-rei de 31 de março de 1560," *Anais da Biblioteca Nacional*, 27 (1906), p. 228.

established in 1604, was particularly significant in Portuguese administrative history because it separated for the first time the administration of overseas affairs from those of the metropolis. The president, secretary, and three councillors of the Overseas Council usually had served in the colonies, and during its history its members included many who had resided in Brazil. The Council divided itself into standing committees to treat various military, administrative, judicial, and ecclesiastical matters. Its primary duty, however, was to advise the king. When, as frequently happened, he requested the advice, the Council's response was known as a *consulta de serviço real*. Otherwise, when the Council advised him on its own initiative, it performed a *consulta de partes*. The Overseas Council was more concerned with commercial matters than its predecessors had been. Its authority in such matters grew accordingly.

Other governmental organs continued to have dual metropolitan and colonial responsibilities. The Treasury Council (*Conselho da Fazenda*) created in 1591 to replace the Treasury Supervisors (*Vedores da Fazenda*) administered public finances and the treasury. The Board of Conscience and Religious Orders (*Mesa da Consciência e Ordens*) established in 1532 by João III advised the Crown on ecclesiastical and Indian matters. After 1551, the Board began to administer the lands and revenues belonging to Portugal's three military orders (Santiago, Aviz, and Cristo). Finally, the *Casa da Suplicação* served as a supreme court for many colonial judicial disputes. Together these bodies formed the principal bureaucratic apparatus which enabled the monarch to rule his scattered overseas domains. Their experience and expertise made that rule more effective—at least in theory.

In Brazil there were representatives of the royal government to administer that colony. At the apex stood the viceroy, "the shadow of the king." When it became evident that the donatory system was failing the king dispatched a governor-general to centralize control of the colony. In particular, the latter saw to it that all taxes were properly collected, that the king's justice was enforced, and that the colony was militarily prepared to repel interlopers. Those governors-general were effective or ineffective as officials largely according to their own strengths and weaknesses. Those who were vigorous dominated the colony. Those who were weak found themselves almost unable to control the capital city, their powers eroded by ambitious bishops, captains-general, municipal councils, and important court justices. Between 1640 and 1718, three of the chiefs of state of Brazil, because of their high noble rank, bore the title of "Viceroy." After 1720, all bore that title. By that time their duties were more or less well defined by customs and law. In theory—and one must continually emphasize the frequent variance in these matters between theory and practice—the viceroys of the eighteenth century as a group were stronger and more effective administrators than their predecessors, with, of course, many exceptions taken into account. Outstanding were the Conde de Sabugosa (1720–1735), the Marquês de Lavradio (1769–1779), and Luís de Vasconcelos e Sousa (1779–1790). The king's chief representative in Brazil served for an average term of six and one-half years in the sixteenth century, three and one-half years in the seventeenth century, and slightly less than six years in the eighteenth century. Most of them were professional soldiers and members of the nobility.

The central government was located in Salvador da Bahia until 1763. By the early eighteenth century the capital boasted of a population of over 100,000, making it, after Lisbon, the second city of the empire. The presence of the viceregal government as well as the capital's location midway along the Brazilian coast and confronting Africa lent considerable military importance to Salvador. Stationed there were one artillery and two infantry regiments, although they were seldom maintained at full strength. The government dispatched soldiers from Salvador to replenish garrisons as far away as Colônia do Sacramento, or even Africa and Asia. In the city also resided the only archbishop in Portuguese America. The capital, furthermore, was a bustling port, the entrepôt of trade with Africa and Europe. Majestically situated on the ample All Saints Bay, the city stood on two levels: pressed between the bay and a sharp escarpment were the docks, warehouses, shipyards, and business houses; high above, crowning the escarpment, were the governmental buildings, homes of the wealthy, and some of the finest religious buildings in the Western Hemisphere. Two immense public plazas graced the upper city. Surrounding one were the impressive Viceregal Palace, the Treasury, the building housing the municipal council and the jail, and the High Court. The magnificent College of the Jesuits dominated the other. One of the native sons, the historian Sebastião da Rocha Pita, rhapsodized about the capital and its environs: "The sky which covers it is the gayest; the stars which illuminate it, the clearest; the climate which envelops it, the most benevolent; the airs which refresh it, the purest; the fountains which water it, the most crystalline; and the fields which embellish it, the most pleasant; it possesses delightful plants, leafy trees, healthy fruits, and temperate seasons. . . ."[15] Despite such eloquent testimony, the seat of the viceroyalty moved in 1763 from Salvador to Rio de Janeiro, another excellent port.

The Southeast had acquired new economic importance because of both mining and greater agricultural exploitation. Rio de Janeiro offered the viceroy, for example, a closer scrutiny over the routes to and from Minas Gerais. At the same time the economic importance of the Northeast diminished. Furthermore, after the Treaty of Taborda in 1654, foreign threats to the Northeast were insignificant. The West Indies thereafter attracted the attention of the European maritime powers. Portugal faced a new challenge in the far south of Brazil. Increasing tension with Spain after the founding of the Colônia do Sacramento in 1680 necessitated greater attention to and protection of claims in the Platine region. Rio de Janeiro was chosen to be the new capital, then, because in the eighteenth century it was geographically closer to this military threat, as well as to the economic activities of the colony. The city had been growing steadily, and the discovery of gold in the hinterlands and the arrival of the viceregal court accelerated that growth. It, too, could boast of imposing civil and religious architecture. Rio de Janeiro became a

15. *História da América Portuguesa* (Bahia, 1878), p. 50.

focal point for colonial wealth where a small, affluent class lived comfortably. A mid-eighteenth-century visitor even described a certain elegance in the streets:

People of fashion here always dress in a very creditable and polite manner. The women never appear abroad, but with a veil of black taffeta, which is fastened behind to their waist, and drawn up over their heads, so as to leave only one eye exposed; thus they see everything, without being themselves distinguished. In their houses they affect to be dressed extremely rich. The gentry here are usually carried in a kind of chair, ornamented in a very grand manner; but instead of two poles, as in Europe, they use but one, to which the chair is suspended, and thus carried upon negroes' shoulders. This vehicle is always followed by at least one or two negro servants, dressed in a fine livery, but bare-footed. A lady is usually attended by four or five negro girls, who, besides a decent clothing, are ornamented with several rows of necklaces, and large gold earrings. If a person is carried in a hammock, he is obliged to lie along it: This hammock is suspended on a Bambou cane, and carried on the shoulders of two negroes. Over it is a curtain, generally of some rich silk, which falls on both sides of the hammock, to keep off the rays of the sun, which are here excessively scorching. Those who are of a lower station and walk on foot, must be poor indeed, if they are not attended by a negro carrying a large umbrella, at least of four feet and a half diameter, which is usually painted green. The governor's state-coach, which might become the governor of Paris, is drawn by four white horses, which, it seems, are always of that colour. Here are also several chariots, and other genteel carriages, all finely ornamented.[16]

As an important leg in the triangular South American-European-African trade and as a staging point for contraband commerce in the Plata, the port throbbed with activity.

The governors-general and viceroys depended on a growing bureaucracy to carry out their primary functions of administering the colony, overseeing its military preparedness, dispensing the king's justice, and enforcing the taxes. Of greatest importance was the High Court (Relação), the first of which was established in Bahia in 1609 under the

16. The Count of St. Malo, A Voyage to Peru (London, 1753), pp. 114–15.

presidency of the governor-general. A second was established in Rio de Janeiro in 1752. Those courts primarily had judicial responsibilities: they functioned as the highest law tribunals in Brazil from which there was limited appeal to the Casa da Suplicação in Lisbon. They reviewed the conduct of all officials at the end of their terms at office and conducted whatever other investigations might be required. Secondarily they served as consultative and administrative organs. When the governor-general absented himself from the capital, the highest member of the court, the chancellor, usually governed in his place. The governor-general often requested the advice of the legally trained judges on a host of judicial and administrative matters. The magistrates who served in Brazil, at least between 1609 and 1759, were highly trained professionals who came from socially middle-rank groups. Between 1653 and 1753, at least ten Brazilian-born magistrates served on the Relação. Like other imperial officials, the magistrates served throughout the vast empire, and there existed a notable exchange of them between West Africa and Brazil. The Relação bore a certain resemblance to the *Audiencias* of Spanish America. Tax matters and the supervision of the treasury fell to the responsibility of another bureau, the Board of Revenue (*Junta da Fazenda*).

The government of the state of Maranhão was similar to that of the state of Brazil, only seemingly less well defined. Nor did the northern state develop the strength of the southern one. It depended even more heavily upon Lisbon. The king appointed a governor-general and a chief justice (*ouvidor*). A slow growth and a scanty population negated the need for a High Court, and none was authorized for Maranhão. In 1737, the capital was transferred from São Luís to Belém, an increasingly active port which for some time had been the effective center of the state. In recognition of the growing importance of the Amazon, the king created in 1755 the captaincy of São José do Rio Negro (the present-day Amazonas), subordinate to the captaincy of Pará. The newly founded town of Barcelos, several hundred miles up the Rio Negro, became the first capital of the subordinate captaincy.

Captaincies were the principal terriorial subdivisions of

the two states. But the Crown regretted entrusting its New World territories to donees. In 1548, starting with Bahia, the monarch set out to reabsorb those hereditary captaincies, giving them the name of royal captaincies. That process was slow and erratic. The Crown purchased some back from their owners; others it simply took over when they were abandoned or left without heirs. Yet at other times reversing its own policies (as so often happened), it awarded new captaincies to private individuals, hoping thus to encourage settlement of distant or neglected regions. Thus policies alternated in a confusing manner over a period of two centuries. At the opening of the seventeenth century, eleven hereditary captaincies existed; ten new ones, five in each state, were created during that century. By the end of the seventeenth century the states of Brazil and Maranhão contained six each.

As representatives and appointees of the king, the governors and captains-general of the principal captaincies and the governors or captains-major of the subordinate captaincies carried out the same responsibilities on a regional scale that the governor-general or the viceroy carried out on the colonial scale. The governor-general was to coordinate, harmonize, and oversee their efforts. Here, as in so many instances, theory and practice diverged. Distance, intrigues, the varying effectiveness of personalities, the vagueness of the law, often meant that the governor-general and later the viceroy exercised little authority over the various governors of the captaincies. In times of crisis, particularly those engendered by the fear of a foreign attack on a coastal city or Spanish expansion in the South, the military authority of the governor-general or viceroy increased. His martial powers may well have been his strongest. Of course aggressive and assertive executives succeeded in extending their authority much further than their more reticent predecessors. Such aggressiveness prompted the chancellor of the High Court of Rio de Janeiro, José Luís França, to comment candidly in a letter written in 1783 to a friend in Lisbon, "The viceroys always try to be independent. . . ." However, more often than not, the lines of communication, seldom passing through the colonial capital, ran from the capital of each captaincy directly to the king. In truth, the governor-general and his later successor the viceroy never exercised the same degree of control or authority as did their counterparts in Spanish America. For that matter, in remote corners of Brazil, the captain-general, governor-general, and king all seemed equally removed and theoretical. Considering the size of the colony, the scant number of small, scattered garrisons, the handful of soldiers, and the few royal officials, almost all of whom resided in a half-dozen coastal cities, the extent of metropolitan control over the colony was nothing short of remarkable. The Crown maintained its authority and control principally through the power of legitimacy. The Brazilians accepted the system, rarely questioned it, and seldom challenged it. When they did question or challenge the system prior to the end of the eighteenth century—for example in the Beckman revolt—they quickly acceded to the forceful imposition of the royal will.

Royal control increased during the eighteenth century. The absolutist tendencies noticeable during the long reign of João V (1706–1750), found their instrument of perfection in the person of the Marquês de Pombal, who ruled through the weak José I, from 1750 to 1777. Portuguese historians contradict one another in their treatment of that powerful prime minister, some praising him as a savior and others damning him as a madman. Brazilian historians have treated him more consistently. They gratefully acknowledge the contributions he made, indirect as some of them might be, to the formation of their country. Indicative of the esteem in which his Brazilian contemporaries held him was the tribute paid him on his death. In May of 1782, Father Joaquim de Santa Ana preached a funeral oration in Salvador praising his justice and patriotism. "The Marquês de Pombal has died, but memory of him will live forever," he affirmed, because "neither the corruption of the times, nor the caprice of fortune" could remove the memory of a "virtuous man."[17]

An ardent nationalist, Pombal hoped to strengthen his

17. "Oração funebre das Exéquias do Marquês de Pombal," by Padre Frei Joaquim de Santa Ana, Monge de S. Bento, May 1782, mss. located in the Museu do Carmo, Salvador, Bahia.

economically moribund country through better and fuller utilization of its colonies, the foremost of which unquestionably was Brazil. To better exploit Portuguese America, he sought to further centralize and standardize its government. He abolished the state of Maranhão in 1772 and incorporated it into the state of Brazil, at least in theory creating, for the first time, a single, unified Portuguese colony in the New World. After the unification of the two states, Pombal encouraged trade between them so that commerce would further cement political integration. Actually the paths the bandeirantes trod through the interior did more to further trade and communication between the areas than did the infrequent and tardy coastal communications. No matter how imperfect the union between the two might have been, it set the psychological tone which helped ensure the future unity of the empire of Brazil. An impatient enemy of the hereditary captaincies, the Prime Minister dissolved the remaining ones and brought them under direct royal control, with the minor exception of Itanhaém, a small private captaincy in the South which lasted until 1791. As a consequence, Brazil in 1800 consisted of the following principal captaincies: Grão Pará, Maranhão, Ceará, Paraíba, Pernambuco, Bahia, Minas Gerais, Goiás, Mato Grosso, Rio de Janeiro, and São Paulo; and the following subordinate captaincies: São José do Rio Negro (Amazonas), Piauí, Rio Grande do Norte, Espírito Santo, Santa Catarina, and Rio Grande de São Pedro (Rio Grande do Sul).

As a further measure to fortify royal authority, Pombal expelled the Company of Jesus from the empire. He had long harbored suspicions that the Jesuits plotted against him and accused that powerful order of challenging the secular government. (Injudiciously they had criticized some of his economic schemes.) An attempt on the king's life provided him with the opportunity he sought to drive the Black Robes from the realm. In 1759, he ordered approximately 600 of them to leave Brazil. Until that time, they had run most of the best schools in Brazil, and colonial education suffered severely after their expulsion. Furthermore, many Indian villages were left unadministered. This situation enabled Pombal to strengthen the government's hand in both education and the care of the Indians. For good or bad, he ended the isolation enforced upon them by the Jesuit villages. By requiring the Indians to speak Portuguese, dress like Europeans, and adopt useful trades and crafts, and by encouraging whites to intermarry with them he attempted to bring them within the Luso-Brazilian community. Many of his ideas were highly impractical. Yet by bridging some of the isolation between the Indian and Luso-Brazilian communities he further unified the colony and modified one of the major differences separating the North from the rest of Brazil. The *aldeia* system, however, by no means disappeared. In 1809, Henry Koster wrote about several of them he knew of in Ceará, one of which he visited and inspected. A priest lived in the former residence of the Jesuits to attend to the spiritual life of the Indians, while a white director oversaw their secular life. Koster noted, "If a proprietor of land is in want of workmen he applies to the director, who agrees for the price at which the daily labor is to be paid, and he commands one of his chief Indians to take so many men, and proceed with them to the estate for which they are hired. The laborers receive the money themselves, and expend it as they please; but the bargains thus made are usually below the regular price of labor."[18] Even the power of Pombal could not eliminate all the exploitation of the Indians.

During the Pombal administration, Rio de Janeiro became the capital of Brazil. That change reflected—as has been noted previously—a greater concern with affairs in the south, where the Prime Minister hoped to settle the boundaries with Spanish America. He favored the principle of *uti possidetis*. Because the Treaty of Madrid violated that principle in the Plata, he worked to annul it; this he accomplished in the Treaty of El Pardo in 1761. Brazilians, of course, have always appreciated Pombal's support of their maximum boundary claims, but their interests affected the Marquês not at all. His interest in a larger Brazil lay in his hope for a richer Brazil, hence a more prosperous Portugal. Always, of

18. *Travels in Brazil*, p. 54.

course, it would be a Brazil subservient to the mother country. For that reason he tried to restrict some of the independence of the municipal governments and, although it is true that those local governments exercised less freedom than they had in their heyday, the seventeenth century, they still continued active and important nuclei of local politics.

The municipal government was the one with which most Brazilians came into contact and the only one in which they participated to any degree. Governing much more than the town and its environs, each municipality extended to meet the boundaries of the next. In sparsely settled Brazil, the municipalities contained hundreds, often thousands, of square miles. European countries seemed dwarfs compared to some of those municipal giants.

The most important institution of local government was the *senado da câmara*, the municipal council. A restricted suffrage of the *homens bons*, which is to say the propertied class, elected two justices of the peace, three aldermen, and a procurator to office every three years. The presiding officer was a *juiz ordinarío* (ordinary judge) if elected by the other councilmen, or a *juiz-de-fora* (outside judge) if sent by the crown. By the end of the seventeenth century, the Crown was appointing a presiding officer in the most important towns and cities. The duties of the council varied. Meeting twice weekly, it meted out local justice, handled routine municipal business and local administration, and passed the necessary laws and regulations. The procurator executed those laws. In cooperation with the Church, the senado helped to oversee local charities. The municipality enjoyed its own sources of income: rents from city property, license fees for tradesmen, taxes on certain foodstuffs, charges for diverse services such as the verification of weights and measures, and fines.

Unlike their Spanish American counterparts, the *cabildo*, the senados exercised considerable independent power. Even after the king's juizes became presidents of the major senados and even after more limitations were placed on the final selection of the council members, they continued to display a remarkable independence. The senado of São Luís during the seventeenth century was particularly ambitious. So often did it summon the governor to appear before it that the king in 1677 ordered it to desist forthwith, reminding the councillors that the governor represented the Crown and could not be ordered around. Even the proximity of the viceroy did not seem to inhibit the activity of the senado although it was under far greater scrutiny. On that point, one of the most powerful and able of the viceroys, the second Marquês de Lavradio, wrote to his successor in 1779, "In the municipal chamber I allowed the President and Aldermen to govern according to their attributes, I meanwhile paying attention to all irregularities, and writing from time to time to the chamber to remind its members of their obligations." Occasionally the senados and governors engaged in power struggles. Such certainly was the case in Paranaguá, Belém, and São Luís. At times the senados dared to challenge the Crown itself. The inauguration of the convoy system in the seventeenth century excited the wrath of the senados of both Bahia and Rio de Janeiro to the point where they defied the king. To protect their interest, the larger cities maintained a representative at the court in Lisbon as a sort of lobbyist.

As Brazil's foremost historian of the colonial period, João Capistrano de Abreu has pointed out, the senado frequently served as an arena—the first one—for the struggles between the *mazombos,* the whites born in Brazil, and the *renóis,* the whites born in Portugal. The Portuguese officials, occupying all levels of government except the municipal, enforced the universal law of the empire. Their point of view was global. They saw Brazil as one part of a larger empire which existed for the grandeur of Portugal. The mazombos sitting on the municipal councils cared only for the local scene; their vision was restricted. It was, in short, Brazilian. They wanted to enforce those aspects of the laws beneficial to them, to their community, and, to a lesser extent, to Brazil. Those different perspectives gave rise to repeated clashes in which the mazombos did not always give ground to the renóis. In the seventeenth century, the senados repeatedly expelled Jesuits, judges, and even governors whom they considered unpopular or unsympathetic to local causes or situations. One of the bitterest struggles was over the Indians. The senados of Belém, São Luis, Rio de Janeior, and São Paulo, to mention only the most vitriolic, were locked in battle for decades with crown officials over the Indian question. The crown officials in alliance with the Jesuits attempted to enforce the altruistic policies of Lisbon. The senados, representatives of the local landed class, refused to surrender their native slaves. They succeeded in persuading the king to modify his policies. In that and myriad other matters they spoke out boldly in favor of local interests.

Furthermore the senado provided Brazilians with an opportunity to gain some governmental experience. According to one student of the institution, C. R. Boxer, it was relatively democratic. Naturally such a description must be understood within the confines of time and place. During the first decades of colonization, qualified or even educated persons were rare and often men of dubious reputation served on the senado. Later, the municipal government became the stronghold of the local aristocracy whose economic power lay in the land and whose political power in the senado. From those senados the landed gentry rose directly to positions of national power after 1831. Membership on the senados was never self-perpetuating, here once again a contrast with the *cabildo*. In fact, the offices rotated rather freely among the *homens bons*. More than that, eventually some of the senados included representatives of the working-class guilds. In Salvador, for example, between the mid-seventeenth century and the early eighteenth century four *procuradores dos mestres* exercised voting rights in matters related to crafts, trades, and the economic life of their city. The king suppressed the people's representatives in the Salvador senado in 1713, after they had incited the masses to demonstrate against a price increase in salt and a suggested 10 percent tax on imported goods. The senado in that same city reflected changing social patterns in the colony. João V in 1740 ordered that the names of prominent businessmen and merchants be included on the electoral roles for the posts of aldermen. He thus confirmed that the business and commercial class was well established and qualified to hold public office. Later, when Pombal reformed the government's fiscal system, he did not hesitate to hire his accountants and financial officials from the local business and commercial community. Both of those changes denoted a certain social mobility which permitted members of the petite bourgoisie to transcend barriers and enter the more privileged classes.

In times of crises, the senado da câmara amplified its membership to become a *conselho geral,* a general council. On those occasions, local military, judicial, and ecclesiastical authorites as well as representatives of the people met with the senado to discuss the emergency at hand. Such a meeting took place in Rio de Janeiro in 1641 after the governor of the captaincy, Salvador de Sá, received word of the Portuguese declaration of independence from Spain. The general council discussed whether or not to acknowledge João IV as the king of Portugal and decided affirmatively.

A second institution of local government deserves mention because of its influence on subsequent Brazilian development. Regional militias developed in which the principal figure of prestige and power in an area, usually the largest landowner, bore the rank of *capitão-mor,* equivalent to colonel. The majority of them seem to have been colonial born. In the absence of regularly constituted governmental officials in the hinterlands, those *capitães-mor* performed a variety of administrative and even judicial tasks. Obviously it was to their own interest to enforce law and order in their region and that they did to the benefit of local tranquillity. Their power varied widely and, as in so many cases, depended mainly on their own abilities and strengths since the distant government could do little to help or hinder them. They often became local *caudilhos,* the precursors of the local *coroneis.*

Such in the most general terms was the structure of government under which Brazil developed during more than three centuries. On the one hand, the great distances and the slowness of communication and travel allowed for considerable local autonomy and many irregularities. It meant that in practice the Crown could only hope to dictate the broad outlines of policy, leaving interpretation and implementation up to colonial and local officials. On the other hand, the Crown exercised a number of checks and controls to limit the degree of latitude permitted to overseas personnel. In theory, at any rate, all the laws were formulated in Lisbon and only needed enforcement overseas. The king sent to Brazil only officials of unquestioned loyalty. At best he suspected that life in the colony of Brazil increased in everyone "the spirit of amibition and the relaxation of virtues." For a long time he refused to appoint any Brazilians to high colonial posts; never did he appoint many, because of that suspicion of their loyalty. For example, in the early seventeenth century, the king refused to appoint Agostinho Rebeiro, a mazombo, as bishop in Brazil. The Crown at this time considered it too hazardous to elevate a native Brazilian to such a high post in his own land. Later the Crown relaxed its policy to permit a number of Brazilians to become judges, governors, and to fill other high offices in Brazil as well as in other parts of the empire, and in the metropolis itself. André Vidal de Negreiros, Alexandre de Gusmão, and José Joaquim da Cunha de Azeredo Coutinho serve as excellent examples. A larger number of Brazilians received appointments to minor posts in Portuguese America.

Since so many officials—the vieroy, the governors, bishops, treasury officials, etc.—had direct access to royal ears, there was considerable reporting and "tattling," which made all the overseas personnel cautious. Furthermore, those officials could expect at any time a *devassa* or a *visitação* or *correição*, an on-the-spot investigation to which all subordinates could be subjected. At the end of all terms of office, each administrator could expect a *residência*, a judicial inquiry into his public behavior. All those checks required an immense amount of paperwork, an abundantly evident attribute of all Luso-Brazilian bureaucracy. A multitude of lawyers, scribes, and notaries in all the major cities testified to the fascination of the Iberian mind with legal and bureaucratic matters. A witness to the efforts made by a merchant marine officer to get his personal effects through customs in Bahia in 1803 bemoaned: "Some trifling articles, the private property of the master he requested by petition to have granted to him. Previously to his obtaining them, he was obliged to justify his claim by three witnesses; and four sheets of paper were filled by an attorney with the process; this, after being recorded in a proper office, had then to pass five different signatures for giving it validity. The expenses thus amounting to nearly as much as the effects were worth."[19] Such complex and slow bureaucracy bespoke an insecure, if not weak, government.

Stronger in organization and authority than governmental institutions were the patriarchal plantation families. Those large, cohesive family units appeared at the inception of the sugar industry, and they grew together. As early as the mid-sixteenth century, a few of those family groups, like that of Duarte Coelho, proprietor of Pernambuco, were evident. Later their number increased and they could be found in all the rural areas. The paterfamilias dominated the household and the plantation, ruling family, slaves, and tenats with unquestioned authority. He and the other males of the household liberally expanded the basic family unit through their polygamous activities to include hosts of mestizo and mulatto children, verifying once again that it was in and around the plantation house that European, Indian, and African cultures blended together most perfectly to create a Brazilian civilization. The traditional godparent relationship (*compadrio*) further ramified and reinforced the family structure. Profoundly Christian and emphatically patriarchal, those family units set the social tone and pattern for the entire colony. The strongest of these families formed a landed aristocracy which dominated the senados da câmara in the colonial period and the newly independent national government in the imperial period.

Brazil by the close of the eighteenth century was widely if thinly settled. Growing at a rate approximated at 1.9 percent annually, the population numberd approximately two and one-third million with Minas Gerais, Bahia, Pernambuco, Rio de Janeiro, and São Paulo the most populous captaincies,

19. Lindley, *Narrative of a Voyage to Brazil*, p. 142.

in that order. The majority lived along the coast or in the rich river valleys. The trend of migration to the interior which was accelerated by the discovery of gold had been stemmed by this time, and in many cases reversed, with some return of the population to the coast. Obviously hollow frontiers still characterized the land settlement.

It was possible to distinguish five different regions of settlement. The far North, which included the vast Amazon valley, was scantily settled, a few villages dotting the river banks and coast. The cattlelands of the sertão stretching from Maranhão to Minas Gerais were the domain of the mestizos. The dry land and light vegetation grudgingly supported cattle, some horses, and a few sheep and goats. Ranches and hamlets were scattered over that vast interior with no concentration of settlement. The lush sugar coast extending from Maranhão to São Vicente included excellent ports and the largest cities in Brazil; the black prevailed in that more concentrated settlement. The mining regions of Minas Gerais, Goiás, and Mato Grosso exported their gold and diamonds but retained enough of the wealth to create a few prosperous towns. Stock-raising, sugar cane, and agriculture played a secondary economic role in the region. The far South boasted of excellent agricultural and pastoral lands. Immigrants, white European stock from the Azores, settled the coastal region. Their small family farms grew grapes, wheat, and olives. In contrast, bandeirante types migrated overland from São Paulo to colonize the interior of the South. There one encountered patriarchal cattle ranches and a profitable business in mule and horse raising.

Chapter Three

The Proclamation and Consolidation of Independence

As the eighteenth century closed, Brazil was formed territorially, although, of course, there were detailed changes thereafter. The Brazilians as a people, the racial composite of Europeans, Indians, and Africans, already existed. Indeed, certain basic types—the gaúcho, vaqueiro, tropeiro, bandeirante, senhor do engenho—were evident. The spiritual formation of the Brazilians had definitely begun and would accelerate rapidly. Some Brazilians had already articulated a desire to alter their relationship with Portugal, a desire from which independence eventually was to spring. The years between the opening and the middle of the nineteenth century marked a period of political and psychological change superimposed upon the continuing colonial economic and social structure.

Spiritual and Intellectual Formation of Nationhood

During the second century of colonization, the Brazilians began for the first time to think of themselves and their surroundings in introspective terms. In 1618 Ambrósio Fernandes Brandão made the first attempt to define or interpret Brazil in his *Diálogos das Grandezas do Brasil* (Dialogues of the Greatness of Brazil). In doing so, he exhibited his devotion to the colony, chiding those renóis who came to Brazil to exploit it and return wealthy to the peninsula. Less than a decade later, in 1627, the Franciscan Friar Vicente do Salvador, a native Brazilian, wrote the first history of Brazil to boast of the colony's favorable position, gigantic size, profitable sugar industry, and, above all else, its enormous potential. Setting the pattern for future self-examination, those two contributed intellectually to the incipient nativism which, a century later, would engulf the elite. The Bahian Jesuit André João Antonil (the nom de plume of João Antônio Andreoni) initiated the eighteenth-century glorification of Brazil with his florid but highly informative *Cultura e Opulência do Brasil* (Culture and Opulence of Brazil), published in 1711 in Lisbon. Royal authorities promptly suppressed it. They reasoned that the treatise revealed too much both to prying foreign eyes and to the mounting native ego, for Antonil sang a hymn of praise to the wealth of Brazil. *Cultura e Opulência* contained much less defensive explanation than *Os Diálogos*, and was far more boasting.

Against that background of increasing nativism, the intellectual life of Brazil accelerated as the colony became more urbanized in the eighteenth century. Growing in number and population, the urban centers brought together diverse peoples, exposing them to wider varieites of experiences, life styles, and opinions. Such a milieu encouraged the introduction, discussion, and circulation of ideas, facilitated by the construction of a new secular intellectual infrastructure which permitted the intellectuals to contribute significantly to change in the colony and eventually to the declaration of Brazil's independence.

That intellectual infrastructure consisted of such formally organized institutions as academies, schools, and public libraries, and of less formal but equally significant ones such as private libaries, bookdealers, and literary gatherings. The formal and informal institutions interconnected frequently, buttressing and strengthening each other. The same intellectuals participated in all of them.

The foundation stone of the intellectual infrastructure rested on the various academies which sprang up and flourished briefly in Salvador and Rio de Janeiro throughout the eighteenth century. Six of them can be identified: Academia Brasílica dos Esquecidos (Salvador, 1724–25), Academia dos Felizes (Rio de Janeiro, 1736–40), Academia dos Selectos (Rio de Janeiro, 1751–52), Academia Brasílica dos Renascidos (Salvador, 1758–60), Academia Scientífica (Rio de Janeiro, 1772–79), and Sociedade Literária (Rio de Janeiro, 1786–90, 1794). The academies provided the perfect forum to ventilate the thoughts wafted westward from Europe. With a baroque flourish, the academicians introduced and discussed a wide variety of ideas in their sessions. Devoting much of their time to environmental and botanical studies, they put considerable emphasis on improving agriculture and exploiting the natural wealth of Brazil, thereby demonstrating their endorsement of the physiocrat doctrines gaining popularity in Portugal. In general, the Brazilian academies, like their counterparts throughout the Western world during the eighteenth century, sought and examined that practical knowledge which promoted people's fuller utilization of, and adaptation to, their surroundings. In doing so, they understood as had never before been understood the potential wealth of Brazil; and in their fulsome praise of that potential, many of the savants contributed significantly to a spirit of nativism which cities nourished. Indeed, in the speeches made and poems recited in the academies, it is possible to trace the development of a new Brazilian mentality, a profound psychological change from a feeling of inferiority to Europeans to one of equality or even superiority.

Libraries, both private and public, were mighty pillars supporting the intellectual infrastructure. Books facilitated the introduction and circulation of ideas, thus contributing fundamentally to the shaping of a new mentality. At least on two occasions, November 13 and 17, 1812, the *Idade d'ouro* of Salvador emphasized to its readers the importance of books "to acquire enlightenment" and knowledge. Information on the book trade remains scarce and vague. Some of the earliest data concern the bookdealer Manuel Ribeiro Santos, who imported books from Portugal and sold them in Vila Rica, Minas Gerais, between 1749 and 1753. He ordered works on medicine, law, literature, history, geography, and classics. Apparently his service was fast (the imprint date on the book and its date of arrival in Minas Gerais were sometimes only one year apart) and frequent (he spoke of books arriving with every fleet). To avoid the disapproval of the censor and the Inquisition and the consequent confiscation of books by customs officials, the Brazilians imported their forbidden books in false covers. It was a method the Portuguese bibliophiles had perfected, and apparently it worked.

The *Almanaques* for Rio de Janeiro prepared by Antônio Duarte Nunes reveal that in 1792 and 1794 there was a bookdealer in the viceregal capital. In 1799, there were two. The American visitor H. M. Brackenridge reported the existence of two bookstores in 1817–18, and Robert Walsh spoke of twelve booksellers in the 1820s, all of whom were French. Salvador boasted of two bookdealers in 1812; nine years later the city still supported two bookdealers.

Private libraries existed in the major Brazilian cities. The library of Canon Luís Vieira da Silva, a participant in the Inconfidência Mineira, contained nearly 800 volumes and 270 titles representing all of Europe's foremost thinkers of the seventeenth and eighteenth centuries. The implication was—and the Portuguese government did not hesitate to draw it—that he was influenced enough by what he read to conspire for Brazil's independence. The remarks of foreign travelers shed additional light on the reading preferences of the Brazilians. Thomas Lindley remembered Father Francisco Agostinho Gomes, whose library in Salvador in 1803 was "very complete" in English and French works. The Englishman mentioned by name Buffon, Lavoisier, and d'Alembert. Andrew Grant spoke of private libraries in Rio de Janeiro and Salvador which contained books by "d'Alembert, Buffon,

Adam Smith, Thomas Paine, etc." In Pernambuco, L. F. de Tollenare commented on the literary preferences before the revolution of 1817: "The French works are the most sought after and among those all the writers . . . of the philosophy of the eighteenth century." John Luccock mentioned a brisk book trade in Rio de Janeiro in 1818, where "French books are in demand." In 1823, Maria Graham visited the private library of a *carioca* judge. Examining the books, she observed, "Of course the greater part is law; but there are history and general literature, chiefly French, and some English books."

The first public libraries date from 1810. On June 4, the library of the Coast Guard Academy (the predecessor of the Naval Academy) was opened to "the elites of the realm [*grandes do reino*] and naval officers." On October 29, Dom João opened to the public the Royal Library, a rich collection of about sixty thousand volumes, although apparently it contained few recently published works. The city of Salvador inaugurated a public library on August 6, 1811, in the former library of the Jesuit College, "with the hope of spreading enlightenment." The *Idade d'ouro* editorialized, "Knowledge of all things put within reach of the curious ought to awaken talents hitherto asleep." The library depended on contributions, both of money and books, from public-spirited citizens. The local inhabitants, including the governor and foreign consuls, responded. By 1818, the library contained between five and six thousand books. The library subscribed to English newspapers and received Hipólito da Costa's *Correio Braziliense*, a monthly journal published in London but intended to keep Brazilian readers abreast of world events.

Essential to the strength of the intellectual infrastructure was the effort made to improve the few schools in the colony after the expulsion of the Jesuits, which seemingly helped to widen the doors for the entrance of the Enlightenment as it had done in Portugal. Much of the Enlightenment filtered through the metropolis where Luís Antônio Verney had published in 1746 his *Verdadeira Maneira de Estudar* (The True Method of Study), Portugal's principal contribution to the literature of the Enlightenment. The Royal Academy of History, founded in 1720, set as its goal the dispassionate investigation of history through documentation. Established in 1779, the Royal Academy of Sciences began to delve in the broadest terms into the scientific aspects of the Enlightenment. Its minutes and monographs outline the profile the Portuguese Enlightenment assumed. Quite unwittingly, Pombal, impressed by the success of the French statesman Colbert and his own travels in Europe, gave the major impetus to the Enlightenment within the empire. His expulsion of the Jesuits with their scholastic approach to education and their reliance on the classic texts cleared the way for experimentation and the latest thought. His reforms of Coimbra University in 1772 substituted practice and observation for the hoary theory that had paralyzed the curriculum for so long. He invited foreign professiors to lecture and built a medical amphitheater and botanical garden. Many of Brazil's future leaders studied in Portugal at the newly reformed Coimbra University, where they imbibed heavily of the wines of European thought. On several occasions the Brazilians petitioned for the establishment of their own university, but the king never responded favorably.

Progress in reforming Brazilian education appears to have been painfully slow and spotty. Critical of scholasticism, in 1776 the Franciscans in their province of the Immaculate Conception of Rio de Janeiro updated the curriculum and put a new emphasis on geometry, natural history, and experimental physics. The professor of rhetoric, Manoel Ignácio da Silva Alvarenga, a graduate of Pombal's reformed Coimbra, came to the attention of crown officials investigating the "Conspiracy of the Intellectuals" in the viceregal capital in 1794, partly because they disapproved of some of his teaching. His library contained a copy of Gabriel Bonnet de Mably's *Direitos do cidadão* (to use the title in the court testimony), a book which seemed to particularly upset the viceregal bureaucrats. His own notes expressed ideas similar to those of the Frenchman, and what seemed even more dangerous to the officials was the fact that he had explained such ideas to at least one student. According to one judge,

Professor Alvarenga was too much a Francophile for the public good. At the end of the century in Salvador the Benedictines in teaching philosophy were using, among others, texts by Antonio Genovesi, Johann Gottlieb Heineccius, and Pieter van Musschenbroeck. Antônio Joaquim das Merces, a sort of itinerant philosophy professor between 1818 and 1823, lectured in Bahia, Alagoas, and Paraiba, where he too used Genovesi and Heineccius, in addition to Etiene Bezout and Rousseau's *Social Contract* (the latter he used apparently only in Paraíba). A Portuguese disciple of Condillac, Silvestre Pinheiro Ferreira, lectured in Rio de Janeiro in 1811 and 1812. His lectures appeared in book form in 1813 under the title *Reflecões filosóficas*.

Bishop José Joaquim da Cunha de Azeredo Coutinho introduced some of the Pombaline reforms of Coimbra into the seminary he established in Olinda in 1800. The curriculum put a new emphasis on the sciences; the bishop persuaded a number of outstanding teachers to accompany him to Pernambuco where he shunned pedagogic methods based on Aristotelian theory in favor of innovations influenced by Cartesian doctrines. The staff of the seminary seemed well aware of its own novel role. Professor Father Miguel Joaquim de Almeida e Castro, at the solemnities accompanying the opening of classes, delivered an impassioned address in which he evoked a new enlightened age of glorification of the sciences and arts to supplant the "dark centuries" of the past. Drawing on a wide variety of European, particularly French, authorities to substantiate his thesis, he asserted that only the sciences could "illuminate the darkness" and dispel ignorance and superstition. The speaker reminded his audience that science eschewed the blind acceptance of life and encouraged man to explore the world around him. The students seemed to welcome those remarks.

Educational institutions multiplied after the Portuguese royal family arrived in Rio de Janeiro in 1808. The crown established naval and military academies, both of which offered courses in engineering, two medical schools, and courses in economics, agriculture, and chemistry. An admirer of French civilization, Dom João invited a French cultural mission to Rio de Janeiro in 1816 to staff the new Academy of Fine Arts. Primary and secondary schools received needed attention and improvement. In 1812, the Colégio da Boa Sorte was offering a modern curriculum in Salvador, placing a new emphasis on geography, history, mathematics, French, and English.

The printing press arrived very late in Brazil, but once installed it too contributed to the dissemination and discussion of ideas. The first printing establishment, the Régia of Rio de Janeiro, was set up in 1808. The second, the press of Manuel Antônio da Silva Serva, began to function in Salvador in 1811. Both presses published some foreign authors in translation, although the Régia did so with greater frequency than did Silva Serva. A press began operation in Recife in 1817, and both Belém and São Luís do Maranhão had presses by 1821.

Finally, mention should be made of the private gatherings, salons, and clubs, which served as a forum for diffusing ideas and debating new concepts. During the closing decades of the eighteenth century in Minas Gerais, the *tertúlias literárias* served as effective means of gathering together the local intellectuals to discuss the current topics of the day. Strictly speaking, the famous Inconfidência Mineira was hardly more than a succession of such *tertúlias*. Perhaps the *oiteiros*, which epitomized the intellectual life of Fortaleza in 1813, exemplified similar activities elsewhere. The governor invited the local intellectuals to his residence to participate in literary discussions and poetical contests.

The salons were not always the exclusive domain of the male. The diary of Maria Graham provides a unique look into the habits of upper-class women at the time of Brazilian independence. Herself well educated and extremely intelligent, she admired the wit and conversation of many of the Brazilian ladies she met in Recife, Salvador, and Rio de Janeiro. Some knew English and most spoke French. In contrast to the silent, shrouded, secluded females mentioned by most nineteenth-century travelers—who happen to have been men—the women Ms. Graham found frequented drawing and dining rooms, contributed to the conversation, and were aware of what was going on in the world.

The secular intellectual infrastructure took shape slowly after the establishment of the first academy in 1724. It grew more rapidly during the last decades of the century, and the pace accelerated markedly during the first decades of the nineteenth century. The flow of new ideas into Brazil increased as the intellectual infrastructure expanded. The input of new ideas and the construction of the infrastructure buttressed each other. The more ideas that entered, the stronger the infrastructure became; and as the infrastructure strengthened, it became easier for ideas to migrate. The entire progress of intellectual change from more traditional ideas to acceptance of much of the thought associated with the Enlightenment took generations; the slowness of the process was by no means peculiar to the Luso-Brazilians but was rather a testimony to the fact that people are more creatures of habit and tradition than of innovation and change.

Obviously, in the process of intellectual change intellectuals themselves figure predominantly. It is difficult to define them precisely. We can use the term "intellectuals" in a general sense to refer to all the educated elite, the teachers, doctors, lawyers, bureaucrats, some military officers, merchants, and priests, those who engaged in literary conversations, read European authors, exposed themselves to new ideas or methods emanating from Europe, and concerned themselves with the world around them. A tiny group, their importance lay not in their size but in their ability to articulate and in their location. They lived in the cities, near the decision-making process. Their skill in expressing their ideas cogently in public oratory, in the classroom, in conversation, and later in books and newspapers made them influential. Unlike their counterparts before the eighteenth century, they were increasingly less associated with the church, more secular in origin and orientation, and above all else, in their professed devotion to reason they were prone to question some of the ideas and institutions which their predecessors had not only accepted but defended.

At the very core of the intellectual elite were the university graduates, or in some cases the ablest graduates of seminaries, *colégios*, and military schools. Brazilian students who had studied in Coimbra (more than 3,000 Brazilians received degrees from Coimbra during the colonial period), Montpellier, and a few other European universities, brought back with them the latest thoughts. Colonial officials regarded those graduates as propagators of seditious ideas. The Visconde de Barbacena expressed the suspicion well in a letter to Maria I after uncovering the Inconfidência: "I cannot help believing that the ideas [of the Inconfidência] came from Coimbra . . . because in that matter I found very dangerous the sentiments, opinions, and influence of the Brazilian university graduates, who have returned to their own land . . . to the self-interests of Europe. They know too well the natural products [of Brazil]. Even more dangerous were those who studied in foreign universities, as some have done without sufficient reason."[1] That group began the construction of the secular intellectual infrastructure, and as it grew it recruited more diverse elements into the intellectuals' ranks. The intellectuals seem a group when they are contrasted with the rest of the population, but among themselves they held diverse opinions and manifested different life styles. They became increasingly divorced from the traditional rural patrician class; of course they were not associated with the slaves or peasants who made up the vast majority of the population. They occupied, then, a middle position between the two extremes of Brazilian society.

The intellectuals of the period understood, perhaps better than anyone else, the conditions of Brazil. They also knew, either through reading, conversation, or travel, about other areas of the world, particularly western Europe, whose progress and achievements they admired, envied, and hoped to emulate. Partial toward the "progressive" countries, they freely drew their ideas from them. The vast difference between reality (Brazil as it was) and desire (Brazil as they

---

1. Quoted in João Camillo de Oliveira Torres, *História de Minas Gerais* (Belo Horizonte, 1962 [?]), III, 685.

wished it were) frustrated them and heightened their advocacy of change. Indeed, by the opening of the nineteenth century, the intellectuals allied with the commercial class—both urban groups—were the foremost partisans of innovation. A convincing case can be made that those two groups were fundamental in bringing about Brazil's nominal independence in 1822.

The intellectuals played a number of significant roles in the late colonial period by ushering new ideas into the country, creating a flattering image of Brazil which was the basis of nativism, and voicing in a cogent and often literary fashion some of the major complaints of the colonials. Likewise, they suggested and championed some major reforms in the imperial system; and they provided much of the leadership for the independence movement.

The intellectuals introduced new ideas into Brazil as a result of their studies and travels in Europe, their reading of books, and quite possibly their encounters and conversations with North Americans, Portuguese, and other Europeans in Brazil. Greater tolerance on the part of royal officials facilitated travel abroad and contact with foreigners. By the end of the eighteenth century, the stern countenance of the Inquisition was relaxing.

It is significant that among the educated much emphasis was placed on the mastery of foreign languages, which provided direct access to European thought. English was known to some degree, but French was especially valued as the language in which all the modern discoveries and ideas were set forth. The higher schools established during the Joanine period seem to have required not only French but other languages as well. The Military Academy taught French, German, and English. Medical students had to pass French and English examinations. The newspapers in Rio de Janeiro and Salvador contained numerous advertisements offering the services of French and English teachers. Books in French—as well as representatives of works in other languages—filled the shelves of private and public libraries. The comments of foreign visitors further testified to the widespread use of French among the Brazilian elite.

This concentration on foreign languages signified that Brazilians preferred to draw from a large European reservoir of ideas. By the end of the eighteenth century, Portugal no longer served as the colony's intellectual mentor. Not surprisingly, French influence dominated. Primarily that influence was exerted through the large number of French books eagerly imported, but by the end of the century, more Brazilians were also visiting and even studying in France. The arrival of the French cultural mission in 1816 consolidated the French intellectual domination. Although disturbed by its excesses, Brazilians followed the developments of the French Revolution with fascination. Indications are that information on the causes, course, and consequences of that revolution circulated widely in Brazil.

English influence among the elites also burgeoned, partially as a result of the commercial dominance Great Britain exerted over Brazil after 1808. Growing numbers of British merchants, diplomats, and visitors entered Brazil after the opening of the ports, and their presence facilitated the circulation and acceptance of Anglo-Saxon ideas. The works of John Locke may have been the first of any English thinker to be introduced into Brazil, where Locke enjoyed considerable respect among intellectuals. In fact, the constitution of 1824 had its roots in the ideas of Locke. The Brazilians translated and published extracts from the works of Edmund Burke in Rio de Janeiro in 1812, and the *Idade d'ouro* recommended his ideas to its readers. However, Adam Smith was the most influential intellectual from the British Isles. We can get some notion of the impact of the Scottish economist when we look at the impressive number of outstanding Brazilian intellectuals, such as José Joaquim da Cunha de Azeredo Coutinho, José da Silva Lisboa, João Rodrigues de Brito, Hipólito da Costa, and José Bonifácio de Andrada e Silva, who cited, praised, and quoted from him. Two editions of *The Wealth of Nations* issued from the new Brazilian presses: the Régia Press brought it out in 1811 and Silva Serva published it the following year. Analyzing Smith's theses, the *Idade d'ouro* applied them favorably to Brazil. On a subsequent occasion, the newspaper returned to his ideas, assuring its readers that their implementation would guarantee Brazil's prosperity. Thus Britain seems to have exerted greater intellectual influence over the mazombos during the waning years of its colonial status than has been ordinarily recognized.

German, Italian, and North American intellectual influences could be discerned as well. In his lectures on philosophy in Rio de Janeiro in 1811 and 1812, Silvestre Pinheiro Ferreira, who had travelled extensively in the German states, outlined the thought of Immanuel Kant, Johann Gottlieb Fichte, Friedrich Wilhelm Joseph von Schelling, and Georg Wilhelm Friedrich Hegel. Beginning with Friedrich Wilhelm Sieber in 1801, an impressive number of German naturalists, explorers, geologists, geographers, and zoologists descended on Brazil. The arrival of Austrian Archduchess Leopoldina, the young bride of Dom Pedro, in 1817, accompanied by a retinue of distinguished intellectuals, further exposed the Brazilians to German thought. The Italian Antonio Genovesi ranked as one of the most widely read European philosophers, and apparently his books circulated among most Brazilian intellectuals. The botanist Alexandre Rodrigues Ferreira was one of his most notable Brazilian disciples. The appearance of works by Thomas Jefferson, Benjamin Franklin, and Thomas Paine in Brazilian libraries indicated curiosity about the United States as well as interest in the intellectual currents there. Apparently Tiradentes possessed copies of laws passed in North America as well as of the Declaration of Independence. Hipólito da Costa, one of the few Brazilians to visit the United States, later commented at length on his impressions. Increasing trade between the United States and Brazil brought Brazilians into closer contact with North Americans and their ideas.

Drawing from a wide variety of sources, the intellectuals imported those ideas which pleased them most into Brazil, where they were discussed, in some cases Brazilianized, in some cases implemented. Exposure to them prompted a more thorough questioning than ever before of concepts long held sacrosanct. Thus skepticism and inquiry challenged the more traditional and less rational aspects of a colonial system which was proving to be less and less satisfactory to the colonials.

As one result of the influx of new ideas, the Brazilians more sharply focused attenition on their own land, its problems as well as its potential. Physiocrat doctrines in particular impelled them to investigate their surroundings, an activity which accelerated the growth of the nativism already manifested. Love of, devotion to, pride in Brazil constituted the cult for which the intellectuals served as high priests.

That cornerstone of the secular intellectual infrastructure, the Brazilian Academy of the Forgotten, established a nativistic pattern which intellectuals would follow and build on. Throughout the prolix prose and poetry of the Academy's sessions, the Luso-Brazilian literati wove abundant references to the beauty, importance, and wealth of Brazil. Nativistic pride reached a climax of sorts in the "Dissertação terceira" of Caetano de Brito e Figueiredo, which describes the bounty of Brazilian geography. In part the judge mused: "Golden Brazil is the depository of the most priceless metal, fertile producer of the sweetest sugar canes, and generous cultivator of the most useful plants. Let me say it boastfully: Brazil is the most precious jewel of the Lusitanian scepter, the most valuable stone in the Portuguese crown, which of itself possesses much majesty and beauty."[2]

The "Forgotten" elected Brazilian history as their subject of study, a theme which lent itself to expressions of nativism. The topic obviously inspired one of the academicians, Sebastião da Rocha Pita. In 1730 he published the best history of Brazil written during the colonial period. His florid *História da América Portuguesa* stands out as one of the classic statements of nativistic sentiment. Rocha Pita also penned a baroque poetic gem entitled "The Shift of the Sunrise," in which he proclaimed that the sun "is born with greater brilliance in the west."[3] During the following century, Brazilian

2. José Aderaldo Castillo, ed., *O Movimento Academista no Brasil* (São Paulo, 1971), I:5, 167.

3. Péricles Eugênio da Silva Ramos, ed., *Poesia barroca. Antologia* (São Paulo, 1967), p. 104.

literature repeated that symbolic allusion to a new sunrise in the west.

Some remarkable poets raised their voices to praise Brazil. Few were more nativistic than José Basílio da Gama and José da Santa Rita Durão. Basílio da Gama's epic poem *O Uraguai* glorified the heroic resistance of the Indians of the seven missionary villages of southern Brazil to Spanish and Portuguese incursions. It painted an alluring picture of the Brazilian landscape. In his exaltation of the noble qualities of the Indians, Basílio da Gama proved to be a precursor of the nineteenth-century romantic Indianist movement. The Indian emerged for the first time as the symbol of what was truly Brazilian. Later the nationalists seized on that convenient symbol and carried the glorification of the Indian to more exaggerated extremes. Santa Rita Durão's epic *Caramurú* traced the history of the colony from discovery to the expulsion of the last foreign invader, mixing political insights with descriptions of lush vegetation.

The theater contributed to nativism as well as to intellectual change. It may be difficult to assess its exact influence in eighteenth-century Brazil, but let us consider its important social function in a society which had no press and high illiteracy rates and in which books were expensive and secular amusements few. It exposed relatively large numbers of people to new ideas, customs, or influences. It was a convenient place to gather and converse as well as to view a spectacle. The audiences of the eighteenth century attended plays written by foreigners and translated into Portuguese. In fact, Spanish, Italian, and French plays proved more popular than those of Portuguese writers to the audiences of Salvador, which applauded the works of Molière, Voltaire, Carlo Goldoni, and Matastasio. One can speculate on the impact those plays might have had on the people in the audience. For example, Antônio Rodrigues Machado, arrested and implicated in the Bahian conspiracy of 1798, frequented the theater constantly.

The Brazilians themselves wrote and produced theatrical pieces reflecting nativist themes. One delightful example was *A Felicidade no Brasil*, presented in the Teatro Público of

Belém in 1808. The author, Bento de Figueiredo Tenreiro Aranha, a singular figure, lived his entire life (1769–1811) in the Amazon region and had only a rudimentary formal education. Self-taught, he wrote poems, plays, and orations. The cast of his one-act drama consisted of the Grande Génio Tutelar e Superior, who presided over the destinies of all Brazil, the Génio Tutelar do Cabo Frio, and a nymph of the Amazon River leading a chorus of other undines. As the curtain rises, the Grande Génio do Brasil promises a bright future for the land, indeed "a new sun." He salutes the fabulous richness of the land, predicting, "You will see your name and commerce flourish." Throughout the short drama, essentially celebrating the arrival of the royal court in the New World, the potential wealth and promising future of Brazil are his themes.

Not content just to sing Brazil's praises, the intellectuals industriously probed their surroundings—with the blessing and encouragement of Portuguese officials, whose motives, however, were quite different from theirs. They produced a remarkably varied series of monographs on Brazilian flora, fauna, geography, minerals, and agriculture. José Vieira Couto wrote a long monograph on Minas Gerais; José de Sá Bettencourt left studies on cotton farming; Bernardo Teixeira Coutinho Alvares de Carvalho prepared a treatise on the manufacture of ink from local resources; and Joaquim Amorin de Castro penned a natural history of Brazil as well as monographs on the tobacco and cochineal industries. The botanists were among the most active students of Braziliana and at least two first-rate scholars emerged. Alexandre Rodrigues Ferreira, a native of Bahia who received his doctorate in natural history from Coimbra, trekked for nearly a decade, 1783–1792, through Amazonia and the interior gathering specimens, sketching, and writing an impressive variety of reports on the area and its inhabitants. Sent by Minister Martinho de Mello e Castro as one of a group of naturalists to ascertain the natural wealth of Portugal's global empire, he reported enthusiastically about the Amazon, "The land itself, Your Excellency, is a paradise; it produces so much that I do not know which way to turn." José

Mariano da Conceição Velloso, a Franciscan from São João del-Rei in Minas Gerais, devoted eight years (1782–1790) to his major study, the *Flora Fluminensis,* the collection and classification of 1,640 different plants from the captaincy of Rio de Janeiro.

Those authors, more often than not recent graduates of Coimbra, were, in the words of a student of their activities, "the first men of this country who had an objective view of the need for national development."[4] Their conclusions, as well as their pride, can be summed up in the results of a debate held in the Academia dos Felizes on the question, "Was Portuguese America the best part of this continent?" They unanimously concluded that it was. Later the *Idade d'ouro* concluded that it was superior to Europe as well! And on November 17, 1812, that newspaper urged its readers, "Let us study our territory, let us explore its possibilities, let us see what it can provide us. Following this method constantly for a period of thirty years, we will see Brazil rise from poverty to become one of the richest and most respected nations of the universe."

One does not have to look far in the early nineteenth century for evidence of native pride. Whereas formerly the Brazilians had only compared their land to paradise, Francisco de São Carlos published a long poem, *A Assumção,* in 1819 in which he pictured paradise as remarkably similar to Brazil. The Brazilian deputies to the Portuguese Cortes in 1822 voiced their nativistic pride repeatedly with a frankness which widened the gap between themselves and the Portuguese. As one deputy reminded the assembly, "There is not a Brazilian who does not boast of the great resources of his land; there is not a Brazilian who is not proud of the potential which Brazil has to be one of the first nations of the universe." The resources and potential of Brazil provided the leitmotif of nativism.

Among the elite and in some vague way among large numbers of the urban masses as well, the intellectuals in-

4. José Ferreira Carrato, "Uma primeira tomada de consciência do desenvolvimento brasileiro," *Revista de História* (São Paulo), 44 (1972), p. 263.

spired an awareness that Brazil not only differed from Portugal and the rest of the world but that it was superior. While eroding confidence in motherland, they created a flattering self-image which was the nucleus of national consciousness. In short, they promulgated the idea of the nation and instilled a sense of nationality in their fellow countrymen. Taking the longest possible historical view, the colonial intellectuals in the eighteenth century accelerated a movement of "Brazilianization" which reached its climax with the proclamation of the majority of Dom Pedro II in 1840.

Growing pride in Brazil, coupled with a knowledge of the enlightened thinking of the eighteenth century, prompted the intellectuals to criticize those aspects of the Portuguese imperial system which they believed inimical to Brazil's wellbeing. Criticism, after all, was and is one of the principal activities of intellectuals. Of course, by later standards their criticism would seem mild: indeed, the majority of the intellectuals appear to be moderates. Hipólito da Costa repeatedly emphasized in his *Correio Braziliense* the need for reform, not revolution, an observation in which succeeding generations of intellectuals concurred. However, moderate as the intellectuals were in their suggestions and aspirations, they proved to be instrumental, given the climate of opinion favoring change, in discrediting some traditional ideas so that it could take place.

Scattered and oblique at first, the criticism did not become really pronounced until the closing decades of the eighteenth century. It intensified during the early years of the nineteenth century and was directed at many targets, economic, political, and social, although perhaps economic complaints have been most familiar to subsequent generations.

Early political criticism tended to be theoretical and idealistic, not directed toward specific issues. The *Paulista*, Matias Aires da Silva de Eça, in his major work *Reflexões sôbre a vaidade dos homens*, published in 1752 in Lisbon, where he lived, discoursed on the equality of man. "Men are born equal. . . . The world was not made for the greater benefit of some than of others," he concluded. That novel idea found scant acceptance in a hierarchical society. Eça's sister, Teresa Margarida Silva e Otra, denounced absolutism in her own book, *Aventuras de Diófanes* (Lisbon, 1753). Praising liberty and reason, scoffing at the divine right of monarchs, she advocated a government of law to which all, the king not excluded, were obedient and responsible. In his "Instrucção para o governo da Capitania de Minas Gerais," an essay on political philosophy composed in 1780, José João Teixeira Coelho, reflecting on eleven years of experience in Minas Gerais, held that a worthy government was one established for the good of the people, one of laws, not of the whims of the executive. In a polite way these writers were questioning the Portuguese political system.

The *inconfidências* of Minas Gerais (1789), Rio de Janeiro (1794), Bahia (1798), and Pernambuco (1801) and the rebellion in Pernambuco (1817) expressed in dramatic form and somewhat more precise language festering political grievances. Unlike the critics before them, the participants in the *inconfidências* and the rebellion were specific: they decried the Portuguese imperial system as repressive, preferred republican to monarchical institutions, and in general subscribed to the political doctrines popular at the time in France and the United States. The extent of republican sentiment has never been adequately measured, and assessments of it range broadly.

In the long political discussions filling its pages, the *Correio Braziliense* mixed general and specific criticism of the Portuguese system. Believing that government was a contract between the governor and the governed, the editor favored a written constitution to limit the powers of government. He argued that the government of Brazil did not conform to enlightened principles. Such political views motivated most of the Brazilian deputies to the Portuguese Côrtes in 1822, whose speeches expressed some of the most important attitudes of the Brazilian elite on the eve of independence. José Lino Coutinho, one of the Bahian representatives, emphasized to the Portuguese deputies the many differences between the kingdoms of Portugal and Brazil, pointing out that laws appropriate for one did not necessarily fit the other. He asked them to recognize those differences in considering legislation. On other occasions, he avocated the separation of powers, autonomy for the courts, a military responsible to the legislature instead of to the executive, and the franchise for freed slaves. The debates of the Côrtes reveal the degree to which the Portuguese political system displeased the new generation of Brazilian spokesmen, who eventually participated in the breaking of ties with Portugal.

In addition to their political complaints, the intellectuals voiced frequent economic criticism, prompted in part by the economic doldrums of the late eighteenth century. Bewilderment over the widespread poverty in Brazil in the midst of potential wealth was best expressed in the pertinent question of Luís dos Santos Vilhena, a Portuguese who lived for twelve years in Bahia: "Why is a country so fecund in natural products, so rich in essence, so vast in extent, still inhibited by such a small number of settlers, most of them poor, and many of them half-starved?" He laid the blame on slave labor, latifundia, and obsolete agricultural methods.[5] In doing so, he castigated the fundamental economic institutions of colonial Brazil. His discussions of the need for greater economic freedom and reform, of "hunger," "shortages," and "poverty" indicated the crisis into which the imperial system had plunged. An anonymous manuscript written in Bahia at the same time, but unpublished until recently, examined at length the colony's economic problems. Critical of Portuguese policies, it voiced the economic complaints of the Brazilians.[6] At the same time, Manoel Antônio writing to the crown from São Luís do Maranhão, spoke out in favor of relaxing restrictions on commerce and in support of free trade.[7]

5. Luís dos Santos Vilhena, *Recopilação de notícias soteropolitanas e brasílicas*, 2d ed. (Salvador, 1922), 2:926.

6. The manuscript bore the title "Discurso preliminar, histórico, introdutivo, com natureza da descrição econômica da comarca e cidade da Bahia." Edited by Pinto de Aguiar, it was published under the title *Aspectos da economia colonial* (Salvador, 1957). Another example of the economic criticism of the eighteenth century is José Gregório de Morais Navarro, *Discurso sôbre o melhoramento da economia rústica do Brasil, pela introducçao do arado, reforma das fornalhas, e conservaçao de suas mattas, etc.* (Lisbon, 1799).

7. Letter dated October 30, 1791, Arquivo Histórico Ultramarino, Lisbon, Maranhão, box 64.

From Lisbon, the Brazilian José Joaquim da Cunha de Azeredo Coutinho commented on the imperial economy. His three economic essays, all of which were published, were widely circulated and became the focus of considerable comment. They suggested some far-reaching adjustments in the Brazilian economy but did not imply that they should be instituted by means other than reform within the empire. Like most of his contemporaries, he preached neither revolution nor independence. Undoubtedly the importance of his three essays lay in the fact that for the first time a series of basic economic reforms highly desired by Brazilians had been classified and clarified. Azeredo Coutinho wanted them to be carried out within the empire, but when they were not forthcoming from Portugal, Brazilians came to realize that only by taking control of their own destiny could change come about. Hence, by indicating a path to economic reform, Azeredo Coutinho's essays had the unexpected effect of increasing the Brazilians' desire to be economic masters in their own house.

In his first essay, *Memória sôbre o preço do assúcar,* published in 1791, Azeredo Coutinho argued that any governmental regulation of the price of sugar would thwart the natural economic order, harming not only Brazil but, in the long run, Portugal itself. The second essay, *Ensaio econômico sôbre o commércio de Portugal e suas colônias,* first published in 1794, was destined to have great importance to Brazilians. Following both nativistic and physiocrat traditions, it first analyzed the rich resources and potential of Brazil and then proceeded to recommend policies which would permit the best utilization of them. Azeredo Coutinho emphasized frequently the physiocrat doctrine that agriculture was the true source of wealth. Gold, a false wealth, instead of enriching the empire had impoverished it. Greater liberty, he reasoned, would help Brazilians tap their potential wealth. He called specifically for the abolition of the salt monopoly and the restrictions on forest industries, permission to manufacture in Brazil, and freer trade outside the empire. A third essay, *Discurso sôbre o estado actual das minas do Brasil,* published in 1804, correctly attributed Brazil's economic distress to overemphasis on mining and the consequent neglect of agriculture. He urged the Luso-Brazilians to take advantage of the new European technology in order to increase their economic efficiency. In the depressed economy of the period, the Brazilians were receptive to the new economic ideas.

Other critics of the economy joined Azeredo Coutinho, one of the most enlightened being the Bahian João Rodrigues de Brito. Writing in the first decade of the nineteenth century, he lamented the backward state of Brazilian agriculture, advising an end to monopolies and restrictions, which, he argued, only inhibited growth. He prescribed the liberty to think freely and to publish those thoughts. The Brazilians' criticism of the economic policies of Portugal seemed to mount in proportion to their optimism about the potential of their land.

A third aspect of the intellectuals' criticism focused on pressing social problems. Slavery aroused some concern, although few advocated the outright abolition of the institution. The Bahian conspirators of 1798 seem to have been the only ones to favor so dramatic a remedy. The *Paulista* judge Antônio Rodrigues Veloso de Oliveira, writing in 1810, supported the manumission of children born of slave women.[8] In that same year, far to the Northeast in Recife, Manoel de Câmara summed up his thoughts on the social iniquities of Brazilian society:

The benightedness of the colored people must be done away with. This must come to an end so that when later men are needed to fill public positions they will be ready, for Brazil will never progress unless they can play their part in its affairs; never mind that degraded and absurd aristocracy which will always try to create obstacles. With a monarchy or without it, the colored people must share in Brazil's prosperity.[9]

8. The manuscript did not reach print until twelve years later (*Memória sôbre o melhoramento da Província de S. Paulo, applicável em grande parte a tôdas as outras províncias do Brasil* [Rio de Janeiro, 1822]).

9. Gilberto Freyre, *The Mansions and the Shanties: The Making of Modern Brazil* (New York, 1963), pp. 262–63.

An impressive, albeit limited, criticism of the harsh treatment of the slaves appeared. The *Idade d'ouro,* published in the heartland of the slave system, editorialized on June 16, 1812, on the necessity of eventually ending the slave trade.

Many of the deputies representing Brazil in the Côrtes in 1822 expressed strong opinions against slavery. Notably effective in his efforts to protect the nonwhite from discrimination—as well as nativistic in his defense of the Brazilian "family"—Cipriano José Barata de Almeida, a deputy from Bahia, reaching an emotional apogee in his oration before the Côrtes, declared:

Mulattos, *cabras,* and *crioulos;* Indians, *mamelucos,* and mestizos are all our people, they are Portuguese; they are honorable and valuable citizens. Throughout history they have proven their value to Brazil, defending it, working for its prosperity whether it be in agriculture, commerce, or the arts. Those races have provided great heroes. . . . They are Portuguese citizens, the sons of Portuguese or Brazilians, even if they are illegitimate. Whatever their color, whatever their status, they were born in Brazil.[10]

Much to its credit, the Côrtes voted unanimously to extend the suffrage to all *libertos.*

The harsh treatment accorded the Indians awaken the social conscience of some intellectuals. José Bonifácio, for one, defended the remaining original inhabitants. The ode he published in 1820 testified to his social concern. Some observed that the Roman Catholic Church had failed to help the Indians because it had neither properly civilized them nor integrated them into the colony. Criticism of the Church's missions, the Church's Indian policy, and even the "indolent clergy" appeared in print.

A long editorial commentary appearing in the *Idade d'ouro* on May 29, 1812, in many ways summed up the criticism of the Brazilian intellectuals. Labeling the Portuguese "inert," it said, "The three centuries since discovery have not been well employed to construct the strong foundation Bra-

10. *Diário das Côrtes Geraes, Extraordinárias e Constituintes da Nação Portugueza,* session August 13, 1822, 7:139.

zil now needs." The editor counseled the building of roads and increased immigration in order to improve conditions in the colony. The newspaper thanked Prince-Regent Dom João for the salutary reforms he had instituted and intimated that they should be expanded.

Throughout the criticism—for that matter throughout all the activities of the intellectuals—it is easy to detect the influence of the Enlightenment. The philosophies of all the European thinkers associated with the Enlightenment are visible, and the intellectuals looked increasingly to reason and science to find solutions for the problems they discussed. Once again it is possible to refer to the Brazilian Academy of the Forgotten to see the establishment of a pattern which would characterize the intellectual activity of the ensuing century. In his address in 1724 inaugurating the Academy, José da Cunha Cardoso paid tribute to some of the tenets of the Enlightenment by recognizing that man's search for knowledge was natural, appropriate, and rational. His fellow academicians echoed that opinion. One reminded his peers that "science is the fundamental base" of their work. For the remainder of the final colonial century speeches and orations resounded with denunciations of scholasticism and superstition and with praises of science, inquiry, and reason. The Luso-Brazilians, then, offered their criticism within the accepted framework of *o século das luzes*.

The criticism provided the explanation as well as the justification for change. The intellectuals suggested those reforms they felt would benefit Brazil. Implied in their criticism or accompanying it, as the discussion above indicates, was a program of reform, most of it based on ideas emanating from those few nations whose government, culture, and/or economic success they most admired.

At this juncture, it is tempting to oversimplify, to point to one current of criticism and one program of reform and show how the first intensified, while the second gained popularity over the course of a century. Events and emotions were far more complex, however. Varying intellectual trends moved forward and backward, intersected, and contradicted one another. Some intellectuals simply sought change within the system; others questioned the system itself and saw change as altering it. On one issue the intellectuals seemed unanimous. They insisted that Brazil's status within the empire be improved. They felt it imperative that the kingdom's overwhelming importance be recognized. After all, at the beginning of the nineteenth century, Brazil had a population larger than the metroplis, furnished approximately three-quarters of the empire's exports, and boasted an economic potential far superior to that of any other part of the empire. In size, Brazil dwarfed the motherland. The inevitable clash between metropolis and colony on the issue of the colony's rising importance was postponed by the unexpected transfer of the court to Rio de Janerio in 1808. The return of the king to Lisbon in 1821 projected the issue to the forefront again.

To summarize the political reforms most frequently advocated, it can be said that on more than one occasion over this long time span, intellectuals suggested the integration of the Indians and manumitted blacks into society, the unification of the sparwling territory by means of better roads, a constitution based on the concept of government as a social contract, a stronger Brazilian voice in the imperial government, and the enhancement of the roles of the legislature and judiciary. A few spoke out for the establishment of a republic. As for the economic aspects of their reforms, they favored free trade, industrialization, modernization of agriculture and mining, and an end to burdensome restrictions, monopolies, and taxes. Their social statements were much more nebulous. They paid lip service to the concept of the equality of all men and talked in vague terms of improving the conditions of the Indians and the slaves; a few even spoke of ending the slave trade. They wanted personal liberties, civil freedom, and religious tolerance. Most emphatically, however, they proposed ambitious plans to reform and expand education. Such, then, in composite was the ideology of change espoused by the intellectuals. It has never been fully implemnted, but it provided the goals of the reformers throughout the nineteenth century.

The influx of enlightened ideas and the growing economic discontent combined to promote rebellion. We have already noted that the Inconfidência resulted partly from a reaction to a threat of improved tax collecting and partly as the imperfect comprehension of enlightened thought. The curious mixture of economics and idealism plunged the Mineiro elite into impractical plotting. The outcome was an aborted rebellion. Brazilian historians have given the Inconfidência far greater significance than it seems to deserve. At best it revealed some romantic dreamers at work, but the plot itself never passed the hypothetical stage. Although they thought in terms of independence, some of the conspirators were republicans, others monarchists; some advocated the abolition of slavery, others favored it. The plot is worthy of consideration only because it proves that many ideas of the Enlightenment penetrated the interior of Brazil to agitate the waters of economic and political discontent.

Less discussed but perhaps more important was the Bahian conspiracy in 1798, which was the unique example of the penetration—imperfect as it may have been—of the Enlightenment into the masses. Confronting his judges in Salvador at the close of the eighteenth century, the twenty-three-year-old soldier Lucas Dantas do Amorim Tôrres stated, "We want a republic in order to breathe freely because we live subjugated and because we're colored and we can't advance and if there was a republic there would be equality for everyone."[11] More than boldness was notable in his statement. Obviously, the young soldier had imbibed the thoughts of the Enlightenment; the revolution of ideas had reached him. Dantas was but one of a larger group of conspirators arrested in Salvador in 1798 for plotting against the crown. By and large those conpsirators were simple folk: soldiers, workmen, aritsans, and so large a number of tailors that the movement sometimes bears the name of the "Conspiracy of the Tailors." The statistics tell the tale. Of the forty-nine arrested, forty-six were male, forty were freedmen, almost all were literate, all were between seventeen and thirty years old, all had modest backgrounds, and all were mulattos.

11. Quoted in Braz do Amaral, *Fatos da vida do Brasil* (Salvador, 1941), p. 28.

As in the case of Dantas, the testimony of the other defendants at the trial revealed that those representatives of the lower classes were acquainted with current European thought. They made accusations against Portugal similar to those of the intellectuals of the time. In general, the conspirators favored independence, a republic, the equal treatment of all men, the abolition of slavery, and free trade. The Bahian rebels proposed far more profound changes than the other colonial dissidents before and after them. They were the only ones to strike at slavery, that institution which was the sinew and muscle of colonial Brazil. In some ways their desires harmonized more with the Enlightenment than did the programs of the intellectuals, who were compromised by their aspirations or association with the interests of the upper class or the Portuguese.

The first signs of the impending rebellion appeared in the form of handwritten posters affixed to public walls on August 12, 1798. One announced, "Courage Bahian People, the happy day of Liberty is at hand, the time when we will all be brothers, the time when we will all be equal." Another affirmed, "Each soldier is a citizen, particularly the brown and black men who are abused and abandoned. All are equal. There is no difference. There will only be liberty, equality, and fraternity." References to "liberty, equality, and fraternity" abounded, as did praises of the French Revolution and the French republic. The plot had its picturesque aspects. A letter addressed to one priest informed him that the conspirators had named him "Future General-in-Chief of the Bahian Church." Another, to the governor, addressed him as "President of the Supreme Tribunal of Bahian Democracy."

A major significance of the Bahian *inconfidência* lay in the revelation that the new ideas had reached the masses as well as the educated elite. Somehow the intellectuals communicated to the lower strata of urban society those ideas of which they were the brokers. Perhaps the transmission testifies to the social fluidity of the Brazilian city by the close of the eighteenth century, which was sufficiently in flux to facilitate interchange betwen various classes. Ideas were probably passed on by word of mouth, since books were expensive and illiteracy predominated. Speaking of the Bahian case in particular, Luís Henrique Dias Tavares also stressed conversations as the major means by which the lower classes might have picked up their notions of the philosophy of the Enlightenment.[12] Some testimony in the trail of the conspirators mentioned word of mouth as the means by which they might have gathered their ideas. There may also have been contacts between the soldiers who participated in the plotting and a few junior officers well acquainted with European thought and also implicated in the *inconfidência*. For example, Lt. Hermógenes Francisco de Aguilar Pantoja, who was known to Lucas Dantas, possessed a private library containing French books. The court testimony pointed out that the young lieutenant would bring his books to the barracks and read aloud from them to his troops. At any rate, by whatever means, the intellectuals did transmit ideas to the masses.

The Bahian conspiracy added the dimension of the common person, almost always overlooked, to the history of ideas in colonial Brazil. As a historian of Bahia, Dias Tavares, noted, "The Brazilian people rarely appear in the histories of Brazil, but in the revolutionary movement of 1798 they are the principal actors." Awareness of that popular dimension in intellectual history is an incentive to broaden future studies of Brazil to encompass wider segments of the population. The urban masses also acted on the ideas of the times. The influence of the intellectuals extended beyond the narrow confines of the elite.

In Recife a third conspiracy climaxed in rebellion in 1817. Some of the elite had read the latest European books and discussed the ideas wafted across the ocean from France and England. Bishop Azeredo Coutinho, already famed for his economic essays, founded a seminary in Olinda in 1800 for the general education of the captaincy's youth. His seminary reflected many of the thoughts of the Englightenment. Since French was taught there, the students had direct access to

12. *Introdução ao Estudo das Idéias do Movimento Revolucionário de 1798* (Salvador, 1959), pp. 50–54.

the primary literature of that intellectual movement. Some years later, in 1814, a Masonic lodge was organized in which discussions frequently touched on republican ideas. The elite was fully cognizant of the successful revolutions in the United States and France as well as of the holocaust enveloping much of Spanish America. Economic considerations also encouraged thoughts of rebellion. During the War of 1812 between Great Britain and the United States and for some years thereafter cotton from Pernambuco sold exceedingly well in Europe. Planters realized as much as 500 percent profit on their shipments. Conscious of their renewed economic importance and hopeful that it would continue, the planters complained ever more bitterly of Portuguese bureaucratic restrictions on their activities. The antipathy between the Brazilians and Portuguese in the area continued unabated from the days of the War of the Mascates. A certain regional pride was involved in the conspiracy, which limited plannning to the establishment of a republic only in the Northeast. Word of the plot reached Governor Caetano Pinto, but his hesitation to arrest military officers implicated gave the rebels an opportunity to execute their plans. They captured the Governor and packed him off to Rio de Janeiro. A provisional government of five men representing the military, the judiciary, and agricultural, religious, and commercial interests took charge. It is worthy of note that a high percentage of the revolutionary leaders had studied in Bishop Azeredo Coutinho's seminary. The republican government dispatched emissaries to Argentina, Great Britain, and the United States and sought vainly to obtain arms and protection from the Anglo-Saxon powers. Delegates also visited Bahia and Ceará to solicit their support. The governors of those captaincies arrested them. Alagoas and Paraíba adhered to the revolution. The initial actions of the revolutionary government revealed much of the philosphy that had brought it to power. It abolished the brazilwood monopoly, all titles of nobility, class privileges, and some taxes. Rio de Janeiro reacted with unusual swiftness. The Royal Navy blockaded Recife and troops under the Conde dos Arcos advanced on the city overland from Bahia. Under those military pressures the revolt collapsed. Less than three months after the republic was proclaimed, Pernambuco returned to the monarchical fold. It was the principal revolt of the colonial period and furthermore testified dramatically to the existence, and even the popularity, of republican ideology. The cause of independence, timidly put forward by the inconfidencias of Minas Gerais and Bahia and boldly proclaimed in Pernambuco, was best served by events far from the coasts of Portuguese America. Struggles in Europe brought about a virtual transformation of Brazil.

The Braganzas in Brazil

In the early nineteenth centiry, Portugal found itself caught between its traditional alliance with Great Britain and the demands of Napoleon, who was determined to close Europe's ports to English trade. Napoleon ordered Prince Regent João, ruling in the name of his demented mother, Maria I, to seal the Portuguese ports, confiscate British property, and arrest British subjects. He reluctantly agreed to close the ports but nothing more, a decision which prompted Napoleon to invade Portugal in late 1807. The army of General Andoche Junot marched on Lisbon. In view of those events, the British minister, Lord Strangford, counseled João to migrate with the court to Brazil, a course of action broached as far back as the sixteenth century and periodically discussed thereafter. The approach of Junot negated any other alternatives in the prince's mind. In return for generous commercial privileges in Brazil, the British agreed to transport the royal family to the New World and to preserve intact the Portuguese empire. The day that Junot entered Lisbon the Braganzas and their court sailed out of the Tagus for their tropical destination.

Historians generally applaud João's decision to move his court to Brazil. Such a migration has been considered a wise political maneuver rather than a cowardly flight before the enemy. Certainly from the Brazilian viewpoint the decision was laudable. On the other hand, the Portuguese soon would complain that the Crown tarried too long overseas. The event remains unique in history: the Braganzas were the only European monarchs to rule an empire from one of the colonies rather than from the metropolis. They were the only European monarchs to set foot on their American domains.

Divided by a storm at sea, the bulk of the fleet stopped first at Salvador da Bahia, while the rest sailed directly to Rio de Janeiro. João and the royal family were aboard those vessels which called at Salvador. One can imagine the joy, the excitement, the surprise of the inhabitants of the former colonial capital as they greeted their monarch on January 22, 1808. The city scrubbed and festively decorated, the inhabitants in their finest attire waited impatiently to view the new course history was opening before them. Within a few days, the Brazilians heard evidence of the changes in store. Already committed to permit the English to trade with Portuguese America, João listened attentively to a petition from the Governor of Bahia, the Conde da Ponte, prompted by the economist José da Silva Lisboa, to throw open the ports to world trade and thereby end the rigorous Portuguese restrictions on and monopolies of external trade. In response, on January 28, the prince announced, "Royal Decrees and other Orders which until now prohibited trade between My Vassals and foreigners are suspended and without vigor." It was a momentous step in Brazil's development, for by one stroke of the pen some three hundred years of mercantilist policy were abandoned. Some historians have enthusiastically embraced the decree as the declaration of Brazil's economic independence, but that claim seems premature.

The effects of the decree, however, were immediate. In the following three years, Bahia increased its exports by 15 percent and its imports by 50 percent. Customs receipts from the five principal ports rose 20 percent. In the port of Rio de Janeiro there were 90 foreign ships in 1808; in 1809, 83; in 1810, 122; in 1815, 217; in 1820, 354. Vessels flying the English ensign predominated. By the end of 1808, about one hundred British merchants resided in Rio de Janeiro. It would be safe to conclude that after 1808 Brazil had little economic contact with Portugal. Great Britain rapidly and completely replaced the mother country in commerce, an economic reality officially recognized by the treaties of 1810. Skillfully negotiated by Strangford, these treatises set the maximum duty for British goods at 15 percent (imports from Portugal itself were required to pay a minimum of 16 percent and for other countries the minimum was 20 percent), provided that a packet line be established between England and Brazil. They also conceded to the English a right to have their own judges in Brazilian and Portuguese ports. In short, it was economic capitulation, the acknowledgement of the shift of Brazilian dependence from Portugal to England. However, the regent had little alternative but to acquiesce to London's demands, a recognition of the obvious. So, freed from Portuguese mercantilism in 1808, Brazil fell at once under the economic control of Great Britain, from whom the Brazilians bought most of their manufactured goods but to whom they sold only secondary amounts of their exports, a situation which would prevail for over one hundred years. The Swedish minister in Rio de Janeiro reported to his government that the treaty made Brazil a colony of Great Britain.

The opening of the ports was followed on April 1, 1808, with a decree revoking all previous prohibitions on manufacturing: "Henceforth, it shall be legal for any of My Vassals in any area in which they live to establish any kind of manufacture, without any exception, to make goods in large or small quantities as best suits them." The decree specifically lifted the onerous restrictions of 1785, that culmination point of Portuguese mercantilism. Some small textile factories were built in the decades that followed and an infant iron and steel industry began. The steam engine made its maiden appearance in Brazil at this time. In 1815 Bahia boasted its first steam-driven sugar mill. Two years later Pernambuco also possessed one. By 1834, there were sixty-four of them in operation. It was also in the All Saints Bay in 1819 that the first steamboat plied Brazilian waters. Among its distinguished passengers was the governor of Bahia who reported the journey to the king: "I traveled on the ship to Cachoeira where it arrived between eight and nine in the evening, having left Salvador at eleven that morning. I was very satisfied with the comfort, elegance, and safety of this ship. . . . It all worked so splendidly that I recommend the construction of more of these ships, hitherto unseen in Brazil, which have many advantages over our old ships."[13] To encourage such enterprises, the Crown appointed the Royal Committee of Commerce, Agriculture, Factories, and Navigation. Among other activities, it awarded prizes for the introduction of new crops. The establishment of the Bank of Brazil in 1808 in Rio de Janeiro with branches in Salvador and São Paulo further stimulated the economy. After centuries of steady but lethargic growth, Brazil's population increased by about one million in two decades. Table 3.1 indicates the growth as well as the approximate composition of the population.

Table 3.1. Population Figures and Components, 1798 and 1818

	1798	1818
Whites	1,000,000	1,040,000
Indians	250,000	250,000
Freedmen	225,000	585,000
Slaves	1,500,000	1,930,000
Total	2,975,000	3,805,000

The cultural changes wrought by the presence of the Crown metamorphosed the intellectual and professional life of Brazil. That was emphatically true of the capital. When the court arrived it found a beautifully located but somnolent city of approximately 60,000 inhabitants. A foreign merchant and resident of Rio de Janeiro during the first year of the court's presence left a valuable socio-economic perspective of the city through his analysis of the inhabitants' employment. John Luccock estimated that there were 1,000 connected in various ways with the court, 1,000 holding public offices, 1,000 men who resided in the city but received their incomes either from their plantations or from shipping, 700 priests or religious people, 500 lawyers, 200 medical doctors, 40 wholesale merchants, 2,000 retail merchants, 4,000 clerks,

---

13. Quoted in Edgard de Cerqueira Falcão, "A Primeira Máchina a Vapor que Sulcou Águas Brasileiras," *Revista do Instituto Geográfico e Histórico da Bahia*, no. 62 (1936), pp. 190–91.

apprentices, and commercial servants, 1,250 mechanics, 100 vendors, 300 fishermen, 1,000 soldiers of the line, 1,000 sailors belonging to the port, 1,000 free Negroes, 12,000 slaves, and 4,000 housewives. The remainder of the population consisted of children.[14] Within a decade after the arrival of the court, the city's population doubled. The influx of an estimated 24,000 Portuguese, a large contingent of Frenchmen and Englishmen, and some European diplomats lent a certain cosmopolitan air to the capital. The desperate need for institutes of higher learning was partially answered: in 1808 a naval academy was established and in 1810 a military academy, both of which offered courses in engineering and drawing; a medical school opened in Salvador in 1808 and another in Rio de Janeiro in 1810; likewise, courses in economics, in 1808, agriculture, in 1812, and chemistry, in 1817, were offered; a library of 60,000 volumes was inaugurated in Rio de Janeiro in 1814. Indicating the fascination with French culture, the Crown invited a French cultural mission to Rio de Janeiro in 1816 and founded the French-staffed Academy of Fine Arts some years later. Most remembered from that group of talented French instructors is the artist Jean Baptiste Debret, whose brush depicted memorable scenes of the epoch. Primary and secondary education received a badly needed impetus to grow and to improve. Law schools did not appear until 1827 when one was organized in São Paulo and a second in Olinda. After several abortive attempts in the eighteenth century, printing presses at last began to operate, principally in Rio de Janeiro, where the first newspaper, *Gazeta do Rio de Janeiro*, appeared in 1808, and in Salvador, which started to publish its first newspaper, *Idade d'Ouro do Brasil*, in 1811.

In addition to those cultural institutions, the colony also witnessed the establishment of myriad governmental bureaus, all new to Brazilian soil. The Brazilians were acquainted with most of them by name and reputation—the Council of State, the Conscience Board, the Treasury Coun-

14. John Luccock, *Notes on Rio de Janeiro and the Southern Parts of Brazil* (London, 1820), p. 41.

cil, etc.—but little had they ever dreamed of seeing them in full operation in their midst. In essence João set up in Rio de Janeiro the same organs that had functioned over the decades in Lisbon, although in certain instances he modified their functions because of their new location. Most notable, the Ministry of the Kingdom paid closer attention to Brazil while the Ministry of Navy and Overseas paid less. The captaincy governments remained unaltered in structure by the transference of the court. However, the presence of the Crown centralized control of Brazil in Rio de Janeiro to a degree unattainable or even unthinkable in the viceregal period. That centralization of power served as a powerful force for the unification of Brazil. Two European visitors observed, "Even the more remote provinces of the infant kingdom, whose inhabitants, led by curiosity, interest, or private business, visited Rio de Janeiro, soon accustomed themselves to recognize that city as the capital, and to adopt the manners and modes of thinking, which, after the arrival of the court, struck them as European."[15] Portuguese officials on all levels surrounded the prince regent. No Brazilian served as minister, nor was any chosen to sit on the Council of State, although they held posts on the secondary level and below. The metropolitans monopolized the government while the colonials financed it. Still, the Brazilians could not contain their pride, especially at the outset, in finding the fountainhead of the empire on their soil. Foreigners who knew Brazil during the first decade of the monarch's residence there, such as Henry Koster, John Luccock, J. B. von Spix, Johan A. Kantzow, and K. F. P. von Martius, commented on the salutary effect the presence of the Crown exercised on the spirit of the Brazilians. Ignácio José de Macedo typified the elation of the Brazilians when he wrote:

In its colonial status, from which it had just emerged, Brazil was known only because of the products of an abundant Nature; and now with its new status within the Empire, it begins to be admired for its political products which foretell its future elevation and long

15. J. B. von Spix and K. F. P. von Martius, *Travels in Brazil in the Years 1817–1820* (London, 1824), I, 143–44.

life. The unexpected transference of the Monarchy brought a brilliant dawn to these dark horizons, as spectacular as that on the day of its discovery. The new day of regeneration, an omen of brighter destinies, will bring long centuries of prosperity and glory.[16]

The changes were not isolated in Rio de Janeiro. Returning to Recife in late 1811 after an absence of only fourteen months, the traveller Henry Koster marvelled, "I perceived a considerable difference in the appearance of Recife and of its inhabitants, although I had been absent from the place for so short a period." The city visibly grew and some of its twenty-five thousand inhabitants shed their traditional habits to experiment with innovation. Koster attributed some of the changes to the influence of the Europeans who recently had settled in the Pernambucan capital and then concluded, "The time of advancement has come, and men, who had for many years gone on without making any change either in the interior or exterior of their houses, were now painting and glazing on the outside, and new furnishing within; modernizing themselves, their families, and their dwellings."[17]

The Brazilians found flattering the regent's personal view of their land. He seemed to have adapted himself perfectly to the new surroundings—certainly he was a model of adaptability in contrast to his wife, Carlota Joaquina, a Spanish princess who did nothing to hide her contempt. As a matter of fact, there can be no doubt that the well-intentioned, portly, and good-natured prince regent became genuinely fond of Brazil.

João showed himself well disposed toward his new home by elevating its political status. True, pressures from Europe helped him to resolve the matter. The delegates to the Congress of Vienna did not disguise their annoyance with a monarch who elected to live in a distant colony rather than speed back to his European capital. Talleyrand suggested that if he chose to linger in his tropical paradise the least he could do would be to make his viceroyalty a king-

16. Ignácio José de Macedo, *Oração Gratulatória ao Principe Regente* (Salvador, 1811), p. 1.

17. Koster, *Travels in Brazil*, pp. 88–89.

dom. João concurred. On December 16, 1815, Brazil became a kingdom, the equal, at least in judicial theory, of Portugal. Thereafter, the monarch was to bear the imposing title of "King of the United Kingdoms of Portugal, Brazil, and the Algarves." The promotion delighted the Brazilians, whose nativism swelled over their new royal status. John Luccock noted the effect: "The event infused into the public mind a sense of independence, a proper consciousness of its own importance, and a determination to support the new dignity." [18] The following year the ill and aged Maria I died and the prince regent ascended the throne in his own right as King João VI. The clamor in Portugal for his return mounted. Yet he dallied.

Political Independence

Brazil's proclamation of independence followed and in a certain sense was a reaction to a revolution in Portugal. Liberal thought disturbed the placidity of the entire Iberian peninsula as the second decade of the nineteenth century matured. The Portuguese liberals hoped to convoke a Côrtes, adjourned nearly a century and a quarter before. They wanted to write a constitution for the empire. While they debated the best method of procedure, a revolt in Spain under the leadership of Colonel Rafael Riego forced King Fernando VII to reinstitute the enlightened Constitution of 1812. Riego's temporary success encouraged the Portuguese liberals, and under their leadership revolt swept southward from Oporto engulfing the nation. The revolutionaries convoked the long defunct Côrtes to which Brazil was to be allowed sixty-nine representatives while one hundred would represent Portugal. The revolutionary junta demanded that João return to Lisbon forthwith. Reluctantly the king realized that his presence was essential in Lisbon if he was to continue wearing the Portuguese crown. On April 26, 1821, he bid a melancholy farewell to the city he had transformed

18. *Notes on Rio de Janeiro*, p. 568.

from a small, quiet viceregal capital into a larger, more cosmopolitan imperial capital. In reality the transformation of Rio de Janeiro symbolized a larger, more fundamental psychological change among the Brazilians themselves. In the space of thirteen years the inhabitants of the colony had entirely modified their attitude, assumed a different outlook. Because of their experience as the seat of a world-wide empire, they could never quite be provincials again. João seems to have sensed that change. Tradition has it that as he bid farewell to his son Pedro, left behind as the regent, he advised, "Pedro, I fear Brazil might separate itself from Portugal; if so, place the crown on your own head rather than allow it to fall into the hands of an adventurer."

The twenty-three-year-old Prince Pedro, heir to the Portuguese throne, enthusiastically took up his duties as regent with authority over internal affairs. He was a talented and complex young man. Unfortunately his education had been neglected during his rather undisciplined childhood. Nonetheless, he exhibited a large measure of common sense and sagacity. His energy was great and not a little of it was spent in amorous escapades. For many years, he lived openly with his mistress, the beautiful Domitila de Castro, who bore him five children and to whom he granted the title of "Marquesa de Santos." Severely criticized by the court—and for that matter in Europe as well—their passionate relationship stands as one of the great love affairs of the Americas. To overemphasize his bedroom behavior, however famous it might be, would be unfair. He engaged in a host of other activities as well. He could be a dashing horseman one hour and a serious composer of music the next. As a matter of fact, he became a friend of Rossini's and at least one of his symphonies was performed in Paris. Impetuous, sensuous, romantic in every sense of the word, he alternated between authoritarian and democratic behavior. Pedro thought of himself as a confirmed liberal; perhaps, considering the time and place, he was.

Aided by a bevy of Portuguese officials, the prince set about to rule Brazil. The challenge was formidable. In the first place, the vaults of the Bank of Brazil were empty; the departing court had withdrawn all the funds. Government income met only half of its expenses, a situation which would not be unusual in the decades ahead. The economy was very weak, dependent as it always had been on the demands, or lack of them, of a few leader nations. Brazil bought more abroad than it sold, and consequently an already high debt mounted. During the decade of the twenties sugar outsold coffee, the former accounting for a third of the exports and the latter for a quarter. In the following decade that ratio altered and coffee became the principal export and hope for future prosperity. Besides relying on a few foreign markets to buy its raw products, Brazil, because of limited capital accumulation, sought foreign investments in initiate new enterprises, thus making the economy doubly dependent on the exterior. Not the least of the prince's problems as he assumed his new responsibilities was the Côrtes. The behavior of that cantakerous Portuguese parliamentary body was rapidly intensifying and solidifying sentiment for independence within Brazil.

The Côrtes, which opened its sessions in Lisbon in January of 1821, quickly displayed its inexperience and amply demonstrated its lack of preparation to lead the empire. Belying the liberal sentiments which had animated them, the Portuguese representatives generally manifested a hostile attitude toward Brazil and verbally abused the forty-six Brazilian delegates who began arriving in August to take their seats. Failing to understand the alteration of Brazil's position vis-à-vis the metropolis, they dissipated much energy in an effort to put Brazil in its place, in other words to relegate the kingdom of Brazil to its colonial status quo ante 1808. Among other vexing restrictions, they refused to permit the establishment of a university there, tried to limit its commerce and trade, and replaced the few Brazilians holding office with Portuguese. In order to break Brazilian unity the Côrtes authorized the establishment of provincial governing juntas dependent directly on Lisbon. Military commanders were ordered to report directly to the metropolis and many governmental agencies established overseas were abolished. The Brazilian press criticized the actions of the Côrtes and inflammatory pamphlets carried the local case to the small but powerful literate segment of the population. Highly influential was a pamphlet entitled *O Despertador Brasiliense* (The Brazilian Awakener) written by Francisco de França Miranda. He attacked the Côrtes for being

illegal, injurious, and impolitic. Illegal, because it was decreed without the cooperation of our representatives, and consequently without the sanction of the nation. Injurious because it revealed the cynicism with which the Côrtes disposed of our existence as if we were a handful of miserable slaves . . . and not an allied kingdom more powerful and with more resources than Portugal herself. Impolitic because it chose this particular moment, when the eyes of the world were on Brazil and Portugal, to make our independence necessary and legitimate.[19]

Clearly the Brazilians had no intention of acquiescing in the authoritarian, humiliating, and damaging rule of the Côrtes.

The first direct confrontation between the orders of the Côrtes and the desires of the Brazilians occurred in late 1821 and early 1822. The Côrtes ordered Pedro to return. Reaction in the Brazilian capital was instant and negative. Officials and inhabitants sought to counter the order. Couriers sped from Rio de Janeiro to São Paulo and Minas Gerais to enlist the aid of those captaincies, important because of their proximity to the center of political power, their growing populations, and their prosperous economies based on sugar, coffee, cattle raising, and mining. Thereafter those three would form a vital political trinity, the core of Brazil. They would provide leadership for the others and as a consequence national Brazilian history would revolve around that heartland. In this case, sentiment within the trio opposed Pedro's departure. A special committee requested an audience with the prince and on January 9, 1822, presented a petition informing him that the consensus favored his remaining. Pedro replied, "As it is for the good of all and the general happiness of the Nation, I am ready. Tell the people

19. Quoted by Percy Alvin Martin, "Brazil," in A. Curtis Wilgus (ed.), *Argentina, Brazil, and Chile since Independence*, 2nd ed. (New York, 1963), p. 160.

that I will stay." The response pleased the people and the words, "I will stay" (the famous "Fico," in the Portuguese) were an open challenge to the Côrtes. The Portuguese garrison in Rio de Janeiro, declaring its loyalty to the Côrtes, prepared to force Pedro to accede to its will. The townspeople, militia, and students organized to oppose the garrison and thereby assert their own challenge to Lisbon. They forced the commander and his garrison to embark for Portugal.

The rapid pace of events required Pedro to reorganize his government. In the new cabinet, the well-educated, vocal, and nationalistic José Bonifácio de Andrada e Silva received the key post of "Minister of the Kingdom," the first Brazilian to hold such a high office. Otherwise Pedro continued to be surrounded by Portuguese who were personally loyal to him and who also had adopted Brazil as their new homeland. But Bonifácio was the most powerful figure in the newly reorganized government and, unlike either the prince or the other functionaries, he possessed a clear vision of what lay ahead. He guided the prince and Brazil toward independence.

A stellar example of the Brazilian intellectual of the period, the patriarch graduated from Coimbra in 1787 and went on to continue his studies in Italy and Germany. He traveled extensively in Europe and met some of the Continent's outstanding intellectuals. Scholarly institutions in France, Germany, and England elected him to membership. He observed the French Revolution at first hand during his residencies in Paris for parts of the years 1790, 1791, 1793, 1794, and 1799. An avid reader of the *philosophes*, he particularly admired Rousseau, all of whose works he owned. In short, he immersed himself totally in the European Enlightenment. He returned to Brazil in 1819, intent upon applying the knowledge gained from his studies, travels, and experience. Few Brazilians could exhibit such a distinguished and extensive education as José Bonifácio, but if we examine the biographies of the leaders of the independence movement, one salient characteristic emerges: a majority of them were educated abroad.

For that period, Bonifácio enunciated a very liberal

ideology. First and foremost, he sought to retain the unity of Brazil and believed that could be accomplished only with a Braganza in Rio de Janeiro. He favored the incorporation of liberal and democratic ideas into a traditional but constitutional monarchy. Bonifácio subscribed to Physiocrat philosophy. Only a stable monarchy could insure that the state encouraged agriculture, industry, and commerce, a necessary goal in the minister's opinion. Although supportive of individual liberties, he felt that in the last analysis they had to be subordinated to social order. In fact, he fretted a great deal about order and the need to defend property. A strong monarch could defend both and thus prevent excesses of liberty, doubtless his reaction to the French Revolution and perhaps to certain events then taking place in Spanish America. The ideal state would be achieved through broad education, moral as well as scientific, which would insure progress and social integration.

As Minister of the Kingdom, Bonifácio declared all the provinces under the control of Rio de Janeiro and moved to convoke a consultative council composed of delegates from all the provinces, thereby negating the vain effort of the Côrtes to decentralize Brazil. His attempt was not immediately successful. Only São Paulo, Minas Gerais, and Rio de Janeiro followed his leadership, and here once again that trio set the course for the rest. Strong Portuguese garrisons in the South and North tempered the reactions there. Prenambuco and Ceará vacillated. The Cisplatine Province, Bahia, Maranhão, and Pará remained loyal for the time being to the Côrtes. A small, radical press began to call for independence. In April, the *Reverbero Constitucional Fluminense* suggested that Pedro make himself "the founder of a new Empire." In May, the prince decreed that no act of the Côrtes would have force in Brazil without his approval and took the title "Perpetual Defender of Brazil." By that time talk of independence could be heard everywhere. Indeed, José Bonifácio was composing a letter to "friendly nations" in which he harshly criticized the colonial administration of the metropolis and asked them to establish direct relations with Brazil.

Having gone that far it was but a short step to formal independence. Even so, it came at an unexpected moment. A messenger overtook Pedro on a journey from Santos to São Paulo on September 7, 1822, and delivered to him letters from, among others, the Côrtes, José Bonifácio, and Pedro's wife, Princess Leopoldina. The Côrtes informed Pedro that it had reduced his powers. Other letters told how the Côrtes had criticized the young prince. Bonifácio urged the prince to defy the humiliating orders from the Côrtes and to heed mazombo opinion, which refused to allow Lisbon to dictate policies for Brazil. Princess Leopoldina, although Austrian by birth, had dedicated her energies and devotion to Brazil after she arrived in Rio de Janeiro in 1817 to marry Pedro. She too urged him to defy Portugal. Her letter stated, "Brazil under your guidance will be a great country. Brazil wants you as its monarch. . . . Pedro, this is the most important moment of your life. . . . You have the support of all Brazil." Angered by the news from Lisbon and encouraged by the advice of Bonifácio and Princess Leopoldina, Pedro unsheathed his sword right there on the bank of the Ipiranga River and gave the cry "Independence or Death!" One man, then, without the backing of a congress or junta, far from the noise of a crowd, declared the independence of Latin America's largest nation. He left no formal, written document of his accomplishment. His declaration was solely verbal. In that solitary act, the personable prince correctly reflected public sentiment. He apparently expressed the will of the majority, or perhaps it is more exact to say the will of the majority of the elite, since the masses had little to do at any time with political decisions. On December 1, 1822, amid a splendiferous ceremony, Pedro was crowned "Constitutional Emperor and Perpetual Defender of Brazil."

The roots of independence burrowed deeply into the past. Imperial reforms in the eighteenth century tightened Portuguese control to the alarm of the Brazilians who felt that greater bureaucratic authority and efficiency threatened their economic interests. The Enlightenment encouraged the Brazilians to know their land and to investigate its potential. Thus awakened, the Brazilians began to protest what they considered to be unjust restrictions on their development. Economic complaints became more audible. Concurrently the literature took on pronounced nativistic characteristics. The rapid changes during the period of João's residency in the New World swelled Brazilian pride. The old hostility between the mazombos and the renóis had not diminished. If anything, the enforced close contact of the Brazilians with the Portuguese in the preceding decade and a half intensified it. The highhanded action of the Côrtes further inflamed passions. Transformed from bucolic nativists into ardent nationalists, the Brazilian elite determined to create and defend a sovereign nation. That national consciousness triumphed in the Cry of Ipiranga in 1822. To fully understand the birth of Brazil, one must also realize that pro-independence sentiment hung heavily in the hemispheric air. The United States and most of Spanish America had gained their freedom from Europe. The kingdom of Brazil lay in the midst of a community of newly independent states and it was inevitable that the hemispheric disposition toward independence would affect Brazilian opinion and action.

Then, too, there converged in the early 1820s three interest groups whose combined impact made independence inevitable. Strongest of these was the mazombo planter aristocracy. Born and bred in Brazil, that landed gentry enjoyed considerable power and social prestige because of its great estates and control over the local senado da câmara. They identified fully with Brazil, Portugal being only a distant abstraction. They favored independence in order to expand their own power and to assure a greater freedom of access to international markets. Conservative by nature, they supported no structural reforms. The only change they sought was to substitute themselves for the Portuguese in power. Perhaps the foremost journalist of the period, Evaristo da Veiga, summed up their viewpoint when he pleaded, "Let us have no excesses. We want a constitution, not a revolution." The second group was the urban dwellers. So long as Brazil remained totally rural there was little possibility of revolt against Portugal. The growth of the cities—modest as they were—in the eighteenth century provided the focal point for agitation: Ouro Prêto in 1789, Salvador in 1798, Recife in 1817, and Rio de Janeiro in 1822. Frequently the municipal council served as the forum of debate and the instrumentality for action by which the cause of independence was furthered. On the one hand, the cities were a means of bringing together the planters; on the other, within the cities a small but vocal class of free persons appeared, neither plantation owners nor slaves, an unstable class anxious to improve its status. Independence offered them that possibility. Finally, the British, eager to expand their trade and to perfect their economic hegemony over Brazil, favored independence. Castlereagh for one, understood the advantage of a Brazil liberated from Portuguese rule but dependent on Britain, and Canning later acted to bring that to pass.

Obviously Pedro played a paramount role in the independence of Brazil. Until December of 1821, he submitted to the will of the Côrtes and of his father. Under the influence of some Brazilians who served him, the prince then began to perceive that the Côrtes really aimed to injure Brazil, the country where he grew up and which he loved. It became increasingly clear as well that his father was a prisoner of the Côrtes and an unwilling spokesman for it. In his powerful ministerial position, José Bonifácio impressed upon the prince the Brazilian point of view and where possible guided his decisions. The minister had the intelligence and ability to foresee the inevitability and desirability of independence. The prince had the flamboyance and dash to declare it. The turning point came in January, 1822, when Pedro resolved to remain and thereby countered the wishes of the Côrtes. By May of that year, he was speaking and writing of "We Brazilians." He had identified his fortunes entirely with the Brazilian cause and served as the perfect instrument to effect national independence.

The fundamental problem confronting the new nation was not so much its need to assert its independence as to maintain its unity. A small navy under the command of Lord Cochrane, Earl of Dundonald, recently admiral of the victorious Chilean squadron, carried word of the declaration of independence to the principal cities along the coast from

Montevideo to Belém. By bluster or force, the navy obtained the allegiance of all the littoral cities even though ports with strong garrisons like Montevideo and Salvador required siege and battle. Before the end of 1823 the navy had overcome all opposition to the declaration of independence, raised the imperial ensign over all the ports, established the authority of Pedro I, and incorporated such distant provinces as Pará and Maranhão into the new empire. The navy's role was an important one, but of course national unity was based on much more than military force.

That so diverse and so immense an area as Brazil retained its unity has intrigued students of the nation's evolution. The unity is all the more miraculous when one compares monolithic Brazil with the fragmented remnants of Spain's American empire. The three viceroyalties of Spanish South America disintegrated into ten republics, the viceroyalty of New Spain into an archipelago of states. An extreme example was the Kingdom of Guatemala, already a subdivision of the viceroyalty of New Spain, which splintered into five microstates. The examples of Spanish America demonstrate that language, religion, tradition, geographic continuity, and common history are not always denominators guaranteeing unity. They may help to solidify a state but they in and of themselves are insufficient to weld a nation together. In the case of Brazil, it is obvious that the vast majority of the inhabitants spoke Portuguese, professed Roman Catholicism, enjoyed the same mélange of Afro-Indo-Iberian traditions, and shared three hundred years of history. They inhabited contiguous territory. Those similarities provided the basis for a superficial cohesion, but Brazil had something more which, taken with these factors, explains its phenomenal unity in the face of diversity and regionalism.

The very fact that Portugal was far less well organized or structured than Spain permitted Brazil to develop at a more natural pace. After all, it was not until Pombal applied his heavy hand that all of Portuguese America was unified—at least in theory—into one colony. It occasionally seemed that the colony acquired or altered institutions as needed, and Lisbon from time to time reformed some of its organs of government. In contrast, the rigid hierarchical administration imposed almost at once on Spanish America minimized flexibility. The only method of change it allowed was destruction. During the passage of three centuries, the government of Brazil gradually became more uniform as it also became more centralized. Power first focused in Lisbon, but after 1808 its focal point was Rio de Janeiro.

The presence of the Braganzas in Rio de Janeiro for thirteen years forged the strongest link of unity. During this period the Brazilians acquired the habit of looking to Rio as the seat of government, the source of power, and the font of authority. Further, there was a Braganza on hand to lend legitimacy to each peaceful transition from viceroyalty to kingdom to empire.

The educated Brazilians and the rest of the elite seemed disposed to accept the monarchy with which they identified. Like José Bonifácio, they saw in the monarch a guarantee of national unity and the preservation of public order. Consequently no acrimonious debates between republicans and monarchists rent the tranquillity of the new nation as was the case in Spanish America. The presence of a sympathetic prince who was not a usurper made monarchy the logical choice, and thus the transition from colony to nationhood was as smooth as anyone could hope for. Pedro's power was at once legitimate. Thus the problem of legitimacy of power, so troublesome in the Spanish-speaking republics, did not beset Brazil. Heir to the long tradition of the house of Braganza, Pedro inherited his authority. He possessed and was surrounded by all the symbols of authority. Historical precedent strengthened his position. In that way, the throne occupied by the Braganza dynasty proved to be the perfect unifier of the new empire.

A consensus, certainly among the elite, favored unity. Manuel de Nascimento Castro e Silva, a deputy from Ceará to the Côrtes, expressed that sentiment well in his remark, "The Supreme Arbiter of empires created Brazil as a single territory from the Amazon to the Plata; and consequently it must never be divided without the very express and solemn declaration of those provinces which intend to separate themselves from the Brazilian union."[20] All the other deputies echoed that sentiment.

The Brazilians possessed a mobility which broke down regional barriers. The interior had for several centuries scattered and mixed people with no distinction as to their place of origin. In the sertão, a single, a truly "Brazilian" society formed. The resultant fusion provided a national nucleus which counterbalanced the regionalism more characteristic of the coast. Foreign threats, real or imagined, strengthened unity during the nineteenth century. From time to time waves of anti-Portuguese, anti-British, and anti-Spanish American sentiment inundated Brazil, and at those times a strong feeling of nationalism surged. Nothing served better to close regional divisions than an external threat. Ill-defined as nineteenth-century nationalism was, it contributed significantly to strengthening unity.

On several occasions, the young emperor had signified his willingness to rule under a constitution. Consequently the single most important political problem confronting the new empire was the writing and implementation of such a constitution. Elections were held for an Assembly which would have both constituent and legislative powers. On May 3, 1823, the Assembly opened with ninety deputies in attendance. Their backgrounds varied: 26 were lawyers; 22 judges; 19 priests; 7 military men; and the rest were medical doctors, landowners, and public officials. With the exception of those few who recently had served in the Côrtes, they lacked legislative experience. By and large it was a liberal group; some of them had served as leaders of the Inconfidência of 1789 and the Revolt of 1817. The Assembly would furnish many of the future leaders of the nation.

Once again in terms of the times, liberal ideology seemed dominant among the elite, particularly those segments associated with the cities and with exports. Not surprisingly, then, they put forth, advocated, and adopted some of the major tenets of early nineteenth-century liberalism, a

20. Session of August 7, 1822, *Diário das Côrtes Geraes, Extraordinárias, e Constituentes da Nação Portuguesa* (Lisbon, 1823), p. 83.

liberalism strongly influenced by the Enlightenment in general but by English ideas and models in particular. They favored free trade; they looked to capitalistic models as guides; they stressed the value and sanctity of private property; they prized education; they argued the advantages of free navigation of rivers. Their loyalty to that type of liberalism revealed their aspirations to duplicate the material successes of those nations from which they drew their ideology. However, removed from its original context, that liberalism had the unfortunate effect of further subordinating the Brazilian economy to the needs of the capitalist markets of the North Atlantic. Free trade and competition, as we shall see, proved disasterous for a majority of the Brazilians. In short, the liberalism of the Brazilian elite had the ultimate effect of deepening Brazil's dependency.

From the start, the legislature and the emperor clashed. Passionately debated was the question whether the laws passed by the Assembly needed imperial sanction before they could take effect. After a close vote, the Assembly decided negatively. The emperor disapproved but upon reflection resolved to say nothing. In its brief history, the Assembly passed only six laws, all of which have been regarded as salutary. But the difference between the legislature and the executive was far more fundamental than that power struggle indicated. The legislators were Brazilian, products of the old landed aristocracy or of the new urban society. The emperor—despite all his generously manifested devotion and dedication to the cause of Brazilian independence and commonweal—was Portuguese. He had been born in Portugal and he surrounded himself with Portuguese-born advisers. The ensuing struggle between the legislature and the executive represented the continuing effort of the Brazilians to rid themselves of lingering Portuguese influence. The legislative debate showed that the legislators were almost pathologically anti-Portuguese and by implication hostile to the emperor. The sensitive and headstrong Pedro resented their attitude and disapproved of their encroachment on what he considered to be his prerogatives and power. As the lack of understanding and good will between the two grew, a rivalry developed in which each sought to curtail the powers of the other. Persuaded that the Assembly not only lacked discipline but scattered the seeds of revolution, Pedro decided to dissolve it. Troops arrived at the Assembly hall on November 11, 1823, to prohibit further sessions. The legislative leaders were sent into exile.

Pedro had promised the Brazilians a constitution, and despite the dissolution of the Assembly he meant to keep his word. He immediately convoked a committee of ten Brazilians who at his behest completed the basis for a constitution by early December. The emperor submitted the projected constitution to the municipal councils for approval. As they had during the days of agitation for independence, they played another significant role in national formation. Most of the municipalities approved. Stating that the voice of the Brazilian people had spoken through their local governments, Pedro promulgated the constitution on March 25, 1824.

Above all else, the new constitution provided for a highly centralized government with a vigorous executive. Although power was divided between four branches—executive, legislative, judiciary, and moderating—the lion's share rested in the hands of the emperor. Assisted by a council of state and a ministry, the emperor exercised the functions of the chief executive, but even more important than that he wielded the moderating power, which made him responsible for the maintenance of the independence of the nation as well as the equilibrium and harmony of the other powers and the twenty provinces. He enjoyed a veto over all legislation as well as the right to convoke or dissolve the General Assembly. He selected the presidents of the provinces, the ministers, the bishops (for he claimed the old royal patronage the pope had conferred on Portuguese kings), and the senators. He could pardon criminals and review judicial decisions. His powers were many—but then so were his responsibilities. In short, the emperor was expected to utilize his moderating power as an omniscient harmonizer in a far-flung empire whose infinite geographic and human diversity challenged the existence of the state. In the final analysis the Crown was the one, pervasive, national institution which could claim to represent all Brazilians. The General Assembly was divided into a senate, whose members were appointed for life from lists presented by the provinces, and a chamber of deputies elected periodically and indirectly by a highly restricted suffrage. The constitution provided for broad individual freedom and for equality before the law. Considering the time, the place, and the circumstances, it is safe to conclude that the constitution was a liberal document. It was also flexible, generously allowing amendments and reforms without the necessity of adopting a new constitution. Proof of the viability of the document lay in its durability: it lasted sixty-five years until the monarchy fell in 1889.

With independence, unity, and the form of government established, the next problem demanding attention was the recognition of the empire by other nations. On August 6, 1822, Pedro had signed José Bonifácio's "Manifestation to Friendly Governments and Nations" and had dispatched diplomatic agents to London, Vienna, and Rome. Serious difficulties complicated Brazil's acceptance into the community of nations. Foremost was the attitude of Portugal. The European states were reluctant to recognize Brazil before the former mother country did. Great Britain, for example, was eager to accord recognition but at the same time reluctant to weaken its influence in Portugal or alienate its profitable Portuguese market. Furthermore, the attitudes of the Holy Alliance dissuaded the European states from welcoming Brazil. The European policies did not influence the course of the United States, which had begun to embrace the new Latin American nations in 1822. The United States became the first to extend the international hand of friendship to Brazil when, in May of 1824, President James Monroe received José Silvestre Rebelo as chargé d'affaires.

Commercial pressures in England pushed the Court of St. James's to extend recognition. Britain wanted to protect its valuable Brazilian market. English exports to Brazil in 1825 equaled those sold to the rest of South America and Mexico combined, and totaled half those sent to the United States. The English hoped to renew the Treaty of 1810 before expiration scheduled for 1825 would elevate the tariff on British goods from 15 to 24 percent. Such a renewal required first the establishment of diplomatic relations. Not strangers to interference in Portuguese affairs, London sent Sir Charles Stuart first to Lisbon to confer with João VI and to apply the necessary pressure on him to accord recognition; he then proceeded to Rio de Janeiro to complete the necessary mediation. Sir Charles executed his mission brilliantly. By the end of 1825, Portugal acknowledged the independence of Brazil in return for 2 million pounds sterling, part as Brazil's share of Portugal's debts and part as payment of João for property and a palace in Brazil. As a sign of respect and love, Pedro permitted his father to use the honorary title of "Emperor of Brazil." Both concessions infuriated the Brazilians and further inflamed their anti-Lusitanian passions. Further, the agreement with Portugal ended the possibility of a union between Brazil and Angola encouraged by their intimate relations over the centuries. Pedro had to promise "not to accept the proposals of any Portuguese colonies to join the Empire of Brazil."

But there was still more to be extracted from the Brazilians. British services and favors were not gratuitous. In return for Sir Charles's efforts in his behalf and for promised British recognition, Pedro had to agree to a series of treaties with Great Britain, none of which offered a promising prospect to the novice nation. First, he consented to a new commercial treaty, a reenactment of the one with Portugal in 1810, to continue the favorable import duty of 15 percent on British goods. In a second treaty, Brazil consented to abolish the slave trade within three years. The recognition by first Portugal and then Great Britain broke the diplomatic impasse. Within a year, Austria, the Vatican, Sweden, France, Switzerland, the Low Countries, and Prussia welcomed the new empire into the community of nations.

From several points of view, Pedro met his downfall because of his inept handling of foreign affairs. First, the unpopular concessions to Portugal and Great Britain in exchange for their recognition aroused public ire. Second, Pedro fell into a diastrous war with Argentina over the east bank of the Plata, the final chapter of that century and a half of territorial struggle. João, taking advantage of the unrest caused by the independence struggle against Spain in the Plata region, had dispatched troops into the Banda Oriental del Uruguay in 1811. He withdrew them the following year under British pressure, but sent them again in 1816 to reoccupy the coveted territory. In 1821, he annexed the area as the Cisplatine Province, which was allowed to keep its own laws, language, and some local autonomy. The annexation to the kingdom of Brazil did not suit most of the inhabitants of the area and elicited cries of protest from the Argentines who were no happier to see the Brazilians in partial control of their strategic Río de la Plata than the Spaniards had been to see the Portuguese there. In 1825 war broke out between Argentina and Brazil over the future of the Cisplatine Province. Neither side distinguished itself on the battlefield. Both exhausted themselves financially, and when neither perceived a clear victory they agreed on a compromise in 1828: the disputed province would become an independent buffer state. Thus was born the Republica Oriental del Uruguay. The loss of money, men, and a province embittered the Brazilians, who blamed the emperor for their reverses.

Pedro's third foreign involvement irreparably alienated the Brazilians. When the death of João VI in 1826 vacated the Portuguese throne, a temptation crossed the emperor's path. As legitimate heir to that throne he would have liked to have worn two crowns. The Brazilians refused to hear of the matter. Reluctantly he renounced the Portuguese crown in favor of his daughter, Maria II, who was to marry his younger brother, her Uncle Miguel. To further complicate matters, Miguel seized the throne in 1828 in defiance of Maria's rights. Civil war resulted, and Pedro devoted more and more of his time to the complexities of that struggle. The Brazilians deeply resented his absorption in those European matters. Anti-Portuguese sentiment, long simmering, began to boil. To the degree that that anti-Portuguese feeling increased, Pedro's popularity decreased.

Internal affairs were not favorable to the emperor either. The financial situation deteriorated under the pressure of war; the foreign debt rose, the exchange rate declined. The

Bank of Brazil resorted to the wholesale emission of paper money to meet budgetary deficits. All too quickly inconvertible, the paper drove gold and silver out of circulation. The unhealthy condition of the Bank forced the government to liquidate it. Its demise did not stem the flow of paper money because the national treasury continued to issue it. Nor was the tariff policy calculated to relieve the financial strain. In a mood of impractical liberality, the government extended the 15 percent maximum tariff to Portugal, France, and others in 1826 and 1827. The Vasconcelos Tariff of 1828 uniformly fixed the tariff at 15 percent on all foreign merchandise.

Pedro revealed scant talent in dealing with the legislature, whose first session opened in 1827. Ignoring the chamber of deputies as much as possible, he drew all of his ministers from the senate. Bernardo Pereira de Vasconcelos, a liberal from Minas Gerais who dominated the legislature, introduced a bill to require ministers to submit annual reports and to attend budgetary hearings. The emperor twice attempted to govern with a ministry in accord with the elected Chamber, but both of those vague attempts at parliamentary government failed. It became apparent that there existed no confidence and even less cordiality between the emperor and the Assembly. Pedro tersely and bitterly confined his speech from the throne closing the First Assembly in 1829 to, "This session is closed." Indeed, he had quarreled with most of the prominent liberal leaders, chief among whom were the Andrada e Silva brothers, José Bonifácio, Martim Francisco, and Antônio Carlos, who spent much of the 1820s in exile.

Several revolts disturbed internal peace. The most serious was in Pernambuco in 1824 where the emperor's selection of the provincial president met opposition. Furthermore, the rebels refused to accept the new constitution and swore their loyalty to the recently dissolved Assembly. Reaction from Rio de Janeiro was immediate. As in 1817, both land and sea forces surrounded Recife and swiftly crushed the rebellion. The so-called Confederation of the Equator represented a vigorous regionalism always a potential threat to national unity. In 1828, two battalions of German and Irish mercenary troops revolted in Rio de Janeiro in protest against inhumane treatment. Their lawlessness shook the capital before they could be disarmed and many of them deported. In 1829 there was yet another rebellion in Pernambuco, this one brief and confined to the interior.

All these events, foreign and domestic, tended to diminish the popularity of the young ruler. The dissatisfaction coalesced into an active opposition to him. The small but outspoken newspapers gave voice to that opposition. Its criticisms stung, and Pedro requested legal means to deal with a press he asserted abused its freedoms under the pretext of liberty. Instead, new journals appeared so that by 1830 the empire counted forty-two of them. Those papers devoted full coverage to the overthrow of Charles X of France in 1830, noting pointedly that any monarch who sought to subvert the free institutions of his country deserved to see his reign end. It was a warning the emperor failed to heed. He boosted his popularity in mid-March of 1831 by appointing a popular, all-Brazilian cabinet, but in early April he replaced it with an unpopular one composed of senators and nobles. The opposition seized that cabinet change as the opportunity to bring pressure to bear on Pedro. They demanded the return of the March cabinet. The emperor retorted that it was his constitutional right to change ministries at will—and legally he was right. However, the legal technicality did not prevent the populace and the military in Rio de Janeiro from demonstrating in the streets. A delegation visited Pedro to demand the reappointment of the dismissed cabinet. He answered with his abdication. He moodily announced:

I prefer to descend from the throne with honor rather than to go on reigning as a sovereign who has been dishonored and degraded. Those born in Brazil no longer want me for the reason that I am Portuguese. I have been expecting this for a long time, have seen it coming ever since I visited Minas. My son has the advantage over me in that he is a Brazilian by birth. The Brazilians respect him. He will have no difficulty in governing, and the constitution will guarantee him his rights. I renounce the crown with the glory of ending as I began—constitutionally.[21]

As his father had before him, Pedro set sail for Europe, leaving a son behind to rule Brazil, in this case the five-year-old Pedro de Alcântara. Back in Europe, he entered fully into the struggle over the Portuguese succession and placed his daughter on the throne as Maria II in 1834. He died shortly thereafter, ending an eventful life of thirty-six years.

Pedro's reign in Brazil, 1822–1831, the period called the First Empire, is not an easy one to evaluate. The loss of the Cisplatine Province rankled Brazilians, and it remains as the major territorial loss the nation has suffered. The consequent failure to maintain at least partial control of the Plata would lead to endless diplomatic maneuvering, military intervention, and the major Latin American war. In general, Pedro's diplomacy failed. Likewise, it is difficult to find much progress in national development during his reign. On the other hand, he gave Brazil independence bloodlessly and obtained prompt international recognition for the new empire (whatever the cost); both were considerable achievements, particularly when one compares them to the long and costly wars the Spanish Americans waged for their freedom and the difficulty they had in getting Spanish recognition of their new republics. His rule, furthermore, maintained order and strengthened unity. Finally, the Constitution of 1824 proved to be a useful and practical document which guided Brazil through its first sixty-five years. The balance of evaluation, then, seems to tip in favor of Pedro I.

Chaos Into Order

The years immediately following the abdication constitute a period of reaction against many events of the preceding decade. Of primary importance is the fact that the Brazil-

21. Quoted in Sérgio Correa da Costa, *Every Inch a King: a Biography of Dom Pedro I, First Emperor of Brazil* (New York, 1953), pp. 166–67.

ians themselves for the first time took control of their own government. Members of the elite with their roots firmly in the plantation economy replaced the Portuguese-born who, under Pedro, in a fashion reminiscent of the colonial era, had continued to monopolize the highest offices in the empire. A majority of the new, nationalistic leaders reacted violently against the highly centralized government of Pedro I. They tended to favor federalism. That principle, widely debated and experimented with throughout Latin America in the nineteenth century, offered obvious appeals in a large and varied country such as Brazil. In addition, many Brazilians desired to broaden the powers and participation of the elected representatives in the government. For the first time masters of their own ship of state, the Brazilian elites were eager to chart their own course. Few thought, however, in terms of a republic. The overwhelming majority gave their allegiance to the infant Pedro II, but there was in the air a willingness—even at this stage a necessity—to experiment in government.

The constitution stipulated that until Pedro reached the age of eighteen and in the event that there was no one else in the family old enough to rule in his name the General Assembly would elect a regency composed of three men, presided over by the eldest. The Assembly elected such a triumvirate but withheld from it some of the imperial powers. For example, the regents could not dissolve the Chamber, nor could they confer royal titles. In the intense political maneuverings initiated by the Assembly's exercise of its expanded power the first glimmerings of future party structure could be discerned. At that early stage of development it is probably safe to observe that there were two political tendencies toward which the politicians gravitated. On the one side stood those of liberal or moderate persuasions. While swearing absolute loyalty to the monarch, they believed that the emperor should reign and not rule. They advocated the biennial election of the popular chamber, an elected senate, suppression of the Council of State, and a federal structure with elected bicameral provincial assemblies. The more radical within that movement preached that illegal acts on the part of the government or breaches of the constitution could be met with armed resistance. On the opposing side, the conservatives supported a strong, centralized monarchy, the core of their political ideology. They recognized no legal form of resistance or change outside of the ballot box. The liberals exercised considerable influence and power during the early years of the regency. After all, their ideology offered the most marked reaction to the immediate past.

The liberals won their major victory with the passage of the Additional Act of 1834, a constitutional amendment. To increase governmental efficiency, the number of regents was reduced from three to one who would be elected by restricted suffrage and hold office for four years. The Act abolished the Council of State, regarded by the liberals as the bastion of conservatism. It also outlawed the entailing of estates. In an agricultural empire such as Brazil, that prohibition provided, at least in theory, for some fundamental future economic changes. To encourage federalism in the provinces, legislative assemblies with power over local affairs replaced the General Councils whose duties had been primarily consultative. This last provision was a major concession to those who favored decentralization. Its passage coincided with, if it did not encourage, a series of disastrous provincial rebellions whose cumulative effect threatened the very existence of the empire.

The experiments in government were carried out during a period of economic difficulties. Tariffs and taxes provided a meager income for the central government. Sugar prices dropped steadily; the return on cotton was even less. Gold mining had fallen to a small fraction of its previous output and as one result the internal demand for cattle declined. As those basic economic activities stagnated, per capita income fell. A general impoverishment beset the nation. The obvious consequence of the economic distress was unrest which in turn fed upon a political structure weakened by uncertain experimentation and the instability of the regency.

In the period between 1831 and 1835, there already had been frequent, shortlived, and tumultuous rebellions. Most of the provinces witnessed some degree of disturbance. In

Pernambuco, Bahia, and Mato Grosso, the trouble stemmed primarily from anti-Portuguese sentiments. The year 1831, in particular, was a restive one in Rio de Janeiro. Those disturbances, however, were but preludes to what was to follow.

Five major provincial revolts erupted between 1832 and 1838 in diverse parts of the empire from the extreme north to the extreme south, but all of them occurred outside of the controlling core of the empire, Rio de Janeiro, Minas Gerais, and São Paulo. This might partially explain their eventual failure. They were the War of the Cabanos in the interior of Pernambuco and Alagoas, 1832–1836; the related Cabanagem in Pará, 1835–1840; the Sabinada in Bahia, 1837–1838; the Balaiada in Maranhão, 1838–1841; and the Farroupilha in Rio Grande do Sul, 1835–1845. These revolts had complex origins which were in each case largely regional, but it is possible to find some common denominators. A varied combination of economic, social, and political dissatisfactions gave rise to all of them. Each of the areas suffered from economic reverses. In at least two and possibly three of the revolts, the antipathy felt by the Brazilians toward resident Portuguese merchants and landlords played a role. Resentment of the provincial president appointed from Rio de Janeiro figured among the causes of three of them. Confusion at the court accompanied by relaxed centralism contributed to the causes of all.

It is also possible to view at least some of the tumult and revolt as genuine expressions of popular discontent or frustration. In fact, the first half of the nineteenth century may well be the period of Brazilian history in which the masses expressed most protest and played their most active political role. Large numbers of the popular classes throughout the provinces resented their status and feared the changes imposed on them. Bahia, in particular, during the years 1824–1840, seethed with social protest. In general terms, it is safe to conclude that the Bahian dissidents were people of color who opposed or fought against "European types." Their ideology was vague and often contradictory. They frequently sacked shops and warehouses in a quest for food and killed military officers and landowners in a challenge to authority.

Three major popular rebellions of the 1830s, the Cabanos, Cabanagem, and Balaiada, further revealed the unrest of the masses. Those rebellions appear to have expressed the frustrations of poor whites, mestizos, mulattoes, black slaves, and Indians. The rebels hoped to improve their standards of living, although their programs were vague, and to share in the exercise of power. The War of the Cabanos was particularly significant because it was entirely agrarian. Vicente Ferreira da Paula commanded the rural masses and can be considered a genuine populist caudilho. The leaders of all three rebellions were revered by their followers who considered them to be one of themselves; however, to the governments, they were "criminals" "bandits," and "outlaws," which they are still termed whenever mentioned in the official histories. For example, in a history text, *História do Brasil* by Hélio Vianna, widely used during the 1960s in Brazilian universities, the author spoke of the Balaiada as "unchecked banditry," and the principal allegation against the rebels was their "audacity to attack private property." The elitist view of popular agitation seems to have changed very little over the course of more than a century.

The regents had neither the prestige nor the authority to hold together a vast empire shaken by revolt. The first single regent, Diogo Antônio Feijó, a radical liberal, was elected in 1835. He had served in the Côrtes, been an early advocate of independence, held the portfolio of Minister of Justice, and sat in both the assembly and the senate. He failed to calm the provincial storms and resigned under heavy criticism in 1837. The second regent, Pedro de Araújo Lima, a conservative, was no less qualified: he too had represented Brazil in the Côrtes and served as a senator and minister. Some notable cultural advancements took place during his regency: the foundations of the elite secondary school, the Imperial College of Pedro II, the creation of the National Archives, and the organization of the Brazilian Geographical and Historical Institute. But the provincial rebellions raged on, if anything increasing in scope. A strong reaction against the mounting chaos prompted the elites, fearful of the very unity of the empire, to turn to the throne as the instrument and symbol of national unity, to duplicate the miracle it had wrought in 1822.

Experience indicated that too much autonomy had been given to the provinces under the Additional Act, an autonomy which they were unprepared to exercise responsibly. In the name of unity, to say nothing of efficiency, it proved necessary to check the centrifugal tendencies. The General Assembly passed the Interpretive Law in 1840 to end the federal experiment and return to centralism. At the same time, a clamor to coronate the young prince rose. The constitution barred Pedro from ascending the throne until he reached eighteen. Since he was born on December 2, 1825, the nation theoretically would have to wait until that date in 1843. Most feared that the spiralling chaos and crises would disintegrate the nation before then. A movement was organized to declare Pedro of age at once and to crown him. Newspapers and public opinion seemed increasingly favorable to the idea. When the legislature failed to come to an agreement on the plan, the liberals took matters into their own hands. They sent a mission to Pedro on July 22, 1840, to ask if he was willing to wear the crown at once. He replied affirmatively. The following day he appeared before the General Assembly to take the oath to uphold the constitution. The appearance of the handsome and dignified adolescent, blond and blue-eyed, sparked deliriums of cheering among the crowds filling the assembly hall and packing the square and the streets around it. The cry of "Viva Senhor Dom Pedro II, constitutional emperor and perpetual defender of Brazil!" rang out repeatedly. Later, in the hushed expectancy of the Chamber, he pronounced clearly his oath: "I swear to maintain the Roman Catholic Apostolic religion, and the integrity and indivisibility of the empire; to observe, and to cause to be observed, the constitution and laws of the Brazilian nation, and to promote the general well-being of Brazil by every means in my power." From the Assembly, Pedro proceeded to his palace in the center of Rio de Janeiro accompanied by the military and the people. A fully illuminated city celebrated the festivities far into the night. The formal coronation took place one year later. As is evident, the premature proclamation of his majority was devoid of any legality. Rather it was a kind of coup d'etat sanctioned by the anxieties of the nation. A foreign resident in Brazil during this period, Daniel F. Kidder, observed: "A revolution has indeed transpired; the constitution has been trampled under foot; but it is a popular revolution, in accordance with the inclination of the people, and therefore it is a glorious event. The monarchical principal is triumphant; but it has become so by means of the most palpable mobocracy."[22] However, the coup calmed turbulent political waters. The presence of the young emperor on the throne provided the authority figure which reunified the sprawling empire. Hierarchy reigned; order slowly returned. His early coronation reaffirmed the patriarchal principle which had dominated Brazil for centuries. The escape from national disintegration also slowed the impact of innovation for at least another generation. Those who lived through the centrifugal dangers of the regency period deeply venerated the monarchy thereafter because it had preserved Brazilian unity during its moment of greatest stress. As long as that generation lived, the monarchy remained an unquestioned institution. Strong centralization was regarded, at least for the time being, as the remedy for the evils of the past. If the abdication of Pedro I had opened the posts of government to the Brazilians, the coronation of Pedro II gave them a genuine national emperor, for the young Pedro had been born and reared in Brazil and was entirely identified with his native land. His coronation was the logical conclusion to the Brazilianization of the government which had begun in 1808 and accelerated in 1831.

The decade beginning in 1840 with the proclamation of the majority was a significant period of transition for Brazil. In many respects those years marked the twilight of the colonial period and the dawn of a truly national state. Further steps toward the Europeanization of Brazil were taken and a new sophistication characterized politics.

22. *Sketches of Residence and Travels in Brazil* (Philadelphia, 1845), II, 367.

Quite logically the emperor's first attention focused on the problem of reestablishing peace in his domains. The Balaiada and Farroupilha revolts raged on, and in 1842 the liberals in São Paulo and Minas Gerais took up arms to protest the investment of a conservative cabinet and the rapid return to centralization. Fortunately for the emperor there appeared at that time an extraordinarily capable military leader, Luís Alves de Lima e Silva, Baron and later Count, Marquis, and Duke of Caxias. Ably and firmly he suppressed the uprisings in Maranhão, Minas Gerais, and São Paulo before going on to quell the rebellion festering in Rio Grande do Sul. Peace returned to the shaken empire, and the entire Brazilian nation gathered around the throne to pay homage to Pedro II.

The empire matured politically during that decade. The emperor did not hesitate to use his moderating power to seat and unseat ministries and thus to alternate the two political parties, the Liberals and the Conservatives, in power. He would select ministers from one party. If that party held a majority in the popular chamber, the ministry governed without difficulty. If that party did not hold a majority, he dissolved the Chamber and called for new elections. Since the new ministry controlled the electoral machinery, its party was certain to win the majority needed in the new Chamber to enable it to govern. Such an arrangement demanded astuteness on the part of the emperor to correctly assess public opinion so that he knew when the nation favored a shift of political parties. In 1840, the emperor nodded to the Liberals, but the following year he reversed himself and brought the Conservatives to power. At once they initiated a concentrated campaign to recentralize the government. They restored the Council of State whose primary duty was to advise the emperor on the use of his moderating power. Curtailing the powers of the provincial legislatures, they even appointed the vice-presidents of the provinces. Furthermore, the central government assumed direction of all the police forces throughout the realm. The Liberals loudly protested these measures—even resorting the violence, as we have seen, in Minas Gerais and São Paulo—but when they returned to power for four years in 1844 they did nothing to negate that recentralization. Sobered by the responsibilities of power, they accepted it as inevitable and necessary.

In 1847, Pedro decided no longer to select the entire ministry but just to name a president of the Council of Ministers who in turn would pick his own subordinates after due consultation, of course, with the emperor. The creation of the post of prime minister facilitated the adoption of a parliamentary system—quite *sui generis*. Under the firm tutorial guidance of their ruler, the politicians learned the give and take of politics, and because they trusted his sagacity they accepted his decisions with a minimum of complaint. On his part, Pedro exhibited unusual skill in balancing the two parties. During his forty-nine-year reign, there were thirty-six different cabinets, most of which received and merited public support.

The decline of rebellion in the late 1840s and thereafter as a political weapon reflected the acceptance of the legitimacy and authority of Pedro II. Still, the policies of the new emperor did not go unchallenged, as indicated by the Liberal revolts in 1842 and in 1848. Mention has been made of the former; the latter occurred in Pernambuco. It partially protested the recall of the Conservatives to power again and partially demonstrated local antipathy toward the Portuguese merchants' resident in the province. The two causes were not divorced in the minds of the disgruntled Pernambucan Liberals who in heated emotion frequently equated the Conservatives and the Portuguese merchants as one and the same. As a matter of fact, the Portuguese did control a considerable share of Brazilian business. It has been estimated that they owned approximately one-third of all commercial houses. Their sentiments tended to favor the Conservative cause. The Liberals resented their presence and influence. In one sense at least, the War of the Mascates was still being fought. Some participants in the Praieira Revolt of 1848 favored a land reform. The articulate mulatto Antônio Pedro de Figueiredo wrote against the abuses of the latifundia class and advocated measures, such as a heavy tax on unused land, to reduce the size of the huge estates and to encourage a rural middle class. Such sentiments found friendly acceptance elsewhere in Brazil but no practical remedies were forthcoming. In 1850, the Crown abolished the centuries-old sesmaria system and prohibited further free distribution of the land. It hoped thereby to check some of the abuses of the past but failed to end the abuses of the latifundia or to aid the rural poor. The Praieira Revolt itself was suppressed in 1850.

Economic changes during the period were impressive. Already coffee had surpassed sugar as the major export, accounting for about half of the exports as compared to a quarter for sugar. Still, imports exceeded exports. As a result of a bare treasury, the Minister of Finance resorted to the frequent issuance of paper money. The statesmen regretted their earlier economic liberality and determined that as soon as the commercial treaties ran out they would raise the tariff with the joint objective of increasing revenue and of encouraging national industry. In the face of powerful English pressure to renew their expiring commercial treaty, the Brazilians stood firm and in 1844 enacted the Alves Branco Tariff, which more than doubled duties. The tariffs thereafter accounted for approximately half of the government's income. Throughout the remainder of the century the government adamantly refused to negotiate any commercial treaties and thereby gained just a shade more of economic independence from Great Britain. The tariff was not really high enough, however, to promote domestic industrialization. In 1846, the government did give a stronger impetus to potential industrialists by permitting the free importation of machinery. Despite the establishment of a few fragile industries and the slow but steady growth of the coastal cities, Brazil remained overwhelmingly rural. Large and generally inefficiently run plantations continued to dominate the countryside. As always they catered to the caprices of an international market, now smiling, now frowning. To all appearances, the fazenda remained the same in structure and operation as it had been for hundreds of years. One observant traveler, Daniel F. Kidder, visited a fazenda at Jaraguá in the interior of São Paulo during the early years of the Second Empire. The estate belonged to an enterprising woman who resided most of the year in the city of São Paulo. The variety of products grown on the fazenda impressed Kidder: sugar cane, manioca, cotton, rice, and coffee. He left this description of part of it:

Around the farm-house as a centre, were situated numerous out-houses, such as quarters for negroes, store-houses for the staple vegetables, and fixtures for reducing them to a marketable form.

The engenho de cachassa was an establishment where the juices of the sugar-cane were expressed for distillation. On most of the sugar estates there exist distilleries, which convert the treacle drained from the sugar into a species of alcohol called cachassa. . . . The apparatus for grinding the cane was rude and clumsy in its construction, and not dissimilar to the corresponding portion of a cider-mill in the United States. It was turned by four oxen.

He went on to describe the customs of the plantation house and of his hosts:

Our social entertainments at Jaraguá were of no ordinary grade. Any person looking in upon the throng of human beings that filled the house when we were all gathered together, would have been at a loss to appreciate the force of a common remark of Brazilians respecting their country, viz: that its greatest misfortune is a want of population. Leaving travelers and naturalists out of the question, and also the swarm of servants, waiters, and children— each of whom, whether white, black, or mulatto, seemed emulous of making a due share of noise—there were present half a dozen ladies, relatives of the Donna, who had come up from the city to enjoy the occasion. Among the gentlemen were three sons of the Donna, her son-in-law, a doctor of laws, and her chaplain, who was also a professor in the law university, and a doctor in theology. With such an interesting company, the time allotted to out stay could hardly fail to be agreeably spent. . . . It is a pleasure to say, that I observed none of that seclusion and excessive restraint which some writers have set down as characteristic of Brazilian females. True, the younger members of the company seldom ventured beyond the utterance of Sim Senhor, Não Senhor, and the like; but ample amends for their bashfulness were made by the extreme sociability of Donna Gertrudes. She voluntarily detailed to me an account of her vast business concerns, showed me in person her agricultural and mineral treasures, and seemed to take the greatest satisfaction in imparting the results of her experience on all subjects.

Kidder spoke favorably of the food. The national diet revolved around the basic staples of rice, beans, manioc flour, sugar, coffee, corn, and dried meat. Apparently the fazenda offered its guests considerably more. Our traveler noted:

> There was a princely profusion in the provisions for the table, but an amount of disorder in the service performed by near a dozen waiters, which might have been amply remedied by two that understood well their business. The plate was of the most massive and costly kind. The chairs and tables were equally miserable. The sheets, pillow-cases and towels, of the sleeping apartments, were of cotton, but at the same time ornamented with wide fringes of wrought cambric. Thus the law of contrast seemed to prevail throughout. Dinner was served at six P.M.; supper at about nine.[23]

Life on the large plantation appeared genteel enough, for the owners that is. As limitless as Brazil seemed, there was a scarcity of tillable, accessible land for the small farmer. Long before the Cry of Ipiranga, that land had been distributed in sesmarias and the tendency had been more toward the consolidation of land holdings than otherwise. The *Diário de Pernambuco* in the mid-nineteenth century summarized and decried the situation as follows: "Now, agriculture is closed by an insurmountable barrier to the less favored man, to anyone who does not have a certain amount of money. Agriculture is the chief source of production, the chief hope of our country. But since agriculture is closed by a barrier it is necessary that that barrier fall, cost whatever it may. . . . And what is that barrier? Large landholdings. It is the terrible curse which has ruined and depopulated many other nations."[24] If the land-holding system had altered not a whit since the colonial period, now two generations in the past, neither had the labor system. The black slave performed all the menial tasks.

23. Kidder, *Sketches of Residence*, I, 239–40, 244–46.

24. Quoted in Gilberto Freyre, *Nordeste* (Rio de Janeiro, 1937), p. 248.

In the 1840s increasing internal objections to the nefarious slave trade arose. Foreign objections were not lacking
either, but then they had been in evidence for many decades. From the beginning of the century, the English, for a
variety of humanitarian and commercial reasons, had applied
external pressure first to limit it and then to abolish it, as
they had done and were doing in the United States and
Spanish America as well. Many Brazilians accused the British
of seeking to eliminate slavery in order to raise the prices of
Brazilian products on the world market, thereby permitting
similar products from English colonies to undersell them.
The North American minister in Rio de Janeiro reported the
existence of such a commercial plot to the Minister of
Foreign Relations and concluded "that, if it should be con-
summated, it would destroy the peace and prosperity of
both [Brazil and the United States], and transfer the production of tobacco, rice, cotton, sugar, and coffee from the
United States and Brazil, to her possessions beyond the
Cape of Good Hope."[25] London coerced Portugal to accept
by treaty a series of restrictions on the traffic: in 1810 the
slave trade was limited to the Portuguese colonies in Africa;
in 1815 all trade was limited to the Portuguese colonies south
of the equator and required to observe a number of ame-
liorative conditions; in 1817 the British navy received permission to stop and search Portuguese vessels believed to be
violating the conditions imposed upon the trade. In return
for British recognition, the Brazilians reluctantly signed a
treaty in 1826 agreeing to terminate the traffic within three
years after the ratification. Furthermore, British ships were to
be permitted to search vessels suspected of engaging in the
trade, and mixed British-Brazilian commissions would judge
all violations. The populace greeted the treaty with cries of
protest. The shaky agricultural economy would have collapsed without the continued importation of slaves. Under
duress, the Brazilians grudgingly passed a law to implement
their treaty obligations. All slaves imported after 1830 were to

25. Henry A. Wise to Ernesto F. França, Sept. 24, 1844, in William R. Manning (ed.),
Diplomatic Correspondence of the United States, Inter-American Affairs, 1831–1860
(Washington, 1932), II, 257.

be *ipso facto* free and the importers punished and forced to repatriate them. Shortly thereafter chaos enveloped the empire and even if there had been the will—which there emphatically was not—there was not the power to enforce that law, although Great Britain quixotically tried. In 1845, the convention permitting British search and establishing the mixed commission to judge cases expired and the imperial government stubbornly refused to renew it. England reacted with the Aberdeen Bill, which unilaterally provided for continued search and seizure of suspected slave ships and appropriate trials in Admiralty courts. That high-handed act offended Brazilian sensitivity. The estimated number of slaves imported yearly doubled after the British announcement. Part of the explanation can be found in Brazilian defiance but more importantly most Brazilians realized that the unseemly traffic must halt soon. As a more enlightened attitude came to prevail, public opinion increasingly opposed the continued importation. Also the Brazilians resented the fact that they bore the blame and shame for the trade while most of the slave ships were foreign-owned, particularly by Portuguese, and earned handsome profits from the impecunious planters. Finally the Brazilians indicated their readiness to suppress the trade, which was effectively done by the Queiróz Law, passed in 1850. The estimated figures of slaves imported (see Table 3.2) reveal how efficient the law was.

In the nineteenth century, the area around Rio de Janiero was the undisputed depot of the slave trade. The termination of the slave trade brought to a close a long phase (over 300 years) in Brazilian history. It heralded many changes. For one thing, money tied up in the slave trade, and it was a stagger-

Table 3.2. Slaves Imported into Brazil, 1845–1851

1845	19,453
1846	50,324
1847	56,172
1848	60,000
1849	54,000
1850	23,000
1851	3,287

ing sum, was freed for other investments. For another, the continuing need for labor dictated a greater encouragement and welcome for European immigration.

A more rapid pace of urbanization began to alter Rio de Janeiro. By the end of the first decade of Pedro II's reign it was the largest city of South America, with a population exceeding a quarter of a million. Pressed between sea and mountains, the city wound its way along beaches and into mountain valleys. Where the land was flat, streets intersecting each other at right angles divided the city, but frequently the terrain admitted only single, crooked streets. Some imposing buildings dominated the city: the National Assembly, Senate, Palace of the Municipal Government, the naval and military arsenals and academies, the customshouses, the former Viceregal Palace then coverted into governmental offices, the National Library, National Museum, and Academy of Fine Arts. Magnificent religious structures such as Candelária, Santo Antônio, Carmo, and São Bento were in full evidence as well. The houses rose three or four stories, with the ground floor commonly given over to business or commerce and the family residing above. Already, however, a migration to the picturesque suburbs of Botafogo and Engenho Velho was under way. Botafogo was revealed in this contemporary description: "The houses are low, faced with colored stucco, and roofed with the old red tile: not a paneled front-door, stoop knocker, or bell-pull, and many windows without glass. Coming to a small garden-plot attached to a showy corner house, I stopped a moment to look at white, red, blue, yellow, green, and gilded screens and trellis-work, vying in colors with the flowers; while the walks, bordered with shells, were crowded with something like a hundred painted statues and statuettes."[26] One of the pleasantest retreats in the city was the *Passeio Público* (Public Promenade). Overhanging trees, a myriad of varied plants, blooming flowers, cool fountains, and refreshing sea breezes offered rest and comfort to the many who entered. On the side facing the bay were magnificent views of the distant ocean, Sug-

26. Thomas Ewbank, *Life in Brazil* (New York, 1856), p. 59.

arloaf Mountain, and the exquisite Gloria Church perched on a hill of the same name. The peaceful quality of this scene would be reflected in Brazilian evolution for some decades.

Urban society enticed ever larger numbers of the planter aristocrats to spend less time on their estates and more amid the conviviality of the cities with their noisy, friendly streets and their sedate salons. The attractions, social or political, of the court in Rio de Janeiro tempted the landed gentry from all corners of the empire to visit the capital, if not to reside in it. That same class began to send some of its sons to study law in São Paulo or Olinda (later to Recife where the law school was transferred in 1854) or to study medicine in Rio de Janeiro and Bahia. Adapted to the ways of the city, those university graduates abandoned the plantations forever.

In the invigorated urban environment literature flowered. Educated Brazilians always had been given to poetry, but in the decade of the 1840s prose assumed a new importance with the appearance of the novel. Antônio Gonçalves Teixeira e Sousa introduced the first with the publication in 1843 of his brief *O Filho do Pescador* (The Fisherman's Son). Five more novels, all of them undistinguished, followed from his pen. The prolific Joaquim Manuel de Macedo (twenty-one novels to his credit) published his first and most successful novel, *A Moreninha* (The Little Brunette) the following year. An instant success, it has gone through more editions than any other Brazilian novel. Sentimental and romantic, it is a classic of middle-class literature in both origin and appeal. The third novelist was Manuel Antônio de Almeida, whose only book, *Memórias de um Sargento de Milícias* (Memories of a Militia Sergeant) appeared first as a serialized novel in the newspapers and then in 1854–1855 as a book. He depicted picaresque *carioca* life of the first quarter of the nineteenth century. The theater also flourished at this time and no one contributed more to its vitality than Luís Carlos Martins Pena, witty satirist of manners and morals. His comedies amused but they also contained telling observations of Brazilian foibles. The *Correio Mercantil,* which began publication in 1843, regularly contained a literary section, which more often than not printed translations of French works, but occasionally Brazilian works too. It was there, for example, that *Memórias de um Sargento* first reached print. *The Correio,* and with it the *Jornal do Commércio,* whose first issue dates from 1827, were for many years the leading newspapers of the realm. They attempted to give full coverage of the news, local, national, and international, and ran pithy as well as influential editorials. Both the quality and quantity of the intellectual life of the empire were increasing.

Brazil already had proved its political viability by triumphing over the threats of disunity, consolidating its territorial integrity, challenging British hegemony, and implementing an effective two-party parliamentary government under the guidance of a benevolent emperor. In the course of a half-century the Brazilians had completely taken over their own government. Starting from their traditional base in the municipal councils they had slowly moved upward until, after 1840, a Brazilian even sat on the imperial throne. The psychological implications were momentous and not the least in consequence was the growth of nationalism. The prohibition of the slave trade constituted the first effort to alter the rigid economic structure of the colonial past. For the first time the prospects of the empire looked bright. An American visitor about that time, Thomas Ewbank, predicted a glorious future: "As for the material elements of greatness, no people under the sun are more highly favored, and have a higher destiny opened before them."

Chapter Four

Change and Continuity

The political changes during the first half of the nineteenth century were significant. A colony became a nation in which the Brazilian elites by stages took control of the government. The coronation of the Brazilian-born Pedro II climaxed that process, and he brought tranquillity, order, and stability to the empire. The succeeding decades witnessed economic changes wrought by the expansion of the lucrative coffee industry. The combination of political stability and economic prosperity facilitated the introduction and consideration of new ideas. Those ideas emanating from the capitalist nations admired by the elites helped initiate and propel a modernization whose goal was to transform Brazil. Indeed, the Brazilians severed two strong ties with the past: sugar and slavery. Coffee eclipsed sugar, and slavery gave way to European immigration. Symbolically of greatest importance was the abolition of slavery in 1888. It indicated Brazil's emergence from its colonial past into a more modern world. Great changes occurred, and yet much continuity with the past still remained.

The Ascendancy of Coffee

The age of sugar, the dominant export of the colonial economy, faded rapidly in the nineteenth century. In the first decade of independence, sugar still ranked as the single most important crop, accounting for over 30 percent of the exports. The following decade it fell to second place behind coffee and never again recovered its preeminence, so that by the last decade of the century it furnished but 6 percent of the nation's exports, although it remained an important crop of internal consumption. In 1852, the newly appointed Minister of the Empire Francisco Gonçalves Martins, Visconde de São Lourenço, a Bahian, decried the bleak future sugar seemed to face. At that time, Brazil possessed approximately 1,651 sugar mills of which 144 operated by steam, 253 by water power, and 1,275 by animal power. A decade and a half later there were only 511 sugar mills, the reduced figure brought about both by the decline in the industry and a consolidation of the mills. Confident foreign competition challenged the empire's shaky position in the world's markets. The new mills in the West Indies mechanized rapidly, and radiating railroad lines increased the size and efficiency of the plantations. These mills produced sugar so economically that it drove the more highly priced, because inefficiently produced, Brazilian sugar off the international market. Also, countries which once had imported sugar freely began to experiment with the sugar beet. In some regions of Brazil, deforestation and impoverishment of the soils further contributed to the decline of the sugar industry. Although the total quantity of sugar exports rose 33 percent in the last half of the nineteenth century, prices for that sugar fell by 11 percent. The sugar statistics seem gloomy when compared to other exports. During that same period, total exports rose by 214 percent and the average price 46 percent. Between 1833 and 1889, the value of foreign trade increased by six to seven times. Coffee made that remarkable record possible.

Although a new and welcome impetus to the national economy, the coffee industry on closer examination proved in fact to repeat many old economic characteristics and, alas, to fall well within those established economic patterns which perpetuated dependency. A part of the large monocultural plantation system, the coffee fazenda was worked, at least in the beginning, by slave labor. It maintained the patriarchal social system initiated by its agricultural predecessor, the sugar plantation. The size and operation of the coffee fazenda, as well, gave it certain other similarities to the sugar plantation. Both centered on the big house with its chapel, slave quarters, storehouses, stables, sheds, and machinery. However, coffee production required even larger investments and consequently was more prohibitive for the small or medium-sized farm.

On the other hand, some basic differences in outlook separated the sugar and coffee producers. The sugar planters, who were spokesmen for conservative doctrines, were intimately allied with the imperial government and were dependent upon protective tariffs. Less prone to change than the coffee producers, they made too little effort to increase their productivity or efficiency. They acted on the assumptions that slavery would always exist, that the sugar aristocracy would always be important to the government, and that the government would always support the sugar industry. Less wedded to the past, the coffee planters tended to hold more adaptable economic and social views. Their heavy dependence on foreign trade made them receptive, for example, to liberal trade-doctrines. They seemed readier to experiment with new techniques, machinery, and labor practices. Since most of the coffee industry began after the cessation of the slave trade, it depended less on slavery than the sugar industry had. In fact, the fazendas relied ever more heavily on immigrant workmen hired at modest salaries. Many representatives of the coffee class favored accelerated immigration, an attitude seldom expressed and rarely acted upon by the sugar class.

Coffee appeared late in Brazil and its cycle in the economy began modestly. The seeds were introduced into Pará from French Guiana around 1727. The coffee tree penetrated the Amazon, but more importantly it spread southward, passing through Bahia and reaching Rio de Janeiro around 1770. At approximately the same time it appeared in Minas Gerais. The coffee industry at first centered on the high terraces and lower mountain slopes on the southern side of the valley of the Paraíba River. There climatic and topological conditions were nearly perfect for the temperamental trees to flourish. The Paraíba River originates just northeast of the city of São Paulo, meanders across the entire length of the state of Rio de Janeiro, at one stretch serving as the boundary with Minas Gerais, and flows into the Atlantic Ocean some twenty miles south of Espírito Santo. Along that course, coffee production reached its peak in the mid-nineteenth century. Careless and wasteful agriculture diminished the harvests in the once-fertile valley, pushing production westward. The green waves of coffee trees soon inundated Minas Gerais and São Paulo.

At the same time, coffee culture had spread through the Caribbean. By the second decade of the nineteenth century, Haiti, Jamaica, Cuba, and Venezuela were exporting the bean. Colombia and Costa Rica began producing coffee for export before mid-century, and Guatemala and El Salvador marketed the beans during the last half of the century. Together they grew far less coffee than Brazil.

To cultivate the Brazilian coffee country, whether in the Paraíba Valley or to the west, the first step was to clear the land. The proprietors employed the traditional cut-and-burn method adopted from the Indians. The workers chopped down all the underbrush and trees and hauled away the usable timber for building purposes. After providing a suitable firebreak for the area, the dried wood and brush were ignited just prior to the September rains. A simple hoe prepared the land for planting. Seedlings planted in even rows climbed the hills or mountain slopes vertically. The laborers weeded those fields semiannually. By the end of the third year, the young trees, then nearly six feet high, began to produce, reaching full production—between three and four pounds of berries—by the end of the sixth year. They could bear fruit for fifteen to thirty years depending on the soil and climate.

Harvesting began in May when the reddish brown berries, a little larger than cranberries, weighed down the tree branches. The harvester encircled each branch with thumb and index finger, pulling toward him to strip the branch of its berries. They, along with twigs and leaves, fell into the screen of woven bamboo each worker carried. Tossed into the air, the berries fell to the bottom of the bamboo strainer and the leaves and twigs remaining on the top were brushed off. The workers then dumped the berries into bags to be carried to a field shed from which they were transported to a drying terrace. On an average, the worker gathered 3 bushels of coffee berries a day, enough to produce approximately 50 pounds of dried coffee. An acre of trees yielded on the average between 400 and 500 pounds of berries.

Each berry was coated with pulp and a tough shell (*casco*), which contained two seeds, the coffee beans. Each coffee bean was enclosed in a thick covering (*casquinho*) and a delicate adherent membrane (*pergaminho*). The task of processing was to remove all the covering from the tiny beans. A vigorous washing removed the pulp and shell. The beans then dried for approximately sixty days in a wide, open expanse of beaten earth or concrete called the *terreiro*. A few progressive planters used steam sheds to complete the drying in a few hours. When the skins became shriveled, hard, and nearly black, the beans were pounded in wooden mortars, either by hand or by water-driven or steam-driven machinery. The blows burst open the covering skins without injuring the tough bean. Sifting then separated the skins from the beans. Finally, the workers sorted them according to size and quality and sacked them.

During the harvesting season, the plantation worked long and hard hours. One traveler to the Paraíba Valley in the 1870s visited a modern and efficient plantation in full operation and reported the following schedule for the slaves:

The negroes are kept under a rigid surveillance, and the work is regulated as by machinery. At four o'clock in the morning all hands are called out to sing prayers, after which they file off to their work. At six coffee is given to them; at nine they breakfast on jerked beef, mandioca-meal, beans and corn-cake; at noon they receive a small dram of rum; at four o'clock they get their dinner, precisely like the breakfast, and, like that served in the field, with the slightest possible intermission from work. At seven the files move wearily back to the house, where they are drawn up to the sound of a bugle. From the tripod at one side a bright fire half illumines, half conceals, the dark figures, sending flashes over the walls beyond, and casting long shadows on the ground. The tools are deposited in a storehouse, and locked up; two or three of the crowd, perhaps, advanced timidly to make requests of the master; after that all are dispersed to household and mill-work until nine o'clock; then the men and women are locked up in separate quarters, and left to sleep seven hours, to prepare for the seventeen hours of almost uninterrupted labor on the succeeding day. On Sunday there is a nominal holiday, which, practically, amounts to but three or four hours; none of the Catholic holidays are celebrated here, and even Christmas is passed unnoticed.[1]

Obviously it was at the cost of enormous inhumanity that the coffee beans were prepared for market.

Mules and railroads carried the coffee sacks to the nearest ports for export. During the heyday of the Paraíba Valley, the port of Rio de Janeiro handled 88 percent of Brazil's coffee exports as compared to 10 percent for Santos, 1 percent for Bahia, and 1 percent for the remaining Brazilian ports. For about half a century the bulk of the coffee traffic headed for Rio de Janeiro. The mules, each with a pair of coffee sacks slung from a rough pack frame, paraded single-file along the paths and good hard roads of the valley to the railroads, which began to penetrate the state of Rio de Janeiro in the 1860s and 1870s. At the railroad stations the mules discharged their cargo, and the coffee bags were piled high on the platform and in nearby warehouses to await shipment. The *comissários,* planters' agents in Rio de Janeiro, received the coffee and sold it for a small commission to the packers; the packers then transferred it by horse carts from the railroad to the huge warehouses in the northern and eastern part of the capital. In the caverns of those ware-

1. Herbert H. Smith, *Brazil: The Amazons and the Coast* (London, 1880), p. 526.

houses the coffee was resacked, each bag being carefully weighed at 130 pounds (60 kilograms). From the packer the coffee went to the exporter, usually an Englishman, to be sent abroad when the market was favorable. Long was the odyssey of the coffee bean from the tree to the cup and complex was the business managing that journey. Many made their fortunes on those beans. The government, too, profited handsomely thanks to taxes it levied on the business.

Coffee exports mounted annually. The first coffee exported left Maranhão in 1731 for Lisbon. Maranhão and Pará continued to ship coffee to the metropolis throughout the rest of the eighteenth century. In 1779, Rio de Janeiro sent its first shipment of coffee to Lisbon, a modest ton and a quarter. By the period of independence, coffee accounted for about a fifth of the exports, a figure which rose to two thirds by the time of the fall of the monarchy, 1889. Those figures indicated an increase from 190,060 to 5,586,000 in the number of sacks of coffee beans shipped yearly to the world markets in a sixty-seven-year period. The value of the coffee sold during those years equaled that of all the exports during the entire colonial period. It is worthwhile to note that of all the major Brazilian exports of the nineteenth century, only coffee met no intense international competition. This reveals, of course, why coffee came to play the dominant role in the economy. By the 1858–1860 period, coffee alone provided half of all the exports. As one result of the rising coffee exports, the country after 1860, for the first time in its independent history, exported more than it imported. Accordingly the balance of trade tipped in favor of Brazil, a novelty which became commonplace over the succeeding decades. The favorable balance was all the more notable because the amount of imports continually rose.

The emperor paid tribute to the producers of the new wealth. In 1841, he first elevated a coffee planter to the nobility: José Gonçalves de Morais became the Barão de Piraí. With each passing decade thereafter, the coffee class figured ever more prominently among the new nobility. Indeed, some of the coffee planters were the wealthiest men of the realm. Joaquim José de Sousa Breves alone harvested 1.5 percent of the empire's total crop in 1860 on his extensive and fertile fazendas and lived in a fashion commensurate with his economic power. Antônio Clemente Pinto, Barão de Nova Friburgo, who could trace his riches directly to coffee exports, enjoyed a home in the capital more luxurious than the royal palace. In fact, his *palácio* became the residence of the president after the proclamation of the republic. Visitors to the coffee regions commented favorably on the vast plantations and the solid, often sumptuous, residences, which like those in the sugar areas embodied an entire way of life.

The Reverend J. C. Fletcher left a vivid description of his visit to the impressive coffee fazenda of Commendador Silva Pinto in Minas Gerais. Containing an area of sixty-four square miles, the fazenda grew cotton, sugar, corn, mandioca, and a variety of fruits, and in its ample pastures herds of livestock grazed. None of these items found their way into the marketplace. They were used to feed and clothe the household and slaves, whose number at one time was 700. The commercial crop was coffee, a source of considerable wealth which enabled the Silva Pinto family to live in grand style. Fletcher pictured this style in part as follows:

At dinner we were served in a large dining-room. The Commander sat at the head of the table, with his guests and the various free members of his family sat upon forms, the *feitors* (overseers) and shepherds being at the lower end. He lives in true baronial style, and I was reminded of the description by Mr. J. G. Kohl of castle-life among the noblemen of Courland and Livonia. A pleasant conversation was kept up during the long repast, and at its close three servants came—one bearing a massive silver bowl a foot and a half in diameter, another a pitcher of the same material containing warm water, while a third carried towels. The newly arrived guests were thus served in lieu of finger-basins, which are rarely seen outside the capital.

.   .   .

In the course of our conversation the Commendador told us that he had his "own music now." He spoke of it very humbly. We desired to hear his musicians, supposing that we would hear a wheezy plantation-fiddle, a fife, and a drum. The Commendador said that we should be gratified in the evening. An hour after vespers I heard the twanging of violins, the tuning of flutes, short voluntaries on sundry bugles, the clattering of trombones, and all those musical symptoms preparatory to a beginning of some march, waltz, or polka. I went to the room whence proceeded these sounds; there I beheld fifteen slave musicians—a regular band: one presided at an organ, and there was a choir of younger negroes arranged before suitable stands, upon which were sheets of printed or manuscript music. I observed a respectable colored gentleman (who sat near me at dinner) giving various directions. He was the maestro. Three raps of his violin-bow commanded silence, and then a wave of the same, á la Julien, and the orchestra commenced the execution of an overture to some opera with admirable skill and precision. I was totally unprepared for this. But the next piece overwhelmed me with surprise: the choir, accompanied by the instruments, performed a Latin mass.[2]

The decade of the 1860s owed its remarkable prosperity to factors other than mounting coffee sales, important as those were. The Civil War in the United States reduced the world's cotton supply and impelled Europe's textile manufacturers to seek other sources. Brazil increased cotton production to meet the new demands. Cotton during the 1860s accounted for 18.3 percent of the total exports, a threefold increase over the preceding decade. Furthermore, burgeoning European and North American industries demanded more raw products. For one thing, Brazil sold rubber, whose export accounted for less than a half of a percent of the total in the 1840s and a full 15 percent in the 1890s. The general trend during the last half of the century, as Table 4.1 indicates, was for coffee, rubber, cocoa, and erva-maté exports to increase, while sugar, skins and hides, and cotton (with the exception of the 1860s) decreased. Tobacco remained about the same, consisting of between 2 percent and 3 percent of the exports.

Great Britain maintained its dominant position in Brazilian foreign commerce. The British supplied the lion's share

2. J. C. Fletcher and D. P. Kidder, *Brazil and the Brazilians* (Philadelphia, 1857), pp. 440–42.

Table 4.1. Brazilian Exports in the Nineteenth Century
(Percent of Total Exports)

Decade	Total	Coffee	Sugar	Cocoa	Maté	Tobacco	Cotton	Rubber	Skins & Hides
1821–1830	85.8	18.4	30.1	.5	—	2.5	20.6	.1	13.6
1831–1840	89.8	43.8	24.0	.6	.5	1.9	10.8	.3	7.9
1841–1850	88.2	41.4	26.7	1.0	.9	1.8	7.5	.4	8.5
1851–1860	90.9	48.8	21.2	1.0	1.6	2.6	6.2	2.3	7.2
1861–1870	90.3	45.5	12.3	.9	1.2	3.0	18.3	3.1	6.0
1871–1880	95.1	56.6	11.8	1.2	1.5	3.4	9.5	5.5	5.6
1881–1890	92.3	61.5	9.9	1.6	1.2	2.7	4.2	8.0	3.2
1891–1900	95.6	64.5	6.0	1.5	1.3	2.2	2.7	15.0	2.4

SOURCE: Hélio S. Silva, "Tendências e Características do Comércio Exterior no Século XIX," *Revista de História da Economia Brasileira* (June 1953), p. 8.

of the imports, the most important of which were textiles, manufactured items for wear, and prepared foods, and controlled and handled most of the empire's export trade. Furthermore, they supplied the loans and foreign investment the empire needed. After 1870, however, the United States emerged as the major customer for Brazil's exports, buying more than 50 percent of the coffee and rubber exported as well as much of the cocoa crop. It was at this time that those two giant countries of this hemisphere began to discover each other. Economic approximation was under way when Pedro II made a visit to the United States in 1876 to see the country and to contribute to the centennial celebrations in Philadelphia. Curious Americans welcomed the philosopher-emperor from the tropics. An equally curious emperor examined the booming North American colossus. Both liked what they saw and Dom Pedro's visit was a great success. The trip marked the opening of a political *rapprochement*.

The prosperity brought about by mounting coffee sales not only influenced Brazil's relations with the outside world but helped to transform the country internally. A variety of material changes resulted.

Material Transformation

The modest Alves Branco Tariff of 1844, permission to import machinery duty-free in 1846, the first laws for the incorporation of commercial companies in 1849, the promulgation of the Commercial Code in 1850, the end of the slave trade in the same year with the consequent liberation of capital for investment, and the establishment of the second Bank of Brazil in 1851 were powerful economic inventives for material expansion. The suppression of the Praieira Revolt in 1850, the long and tranquil government of the Conservatives which began in 1848, and the strength and assurance which the able young emperor brought to his realm were political stimuli to the same end. Addressing his subjects from the throne in 1850, Pedro called for the strengthening of the army and navy and the stabilization of currency. The following year, he noted jubilantly the tranquillity which reigned throughout the realm and urged the further strengthening of the national institutions because "the innumerable natural resources of the soil need only the impulse of authority to produce great social advantages." Already, good and strong government, public order, favorable economic laws, and prosperity, thanks chiefly to increasing coffee sales, were giving an impetus to the material transformation of the empire.

The decade of the 1850s was one of unprecedented activity. Capistrano de Abreu characterized the decade as "the most brilliant of the empire." The organization of credit, the better circulation and wiser investment of capital, and the increased emission of money, all made possible by the establishment of banks, contributed to that change. In 1845, there existed only one bank in the empire, the Commercial Bank of Rio de Janeiro. That year, with the foundation of the Commercial Bank of Bahia, initiated the beginning of the rapid expansion of the banking network. In 1846, the Commercial Bank of Maranhão and in the following year the Commercial Bank of Pará opened their doors. In 1848, a second bank was established in Salvador da Bahia. Three years later, the Commercial Bank of Pernambuco, the Rural and Mortgage Bank of Rio de Janeiro, and the Bank of Brazil, founded by Irineu Evangelista de Sousa, Visconde de Mauá (1813–1889), began to operate. Mauá's bank and the Commercial Bank of Rio de Janeiro merged in 1853 and continued to bear the name Bank of Brazil, the first large-scale institution of its type. It monopolized the emission of bank notes for the government for a few years. The Mauá, MacGregor and Company Bank was formed in the capital in 1854. The year 1857 saw the establishment of the Commercial and Agricultural Bank of Rio de Janeiro, the Bank of the Province of Rio Grande do Sul, the New Bank of Pernambuco, the Savings Bank of Pernambuco, and the Bank of Maranhão. A world financial crisis in 1857 briefly shook Brazil, but after calm returned the confident government extended to other banks the privilege of emitting money. Abuse of the new privilege flooded the empire with currency, a scandal in which the Bank of Brazil was deeply implicated. As a result, in 1866, the government assumed the responsibility for the issuance of money, a monopoly it exercised until 1888. Foreign banks made their appearance in Brazil for the first time with the inauguration of the London and Brazil Bank in the capital in 1862. In the next two years, it opened branches in Recife, Salvador, Santos, Curitiba, and Pôrto Alegre. The Brazilian and Portuguese Bank was chartered in 1863. The banks ended most of the personal financial transactions characteristic of the early decades of the empire. Impersonal institutions of growing resources, they multiplied the power and importance of the city and conversely diminished the prestige of the landowners, particularly the sugar planters, whose debts to the urban banks increased.

The telegraph initiated a communications revolution in Brazil in 1852. The first line connected the imperial palace at São Cristóvão, on the outskirts of the capital, to the military headquarters at Campo Santa Ana in the capital. Later, more lines linked the palace with the other public buildings. By 1857, Petropolis, the cool summer capital in the mountains behind Rio de Janeiro, communicated telegraphically with Rio de Janeiro. The outbreak of the Paraguayan war initiated a flurry of activity to string lines southward to the theater of action. In a record time of six months a telegraph line connected the southern provinces to the court. In the opposite direction, the lines reached Belém in 1886 and thereafter penetrated into the interior: they reached Goiás in 1890,

Mato Grosso, in 1891, and the capital of the Amazon, Manaus, in 1896. The number of stations increased. In 1861 there were 10 stations with 40 miles of lines transmitting 233 messages. By 1885 there were 171 stations with 6,560 miles of lines handling over 600,000 messages. The progressive Visconde de Mauá formed a company with an English partner to lay a submarine cable from Europe to Brazil. The idea of not only direct but instantaneous communication with Europe titillated the Brazilian imagination. A grand festivity inaugurated that line. Seated before a special machine in the National Library, on June 23, 1874, Pedro II dictated the first message to be cabled to Europe, as, very significantly, Rio de Janeiro was linked to Europe by telegraph long before it could similarly communicate with other parts of its own empire. The next stage in international communications was to establish telegraphic contact with the Plata neighbors. The lines reached Montevideo in 1879 and Buenos Aires in 1883.

A revolution in transportation accompanied that in communications. Historically the water routes had been the most important means of transportation and so they continued to be throughout most of the nineteenth century. The steamship first appeared in Bahia de Todos os Santos in 1819 to serve Salvador and neighboring settlements. Gradually the shipping companies adopted steam power for coastal trade. By 1839, a steamship line plied between the capital and the northern provinces. The navy also purchased steam vessels. The nation understood the dramatic significance of the steamship in 1843, when the puffing and chugging *Guapiassú* churned the waters of the Amazon for the first time. That steamship journeyed from Belém to Manaus, 900 miles upstream, in nine days and returned in half the time, a remarkable record considering that hitherto the sailing vessels required two to three months to ascend and a month to descend. In 1852, Mauá formed the Amazon Steam Navigation Company to exploit the entire Amazon basin with the benefit of the steam engine. In the previous year, the Royal English Mail Line established regular steamship service between European and South American ports. Steam navigation proceeded at a modest pace. By 1875, some 29 percent of the vessels entering Brazilian harbors were steam propelled; the rest were still sailing ships.

For many years the government eagerly had hoped that some entrepreneur would undertake to construct a railroad. A new law in 1852 provided favorable conditions for anyone who would do so. Mauá accepted the challenge. Completed in 1854, the first line ran ten miles from the head of Guanabara Bay to the foot of the mountains in which Petropolis nestled. This contemporary account described the first official rail journey in Brazil, which took place on September 5, 1853, some months before the line formally opened:

A few paces distant we saw a single, graceful looking locomotive, with a certificate of the year of its birth and the name of its worthy father engraved on the central wheels. The letters in yellow metal were as follows: "William Fairbarn & Son, 1853, Manchester." The proper carriage was not yet attached; they substituted for it a rough wagon, used for the conveyance of materials, and without further delay we squatted at the bottom of this impromptu vehicle. Suddenly a prolonged and screeching shriek, a whistle with the force of fifty sopranos, rent the air, deafening the hearers, and causing us to put our hands over our ears. It was the signal for departure, the warning to those who might be on the line to guard against a mortal blow, an announcement made by a tube attached to the locomotive itself. Swifter than an arrow, than the flight of a swallow, the locomotive threaded the rails, swung from side to side, raced, flew, devoured space, and passing through fields, barren wastes, and frightened animals, it stopped at last breathless at the point where the road does not yet afford safe passage. The space traversed was a mile and three quarters, and the time occupied in transit was four minutes.[3]

It was a modest start and came less than two years after the first rail line in South America was inaugurated in Chile. In 1858 Brazil's second and third railroad lines commenced operation. One in the province of Pernambuco running from Recife to Cabo, a distance of 20 miles, the first stage of a line which would link Recife with the São Francisco River and its commerce, crossed rich sugar lands. The other connected

3. *Jornal do Commércio* (Rio de Janeiro), Sept. 7, 1853.

Rio de Janeiro with Quemados, a distance of 30 miles, the first stretch of the Dom Pedro II railroad, which reached São Paulo in 1877. By 1874, there were approximately 800 miles of tracks, which meant that in the twenty years since Mauá inaugurated the first line only about 40 miles of track had been laid each year. After 1875, construction increased rapidly: in 1875–1879, 1,023 miles of track were laid; in 1880–1884, 2,200; in 1885–1889, 2,500. In 1889, then, trackage totaled approximately 6,000 miles. Fourteen of the twenty provinces had at least some rail service, although most of the trackage was concentrated in the southeast. There, as the plantations moved rapidly inland to exploit virgin soil, the coffee interests needed fast and efficient transportation to get the coffee beans to the ports. The governments, both provincial and national, catered to their needs. One emerging characteristic of rail construction was that the new lines generally ran from plantation to port. Thus, they helped to speed exports to market rather than to unify the empire or to create an internal economic infrastructure. Whatever the residual benefits for Brazil, the railroads further linked Brazil to world markets and thereby deepened dependency.

Along the new tracks and at rail junctures and heads, new villages and towns sprang up and older ones took on a new life. Hastings Charles Dent, an English engineer in Brazil in 1883–1884 to survey the route for the Minas Gerais Railroad, observed one such impact of the railroad on urbanization. He commented on the phenomenal growth of the town of Queluz, Minas Gerais, during the short span of eleven months. "There are great changes in this place since I was here on July 1, last year. The town of Queluz is up on a hill; the station Lafayette . . . which last July was in course of construction, and an isolated building, is now the centre of a large colony of houses, inns, 'armazens,' etc."[4] Elsewhere, too, the railroad brought such changes in its wake.

Other means of transportation developed slowly. The bandeirante tracks provided the most widespread network for travel. The more densely populated areas had narrow dirt

4. *A Year in Brazil* (London, 1886), p. 179.

roads, more often than not rough and unusable after heavy rains. Over those, horses, carts, coaches, and mule trains passed. A singular experiment in road construction was the Union and Industry Highway built to connect Petropolis and Juiz de Fora, the gateway to the province of Minas Gerais. In 1861 the Government completed the ninety-mile road begun in 1856. Eighteen feet across, it rested on a roadbed of crushed rock with roadside ditches of brick. Its builders had employed the latest principles of road engineering. Coaches sped along the road at an average of twelve miles per hour. With time out to rest, they could cover the distance between the two towns in a record nine hours. One English visitor, William Hadfield, referred to the highway as a "splendid road," a compliment which, given local deference to English opinion, must have delighted the Brazilians. In the decade of the 1860s two other highways were built, both connecting the lowlands with the highland interior, one in Paraná and the other in Santa Catarina. In the immensity of Brazil, those short roads were significant only because they were built in areas of accelerating economic growth.

Once the process of growth had begun the effects were cumulative. The expanding transportation system opened new markets and tapped new resources. Coffee sales and profits from other agricultural sales, such as the high prices received for cotton in the 1860s, introduced new wealth into the economy, which in turn increased demands and provided capital for investment. After 1860, the favorable balance of trade infused greater sums into the economy. The new banking system provided the instrument for both investment and credit. The lengthy struggle against Paraguay, 1865–1870, revealed many inherent weaknesses in the Brazilian economy, not least of which was the need for industries which could support an active army. The world financial crisis of 1875, the repercussions of which sent the Brazilian economy reeling, and a decline in coffee prices between 1880 and 1886 caused the most thoughtful Brazilians to reassess their vulnerable economy and intensified their first aspirations toward an economy diversified and strengthened through industrialization. Thanks to steamships, railroads, telegraphs, banks, an enlightened and stable government, and the prosperity provided by coffee, industrialization was for the first time within the realm of possibility.

In the 1850s it was already possible to discern the first faint glimmerings of industrialization and to observe a hitherto unprecedented growth of business. In that decade some 62 industrial firms were founded as well as 14 banks, 20 steamship companies, 23 insurance companies, 4 colonization companies, 8 mining companies, 3 urban transportation companies, 2 gas companies, and 8 railroad lines. Many of those enterprises represented pure speculation which led to financial crises in 1857 and 1864. Discounting such paper activity, a tiny but expanding industrial base was laid. In 1850, there were approximately 50 factories in Brazil; in 1889, there were 636. The textile industry was the most important. The 9 cotton mills in 1865 multiplied into a hundred before the end of the empire, centered in Rio de Janeiro, Recife, Salvador, São Paulo, Caxias in Maranhão, and Juiz de Fora in Minas Gerais. Other important industries were food processing, clothing manufacturing, and woodworking, as well as chemical and metallurgical industries. Even the sugar barons stirred themselves in an attempt to revive their moribund industry by introducing steam power into their operations. By 1878 many of the inefficient if picturesque sugar mills had been replaced by the *usinas,* mechanized refineries. Some limited industrialization began in the traditionally sugar-oriented Northeast after the ports were closed to the slave trade. In the quarter century thereafter, Recife acquired 9 textile mills, a candle factory, a tobacco factory, a soap factory, and a biscuit factory along with some other industries. The Conservatives enacted a frankly protectionist tariff in 1885 with the aim of encouraging national industry. On the one hand it reduced duties on primary materials needed by Brazilian manufactureres, while on the other it raised the tariff to an average of 48 percent on goods competing with those made locally.

In the vanguard of those concerned with encouraging business and industry stood the Visconde de Mauá, whose biography follows the classic Horatio Alger format. Born of humble parents in Rio Grande do Sul, he worked his way up from clerk to manager of a British commercial house in Rio de Janeiro. His name was connected with almost every phase of the progress and transformation of Brazil during his lifetime. In the mid-1840s, he began to lay the foundations for a vast economic empire which included shipyards, steamship companies, banks, and railroads. In Rio de Janeiro alone he built floating docks, increased the city's water supply, installed gas lighting in the public streets, and initiated a streetcar system. "The spirit of association," he told one group of stockholders, "is one of the strongest elements of the prosperity of any country. It is, so to speak, the soul of progress." His enthusiasm, as well as his efficiency, brought new foreign capital into Brazil. "Credit is the basis of capital and the source of new wealth," he proclaimed. Elsewhere the idea might have been conventional, but the Brazilians remained somewhat wary of his capitalistic ideas. Unfortunately he overextended himself and the government refused to come to his aid during the financial crisis of 1875. His economic empire came tumbling down around him. No doubt Mauá would have felt much more at ease among the captains of industry who were then at the helm of the United States economy—Fisk, Frick, Vanderbilt, Gould, et al.—than he did in the neocapitalist economy of Brazil where few appreciated his efforts and many suspected him of questionable practices. Yet in his very active lifetime, this one man did more than any other individual, or group for that matter, to orient the empire's steps along the path of industrialization. Furthermore, his railroads, steamship lines, and banks contributed to national unity.

The capital faithfully reflected the changes affecting the coastal belt of Brazil. In the 1850s and early 1860s, Rio de Janeiro became a bustling metropolis. The English traveler William Hadfield, returning there in 1868 after a sixteen-year absence, stood in admiration of the metamorphosis. He confronted a city with a population, including all the suburbs, of over 600,000. All the principal streets had been paved and an efficient drainage system installed. The new streets were wide and lined with buildings whose beautiful architectural style he commended. New public markets and an increased number of shops provided a greater variety of wares than ever. Omnibuses drawn by mule teams, carriages, and Tilbury coaches crowded the main streets which, along with principal buildings and comfortable homes, were illuminated with gas. At night both city and suburb appeared well lighted. A city he had always admired for its beauty had been graced with more public gardens and ornamental squares, one of the most impressive of which was the Praça da Constituição with a handsome new statue of Pedro I proclaiming the nation's independence. Hadfield also spoke well of São Paulo. He wrote:

A ramble over the city impresses one favorably: good wide streets, paved with a material resembling macadam. . . . There are several fine churches, an extensive new public market, and, as a rule, the houses are well and substantially built. The shops are also numerous and well appointed with all the requisites for conveniences and comfort suited to a city of 20,000 to 25,000 inhabitants. There are several national colleges here, with a number of young students, who help to enliven the place.[5]

Undeniably the decade of the 1850s stands out as a period of innovation. It was a propitious start heralding other changes which, as we shall see, continued to transform the empire. Much of the financial burden to underwrite the changes fell on the government, which levied a wide array of taxes to meet its expenses. Taxes were placed on official stamps, the salaries of government employees, water service, stores, buildings, professions, lotteries, vehicles of transportation, stock transfers, promissory notes, exports, imports, slaves, cattle, transfer of property, mining, storage, docks, anchorage, transportation, alcoholic beverages, and the mail and telegraphs. National income rose rapidly. In 1838, it had totaled 20,000 *contos;* in 1858 it exceeded 100,000. During that same period, the income from import duties tripled. Periodically the government found it necessary to borrow money for extraordinary purposes and cus-

5. *Brazil and the River Plate in 1868* (London, 1869), p. 67.

tomarily these loans came from British bankers. Prior to 1858, the government contracted loans to finance the indemnization to Portugal, to cover budget deficits, or to pay the service on previous loans. The loan of 1858 marked a turning point and demonstrated once again the progress being made: it was the first loan secured for a productive purpose, railroad building, and the first liquidated strictly according to the terms of the contract.

The monarchy continued to do whatever it could to encourage the growth. In 1860, the government authorized its seventh ministerial post, for Agriculture, Commerce, and Public Works. The Central School opened its doors in Rio de Janeiro in 1858 to train engineers, an education hitherto available only in the military academies. In 1874, it was reorganized and became the Polytechnical Institute. The School of Mines was established in Minas Gerais that same year. São Bento das Lages, the first agricultural school, began to offer classes in 1877. Agricultural societies were formed throughout the empire, and national and regional fairs and exhibits increased in number. These accomplishments attested to the official policy favoring modernization by which the elites hoped to reshape their country.

Progress and Dependency

The Brazilian elites boasted of their European heritage and even those with Indian and/or African ancestors dwelt more on their European ties than otherwise. They readily understood what was happening in Europe and ably discussed the latest ideas radiating from the Old World, which they welcomed to their shores. But European thought was no intellectual spring; it proved to be an ideological flood which swept before it most Brazilian originality. Generally speaking, three major European philosophies shaped the ideology of the elites during the nineteenth century: the Enlightenment, the ideas of evolution put forth by Charles Darwin and Herbert Spencer, and Positivism. The concept of "progress," perhaps the key word for the understanding of nineteenth-century Brazilian history, linked the three.

Stressing the vincibility of ignorance, the Enlightenment philosophers concluded that if people had the opportunity to know the truth, they would select "civilization" over "barbarism." Adherents to the Enlightenment believed in a universally valid standard to judge "civilization," and the criteria for such a judgment rested on European concepts of progress. Civilization and the progress which led to it became identified with Europe, or more specifically with England, France, and Germany. Moreover, a burgeoning faith in science directed judgments on progress as well as progress itself away from philosophical and moral matters toward material change. The popularized ideas of Darwin that organic forms developed over the course of time and represented successive stages in a single evolutionary process toward perfection further heightened the interest in progress, giving it in fact a scientific veneer. Very propitiously, Spencer, who commanded considerable attention in Brazil, applied the same principle of evolution to society. To Spencer, progress signified a march toward "the establishment of the greatest perfection and most complete happiness." However, that march subsumed a great many economic changes and adaptations. As one example, Spencer advocated railroads as a vital part of the organic system of a modern society. As another, he regarded industrialization as a certain manifestation of progress. Many Brazilians drew from Spencer the interrelationship of science, industry, and progress, a combination pointing to future glory through societal evolution. Like most European thinkers, Spencer said much that damned Brazil, his racist statements for example. But the Brazilian elites proved to be selective readers, choosing to ignore what displeased—or frightened—them.

Many of the ideas on progress pulled from the Enlightenment, Darwin, Spencer, as well as from other sources, seemed to converge in the form Auguste Comte's Positivism assumed in Brazil during the last quarter of the century. Positivism affirmed the inevitability of social evolution and progress. To Comte that progress was attainable through the acceptance of scientific laws codified by Positivism. Outward manifestations of progress—again railroads and industrialization—assumed great importance in Positivism and emphatically so among the Brazilians, whether they acknowledged Comte or not.

Clearly those distant intellectual mentors provided powerful arguments for those elites desiring to replicate European civilization in Brazil, which to their thinking evinced all too many "barbaric" Indian and African traits. In the first issue of the literary and scientific magazine *Minerva Brasiliense* (November 1843), Sales Tôrres Homem saluted the progress of the nineteenth century. The breathtaking advances in science as well as the achievements of "political and moral sciences" excited him. He believed Brazil would participate in the progress emanating from Europe. He expressed tremendous faith in the future, a faith shared by many of the elites who constructed a philosophic overview echoing the European concept of "progress." Politically, they required order to implement it. Economically, they adopted capitalism, which seemed to have transformed the North Atlantic states into modern nations, to finance it.

In the last half of the century, the elites sharpened their awareness of the material progress being made on the continent. Many of them had mastered French, the second language of the Brazilian elites, and some had a knowledge of English or German, so that they had direct access to the information and literature of the nations whose progress impressed them. The newspapers carried accounts of what was happening in the leading nations of the Western world, and the programs of the learned societies featured discussions of the technical advances of the industrializing nations. Many members of the elites traveled abroad, thereby exposing themselves first hand to the innovations. They returned to Brazil with a nostalgia for Europe, particularly Paris, and the irrepressible desire to copy everything they saw there. Of course, the imports bore testimony to larger segments of the population of the manufacturing skill and ingenuity of those technologically advanced societies.

As the century matured, many Brazilians interpreted the experience of the United States as a verification of the wisdom of implememting European ideas in the New World. After all, the United States once had been a colony too, and yet by mid-century, not even three-quarters of a century after achieving independence, it seemed to exemplify progress itself, certainly the material manifestations of it. Progress seemed most obvious in the post-Civil War period, which boasted of the transcontinental expansion of the railroads and the triumph of industrialization. The Brazilian elites attributed the success of the United States to two factors: the preponderance of Europeans in the racial composition and the adoption of European ideology, political as well as economic. In short, the United States represented in their eyes the triumph of progress in the New World and further demonstrated the means of achieving it.

The elites' perception of progress is perhaps more correctly and easily defined by example rather than more complex social science terminology and concepts which have marginal value in understanding the Brazilian experience. Later generations of scholars substituted the word "modernization" but such a replacement did little to clarify events in nineteenth-century Brazil. Both words, used interchangeably hereafter, implied a questioning and rejection of habits, patterns, and values associated with the Luso-Brazilian past and an admiration for the ideas, modes, technology, and styles of Europe and the United States and a desire to adopt—rarely to adapt—them. Consequently, to those elites, "to progress" meant to recreate their nations as closely as possible to their European and North American models. So, they set out to diffuse education, to raise the level of technology, to industrialize, and to urbanize. They felt certain they would benefit from such a program, and by extension they assumed that their nations would benefit as well. They tended to identify (and to confuse) class well-being with national welfare.

As it turned out, the progress pursued by the Brazilians was superficial. They preferred the façade to the risk of tampering with basic neocolonial institutions—the land structures, for example—whose transformation might have instituted a more meaningful form of progress but might also have threatened the privileges of the elites. They relied, for example, on monoculture and the export of coffee to finance most of the progress they sought and thereby they tied their modernization to neocolonial practices which previously had not benefited the majority of the Brazilians. "Progress" in nineteenth-century Brazil was measured largely in quantitative terms. It could be measured—at least according to the elites, politicians, and scholars—by the number of miles of railroad tracks or telegraph lines, no matter where they went or what ends they served. The expansion and renovation of port facilities have been equated ipso facto with progress, even though in the final analysis those ports more tightly linked Brazil with foreign markets, strengthening the mono-export sector of the economy and further contributing to Brazil's dependency. The large cities sought to transform themselves into copies of admired European cities, and Paris was the primary model. To the extent that Brazil was able to ape Europe, the elites classified themselves, their cities or regions, and Brazil as "cultured," "civilized," or "progressive." The arrival of increasing numbers of European immigrants in the last quarter of the century signified the acceleration of the progress cherished by the elites since the newcomers brought with them much admired tastes and skills.

The establishment of peace and stability after 1850 and the prosperity infused by coffee exports permitted the acceleration of the process of modernization. Brazilian progress paralleled similar advances in the other major Latin American nations. Chile after the promulgation of the conservative constitution of 1833, Argentina after the unification of Buenos Aires with the other provinces in 1862, and Mexico after the execution of Maximilian in 1867 followed similar courses.

In speaking of "progress" a serious confusion can and does often arise since progress signified to many some form of development. Here a semantic confusion intrudes which confuses development and growth. They are quite distinct and must be separated to understand better the economic fate of Brazil. Growth indicates simply and exclusively numerical accumulation and in no way indicates how it occurred, or what grew, or who benefited. The part of Brazil associated with coffee exports grew wealthier in the last half of the nineteenth century, but that wealth concentrated largely in one region, the Southeast, and even there in the hands of relatively few. One could argue that such growth through monoexportation undermined the wellbeing of Brazil. Development, on the other hand, signifies the maximum use of a nation's potential for the greatest benefit of the largest number of the inhabitants. Development can imply or include growth, although it is conceivable that a nation can develop without growing. Nor does modernization or "progress" necessarily denote development.

The study of the efforts to modernize the moribund sugar industry by Peter L. Eisenberg, *The Sugar Industry in Pernambuco, 1840–1910: Modernization without Change,* perfectly illustrated the insidious aspect of modernization without basic institutional changes. Modernization in the sugar industry meant the use of the latest technological advances and the abolition of forced labor. Governmental subsidies facilitated the planters and mill owners' conversion to modernization. They managed to survive and prosper to a certain extent, but they transferred losses suffered in the export market to the workers in the forms of low wages and dismal working conditions. Eisenberg found that after 1870 the daily wage for unskilled rural labor fell while the cost of living continued to rise. He concluded, "One cannot escape the conclusion that the free rural laborer in the later nineteenth century enjoyed little material advantage over the slave." The declining standard of living for the rural worker in the Northeast was reflected in the growing number of deaths per one-thousand inhabitants in the later years of the century. Apparently urban workers in Rio de Janeiro, to cite another example, suffered a similar restriction in their quality of life. Professor Eulalia M. L. Lobo, who has conducted lengthy investigations of salaries and prices in the capital during the nineteenth century, emphasized the general trend toward the lowering of the real buying power of the workers' salaries in the last half of the century.

Scant evidence exists that Brazil developed in the nineteenth century. The type of progress selected or imposed complemented the export sector and benefited the elites associated with it. By spending accumulated capital on luxuries and "show pieces" of progress, by draining away potential capital in the form of interest payments on foreign loans or as profits on foreign investments, the elites seem to have further impoverished the majority of the Brazilians. Brazil testified to the harsh reality that when growth occurs in an agrarian economy through the expansion of a narrow modern sector linked to exports, inequality in the distribution of income multiplies. Progress helped to perpetuate the glaring social inequalities which already had characterized Brazil because it took place within the framework of old institutions which previously had given ample evidence of their inability to provide socio-economic justice to the majority. "Progress," thus, should be understood as a most subjective concept, which in the nineteenth-century Brazilian experience contributed to retarding development, impoverishing the masses, and increasing dependency.

Statesmen and Diplomats

The empire matured politically under the guidance of Emperor Pedro II. In nearly every way he contrasted with his dashing and romantic father. Pedro II was calm, deliberate, and serious. He eschewed military uniforms for somber black suits and preferred books and study to the active life of the outdoors. He practiced a morality in both private and public life which few could equal. The empress, Tereza Cristina Maria de Bourbon (1822–1889) of the Kingdom of the Two Sicilies, whom Pedro married in 1843, was the model of domesticity. By their example, the two monarchs impressed a Victorian morality on the court and government in an otherwise relaxed nation.

By all accounts, and his portraits and photographs do not contradict it, the emperor was an imposing and handsome man, simple in manners and unaffected in appearance. He seldom failed to win the sympathy of those who met him. Certainly all the foreign visitors exuded praise. The clergymen D. P. Kidder and J. C. Fletcher, whose accounts of nineteenth-century Brazil are among the best written and most informative, were no exceptions. In the early 1850s, they witnessed the emperor's behavior at the gala opening of the legislature. For that occasion, banners of silk and satin brocade decorated the main streets of the capital to provide the festive setting for the impressive procession from the royal palace to the legislative chambers in the Campo de Santa Ana. The guards, mounted and on foot, wore bright uniforms and the mounted military band blared out martial music. Six state coaches—each with its six caparisoned horses and liveried coachmen and postilions—carried officers of the imperial household. An elaborate carriage drawn by eight iron-gray horses transported Empress Tereza and her maids of honor. A magnificent imperial carriage drawn by eight milk-white horses decked with Prince of Wales plumes bore the emperor. The stately pageant elicited this commentary from the two Americans about Pedro II:

The Emperor is indeed a Saul—head and shoulders above his people; and in his court-dress, with his crown upon his fine, fair brow, and his sceptre in his hand, whether receiving the salutes of his subjects of opening the Imperial Chambers, he is a splendid specimen of manhood. His height, when uncovered, is six feet four inches, and his head and body are beautifully proportioned: at a glance one can see, in that full brain and in that fine blue eye, that he is not a mere puppet upon the throne, but a man who thinks.[6]

When Pedro had agreed to mount the throne at the age of fourteen, he was a puppet in the hands of the courtiers. He achieved political maturity within a few years. By 1847, he

6. *Brazil and the Brazilians*, p. 212.

had consolidated his position and was virtually independent of political forces and influences. When Kidder and Fletcher witnessed his appearance before the legislature, he was tightly controlling the reigns of government. As the constitution prescribed, he functioned on a plane above political factions, the grand manipulator of all the instruments of government. Those responsibilities, as well as all his duties, the emperor took very earnestly. Perhaps one of the tersest and surest guides to his conception of his role as emperor can be found in this poem he penned in 1852:

> If I am pious, clement, just,
>   I'm only what I ought to be:
> The sceptre is a weighty trust,
>   A great responsibility;
> And he who rules with faithful hand,
>   With depth of thought and breadth of range,
> The sacred laws should understand,
>   But must not, at his pleasure, change.
>
> The chair of justice is the throne:
>   Who takes it bows to higher laws;
> The public good, and not his own,
>   Demands his care in every cause.
> Neglect of duty,—always wrong,—
>   Detestable in young or old,—
> By him whose place is high and strong,
>   Is magnified a thousandfold.
>
> When in the east the glorious sun
>   Spreads o'er the earth the light of day,
> All know the course that he will run,
>   Nor wonder at his light or way:
> But if perchance the light that blazed
>   Is dimm'd by shadows lying near,
> The startled world looks on amazed,
>   And each one watches it with fear.
>
> I likewise, if I always give
>   To vice and virtue their rewards,
> But do my duty thus to live;
>   No one his thanks to me accords.

But should I fail to act my part,
   Or wrongly do, or leave undone,
Surprised, the people then would start
   With fear, as at the shadow'd sun.[7]

Fortunately he ruled better than he rhapsodized. The poem would scarcely last as a piece of literature, but as an indication of the emperor's own perception of his role it has considerable political value. Pedro ruled benevolently but firmly. As the years of his long reign waxed, he preferred to exercise power more indirectly but nonetheless his presence was always felt. The emperor was known to believe that if power was shared by too many it was effectively exercised by no one. An immigrant leader of the German colony in Rio Grande do Sul observed in 1885 that the emperor "reigns, governs, and administers," exercising more power than most other sovereigns of the epoch.

As Brazil moved from its ambivalent neofeudalistic/neocapitalistic stage toward a more fully developed capitalism, the emperor served as both a symbolic and effective guarantee of order and prosperity for the varied regional, rural groups. He watched over the interests of the sugar, cacao, and coffee classes in return for their loyalty. Rarely did he restrict their local autonomy or threaten their patrimonial domination. After all, Brazil was overwhelmingly rural, and Pedro calculated correctly that he needed the loyalty and support of those who exercised authority in the countryside if he was to reign peacefully.

Historians praise the honesty, integrity, and moderation of Pedro II. His rule probably benefited Brazil. Some critics, then as well as later, have considered him a man of mediocre intelligence, who hesitated to propel the empire into the modern world. Arguments can and have been made that such caution was salutary. Pedro tried to rely on national opinion, which he distinguished from public opinion, as his guide. He seemed to equate national opinion with national well-being and thus divorced it in his mind from public opin-

---

7. Ibid., p. 595.

ion, which was, according to his thought, often misguided, erroneous, and emotional and therefore not always in accord with the best interests of the realm. In short, he relied on elitist views to guide him. He pointed out to his daughter, Princess Isabel (1846–1921), who on occasion served as regent, that the surest way to ascertain national opinion was "to hear honest and intelligent men of all political views, to read fully everything the press throughout Brazil has to say, and to listen to what is said in the legislative chambers both on the national and provincial levels." More often than not, the emperor sought his advice in the Council of State, in theory—and probably in practice as well—an august body of wise men.

The liberals regarded the Council with suspicion as a bastion of conservative, if not reactionary, thought and the bulwark of centralized authority. It had been abolished during the radical heyday of 1834 only to be reestablished again in 1841 during the Conservatives' ascendancy. Twelve regular members and twelve extraordinary members composed the Council. They met in plenary session to discuss matters of the greatest importance but otherwise they sat in committees to handle routine work. Their primary duty was to advise the emperor on the use of the extensive moderating power which he wielded. From 1842 to 1889, Pedro appointed 72 councilors. The largest number, 17, came from the province of Rio de Janeiro; Bahia furnished 14 and Minas Gerais 13. Indeed, the preeminence of the triumvirate of Rio de Janeiro, Minas Gerais, and São Paulo stood out. Together they provided 33 of the councilors, considerably outweighing the Pernambuco-Bahia axis and their satellite provinces from which came 24 councilors. Effective power, economic as well as political, gradually was shifting to the Southeast. The preferential treatment of the Southeast elicited complaints from a jealous Northeast. The *Diário de Pernambuco* editorialized: "Only the south is taken care of, just the south. There the light radiating from the center of our political system shines most brightly, and also there the heat of government attention warms everyone and everything. The north, on the other hand, is a miserable outcast, whose only privilege is to wait for crumbs from the banquet table of the gods."[8]

During the first decades of his reign, Pedro tended to rely on a handful of politicians whose honesty, skill, and long service to the nation impressed him. Principal among them were Honório Hermeto Carneiro Leão, Marquês de Paraná (Minas Gerais, 1801–1856); Pedro de Araújo Lima, Marquês de Olinda (Pernambuco, 1793–1870); José da Costa Carvalho, Marquês de Mont'Alegre (Bahia, 1796–1860); and Joaquim José Rodrigues Tôrres, Visconde de Itaboraí (Rio de Janeiro, 1802–1872). All four were Conservatives, representatives of the old landed class, whom Pedro elevated to the nobility. Their political experience reached far back into the nation's history: Olinda had been a deputy to the Côrtes; all four served in the legislature of the First Empire and played active roles during the Regency, Mont'Alegre serving as one of the triumvirate of regents and Olinda as the single regent from 1837 to 1840. All four served on the Council of State and organized at least one cabinet. Olinda organized four cabinets and held portfolios in ten others; Itaboraí served as president of the Council of Ministers twice and as a minister ten times. Three of them died before the end of the Paraguayan war, and the fourth, Itaboraí, left office in 1870. One Liberal provided perhaps the most perfect political and historical continuity. Antônio Paulino Limpo de Abreu, Visconde de Abaeté, was born in Portugal in 1798, came to Brazil with the royal court in 1807, began to serve as a minister during the Regency, held twelve portfolios during his political career, presided over the Council of Ministers from 1858 to 1860, became a councilor of state, and was elected president of the senate in 1860, a post he held with distinction until his death in 1883. Statesmen such as these provided the perfect continuity with the past and gave a solid cohesion to the first decades of Pedro's reign.

Using his moderating power and relying on the consensus of national opinion, the emperor alternated the Con-

8. May 24, 1884.

servative and Liberal parties in power. That alternation produced the following political pattern: 1840–1841, Liberals; 1841–1844, Conservatives; 1844–1848, Liberals; 1848–1853, Conservatives; 1853–1857, the Period of Coniliation in which both parties shared power; 1857–1862, Conservatives; 1862–1868, Liberals; 1868–1878, Conservatives; 1878–1885, Liberals; 1885–1889, Conservatives; and the Liberals had taken power again just prior to the overthrow of the monarchy. Cabinet approval rested with the Assembly. Until 1881, deputies to the Assembly were elected indirectly by electoral colleges. Reforms in that year mandated direct elections of deputies for three-year terms by all males who met the income requirements. Pedro used his power to dissolve the Assembly and thereby obtain support for a newly appointed cabinet eleven times during his reign. During those forty-nine years, the two parties formed thirty-six different ministries. The longest-lived was that of José Maria da Silva Paranhos, Visconde do Rio-Branco, from early 1871 to mid-1875. The briefest lasted but six days in May of 1862, the first cabinet organized by Zacarias de Góes e Vasconcelos. After the creation of the post of President of the Council of Ministers in 1847, the Liberal party formed the government sixteen times, to hold power for 17 years, 3 months, and 28 days; and the Conservatives, twelve times, for 20 years, 8 months, and 19 days. Omitted here is the Period of Conciliation, 1853–1857, when Paraná organized a nonpartisan government. That period witnessed such genuine cooperation among the leading men of both parties that it can be considered as apolitical. Eleven of the thirty *Presidentes do Conselho de Ministros* (Prime Ministers) came from Bahia, a monopoly unapproached by any other province. Second place fell to Pernambuco, natal province of five. Four originated in Rio de Janeiro, and São Paulo contributed only two.

    With the notable exception of the Period of Conciliation, the party out of power engaged in unrestricted criticism of the party in power. Freedom of expression in all forms was fully guaranteed, respected, and exercised. After 1850, the opposition no longer resorted to violence (at least not for thirty-nine years), but relied on constituted and orderly channels to voice disagreement. In short, discussion replaced violence.

The clientel of the two dominant political parties, the Liberals and the Conservatives, by no means espoused unanimous opinions. In fact, there might have been more differences of opinion within each party than between them. The powerful rural elites split between the two parties, just as the urban elites did. In general the Conservatives attracted landowners largely from areas of economic decline, the Northeast, Bahia, and Rio de Janeiro as well as most bureaucrats in the cities. On the other hand, the Liberals seemed to draw landowners from areas of economic expansion such as Minas Gerais, São Paulo, and Rio Grande do Sul and urban professionals. The major issue clearly dividing those two parties focused on questions of centralization of power. The Liberals sought to diffuse power, giving greater strength to the provinces, an attitude firmly opposed by the Conservatives. Little was done to diminish central authority during the Second Empire. The crown exercised tight control over the provinces through appointments. The monarch named the provincial senators and presidents, for example. Local electors selected provincial legislatures as well as national deputies. In the course of the long reign of Pedro II, the Conservatives found their most steadfast support in the province of Rio de Janeiro; the Liberals in Minas Gerais, São Paulo, and Rio Grande do Sul. Bahia and Pernambuco divided almost equally between the two parties.

Since similarities rather than differences characterized the two parties, a change of party in power did not signal a great change of policy. The Liberals seldom advocated anything so drastic that it could not eventually be enacted by the Conservatives, a procedure frequently followed. For example, the Conservatives terminated the slave trade in 1850, passed the Law of the Free Womb in 1871, and finally abolished slavery in 1888, all goals originally suggested by the Liberals. Such continuity prompted the observation of the Visconde de Albuquerque that there was nothing so like a Conservative as a Liberal in power. The playwright Joaquim José de França Junior joked knowingly about the political similarities of the parties in his humorous play *Como Se Fazia Um Diputado* (How a Deputy Was Created, 1887). One of the characters in the play accused of changing his party affiliations replied, "I changed my opinions for the soundest reasons of social order. Look here, my friend, if changing party labels were a crime, our jails wouldn't be big enough to hold all the criminals now on the loose." The same character later confessed, "My friend, I don't know of two beings more similar than a Liberal and a Conservative. They are both the offspring of the same mother, Lady Convenience, who rules everything and everyone in this world. Anybody who thinks otherwise had best leave politics to become a cobbler." The men who belonged to the parties were far more important then the platforms. Clashes between parties were, more likely than not, conflicts of personalities.

In the final analysis both parties were deeply rooted in the landowning oligarchy. After all, Brazil remained throughout the nineteenth century an overwhelmingly agrarian nation. Because of the basic similarity of their clientel, neither party ventured beyond well-circumscribed political boundaries, never desiring to deal with certain basic socio-economic issues. Land reform, for example, was taboo. Yet, a basic political complexity was emerging in the final decades of the Second Empire, which sooner or later would challenge traditional political patterns and behavior. Within an agrarian nation with strong patriarchal and folk customs, the government became increasingly Europeanized in form and mentality. While sympathetic to the interests of the rural elites, the government became increasingly molded by urban interests which strengthened greatly in the last years of the empire. Those urban interests were more congenial to the dynamic sector of the economy, coffee exports, and became more alienated from the older and declining economic center, the Northeast. As the Northeast and Southeast competed for the favors of the government, the urban interests tended to weigh in with the coffee class. The potential for a more fundamental political conflict increased.

The weaknesses of the parliamentary system were many: among them were its limited representation, its reluctance to come to grips with some of the nation's major problems, its ritualized, stilted behavior, and its exclusivity. Still, it did implant in the politicians a respect for their adversaries, a willingness to accept electoral defeat, and in general an attitude of fair play and sportsmanship in politics. Furthermore, since the parties prepared younger men for responsibility, the system provided political continuity. It seemed a practical step toward self-government after three centuries of authoritative colonial rule in which the Brazilians gained a minimum of experience. The advantages of the imperial political system are more visible when one compares it to its counterparts in the Spanish-speaking republics. Under the parliamentary system guided by Pedro II there was a peaceful rotation of parties and personalities in office. This contrasted dramatically with the force and violence accompanying the change of governments in many of the Spanish-speaking republics. In short, Brazil had a workable and acceptable political system in contrast to the troubled search for such a solution in most of the Spanish American nations.

The principal dividing point in the political history of the Second Empire seems to be the fall of the Liberal ministry of Zacharias de Góes e Vasconcelos in 1868. He thoroughly controlled the Assembly, and when a vacancy in the senate occurred he informed the emperor that he would like the Liberal chief of the province of Rio Grande do Norte appointed from the customary triple list. The emperor, of course, had the final voice in those nominations; he preferred Sales Tôrres Homen, a well-known orator, writer, and intellectual. When Pedro insisted on making his choice, Zacharias resigned. As was customary when the prime minister left office, the entire ministry followed. Pedro invited Itaboraí, a Conservative, to form a new cabinet. Because the Conservatives did not have a majority, the emperor dissolved the Assembly and ordered new elections. Predictably the Conservatives, in charge of the electoral machinery after the appointment of Itaboraí, won those elections. The loss of power infuriated the Liberals. They regarded the events as nothing short of a coup d'état manipulated by the emperor himself. Their anger united the Liberals more strongly than they hitherto had been and impelled them to reconsider their program. As a result, in 1869 they issued a reform manifesto calling for the abolition of the moderating power, the Council of State, the National Guard (they disliked its privileged officers), and slavery. The manifesto favored the establishment of direct elections, expanded suffrage, periodical elections for senators for a limited term of office, popular election of provincial presidents, an independent judiciary, more educational institutions, and other reforms. If enacted, their program would have weakened the government in Rio de Janeiro because in effect what they envisaged was federalization with its consequent decentralization. The new Liberal program harked back to the early years of the 1830s. Indeed, the generation which had lived through the chaos, anarchy, and threatened disintegration of that critical period in Brazilian history had passed, or was passing rapidly, from the political scene. A new group of politicians appeared in the 1860s and early 1870s who were perfectly loyal to the monarchy but who had not experienced the rebellions of the Regency period.

Although impossible to pick out a politician typical of that new group, it nonetheless would be instructive to review the ideology of at least one. Aureliano Cândido Tavares Bastos (1839–1875), an articulate national deputy from Alagoas, wrote and spoke passionately for the ideas he believed in and fought for them in the Assembly. His background placed him well within the emerging middle sectors. First as a Conservative and later as a Liberal, that young intellectual advocated a "progress"—he often referred to it as "unlimited progress"—derived from British and North American experiences from which he insisted Brazil could benefit: "I am an enthusiastic fanatic of England, but I understand the greatness of that people only when I contemplate the republic the English founded in North America. It is not enough for us to study England; it is necessary to know the United States. It is from this second country that we can derive practical lessons to improve our agriculture and our economy."[9] He called for closer relations with the United States.

9. Carlos Pontes, *Tavares Bastos* (São Paulo, 1939), p. 160.

Tersely he summed up the three urgent necessities of Brazil as "education, emanciptation, and transportation," but he elaborated complex plans to engineer Brazil's progress. Agriculture was to be the business of Brazil, and in his campaign to develop agriculture he linked himself closely with the coffee planters. He adhered to the old ideas of Adam Smith that each nation should engage in what it did best, and therefore he believed others should supply Brazil with the manufactured goods it needed and even provide the ships to carry on the trade. Tavares Bastos defended private initiative and property, yet believed the government should undertake public works projects so long as they contributed to expanding exports. Progress could be measured, in fact, by foreign commerce, and to him mounting coffee exports were a sure sign of such progress. However, inefficient and retrograde slavery doomed Brazil's agriculture, and thus Tavares Bastos urged gradual emancipation of the blacks and their incorporation into the nation through education. Free coastal navigation and the opening of the Amazon to international trade—first advocated by him in 1862 and enacted by the government five years later—were other methods he lauded as necessary for increased commerce and thus certain progress.

Tavares Bastos worried a great deal about unbalanced budgets; he advocated strengthening the currency and reducing debts. Education should be practical, useful, and wide-spread. Immigration should be encouraged, particularly from the United States and Northern Europe. He advised, "Without the immigrants of Germany and Great Britain, Brazil will never progress. It is necessary that the pure blood of the Northern races some to develop and renovate our degenerate race."[10] The Brazil the Alagoan envisioned was largely agrarian; it engaged in a lively international commerce; and it was strengthened and refined by emancipation, education, and immigration. Other younger politicians might adhere to parts of this program but one certain variation would be encouragement for industrialization.

In the 1880s even a greater number of rising politicians participating in national life had little but the remotest child-

10. Luiz Pinto, *Tavares Bastos, Idéias e Diretrizes* (Maceio, 1967), p. 52.

hood recollections of anything before the political stability of the Second Empire. Among the statesmen whose careers were associated exclusively with the Second Empire were José Tomás Nabuco de Araújo, José Antônio Saraiva, José Maria da Silva Paranhos, Visconde do Rio-Branco, and Afonso Celso de Assis Figueiredo, Visconde do Ouro Prêto.

Reflecting the temper of their times, the new statesmen showed themselves to be reformist in outlook and, regardless of their political party differences, instrumental in implementing many of the reforms called for by the Liberal Manifesto. The emperor stepped into the political background to allow his ministers more prominence. The Council of State became more administrative and less political in its operation. Slavery was gradually abolished until its final extinction in 1888. Judiciary reforms made that branch of government increasingly more independent. The Saraiva Law of 1881 provided for direct elections. Although it did not remove property qualifications for voting, it did lower them. However, with the possible exception of the elections immediately following the reform and despite the best intentions of the law, the elections continued to be manipulated by the party holding power to ensure the victory of its candidates for the legislature. The electorate continued to be but a fraction of the total population. In 1881 it numbered only 142,000 out of a population of approximately 15 million. The enactment of these reforms by both the Liberals and Conservatives again blurred the distinctions between the two parties.

The crisis in 1868 reawakened republican sentiment which had manifested itself periodically if weakly in the past, particularly in the inconfidências of 1789 and 1798, the revolts of 1817 and 1824, and throughout the Regency period. A Republican Club was organized in Rio de Janeiro in November of 1870 and the following month it published its manifesto calling for the abolition of the monarchy and the establishment of a federal republic. In other respects, its program resembled that advocated by the Liberals except that the Republicans tended to be vaguer on the question of slavery. The early Republicans inherited much of their thinking from the Enlightenment and were strongly influenced by federalism as practiced in the United States. A later breed of Republicans, however, adhered more to Comte's Positivist concept of a dictatorial republic ruled by an elite. Naturally they regarded themselves as that elite. Republican leaders, men like Antônio da Silva Jardim, Quintino Bocaiúva, Lafayette Rodrigues Pereira, Aristides Lobo, Salvador de Mendonça, Rangel Pestana, Manuel Ferraz de Campos Sales, and Américo Braziliense, were talented and enthusiastic, but they failed to attract a popular following. Almost exclusively urban in orientation, the party's strength centered in the cities of Rio de Janeiro, Minas Gerais, São Paulo, and Rio Grande do Sul. Of those provinces, São Paulo boasted the strongest and best organized branches of the Republican party. In 1884, São Paulo elected three Republican deputies to the national legislature, among them Campos Sales and Prudente José de Morais e Barros, both of whom were destined to become presidents of the republic. They were the first Republicans to sit in Parliament. The Republicans abjured the use of force to implement their program. Instead, they hoped to educate public opinion to accept it. In their program they considered federalism paramount, the panacea for the ills besetting their country. They, too, were of a generation which had known neither the Regency nor its turbulence.

One of the major issues to disturb the political tranquillity of the Second Empire had little to do with the political parties. Nascent ultramontanism among the clergy challenged the regalist doctrines of the state. An acrimonious struggle jolted the customarily amiable relations between Church and State, unusually harmonious in Brazil, especially when compared to the habitual strife between the two which disturbed nineteenth-century Spanish America. Most of the clergy in Brazil had supported independence and all had sworn allegiance to the new emperor. Although permitting religious liberty, the Constitution of 1824 established Roman Catholicism as the state religion and the emperor continued to exercise royal patronage over the Church within his domains as his Portuguese ancestors had done for centuries. The Vatican remained silent on the question of patronage, accepting Pedro's interpretation rather than overtly conceding to him the privileges and responsibilities of the patronage. The first major dispute between Rome and Rio de Janeiro erupted in 1834 over the nomination of Antônio Maria de Moura as bishop of Rio de Janeiro. Moura advocated the abolition of clerical celibacy and held other ideas the Church fathers regarded as radical. The government, encouraged by the radical priest-politician Diogo Antônio Feijó, supported his candidacy; Rome refused to install him. The question was resolved in 1835 when Moura himself withdrew his candidacy. Relations between the Vatican and Rio de Janeiro returned to normal.

Pedro II was an uncompromising regalist and the ecclesiastical hierarchy acquiesced timidly. In truth the State was far stronger than the Church, whose lamentable physical and moral condition within Brazil weakened its position. The buildings were in a sad state of disrepair and deterioration, the morality of the clergy was embarrassingly loose, and there was a dire shortage of priests. The puritanic emperor appreciated the subservience of the clergy to the throne but deprecated their immorality. He resolved to purify the Church by sending promising candidates for the priesthood to Europe for study. They returned morally stronger, much to his gratification, but they had drunk headily from ultramontane ideology as well, a consequence of their European sojourn which Pedro had not considered. The inevitable contest of strength between the regalist monarch and a new ultramontane Church hierarchy occurred in the 1870s as a result of conflicting views on Masonry.

An encyclical of Pope Pius IX denounced the Masonic Order in 1864. The emperor never sanctioned its publication, realizing that the rabidly anticlerical Masons of Europe had little in common with the fraternal Masons of Brazil, most of whom were devoted servants of the Church and many of whom were clergymen; and hence the encyclical should not have circulated in Brazil. But the new ultramontane bishops thought otherwise. In 1872 a priest in Rio de Janeiro, after speaking enthusiastically in a Masonic lodge to commemorate the Law of the Free Womb promulgated a year earlier, received an ultimatum from his bishop either to sever his

Masonic relationships or be suspended from the Church. The priest refused to renounce his Masonic ties and thereby challenged the Church. Bishop Vital Maria Gonçalves de Oliveira of Pernambuco, educated in France in ultramontane doctrines, took up the challenge. He ordered the religious brotherhoods, significant religious and social institutions composed of laymen, to expel their Masonic members, who more often than not happened to be some of their most prominent members. When the brotherhoods refused, the bishop suspended the religious functions of the Brotherhood of the Santíssimo Sacramento. Here now was a direct challenge to the Crown since the bishop resolved to enforce an encyclical that the emperor had not allowed into the country. The brotherhood appealed to the throne in June of 1873, and the emperor ordered the bishop to remove the interdict forthwith. Bishop Vital defied the emperor's order, and the Government was left with no alternative but to institute legal action against the recalcitrant churchman, charged with violating the criminal code and the constitution. He stood trial in Rio de Janeiro in 1874 amid Byzantine diplomatic maneuverings between the pope and the emperor. The court found the bishop guilty and sentenced him to four years of hard labor, a sentence commuted by the throne to simple imprisonment. A similar case involved Bishop Antônio de Macedo Costa of Pará, also educated in France. Eventually the Vatican and Rio de Janeiro came to an agreement. The emperor issued a decree of amnesty in 1875, and the pope ordered the interdicts against the Masons lifted and the brotherhoods restored to their positions prior to 1873. In that overt challenge of the State, the Church lost; regalism triumphed. Many in the Church hierarchy brooded over the defeat. Their enthusiasm waned for the regalist monarch whom they regarded thereafter as unfriendly. Politically the struggle between Church and State was nonpartisan. Politicians of all hues and beliefs supported the emperor.

Foreign relations were another nonpartisan matter. After obtaining recognition with relative ease, the empire turned its attention to establishing friendly relations with its neighbors, and, above all else, to demarcating favorably its extensive frontiers, believed to border all the republics and colonies of the South American continent save Chile. Attention focused on the headwaters of the Amazon and on the Plata River network. Brazil possessed the course of the Amazon and its tributaries but not their headwaters. Vague geographical knowledge about the trackless Amazonian hinterland complicated efforts to settle frontiers there. Brazil guarded its South American heartland jealously, preoccupied with the thought that a neighbor might expand and fearful that some stronger, extracontinental power might trespass. For many decades Brazil kept the Amazon River closed to international traffic and used the promise of opening it to coax the other riparian nations to agree to a boundary settlement. When that tactic proved unsuccessful, Brazil bowed before international pressure and in 1867 permitted the vessels of all nations to ply that river.

Unlike the vast, unoccupied Amazon region, sizable population concentrations with differing loyalties confronted one another along the banks of the Plata, an area historically disputed by Spain and Portugal. In the national period, Argentina and Brazil, both potential powers, faced each other there to vie for dominance. Geopolitically Brazil needed to have the Plata open to commerce and communication so as not to isolate the immense province of Mato Grosso, which was underpopulated, weakly held, and tenuously tied to the effective national territory. As long as the Cisplatine Province (the Banda Oriental del Uruguay) remained within the empire, Brazil exerted control over the left bank of the mouth of the Plata and could ensure that that river network was kept open to its vessels. The loss of the Cisplatine Province as a result of the war with Argentina complicated the situation. Brazil found itself owner of the headwaters but without control over the main courses and mouth of the Plata waterway, quite the reverse of the position in the Amazon. Brazil's use of the Plata remained at the mercy of Argentina, Uruguay, and Paraguay. The confrontation with those Spanish-speaking republics over the use of the river and over unresolved boundaries required Brazil to concentrate most of its nineteenth-century diplomacy on the

Plata basin where an intensely dramatic and complex power struggle took place.

At stake for Argentina and Brazil in that struggle were control of the Plata and domination of Paraguay and Uruguay and to a lesser extent of Bolivia. Argentina remembered only too well that Brazil had once annexed the left bank of the Plata and suspected that the empire would be only too eager to reabsorb that strategic area. Brazil likewise believed that Argentina entertained expansionistic designs in the region. The authorization which the legislature of Buenos Aires gave Juan Manuel de Rosas, the Argentine caudillo, in 1850 to incorporate the "province" of Paraguay into the Argentine Confederation by any means possible only heightened Brazilian anxieties. For that matter, during his long administration, 1829–1852, Rosas spoke often of a "Greater Argentina" which would encompass the territory of the former viceroyalty of La Plata, that is Argentina, Uruguay, Paraguay, and part of Bolivia. Brazil did not desire such an overwhelming neighbor as an Argentina of that size would be. Furthermore, Brazil feared that Argentina might like to annex the province of Rio Grande do Sul, over at least part of which Spain and Portugal had contended. Brazilian concern mounted when French and British blockades of Buenos Aires not only failed to humble Rosas but, if anything, strengthened the internal position of the Argentine leader.

The empire's first move to counter Argentine pretensions in the Plata was to recognize Paraguay's independence in 1844, a move which infuriated Rosas. Brazil maneuvered thereafter to exert a maximum amount of influence in that landlocked nation in order to check any Argentine designs. As one Brazilian diplomat explained in 1846, "The annexation of Paraguay to the [Argentine] Confederation would give to the latter, in addition to the pride of conquest, an increase of territory and forces such that the equilibrium would cease to exist, and all of the sacrifices made by Brazil when it adhered to the independence of Montevideo would be entirely fruitless." The second move of the empire to counter Argentine pretensions in the Plata was the extension of Brazilian influence into Uruguay, a move complicated by the perennial chaos engulfing that country. Civil war between the Blancos (Conservatives) and the Colorados (Liberals) seemed to be the order of the day in Uruguay. Nonetheless, the Brazilian presence was inescapable. In 1842, approximately 20,000 Brazilians lived in and around Montevideo, and by 1864, fully a fifth of the population of the nation was Brazilian. As was inevitable in those endless civil wars, some estates owned by Brazilians in Uruguay were invaded, sacked, and at times confiscated. To further complicate the matter, Uruguayan bandits frequently crossed the frontier into Rio Grande do Sul to carry out their crimes. The extensive cattle ranches particularly attracted them. The imperial government claimed that such border raids had cost the ranchers some 800,000 head of cattle.

Rosas kept a sharp eye on Uruguay, not only because it had once formed a part of the viceroyalty of La Plata but also because Argentine exiles settled in Montevideo, where they ceaselessly plotted his overthrow. In the internal political struggle, the Argentine caudillo threw his support behind the leading Conservative politician, Manuel Oribe. In its turn, Brazil aided the leading Liberal politician, Fructuoso Rivera. The intricate political dance reached a climax in 1851 when Brazilian military forces marched into Uruguay to strengthen Rivera. Once military intervention in the Plata had begun, the Brazilians resolutely carried it to its ultimate conclusion. They allied with the new government of Uruguay and the dissident Argentine provinces of Entre Ríos and Corrientes to attack Rosas. The Argentine regional caudillo, Justo José de Urquiza, led the combined forces to victory at the battle of Monte Caseros in 1852. To the relief of the Brazilians, the defeated Rosas fled his homeland for a European exile. Diplomatic relations between the two Plata powers were reestablished in 1856, when they signed a treaty of friendship, commerce, and navigation. The ingrained suspicion, distrust, and rivalry could not be disguised by the cloak of momentary cooperation. Argentina and Brazil eyed each other warily through the chaos in which Uruguay continued and over the fortress into which Paraguay had built itself.

In the early 1860s, a new complication threatened the

delicate Platine balance of power. As a small country whose boundaries had not been recognized by its neighbors, Paraguay historically lived in a state of anxiety, if not impending danger. Repeated Argentine threats, even efforts, to annex their country did little to allay Paraguayan fears, which amounted almost to paranoia. Brazilian meddling in the other small Platine republic, Uruguay, only served to augment Paraguayan distress and concern. Being buffeted about by its two immense neighbors, Paraguay naturally felt insecure. Such insecurity had prompted the first chief of state, José Gaspar Rodríguez de Francia, to isolate his country from most foreign contacts for a generation. Although opening the frontiers, the second chief-of-state, Carlos Antonio López, was hardly less suspicious of his neighbors. For one thing, he feared Brazilian imperialism. To become master rather than victim of the situation, Paraguay resolved to take greater control of its own destiny. The nation methodically armed itself and trained the largest army in South America.

In the meantime, Brazil seemed to have defined more sharply its Platine policy: Paraguay and Uruguay must be kept as independent buffer states friendly to the empire and the Plata River must be kept open to Brazilian traffic. Careful and generally able Brazilian diplomacy seemed for a time successful in its labyrinthine maneuverings in that volatile region. The same imperial hand which on one occasion proffered aid could, on another, administer a slap. The methods varied, but the aims were uniform. The always delicate situation on the Uruguayan-Brazilian frontier deteriorated in late 1863. Renewed border incursions into Rio Grande do Sul on the part of the Uruguayan bandits annoyed the government in Rio de Janeiro. To emphasize the exhaustion of Brazilian patience, the emperor dispatched José Antônio Saraiva to Montevideo in April of 1864 to present Blanco President Atanasio Cruz Aguirre with an ultimatum: either Uruguay would pay for the damages suffered by the Brazilians and punish the guilty or the Brazilian army would be dispatched to Uruguay to seek satisfaction. Aguirre refused to bow to Brazilian demands. As an alternative he turned to Francisco Solano López, since 1862 chief-of-state of Paraguay.

The idea of serving as a mediator and of maintaining an equilibrium of power in the Plata obsessed López. He believed that peace and Paraguay's well-being in the Plata required a balance of power between Argentina and Brazil, an equilibrium which Paraguay had the obligation to force if necessary. López felt that Brazil's threat to Uruguay if carried out would upset the Platine balance. The strange concurrence of Brazilian and Argentine policy, both seeking to overthrow the Blancos, further aroused his suspicions. Indeed, rumors circulated that Brazil and Argentina had reached an agreement whereby the former would absorb Uruguay and the latter would absorb Paraguay. With such fears in mind, López let Aguirre understand that Paraguay would support Uruguay's defiance of Brazil. Receiving no satisfaction from Aguirre, Saraiva then returned to Rio de Janeiro. Clearly the Brazilian foreign minister had expected the Uruguayan to meet his demands, and because he did not Brazil found itself in an inflexible position. It seemed necessary to make good the threat. Obviously at that point the usually perceptive Brazilian diplomacy had failed, and not the least of its failures was an inability to link events in Uruguay with those in Paraguay.

Brazil rendered support to Aguirre's rival, Venancio Flores, who had declared himself favorable to the Brazilian cause. The Imperial Navy blockaded Uruguayan ports and the Imperial Army invaded that neighboring republic without a formal declaration of war, an act openly violating international law. Before such a use of force, Aguirre quickly fell. Flores assumed the presidency and promptly agreed to restore confiscated Brazilian property and to recognize Brazilian claims.

López watched the drama with mounting concern, more convinced than ever that the fate of his nation was linked to that of Uruguay. He saw in Aguirre's fall the first act of a tragedy which would end with the disappearance of the two smaller Platine states. To his mind, the precarious balance of power had been tipped to favor Brazil and it was essential for him to right it. In the words of his official newspaper, *El Semanario*, the Brazilian occupation of Uruguay was "a threat to the liberty, independence, sovereignty and territorial integrity of the Republic of Paraguay, and of the other states in this part of America." With the determination to challenge his large neighbor, he selected Brazil's most vulnerable point to display his strength. On November 11, 1864, he closed the Paraguay River, a vital branch of the Plata network, to Brazilian traffic. Furthermore, he ordered one of his gunboats to capture the *Marquês de Olinda*, an Imperial river steamer then transporting the provincial president to Mato Grosso. López then informed the emperor's minister in Asunción that Paraguay was breaking diplomatic relations with Brazil because of the intervention in Uruguay.

A Paraguayan army unit at once invaded Mato Grosso, but the real objective of López was to unite his main forces with those of Aguirre in Uruguay. To do so required crossing Argentine territory. He requested such permission from Buenos Aires. Argentina had everything to gain from the struggle between the three neighbors and common sense dictated that the nation should impartially observe and emphatically not participate. Following the dictates of such a policy of neutrality, President Bartolomé Mitre refused to concede the permission López sought. Just as Brazil had misjudged the situation earlier, Argentina did so now. To the amazement of the Argentines, López boldly captured their vessels on the inland waters and invaded the province of Corrientes. Argentine hopes of neutrality evaporated and quite unexpectedly the government in Buenos Aires found itself signing a treaty of alliance with Brazil, along with the puppet government of Uruguay, on May 1, 1865. Those allies accused López of wanting to create a Platine empire made up of Paraguay, Uruguay, and the Argentine provinces of Entre Ríos and Corrientes.

No adherent to this Triple Alliance was prepared for war. Brazilian troops were scattered throughout the length and breadth of a vast empire. It was necessary first to collect and transport them to the south and the problem of supplying them was never satisfactorily resolved. Still, the sheer weight of the Allies pressed down on small, landlocked Paraguay. In the naval engagement of Riachuelo on June 11, 1865, the

Allied fleet destroyed the Paraguayan squadron and took command of the inland waterways. It was not, however, until April of 1866 that the Allies first invaded Paraguayan territory. The key to the defense of Paraguay was the solid fortress of Humaitá which guarded the ascent of the Paraguay River and stood as a formidable block on the road to Asunción. The siege of Humaitá got under way in July of 1867, when the Allies brought all their strength to bear upon that fortress. Yet it stood in heroic defiance of the impressive forces arrayed against it. The war lengthened beyond what even the most pessimistic among the Allies dreamed possible. Convinced that they were defending the very existence of their homeland, the Paraguayans demonstrated uncommon courage. Their pluck was well illustrated by Commander Estigarribia, trapped in Uruguaiana, Rio Grande do Sul, by an overwhelming Allied army. The Allied commander requested his surrender, stating that the Allies had no quarrel with the Paraguayan people but rather sought to overthrow the tyrant López who commanded them and treated them as slaves; and that the Allies would give them liberty and the right to a government of their own free election. Estigarribia pointedly replied, "If Your Excellencies are so anxious to grant freedom to Paraguay's peoples, why haven't you commenced by liberating the unhappy Negroes of Brazil who compose the majority of the population and who exist under the hardest and most frightful slavery in order to enrich and provide idle time to some hundreds of the empire's principal figures."[11] Such was the spirit which made the Paraguayans a formidable foe.

As the war stretched on, opposition to it within Brazil mounted. The empire bore the chief responsibilities for the conduct of the war, furnishing most of the money, materiél, and men for the Allied cause. The rapid material development of the realm was hindered by the military sacrifice. The mounting costs—in total over $300 million—weakened the national currency and required the government to contract

11. This exchange is quoted by Charles J. Kolinski, *Independence or Death* (Gainesville, Florida, 1965), pp. 104–5.

debts abroad. The casualty lists, which accounted for between 33,000 and 50,000 men, sobered the enthusiasm of the populace. Despite much complaint at home, the Allied governments determined to press on and refused anything except an unconditional surrender.

The fall of Humaitá in August of 1868, after a prolonged siege, opened up all of Paraguay to the Allied armies. They descended on Asunción and took the capital on January 5, 1869. In the process they destroyed most of the remaining Paraguayan army. However, López miraculously escaped to the mountains far to the northeast of the capital. There his fragmented forces continued to display the courage which characterized the Paraguayan soldier throughout the long war. A pursuing Brazilian army defeated the Paraguayans again at Cerro Corá on March 1, 1870. Among the dead in that battle was Marshal Francisco Solano López. The war was over. To the Paraguayan people, López still remains their national hero. He is the leader who saved the republic from extinction. Outside of Paraguayan histories, he has been accorded quite a different treatment. Brazilian historians traditionally and uniformly regard him as a "mad and insane despot," if not worse. As one Brazilian historian candidly admitted, "It is exceedingly difficult to find anything good to say of this man."[12]

Paraguay's defeat—its near destruction—removed all pretensions that nation might have had as a Platine power and relegated it once again to its position as a buffer state. The war reduced the population to less than half its former size, and of those probably no more than 28,000 were adult males. Nonetheless, López seems to have achieved one of his major objectives: the war ended the direct interventions of Argentina and Brazil in Uruguay. Moreover, the two major powers seem to have understood more clearly thereafter the useful purpose served by the independence of the two buffer states. Argentine and Brazilian imperialist ambitions to

12. João Pandiá Calógeras, *A History of Brazil* (New York, 1963), p. 208. Textbooks on Latin American history written by North Americans uniformly support the Allied cause and cast López as a villain.

absorb one or both of them disappeared. One of the major causes for Brazilian intervention in Platine affairs was removed with the definitive opening of the river network to world commerce. Contrary to the pledges of the other parties of the Triple Alliance, Brazil signed in 1872 a separate treaty of peace with Paraguay which, among other things, delineated their common frontiers to Brazil's advantage. By conceding a small amount of territory to Brazil, Paraguay enlisted the empire's support against exaggerated Argentine claims. Argentina reacted adversely to the treaty, accusing Brazil of violating Article Six of the Treaty of the Triple Alliance which forbade separate peace treaties with Paraguay. In the disagreement which ensued, the Paraguayans cleverly played off one power against the other and in the process saved some of their own territory coveted by Argentina.

An exhausted Brazil turned its attention inward again after the successful conclusion of the war. The traumatic international involvement had had severe internal effects which in the long run would modify the course of national evolution. Those effects would be most noticeable in the 1880–1890 period. Of major significance for the future, a new national institution emerged as a consequence of the war: the military. With no war for independence to fight comparable to the protracted and bitter wars which ravaged much of Spanish America, the Brazilian military had been weak and inconsequential. Pedro I even had to rely on mercenaries to fight against Argentina in the 1825–1828 war over the Banda Oriental. In fact, not until a decree of 1839 was the army even systematically organized. Five years of long struggle with Paraguay necessarily changed all that. A large, well-organized, powerful, and above all else professional military emerged from that war. Of further significance, that new institution did not represent the rural aristocracy who from the beginning had controlled Brazil. The officer class instead originated in the newly formed urban middle groups. Their loyalties, values, and ambitions were markedly different from those of the landed oligarchy. As long as war absorbed their attention, the officers exerted no influence on the structure and functions of the state, but the long years of peace after

1870 made the army restless, ambitious for political participation, and consequently vulnerable to Republican and Positivist propaganda.

To arouse public support for the long war, it was necessary to engender among the civilians a respect for the military they never before had demonstrated. Considerable propaganda lauded the soldier as the true patriot fighting in
defense of the fatherland. It is interesting to observe the
changing attitude of the august Brazilian Historical and Geographical Institute, an elitist club influential in forming the
opinion of the educated public. Prior to the war, the
members of the Institute in their meetings and in the pages
of their prestigious *Revista* spent most of their energy glorify-
ing the Indian past of Brazil. The war worked a sudden
change. They turned their attention to the military hero. Military biographies filled the pages of their journal. A once neglected institution became the worthy topic for their dis-
courses. From the war, then, emerged not only a
well-established military institution but also a new respect
for the military.

It had been the use of force which permitted Brazil to
advantageously mark its frontiers with Paraguay in 1872, just
as it had been the judicious use of the presence of force
which accomplished the same end with Uruguay in 1851.
Those boundaries with the two Platine states were the only
ones delineated during the Empire despite the tireless efforts
the diplomats dedicated to fixing the distant limits of their
nation. One of the ablest of the foreign ministers was Paulino José Soares de Souza, Visconde do Uruguai, who held
the portfolio from 1849 to 1853, years of an intensive diplomatic offensive in both the Amazon and Plata. Uruguai made
aggressive efforts to settle all Brazilian territorial claims on
the basis of *uti possidetis,* the concept, introduced onto the
continent by the Treaty of Madrid of 1750, which dominated
all Brazilian border diplomacy. The imperial diplomats did
succeed in laying the groundwork upon which future favorable settlement could be made.

Throughout the imperial period Great Britain continued
to be the paramount foreign power exercising influence over

Brazil. Elsewhere we have noted the intimate commercial and financial ties between the two nations. The Brazilians were sensitive to that British presence, but in the nineteenth century they had little alternative but to accept it. Twice, however, the Brazilians challenged the British and on both occasions triumphed—at least temporarily. The first incident was over the renewal of the commercial preference, and as we have seen Brazil not only refused to renew it in 1844, but enacted a modest tariff increase. The second, the so-called Christie question, involved several complicated but usually mundane matters. In 1861, the cargo of a British ship wrecked on the coast of Rio Grande do Sul was pillaged. The following year three drunken British sailors out of uniform insulted a Brazilian official and were arrested. Upon learning their identity, the Brazilians released them. The highhanded British minister, William D. Christie, demanded indemnization for the pillaging and full satisfaction, including the punishment of those responsible, for the arrest. To enforce his demands, Christie ordered British warships then in Brazilian waters to blockade the port of Rio de Janeiro, which they did for six days. Under protest, the government reluctantly paid the indemnization, but it refused to accede to British demands for satisfaction. Furthermore the government requested an apology and compensation for the Brazilian ships seized during the blockade. Britain declined both. The Brazilians asked that Christie be recalled and then broke diplomatic relations with the Court of St. James's. Meanwhile, the question of the three sailors was submitted to the king of Belgium for arbitration. His decision favored Brazil. Britain presented its excuses to Brazil and asked to renew relations. The events gave Brazil some moral satisfaction but Great Britain continued to exercise its commercial and financial hegemony.

Although challenging Britain's position in the Caribbean, the United States was unable to do so with much authority in South America during the nineteenth century. In mutual recognition of each other's growing importance, Brazil and the United States elevated their diplomatic representatives in Rio de Janeiro and Washington from chargés d'affaires to envoys extraordinary and ministers plenipotentiary in 1842. Both nations, however, were too engrossed in continental matters to pay much heed to distant hemispheric neighbors. The decade of the 1860s proved to be an unusually trying one in the relations of the two. Brazil recognized the belligerency of the Confederacy in the Civil War, and with that status Southern ships were able to use Brazilian harbors, which they occasionally did, much to the chagrin of the government in Washington. Eventually the presence of a Confederate war vessel in a Brazilian harbor led to the violation of Brazilian sovereignty by the United States. The *Florida* put into Salvador da Bahia for supplies and repairs. A Union warship then entered the harbor and captured the Confederate ship. That bravado angered Brazilians sensitive to the insult it implied. Eventually the United States offered its excuses, but only long after the triumph of the Union did it salute the Brazilian flag in the port of Bahia as the imperial government had required. The War of the Triple Alliance brought new diplomatic complications to the relations between the two nations. In 1867, during the siege of Humaitá, the Brazilians refused to permit the United States minister to Paraguay, Elihu Washburn, to pass upriver to Asunción. That refusal ruffled diplomatic sensitivities for some time. Nor could the behavior of the United States minister to the imperial court, General James Watson Webb, 1861–1869, be considered the model of diplomatic propriety. It came to light soon enough that he had grossly abused his official position by extorting some $50,000 from the Brazilian government, a sum promptly returned with interest when the Department of State uncovered the irregularity. In the 1870s relations between the two nations improved. By then, the United States had emerged as the principal market for Brazilian coffee and other products. Closer commercial relations called forth better diplomatic harmony which began with the visit to the United States of Pedro II in 1876.

New Social Groups and New Ideas

After 1865, the Brazilian intellectuals, under the influence of European realism, indoctrinated—at least informally—by Positivism, and awed by the century's scientific advances, began to reflect a new concern with their own national reality. Not surprisingly that concern involved them in national crises which increasingly disturbed the tranquility of the empire. The expensive and long war with Paraguay, the rise of republican sentiment, the church-state conflicts, and the abolitionist campaigns which challenged the hoary institution of slavery excited debate and prompted the rise and fall of several governments. Those crises stimulated literary production and were in turn aggravated by social criticism from the intellectuals who increasingly occupied themselves with questions of national self-examination.

The surge of new ideas resulted to a large extent from the emergence of a new element in society, the urban middle groups, sizable enough for the first time to exert influence, flexible enough to welcome innovations, and strong enough to challenge the traditional powers of the rural aristocracy. To the merchants, commercial agents, exporters, artisans, government bureaucrats, lawyers, doctors, priests, teachers, bankers, and military officers who made up the core of the urban middle groups were added in large numbers during the last third of the century a salaried labor force of stevedores, mechanics, factory workers, and shop clerks. In short, in the last half of the nineteenth century it was possible to talk unmistakably in terms of a middle segment of the population, never cohesive—many times interrelated with the planter class—but increasingly vocal and influential. The intellectual and professional components of the middle groups were the most articulate and effective, if not the most representative, spokesmen. Much separated the various layers of those middle groups, but they more or less shared a perspective incorporating the values, attitudes, and behavior of their European counterparts who exerted increasing influence over them. They participated in sundry ways in a modern life characteristic of the city and contrary to the more traditional rural ways. They complained of their difficult position, wedged between the landowners above and the slaves below. They evinced ambitions to improve their status and favored whatever reasonable means would widen their future social horizons and strengthen their present base. Education they quickly realized was one of the surest steps toward upward mobility. Yet, despite these random similarities, they were still not cohesive enough or sufficiently defined to compose a "class," and for that reason the purposely chosen, more nebulous term "middle groups" is applied to them.

Even in the quainter backland towns and middle groups had their representatives. The merchants together with the local telegraph operator, teacher, priest, and the municipal clerks and tradesmen constituted a small buffer society between peasants and planters. Tobias Barreto estimated that in Escada, an inland city of Pernambuco with a population of 20,000 in 1877, approximately 10 percent of the inhabitants lived adequately or better, an indication of the size of the middle groups in one provincial *cidade*. Those provincial middle groups were not ignorant. They too shared the belief in progress, even though their opportunities to learn about the modern world might have been more limited. Nonetheless, they demonstrated their desire to change.

The cities, larger, more important, progressive, and receptive to change, steadily eroded the influence of the rural aristocracy. Indeed, when the landowners themselves began to maintain residences in the city and to spend more time in them, they lent prestige and authority to the city which enhanced its position. The government bureaus, export agencies, and banks, rooted in the cities, branched out to exert economic control in the rural areas, a trend which accelerated throughout the nineteenth century. The landowner could make fewer decisions in the confines of his fazenda. He had to go to the city to consult his banker or his agent; he had to petition a government official for a favor. If his children were to receive a higher education, they had to be sent to the cities. There the sons of the rising bourgeoisie as well as of the plantation aristocracy enrolled in ever larger numbers in the law, medical, engineering, and military schools. Upon graduation, they pursued urban careers, adding their numbers and ability to the strength of the city. After 1870, greater currents of immigration flowed into Brazil. A high percentage of those foreigners chose to settle in the cities, where their differing customs and thoughts contributed to the changing milieu. Table 4.2 shows both the growth of Brazil's major city, Rio de Janeiro, and the very high percentage of foreign-born who came to make up the population. A prosperous economy afforded the new generation more time for thought and reflection than their ancestors had enjoyed. For the urban dwellers there was not only more time to read but a wider selection of material to choose from, and they showed a strong preference for European authors.

Table 4.2. Rio de Janeiro: Population Growth and Presence of Foreign-Born

	Population		*Percentage of Foreign-Born*
1799	43,376	1836	7%
1807	50,000	1856	35%
1815	100,000	1870	34%
1821	112,695	1890	30%
1838	137,078		
1849	226,466		
1856	181,158		
1870	235,381		
1890	552,651		
1895	650,000		

Always susceptible to the influence of European thought, the Brazilian elite, particularly in the cities, was brought into closer contact with it by the more frequent and more rapid steamship service and by the submarine cable. The expanding middle groups also succumbed to European influence. France continued to shape Brazil's intellectual and cultural life. Three French cultural missions—the first in 1816 and the last in 1840—succeeded in strengthening a preference for Parisian values. French became the second language of the educated classes, who read French literature avidly and knew it better than their own. Polite society as well as the intellectuals animatedly discussed the novels of Gustave Flaubert, Honoré de Balzac, and—especially among the new generation—Emile Zola. Their works dominated the bookshops. In the stores of the major cities, every Parisian luxury could be found. One of the principal streets in the capital, Ouvidor Street, was almost exclusively French. The ladies vied with one another to copy the latest Parisian styles.

On a more mundane level—commerce, banking, and politics—the influence of Great Britain held sway. Although Brazil's parliamentary monarchy was *sui generis,* it found a vague model in the British system whose order and stability appealed to the aristocrats. Britain's economic predominance already has been noted. Regarding anything foreign as superior, the elite aped Europe to the fullest extent possible and the middle groups followed suit. Consequently they deprecated national products and culture and averted their eyes from the local scene. In his memoirs, Gilberto Amado vividly depicted one foolish aspect of that blind copying of European customs:

At that time, that is some seventy years ago [circa 1880], Brazil did not manufacture a yard of silk, a shoe, a spool of thread; everything was imported. The names on the packing boxes were indecipherable to me. . . . Men's clothing for a tropical climate was made of English wool suitable for life in the unheated homes of an English winter. I asked myself: how did they stand the heat? The ladies when they took off their shoes at home used slippers of heavy wool, as if they were in Siberia. Years later, I saw in Rio, Quintino Bocaiúva at the door of Watson's on the corner of Rua do Ouvidor dressed in a frock coat of heavy material and using gloves. When I look at a photograph of José do Patrocínio, I note the collar of twill and I ask myself how he could stand during the abolitionist campaign to give his speeches in the Recreio Dramático with that pressure on his body? Imagining the rivers of sweat pouring down, I sweat with him. In Pernambuco, we students of the Faculty wore morning coats and riding coats. In Rosa dos Alpes, a shop of Castro Alves, I saw at the door a well-known doctor, Artur Costa, with a glistening top hat just like those I later saw in Europe during the winter. Senator Rosa e Silva also went around in a top hat. Aníbal Freire never arrived at the office of the *Diário de Pernambuco* without his morning coat and top hat. How did he stand it? . . . Except for the poor, I never saw in the Pernambuco of my time anyone dressed in light clothing.[13]

13. Gilberto Amado, *História da Minha Infância* (Rio de Janeiro, 1954), p. 40.

Hypersensitivity to foreign criticism was what probably prompted the elites and middle sectors to adopt unquestioningly in the tropics all the trappings of a temperate-climate civilization. Beset with a feeling of inferiority, they sought to be more European than the Europeans. In the process, of course, they imported many new ideas—Positivism, for example—whose influence would go far toward the modification of the traditional society.

A few voices protested the slavish imitation of foreign cultures. The literary critic Sílvio Romero (1851–1914) and the historian João Capistrano de Abreu (1853–1927) began in the decade of the 1870s to advise their compatriots that much could be gained from introspection. They suggested that more harm than good resulted from the unrestricted and unselective importation of ideas, and they encouraged their countrymen to exert some intellectual originality. Their admonitions formed the headwaters of a stream of cultural nationalism which, within two generations, would become a turbulent river.

Although himself under the influence of European ideologies of his day, Romero attempted to free himself so that he could see his own country through Brazilian eyes. He condemned blind imitation and called for intellectual—and literary—independence. He aimed his critical barbs at "the figure of the imitator, of the slavish and witless copier of each and every trifle that the ships from Portugal or France or any other place bring us." Advocating national introspection, he crusaded for a Brazilian literature with its roots in the people, one which would interpret the national environment, traditions, and sentiments. The major obstacle to such national expression, he concluded, was that "we do not know ourselves."

Romero wrote prolifically but no work exceeds in importance his monumental *História da Literatura Brasileira* (1888). Of lasting value, it is as essential today for an understanding of Brazil as it was when first published. Following the thought of Taine, Romero considered literature as a national expression, an integral part of society, an inescapable conclusion in Brazil where the literati played multiple roles in society. Romero lamented that Brazilian literature had placed excessive emphasis on the elite to the neglect of the people, whom he considered the basic force of society. In one effort to bring the masses and literature together; he published two anthologies of folk poems and songs: *Contos Populares do Brasil* (1885) and *Estudos sôbre a Poesia Popular do Brasil* (1888). He had to deal with European racist doctrine which influenced and would continue to influence so many Brazilian intellectuals. Still, he repeatedly affirmed that Brazil was not the exclusive product of Europe but the joint effort of Indians, Europeans, and Africans, a truly revolutionary thought at that time. Romero had a vision of the future as well as of the past. He understood a reality which still eludes most: before Brazil could develop, it would be necessary to reform basic agrarian institutions by abolishing slavery and redistributing the land. Such a realistic blueprint for the future required fundamental changes which the elites stubbornly resisted.

Brazil's foremost historian, João Capistrano de Abreu, emerged at the same time as Romero and his message was much the same: Brazilian culture in its imitation of Europe modes was not expressive of the national soul. Isolated from its own environment, it did not represent the "conscious expression of the people." He revolutionized historical studies in Brazil by turning attention from the coastal band with its obvious link to Europe and examining the previously little known interior. He presented his major thesis in 1889 in a short but brilliant essay, *Os Caminhos Antigos e o Povoamento do Brasil* (Old Roads and the Peopling of Brazil), the single most important statement on Brazilian history yet made. Neglecting the archbishops, generals, and viceroys who had populated the histories of Brazil to that date—even refusing to treat the official national hero, Tiradentes, whom he considered more the creation of the elites than representative of the Brazilian people—he concentrated on the contributions of the masses, meaningful periodization of the past, and significant themes. He wrote:

In history we only point to the dominant figures, those who destroyed or constructed, leaving behind a trail of blood or a ray of hope. We do not remember the shoulders which bore them, or the courage of the masses which gave them their strength, the collective mind which exalted their minds, the unknown hands which pointed out to them the ideal which only the most fortunate attained. And often the unknown person is the one whose cooperation was most vital in bringing about the great event.[14]

If the masses made history, it was the vast interior which constituted the true Brazil, the valid national reality. Only when the coastal inhabitants turned their backs on the sea and penetrated the interior did they shed their European ways and become Brazilianized. His *Caminhos Antigos* contained a remarkable global vision of the Brazilian past which emphasized the themes of exploration and settlement of the interior, the creation of overland and fluvial transportation networks to weld the vast nation together, the significance of cattle raising and gold mining growth, unity, and change, and the psychological changes those events wrought in the Brazilian people. Capistrano de Abreu focused attention on the national heartland and the people who opened and settled it. In doing so, he Brazilianized the study of Brazilian history.

Some literati did select native themes which gave their works a nationalistic cast. Obviously the most Brazilian themes possible in literature were nature, the exuberance and grandeur of the tropics, and the Indian, the original inhabitant of the land. Both distinguished the New World from the Old. It was to those themes that writers turned for nationalistic inspiration. The Romantic school in Brazil, ushered in by Domingos José Gonçalves de Magalhães (1811–1882) with the publication of his *Suspiros Poéticos e Saudades* (Poetic Sighs and Longings), adopted the Indian as one of its preferred subjects. The foremost Romantic poet, Antônio Gonçalves Dias (1823–1864), portrayed the Indians in some of his best poems,"I-Juca-Pirana" and "Os Timbiras" for example, as courageous warriors endowed with every noble

14. João Capitstrano de Abreu, *Ensaios e Estudos* (Rio de Janeiro, 1931), I, iii.

quality. He sang of their feats of valor, to which by implication the Empire of Brazil fell heir. His interest in the Indians prompted him to prepare a *Dicionário da Língua Tupi* (Dictionary of the Tupi Language). The contributions of Gonçalves Dias to nationalism had another poetic facet. While a law student at Coimbra University in 1843, he penned his most famous poem, "Song of Exile," whose theme of the glorification of Brazil was in the best tradition of the eighteenth-century nativists. He mused with nostalgia upon his homeland. The opening lines, "Land of mine, with waving palms! / The sabiá is singing there," became the ritual salutation to Brazil which millions of school children have learned by heart ever since.

In prose, José de Alencar (1829–1877) was the master exponent of Romanticism, and in three of his novels, *O Guaraní, Iracema,* and *Ubirajara,* the Indian figured predominantly. The handsome, brave, noble savages of Alencar shared much in common with those of Chateaubriand and James Fenimore Cooper. Alencar's masterpiece of Indianist literature, *O Guaraní,* appeared in 1857. It mattered little to his readers that the novel's Indians spoke and acted like Europeans garbed in feathers. They conformed to the stereotype of how the elites thought the native should be. Amid splendid descriptions of the natural beauty of Brazil, Alencar treated the relationship between the Indians and Portuguese in the sixteenth century, in particular between Peri, an Indian chief, and Cecília, the daughter of a Portuguese nobleman. An affection between the golden-haired European and the bronze savage flowered into an exemplary love before the end of the novel. To Peri the author ascribed a catalog of desirable virtues—honesty, trustworthiness, courage, strength, bravery, et al.—while most of the Portuguese in the novel (Cecília, of course, excepted) displayed serious personality defects. Beneath the heavy romanticism of *O Guaraní* lies a profound nationalist message: Brazil is the product of the union of the New World with the old. But the domination of the values of the Old World was explicit.

The foremost composer of the imperial period, Carlos Gomes (1836–1896) picked up the theme of *O Guaraní* and composed a melodic opera of the same name whose rousing overture is as familiar to Brazilians as their national anthem. The music sounded Italian (after all Gomes studied in Verdi's Italy), but the plot was undeniably Brazilian. The same combination was visible in his *Lo Schiavo* (The Slave). While serious music remained indebted to Europe for its form if not always its content, a Brazilian style in popular music began to be played and danced to. Around 1870, the *maxixe* appeared. A mixture of European polka and African *lundu*, it was the first truly national dance in both movement and music.

The painters of the period never discovered the light, coloring, or drama of their own national habitat. The two best known artists, Pedro Américo (1843–1905), who painted many historical scenes, best known of which may be his *The Cry of Ipiranga,* and Victor Meirelles (1832–1903), whose historical canvas *The First Mass in Brazil* earned him a national reputation, studied in Europe and unquestioningly accepted European artistic values. Although they sometimes searched their country's past for subject matter, they neglected the alluring landscape surrounding them and refused to experiment or innovate.

The Brazilian Historical and Geographical Institute played the prominent role in encouraging the intellectuals to focus attention on the past. In its solemn sessions, often in the presence of the scholarly emperor himself, members delivered papers on their investigations and studies. On the pages of its periodical appeared essays, articles, and commentaries on national history with large sections of each issue dedicated to the printing of archival documents. Jointly with the government, the Institute sponsored archival missions to Europe with the objective of copying from the Old Wrold sources documents germane to Brazilian history.

A few notable historians began to publish. João Francisco Lisboa delved into the past of his natal province, Maranhão, to write an important regional history, *Apontamentos, Notícias e Observações para Servirem á História do Maranhão* (Notes, Notices and Observations on the History of Maranhão). Joaquim Felício dos Santos (1828–1895) published a brilliant historical study of the diamond industry and Minas Gerais, *Memórias do Distrito Diamantino* (Memoirs of the Diamond District). José Inácio de Abreu e Lima (1796–1869) broadly outlined Brazilian history in several books and was the center of considerable controversy over his accuracy and points of view. Standing head and shoulders above all his contemporaries was Francisco Adolfo de Varnhagen, Visconde de Pôrto Seguro (1816–1878). He indefatigably explored archives in both South America and Europe where he discovered such historical treasures as the *Diário da Navegação* (The Navigation Diary) of Pero Lopes de Sousa, a record of the first efforts at colonization, 1531–1532. Varnhagen wrote prolifically. An unimaginative style could not hide the wealth of data he brought to his studies. His major contribution, *História Geral do Brasil,* published in two volumes in 1854 and 1857, was a major compendium of facts on Brazil's colonial past.

Literature felt the effect of intensified intellectual probing. Romanticism passed out of vogue in a society struggling with new ideas. Realists and naturalists rushed in to fill the literary void. In the process, the novel of manners gave way to works of social implication, "slices of life" depicting people's struggles. The first exponent of the naturalist novel was Aluísio Azevedo (1857–1913), whose *O Mulato* (The Mulatto), published in 1881, explored the always intriguing question of racial relations in Brazil. The plot concerned the love of a mulatto for a white girl, and, of course, the bigoted views of the girl's family toward the handsome and talented young man of mixed blood thwarted that pristine love. Azevedo poignantly conveyed the feelings of Raimundo, the light-skinned, blue-eyed mulatto, an exposé of the subtleties of racial prejudice. Eventually Raimundo was assassinated, a vengeance society wreaked upon him because he dared to be the equal of the "white" Brazilians. The plot exposed the violence which characterized one aspect of Brazilian life. In a second novel, *O Cortiço* (The Tenement), Azevedo treated naturalistically life in a Rio de Janeiro slum. Significantly, then urbanization had reached a point—as Azevedo's work indicated—where it was creating new social problems unique in a hitherto rural nation.

The new trend in literature emboldened young writers to experiment with other themes unexplored in Brazil in print before. The models were European. Raul de Avila Pompéia (1863–1895) satirized the private educational system in the capital in *O Ateneu* (The Athenaeum). Herculano Inglês de Sousa (1853–1918) depicted a Roman Catholic priest falling victim to his sensuous tropical environment in *O Misionário* (The Missionary). And *A Carne* (The Flesh) by Júlio César Ribeiro (1845–1890) analyzed an intellectual woman succumbing to all her carnal desires. At the same time, Brazil's most gifted novelist, Joaquim Maria Machado de Assis (1839–1908) strode to the center of the literary stage. Son of a mulatto housepainter and a Portuguese woman, he was orphaned at the age of ten. Always sensitive about his racial mixture and his humble origin, a victim of epilepsy, he lived an introverted, conventional life, much devoted to his wife. That outward calm disguised a drive which caused him to write drama, criticism, poetry, short stories, and novels over a period of nearly half a century. Best known of his literary output are his last five novels: *Memórias Postumas de Bras Cubas* (translated into English under the title *Epitaph of a Small Winner*), *Quincas Borba* (bearing the English title *Philosopher or Dog*), *Dom Casmurro* (translated under the same name), *Esau e Jacob* (the English translation is *Esau and Jacob*), and *Memorial de Aires* (rendered into English as *The Memorial of Ayres*). Rio de Janeiro in the nineteenth century served as the setting for these novels of urban society. Their treatment of the individual's relations to society gave them an application to all people, everywhere, at all times. His superb style cleverly combined humor and pessimism. *Epitaph of a Small Winner* wittily displayed that ironic pessimism characteristic of its author, and in one of his short chapters he summed up his negative attitude toward life:

> As some of my readers may have skipped the preceding chapter, let me observe that one must read it in order to understand

what I said to myself just after Dona Placida left the room. I said the following: "And so the cathedral sacristan, helping at Mass one day, saw the woman come in who was to be his collaborator in producing Dona Placida. He saw her on other days, perhaps over a period of several weeks; he liked her; he said something flattering to her, he touched her foot with his, while lighting the altars on holy days. She liked him, they drew near to each other, they fell in love. From this conjunction of vagrant lusts, issued Dona Placida. Probably Dona Placida did not speak when she was born, but if she did, she might have said to the authors of her day, 'Here I am. Why did you summon me?' And the sacristan and his lady naturally would have replied, 'We summoned you so that you would burn your fingers on pots and your eyes in sewing; so that you would eat little or nothing, rush around, become sick and then get well so that you might become sick again; sad today, desperate tomorrow, finally resigned, but always with your hands on the pot and your eyes on the sewing, until you wind up in the gutter or in a hospital. That is why we summoned you, in a moment of love.' "

He concludes the novel by revealing how it is possible to exercise one-upmanship in life:

This last chapter consists wholly of negatives. I did not achieve celebrity, I did not become a minister of state, I did not really become a caliph, I did not marry. At the same time, however, I had the good fortune of not having to earn my bread by the sweat of my brow. Moreover, I did not suffer a death like Dona Placida's nor did I lose my mind like Quincas Borba. Adding up and balancing all these items, a person will conclude that my accounts showed neither a surplus nor a deficit and consequently that I died quits with life. And he will conclude falsely; for, upon arriving on this side of the mystery, I found that I had a small surplus, which provides the final negative of this chapter of negatives: I had no progeny, I transmitted to no one the legacy of our misery.[15]

The Brazilian reading public enthusiastically greeted his novels of pessimism and realism, and critics and readers abroad have been slowly according them their merited place of honor.

15. Machado de Assis, *Epitaph of a Small Winner* (New York: Farrar, Straus and Giroux, 1959), pp. 136–37, 223. Quoted with the permission of the publisher.

Literature was the luxury of a small, privileged group, for few knew how to read, let alone write. The illiteracy rate during the imperial period never dropped below 85 percent among the free population, and it was considerably higher if one took into account the slaves. Schools were few and those that existed tended to be concentrated in the cities. The provincial governments controlled primary and secondary education. Rio de Janeiro with its more affluent society, scholarly institutes, academies, printing presses, book stores, and National Library was the principal educational center. Approximately 12,000 students attended the capital's primary schools in 1879. There was only one public secondary school, Dom Pedro II College, with an enrollment of 418, but 2,706 other students attended 62 private secondary schools. Such was the record for the cultural center of the empire. The conditions in the provinces were poorer. In 1879, Mato Grosso, a province nearly twice the size of the state of Texas, had only 30 primary schools attended by 1,375 pupils; there was no secondary school. In the 1880s, with a population in excess of 13 million, the total national enrollment in primary schools was less than a quarter of a million. However alarming the record might seem, the facts testify that school attendance had multiplied during the Second Empire. In 1869, there were 3,516 schools with 115,735 students; three decades later the schools numbered 7,500 and enrollment was 300,000. School population tripled, although national population did not quite double during that period. Still, the number privileged to attend school was tiny in comparison to the total population. The unschooled masses silently witnessed the events which surrounded and affected them but in which they could play only the most limited role. A small minority, the emerging urban middle groups and the staid rural aristocracy, controlled the nation. They wrote and read the literature of the period.

Dutifully mirroring the intellectual modes of Europe, that minority warmly welcomed Positivism as a convincing formula for progress. Auguste Comte, the French founder of Positivism, held that human thought had evolved beyond its theological and metaphysical stages and was then reaching its highest level, the scientific or positivistic stage. In that stage people eschewed purely speculative knowledge for that based on experience. By synthesizing the whole of human knowledge and reducing social facts and events to laws, Positivism promised to reconstruct society.

The Brazilian intelligentsia acclaimed the ideas of Comte with a degree of acceptance they had scarcely enjoyed in Europe. In particular the young bourgeois Brazilian intellectuals embraced the ideology. It is not surprising, therefore, that the focal points for the discussion and dissemination of Positivism were the schools—especially the engineering and military schools—where the sons of the commercial and bureaucratic middle groups studied in order to advance their social and economic positions.

Positivist ideas were manifest in Brazil as early as 1850, and as might have been expected they appeared first among the new bachelors of the technical and military schools of Rio de Janeiro. The first important Brazilian sociological statement of Positivist ideas appeared in Francisco Brandão Júnior's *A Escravatura no Brasil* (Slavery in Brazil), printed in 1865. Nine years later a trenchant statement of Positivist thought appeared in *As Três Filosofias* (The Three Philosophies) by Luís Pereira Barreto. His introduction revealed the profound characteristic which Positivism already had assumed in Brazil: "Brazil already harbors in its midst a small group of Positivists recruited principally from the middle class and the profession of engineering. This group, far from diminishing in size, grows quickly and will continue to do so." In 1876, the young disciples of Comte founded the first Positivist Association of Brazil. Similar Positivist approaches to change and material progress characterized the intellectual development of most of Latin America in the last half of the nineteenth century.

Doubtless the most influential devotee of Comte among the Brazilians was Major Benjamin Constant de Magalhães (1836–1891), a popular professor of mathematics at the military academy, who cannot be considered an orthodox Positivist. Energetically he advocated republican doctrines, to which many of the Positivists paid lip service only, and infused among the young cadets in his classes a similar enthusiasm for republicanism. His students, mostly sons of the bourgeoisie, saw in a republic their best hope for the future. Like their professor, they drew only from a part of Comte's philosophy and were often better republicans than Positivists.

During the last quarter of the nineteenth century, Positivism assumed an importance belying its numerical following because it appealed to and influenced members of key urban groups which exercised power far beyond their size and because it codified a program sanctioned by the changing times and attitudes. Many favored parts of the Positivist doctrine without being practicing Positivists or conceivably even knowing that their preferences coincided with the Positivist doctrine.

For many, Positivism summed up the longing for progress and gave them a recognizable philosophical base. It provided for change within an acceptable and familiar framework. The essentially conservative middle groups found in Positivism a way to incorporate themselves into the national institutions without destroying their elitist essence, that is their projected reforms tended more to conserve the social order rather than to alter it radically. In general, Brazilian Positivism advocated governmental planning for progress and industrialization, restricting foreign economic influence and penetration, modernizing agriculture, expanding the communications and transportation infrastructures, encouraging education, controlling immigration, and enacting social legislation. Positivism hoped to insure social stability by incorporating the proletariat into society by means of education, higher wages, and regulation of wages, hours, and working conditions. The Positivists held conservative economic and monetary policies based on the defense of private property and yet they challenged some prevailing notions of laissez-faire policies. They felt the government should intervene in the economy to provide those essential services which the private sectors could not or would not provide. They denounced foreign economic domination, colonialism, and imperialism. Their ideas of racial equality were extremely enlightened. They regarded women as superior to men. They favored the abolition of slavery, establishment of a republic, and the separation of Church and State, changes which eventually occurred in Brazil. The principal contribution of the Positivists seems to have been to codify the diverse yearnings for progress expressed in many sectors of Brazilian society and to present an appealing program to implement them. Further, Positivism provided one insight into the mentality of the middle sector of society as it emerged into political prominence. Positivism unwittingly synthesized the ideas of a new class taking shape in urban Brazil.

Abolition, Immigration, and Labor

The termination of the slave trade in 1850 aggravated one of Brazil's most serious problems, unsolved since the first years of colonization: the acute labor shortage. At that time, there were approximately 3 million slaves in a total population of 7 million. The land was vast; nature was generous; but only labor could turn the land and its products into wealth. Africa had been Brazil's principal source of labor, and the planters counted almost exclusively on the brawn and skill of the imported blacks to plant, harvest, and prepare their crops for export. The slaves worked as artisans and mechanics in the city as well as on the plantation. On many levels they constituted the most important part of the population. Slavery had existed in Spanish America as well, but only in a few places—Cuba would be the best example—did it become the warp and woof of the economy and society as it did in Portuguese America. In fact, some authorities claim Brazil imported about a half million to a million more slaves than did all of Spanish America.

The institution of slavery patterned the entire social-economic-political fabric of the nation. Numerically the slaves had predominated. At the opening of the nineteenth century, for example, slaves constituted a majority of the population. So dominant were the blacks and their influence that a statesman like Bernardo Pereira de Vasconcelos could proclaim in the chamber of deputies during the early years of the Second Empire that Brazil owed its civilization to Africa. He reminded his startled listeners that the African provided the leisure for the aristocracy to pursue the arts and to govern. Consequently the civilization that had developed in Brazil rested squarely on the blacks' labor.

Slowly intellectuals began to point out the invaluable contributions made by the Africans to Brazilian development. When the Brazilian Historical and Geographical Institute sponsored a contest to find out how the history of Brazil should be written, the German naturalist, Karl Friedrich Philipp von Martius, who had spent three years traveling extensively in Brazil, responded with the prize-winning eassy. Published in the Institute's *Revista* in 1844, it called attention for the first time to the need to investigate the blacks' influence and contribution to Brazil. Later, the perceptive Sílvio Romero assigned the blacks their just place in the formation of Brazilian civilization. He emphasized the adaptability of the Africans to the New World, their ability to learn quickly and their miscibility with the European. Concluded Romero, "We owe much more to the Negro than to the Indian; he entered fully into all aspects of our development." In the 1870s, Romero and Capistrano de Abreu carried on a discussion—not quite a debate—in the pages of the *carioca* newspaper *O Globo* on the extent of the black contribution to the formation of Brazilian civilization. They constantly contrasted and compared it with that of the Indian. Later, in his important history of the colonial period, *Capítulos de História Colonial,* Capistrano reaffirmed the economic and social importance of the African to Brazil.

The Brazilians closed their principal source of labor in 1850 without finding another, just at the time when the increasing number of coffeee plantations began to intensify the need for workers. Planters and deputies talked of plans for importing Chinese coolies and for encouraging European immigration. For the meantime, such plans remained only theoretical. The government never sought the coolies, and the flow of European immigrants barely trickled into the immense and underpopulated empire. The slaves retained their vital importance in the economy. With the planter aristocracy in firm control of the government throughout the First Empire and the Regency, and for the first decades of the Second Empire, a propitious political atmosphere certainly did not exist for the discussion of abolition. An economy pinched by a labor shortage further discouraged such discussion. Nonetheless, a few distinguished liberals dared to speak out for abolition. Many of Brazil's delegates to the Côtes in 1822 damned the institution of slavery. Such eminent statesmen as José Bonifácio labeled it a "crime" and a "sin." In 1831 and 1852 projects to emancipate the slaves were presented to the chamber of deputies, which refused on both occasions to discuss the subject. Various writers denounced slavery in print: Hipólito da Costa did so in his peridoical *Correio Brasiliense* (Brazilian Mail), published between 1808 and 1822; Antônio Rodrigues Veloso de Oliveira in his *Memória sôbre o Melhoramento da Província de São Paulo* (Memorial on the Improvement of the Province of São Paulo), in 1822; and Henrique Velloso de Oliveira in his *A Substituição do Trabalho dos Escravos pelo Trabalho Livre* (The Substitution of Free Labor for Slavery), in 1845. The usually very conservative Brazilian Historical and Geographical Institute published a "Memória Histórica" by Joaquim Norberto de Souza Silva, in 1854, which opposed slavery and detailed its pernicious effects on the nation.

No one seriously advocated an immediate end to slavery. The economy could not absorb the shock of so radical a move. All the abolitionists favored a gradual emancipation, to take place over a lengthy period. That moderate solution to the problem steadily gained supporters. Still, with considerable sums tied up in their slaves, the planters rallied to the defense of their investment. They pointed out that the shortage of laborers was already grave enough and indicated their apprehension that, once freed, the blacks would abandon the plantations in a mass exodus, with disastrous economic results for the nation. Hence for a long time the planter aristocracy from both the traditional coastal sugar lands of the Northeast and the newer coffee lands of the Paraíba Valley refused even to consider the subject of abolition, no matter how gradual. Mass public opinion, still amorphous, had little to say on the subject.

The cause for emancipation had an effective ally, however, in the person of the emperor, who quietly opposed slavery. In 1840, he liberated all his own slaves. Nonetheless, he understood the importance of the institution to the economy and realized that for the time being nothing must be done to frighten the planters and thus to harm the newly invigorated economy or to alienate his loyal rural supporters. He waited patiently for opinion in favor of gradual emancipation to solidify, a course he deemed inevitable after the termination of the nefarious slave traffic. In the early 1860s, he perceived that national opinion was ready to accept preparations for the first stage of emancipation. Accordingly, in January of 1864 he wrote to Prime Minister Zacarias de Góes e Vasconcelos to suggest that the first step be taken:

> The success of the American Unionists has led me to believe that we must seriously consider the future of slavery in Brazil to avoid a repetition of the events that followed the prohibitions of the African traffic. A measure which seems to me to offer advantages is the liberation of the offspring of all slave women a few years hence. I have given much thought to the means of carrying out this measure; but it is of the order that requires firm execution, the evils that will necessarily arise from it being dealt with as circumstances permit.[16]

Pedro cautiously counseled gradual emancipation to avoid disturbing the economy. After the close of the Civil War in the United States, new pressures for emancipation were exerted from the exterior. Only Cuba and Brazil in the Western Hemisphere still tolerated slavery, to the undisguised disgust of the rest of the Western world. Those pressures were persuasive in Brazil, sensitive to such mounting foreign criticism, and prompted the emperor to speak out, this time publicly, in favor of reforming the moribund institution. He signified his hope for change in a speech from the throne in 1867 opening the legislative session:

16. Quoted in João Cruz Costa, *A History of Ideas in Brazil* (Berkeley, California, 1964), pp. 77–78.

The slave element in the Empire cannot fail to receive your consideration at the oppportune moment. The subject of emancipation should receive your attention in such a way that the treatment of it will respect existing property rights and not threaten our primary industry which is agriculture.

The promotion of immigration ought to be the subject of your special attention.[17]

Brief and certainly moderate in tone, his statement directed the nation's attention to the question of emancipation and made it the subject for general discussion. He thereby publicly committed his immense prestige to the cause of emancipation.

During the Paraguayan War the government considered it unwise to take any action on the question, but it began preparing public opinion. Slaves volunteering for military duty during the war were given their liberty and some 6,000 gained freedom in that manner. The army then and thereafter played a significant social role by absorbing emancipated slaves, training them for new tasks, and in that way facilitating their integration into a free society. As has been mentioned, the abrupt change of government in 1868 which brought the Conservatives back into power so angered the Liberals that they strengthened their flagging unity and issued a far-reaching reform program which, among other things, called for gradual emancipation.

After the defeat of Paraguay, the empire's attention once again focused fully on internal matters, among them the slavery question. Events in the Caribbean intensified foreign pressure on Brazil to free its slaves. In 1870, the Spanish government promulgated the Moret Law, which retroactively emancipated all children in Cuba born of slave mothers after September 1868, and all slaves who reached sixty-five years of age (later amended to sixty years). In Brazil shortly thereafter, the government headed by the Conservative Visconde do Rio-Branco resolved to carry out the suggestion made by the emperor in 1864. The legislature enacted the Law of the Free Womb in 1871 declaring free all children born to slaves:

17. *Fallas do Throno* (Rio de Janeiro, 1889), p. 627.

The children of women slaves that may be born in the Empire from the date of this law shall be considered to be free.

The said minors shall remain with and be under the domination of the owners of the mother, who shall be obliged to rear and take care of them until such children shall have completed the age of eight years.

When the child of the slave attains this age, the owner of its mother shall have the option either of receiving from the State the indemnification of 600 dollars, or of making use of the services of the minor until he shall have completed the age of twenty-one years.[18]

At the time this law was passed there were approximately 1.5 million slaves and a free population of 8.6 million. The law slowly doomed slavery. Africa as a source of slaves had long been closed; after 1871, the other source, the womb, would bring forth no more slaves. At about the same time, several pieces of legislation were enacted to mitigate some of the harsher aspects of slavery. A law of 1869 prohibited the separate sale of husband, wife, and minor children. Another of 1871 compelled masters to accept the self-purchase of a slave at his market price. The promulgation of these laws quieted for the time being the agitation in favor of emancipation. The empire settled back to adjust to the new situation.

As the emperor's speech from the throne in 1867 indicated, considerations of emancipation were not made without giving thought to European immigration. The two were inextricably intertwined. As Henrique J. Rebello noted in his "Treatise on the Population of Brazil," written in 1836 and published in 1867: "If Brazil wants to increase its population, it ought to encourage German, Swiss, and immigrants from other civilized nations to come to our land. In this way, we will not feel the lack of the Africans, and our own civilization will become greater."[19] Others were of a like mind. The enlightened Miguel Calmon du Pin Almeida published in Bahia,

18. Quote in E. Bradford Burns (ed.), *A Documentary History of Brazil* (New York, 1966), pp. 257–58.

19. "Memória sobre a População do Brasil," *Revista do Instituto Histórico e Geográfico Brasileiro*, 34 (1867), p. 37.

one of the centers of Brazilian slavery, his *Memória sôbre o Estabelecimento duma Companhia de Colonisação* (Memorial on the Establishment of a Colonization Company) to urge the formation of an organization to encourage European immigration so Brazil would depend less on slavery.

It is worthwhile, although not surprising, to observe that with each step taken to end the institution of slavery, European immigration increased proportionately. Certainly as long as slavery remained a vigorous institution, the Europeans were not going to be attracted to Brazil, where most of them in effect would be competing with the slaves. In addition to that major socio-economic handicap, Brazil had other disadvantages, at least in the minds of the Europeans, which tended to dissuade them from migrating there. Most Europeans believed that all of Brazil suffered an enervating tropical climate. The fact that the Roman Catholic Church was the established state religion dissuaded Protestants. The restricted political system with its limited vote and oligarchical domination discouraged many. Nonetheless, despite these negative factors, some Europeans immigrated. Aided by the government of João VI, about 2,000 Swiss settlers arrived in 1819 to establish a colony, the first such non-Portuguese colony, at Nova Friburgo in the cool, mountainous region of the province of Rio de Janeiro. Four years later, German immigrants founded a colony at São Leopoldo in Rio Grande do Sul. In 1827, some Germans settled in Santa Catarina, and two years later others arrived in Paraná. By 1830, approximately 7,000 Germans had entered Brazil. Then and thereafter the majority of the European immigrants settled in the South, where the climate most resembled that of Europe. In order to encourage immigration, the government prohibited the employment of a free man in the same job as a slave, set up an immigration center in Europe, and provided reception centers for the new arrivals in Brazil.

Access to land—or rather the lack of it—dissuaded some ambitious Europeans from migrating. The prime lands long before had been claimed, although claims to extensive tracts were vague, and the immense estates never developed a notable efficiency. In 1822, the state had stopped granting land in sesmarias, but those who wanted land thereafter simply squatted and/or declared their possession of it. They developed an impressive repertoire of means to show or prove they owned public lands. Under pressure from those who claimed such lands, the government in 1850 legitimized the claims. Whatever public land remained continued to be usurped by new encroachments. After 1854, the *Repartição Geral das Terras Públicas* (General Bureau of Public Lands) tried to exercise a monopoly over the sale and distribution of public lands which benefited, at least theoretically, those new arrivals who sought farms for themselves. Unfortunately none of the procedures or laws worked satisfactorily. In the last analysis, the powerful who through force could make good their claims and through influence further protected them took advantage of the situation to increase the size and number of their land holdings.

In the search for a substitute for slave labor on the coffee plantations, the progressive Nicolau de Pereira de Campos Vergueiro began to experiment with a system which combined features of indentured service and sharecropping. A Portuguese who arrived in Brazil before João VI, Vergueiro favored and promoted the independence of his adopted land. He served as deputy to the Côrtes, and after independence served constantly as either a deputy or a senator and was a minister of the empire under Pedro I. He generally supported liberal policies and was highly praised for his enlightened ideas. In 1840, he began his planning to induce European laborers to migrate to his plantations, an idea he had to abandon the following year because of the intense strife between the Liberals and the Conservatives and the resultant revolt in Minas Gerais and São Paulo. He returned to his plans in 1845, this time with governmental approval, and in the following year the first immigrants started to arrive on his coffee plantations.

Vergueiro's agent in Europe made contact with peasants willing to emigrate. The emigrant either paid his own passage or Vergueiro paid for him under an agreement that he would repay the loan over a long period at a small rate of interest. To further decrease costs, the agent chartered a vessel to transport the emigrants. Vergueiro paid the transportation from the coast to the plantations, furnished housing, and supplied at cost all the necessary provisions and clothing. The colonist then received a specified number of coffee trees proportional to the size of his family. He agreed to tend those trees and to share the profits from the coffee harvest with his employer. He was obliged to repay any debt and to give one year's notice before he could leave the plantation. The senator found his system, in which each man had a stake in the success of the coffee harvest, to be much more profitable than slave labor. He thought his plan also instilled in the European peasants a brighter hope for the future and an opportunity, hitherto missing, to raise their standard of living.

The Reverend J. C. Fletcher visited one of Vergueiro's coffee plantations, Ibicaba, in 1855, and was enthusiastic about what he witnessed. As plantations went, Ibicaba was small, measuring only five or six square miles. Some 177 peasant families from Germany and Switzerland, in total nearly 1,000 Europeans including children, dwelt in "neat little cottages." The majority were Roman Catholics. The cheerfulness of the homes, the industry of their inhabitants, and the high morality of the community (not one illegitimate child had been born into it) impressed Fletcher. The efficiency of those workers in addition to the use of the best techniques and latest equipment brought forth from Ibicaba a harvest of 1.6 million pounds of coffee in 1854, which was divided equally between the landowner and the immigrants. As a result some of them had thrived and earned between $2,500 and $3,500 in five years. Fletcher believed that Vergueiro had found the solution for Brazil's dual problems of slavery and labor and pronounced the idea "a great blessing to Brazil."

Others apparently thought so too. In the decade between 1847 and 1857 some seventy similar efforts were made, often with governmental financial aid, in the São Paulo area. Before the plan spread more widely some defects marred its further acceptance. Some agents in Europe recruited unscrupulously and deceived both planter and emigrant so that the two scarcely knew what to expect of each other; consequently misunderstandings multiplied. One such immigrant, Thomas Davatz, a Swiss, condemned the system in his memoirs, *Memórias de um Colono no Brasil* (Memoirs of an Immigrant in Brazil), as too favorable to the planters and oppressive of the immigrants who really wanted to own their own land. What they did not realize when they arrived was that most of Brazil, certainly the most accessible and best lands, had already been divided up into huge estates for a privileged few. The immigrants, when literate and articulate as Davatz certainly was, sought to replace the latifundia system with family-sized and family-operated farms. Eventually the government took charge of the search for immigrants in Europe, soliciting them as well as paying their passage. By the mid-1870s a system which made use of salaried workers replaced the sharecrop system. The fixed salary earned by the immigrants guaranteed them a greater measure of security, although the low wages provided for nothing more than the basic existence of the workers and their families. Coffee workers never organized, but nonetheless some bitter strikes disturbed the countryside from time to time.

Table 4.3 indicates the flow of immigrants into the empire after the termination of the slave trade and until the abolition of slavery. That immigration increased rapidly after 1871. Thereafter, only five times did immigration fall below 20,000

Table 4.3. Annual Arrival of Immigrants in Brazil, 1850–1888

(Prior to 1850 the annual number of immigrants rarely exceeded 1,000)

1850	2,072	1863	7,642	1876	30,747
1851	4,425	1864	9,578	1877	29,468
1852	2,731	1865	6,452	1878	24,456
1853	10,935	1866	7,699	1879	22,788
1854	9,189	1867	10,902	1880	30,355
1855	11,798	1868	11,315	1881	11,548
1856	14,008	1869	11,527	1882	29,589
1857	14,244	1870	5,158	1883	34,015
1858	18,529	1871	12,431	1884	24,890
1859	20,114	1872	19,219	1885	35,440
1860	15,774	1873	14,742	1886	33,486
1861	13,003	1874	20,332	1887	55,965
1862	14,295	1875	14,590	1888	133,253

SOURCE: Instituto Histórico e Geográfico Brasileiro, *Diccionário Histórico, Geográphico, e Ethnográphico do Brasil* (Rio de Janeiro: Imprensa Nacional, 1922), 1, 295–96.

and even then it was far higher than the yearly average between 1850 and 1870. Not only was there a continual numerical increase but an ethnic change soon occurred as well. The Italian immigrants outnumbered the Portuguese for the first time in the 1870s, and throughout the remainder of the century Italy supplied the greatest share of the new arrivals. Portugal, Germany, and Spain also contributed heavily. Russians, French, English, Syrians, Austrians, and Swiss immigrated in smaller numbers. The inclusion of non-Iberians as well as non-Catholics among the immigrants introduced possibilities for social change in Brazil. Most of the immigrants went to the South or Southeast. Many remained in the cities. By the end of the century, practically all the industrial workers were foreigners. Although the *senhores de engenho* of the Northeast paid some attention to the thought of attracting foreign immigrants, they had scant success. Disenchanted with what they found or unable to adjust to their new surroundings, many immigrants either returned to Europe or moved on to a Spanish American republic to try their luck again. Many went to Argentina, the Latin American nation which received the largest number of immigrants. In a population of 9,723,604 in 1872, Brazil counted 388,459 foreigners, about 3.9 percent of the population; in 1890, the population was 13,982,370 but the number of foreigners had dropped to 351,545, or 2.5 percent. The immigrants who remained scorned slavery and contributed to the opinion favoring its abolition.

Patience with the long-term results of Rio-Branco's Law of the Free Womb wore thin. After 1871, the question was not whether slavery should be abolished. All agreed that it should be. The question, then, was how quickly abolition should take place. The Conservatives hoped to make it as gradual a process as possible. The Liberals sought to speed it up. When the Liberals returned to power in 1878, they again pressed the slavery question on the nation. By then, the Positivists were attacking slavery as incompatible with the scientific progress of man. Under the prodding of the Liberals and Positivists, abolitionist sentiment welled up within the middle groups. The movement to abolish slavery was primarily urban, finding its greatest support among those least connected with the institution. In short, the urban middle groups overtly challenged the traditional rural oligarchy. The cities once again served as the bellwether of change.

The concern for the welfare of the remaining million and a quarter slaves called forth some mesmeric spokesmen. Joaquim Nabuco (1849–1910), lawyer, diplomat, and statesman, served in the chamber of deputies as a representative of his natal province, Pernambuco, on several occasions beginning in 1878, and eloquently supported the cause of emancipation. A *bacharel* from the Law School of Recife in 1870, he exemplified the nineteenth-century university graduate who spurned his rural background to adopt the mentality of the city. Nabuco compiled his most cogent arguments against slavery in his fiery book *O Abolicionismo* (Abolitionism), in one paragraph of which, with telling mathematics, he ridiculed the Rio-Branco Law by pointing out that a black girl born on the eve of the proclamation of the law might give birth to a child in 1911 who would remain in provisional slavery until 1932. In 1880, he became president of the newly organized Brazilian Anti-Slavery Society, the most important of many such societies which sprang up throughout the empire in that decade. Several highly articulate black leaders contributed to the leadership of the abolitionist campaign: José Carlos do Patrocínio (1854–1905), a persuasive journalist, wrote ceaselessly for the cause and became a symbol of the campaign; André Rebouças (1838–1898) organized abolitionist clubs and spoke and wrote profusely in support of abolition; and Luís Gonzaga de Pinto Gama (1830–1882) spent his youth as a slave and later became a distinguished lawyer who specialized in defending slaves in court. He claimed credit for freeing 500 slaves through the courts. A fiery advocate of immediate abolition, he declared, "Every slave who kills his master, no matter what the circumstances may be, kills in self-defense." He also preached "the right of insurrection." A poetaster, one of his better-known verses began, "My loves are beautiful, the color of night."

Poets contributed significantly to the abolitionist cause. Two mulattoes, Gonçalves Dias and Castro Alves (1847–1871), wrote some of the most beautiful poetry produced in Brazil in the nineteenth century. Although Goncalves Dias was chiefly concerned with the Indian, he also touched very eloquently on the theme of slavery. Castro Alves dedicated himself fervently to the cause of the slaves. He depicted the plight of the slave with such moving verses that he awoke the social conscience of his readers to the injustices inflicted on the slaves. One of his best known poems, "Navio Negreiro" (The Slave Ship), evoked the inhuman suffering of the captives during the crossing from Africa to Brazil. Life on the slave ship recalls some of the scenes of Dante's *Inferno*.

The slavery question forced itself to the forefront of politics. The Liberals called for a second step toward the ultimate goal, if not the *coup de grâce* itself. The Conservatives fought a delaying action. In 1884, the provinces of Ceará and Amazonas freed all their slaves. Voluntary manumissions became increasingly frequent. In the province of Rio de Janeiro, a slavery stronghold, approximately 15,100 slaves received their freedom from their masters between 1873 and 1885. The newspaper *O Provinciano* of Paraíba do Sul listed on January 24, 1884, the following manumissions:

Dona Anna S. José, 16 slaves liberated, and a farm given to them for their own use.

Dona Maria de Caula, 16 slaves liberated, with the condition they serve five years on works of charity in the local Casa de Caridade (Charity House).

Condessa do Rio Novo, 200 slaves liberated by her will and the Cantagallo Plantation given them for a home.

José Eunes Baganha, Portuguese, died in Lisbon and left $100,000 for the liberation of his old slaves.

Barão de Simão Dias, 163 slaves liberated, who remain on his plantation as workers.

Barão de Santo Antônio, 168 slaves liberated by his will and two plantations given to them for their own use.

In 1887, two of the province's largest landowners, the Condes de São Clemente and Nova Friburgo, manumitted 1,909 slaves. Furthermore, a sympathetic public extended every possible facility to aid and encourage runaway slaves.

The Conservatives, in power in 1885, faced up to the issue as they had in 1871 and enacted yet another measure to forestall the total abolition of slavery. The Saraiva-Cotegipe Law liberated all slaves who reached the age of sixty. At the time of its passage this law affected some 120,000 slaves. Slavery was then cut off at both ends. Blacks who were not born into freedom could look forward to retiring into it.

Discredited as slavery was, the rural aristocracy continued to apologize for it. They argued that their slaves lived better than most European workers and accused the abolitionists of painting far too gloomy a picture of the institution. They regarded the Brazilian brand of slavery as extremely mild. On this point of the severity or leniency of the institution arguments still rage. Certainly a large number of foreign visitors to Brazil wrote in their memoirs accounts of the mitigating aspects of the Brazilian slave system, with its permissive and indolent masters. They emphasized the possibilities for the slaves to achieve their freedom as well as their acceptance into society once free. Kidder and Fletcher noted, "The comparative ease with which a slave may obtain his freedom, and, by the possession of property, the rights of citizenship, will probably in twenty years put an end to servitude in this South American Empire." Drawing on the experience of thirteen months in Brazil, H. C. Dent affirmed, "I never came across any other than considerate kindness from master to slave, sometimes even far greater benevolence and consideration than is exercised towards servants in our own country [Great Britain] which boasts of its freedom." Other travelers such as John Codman, Walter Colton, John Esaias Warren, and Thomas Ewbank also emphasized the mildness of Brazilian slavery. They usually coupled those remarks with comments on miscegenation and racial tolerance in Brazil. Thomas Ewbank, doubtless with thoughts of what he had witnessed in the United States, observed: "As the omnibus from Boto-Fogo stopped at the door, I observed three blacks seated among white gentlemen. This is common. A free negro in decent attire—implied by the expression 'wearing shoes and a neckcloth'—can take his seat in places of public resort and conveyance as freely as persons of the lightest complexion. The Constitution recognizes no distinction based on color." Surprise pervaded Ewbank's tone, and he returned repeatedly to the theme of comparative social and racial fluidity. On visiting a restaurant in Rio de Janeiro, he marveled, "Young colored men came in, sat down without hesitation at the same table with whites, and on a perfect equality took part in the conversation." The wealthy and well-placed colored people of imperial Brazil were a never-ending source of amazement to him, and he commented on everything from black ladies attired in expensive silks and bedecked with costly jewels to the number of black men who had mastered the professions or who served in high political posts. Such foreign commentators and subsequent students who adopted similar points of view dwelt on the humanitarian customs surrounding the institution of slavery in Brazil.

The attitudes toward slavery taken by the more enlightened Brazilian patricians added weight to that point of view. At worst, they regarded slavery as a necessary evil—the sole source of labor—to be mitigated by compassionate treatment of the blacks. At best, they gradually manumitted their slaves. José Lino Coutinho, a well-to-do Bahian physician who served in both the Portuguese Côrtes and the Brazilian legislature, represented that group. Lamenting the necessity of slaves, he advised his daughter: "As I have said, dear Cora, be humane and charitable with them [the slaves]. When they are well, see that they are well fed and dressed; when they are ill, see that they receive treatment. Even though they are our slaves, they are also our fellow human beings. Whoever shows kindness and consideration to them will be rewarded with their gratefulness."[20]

The slave in Brazil was at least partially integrated into society and possessed rights, quite a legal contrast to the plight of the slave in the United States. Hence his transition from slave to freedman was facilitated. One paramount privilege the slave enjoyed was his ability to purchase his own freedom. Blacks, taking advantage of the many Catholic holi-

---

20. José Lino Coutinho, *Cartas sobre a Educação de Cora* (Bahia, 1849), p. 166.

days to work on their own, saved money for that purpose. They occasionally formed their own mutual aid societies to facilitate their purchase of freedom. The bylaws of the Negro Brotherhood of St. Anthony of Catagerona in eighteenth-century Bahia stated, "Chapter XIII provides that any member who is a slave, either male or female, shall whenever possible be helped financially by the brotherhood to secure his or her freedom." In general Brazilian historians have concluded that the Brazilian brand of slavery was less rigorous than that practiced by the French, English, North Americans, or Dutch. Manuel de Oliveira Lima represented that position very well. He held that the patriarchal aspect of Brazilian slavery in which the slave was but an extension of the master's family, fondly looked after and cared for, eliminated much of the harshness and cruelty attendant upon the institution in other lands. To his thinking, humaneness was the primary characteristic of the Brazilian master.

The opposite school of thought, the revisionists as it were, put its emphasis elsewhere. Those historians called attention to the immense gap between the beneficent theory of the law and the brutal practice of the masters. Slaves in the Northeast worked fifteen to eighteen hours a day, seven days a week, eating on the job, during the sugar harvest. The coffee harvest required the same exhausting effort. Little wonder the life span of a slave averaged only fifteen years (some authorities calculate only seven years)! Cruel punishments constituted another sad chapter in the history of slavery. Chains, iron collars, tin masks, wooden stocks, whippings and brandings were but a few of the better-known and more widely used methods of punishment. Herbert H. Smith, one of the most intelligent foreign observers of the Brazilian scene in the late imperial period, damned slavery without reservation. He testified, "Around Rio and Bahia, where the vast majority of the slaves are now owned, there are masters who treat their servants with a severity that is nothing short of barbarism." His experiences convinced him that "all other evils with which this country [Brazil] is cursed, taken together, will not compare with this one [slavery]; I could almost say that all other evils have arisen from it, or been strengthened by it." In his opinion, slavery induced indolence, pride, sensuality, and selfishness among the owners and physically and mentally debilitated the blacks, making them unfit for civilization.

Slave revolts against inhumane treatment and the ubiquitous quilombos provided convincing arguments for the historical revisionists. The major revolt of the nineteenth century took place in Bahia in 1835, scene of nine revolts or attempted revolts since the opening of the century. Well organized and directed by Nagos slaves, the rebels sought to kill all whites and free all slaves. The revolt failed, but it sent shivers of fear throughout the white community which never abated until slavery was abolished.

Slaves sometimes murdered their overseers, masters, and their families. To take revenge on the brutal system which exploited them, the slaves frequently put the torch to the masters' houses, barns, warehouses, sugar mills, forests, and cane fields. Many turned their backs on the system, fleeing into the vast and underpopulated interior. Still others, unable to bear the burden of their slavery any longer, committed suicide. The blacks thus met violence with violence on such an intense level as to cast into doubt the bucolic legends of plantation harmony.

Brazilian society lived in a state of tension, fearful of slave revolts or reprisals. In his authoritative study, *A Escravidão no Brasil* (Slavery in Brazil) published in 1866, Agostinho Marquês Perdigão Malheiros described the slave as "a domestic enemy" and "a public enemy." He cautioned, "He is a volcano that constantly threatens society, a mine ready to explode at the least spark." Foreign travelers sensed the tension. Prince Adalbert visited one large and well-run plantation which he praised as a model. After noting the friendly relations between master and the slaves, he revealed, "The loaded guns and pistols hanging up in his [the owner's] bedroom however, showed that he had not entire confidence in them [the slaves] and indeed, he had more than once been obliged to face them with his loaded gun." The abolition movement increased rather than diminished that tension. Evidence indicates that the fazendeiros lived in fear of attack from their slaves as their day of deliverance approached. In June of 1887, the minister of agriculture confessed that the large number of escaped slaves in Santos constituted a "grave and imminent danger to public order and property." He reported that the government had dispatched troops to São Paulo not to recapture slaves but "to maintain public order and calm the frightened agricultural and commercial interests" of that province. In his official message the following year, the president of São Paulo spoke with alarm of the increasing number of slaves who fled their plantations "armed." The picture which emerges is far from that of the docile slave faithfully and good-naturedly attending his master on the plantation.

The revisionists—like the abolitionists—concluded that slavery at best was a despicable institution contrary to human reason and without defense. Henry Koster, after a long discussion of the institution based on both observation and experience, concluded that nothing good could be expected from slavery. The natural desire of the slave, he concluded, was to get his freedom. Visiting a plantation run by a religious order in Pernambuco, he noted,

I had great pleasure in witnessing the most excellent arrangements of this plantation; the Negroes are as happy as persons in a state of slavery can be; but although the tasks are, comparatively speaking, easy, and corporal punishments are only resorted to for children, still the great object at which they aim is to be free, and to purchase the freedom of their children. One man, who was a fisherman by trade, had obtained manumission of his wife, though he was still a slave himself, with the intent that if she should still have any more children, they might be free; and he purposed afterwards purchasing his own freedom, and that of his young ones. Several instances of the same behavior are frequently occurring upon the estates belonging to these and other friars. Thus everyone wishes to be a free agent; and it is this feeling alone which makes a São Bento Negro do all in his power to be able to act for himself; for very probably he may be obliged to labor with more diligence to obtain his living as a free man than as a slave.[21]

21. *Travels in Brazil* (Carbondale, Illinois, 1966), pp. 113–14.

With abolitionist sentiment aflame, the days of slavery in Brazil were clearly numbered. At the same time, the economic arguments against the institution were beginning to carry the same weight as the emotional appeal. It became obvious to more and more concerned Brazilians that for the long run salaried labor was more economical than paying the rising price of slaves and their upkeep, to say nothing of the capital loss if a slave died young or proved to be recalcitrant or inefficient. After 1850, many planters in the Northeast found it cheaper to pay wages than to keep slaves. Within two decades free workers outnumbered slaves on the sugar plantations. Efficient and well-organized exploitation of slaves in some new coffee regions made the system temporarily profitable for some fazendeiros, but, in contradiction, other statistics appeared to show that a sack of coffee produced by free labor cost approximately half of that produced by slave labor. The declining numbers of slaves meant that by 1880 most new coffee plantations (and many older ones as well) had to depend heavily on free, salaried labor. In some instances modern plantation owners were introducing labor-saving machinery. The president of São Paulo boasted in 1871 that some planters in his province were no longer "stubbornly sticking to tradition and routine." Rather, they experimented with and adopted machinery which could replace scarce and expensive labor. The Republican party in São Paulo, composed primarily of coffee planters, resolved in 1887 to favor total emancipation, and its members agreed to free their own slaves within a two-year period. In the same year, the army, through the influential Military Club, petitioned the Crown that it be relieved of the irksome and humiliating duty of chasing down runaway slaves. Slavery had lost its basis of support. Many slave owners continued to apologize for the institution, more in the hope of obtaining a handsome indemnification from the government than in the folly of stemming the crescent abolitionist tide.

It could come as a surprise to no one when on May 13, 1888, to cries of approval from those in attendance, the parliament passed the Golden Law liberating the remaining three-quarters of a million slaves. The final vestiges of slavery had been eliminated in Cuba in 1886, and so with the passage of the Law of 1888, slavery finally disappeared from the Western Hemisphere. Ironically it fell to the Conservatives to act once again on the matter, and it was they—as it had been in 1871 and 1885—who passed the legislation. The law contained no provision to indemnify the owners for their slaves, although the government established a new agricultural bank to extend credit to landowners suffering from the effects of emancipation. In the absence of her father, Princess-Regent Isabel, a committed abolitionist, signed the law. The crowds shouted their approval. Band music erupted. Dazzling fireworks exploded. Speeches resounded. And people merrily danced and sang in the streets of Rio de Janeiro.

While those joyous scenes took place in the capital and other major cities, a deafening silence greeted the Golden Law in much of the countryside. Confusion, uncertainty, and concern for the future troubled those directly connected with the abolished institution. The slaveholders sulked moodily over their sudden capital loss and the threat to their economic position. They blamed the monarchy for the financial blow. If the slaves expected the rapidly penned signature of Princess Isabel at the foot of the Golden Law to transport them forthwith to a promised land, they became disillusioned. Life continued to be hard for them, as they lamented in this popular verse:

> Everything in this world changes,
> Only the life of the Negro remains the same:
> He works to die of hunger,
> The 13th of May fooled him!

Indeed some of the literature in the decades after emancipation would have the reader believe that not a few of the ex-slaves looked back nostalgically to the "good old days" of security and the paternalism of the plantation. Witness this passage from Graça Aranha's much-praised novel *Canaan*, published in 1902, in which an old former slave reminisces:

> And in his rough dialect he murmured, as if in ecstasy, his sorrowful recollections.
> Ah! All that, my young gentlemen, is gone. . . . Where is the

ranch? My late master died. His son continued to live there until the government deprived him of his slaves. Everything went to pieces. The master went to Victoria, where he has a job; my mates went into the forest and each built a house here, there, and everywhere, just where they pleased. I, with my people, came here, to the colonel's land. Things are sad now. The government finished up the ranches and flung us into the world to look for something to eat, to get something to dress with and to work like oxen in order to live. Ah! Those were good times at the ranch! We all worked together, good people, mulatto women. . . . Who cared for the foreman? . . . A whipping never killed anyone. There was always plenty of food, and on Saturday, Sunday's eve, the old drum used to beat until the early morning. . . .

In this fashion the former slave went on mixing, in the bitterness of his nostalgia, recollections of the pleasures of the communal life of yesterday, protected by the paternal influence of the ranch, with the despair of the present isolation and the melancholy of a world gone to pieces. . . .[22]

Adjustments were necessary for all involved. Most would make the necessary transitions or adaptations within a few years.

Once during the abolitionist campaign Joaquim Nabuco warned his constituents in Pernambuco of the retrograde effects of slavery on their society, and what he said could be applied to the entire nation:

Ah! Pernambuco has a great past, but it seems that its sons do not wish it to have a great future! . . .
Slavery is an institution which destroys and degrades everything that it is the purpose of social institutions to build and develop. . . . The city of Recife has awakened from the profound sleep of many years of indifference and callousness. In this place where I now speak, the center of so many traditions and so much heroism, which were it not for slavery would today be a strong and respected republic.[23]

Nabuco happily proclaimed the abolition of slavery as a landmark in Brazil's evolution. For him the year 1888 heralded the

22. José Pereira de Graça Aranha, *Canaan* (Boston, 1920), p. 25.

23. Quoted in Carolina Nabuco, *The Life of Joaquim Nabuco* (Stanford, California, 1950), p. 125.

birth of a new Brazil. The eminent historian Sérgio Buarque de Holanda has approved that conclusion, declaring, "The year 1888, the most decisive year in the evolution of the Brazilian people, divides two epochs." Abolition signaled Brazil's emergence into the modern world. Slavery was indissolubly linked with the colonial past. That institution was one of the trinity, together with the latifundium and monoculture, perpetuating the traditional agrarian society. In fact, slavery made the archaic agricultural system function since it contributed the most vital ingredient, labor, which turned the land into wealth. Hence the opponents of slavery felt that the institution was the strongest cord tying the nation to its colonial past, and slavery thus stood accused of having retarded national development. The younger generation charged it with the most heinous and unforgivable of crimes: preventing modernization. In their opinion, it inhibited the mechanization of agriculture, dissuaded Europeans from migrating to Brazil, and restricted economic development, especially industrialization, already regarded as the magic key to the future. As early as 1861 at the National Exposition in Rio de Janeiro, where a minimum of industrial products were on display, slavery bore the blame for the fact that domestic manufacturing had failed to prosper. Successful industrialization required, among other things, the capital wastefully invested in slaves. Further, the slaves earned no wages and hence constituted no market, while industrialization required a free proletariat class demanding and able to pay for the manufactured products. On a wider plane than that, slavery and modernization were simply incompatible, indeed, contradictory. The abolition of slavery thus struck the chains of a nation linked to the past and permitted it to step toward the future. The optimistic predicted immediate change and progress on an ever-accelerating scale.

Recife. One of Brazil's Earliest Movie Theaters,
c. 1910.

Itamratí Palace, Brasília

Palace of the Dawn, Presidential Residence, Brasília

Palace of Justice on the Square of the Three Powers, Brasília

Rio-Branco Avenue, Rio de Janeiro, 1916

The Opera House, Teatro Amazonas, in Manaus

An Interior View of the Opera House, Manaus

São Francisco Church, Salvador, Bahia

Altar of the São Francisco Church

Street Scene in Salvador, Bahia

The Rua do Ouvidor in Ouro Prêto, Minas Gerais

The Redemption of Ham,
by Modesto Brocos,
from the Museu
de Belas Artes,
Rio de Janeiro

Cowboys of the Rio São Francisco, 1941

School Children in Rio de Janeiro Watching a Puppet Show, c. 1950

School Children, Rio de Janeiro,
1941

Farm Families Watching an Outdoor Play, São Paulo State, 1941

Waiting to See the Mayor. São Joao d'El Rei, Minas Gerais, 1941

Rural Folk. State of Rio de Janeiro, 1941

A Farm Family of Minas Gerais, c. 1950

Bahianas,
the Women of Bahia
in Festive Costume,

Students March
through the Streets
of São Paulo
in Protest Against
the Old Republic,
1930

Rebels in Recife
Participate in
the Overthrow
of the Old Republic,
1930

The Imperial Family
at the End of the
Second Empire. Comte
d'Eu (extreme left),
Emperor Pedro II (center),
Princess Isabel
(on the Emperor's arm),
Empress Teresa Cristina
(seated).

Emperor Pedro II
in the Second Decade
of his Reign

Emperor Pedro I

King João VI

Getúlio Vargas (center) Flanked by his Cabinet
After his Election to the Presidency, 1934

The Inauguration of President Jânio Quadros
(center), 1961. At the left is the
outgoing President, Juselino Kubitschek.
Vice-president João Goulart stands on the right.

Picking the
Coffee Berries,
São Paulo,
c. 1900

A Coffee Plantation
in the State of
São Paulo

Panorama
of a Coffee
Plantation,
São Paulo, 1962

Coffee Drying
Platform
São Paulo

The Drawing Room
of a Coffee Planter's
Home, c. 1930

The Planter's House in the Interior of São Paulo

"Coffee" Mural by Cândido Portinari

Chapter Five
The New Brazil

The abolition of slavery in 1888 and the overthrow of the monarchy in 1889 initiated a period of social, economic, and political change in Brazil. Those changes accelerated modernization. One student of Brazil during the early years of the twentieth century pointed out that "phenomenal growth and progress" were in the process of transforming the new South American republic. Continuing her observation, Marie Robinson Wright remarked,

The development of an essentially modern spirit of progress and enterprise, which has placed the people of Brazil in the front rank among the leading powers of the New World, and which so dominates the national life at the present moment that every part of the vast republic is responding to its stimulating influence, shows an awakening to new conditions and a realization of larger responsibilities such as necessarily distinguish a great nation thoroughly aroused to the importance of its high density. It is this spirit which has created the new Brazil.[1]

The period in which "the New Brazil" emerged, 1888–1922, forms a part—a major part—of a longer political era in the

1. *The New Brazil* (Philadelphia, 1907), p. 13.

traditional periodization of Brazilian history. Known as the Old Republic, it began with the fall of the monarchy on November 15, 1889, and continued to the rebellion which placed Getúlio Vargas in power in 1930. Since the years from 1922 to 1930 mark the overt challenge to the power structure of the rural oligarchy, a challenge which triumphed in 1930, discussion of those eight years will be considered as part of a longer discussion on the Vargas years in Brazilian history. The discussion of the New Brazil concerns itself primarily with the identification of significant forces for change appearing or forming in Brazil between 1888 and 1922.

The Middle Groups and the Military

The difference in the composition of Brazilian society between the eras of the declaration of independence and the emancipation of the slaves illustrated some of the changes wrought by the nineteenth century. In 1822 the new nation counted barely 4 million inhabitants, of whom probably half were slaves of African birth or descent. When Princess Isabel signed the Golden Law in 1888, roughly 600,000 slaves gained their freedom. They constituted about one twentieth of the population of 14 million. At the opposite end of the social scale stood 300,000 large plantation owners and members of their families. The vast majority of the population fell between those two extremes. True, most of them were impoverished peasants or rural proletariat wedded to the soil, who were unknowing contributors to the maintenance of the status quo. There was an inarticulate group who ran small and medium-sized farms. Of greatest significance, however, within the large body between the two extremes were the urban middle groups, already introduced as the principal agents bringing about the mental transformation of Brazil in the nineteenth century. Among its members the consensus grew that their well-being required the modification if not the eradication of many colonial vestiges which were still intimately associated with national life. With fewer and more tenuous roots in the agricultural past, these urban-based middle groups showed a growing impatience with tradition and a fascination with innovation. Change offered them the best opportunity to improve their status. They would soon challenge the planter elite for the power to effect the improvements they desired.

Despite the many and even the dramatic changes which had taken place in Brazil during the Second Empire, the colonial past still formed a significant part of the present. The agricultural economy characterized by latifundia and monoculture still predominated. The principal class continued to be the landowners. With twenty-five years of residence and travel in South America, Albert Hale observed of Brazil in 1906, "There exist traces of a feudal system, in that sharp line which divides the upper class, the aristocracy, from the lower class, the laborers . . . The monarchy was so recently destroyed that in their [the laborers'] minds an aristocracy of blood still prevails, but this aristocracy is really one of land, of money." When James Bryce visited Brazil in 1910, he vividly described the large planter as living "in a sort of semi-feudal patriarchal way" in his "little principality." He compared the situation to the England of a century earlier, when county squires controlled local affairs and selected the members of Parliament. By the time the slave system ended, the plantation owners already had devised a patrimonial regime in which the small producers and laborers were held to the plantation by noninstitutionalized ties, one of the most common of which was debt. The landed class exploited the countryfolks' ignorance and isolation to augment their power. The patriarchal chiefs of the landed gentry customarily bore the title *coronel*, a title derived from the service they or their forebears gave to the National Guard. They firmly controlled the countryside. Ownership of immense tracts of land conferred on them authority over the people dependent on that land. With their economic advantages and social prestige, they also exercised local political control. Some employed private armies to enforce their will, others hired the backlands bandits for that purpose. Friendship or familial ties with local, state, and national politicians and with neighboring *senhores de terras* buttressed the power structure of each coronel. In contrast to the ideas held in that part of the still neofeudalistic/neocapitalist countryside, the new coffee planters of São Paulo and Minas Gerais increasingly came to represent a rural capitalist class more tightly integrated than ever into the markets of the United States and Western Europe. Their ideas as well as their agrarian practices were increasingly "modern." They favored a liberal democracy which they correctly regarded as more sympathetic, more complimentary to their capitalist inclinations than the monarchy had been.

Along with the capitalist coffee planters, the growing urban centers, particularly in Southeastern Brazil, challenged the neofeudalism of the countryside and the power of the moribund *fazendeiro* class. The struggle between those two sharply different elements was inevitable and set the tone for the future.

The gulf between the neofeudal countryside and the more progressive cities and coffee planters widened rapidly during the closing decades of the nineteenth century. Eventually the urban middle groups and coffee planters realized that the emperor, revered and respected as he might be, represented primarily the entrenched landed class, whom he favored with titles of nobility and political power. Many of the city dwellers viewed the emperor as the embodiment of the planters' desire to retain most of what was colonial in Brazilian society and in the economy while still rejecting, in the stricter legal sense, colonial status. In short, the aging emperor symbolized the past. He did not represent the emerging middle groups or the emergent capitalism. Pedro gave every indication of being reluctant to recognize the increasing importance of the merchants and industrialists. In 1875, for example, he failed to come to the support of the enterprising Mauá and allowed his economic empire to collapse. Of singular importance, he ignored the restless military officers whose desires and ambitions often reflected those of the middle groups from whose ranks they came. Clearly the monarchical regime revealed its increasing incompatibility with the changing times.

Removed from the new elements of society, the monarchy magnified its isolation by offending two of its staunchest supporters. The emperor's liberalism did not please many within the Roman Catholic Church. The display of regalistic ire toward the Church and the imprisonment of the two bishops in 1874 had prompted some in the ecclesiastical hierarchy to reassess their relations with the throne. While the Church did not withdraw its loyalty, many of its leaders did manifest increasing indifference toward the monarchy's fate. On the other hand, churchmen hesitated to embrace the Republican cause since the Republican party was strongly anticlerical. One official Roman Catholic newspaper, *O Apóstolo,* sought to resolve the dilemma by calling for "the re-formation of an honest republican party." An editorial in that paper characterized the government as "pagan Caesarism" and predicted that a new republican party would "serve as a powerful brake on this political monster." Some Catholic priests did find it possible to support the historic Republican party. The first bishop of Diamantina, João Antônio dos Santos, was a Republican; Father Miranda Cruz of Santa Catarina joined the party and in 1886 founded a Republican newspaper; and Father João Manuel de Carvalho, a conservative deputy from the North, publicly supported the Republicans in the last parliament of the empire. During the session of June 11, 1889, he cried out in the Chamber, "Down with the monarchy! Long live the Republic!" In general, however, the hierarchy did not wave the banner of republicanism. The churchmen simply cooled toward the empire and displayed more interest and concern in formulating a new relationship with the civil authorities than in propping up a teetering throne.

Royal favor—and, in the case of the heir presumptive, royal fervor—for the abolitionist movement, and finally the Golden Law's failure to compensate the owners for their freed slaves aroused the hostility of the old landed class. Particularly hostile was that segment, comprising the older sugar and coffee planters, which once had supported the Crown most enthusiastically. After emancipation took place, angry planters joined the Republican party in large numbers. Abolition of slavery in Brazil precipitated the fall of the monarchy, just as abolition in Cuba foretold the end of Spanish dominion there.

At the same time that the base of support for the old emperor diminished, the people's psychological disposition toward a monarchy lessened. A continent of republics encompassed the empire, and Brazilians, because of the uniqueness of their political institutions, felt alienated from their neighbors. The trends of the time seemed to favor the republican system of government. The intelligentsia, always conscious of what was occurring in their beloved France, watched with interest the rapid dissolution of Napoleon's monarchy in 1870 and debated the ideas Leon Gambetta put forth. Furthermore, many began to equate republicanism with progress and, conversely, to equate monarchy with backwardness. They were fully aware of the great progress of Argentina since its unification in 1862 and of the astounding rate of industrialization of the United States since the end of the Civil War. With those records imperial Brazil contrasted poorly. For that, the monarchy bore part of the blame.

During the long process in which indifference or even hostility toward the monarchy overtook greater numbers of the Brazilians, two philosophical currents, Positivism and republicanism, gained adherents among the middle sectors of the cities. Both advocated the abolition of the monarchy. The enthusiasts for those ideas spoke out loudly and frequently, although they alone did not possess the strength to bring down the monarchy. They depended on their growing influence in the army officer-corps to persuade the military to overthrow the emperor and establish a republic.

The military as an institution made a belated appearance in Brazil. It played an insignificant role until the protracted war with Paraguay. Five years of fighting increased both its size and its importance. The 17,000 soldiers in the army in 1864 multiplied to 100,000 by 1870. Restless after peace returned to South America in 1870, the officers focused their attention on politics. The Duque de Caxias, of unquestionable loyalty to Pedro II and the supreme commander of the army, held the military in check. His death in 1880 gave license to greater political activity among the officers. Petty disputes, considered by those in uniform as "affairs of honor," marred the relations between cabinets and the soldiers. To a certain degree those differences reflected a class conflict. The cabinets represented the landed aristocracy and their traditional point of view. The bulk of the army officers came from the middle groups and unconsciously spoke for them or for part of them. In another sense, as a solidifying corporation, the army on many matters spoke only for itself and its interests. Many officers followed a military career because of the mobility and prestige it offered. In the military academy, they received an excellent education. Dressed in splendid uniforms and favored with the aura of victories they or their predecessors had won for the fatherland on the battlefields of Paraguay, they enjoyed a privileged social position which birth or background might otherwise have denied them. Their rank and uniforms admitted them to new opportunities and situations where they did not always feel comfortable or at ease. Increasingly inflated with their own importance, the officers often felt that the politicians—more often than not the imperial nobility or its representatives—scorned, neglected, and, when possible, humiliated them. Their collective paranoia prevented them from maintaining satisfactory relations with the civilian, imperial government.

The military first began publicly to debate governmental policies in 1879. The officers vehemently opposed a bill to reduce the size of the military and did not hesitate to voice their disapproval. Their activities were contrary to two regulations, one issued in 1859 and a second in 1878, prohibiting officers from criticizing their superiors or debating service matters in the press. The officers nonetheless expressed their opposition with impunity, and eventually the bill was abandoned. The civil-military conflict attracted wider national attention in 1883. Over the issue of compulsory payment to an insurance fund, the officers again debated in public questions which were related to the service and the government. When the government proscribed such discussions, reprimanding some senior officers and punishing others, the officers united to defend what they considered to be their rights. One of those who rose to defend the military's position was Marshal Deodoro da Fonseca, a highly respected officer who enjoyed considerable prestige among his colleagues and popularity in the ranks. In 1886, he again intervened in a dispute—this one between some officers stationed in Pôrto Alegre and the government—to support the military point of view. Embittered toward the politicians, Deodoro accused them of furthering their own individual interests to the detriment of the country and of neglecting, even maltreating, the army despite its sacrifices for the fatherland. The marshal decried the sad state into which the nation had fallen politically. His outspoken defense of military in its petty quarrels with the government made him the hero of those in uniform.

In their quarrels with the government in 1886, the officers agreed that the civilians had sullied military honor and determined that the insults must be avenged. In the following year they founded the *Clube Militar* to speak for military interests and to voice military grievances. The members promptly elected Deodoro as the first club president. Thereafter the military's political activities were centered within its salons. All these seemingly minor incidents were significant as indications of the army's fear of neglect, and its determination to regain for itself at any cost the position of prestige it once had enjoyed.

Aware of the mounting dissatisfaction among the officers, the Republican party moved to exploit it to their own advantage. They understood that the military held the key to the establishment of the republic. Unlike any other group in Brazil, the military had both the organization and power to effect change. The young officers, concerned not only with questions of honor but with problems of national development, listened attentively to Republican party and Positivist propaganda, both of which advocated an end to the empire. The military school in Rio de Janeiro resounded with discussions of Republican ideology. In the popular classes of Benjamin Constant, the cadets heard enthusiastic lectures on Positivism. Those young officers reflected the widening distance between the class from which they sprang and the imperial government. The support of the cadets and junior officers was helpful to the Republican cause, but nothing could be done without the cooperation of their seniors. In the late 1880s those ranking officers moved toward the Republican camp as the logical alternative to supporting an empire which they felt had mistreated them. When the most powerful figure in the army, Marshal Deodoro, was convinced by fellow officers and Republicans that the only method of "purifying" the political body was to replace the moribund empire with a vigorous republic, the fate of the empire was decided. Deodoro commanded the loyalty of the entire army, and with him it turned on the empire.

Under Deodoro's orders, on November 15, 1889, the army marched from the barracks, surrounded the Royal Palace, occupied the principal governmental buildings, and silenced Rio de Janeiro. In a dry, authoritative tone the marshal informed a surprised nation, "The people, the army and the navy, in perfect harmony of sentiment with our fellow citizens resident in the provinces, have just decreed the dethronement of the imperial dynasty, and consequently the extinction of the representative monarchical system of government." The empire had fallen.

The nation acquiesced in the change. The masses were indifferent to the events. The former supporters of the monarchy among the planters and the Church hierarchy raised no voice of protest. Of the provinces, only Maranhão and Bahia offered some minor protest and resistance. Those were token demonstrations. Tranqullity generally prevailed throughout the novice republic. Indeed, the evidence seemed to indicate that structurally the empire had been weak and that in the penultimate decade of the nineteenth century its vitality had been sapped. Consequently, more from its own infirmities than anything else the empire expired. The military, then, simply provided the necessary *coup de grâce* and did so without meeting any opposition.

Despite all the talk of a republic over the years, the nation was little prepared to put into practice the elaborate and varied republican theories. The principal question after the coup was whether a republic would be established or anarchy would hold sway. The populace asked anxiously if the new regime could maintain order, insure national unity, and offer the same comfortable liberties as its predecessor had done for nearly half a century. Machado de Assis' novel of the period, *Essau and Jacob*, well captures the prevailing mood of apprehension.

The military, the only really national institution in scope, organization, and program—and the self-appointed guardian of patriotism—immediately took charge of the nation. The emperor abdicated and sailed into European exile, dying in a modest Parisian hotel on December 5, 1891. Deodoro with the unanimous backing of the army kept command of the government as chief of state. At a military parade two months after the coup, he accepted the sonorous rank of "Generalissimo of the Forces of the Land and the Sea." He was a long way from his modest childhood as the son of an army officer in provincial Alagoas. He behaved himself in the presidential palace very much as he had in the barracks, with an unquestioned reliance on discipline, order, hierarchy, and command. Military influence could be seen everywhere. The officers abandoned the secondary role assigned to them during the imperial period to assume a primary role in the new republic. The army increased in size from 13,000 to 20,000. Army officers governed ten of the twenty states. Deodoro's cabinet was essentially civilian in composition, but no one doubted that the military exercised final authority. One bizarre aspect of the military influence was the conferring of the rank of brigadier general on all civilian members of the cabinet, most of whom had never held a rifle or been inside a barracks.

Titles of nobility were abolished, and the holders of them were eclipsed at least momentarily. "Doctor" and "Colonel" were the appellations most prized as the university and service-academy graduates assumed greater political and social importance. The first republican cabinet evinced that trend unmistakably. Quintino Bocaiúva, a respected journalist and doctor of law, held the portfolio of Foreign Affairs; Manuel Ferraz de Campos Sales, a doctor of law, was minister of justice; Demétrio Ribeiro, a young engineer, took charge of the Ministry of Agriculture, Commerce, and Public Works; Aristides da Silveira Lobo, a journalist as well as a doctor of law, directed the Ministry of the Interior; Ruy Barbosa, yet another lawyer, assumed the portfolio of Finances; Colonel Benjamin Constant was minister of war; and Vice Admiral Eduardo Wandenkolk was minister of the navy. The appointment of new officials in the states also mirrored that trend.

Since advocating a republican ideology was a *sine qua non* requirement for the holding of office on any high level, one encountered at least nominal Republicans in all the important posts. However, those Republicans were by no means a homogeneous group. At one extreme end, there was a small group of Positivists who favored a "scientific dictatorship" with the trappings of a republic. However, a much larger body of less doctrinaire Republicans supported a democratic, federal republic. Diverse elements composed that larger group: the historic Republicans who faithfully had pursued their goal since 1870, the ardent young radicals, the young quasi-Positivist army officers inspired by Benjamin Constant, and the senior officers who, for reasons of their own, adopted republicanism at the last minute. Such diversity inhibited the effectiveness of the Republicans and strengthened the hand of the more cohesive military.

The task of creating a republic on the ruins of the empire was challenging. However, once again the Brazilians demonstrated a capacity to make a major change with minimal strife. In direct contrast to the experience of most of the Spanish American nations in the nineteenth century, Brazil altered its government without fighting, without bloodshed, and, what is even more amazing, without imprisonments. In that manner, the nation consolidated the tradition it had established in the nineteenth century of bringing about major changes peacefully, the "conciliation and reform" theory which the historian José Honório Rodrígues has elaborated so convincingly. On the surface at any rate, compromise, accommodation, and conciliation were the mode. But in the months and years after the *fait accompli* of the military, the necessary adjustments did not always come easily.

By decree on November 16, 1889, Deodoro created a federal republic. He then summoned a constituent assembly. Further, he decreed the separation of Church and State, an action applauded by the Brazilian ecclesiastical hierarchy, who sought a freedom for the Roman Catholic Church similar to that insured it in the United States. A collective pastoral letter of March 19, 1890 had expressed the Church's willingness to come to terms with the republic and had criticized the empire severely. The separation of the Church from the State and the attendant freedom it enjoyed satisfied Pope Leo XIII, who in 1898 publicly stated that the position of the Church in the republic was superior to its status under the empire. Deodoro's unchallenged position as the nation's most powerful and prestigious military figure increased the strength of his regime, which quickly displayed an ability to keep order and maintain unity. He rapidly regularized the administration.

A major test for the new republic was to obtain foreign recognition. Much to its relief, the government encountered little difficulty. Neighboring Uruguay and Argentina accorded it on November 20. On the same day, President Benjamin Harrison instructed the United States minister in Rio de Janeiro to maintain relations with the new government. A lengthy debate in the Senate delayed official United States recognition until January 29, 1890. That summer an American naval squadron called at Rio de Janeiro to salute the new sister republic. The Brazilian Navy reciprocated at once with a courtesy visit to North American ports. Meanwhile, Bolivia, Chile, Paraguay, Peru, and Venezuela had given their recognition. The remainder of the hemisphere followed suit. The European nations delayed a little longer. On June 2, 1890, France became the first of the Old World states to welcome the new republic into the community of nations. Great Britain recognized the republic on May 4, 1891. Russia was the last European state to do so. The tsar waited until after the death of Pedro II. The republic, upon entering into friendly relations with the outside world, indicated that there would be no change in traditional Brazilian foreign policy.

The government, always legalistic in its outlook,

promptly gave attention to the writing of a constitution. On December 3, 1889, Deodoro appointed a special committee of five jurists to prepare the bases for a new constitution. The committee drew heavily on the constitution of the United States and also found a useful model in the Argentine constitution. Minister Ruy Barbosa, impressed by the North American document, reviewed the work of the committee for the government and made extensive revisions. Because of him, the proposed document assumed a strong presidential flavor. Thus revised, the proposed constitution was submitted to the Assembly which met on November 15, 1890. The electoral machinery, well oiled in the traditional fashion by the government, had produced an Assembly composed of delegates who were mainly Republicans of one shade or another. It has been characterized as a gathering of novices since the old familiar political faces were absent, having been replaced by younger men. Many of these were military officers participating in politics for the first time. Joaquim Francisco de Assis Brasil, diplomat, statesman, and political commentator, noted with some dismay, "The ignorance of almost all of them concerning the most elementary political questions was fantastic." The only truly coherent group— and one of the most vocal—within the Assembly was the Positivists, small in number but still influential. They encouraged the pronounced federalist sentiments prevalent among the Republicans. Assis Brasil, himself not a Positivist, had done much to popularize the federal idea in his widely read and much discussed book, *A República Federal,* published in São Paulo in 1887. His persuasive arguments weighed heavily in the minds of the impressionable young legislators.

While the concept of federalism excited the imaginations of many who saw in greater local autonomy the end of a stifling unitary embrace, it sent chills of fear through the minds of a minority who looked back to the disastrous experiment with it during the Regency. They foresaw unhappy if not unfortunate results in its reinstitution. Eduardo Prado predicted a splintering of the nation. The Baron of Rio-Branco was equally pessimistic, fearing also that federalism would weaken national unity. However, the question as to whether the republic would adopt federalism was no longer open to debate. What the Assembly had to decide was the degree to which it would be carried. Considerable debate focused on that point, with the Positivist delegates from Rio Grande do Sul advocating the most extreme degree of state autonomy.

The constitution promulgated on February 24, 1891, provided for a federal, republican, presidential form of government. It was the legal base for a liberal, democratic, capitalist state which in practice would permit a system of regional alliances favorable to the dynamic coffee-exporting capitalists of the Southeast. Although weaker than during the Second Empire, the central government still retained some impressive powers. It reserved for itself abundant sources of income and the right to intervene in the states. Of great importance, it could mobilize the armed forces to enforce its will. Within the traditional Latin American framework, the president was not only the executive but the mainspring of all power, dominating and subordinating to his will the other branches and levels of government—and so it had to be if he was to be at all effective and maintain his authority. Essentially he served as a unifying force to balance and neutralize the many centrifugal tendencies of the nation. The national legislature consisted of a chamber of deputies, whose members were elected for three-year terms on the basis of population, and a senate, composed of three delegates from each state elected for nine-year terms. Contrary to the document of 1824, the new constitution disenfranchised the illiterate, a precedent followed by all succeeding constitutions. It vaguely modeled the judicial system on that of the United States. The twenty states governed by popularly elected governors and legislatures had power over exclusively state matters. They could enact an export tax on any of their products, an extremely lucrative source of income in rich states such as São Paulo and Minas Gerais. The states maintained militias which provided them additional leverage in dealing with the federal government.

In general the constitution was liberal and well written,

but, unfortunately, it was not Brazilian. In an effort to repudiate the past, the provisional government had imported a constitution, primarily from the United States, alien to the nation's experience. The past could not be so easily forgotten or ignored. Brazil quixotically hoped that its liberal, democratic institutions would function under the crushing weight of its backward, patriarchal, patrimonial, agrarian structure. To the disappointment of many, authoritative, paternalistic government continued under the guise of an enlightened republic.

The hiatus between the rebellion and its institutionalization through a constitution was comparatively short, from November 15, 1889, to February 24, 1891. It compares favorably with other lapses between rebellion and reinstitutionalization in Brazilian history: 1822–1824, 1930–1934, and 1964–1967. Nonetheless the interim was sufficient to establish a military dictatorship.

After approving the constitution, the Assembly turned its attention to the election of the first president and vice-president of the republic, both to serve until 1894. The military pressure to elect Deodoro as president minimized serious consideration of any other candidates. Still, opposition to him abounded in the Assembly. The marshal already had proved himself to be an inept administrator. With little knowledge of the give and take of politics, and even less interest in it, he preferred the barracks order fulfilled without hesitation or question. He experienced repeated difficulties with Republican party leaders and with the Assembly. Some within the Assembly nominated the old-time Republican Prudente José de Morais e Barros for the presidency. However, the Assembly felt obliged to elect Deodoro since he still commanded the loyalty of the army, and the assemblymen were wise enough to realize that they could not offend the military at this point. The election turned out to be closer than most predicted it might be: Deodoro received 129 votes and Prudente 97. An extremely sensitive man, Deodoro resented his perfunctory and lackluster election, which he rightly perceived to be more the result of a sense of duty than a feeling of enthusiasm. His pride suffered a further blow when the vice-president received more votes than he did. With 153 votes, the Assembly chose Marshal Floriano Peixoto as vice-president. The Assembly once more affronted Deodoro when it greeted the vice-president with more applause than it had given him. Hence, the beginning of constitutional government under the republic was inauspicious. The constitution promulgated and the elections over, the Assembly then changed itself into the first republican legislature and began to enact laws.

Without delay, the president and Congress clashed. Deodoro resented all dissent within the legislature, regarding it as a personal challenge. Affairs in 1891 closely resembled those in 1823, and the similarity did not diminish. Certain of the support of the army as well as of public indifference, Deodoro arbitrarily dissolved Congress on November 3, 1891, and proclaimed a state of siege. The president rationalized his action by accusing the legislature of endangering the safety of the republic and pointing out the threat of monarchical plots afoot. The state governors, with the exception of Lauro Sodré of Pará, supported his action. However, in both Rio Grande do Sul and São Paulo there were strong currents of opinion vociferously opposed to the highhanded action. The navy, whose officers evidenced strong aristocratic tendencies and lacked enthusiasm for the republic from the beginning, challenged the arbitrary action of the president. Led by Admiral Custódio José de Melo, the navy threatened to revolt unless Congress was reconvened. Deodoro could not resolve his dilemma: he would neither give in nor countenance bloodshed. Instead, he resigned from office bitterly convinced that the nation did not appreciate his efforts and sacrifices. The old marshal who had led the nation in its passage from an empire to a republic quickly faded from public view. He died in August of the following year, and in accordance with his own wishes the generalissimo was buried in civilian clothes and without military honors.

The multiple crises of November disturbed the republic. Vice-President Floriano Peixoto, strong and unflappable, strode to the center of the political stage and forcefully took charge of the explosive situation. He declared that Congress had never been dissolved, thereby returning events to the status quo before November 3. With the exception of Sodré, the new president replaced all the state governors because they had supported Deodoro's second coup. The resistance of some to their deposition precipitated outbreaks of violence which contributed to the general unrest. Floriano, however, proved master of the situation, showing that he merited his epithet "the iron marshal." The federal government won in that early display of strength against the states.

At the same time, Floriano's enemies questioned the constitutionality of his right to the presidency. They pointed out that Article 42 of the constitution required that a new election be held if the president should leave office before the expiration of two years of his four-year term. Floriano retorted that Article 42 was invalid in this case since Congress had elected the first president and vice-president and the special nature of the election removed it from the dicta of that article. Congress concurred with his interpretation.

The acceptance of Floriano's succession signified the continuance of direct military control of the government. In another sense—to the degree the military embodied the vague ideology of the urban middle groups—it extended their hold over the government. Floriano, like his predecessor, came from a modest background. He also surrounded himself with many university graduates who proclaimed their Republican and/or Positivist preferences. The republic, therefore, continued to be identified with the military and urban middle groups more than the monarchy had ever been.

A vision of industrialization mesmerized those new elements in power. Awed by the transformation industrialization had brought to Germany, France, Great Britain, and the United States, they imperfectly pictured a new Brazil altered through the same process. They never fully crystallized their ideas and failed to conceive a rational plan to industrialize their country. At best they followed a piecemeal policy with weaknesses that forecast failure in attaining their goal and that in the long run probably retarded rather than accelerated industrialization. Symbolic of the ambitions of the middle groups, the provisional government changed the name of the Ministry of Agriculture, designating it the Ministry of Industry. As further encouragement, the government promulgated a protective tariff in 1890 in the hope of promoting manufacturing. It raised to 60 percent the duty on 300 items, principally textiles and food products, which competed with national output. Conversely it lowered the duty on primary goods used in national manufacturing. Even steeper tariffs were promulgated in 1896 and 1900. Fundamental to any industrialization, new engineering schools were established in Recife in 1892; São Paulo, 1894; Pôrto Alegre, 1894; and Bahia, 1896. They would augment the number of available technicians which would be required by any development of industrialization.

Industrialization required greater capital formation. The abolition of slavery seemed to encourage that. From the date of the Golden Law until the advent of the republic, there already had been an increase of 402,000 *contos* in the capital of corporations formed in Rio de Janeiro. It was reminiscent of a similar movement following the termination of the slave trade. The doubling of coffee prices between 1887 and 1892 further increased Brazilian capital. The first minister of finance under the republic, Ruy Barbosa, hoped to encourage capital formation by the freer emission of bank notes and the consequent loosening of credit. He prepared a new banking law, promulgated on January 17, 1890, which divided the nation into three regions, each with a bank empowered to emit paper money. Further, he authorized the printing of a quarter of a million dollars of *contos* (a considerable sum given the time and place), guaranteed not by gold but by government bonds. Subsequently, his plan was modified many times: gold as well as bonds later guaranteed the emissions and the policy of decentralization was abandoned for the single Banco da República. Despite those changes, there was an influx of new currency which created for a brief period an illusion of prosperity. Between 1888 and 1891, the amount of money in circulation more than doubled. Inconvertible paper money rose from 192,000 contos in 1889 to 712,000 in 1894. The jump from a period of difficult credit to one of easy credit animated economic activity to a feverish pitch. Speculation became the order of the day. That whirlwind of speculation, bogus companies, and unsound finance has been dubbed the *Encilhamento*.

To the dismay of the urban middle groups and the anger of the planters, and contrary to the hopes of the government, Brazil gained little from the Encilhamento. The rate of foreign exchange plummeted. Unprecedented inflation robbed the money of its former value. Fiscal instability unnerved the nation's confidence. At the same time and following a traditional pattern, governmental expenditures exceeded revenues, prompting the printing of still more money in order to balance the budget. The severe economic instability of the 1890s exerted a painful pressure on the wage-earning classes in the urban areas, thereby contributing to the general unrest of the decade.

Unrest erupted into full-scale revolt in 1893, the first major challenge to the republic. For some time, chaos had enveloped Rio Grande do Sul, where the so-called Federalists led by Gaspar da Silveira Martins, a politician who had enjoyed high office and prestige during the empire, challenged Júlio de Castilhos, the ultra-Positivist caudilho of the state, and his followers. Within the Federalist ranks were vague monarchical sentiments subordinated to an intense hatred of Castilhos. In early 1893 fighting between the two Gaúcho rivals erupted. Floriano gave his support to Castilhos, president of the state. In September of the same year, a second naval revolt broke out, this one far more serious than its 1891 predecessor. Admiral Custódio de Melo again exercised the leadership. If the myth of military unity still lingered, this schism of the services dispelled it. The jealousy between the navy and the army no longer could be concealed. Immediately the admirals demanded that Marshal Floriano resign, for they long had felt that he minimized the importance of the navy. With his retirement, they hoped to diminish the vast power wielded by the army in the republic. The navy's position was strengthened in December, when the respected and cautious Admiral Luís Felipe Saldanha da Gama, commandant of the Naval Academy, joined the naval rebels, bringing his immense prestige as well as the youthful vigor of the cadets with him. The navy's motives and objectives appeared at this point to be something more than mere jealousy and a desire to increase its voice in the government. Many of the naval officers could not conceal any longer their aristocratic disdain for the republic. Saldanha da Gama issued a cryptic proclamation to the nation which in one passage declared, "Both logic and justice warrant us in seeking by force of arms to replace the Government of Brazil where it was on the 15th of November of 1889. . . ." The degree to which his monarchical preferences represented the true sentiments of the rebellious navy has been the subject of protracted historical controversy. The navy's monarchical tendencies and its dislike of Floriano were sufficient cause for it to cooperate with the Federalists led by Silveira Martins in the South. The admirals and the Federalist chief concurred, for example, that the nation should hold a plebiscite to choose between a republic and a monarchy. The two rebel forces combined to invade Santa Catarina, and in January of 1894 they attacked Paraná, planning to march northward into São Paulo. But a delay was caused by heavy fighting at Lapa in Paraná. This gave the federal government the time to gather its strength sufficiently to repel the rebels and to push them southward again.

Meanwhile, the heavily armed ships in Guanabara Bay threatened to bombard a virtually defenseless capital, a menace which rallied republicans behind Floriano. The situation looked grim for the government, but the president stoically faced the naval firepower and refused to capitulate. At that point outside forces intervened to strengthen his position. The commanders of foreign warships in the harbor—units of the United States, British, French, Italian, and Portuguese navies—declared for obviously humanitarian reasons their opposition to the shelling of the capital. Also, they indicated their intention to protect the property, such as merchant ships, of their own nationals. Their activities restricted the movements of the rebellious fleet. In Washington, the Brazilian minister, Salvador de Mendonça, a dedicated, historic Republican, importuned the government of President Grover

Cleveland to come to the aid of the fledgling sister republic. The United States responded by dispatching more cruisers to the harbor of Rio de Janeiro. Determined not to allow the rebel ships to interfere in any way with commerce in the port, the American naval commander stationed the cruisers between the rebels and the capital in such a way that in order to fire on the city the Brazilian Navy would have to send its shells over the American vessels, a risk the admirals were unwilling to take. Consequently the maneuver prevented the feared bombardment, and the navy's position was reduced to helplessness or to that of a nuisance. Floriano's government proceeded to purchase some warships abroad and prepared a loyalist fleet in Pernambuco. The rebellious naval officers then understood the hopelessness of their situation and abandoned their ships to take asylum aboard the small Portuguese warships in the harbor. With the collapse of the fleet revolt in May of 1894, the government turned its full attention to the south, where after a series of victories it confined the Federalist rebels to the interior of Rio Grande do Sul. They continued to offer sporadic resistance until August of 1895, when the last participants in the revolt surrendered.

Floriano remained unshakable during the revolt. His determination saved the republican government from collapse and the nation from threatening anarchy. Indeed, the early record of the republic had been one of disturbing instability: financial chaos, the dissolution of congress and resignation of the president, two naval revolts, and a rebellion in Rio Grande do Sul. Yet the new republic managed to triumph over those challenges to prove the viability of the new regime. For his leadership through most of the critical period, Floriano earned for himself another epithet, "the consolidator of the Republic."

The general instability contributed to a loss of power by the urban middle groups. Their temporary prominence had been due in part to the vacuum created by the shifting of economic and political power from the old sugar barons and coffee fazendeiros to the new coffee class. This class was demonstrating its vigor—principally in São Paulo, but in

Minas Gerais as well. The urban middle groups had also gained a temporary prominence through their informal relations with the military. The military proved to be an unreliable ally, however, since it was torn by disunion and jealous bickering absorbed much of its energy. Even in the Constituent Assembly some of the military officers had voted against Deodoro and for a civilian candidate for president, while two naval revolts had displayed the enmity between its two branches.

The disunity which plagued the otherwise potent institution of the military favored the cause of the Paulistas who sought to control the government. The prosperous coffee planters for some decades had hoped to grasp the reins of political power in order to insure favorable treatment for their interests. Many of them had supported republican ideology with the expectation of gaining hegemony over a new government, and they strongly favored federalism in order to free their wealthy state from the burden of financing the rest of the nation. The beginnings of the republic disappointed them. They decried the financial mismanagement, the revolts, and the instability.

The crisis of 1893 provided the leaders of São Paulo with an opportunity to assert their authority over the republic. The military, the only institution capable of checking their interests and control, was seriously divided. Floriano needed allies at that crucial moment, and none would have been more effective than the Paulistas with their fat coffers and well trained militia. Furthermore, their strategic position between the capital and the rebellion in the south made their loyalty essential if the federal government was to win. The Paulista politicians carefully made their bargain with Floriano: money, militia, and loyalty in return for the scheduled presidential elections. The well-organized Republican party of São Paulo was confident that in such elections its candidate would win. Once in control of the government in Rio de Janeiro, the Paulistas were certain they could shape the federal system to suit their own interests and guarantee the order and stability their business and trade required to prosper. At any rate, the alternative to Floriano's success and the consequent suppression of the rebellion would be—to the Paulista's thinking—to plunge Brazil into a never-ending cycle of political chaos of a type which bedeviled many Spanish-American republics.

The Paulistas reaped the reward they sought. In the midst of a tense national crisis, Floriano made no effort to keep the electoral machinery from being set in motion. A large group of senators and deputies led by Francisco Glicério of São Paulo organized the Federal Republican party, composed of state republican parties. The party pledged itself to implement and defend the constitution, to support federalism, and to enforce fiscal responsibility, all goals highly desired by the Paulistas. In September of 1893 the party convention unanimously nominated Prudente de Morais of São Paulo for president and Manuel Vitorino Pereira of Bahia for vice-president. They won the elections that were held on March 1, 1894, and took office in November of that year.

The first civilian president had been the first republican governor of São Paulo. He understood perfectly the desires, interests, and ambitions of the Paulista coffee elite to which he gave preference. Consequently the new government often countervened those goals sought by the urban middle groups, whose influence waned rapidly after Floriano left office. President Prudente de Morais, for example, did not encourage industrial expansion. Rather, echoing São Paulo's preoccupation with agriculture, he maintained that the soil— with São Paulo's rich *terra roxa* for coffee clearly in mind— was the nation's chief source of wealth. Those who supported that argument considered industry as an artificial and undesirable form of wealth. Those ideas smacked quaintly of Jeffersonianism and were the last expression of a noble Physiocrat tradition implanted in the eighteenth century. In order to provide the propitious conditions for the Paulistas to exploit their agricultural wealth, to increase trade, and to attract foreign credit, investments, and immigrants, he pledged his government to political stability, financial rehabilitation, and decentralization. Thus able to orient the policies of the government, the coffee interests assumed the dominant political role to match the economic monopoly they had exercised for over a generation.

The sudden, unexpected emergence of the middle sectors as a political force and their brief exercise of power with the military, 1889–1894, was unique in Latin America, a harbinger of what would transpire elsewhere in the early decades of the twentieth century. The middle sectors did not have another opportunity to wield national power in Latin America until President José Batlle took office in Uruguay in 1903. Pushed aside in 1894, the Brazilian middle sectors nursed their political bruises and intensified their economic complaints. For the time being, however, the dynamic coffee interests overshadowed them and forced them to accept a secondary role.

The Heyday of the Old Republic

Brazil's expanding agricultural activities drew inhabitants into hitherto unexploited regions of the country as economic activities increased throughout the nation. Coffee culture moved into new areas of Minas Gerais and western São Paulo. Cattle raising spread into new regions and became the dominant occupation of southern Mato Grosso. The lure of rubber attracted hardy adventurers into Pará, Amazonas, Acre, and northern Mato Grosso. The cultivation of maté increased in the south and the cacao industry expanded along the Bahian coast as far south as northern Espírito Santo. As important as each one of these economic pursuits was, no one of them—nor for that matter any combination of them—could equal the preponderant importance coffee had assumed in the national economy.

Coffee production rose spectacularly during the last decade of the nineteenth century, from 5.5 million 60-kilo bags in 1890–1891 to 16.3 million in 1901–1902. High profits explained much of the increase, but there were other factors favorable to the expanding industry as well. Abundant suitable land was available and accessible; the credit inflation of the period made money for investments easy to obtain; ever-greater numbers of immigrants provided a ready labor force. At the same time, Asian production declined because of diseases which practically wiped out the coffee plantations.

As production rose, coffee came to dominate Brazil's export trade. By 1901, it accounted for approximately 46 percent of the total exports and by 1908, 53 percent. During the first decade of the twentieth century, the Brazilian production of coffee composed approximately 77 percent of the world's total (see Table 5.1). The importance of coffee in Brazil's international trade assumes even greater dimensions when its success is compared to the fate of sugar, which once dominated Brazil's exports. In 1901, sugar barely reached 5 percent of the total exports, and in 1912 sugar accounted for only .007 percent of Brazil's international trade.

Table 5.1. Brazilian Coffee Production, 1901–1940

	Index Numbers 1901–1905 = 100		Brazilian Production in Percent of Total	Percent Increase in Volume of World Consumption Over Preceding Five-Year Period
	World	Brazil		
1901–1905	100	100	76	17
1906–1910	109	113	78	14
1911–1915	105	103	74	6
1916–1920	105	99	72	−6
1921–1925	120	107	67	15
1926–1930	138	119	65	12
1931–1935	219	182	63	5
1936–1940	232	183	60	7

SOURCE: Henry W. Spiegel, *The Brazilian Economy* (Philadelphia, 1949), p. 170.

A large internal market consumed nearly all of the sugar crop. During the same period, coffee far outdistanced the second most important export, rubber. In 1901, rubber provided 28 percent of Brazil's exports, whereas in 1912, although it maintained its importance, the percentage had declined to 22. These statistics indicate the overwhelming predominance coffee assumed in the national economy during the first decades of the republic.

As had been true throughout its history, Brazil depended—or gambled—once again on a single raw product for sale on a capricious world market. As long as coffee sold well, the nation prospered, but provisions had not been made, as they never had been made in the past, to lessen the economy's vulnerability. The potential danger grew as the coffee planters concentrated their sales in a few countries. The United States, Great Britain, and Germany bought fully three quarters of the coffee. The possibility was all too real that any decline in demand from those purchasers would immediately affect the price and have drastic repercussions on the Brazilian economy. Some Brazilians noted the latent threat but none did anything about it. To the contrary, the planters went on expanding, as they hoped blithely that with their superproduction they could monopolize the world market and hence control it. At least for a limited time, the fazendeiros did manipulate it to their advantage.

The influence of coffee extended beyond the realm of economics into both national and international politics. The once-dominant sugar barons had partially set the tone of nineteenth century diplomacy. They sold their sugar to Europe and looked to the Old World as a mentor, seeking spiritual inspiration in Portugal, cultural orientation in France, and commercial and political guidance from Great Britain. The coffee producers, on the other hand, found their best market in the United States, as did the rubber and cocoa exporters. Since 1865, the United States had taken the single largest share of Brazil's coffee; and after 1870, with the abolition of import duties on coffee, the United States bought more than half of the Brazilian coffee beans sold abroad. By 1912, New York had become the world's largest rubber market and nearly 60 percent of the rubber traded there came from the Amazon. Likewise, the United States consumed more Brazilian cocoa than any other country. The result was that by 1912 the United States bought 36 percent of Brazil's exports, while the second most important market, Great Britain, purchased only 15 percent. The emergence of the United States as the best customer of Brazilian exports helped to shift Brazil's diplomatic axis from Europe to the United States. By 1905, Washington had replaced London as Brazil's principal diplomatic post.

Coffee's dominance over the national economy concentrated economic power in the region best suited to coffee production. The peculiar *terra roxa* soil in the states of São Paulo, Minas Gerais, and Rio de Janeiro, because it was deep and porous and contained humus, was particularly given to the growing of healthy coffee trees. Mild temperatures and adequate rainfall also contributed to coffee development in that region. Consequently, for topographic and climatic reasons, the production of coffee concentrated in southeastern Brazil, giving the three coffee-producing states of that area a formidable influence over the economy of Brazil. That influence seems all the more impressive when one considers that geographically the Southeast constituted only a small parcel of the immense national territory. Yet, those states counted nearly half of Brazil's population; they contributed over half the national revenue; they boasted of the best transportation and communication networks in the country.

Within the tripartite control of the economy, the state of São Paulo played the leading role. Of the total exports of Brazil for 1916, São Paulo furnished 46 percent, whereas Minas Gerais supplied only 22 percent, and Rio de Janeiro 18 percent. During optimum years, the bandeirante state alone harvested between 65 and 70 percent of all the coffee and provided 30 to 40 percent of all the revenue to the national treasury. The economic importance of São Paulo promoted a notation in an official report of the Ministry of the Treasury in 1912 that, "as is always the case," São Paulo held first place among the states as the chief exporter. In that year, São Paulo furnished 50 percent of the nation's exports. In striking contrast, the formerly dominant sugar area of Pernambuco barely contributed 1 percent of Brazil's exports.

In truth, a green wave of coffee trees swept westward across São Paulo inundating the state. Moving inland by train, the traveler passed endless rows of coffee trees. At the end of the nineteenth century, Frank G. Carpenter left this description of the world's largest coffee fazenda, the Dumont plantation, some 300 miles inland from São Paulo:

The estate itself comprises thousands of acres. It has over 13,000 acres of coffee fields and 2,500 acres of pasture land. It is planting more trees every year and is kept like a garden. To go round the estate one would have to travel 40 miles, and more than 40 miles of railroad track have been built upon it to transport coffee.

The estate supports 5,000 people. It has 23 colonies, ranging in size from 70 families downward. It has great stores to supply its workmen with food. It has a bakery, a drug store, a saw mill, a planing mill, and at one time it had a brewery. It has vast factories for cleaning coffee and preparing it for market, and it has offices in which there are bookkeepers taking account of every item of expense, so that they can tell you how much coffee each of the 5,000,000 trees is producing, and give every item connected with picking the coffee and sending it to the seaports.

The labourers on the estate are thoroughly organized. Each man has his own work, the employees being directed by administrators, each of whom has charge of a block of trees, ranging up to a million; these trees are divided among families, each family taking charge of from 3,000 to 4,000 trees, planting them and keeping them clean.

. . .

Within the last ten years great changes have taken place in coffee-growing in Brazil. Formerly, everything was done by slaves, who worked under overseers and who put in nearly fifteen hours a day. . . . Now that the slaves are emancipated, most of them have left the coffee regions and Italians have been imported to take their places. The labourers on the Dumont fazenda are nearly all Italians. I am told they make far better workmen than the negroes.[2]

An influx of Italian workers was part of a population boom which accompanied the economic prosperity of São Paulo. Owing both to foreign immigration and to internal migration, the state's population more than tripled in three decades, increasing from 1,384,753 in 1890 to 4,592,188 in 1920. The capital of São Paulo state, also named São Paulo, became the dynamic financial and managerial center of the Southeast. Santos, the port of São Paulo, shipped most of Brazil's coffee to the burgeoning markets of the United States, England, Germany, and France. Between 1900 and 1914, the annual quantity of coffee handled by Santos dou-

2. *South America: Social, Industrial, and Political* (Akron, Ohio, 1900), pp. 494–95; 449.

bled from 5,742,362 sacks of 130 pounds each to 11,308,784. Santos testified eloquently to the fact that São Paulo consistently harvested and exported more coffee than any other state.

The economic strength of the Southeast conferred political power on the coffee triangle of São Paulo, Minas Gerais, and Rio de Janeiro during the Old Republic and particularly on the state of São Paulo. Control of the presidency unlocked the door to economic legislation and patronage. So, throughout the Old Republic, the dynamic coffee states successfully maneuvered to gain the presidency and thus to enhance their local economies. The first three civilian presidents, who governed from 1894 to 1906, were Prudente José de Morais, Manuel Ferraz de Campos Sales, and Francisco de Paula Rodrigues Alves, all from São Paulo. The next two presidents, governing from 1906 to 1910, were Afonso Augusto Moreira Pena and Nilo Peçanha, respectively from Minas Gerais and Rio de Janeiro. With two exceptions the other presidents down to 1930 came from either São Paulo or Minas Gerais. Coming from areas in which coffee dominated, those presidents carried out programs favorable for their elections. The First Secretary of the United States legation, G. L. Lorillard, aptly reported this reciprocity between coffee and politics:

All the Northern States are bitterly opposed to the hold the coffee planters have over the Government and complain that their legitimate needs are being sacrificed in favor of the planters. The Executive, however, clings to its purpose of doing everything to please the coffee interests. The President fully realizes that he was elected by the planters and that he must now return the favor.[3]

It was obvious, much to the displeasure of the rest of Brazil, that the coffee interests dictated most of the policies of the government. Commenting on that situation, Lorillard wrote:

3. Lorillard to Root, Feb. 4, 1907, Vol. 120, No. 103, Brazilian Dispatches, National Archives of the United States of America, General Records of the Department of State, Washington, D.C. (hereafter abbreviated as NA).

At the present time, however, there exists a group of persons which is stronger than the Executive and Congress combined. As is universally admitted here, never before has the country and especially everyone connected with the Government been so much under the influence of the coffee planters as at the present and any measure which is seriously desired by that element is sure of immediate passage by Congress.[4]

That alliance of the coffee planters and the federal government came quickly after 1889, and it superseded all previous political arrangements, so that political control by the coffee interests was one of the principal characteristics of the Old Republic. Because São Paulo played the dominant role within that alliance, this period of Brazilian history has been designated as one of Paulista control.

The coffee interests of the triangular alliance managed to govern Brazil through agreements, cohesion, coalitions of state parties, and political maneuvering, usually with the implicit or explicit backing of the army. One of the curious aspects of the Old Republic was that no national political parties developed. The old Liberal and Conservative parties of the Second Empire disappeared without leaving any heirs. The Partido Republicano Federal (Federal Republican party) held some initial promise as a nationally based party. Soon after the party nominated Prudente de Morais in 1894, it began to disintegrate because of internal quarrels. Glicério and Prudente argued and separated, and the president eventually triumphed over the party leader. As Glicério's prestige plummeted so did his power. The party fell with him so that by 1897 it ceased to be significant politically. Governor Luís Viana of Bahia publicly nominated Campos Sales for the presidency in 1898. The governing hierarchies of São Paulo, Minas Gerais, and Pernambuco seconded the nomination. President Prudente de Morais bespoke his approval. Campos Sales declared himself to be the candidate of the "traditional Republican party," that historic but weak party which traced its roots back to the Republican Manifesto. Indeed, both Prudente and Campos Sales were "historic republicans."

4. Lorillard to Root, Jan. 28, 1907, Vol. 119, No. 101, Brazilian Dispatches, NA.

Campos Sales showed a growing ambivalence toward political parties. He claimed his political ideas to be his own and boasted that he was above party politics, emphasizing on more than one occasion that the president of Brazil should not at the same time be the chief of a political party. But on the practical political plane, he began to deal with the governors of the most important states to assure their support. He once confessed, "In all the struggles, I try to strengthen myself by getting the support of the States because in them resides the true political force." It was a political philosophy he repeated on several occasions.

The political tone was quickly set for the following decades. The incumbent president with the approval and support of the large states selected the presidential candidate. The successful candidate in turn dealt with the principal state governors, promising them favors in return for support. Under the system of the "politics of the states" the governors sent congressmen to Rio de Janeiro favorable to the president's programs, and in return the president neither intervened nor interfered in the governments of those states. On the one level, then, the president and governors depended upon each other's good will and cooperation. A similar reciprocity existed on another level between the governors and the *coroneis*. The latter regimented the local vote which elected the former. The governors in turn respected the local authority of the *coroneis*. Some *coroneis* of course opposed some state governments, but that position generally lessened their authority and prestige and was to be avoided if at all possible. Politically the Old Republic rested firmly on a rural base.

James Bryce noted with amazement in 1910 that there were no organized national political parties in Brazil and observed that state issues crossed and warped federal issues, which in turn confused state policies. He concluded quite rightly that politicians were more important than parties. Failing to organize a strong party, the traditional republicans abdicated their brief hegemony in politics. It was not long before some of the older and more experienced imperial politicians returned to power. Both presidents Rodrigues

Alves and Afonso Pena, 1902–1909, for example, had been Counselors of the Empire.

From time to time new efforts were made to organize national parties, but the results were inconclusive at best. José Gomes de Pinheiro Machado, a Gaúcho politician, was among the most energetic in making those efforts. He organized the new *Partido Republicano Federal* in 1905 and later the *Partido Republicano Conservador* (Conservative Republican party). Neither party became truly national; instead, they remained organized on a state level with little connection between the state organizations. The nomination and endorsement of presidential candidates remained in the hands of either the incumbent president or an informal congressional caucus. A lack of institutionalized procedures was but one of the many disadvantages the system evinced. As the system functioned in practice, federalism became regionalism and national interests were sacrificed to regional ones. However, on the positive side, that system did manage to provide a candidate for the presidency and guarantee his election. Hence the political process was continuous. It did not break down into the chaos characteristic of the political system of so many of Brazil's republican neighbors.

The masses, of course, played no role in the political process, their interest being subordinated, as it always had been, to the well-being of the oligarchy. For their part, the middle sectors increasingly resented their own political impotence, a condition which encouraged frustration. The literacy requirement to vote enfranchised a minority: adult literate males. Now, it so happened that since the president was chosen by direct vote of those few male literates and since the economically powerful states tended to be those with the largest populations and the best educational systems, São Paulo, Minas Gerais, Rio de Janeiro, and Rio Grande do Sul held a distinct command in the presidential elections. By 1910, slightly over fifty percent of the electorate resided in those four states, and those voters cast over half the ballots. The representative system of government proudly proclaimed in the Constitution of 1891 represented only the upper echelon of Brazilian society and only one limited geographic region.

Through control of the government, the coffee interests sought to maintain the political stability necessary for the progress of the nation or, perhaps more realistically stated, of the Southeast and for profitable international trade. They succeeded remarkably well for a generation. Prudente de Morais quelled the rebellion in the South in 1895. Some local rebellions flared up periodically but they were easily handled. During the heyday of the old Republic, civil order reigned and Brazil remained generally peaceful.

Clearly it was in the best interests of the coffee class to encourage economic stability and progress. The *Encilhamento* had set in motion an inflationary and speculative spiral which disturbed the planters, who felt it essential to reestablish Brazil's international credit, strengthen the national currency, and balance the budget. The financial crisis reached its peak in 1898. To stave off disaster, President-elect Campos Sales visited European bankers and governments to reach an understanding with Brazil's creditors and to negotiate new loans. He obtained a funding loan of £10 million from the house of Rothschild which saved the government of Prudente de Morais from bankruptcy. A sworn enemy of inflationary policies, Campos Sales entered upon his term of office determined above all else to rehabilitate Brazil's finances. He named as his minister of finance the able Joaquim Murtinho, who shared his determination. Murtinho also shared the belief that Brazil had misspent its capital foolishly in the previous decade on an irrational attempt to industrialize. Brazil's wealth, he and the president agreed, came from agriculture, not industry. While the president judiciously balanced the budget by cutting expenses and abandoning public works projects, the finance minister halted further emission of money, increased taxes, and concentrated on the redemption of paper money. To earn more money, the government raised tariff rates in 1900, which were further augmented in 1905 and 1908, and encouraged greater exportation. The program showed the success the government hoped for. The amount of inconvertible money in circulation dropped and the rate of exchange improved. The budgets began to reveal a surplus. The government improved its international credit rating by paying off its loans. An immediate influx of foreign funds resulted. Rodrigues Alves and his own skillful finance minister, Leopoldo de Bulhões, continued the policies of their predecessors. Obviously, the program of financial stabilization required sacrifices, which did not endear it to the majority of the Brazilians.

Always with an eye on the world markets, the coffee planters continued to urge the government to stabilize the national currency and to fix the rate of exchange. Very early in his administration, President Afonso Pena turned his attention to those problems. On December, 1906, he signed a law establishing the *Caixa de Conversão* (Conversion Office). Primarily concerned with external financial transactions, it received deposits of gold and issued against those deposits convertible paper bills with a fixed exchange value. The paper bills it issued always equaled the amount of gold held by the Conversion Office. The principal advantages of the plan were that a fixed rate of exchange strengthened Brazil's links with the financial centers of the world, halted the constant rise in running expenses which weakened the planters' economic position, and improved Brazil's place in the world markets. The coffee planters endorsed the Conversion Office, and other business groups quickly echoed the praise when they saw the steady rate of exchange it maintained. Before the untimely death of Pena in mid-1909, almost one quarter of the currency of Brazil was backed by gold. The financial health of the nation continued to improve until war in Europe upset Brazil's exchange rate again.

With the encouragement of state and federal governments, coffee production continued to increase. By 1900, 10 million bags left Brazilian ports for overseas consumption. The increasing supply regularly lowered the price, but still profits remained sufficiently alluring to attract greater and greater investment in coffee planting. In the last decade of the nineteenth century, the number of coffee trees under cultivation in São Paulo increased from 220 to 520 million. By the opening of the twentieth century the planters realized that they faced a serious threat of overproduction. The threatened coffee interests presented their problems to the government, which undertook to help them. In 1902, the government forbade any new coffee-tree plantings for five years. Nonetheless, because of considerable speculative planting before that date, coffee production rose at a much faster rate than world consumption. By 1905, Brazil had 11 million sacks of coffee in warehouse storage, and productivity was still rising as new trees matured. In 1906, Brazil produced a record coffee crop of 20 million, and Brazil was not the only country with coffee to sell. Clearly Brazil was headed toward economic trouble, and the coffee alliance expected the government to come to its rescue.

In order to avoid the financial debacle forewarned by such overproduction, the government took steps to regulate the production and sale of coffee. The prohibition of new coffee tree plantings was extended to 1912. By means of the Convention of Taubaté, signed on February 26, 1906, the governors of São Paulo, Minas Gerais, and Rio de Janeiro sought to control the marketing of coffee. The convention authorized a valorization scheme whereby, if the coffee prices fell below a minimum level, the state and federal governments would remove the beans from the market by purchasing and holding them until the price rose again. President Rodrigues Alves opposed it, but Congress approved the convention and pledged federal cooperation. Valorization was popular with the three coffee states, and it was their influence which enlisted federal support. Other states complained loudly, but ineffectively, that valorization was governmental favoritism.

Both the Rodrigues Alves and Pena administrations made strenuous efforts to limit the production of coffee and to withhold it from the market so that the enormous surplus could be sold at reasonable prices. With the aid of loans from foreign and national banks and the cooperation of the federal government, São Paulo alone held 8 million sacks of coffee off the market in 1907. The following year São Paulo harvested one of the smallest crops in a decade, thanks to the policy of restricted planting as well as to adverse weather conditions. Between 1908 and 1912, the harvests were small, permitting the government gradually to sell its stored coffee and thus liquidate its investment. The government and the planters judged the valorization scheme a success, and with various modifications it was used until 1929.

The transportation of coffee to market was another problem facing the planters as well as other producers of agricultural exports. The 9,500 miles of railroad tracks laid in the nineteenth century were insignificant in such a large country as Brazil. Aware of the pressing need for more transportation, the republican chiefs of state accelerated railroad expansion. Of the approximately 7,000 miles of rails laid during the first decade and a half of the twentieth century, half was laid during the Pena administration. In a single year, 1910, the addition of 1,200 miles of new rails increased trackage by 10.8 percent. Between 1906 and 1910, four important railway lines were built: Madeira-Mamoré, São Luís de Maranhão-Caxias, Sáo Paulo-Mato Grosso, and São Paulo-Rio Grande de Sul. The last mentioned route connected Rio de Janeiro and São Paulo by rail with the Rio de la Plata. By 1914, the railroad traversed southern Mato Grosso, linking that distant western state with the federal capital. Rails replaced the traditional water route which had for centuries connected that area with the capital. The opening of that line thereby diminished the importance of the Rio de la Plata network as a means of unifying the nation. By the outbreak of World War I, Brazil had increased its railroad network to 16,000 miles, most of which—it should be no surprise—could be found in the coffee-producing states. São Paulo, Minas Gerais, and Rio de Janeiro accounted for well over half the total national trackage. Certainly one of the most profitable of the railroad lines was that connecting the capital of São Paulo with Santos. With a monopoly over coffee transportation, it carried so much that it frequently paid dividends of 50 percent per annum. Thus, the pattern well established during the first decades of railroad expansion continued: the rails tied the plantations to foreign markets, facilitating exports but also deepening dependency.

The renovation of ports received the full attention of both state and federal governments. Between the end of the century and World War I major improvements were made in the harbor facilities of Manaus, Belém, Recife, Salvador, Vitória, Rio de Janeiro, Santos, Paranaguá, Pôrto Alegre, and other smaller ports. Channels were deepened, new wharfs and piers added, and more warehouses built, all with the object of facilitating the shipment of coffee, rubber, cacao, tobacco, cotton, maté, and hides to the world's markets.

Brazilians were obsessed with the idea of material progress during the Old Republic. The nation paused in 1908 to commemorate the centenary of the opening of the ports. None of the celebrations surpassed the grandiose exposition held in Rio de Janeiro. It delighted the Brazilians, who proudly viewed in the exhibits the impressive progress they had made in a hundred years.

More than anything else, the cities testified to that progress. On the one hand, new towns appeared on the map. Approximately 500 new municipalities were established during this period. In 1897, the Mineiros began to build their new capital, Belo Horizonte. On the other hand, old cities showed new vigor. Table 5.2 indicates the rapid population growth of the major cities. São Paulo recorded the most phenomenal growth, increasing at a rate above 25 percent every five years after 1895. Bryce described the bandeirante capital in 1910 as "the briskest and most progressive place in all

Table 5.2. Population Growth of the Capitals of the Major States, 1890 and 1920

State Capital	1890	1920
Salvador	174,412	283,422
Belo Horizonte	——	55,563
Recife	111,556	238,843
Niterói	34,269	86,238
Pôrto Alegre	52,421	179,263
São Paulo	64,935	579,033
Rio de Janeiro (federal capital)	552,651	1,157,873

Brazil. . . . The alert faces, and the air of stir and movement, as well as handsome public buildings rising on all hands, with a large, well-planted public garden in the middle of the city, give the impression of energy and progress." The English diplomat commented on the high percentage of foreign immigrants: Italians, Portuguese, Spaniards, Germans, English, and French. The developing industry and commerce of the state added to its notable prosperity. A rapid and constant construction program altered the physiognomy of the city. In 1906, the imposing Municipal Theater opened its doors and thereafter contributed mightily to the cultural formation of the state and nation. The new Polytechnical School (1895), Conservatory of Music and Drama (1906), and Faculty of Medicine and Surgery (1913) also made significant local and national contributions.

Rio de Janeiro, too, underwent change. Shortly after his inauguration, President Alves focused his attention on the renovation of the unhealthy and underdeveloped national capital, initiating a program to beautify the city, build a first-rate port, and eliminate yellow fever. The president entrusted the eminent Dr. Oswaldo Cruz with the task of eradicating yellow fever in the unhealthy lowlands upon which parts of the capital were built. Yellow fever first had appeared in Rio de Janeiro toward the end of 1849 and in the years thereafter became the scourge of the city, making life there hazardous for both residents and visitors. Fortunately, the years marking the turn of the century witnessed scientific advances which conquered that tropical disease. Taking his cue from the accomplishments of North American scientists and doctors in Cuba and Panama, Dr. Cruz vigorously undertook a four-point program to kill mosquitoes, destroy their breeding ground, isolate the sick, and vaccinate all the inhabitants. In the year in which he began his campaign, 1903, there were 584 recorded deaths attributed to yellow fever. The following year the figure dropped to 53 and, in 1906, to zero. Cruz's energetic and effective campaign made the capital as healthy as any contemporary European city.

Concurrently, the newly appointed prefect of the Federal District, Pereira Passos, set about to rebuild Rio de Janeiro. He brutally cut a wide swath through the old business district to create the ample Avenida Central (today named Rio-Branco) and laid out the pleasant Avenida Beira Mar which skirted the seashore. He enlarged and redesigned the parks, constructed new buildings to which the Municipal Theater, inaugurated in 1909, bore splendid testimony, and cleaned up the most unpleasant parts of the capital. Meanwhile, engineers were rebuilding and expanding the capital's port facilities, for which modern equipment was purchased and installed. Aided generously by a luxuriant and verdant nature, Pereira Passos created the modern wonder of Rio de Janeiro, which has been a source of admiration and awe for natives and tourists alike. After giving a lengthy description of the new Rio de Janeiro in its 1908 edition, the *Almanaque Brasileiro Garnier* rhapsodized, "The rapid transformation . . . turned this capital into one of the most beautiful cities and perhaps, without exaggeration, the most beautiful city in the world." Foreign visitors have tended to agree with that evaluation.

As the intellectual and political center of the republic, Rio de Janeiro vibrated with activity. The quaint colonial street, Rua do Ouvidor, which threaded its narrow way through the heart of the business district, provided the locus of intellectual and political discussion. Pedestrians were crowded together between the buildings, one, two, and three stories high, lining the famed street. Their walls painted white, pink, blue, yellow, and pastel shades were as colorful as the crowds they framed. The women paused to gaze into the elaborately decorated shop windows displaying the latest French and English imports; they still expressed an old preference for French styles, demonstrated by the fact that two of the foremost shops for the carioca elite were French, Madame Coulon's and *Au Printemps*. The men, newspapers in hand, ambled toward their favorite restaurant or coffee bar for yet another cup of coffee and still more conversation. The ubiquitous coffee bar was a notable and essential feature in every town or city, for Brazilians were much given to coffee and conversation, and more business was transacted over a demitasse of strong, sweet coffee in a corner coffee bar than was ever done in any office. The price for a small cup of the always freshly made beverage was a penny and a half. The steaming jet-black coffee was poured directly from the stove into the cup, already half filled with sugar by the customer. There was great truth to the Brazilian proverb that good coffee should be "as strong as the devil, as black as ink, as hot as hell, and as sweet as love." The coffee animated conversation as it relaxed the drinkers. They tarried in energetic discussion, pausing frequently to shake the hand of a passing acquiantance and to inquire into his health and that of his family. For intimates there was a warm embrace, given with genuine cheer and enthusiasm.

Poets and politicians jostled one another in the Rua do Ouvidor and its restaurants. The politicians were distinguishable by their tall, black silk hats. They held daily receptions, feeling the pulse of the populace, carrying on debates begun in the chambers. Crowded around the small circular tables, poets read and explained their works while friends and rivals criticized or complimented. They filled their conversations with French and occasionally English expressions and displayed a thorough knowledge of what the European publishing houses had been turning out. Such serious tones were enveloped in a symphony of cries from lottery-ticket peddlers and hucksters selling a wide variety of wares. Added to that cacophony was the babble of French, English, German, Spanish, and Italian, for Rio de Janeiro had become a gathering point for foreigners, who also showed a preference for the Rua do Ouvidor.

The cities nurtured a cultural life of ever-widening dimensions and importance. Machado de Assis had already reached a position of eminence in the Portuguese-speaking world. He was instrumental, in 1897, in founding the Brazilian Academy of Letters, of which he was president until his death in 1908. Meanwhile, his pen produced *Dom Casmurro* (1900), considered by most critics to be Brazil's finest novel. *Dom Casmurro* enjoyed considerable popular success; it was a best-seller, a category which permitted the printing of 2,000 to 2,500 copies per edition and guaranteed a sale of between 600 and 800 copies the first year. Worthy to be Machado's successor was Afonso Henriques de Lima Barreto, a writer of great sensitivity and insight, whose biting prose dissected the manners and mores of urban and suburban life.

The year 1902 became a literary landmark with the publication of two remarkable books. The first was *Os Sertões* (translated into English as *Rebellion in the Backlands*), one of the most significant works of the new analytical school of literature. Critics hailed it as a classic. The author, Euclides da Cunha, described in it the armed rebellion of Antônio Conselheiro, a religious mystic, which had taken place in the 1890s in the backland town of Canudos in Bahia. To da Cunha, the rebellion symbolized the struggle of man against nature, of civilization against barbarism. The tragedy of the backlands, he believed, was that civilization had abandoned both the area and its inhabitants to barbarism. The villain of the plot was the cities; the victims were Antônio Conselheiro and his rustic followers. Da Cunha impressed upon his compatriots the immense difference between the coast and the hinterlands, the two Brazils. In the interior, da Cunha saw the "bedrock" of the Brazilian race. He observed,

> As we make our way deeper into the land, we come upon the first fixed groupings—in the *caipira* of the south and the *babareo* of the north. The pure white, the pure Negro, and the pure Indian are now a rarity. The generalized miscegenation, meanwhile, has given rise to every variety of racial crossing; but, as we continue on our way, these shadings tend to disappear, and there is to be seen a greater uniformity of physical and moral characteristics. In brief, we have struck bedrock—in the man of the backlands.[5]

That theme would soon be taken up by the nationalists, who felt they saw in the interior the "real" Brazil, untainted and uncontaminated by foreign influences. But in addressing the theme of civilization versus barbarism which had haunted intellectuals for a century, da Cunha expressed ambivalence and wrestled heroically with mental dilemmas. His book reflected the conflict evident between European theory so willingly imbibed by the intellectuals and the reality imposed by

5. Euclides da Cunha, *Rebellion in the Backlands* (Chicago, 1944), p. 481.

their own observation of Brazil. Da Cunha could not reconcile the two. His admiration of the people of the sertão and of their ability to adapt to their environment pervaded the text, and yet he concluded in accordance with European ideas a la Spencer that "progress" emanating from the Europeanized city must redeem those people through education.

The second book, an analytical novel by José Pereira da Graça Aranha, studied Brazilian society, examining it through the eyes of both foreign immigrants and natives. Highly critical of his society, Graça Aranha observed that the nations of the New World suffered from all the evils afflicting the Old. He also concluded that the only "true Brazilian" was the mulatto. Contributing to the intensifying feelings of nationalism, he bitterly attacked Brazilian dependency. In one passage, his characters debated that dependency in these sharp words:

"You gentlemen speak of independence," observed the municipal judge caustically, "but I don't see it. Brazil is, and has always been, a colony. Our regime is not a free one. We are a protectorate."

"And who protects us?" interrupted Brederodes, gesticulating with his monacle.

"Wait a minute, man. Listen. Tell me: where is our financial independence? What is the real money that dominates us? Where is our gold? What is the use of our miserable paper currency if it isn't to buy English pounds? Where is our public property? What little we have is mortgaged. The customs revenues are in the hands of the English. We have no ships. We have no railroads, either; they are all in the hands of the foreigners. Is it, or is it not, a colonial regime disguised with the name of a free nation. . . . Listen. You don't believe me. I would like to be able to preserve our moral and intellectual patrimony, our language, but rather then continue this poverty, this turpitude at which we have arrived, it is better for one of Rothchild's bookkeepers to manage our financial affairs and for a German colonel to set things in order."[6]

Important studies in history and literary criticism accompanied the brilliant achievements in literature. João Capis-

6. José Pereira da Graça Aranha, Canaan (Boston, 1920), p. 196. Copyright 1920 by the Four Seas Company. Quoted by permission of Bruce Humphries.

trano de Abreu, raising Brazilian historiography to a new height of sophistication, meditated on the nation's past and suggested several cogent theories of its evolution as well as a meaningful periodization of it. He wrestled with the problems of explaining the maintenance of Brazilian unity and was the first to perceive the importance of the sertão as a major factor in the unification and "Brazilianization" of the nation. Rodolfo Garcia and Afonso Taunay explored more fully some of the paths indicated by Capistrano. João Ribeiro and João Pandiá Calógeras were less successful in their attempts to write interpretive histories of their country, but Manuel de Oliveira Lima made an important revisionist contribution in 1908 when he rehabilitated a former monarch in his *D. João VI no Brasil* (King Jõao VI in Brazil). An exceptionally fine history of the Second Empire came from the pen of Joaquim Nabuco in 1899 in the form of a four-volume biography of his father, Senator Nabuco de Araújo. *Um Estadista do Império* (A Statesman of the Empire) has remained a standard classic for the study of nineteenth-century Brazil.

In the field of literary criticism three scholars predominated. Sílvio Romero chided his compatriots for their unquestioning aping of European literary styles and urged them to create a national literature. His massive *História da Literatura Brasileira* (History of Brazilian Literature), published in 1888, was the first serious evaluation of Brazilian literature. José Veríssimo published a six-volume *Estudos da Literatura Brasileira* (Studies of Brazilian Literature) between 1901 and 1907 and a *História da Literatura Brasileira* in 1916. The third of the triumvirate was Tristão de Alencar Araripe Junior, distinguished for his critical essays on literary luminaries.

The intellectuals awoke fully to the economic, political, and social realities of a changing Brazil. They identified and discussed many of the problems and innovations, and thus helped to make Brazil not only conscious of itself but better known abroad. By so doing they contributed at the turn of the century to the wave of nationalism inundating Brazil, a nation confident for the first time of its new republican institutions.

In retrospect, the era which began with the return of the government to civilian rule and continued through the first

decade of the twentieth century emerges as one of the fruitful periods in Brazilian history. The few revolts which marred
the period were minor, localized, and swiftly quelled. They
were exceptions to a general tranquillity and to the stability
which characterized the period. Most historians pay tribute
to the good order and material progress during the Paulista
domination. Perhaps the situation was best summarized by
the Mexican diplomatic representative in Rio de Janeiro who
informed his government in 1910, "The development of the
vast wealth of Brazil is visible. In almost every case, the progress in these last years has been greater than even the most
optimistic had hoped for."[7]

The Triumph of Diplomacy

Prosperous and peaceful at home, Brazil for the first
time in several decades could turn its full attention to international affairs and concentrate its energy on the formation
and execution of a constructive foreign policy. When the
republic replaced the monarchy, Brazil still had not demar-
cated its lengthy frontiers, save those with Uruguay in 1851
and with Paraguay in 1872. The republican ministers of
foreign relations turned their full attention to the boundary
questions.

The first order of business was the Missions territory
disputed by Argentina and Brazil. Foreign Minister Quintino
Bocaiúva had suggested that the two nations divide the territory, but the Brazilian congress adamantly refused to ap-
prove such a treaty. The two neighbors then agreed to submit their claims to an arbiter and chose President Grover
Cleveland. The death of Baron Aguiar de Andrade, the chief
of a special mission which had just arrived in Washington to
begin the preparation of Brazil's case, left the Brazilian government in a quandary as to whom it should appoint to lead
the important mission. It was then that official circles began

7. Mexican Chargé d'Affaires in Rio de Janeiro to the Secretary of Foreign Relations,
May 15, 1910, Folder No. 3053-12, Archivo de la Secretaría de Relaciones Exteriores
del México, Mexico City.

to remember Brazil's historian of the Plata, José Maria da Silva Paranhos Júnior, the Baron of Rio-Branco. Years of research, firsthand experience, and a reputation among Brazil's intellectuals for his studies of the Plata qualified him to head the mission. The Floriano government summoned him from his European diplomatic post. In his preparation of Brazil's case, he based his arguments on eighteenth-century documents and maps as well as on Brazilian settlement of the area. So skillfully had he mastered the material that he was able to use Argentine arguments to strengthen the Brazilian claim. When President Cleveland delivered the arbitral award on February 6, 1895, Rio-Branco won an overwhelming victory. The Missions territory, 13,680 square miles, fell to Brazil.

The government then assigned Rio-Branco to work on the troublesome boundary between Brazil and French Guiana. France made broad claims which extended down to the mouth of the Amazon. The two nations agreed to submit their dispute to arbitration and chose the president of Switzerland as arbiter. Once again Rio-Branco had to write detailed memorials in which he employed history and geography as the handmaidens of diplomacy. On December 1, 1900, the Swiss president awarded the controversial territory, approximately 101,000 square miles, to Brazil. Rio-Branco had triumphed in both the north and the south, permitting Brazil to expand peacefully in both directions and to mark the frontiers which had vexed it for four hundred years. The two diplomatic triumphs made him a national hero. The Brazilians rejoiced to see themselves twice vindicated internationally, first with a victory over their archrival, Argentina, and then with an award over a major European nation, France. After more than two decades, during which time the once-brilliant imperial diplomacy had declined to banal routine, Rio-Branco successfully projected national interests into the international sphere.

In December of 1902, Rio-Branco returned to Rio de Janeiro from his post in Berlin to assume the portfolio of foreign affairs in the new government of President Rodrigues Alves. As foreign minister, he resolved to complete the task he had begun so auspiciously as a diplomat, that of marking the Brazilian frontiers. He faced at once the acrimonious dispute with Bolivia over the Acre territory in the heartland of South America. By firm pressure and adroit maneuvering, Rio-Branco brought Bolivia to negotiate the quarrel and in 1903 to sign the Treaty of Petropolis by which Brazil acquired the rubber-rich Acre, approximately 73,000 square miles. In return, Bolivia received a small strip of territory which gave it access to the Madeira River and thus to the Atlantic, as well as a perpetual pledge of freedom of river navigation, 10 million dollars, and Brazil's promise to construct a railroad on the right bank of the Madeira which would bypass the rapids and give Bolivia ascess to the lower Madeira. The Treaty of Petropolis completed the demarcation of the frontier from the Atlantic Ocean in the south to Peru in the far west.

Peru, claiming Acre for itself, as well as a large part of Brazil's Amazon basin, vociferously protested the settlement provided by the treaty. Rio-Branco then focused his attention on the Peruvian claims. Peru proved to be more difficult than Bolivia to bring to the negotiating table. Finally, with a treaty signed in mid-1904, the two nations found a modus vivendi. Lima, however, persisted in using delaying tactics in the hope that somehow time would favor its case; but if time favored anyone it was Brazil. The constant change of Peruvian foreign ministers and diplomatic representatives to Brazil weakened the presentation of the Peruvian case, whereas the five years of negotiations of Brazil under one minister provided a continuity which strengthened its position. On September 8, 1909, Lima consented to sign a treaty defining the boundaries. Once again, the principle of *uti possidetis* determined ownership. Brazilians inhabited the extensive area claimed by Peru. Approximately 63,000 square miles were awarded to Brazil and the newly acquired Acre confirmed as Brazilian. The Spanish-speaking neighbor received less than 10,000 square miles. In addition, Rio-Branco defined the 972-mile frontier, thereby closing Brazil's far-western boundaries.

While the protracted negotiations with Lima were running their course, Rio-Branco attended to other frontier problems. The boundary with British Guiana was resolved in 1904 by a division of the territory in dispute. In the same year, Brazil and Ecuador (then neighbors) signed a treaty resolving their boundary problems. A treaty with Venezuela in 1905 settled the northern frontier. Brazil and the Netherlands negotiated an agreement in 1906 which determined the limits of Surinam; in 1907 Colombia and Brazil reached an understanding which later would permit them to mark their frontiers. Rio-Branco capped the final demarcation of frontiers with the magnanimous Treaty of 1909 with Uruguay, assenting to that small neighbor's petition to redraw the boundaries between the two countries, to give Uruguay the right of navigation on the Jaguarão River and Lake Mirim.

In fifteen years, Rio-Branco had marked Brazil's boundaries, the cause of debate and conflict for four centuries. The most obvious result of his settlements was the addition to Brazil of approximately 342,000 square miles of territory, an area greater in size than France. Somewhat more difficult to measure, and likewise of greater importance, were the potential causes for war, misunderstanding, and dispute which he eliminated.

At the same time that he was defining frontiers, Rio-Branco was initiating new foreign policy goals which set the course for Brazil's twentieth-century diplomacy. He had the ability to attend to the mind-numbing details of diplomatic controversy and at the same time to envision the broadest scope of diplomatic strategy. If the boundary settlements demonstrated his ability to master minutiae, his new foreign policy goals showed him as an expert in grandiose schemes. He envisioned a leadership role for Brazil on a larger world-stage. Such an expanded role contrasted sharply with the parochial nineteenth-century preoccupation with boundaries in general and with the Plata region in particular.

The new foreign policy consisted of four related goals. First, Rio-Branco sought to increase national prestige abroad. Sharing the invigorated nationalism of the new century, he aimed to make Brazil known and respected in the international community. The newly renovated and augmented navy called at more foreign ports to show the flag. The number of foreign diplomats in Rio de Janeiro and the number of Brazilian diplomats abroad increased, as did Brazil's participation in international congresses. Rio de Janeiro played host to the Third Pan-American Conference and the Third Latin American Scientific Congress. During the Rio-Branco ministry, more distinguished foreigners visited Brazil than during any previous decade. The foreign minister greeted and entertained all of them. Among others, he welcomed Sarah Bernhardt, William Jennings Bryan, Georges Clemenceau, Paul Doumer, Guglielmo Ferrero, Anatole France, Roque Saenz Peña, Julio Roca, and Elihu Root. From their statements to the press and from their own writings, it was apparent that those visitors carried away with them a favorable impression of the country. In France during this period a stream of books about Brazil cascaded off the press, of which these titles are representative: *Le Brésil d'aujourd'hui* by Joseph Burnichon, *Le Progrès Bresilien* by the Baron d'Anthourd, *Notes de Voyage dans l'Amerique du Sud* by George Clemenceau, and *Visions du Brésil* by L. A. Caffe. English, German, and North American writers joined in the literary discovery of Brazil. Meanwhile, German and Belgian universities began to offer courses in the Portuguese language and Luso-Brazilian literature. The diplomat Joaquim Nabuco was speaking at civic clubs and universities across the United States, while the historian Manuel de Oliveira Lima lectured at Stanford University, Williams College, and the Sorbonne. José Veríssimo noted proudly in his prologue, written in 1911, to Oliveira Lima's *Formation Historique de la Nacionalité Bresilienne* that Brazil was being considered by the nations of Europe as a cultured country worthy of serious study. He pointed with pride to the fact that a recent scientific congress in Vienna had accepted Portuguese as one of the official languages and that in a music festival in the same capital compositions of the colonial Brazilian musician José Maurício had been played. Much to the satisfaction of the Brazilians their country was being recognized abroad.

Foreign Minister Rio-Branco foresaw the prestige which would accrue to Brazil if it were the first Latin American nation to receive a cardinalate. As late as 1904, there was not

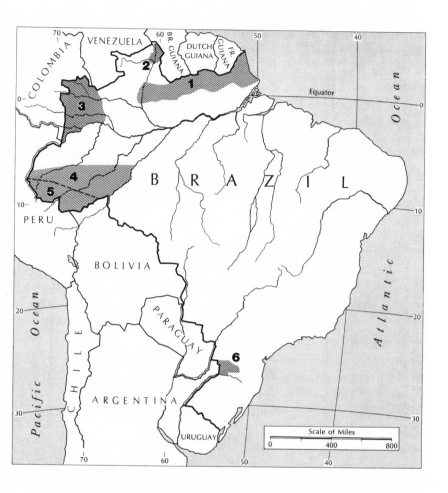

Map 4. Territorial Settlements Made by Rio-Branco

1. French Guiana, Territory of Amapá
   Arbitral Award of the Swiss Federal Council, December 1, 1900
2. British Guiana
   Arbitral Award of King Victor Emmanuel III of Italy, June 6, 1904
3. Colombia
   Treaty of Limits and Navigation, April 24, 1907
   Clarified by the Treaty of Limits and Navigation, November 15, 1928
4. Peru
   Treaty of Demarcation of Frontiers, September 8, 1909
5. Bolivia, Territory of Acre
   Treaty of Petrópolis, November 17, 1903
6. Argentina, Treaty of Missões
   Arbitral Award of President Grover Cleveland of the United States, February 5, 1895

one Latin American cardinal, a curious fact when one realizes that the area was a bastion of Roman Catholicism. Pressure was mounting on Rome to elevate a Latin American to that eminent position. The first Latin American nation to receive the honor would enjoy a singular distinction. The foreign minister ordered the Brazilian diplomat at the Vatican to inform the pope that Brazilian Catholics would be pleased to have a cardinal. By comparison with the rest of Latin America, Brazil had maintained good relations with Rome. Indeed, Brazilians were not reticent in pointing out that they had displayed more loyalty and consideration than other Latin Americans. They also employed the effective arguments of size and population. The reasoning was sound, and the decision of Rome was not long in coming. In the consistory of December 11, 1905, Pope Pius X created as cardinal the distinguished archbishop of Rio de Janeiro, Joaquim Arcoverde de Albuquerque. The announcement was a diplomatic triumph for Brazil. For thirty years thereafter, Brazil was the only Latin American state with a cardinal.

As a second goal in the new policy, Rio-Branco wanted Brazil to exercise leadership in Latin America in general, but in South America in particular. He began by strengthening his nation's diplomatic ties throughout Latin America. Discovering that Brazil had no representative in either Quito or Bogotá, he corrected that oversight in 1904 by dispatching resident ministers to both capitals. In 1906, Brazil accredited a diplomatic representative to Costa Rica, Cuba, Guatemala, Honduras, El Salvador, Nicaragua, and Panama for the first time. The only Latin American capitals to which he did not accredit a diplomat were Port-au-Prince and Santo Domingo. When necessary, the Baron conducted his diplomatic intercourse with those insular republics in Washington. Buenos Aires, Santiago, and Lima became the most important posts in Latin America, and he assigned to those three capitals his ablest diplomats and closest associates. Recognizing the importance of Mexico in the Pan-American community, he established a legation there in 1906, thereby separating the previously joint Washington-Mexico City diplomatic post.

The examples of Rio-Branco's and Brazil's leadership in

Latin America were numerous. Nowhere is it better illustrated than in the coordination by *Itamaraty* (the name given the Foreign Ministry) of the Argentine-Brazilian-Chilean-Mexican recognition of Panama in late 1903 and early 1904, a perfect example of the foreign minister's ability to direct the international participation of the major Latin American nations. Brazil's leadership at the Second International Peace Conference at The Hague in 1907 was another cogent example. There, Ruy Barbosa spoke with the support of all of Latin America when he demanded the equality of all nations on the arbitration court debated at The Hague. Itamaraty also helped to mediate the conflict between Peru and Ecuador over frontiers, found a solution for the impasse over the Alsop claims threatening Chilean-United States relations, and urged the United States to send a permanent diplomatic representative to Paraguay. Brazil came to regard itself as the diplomatic bridge between the United States and Latin America. The Brazilians sought to interpret the United States and its actions to the Latin American community and in turn to serve as the mediator for Latin America before the Department of State. Its efforts at leadership did not go unobserved. The Chilean minister in Rio de Janeiro wrote to Santiago:

Brazil believes itself, because of its enormous size, population, geographical position, and evident rich future, to be the country destined to exercise in South America part of the hegemony which the United States now exercises over all America. That line of thought has the publicly declared approval of the United States. Brazilian politicians do not hide their thoughts and they have stated them in documents.[8]

As the Chilean diplomat hinted, much of the success of new foreign policy depended on Rio-Branco's skill in closely aligning Brazil and the United States. He succeeded during the early years of his ministry in shifting Brazil's diplomatic

8. Chilean Minister, Rio de Janeiro, to Minister of Foreign Relations, Santiago, June 1, 1907, Oficios from the Chilean Legation in Brazil, 1904–1908, Archivo del Ministerio de Relaciones Exteriores de Chile, Santiago.

axis from London to Washington. Throughout the nineteenth century, Great Britain enjoyed a commercial and financial monopoly over Brazil, and the British government served as the unofficial model for the Second Empire. In contrast, the republic modeled its Constitution of 1891 upon that of the United States, the new political mentor. Also, by the last decades of the century, the North American market was by far the prime purchaser of Brazil's exports. Moreover, the elite had been prepared to accept such a shift because of the convincing arguments put forth throughout the nineteenth century by such precursors of the idea of United States-Brazilian approximation as the Marquês de Aracati in 1827, Sérgio Teixeira Macedo in 1848, Tarvares Bastos in 1862, and Salvador de Mendonça in 1891. Rio-Branco, then, picked up and pursued that trend. Furthermore, he clearly understood that the newly emerged world power, if properly cultivated, could serve Brazilian interests well. By an intimate relationship with the United States, he hoped to tip the balance of power in South America to favor Brazil, to add to his diplomatic strength, and to increase his international maneuverability. Washington became the "number one" post, and the foreign minister counseled his diplomats there to maintain the closest contact with the State Department.

The United States, gladly accepting the proffered friendship of the largest Latin American republic, reciprocated Brazil's good will. The two nations exchanged ambassadors in 1905; Washington thereby received the first Brazilian ambassador, the distinguished and pro-American Joaquim Nabuco, and Rio de Janeiro welcomed the only United States ambassador accredited to South America. Together the foreign minister and his ambassador won the understanding and cooperation of Secretary of State Elihu Root and President Theodore Roosevelt, who insured North American support of Rio-Branco's new foreign policy. At one point the ebullient Roosevelt, always intrigued by the size of Brazil, was quoted as remarking to a Brazilian official, "For your great country is reserved a brilliant future toward which, as representative of this Government, I hope to be able to contribute." Root made his own contribution in the form of an official visit to Brazil in 1906, the first visit abroad of a United States secretary of state. There is every reason to believe that Root regarded Brazil as the keystone of his Latin American policy. Certainly his enthusiastic reception throughout Brazil sealed the bonds of an unwritten alliance which then seemed to unite the two giant republics of North and South America, and the visit served notice to the rest of the hemisphere of the special relationship existing between them. Brazil's principal rival, Argentina, took note of that unofficial but nonetheless firm alliance. The Baron's new policies were already beginning to strengthen Brazil's hand in international politics.

For the final point of the new foreign policy, the Baron placed a new emphasis on Pan-Americanism. Set apart from the rest of the hemisphere for nearly a century because of its unique monarchial institutions, Brazil joined the fraternity of republics in 1889, the same year in which the modern Pan-American movement got under way. The amicable settlement of the frontier problems put to rest the major potential source of conflict between Brazil and its neighbors so that inter-American friendship could become a reality. Whatever the personal feelings of the Brazilians toward their sister republics, all responsible leaders understood the importance of friendly relations with them. On Pan-Americanism, Rio-Branco wrote, "I express the deep hope which we have that the spirit of cooperation and good will manifested in the American conference will produce the practical results we all ought to desire to see realized in America." He organized the highly successful third Pan-American conference in Rio de Janeiro in 1906, which consolidated and gave permanence to the Pan-American movement.

Pan-Americanism, close relations with the United States, Latin American leadership, and international prestige became the four cardinal points of a new foreign policy which showed increasing vigor as Itamaraty brought the former frontier diplomacy to a successful conclusion. The Brazilians were delighted to find their country embarked upon new international policies. As they lifted their former limited diplomatic vision from the frontiers to the world scene, they determined for the first time to take their place on the global stage. There was an apt example to illustrate their change. In 1899, Brazil, still very much engrossed in its boundary disputes, refused an invitation to attend the First Hague Peace Conference, claiming that no national interests of Brazil would be discussed. In 1907, Brazil, then engaged in its new policy of aggrandizement, not only eagerly accepted an invitation to the Second Hague Peace Conference but requested an official position for its chief delegate, Ruy Barbosa, who played an active role in the discussions.

Only eight years had elapsed between the two conferences, but during that time the diplomacy of Brazil under Rio-Branco's guidance had changed completely. The new international attitude and the foreign policy accompanying it constituted the legacy of the Baron of Rio-Branco. In the decades following his death, his policies became traditional and his successors proudly and unquestioningly carried them out. Concluding the diplomacy of the empire and setting the course for the diplomacy of the republic, his ministry was the decisive transitional period in Brazilian diplomacy. Furthermore, by studiously avoiding politics, Rio-Branco raised foreign policy above partisan polemics, so that instead of representing one or another party or faction it reflected the desires of the entire nation. Foreign policy became identified with the idea of unified nationality and an external manifestation of growing nationalism.

Exploiting the Amazon

The prosperity and progress of the New Brazil extended even into the distant Amazon Valley, many times regarded as promising and many times failing to fulfill that promise. Hopeful of a brighter future for the valley, the emperor created the province of Amazonas in 1850. The government was installed two years later under the presidency of João Batista de Figueiredo Tenereiro Aranha at Manaus, a small collection of mud huts on the Negro River, a few miles from where it emptied into the Amazon. Shortly thereafter steamships began to ply the waters of the "river-sea," contributing notably to the opening of the valley and to its future exploitation. Mauá's steamship line in 1853 connected Belém with Manaus, providing scheduled service on the eight-day run with stops at Breves, Gurupá, Prainha, Santarém, Óbidos, Parintins, and Itacoatiara. In 1855, scheduled steamship service linked Manaus with Nauta in Peru. Under foreign pressure, the imperial government opened the Amazon to unrestricted international traffic in 1867. Regularly established steamship service appeared in the years thereafter on the major tributaries of the Amazon: the Purús in 1869, the Madeira in 1873, and the Juruá in 1874. Settlements all clung to the edge of the rivers, and hence a network of steamship lines could unite the inhabited regions of the Amazon quite well. Logically, then, the river dominated the lives of all the inhabitants of the North. As the Amazonian poet, Paulino de Brito, sang of it in his *Cantos Amazônicos* (Amazonian Songs), "Oh, river of my birth!/How much, oh, how much I identify with you!" From the shores of that great river came a wide variety of natural products: gums, roots, drugs, woods, animal skins, and rubber. It was rubber which would transform the Amazon.

Rubber remained unimportant until in 1840 Charles Goodyear discovered a vulcanizing process to keep it from becoming sticky in hot weather and brittle in cold. Rubber then proved useful for rainwear, electric insulation, carriage and bicycle tires, and finally automobile tires. With the increased practicality of rubber, the demand for it multiplied. Belém exported 69,174 pounds of rubber in 1827, but by 1853 those exports had reached 5,214,560 pounds and showed every indication of rising. The Amazon was on the threshold of a boom.

The speculators searched out the rubber tree along the courses of the Amazon and its tributaries, claiming gargantuan tracts of land with the hope that they would contain the precious tree. No one thought to plant the tree, which took over twenty years to mature. Popular belief held that wild rubber was superior. Anyway there seemed no limit to what Nature had provided. The entrepreneurs of the burgeoning industry lived in either Belém or Manaus, from which they directed their operations and exported the crude rubber to eagerly waiting world markets. The principal problem was an old one for Brazil, a labor shortage. The dwindling number of Indians was pressed into service as *seringueiros* (rubber gatherers). Many of the seventeenth and eighteenth centuries' worst scenes of enslavement and abuse were reenacted. A large percentage of the population of the Amazon during the rubber boom came from the Northeast, particularly Ceará, driven there by the recurring droughts and held there by a cruel form of debt peonage. But those men who were among the most heartless exploiters of the Indians were forced to borrow heavily from the simple Indian civilizations in order to survive. In the short story "Hospitalidade" in his book *Inferno Verde* (Green Hell), Alberto Rangel depicted the relations between the two groups and the necessity of the invader to adopt indigenous ways. Rubber profits also enticed many foreigners to the tropics, but they stayed principally in the two cities, Belém and Manaus. The English, French, Germans, and Portuguese arrived to direct the rubber operations, while the Spaniards, Italians, Syrians, and Lebanese immigrated to conduct other types of business in the two state capitals. In the entire Amazonian North, the population rose from 250,000 in 1853, to 330,000 in 1872, to 380,000 in 1890, and reached nearly a million in 1910. Never, however, was there a satisfactory number of seringueiros.

The isolated, difficult life of the exploited seringueiro explained the recruitment problem. Euclides da Cunha in his perceptive essays on man in his Amazonian environment repeatedly stressed the theme, "Man is alone." Indeed, the seringueiro was engulfed by the jungle. Each gatherer was assigned a path which, leading through dense undergrowth and swamps to the scattered rubber trees, exposed him to all the dangers which the Amazon could offer. His path might require attention to as many as 200 trees. Early in the morning he tramped along it to tap the rubber trees. He gashed the bark to draw the milk-white fluid which he collected in a cup fastened to the trunk. The seringueiro returned later to gather the offering of the tree. His next task was to smoke the rubber. To produce the best rubber the sap had to be smoked the day it was gathered. The dense smoke of a palm-nut fire quickly coagulated the white fluid into the marketable black rubber ball. Those balls were then stored to be shipped later to either Manaus or Belém for export. The rich profits of the trade did not fall to the seringueiro, who was fortunate to earn a dollar a day. The wage was high, but the cost of living in the Amazon was astronomical. In 1910, prices for coffee, sugar, rice, and beans, the mainstays of the workingman's diet, were about four times what they were in New York City. Coffee sold for 20 cents a pound, sugar for 15 cents, and rice and beans for 12 cents. Because the population refused to farm, nearly everything they ate was imported, In addition to the cost of transporting food into the Amazon, the federal government exacted a high tariff on foreign imports, including imports of food. The expense of importing the food naturally was passed along to the consumer. Little wonder that the seringueiro, no matter how hard he worked, could not rise from poverty and servitude.

Over the years the rubber gatherers fanned out along the many tributaries, large and small, of the Amazon, into the most remote regions of the interior. By so doing, they not only tapped new trees and increased rubber exports but they also carried Brazilian territorial claims into hitherto uninhabited regions of the South American hinterlands. They functioned as modern bandeirantes; their settlement of the Amazonian interior validated Brazil's claims of *uti possidetis,* establishing the basis upon which Rio-Branco made the definitive and advantageous settlement of the frontiers.

Along the Negro River from Venezuela, the Ica and Japurá from Colombia, the Solimões from Ecuador, the Juruá, Purús, and Javarí from Peru, and the Acre and Madeira from Bolivia, the rubber floated into Manaus or on downstream to Belém, leaving the interior no richer for the extraction, but augmenting the wealth and ostentation of those rapidly growing ports.

The price of rubber rose steadily if erratically. In April of 1910 it reached a peak, $2.90 per pound, a record never again equaled. The joy of the rubber barons was brief. In May, the price began to decline just as steadily as it had risen. The sagging prices throughout the remainder of the year, however, did not prevent 1910 from setting income records. The average price for the year, $2.01, was considerably more than the $1.60 average of 1909 and about double the 1908 average, $1.18. The lucrative profits in 1910 set the record for income from rubber sales, even though more rubber had been exported during several previous years and 1912 marked the apogee of rubber exports.

The increasing income from the rubber industry made possible comfortable budgets for the governments of Amazonas and Pará. The principal interest both of those governments displayed in the industry was to levy taxes. A 20 or 25 percent export tax on each kilo of rubber enriched the treasuries. For Amazonas, the state budget in 1910 of 15.561:000$000 was exceeded by an income of 18.069:162$372. Rubber provided 82.11 percent of that income. In the previous year it had furnished 79.04 percent and in 1911 it would provide 77.50 percent.

In many respects the prosperity extended beyond the jungle confines. All Brazil benefited. In the first decade and a half of the twentieth century rubber was second only to coffee in furnishing the country with foreign exchange. In the period from 1910 to 1912, coffee brought some 25 million pounds sterling, while rubber brought nearly 22 million. From 1900 to 1912, rubber made up about one third of Brazil's export trade. The taxes paid on rubber exports sustained in grand style the states of the North and also provided prosperity for several of the states of the Northeast, many of whose citizens were involved directly or indirectly in the industry. In turn, the Southern states benefited by the lively sale of their cereals, meats, coffee, and textiles to the North. The many imports which the northerners could afford to buy also contributed to the national treasury through the high import duties collected by the federal customs service.

The mounting wealth, as rubber exports jumped from 10 percent of the national total in 1890 to 39 percent in 1910, transformed the provincial riverine capitals of Manaus and Belém into modern cities. Situated (or as some thought, imprisoned) in the midst of a vast and alluring jungle, Manaus in the first decade of the twentieth century proudly boasted all the amenities of any European city of similar size or even larger. In 1896, Manaus became the first large Brazilian city to introduce electric street lighting. An excellent system of waterworks, an efficient garbage collection and disposal system, telephone service, handsome public buildings, and comfortable private residences attested to the modernity of the city. The crowning glory of the city was the magnificent Amazonas Theater, one of the splendid opera houses of the day. Built entirely from rubber money during the years 1891–1896, it was reputed to have cost 2 million dollars, an astonishing figure for the period. Like most Brazilian buildings constructed in the nineteenth century before French gingerbread styles became the vogue, the theater showed a solid, simple exterior and gave vent to wild baroque imagination in the interior. Stone furnished the main substance for the construction but the entrances and supporting pillars were finished in Italian marble. Colorful tiles adorned the dome. The rich elaborate interior was brilliant with gold leaf and lush with red velvet. Classical Greek and Roman mythological figures vied for attention with Indian and local motifs in the decorations, painting, and sculpture. Indian heads protruded from the balustrade of the staircases, and palm leaves interlaced in the friezes. Murals depicted European gods and goddesses frolicking in the Amazon. De Angelis, a popular Italian artist of the time, decorated the ceilings. Large gilded mirrors reflected the splendor of the chandeliers. The orchestra pit easily could hold sixty musicians, and the stage in its day was considered immense. Elegant crowds converged on the theater for the many dramatic, operatic, and musical events it offered during the winter season.

The newly expanded harbor bustled with activity. Foreign flags, particularly British and German, mixed freely with Brazilian ones in port. The year 1910 saw the arrival of 151 British and 23 German ships. That year also set a record for ship movement, unequaled for a decade and a half thereafter. Approximately 1,675 ocean-going steamships, river launches, and sailing vessels called at the port. Of that number, 144 arrived directly from abroad, either from Europe or the United States. The rubber merchants were just finishing their biggest decade of export. They had shipped some 345,079 tons of crude rubber abroad, well over a hundred thousand tons more than they had sold the previous decade or would sell the following. The rubber went to New York, Liverpool, Le Havre, Hamburg, and Antwerp, the principal world markets of that product (see Table 5.3).

Table 5.3. Rubber Sales Abroad, 1841–1947

Decade	Tons
1841–1850	4,693
1851–1860	19,383
1861–1870	37,166
1871–1880	60,225
1881–1890	110,048
1891–1900	213,755
1901–1910	345,079
1911–1920	228,754
1921–1930	202,634
1931–1940	115,560
1941–1947	89,429

SOURCE: Cosme Ferreira Filho, *A Borracha na Economia Amazônica* (Manaus, 1952), pp. 10–11.

Belém, a city which had grown from 40,000 in 1875 to over 100,000 by 1900, also bore ample testimony to the rubber riches. It too boasted electricity, telephones, streetcars, comfortable residences, splendid public buildings, and—as one contemporary North America visitor said—"an amount of vice that would shock our modern reformers." The low city of predominantly white buildings possessed several fine cultural institutions as well. The Teatro da Paz opened its doors in 1878 and in 1891 the Paraense Museum, founded some decades earlier, was restored. The river harbor played host to steamships from various continents. In fact, the port in its heyday was one of the busiest in South America. Around it, the very smell of rubber hung in the air. Vessels of all descriptions arrived from upriver with their rubber balls. They were carried to the warehouses, chopped up, and packed in boxes for shipment. The huge wooden and corrugated iron warehouses bulged with rubber. Indians, blacks, and mulattoes carried the great boxes from the warehouses to the awaiting ships.

The rubber merchants exuded confidence as they watched the fleets of ships carrying away their product, and the entire economy of the North vibrated with their enthusiasm. The First Commercial, Industrial, and Agricultural Congress of the Amazon, which met in Manaus in February of 1910, boasted, "The superiority of this country as a rubber producer is guaranteed for some time because of the exceptional quality of its product, and also by the possibility of increasing, one might say indefinitely, the output of the forests." Optimism pervaded this congress just as it characterized the general business attitude in the North. Still, those who were realistic and also possessed a gift of vision—and there were a few—saw forming on the horizon clouds which threatened to cast a shadow of dark despair over the Amazon. The governor of Amazonas, in his annual message given in 1910, complained that increasing attention, energy, and investment focused on the rubber industry to the neglect of such other forest products as castanha nuts, pirarucu fish, cacao, woods, and guaraná. In a vain echo of an earlier message by the president of the province of Pará in 1854, he warned that such a concentration created a potentially dangerous situation. The warning went unheeded. Anyway it was too late.

Asia already had begun to produce rubber in quantity. In 1876, the Englishman Henry Alexander Wickham surreptitiously had taken seeds of the hevea brasiliensis from the Amazon to Kew Gardens in London. From there, seedlings were transplanted to Ceylon, where well-planned plantations were laid out by the Europeans. Asian labor cost a quarter of Amazonian labor and one Asian could tend over 500 trees on a plantation, while one Brazilian with great effort tapped 200 trees in the jungle. The first young rubber trees flowered in 1881. Initial exports from those efficiently organized plantations were modest. In 1900 Asia exported only 4 tons but the figure grew rapidly: in 1905, it reached 145 tons; in 1910, 8,000; and by 1915, 107,000. In other words, the percentage of plantation-grown rubber from Asia entering the world market grew from 0.3 in 1905 to 9.0 in 1910 to 67.6 in 1915. By 1922, plantation rubber accounted for 93.1 percent of international sales. The sharply rising supply of rubber on the world market, together with the low overhead of the European-owned and -managed plantations in Asia brought the price of rubber down. Consequently, in May of 1910, the price of Brazilian rubber began a slow and steady decline which eventually would bring stagnation to the Amazon.

The falling prices pinched the rubber barons. They awoke at once to the changing realities of the world market. By the end of 1910, despite the fact that their total income for 1910 exceeded that of 1909, they were in full panic. They complained bitterly of the plight of rubber, and in pessimistic tones predicted even lower rubber prices in the years ahead. Those predictions proved accurate. The merchants were loath to blame their own haphazard and inefficient production methods for their predicament. Instead, they sought more distant causes. They accused the federal government of lavishing its attentions on coffee to the neglect of the remainder of the economy. Another handy target for their ire was the United States, the world's largest rubber market. "Yankee speculators" were charged with causing falling prices. Even so staid an institution as the Amazonian Bank pointed a finger of blame at American manufacturers, whom it accused of tampering with the world rubber market for the purpose of bringing about a decline of prices—to the great advantage of their own businesses. In doing so the merchants tended to neglect or underestimate the most important cause of their plight: efficient, large-scale Asian plantations which could produce more rubber more cheaply than the Amazon. In truth, Asian rubber had succeeded in breaking the monopoly Brazil had enjoyed for so long in the world's market.

However they might diagnose their problems, the merchants realized by the end of 1910 that the rubber boom was ending and that they needed help and needed it quickly to prevent a further decline. They recalled that a similar problem of overproduction and falling prices had beset the coffee industry about a half-decade before. Restricted plantings and the Convention of Taubaté (in addition to bad weather which diminished the crop) had caused a renewed price rise for coffee. Since Brazil was the major producer of coffee, national action in that case did affect the world market.

The rubber barons, refusing to recognize that they no longer held a world monopoly in the face of Asian productivity, spoke out for a "Convention of the Amazon." This was to be signed by the states of Amazonas and Pará and the federal government, giving to rubber a valorization similar to that enjoyed by coffee. Their aim was to stabilize the price of rubber. As an emergency measure, the state of Amazonas passed an unrealistic law for intervention in the rubber industry. The merchants, though, continued to look to the federal government as the only possible source of a solution to their problem. Rio de Janeiro vacillated. The politicians there seemed to have had a wider perspective upon the global scene than did the rubber merchants and doubtless understood the hopeless situation of their national rubber industry. The belated Rubber Defense Law of 1912 encouraged the creation of plantations, the improvement of transportation, and the attraction of immigrants, and ordered a 50 percent reduction of export taxes. It brought no results. Valorization schemes proved equally ineffective. The Bank of Brazil nearly went broke buying rubber and waiting for a price rise which never came.

The rubber boom was over. Panic replaced prosperity. The frantic activities so characteristic of a boom subsided. Belém and Manaus settled back into somnolence. The docks and warehouses deteriorated; banks closed; foreign merchants moved away; the two great opera houses fell into disrepair. Belém and Manaus took their places beside Olinda and Ouro Preto as cities of the past.

The boom and collapse of the rubber industry followed a pattern well established by dyewood, sugar, gold, diamonds, tobacco, cotton, and cacao. The story of those industries points out one of the major themes in Brazilian history, so evident throughout the colonial period and the nineteenth century and still visible in the twentieth century:

the recurrence of economic cycles during which one product of the soil determined the well-being of the entire economy or a large part of it. The history of the Brazilian economy has been one of the rise and decline of entire industries one after the other. The single-product agricultural economy was the pattern followed for over four hundred years. Each cycle did leave some residues and effects. The cycles often populated new regions of the country and the product continued to be produced, albeit in diminished amounts and for lower prices, providing at least some source of wealth.

Nor did the rubber cycle, which lasted a generation, end without leaving its impress on the Amazon. Human activity stirred the slumbering river valley. The adventurous seringueiro criss-crossed the hinterland in search of his livelihood, and in doing so expanded the Brazilian frontiers. The skilled river pilot navigated uncharted tributaries and streams, thereby extending the effective national territory. The population increased. Belém and Manaus grew from riverside towns to cosmopolitan cities.

The Decline of the Old Republic

The proper functioning of the constitutional machinery in June of 1909 elevated Nilo Peçanha to the presidency to complete the sixteen months of office of the deceased Afonso Pena. Only forty-one years old when he unexpectedly became chief of state, he was the first president who had not received his political education under the empire. As a citizen of the coffee state of Rio de Janeiro and a signer of the Convention of Taubaté, Peçanha was expected to continue the policies of his predecessors. One of the most important acts passed during his administration was the creation in September 1910 of the Indian Protection Service, whose aim was to incorporate the diminishing Indian population of the hinterlands into the national family. In reality, the limited time in which Peçanha held the helm of state was too brief for him to demonstrate his abilities—or lack of them. Basically he presided over a caretaker government.

The first hotly contested presidential campaign in the short history of the republic overshadowed his administration.

Afonso Pena, like the presidents before him, had indicated his successor, the astute finance minister, David Campista. The unexpected death of the president robbed that favorite of the strong support he needed to claim the election. In the novel political vacuum thus created, a variety of factions maneuvered to seize the political prize of the presidency. First some young officers and then some politicians had spoken of Marshal Hermes da Fonseca as a candidate. An informal caucus of a few senators and deputies officially nominated him. Hermes had served as minister of war in the Pena cabinet and, as a representative of the conservative elements of Brazilian politics, could count on the support of the government. But his election was by no means a foregone conclusion.

The nomination of Hermes da Fonseca, a native of the southernmost Brazilian state, Rio Grande do Sul, expressed the ambitions of that rich and maverick state. The economy of Rio Grande do Sul rested on cattle ranching, rice cultivation, and industry. Its interests dictated a far greater preoccupation with internal rather than international trade. The Gaúcho politicians cooperated easily with the military. Fully a quarter to a third of the army was posted in that strategically located state, and Pôrto Alegre boasted of the only professional military academy outside of Rio de Janeiro. At times that academy enrolled more cadets than the better known one in the federal capital. Traditionally Rio Grande do Sul contributed a disproportionate number of officers to the military. Further, ideological bonds, namely Positivism, tied the military and the state Republican Party together. The Gaúcho congressional delegation always defended military appropriations and interests in the federal legislature. For these reasons, it seemed logical that Rio Grande do Sul would put forth the nomination of Marshal Hermes da Fonseca in a bid to achieve national leadership.

Protest against a military candidate called forth an organized opposition which nominated Ruy Barbosa of Bahia. Statesman, jurist, and orator, Ruy had earned a splendid reputation among his compatriots for his role at The Hague Peace Conference in 1907, where according to Brazilian legend he dazzled the world's diplomats with his erudition. As a candidate, Ruy indefatigably toured the states to arouse support. In his lengthy and emotional campaign speeches, he criticized the concentration of political power in the hands of a small political clique, lamented that the government did not represent the people, and above all else warned of the menace of growing militarism. His liberalism was of an old school, but he stated his objectives more clearly and forcefully than most of his predecessors in that school ever had. He appealed to the urban middle sectors.

In his ambitious campaign, the mistake which perhaps cost the Bahian the victory was his oversimplification of the issues. Opposing militarism and most specifically decrying a military man as president, Ruy characterized the election as one which would choose between military and civilian control of the government. He heaped abuse on the military and charged, "Militarism is the common scourge of all opinions, all interests, all national rights. It is the extortion of liberty, the obliteration of intelligence, the prohibition of civic pride, the destruction of credit, the negation of constitutional government, the rule of authority without law, responsibility, culture, redress, or hope." Many military leaders had opposed Hermes, but angered by the vehement anti-military tirades of Ruy, they gave their support to Marshal Hermes as a means of self-protection. One of the major effects of Ruy's campaign appears to have been his complete alienation of the military, a powerful and influential group since the coup of 1889.

As the campaign progressed, it assumed significance in Brazilian history for several reasons. It provided a blunt discussion of the role of the military in which a sizable portion of the politically aware expressed a firm opposition to the participation of officers in politics. Further, a careful reading of the platform and speeches of Ruy reveals one of the early calls for democratic reform and purification of the political body. It was a protest, doubtless quixotic, against the traditional oligarchical establishment dominating Brazil. In that protest, Ruy attempted to present the issues to the people, and in doing so he conducted the first really big and important electoral campaign in Brazilian history.

Marshal Hermes' campaign, on the other hand, was a lackluster one, but he had the government, Congress, Rio Grande do Sul, and Minas Gerais on his side. São Paulo and Bahia supported Ruy. The two principal coffee states split in that election—Ruy's running mate was Governor Albuquerque Lins of São Paulo and Hermes' was Governor Venceslau Brás Pereira Gomes of Minas Gerais. The election held on March 1, 1910 generated great enthusiasm and excitement. Congress took a little less than three months to count the popular vote: Hermes received 233,882 to 126,292 for Ruy. Not even half a million out of a population of 22 million had voted, something like 2.8 percent of the Brazilians. The highly restricted electorate was a graphic commentary on Brazilian democracy. Marshal Hermes received a far lower percent, 64.4, of the votes than any of his victorious predecessors had. (Prudente de Morais had received 84.3; Campos Sales, 90.9; Rodrigues Alves, 91.7; and Afonso Pena, 97.9!)

The election of a soldier to the presidency climaxed a period of growing militarism in Brazil. In late 1905, the alleged German violations of Brazilian sovereignty, when an excited press announced that sailors from one of the Kaiser's warships, the *Panther*, had disembarked in Santa Catarina to apprehend a German immigrant there, impressed upon the Brazilians their military inability to meet foreign threats. Shortly thereafter the energetic ministers Admiral Júlio de Noronha and Marshal Hermes da Fonseca reorganized the army and navy with the encouragement of Minister of Foreign Affairs Rio-Branco. Arms purchases increased. Growing rivalry with Argentina prompted Brazil to buy new warships, and soon the two neighbors were engaged in an arms race neither could afford. The Kaiser's invitation to Marshal Hermes to attend the annual German army maneuvers in 1909 proved to be the capstone. The efficient German army fascinated Marshal Hermes, and he returned to South America with some grandiose ideas. Overlaying these specific causes for the rebirth of militarism in Brazil was the general military spirit abroad in a world noisily arming itself for the Grand Conflict. Brazil was simply following the trend of the times.

Ironically, one of the major consequences of Brazil's overt militarism was a series of naval revolts, in late 1910, whose potential seriousness startled the nation. President Hermes hardly had settled into the Palace of Catete when the sailors of the renovated navy mutinied. On November 23, 1910, the enlisted men of three battleships and a scout expelled their officers, killing several in the process. The crews of seven other warships in Guanabara Bay abandoned ship. The capital waited nervously as the "black" mutineers turned landward the powerful guns of the "great white battleships." The ships fired only sporadically at the virtually defenseless capital. The revolt proved to have no political significance. The sailors, exhausted and overworked, had resolved to take dramatic steps to air their grievances. They complained of harsh corporal punishment, excessive hours of work, insufficient pay, and the bad quality of rations. A later congressional investigation substantiated those charges of overwork and frequent flogging. After an amnesty and a promise of improved conditions, the sailors surrendered meekly and allowed their officers back on board on November 25. At once the government landed all the munitions and the breechblocks of the principal guns, rendering the expensive warships as harmless as steamboats. More trouble, however, was in store. Hardly had the battleships been disarmed when the 500 marines stationed on the Isle of Cobras, situated just off the waterfront of Rio de Janeiro, revolted. On the evening of December 9, 1910, they began firing at the Naval Arsenal. Sailors aboard one warship mutinied and adhered to the cause of the marines. The critical situation required the government to use force as well as to grant another amnesty before the marines would surrender. After quelling the revolt, the government announced that it was devoid of any political significance but declined to give any additional explanations.

Those disquieting naval revolts were but a part of the violence which erupted during this era to disturb the placidity of the nation. A renewed propensity to federal intervention in state affairs brought immediate hostile reactions. The Paulista and Mineiro presidents had avoided those interventions, knowing that their states preferred to pursue their own courses and assuming that the others did too. Such, however, was not the case after 1909. The emerging leadership from Rio Grande do Sul, directed in the federal capital by Pinheiro Machado, was considerably less cautious in interfering in the states to impose its will. Intrigue and intervention accompanied the *riograndense* predominance in Rio de Janeiro in the 1909–1914 period.

The state of Amazonas provided the first example of the new violence fed by political intrigue. For decades the oligarchical Néri family had controlled the politics of Amazonas, much as similar patriarchal families did in other states. For governor, the Néris had handpicked Antônio Clemente Ribeiro Bittencourt and installed him in office, only to find that he displayed a surprising and, to the Néris, disconcerting tendency toward independent action. They resolved to remove him and called upon their political friend, Pinheiro Machado, then at the pinnacle of his national power, for aid. Pinheiro Machado obligingly arranged for a trusted army officer from Rio Grande do Sul to be dispatched to Manaus to take command of federal forces stationed there. With that support, the Néis convinced the usually obedient state legislature to depose the governor for "conflict of interests." Bittencourt, however, refused to step down. The armed forces thereupon shelled the city on October 8, 1910, and the governor fled the following day in order to spare the city further attack.

The bold bombardment by the federal forces shocked and angered all Brazil. The president, already opposed to Pinheiro Machado, took the side of Bittencourt. He recalled the culpable military officers to Rio de Janeiro, and Governor Bittencourt returned triumphantly to Manaus. The events in the distant Amazon reflected the political maneuvering in Rio de Janeiro. Pinheiro Machado wanted allies in power in Amazonas—as elsewhere in the republic—while the president sought to deprive his political enemy of a stronger national base.

Those political machinations continued in the Hermes da Fonseca administration, providing ample evidence that the federal system was faltering. Hermes felt it necessary to overturn the state governments which did not pledge their support. In the state of Rio de Janeiro, rivalries had produced two legislative assemblies and two governors. Federal troops were employed to implant the legislature and executive favored by Hermes. Other maneuvers brought about the downfall of the traditional ruling groups in Pernambuco, Bahia, and Ceará. The bombardment of Salvador by the anti-Pinheiro faction constituted one of the most unhappy chapters of that era's violent history. Considerable damage was done to the old city and shells ripped apart the precious state library. The whole Northeast shook with plots and counterplots, and even Rio Grande do Sul and São Paulo did not escape the intrigues. Part of the troubles can be blamed on the heavy-handed politics of Rio de Janeiro, but another part resulted from the local resentment of the oligarchy and a desire to remove those privileged few from office. In the larger sense, then, the violence stemmed from the growing desire to modernize the country, one step toward what would be greater democratization.

Trouble in the backlands also convulsed the nation. The rural disturbances arose from the gross iniquities of Brazilian society, aggravated by the steady expansion of capitalism inland as communications and transportion networks reached out from the ports with increasing effectiveness. Capitalism brought new cultural values which challenged the folk ways of the interior. Two very different Brazils came into closer contact and on occasion clashed.

The despair of the rural masses, their rejection of the present, and their longing for a better life in the future had given rise to numerous millenarian movements in the nineteenth century. Thanks to the conceptual framework offered by E. J. Hobsbawm, it is possible to consider millenarianism as a type of popular revolution, the rejection of the present for a total restructuring of the future. The first such millenarian movement of the republican period was the one which provided the basis for da Cunha's novel, *Rebellion in the Backlands*. It took place in the sertão of Bahia, where the mystic Antônio Conselheiro had gathered his impoverished followers into the rustic settlement of Canudos. The growing settlement eventually came into conflict with the state government as well as with the religious hierarchy in Salvador. The governor determined to punish what he regarded as the lack of respect for the state's authority. In 1896, he dispatched a police unit to Canudos, only to see it suffer humiliating defeat at the hands of the simple *sertanejos*. The Bahian officials then called upon the federal government for troops to disband the followers of Antônio Conselheiro. Rio de Janeiro took up the cause with a vengeance, believing that those miserable peasants paid loyalty to the monarchy and defied the republic. But the federal army showed no greater skill than the state forces had. The sertanejos overwhelmingly repelled two federal attacks. Finally, the minister of war, Marshal Machado Bittencourt, embarrassed by the defeats, went to Bahia to direct a fourth campaign. Equipped with artillery and well-supplied with munitions, the fourth expedition laid siege to Canudos and in a titanic struggle took the settlement shanty by shanty, completely devastating it in the process. On October 5, 1897, the last resistance was wiped out. The long and bloody struggle (the army alone lost 5,000 men in 1897) awoke the concern of the nation.

While the bloody drama of Canudos was being enacted, a second manifestation of religious fanaticism rocked Ceará. A "miracle" in the Cariri backlands in 1889, repeated in 1891, turned a humble parish priest, Padre Cícero Romão Batista, into one of the most powerful political figures of the Old Republic. A hard-working and dedicated servant of mankind and the Church, Padre Cícero became legendary in the Northeast after the communion wafer he had administered to one of the faithful turned to blood in her mouth. Overnight, the dusty village of Joaseiro become the focal point for religious pilgrimages. The Church cast disapproving eyes on the "miracle" but never removed Padre Cícero from the interior, although it restricted his religious activities. But the peasants of the interior regarded him as their saint. Although his control in Ceará remained unshaken throughout his long lifetime (he died in 1934), some of the priest's most blatant political activity took place during the administration of Hermes da Fonseca. At one point his rural followers marched on Fortaleza and brought about the downfall of the state government. Through his political adviser, Floro Bartolomeu, Padre Cícero allied himself nationally with Pinheiro Machado.

In the extreme south of Brazil, a messianic movement among German immigrants occurred between 1872 and 1898. Jacobina Maurer, the self-proclaimed reincarnation of Jesus Christ, announced the end of the world and life everlasting for her followers. Parenthetically, this movement offers one of the very few examples of female leadership during the nineteenth century. Later, in the Contesatado, an interior area claimed by both Paraná and Santa Catarina, a religious mystic who called himself João Maria, the Monk, agitated the simple folk. Between 1912 and 1915, he put himself above the civil and religious authorities to offer his followers a new and better life. There, as in Bahia, the state militia and police fell in defeat before the rural forces and the federal government found it necessary to dispatch an army to wipe them out, a task which occupied a full division of 6,000 heavily armed men.

Periodically, small messianic movements flourished in the Amazon basin. In the tribes deculturated by missionaries and explorers, the Indians developed a syncretic religion, part Roman Catholic, part that of their ancestors. They turned to religion for unity and hope. The messianic movements which appeared denounced "white civilization" as the source of local misery, and announced a new and perfect life in which the whites would not be present. The masses often conceived of the millennium as a world without whites, whom they universally equated with exploitation and associated with their misery. The many and varied millenarian movements revealed both the spiritual and temporal needs of the people who subscribed to them, a denunciation of the society in which they dwelled and a longing for a better life.

Banditry plagued the interior, particularly the Northeast, where at times state and local officials were unable to guarantee the security of life or property. It attracted the desperate, those who had lost out in the system whether they were poor or members of the impoverished gentry. Whatever else banditry might have included or meant, it also was as much a means of protesting an injustice or righting a wrong as it was of equalizing the wealth or taking political revenge. To the rich and powerful, bandits were outlaws meriting severe punishment; to the poor rural masses, however, they often represented justice and liberation. Bandits roamed the Brazilian interior in the nineteenth century, particularly the impoverished Northeast, where many won the admiration of the poor and the respect of the wealthy, who not infrequently coopted them and utilized their services. Some scholarship correlates the rise of banditry in the late nineteenth century with the breakdown of patriarchal order in the countryside. Brazilian popular poetry abounds with tales of the bandit hero. A well known one, sung at the beginning of the twentieth century, related the history of Antônio Silvino (1875–1944), who became a *cangaceiro* in 1896 to avenge an injustice: his father was slain by a police official who went unpunished by the government. Others related the adventures of Josuíno Brilhante (1844–1879), also seemingly pushed into banditry to avenge local injustices against his family. He assaulted the rich and distributed their goods and money among the poor, boasting that he never robbed for himself. Such "Robin Hood" type robberies and redistributions of wealth received the approbation of the newspaper *O Cearense* in 1878 which huffed, "These bandits loot properties in the most unrestricted fashion as if communism had already been proclaimed among us." The most famous cangaceiro of the twentieth century was Lampião (Virgolino Ferreira da Silva, 1898–1938), whose adventures in the sertão extended over decades until he was killed in 1938. The motives and activities of the cangaceiros varied widely, but at least in part they could be explained as protests against the wrongs of society, as they viewed it. Because of their strength and because they often opposed the elites and official institutions, they received the support, indeed the admiration, of large numbers of the humble classes who often hid them, lied to the authorities to protect them, guided them through strange terrain, and fed them. In short, the disturbances in the backlands were only symptoms of the sterility of the social and economic systems which had been inherited from a distant past.

Assassination was yet another form of violence which disturbed the Old Republic. In 1897, while awaiting in the Arsenal of Rio de Janeiro the disembarkation of troops returning from Canudos, President Prudente de Morais was confronted with a young soldier who pulled a gun. The pistol misfired. Minister of War Machado Bittencourt and several other officers jumped the would-be assassin to disarm him. In the scuffle, he stabbed Bittencourt to death and wounded two others. The other high-level assassination occurred in 1915. The political animosity toward Pinheiro Machado had reached vehement proportions. His heavy-handed methods in Congress stirred one resentful deputy from Pernambuco to introduce a bill commanding, "Let General Pinheiro Machado be eliminated." That command was executed. One September afternoon as the Riograndense politician entered the Hotel dos Estrangeiros an unknown assailant who nurtured a grudge against him stabbed him in the back. Both assassinations profoundly disturbed the nation.

Assassination, banditry, revenging armies marching on Canudos and into the Contestado, the brutal bombardments of Manaus and Salvador, and the naval revolts revealed a violence which has usually been disregarded in studies of Brazil. The tendency in Brazilian historiography is to emphasize peaceful evolution. Perhaps in comparison with the historical experience of Mexico, Venezuela, or Paraguay this emphasis is just. Certainly some momentous changes occurred in Brazil without accompanying bloodshed: independence, the abolition of slavery, and the establishment of the republic. Yet, beneath the tranquil surface of Brazilian evolution, some disquieting currents of violence eddy. Taken as a group, the turbulent incidents provide the basis for a certain amount of skepticism as to the traditionally accepted concept of Brazilian leanings toward conciliation and compromise. This propensity is present, perhaps even dominant, in Brazilian history. But it does not exclude the possibility of violence, which, beginning with the slave revolts and the bandeirantes' treatment of the Indians, continues to the present day. At any rate, President Hermes da Fonseca presided over a restive nation between 1910 and 1914. Indeed, his actions contributed to the rising level of violence.

The president did little to fulfill the growing desire of the prospering citizens of his natal state, Rio Grande do Sul, to shift the political axis of the nation farther southward to their state. The most powerful figure in his administration, Pinheiro Machado, had attempted to force just such a shift. In addition to Machado and the president, Dr. Barbosa Gonçalves, the second minister of public works, Rivadávia Correia, the minister of the interior, and General Mena Barreto, the minister of war, were from Rio Grande do Sul. They formed an impressive body in the top echelon of government. But neither as individuals nor as a group did they possess the ability or strength to effect such a shift, at any rate not while coffee ruled supreme. Clearly it was still too early to challenge Minas Gerais and São Paulo successfully.

Marshal Hermes proved to be a careless administrator of the treasury. As a result, methods more characteristic of the free-spending days of the early 1890s replaced the stringent measures imposed by Murtinho and Bulhões. The national debt mounted. In 1914, the treasury fell back on an old expediency: it issued inconvertible paper money. The government was forced to contract a second British funding loan.

Few doubted that the government of Hermes da Fonseca was inferior to those before it. Lack of ability and lack of action characterized it. The Brazilians became increasingly restive about their choice as a president and dissatisfied with the course of events. Lest the history of the Hermes da Fonseca administration appear too gloomy, however, it should be pointed out that coffee continued to sell well and managed to keep the economy buoyant. A large number of immigrants continued to arrive. The railroad network continued to expand. Little else, however, was accomplished. The gathering war clouds in Europe darkened Brazil's horizon and the storm which burst in August of 1914 disturbed Brazilians in many ways. Clearly the nation's sympathy lay with the Allies, particularly with France, the cultural mentor of the elite. Still there were the sizable colonies of German immigrants in the south, especially in Rio Grande do Sul and Santa Catarina, and not a few Brazilians questioned the loyalty of those new arrivals. The government resolved at once to maintain a "rigorous neutrality," to use the words pronounced by President Hermes on August 4, 1914. It fell to the newly elected president, Venceslau Brás of Minas Gerais, to enforce that neutrality.

The initial impact of the conflict on Brazil's economy was staggering. In 1914 imports plummetted to half the amount in the previous year. Since the government earned a large share of its income from import duties, the national treasury suffered severely. Exports fell as well, which proved disastrous for the state treasuries whose income derived chiefly from the export duties. President Brás reacted to the emergency by cutting back on federal spending. Then, in 1915, the heavy demands of the Allies caused exports to rise spectacularly. Brazil's income mounted as it sold increasing amounts of its national products abroad. These examples illustrate the increase (given in dollars) of three exports from 1915 to 1917: the sale of beans rose from $24,000 to $10,000,000; sugar from $3,000,000 to $17,000,000, and refrigerated beef from $1,500,000 to $15,000,000. The export of these and other agricultural essentials mounted during the war years, while the overseas sales of coffee, a luxury item, declined.

As the war dragged on, Brazil found it ever more difficult to maintain a neutral posture. Pro-Allied sentiment welled up. The government vigorously protested the German blockade of Allied nations declared on January 31, 1917. Only a few months later, on April 5, a German submarine sank a Brazilian freighter. The news stunned the Brazilians. To protest that violent act and to demonstrate its sympathy with the Allies and its solidarity with the United States, which had just declared war on Germany, the government severed relations with Berlin. On June 1, the government took further steps, revoking Brazil's neutrality and authorizing the use of German ships anchored in Brazilian ports for its own purposes. The torpedoing of a fourth Brazilian ship on October 23, 1917, prompted the government to declare war on Germany, the only South American nation to do so. Participation in World War I was limited to furnishing supplies to the Allies, sending some army officers to Europe and a medical mission to France, and assigning a naval mission of two cruisers and four destroyers to patrol the South Atlantic with the English squadron.

Cooperation with the Allies enhanced Brazil's international position and augmented the prestige which Rio-Branco had thought so desirable. Both Great Britain and Italy raised their legations in Rio de Janeiro to embassies in 1918. Further, Brazil as a belligerent participated in the peace conference at Versailles. The delegation under the leadership of Epitácio Pessôa pressed two claims against Germany. First, Brazil wanted Germany to pay at the 1914 value for the coffee stored in German ports which the Germans had sold at the opening of World War I. With the support of President Woodrow Wilson, Brazil's claim was recognized. Second, Brazil sought to purchase at a suitable indemnity the 70 German ships seized by the government in 1917 in its ports. The Allies, on the other hand, wanted to divide those ships among themselves in accordance with their naval losses, a proposal which would have deprived Brazil of them. Once again the United States intervened on Brazil's behalf and effected an agreement which permitted the Brazilians to keep the ships.

In the organizational discussions for the League of Nations, Brazil spoke for the other Latin American states represented in Paris. Epitácio Pessôa, in a manner reminiscent of Ruy Barbosa at the Second Hague Peace Conference, enunciated Latin America's preference for equality of nations in the League with each continent represented on each committee. But Epitácio's stay in Paris was brief. Rodrigues Alves, elected president for the second time in 1918, was prevented by illness from taking the oath of office. When he died on January 18, 1919, Vice President Delfim Moreira of Minas Gerais assumed the first office of the land. In such cases, the constitution prescribed that new elections be held. At that point, Governor Artur Bernardes of Minas Gerais and Governor Washington Luís of São Paulo came to a political agreement, which history records as the "policy of large states." They resolved to select a prominent figure from one of the small states to complete the presidency of Rodrigues Alves. Then the two major states planned to alternate the presidency between them with first a *mineiro* serving the four-year term and then a *paulista* being elected the chief executive. Recognizing the overwhelming power of the two principal coffee-producing states, the plan not unexpectedly annoyed the other states as a blatant reminder of their own political weakness. Epitácio Pessôa, a former minister, congressman, and Supreme Court justice, was selected by the two coffee governors in 1919. After his success at the peace conference, Epitácio visited Italy, Belgium, England, and the United States, returning to Rio de Janeiro on June 21, 1919, aboard the USS *Idaho*.

Brazil won for itself a place of honor in the League of Nations. Although not a permanent member of the Executive Council, Brazil was reelected repeatedly to a seat on that prestigious and powerful body between 1920 and 1926. Several distinguished Brazilian diplomats, Gastão da Cunha, Domício da Gama, and Afrânio de Melo Franco, presided over the Council. Their position on the Council allowed the Brazilians to continue to play the role taken at the peace conference as the leader of the Latin American nations. Brazil persistently demanded that a Latin American nation be represented on the Council with a permanent seat, a post for which Brazil, of course, felt itself eminently qualified. The European nations failed to heed that demand, to the mounting chagrin of the government in Rio de Janeiro. Then the other hemispheric republics switched their support from Brazil's demand for a permanent seat for a Latin American nation to a plan for three temporary, rotating seats. At that point, Brazil, vetoing the admission of Germany, withdrew from the League in 1926. The rationale apparently was that it would be more honorable to play no role at all than to play an insignificant one. The withdrawal signaled a return to a phase of hemispheric isolation, an isolation not unlike that of its North American ally. Thereafter, Brazil concentrated its diplomacy on affairs of the New World.

The years marking World War I witnessed changes in Brazil which tended to increase that nation's independence and self-reliance. Some of them owed little to the war itself. The promulgation of the Brazilian Civil Code, for example, on January 1, 1916, was the result of years of study and preparation; it eradicated once and for all the many vestiges of Portuguese colonial laws Brazil had clung to. However, the war instigated some changes too. It broke the century-old financial and commercial dependence of Brazil on Great Britain, a process under way since the end of the nineteenth century, when the United States began to exert its authority throughout the hemisphere.

A significant economic change increasingly characteristic of Brazil during the three decades after the fall of the empire was rapid industrial growth. Industrialization expanded parallel to the phenomenal rise of Brazilian exports, particularly coffee.

The tardy arrival of industrialization in Brazil had been due to many formidable handicaps: the lack of liquid capital, of an adequate system of currency, credits, and banking, of skilled workmen and technicians, and of a satisfactory transportation network; the failure to erect high enough tariff barriers or to meet competition from Great Britain; the effects of slavery, of the elite's ingrained mercantilist mentality, and of the rivalry of agricultural interests. All these explain to a large extent why Brazil had been so little affected by the long industrial revolution which by then had transformed England, the United States, Germany, and France. Once industrialization did get under way, however, Brazil was able to learn from Europe and the United States, benefiting from the lessons of their experience and freely adopting European and American inventions.

To the degree that industrialization offered an alternative to the purchase of imported items and diversified the economy, it seemed to challenge the powerful grip of dependency. Each new factory promised some degree of local independence; each augmented the wealth of the nation. Nonetheless, industrialization could not be expected to eradicate dependency so long as the fundamental social, economic, and political institutions went unchanged. The quicker and cheaper production of goods could supply the needs of more people. Thus it smoothed the way for the phenomenal growth of the Brazilian population in the twentieth century. The concentration of the factories in a few cities increased both the size and the importance of those cities, and as they grew the complexion of Brazil altered. Hence the factories and the cities contributed to the questioning of a traditional society implanted in the sixteenth century and unchallenged until the last half of the nineteenth.

At the Exposition of 1908 the national industries proudly displayed their wares, a display which afforded the nation an opportunity to take stock of its industrialization. The authorities estimated that Brazil possessed approximately 3,000 industrial establishments, large and small—but preponderantly small. Just as in the industrialization of Great Britain and the United States, textiles were the first important industry. The most industrialized areas were Rio de Janeiro (the Federal District) with 35,000 workers, São Paulo with 24,000, Rio Grande do Sul with 16,000, Rio de Janeiro (state) with 14,000, and Pernambuco with 12,000. In that year, Brazil was in the midst of a modest industrial expansion. Between the fall of the empire and the outbreak of World War I approximately 7,000 new industrial establishments were created, a remarkable record when one considers that prior to 1889 there had been only 626.

The volume of industrial production doubled during World War I and tripled by 1923. The number of new industrial enterprises grew by 5,940 between 1915 and 1919. Two industries, foodstuffs and textiles, accounted for nearly three-quarters of the total factory production. By 1920, the industrial production was valued at $153,060,000 (U.S. dollars), an increase of nearly fivefold since 1907. Table 5.4 illustrates the industrialization under way.

Table 5.4. The Growth of Industrialization, 1907–1940

Year	Number of Industrial Establishments	Capital Invested (1,000 contos)	Value of Production (1,000 contos)	Number of Employees
1907	2,988	665	669	136,000
1920	13,336	1,815	3,200	276,000
1940	70,026	12,000	25,000	1,412,000

SOURCE: U.S. Tariff Commission, *Mining and Manufacturing Industries in Brazil* (Washington, 1949), p. 13.

The processes of industrialization and modernization went hand in hand. Both made themselves felt within the citadel of traditionalism, the plantation. Once the fazendeiros had ruled their own plantations according to their will and whim and upon occasion interposed a formidable barrier between the distant federal government and the humble plantation worker. But now the railroads and road networks had expanded to make possible a challenge to their authority and an end to the peasants' isolation. The rails and the roads led directly to the cities and ports, where the need for stevedores, service labor, and construction workers offered the ambitious rural arrivals a means of escape to a better life. Second generation migrants with some education might hope for industrial jobs. The opportunity to make a choice, however limited, was in itself a novelty. For the country folk who migrated there, the cities were symbols of a hope which was often frustrated and unrealized but never forsaken.

Industrial expansion increased the size of the urban working force. Whereas the factories employed approximately 136,000 workers in 1907, they employed 276,000 in 1920. The rise in the number of workers in the two principal industries during those same years reflected that growth: the textile industry employed 53,000 in 1907 and 104,000 in 1920; the food industries, 29,000 and 41,000. By contrast, the 1920 census showed that federal, state, and local governments together employed 140,000 persons. The civil service, traditionally a big employer in Latin America, was being rapidly outranked in Brazil by industry.

Efforts to unionize labor accompanied industrial growth. The working conditions were abysmal: long hours, a pittance of a salary, dangerous machines, poor lighting, no vacations, no security, a dismal list almost without end. Women suffered worse conditions than men as well illustrated in this call for action by three São Paulo seamstresses to their co-workers in 1907:

Comrades! It is essential that we refuse to work night and day because that is disgraceful and inhuman. Since 1856 men in many places have attained the eight-hour day. But we members of the weaker sex have to work up to sixteen hours a day, double that of the stronger sex! Comrades, think about your futures; if you continue to allow yourselves to be weakened and the last drop of your blood drained off, then, after you have lost your physical energy, motherhood will be martyrdom and your children will be pale and sickly. . . .

You should speak about these matters not only with your families, but also with our inhuman employers, face to face. After all, their businesses grow and prosper day by day. Go at night to protest and give these thieves a canning if necessary! Come, without delay and energetically pull out the claws of those greedy exoloiters! Do you have much to lose? What do they give us—those vultures—in payment for our toil? A ridiculous salary. A miserable pittance!

We too would like to have leisure time to read or study, for we have little education. If the current situation continues, through our lack of consciousness, we shall always be mere human machines manipulated at will by the greediest assassins and thieves.

How can anyone read a book if he or she leaves for work at seven o'clock in the morning and returns home at eleven o'clock at night? We have only eight hours left out of every twenty-four, insufficient time to recuperate our strength and to overcome our exhaustion through sleep! We have no future. Our horizons are bleak. We are born to be exploited and to die in ignorance like animals.[9]

Although Congress passed a law in 1907 recognizing the organization of industrial and commercial employees as well as professionals, union activities were commonly regarded as subversive, doubtless because the socialists and anarchists

9. *Terra Livre* (São Paulo), July 29, 1906, quoted in June E. Hahner, *Women in Latin American History: Their Lives and Views* (Los Angeles, 1976), pp. 115–16.

paid the most attention to the workers. In fact, the anarchists dominated the labor movement until the early 1920s. A workers' congress met in Rio de Janeiro in 1906, and the delegates initiated the steps toward national unionization. The result, the *Confederação Operária Brasileira* (Brazilian Labor Confederation), appeared two years later. The confederation established affiliates in all the major states and in 1913 began to publish *A Voz do Trabalhador* (The Voice of the Worker), a journal with a circulation of 4,000.

The first major strike occurred in 1907. Its objectives were to reduce the working day to eight hours and to raise wages. Starting in São Paulo, it quickly spread to Minas Gerais, Rio Grande do Sul, and Rio de Janeiro. Management met most of the demands. In an unusual show of organization and determination among rural laborers, many of whom apparently were foreign-born, workers on the coffee plantations in Riberão Preto in São Paulo struck for better wages and working conditions in April and May of 1913. Reports circulated that as many as 10,000 were on strike. Significantly, the federal government cooperated with the coffee planters to suppress the strike. Increasing prices and stagnant wages during the war years touched off a general strike in São Paulo in 1917. It affected the entire state and completely paralyzed the city of São Paulo for several days. The government attempted to use the military against the strikers but desisted when the soldiers manifested sympathy toward them. Amid a hostile atmosphere, the unions grew slowly and erratically.

Much of the capital for the new industrialization came in part from successful merchant-importers who could mobilize credit and in part from coffee, as coffee profits were channeled into industrialization through banks. Thus many of the coffee planters were involved in the transition to industrialization, supplying, directly or indirectly, the funds for its growth. It is not surprising, therefore, that the principal coffee state, São Paulo, emerged as the foremost industrial region by 1920. For the first time, that state seemed psychologically disposed to assume national leadership in industrialization, a role it previously had left to Rio de Janeiro; the state's leading newspapers spoke out in articles and editorials to encourage the increasing industrialization. In truth, São Paulo possessed most of the ingredients for successful industrialization. Coffee money provided capital. Labor was plentiful since the state attracted immigrants both from abroad and from other poorer states within the federation. The state possessed a wide variety of raw materials and considerable potential for hydroelectric power. It had developed a railroad network and a reasonably good road system. Furthermore, within the state was an accessible, populous market with buying power. Little wonder then that São Paulo grew in population and wealth. In addition to the coffee wealth, more money became available for investment in industry as the trade balance grew increasingly favorable to Brazil during the war years. The value of exports rose from £26,470,000 in 1914 to £78,177,000 in 1919. In that year, the trade balance in Brazil's favor amounted to £52,000,000.

The heady days of wartime boom ended quickly after 1918. Brazil, like the other nations that had participated directly or indirectly in the war, had to make adjustments to a normal international economy of peace. As the European nations regained their equilibrium, their dependence on Brazil as both the source and supplier of many raw materials and agricultural products lessened. Consequently, Brazilian exports declined. The rate of exchange diminished. The price of coffee fell. By 1920, there was a trade deficit of £17,484,000, a fiscal reverse which Brazil had not experienced in many years. President Pessôa found it necessary to reinstitute the valorization of coffee in an attempt to strengthen the mainstay of the nation's economy. Clearly the 1920s began amid considerable economic uncertainty, soon to be accompanied by political uneasiness. The stress of a turbulent decade would test the foundation of the Old Republic.

New Themes in History

Changes, large and small, altered some of the basic patterns of Brazilian evolution during the last decades of the nineteenth century and the first decades of the twentieth. Mental attitudes underwent modification. The traditional patriarchal system withered in the growing cities, which were a fertile breeding-ground for new ideas. French influence had to yield its exclusivity among the intelligentsia, who found the English language of new interest and fell increasingly under the sway of Anglo-Saxon culture. English theories of Positivism as propounded by Herbert Spencer gained adherents at the expense of the more orthodox theories of Comte. The foremost novelist, Machado de Assis, turned to England for literary models and inspiration. Brazilians admired not only the Constitution of the United States, so important in the writing of their own basic document of 1891, but they also stood in awe of the rapid industrial progress of the northern republic, an achievement they very much hoped to imitate. The commercial ties between the two hemispheric giants continued to tighten. Brazil inaugurated a direct steamship service with New York in 1906; the National City Bank of New York, the first North American banking house in Brazil, established two branches in that country in 1915, and in the same year the American Chamber of Commerce established an office in Rio de Janeiro. Until World War I, American investments in Brazil were practically nonexistent, but thereafter they grew steadily. For practical reasons, then, English became a more widely spoken language among the educated, who increasingly turned to the United States as a commercial and political mentor.

An intensified interest in the United States reflected a broader concern with world affairs in general. The favorable demarcation of the disputed frontiers released Brazilian energies; lifting their eyes to wider, global horizons the Brazilians acquired a greater interest in international affairs. A grandiose foreign policy, aimed at increasing Brazil's prestige in the world and enabling it to assume the leadership of South America, absorbed the nation's attention and set the international course for the future.

The new attitudes characterized the cities, growing both in size and number. The ever larger urban society favored a quicker pace of modernization. The vocal middle groups concentrated in those cities spoke out to suggest reform. These restive groups had a tantalizing taste of power between 1889 and 1894. A new landed class representing the coffee interests replaced them in that year, but they continued to hunger for power and would be heard from again in 1922 and thereafter. Industrialization accompanied urbanization, accounting for some of the city's growth and contributing to the increase in the size of the middle groups. The new factories offered employment to greater numbers of workers. Industrialization centered in the Southeast, roughly in the same region where the coffee culture had predominated. That region emerged as the fastest-developing area in the country, while the prosperity and population of the once dominant sugar-growing Northeast declined proportionately. Thus the Southeast replaced the Northeast as the economic and political heartland of the nation.

A combination of prosperity and the abolition of slavery enticed larger numbers of immigrants into Brazil. The last quarter of the nineteenth century was a period of intensive European immigration, when approximately 40 percent of all immigrants arrived. Between 1891 and 1900 the yearly average reached 112,500. The trend continued and reached record yearly averages just before World War I. From 1911 through 1913, about 500,000 immigrants entered. The figures for the total number of immigrants arriving in Brazil between 1820 and 1930 vary, but a conservative estimate would place the number between 4.5 and 5 million of whom roughly 3.5 million remained. Italians composed the largest group of immigrants, 34.1 percent; the Portuguese were second with 30 percent; the Spaniards third with 12.2 percent; and the Germans fourth with 3.5 percent. The proportion of immigrants to the total population in Brazil never was very high. In 1872, 3.9 percent of the entire population was foreign-born. The percentage rose to 6.4 in 1900, dropped to 4.8 in 1920 and continued to decline thereafter. However, a majority of those immigrants clustered in the four southern states, where they formed a large and influential percentage of the total population.

The number of European immigrants making their

homes in Brazil during the period 1820–1930 approximated the number of Africans imported between the early sixteenth century and 1850. After the passage of the Queiróz Act and its enforcement few if any Africans arrived in Brazil. A definite opinion against admitting them solidified. In fact, by Decree Number 528 of June 28, 1890, Africans and Asians were prohibited from entering Brazil without special congressional approval. That prejudice against Africans and Asians continued, while, on the other hand, the government went to great lengths to encourage Europeans.

In truth, the Brazilian intellectuals, like their counterparts throughout Latin America by the end of the nineteenth century, had fallen victim to specious racial doctrines imported from Europe. The richness of biological thought in the nineteenth century, the popularity of Darwinism, and the complex ethnic composition of Latin America aroused a lively interest in race and racial theories. Much talk circulated about superior and inferior races, and Spain's humiliating defeat in 1898 by the United States seemed to some Cassandras to be the final argument to prove the superiority of the northern European. Brazil's cultural mentor, France, provided an impressive array of pseudoscientific books attesting to that superiority. Joseph Arthur de Gobineau forcefully put forth that argument in his sociological treatise *Essai sur L'Inegalité des Races Humaines*. Widely read at the end of the century was the French social psychologist, Gustave Le Bon, who methodically classified all mankind into superior and inferior races with the Europeans indisputably at the top. Of particular concern to the Brazilians was Le Bon's assertion that miscegenation produced an offspring inferior to either parent. Another champion of the Aryan, the French anthropologist Georges Vacher de Lapouge, minced no words in his chief work, *L'Aryen, son Rôle Social*, published in 1899 to support the theory of racial significance in cultural development. He characterized Brazil as "an enormous Negro state on its way back to Barbarism."

Owing to that French influence, many Brazilians equated whiteness with beauty, intelligence, and ability. Conversely, the darker the people the less possibility there was that they would possess those desired characteristics. Books such as Manoel Bonfim's *O Parasitismo Social e Evolução: A América Latina* (Social Parasitism and Evolution: Latin America), published in 1903, admitted the racial inferiority of Latin America. Graça Aranha's novel *Canaã* (Canaan) suggested the inferiority of people with mixed blood, even as he indicated that the future Brazilian race probably would be mulatto. The self-taught sociologist Oliveira Viana accepted the idea of the superiority of the white in his *Populações Meridionais do Brasil* (The Southern Populations of Brazil). Not at all unusual was this castigation of the Brazilian "race" which appeared in a leading cultural review in 1895:

The Brazilian is the product of three races, each of which differs considerably from the other.

The Negro is of all the races, as everyone knows, the most backward. . . .

The Portuguese race, which once occupied one of the highest positions in the world's history, quickly fell into decadence to the point of being today one of the most exhausted and incapable of all peoples. . . .

The Indian or the primitive among us is inactive and we believe unable to change from his tribal life.

The ruinous combination of these three races is further weakened by an irregular climate, a bad diet, and the adoption of customs and habits contrary to our tropical nature. The Brazilian is an atrophied product, without will, stability, and initiative. Corrupted by Nature, stunted by the colonial process, without physical education which would develop his muscles and tone his nerves, he is a sick man, disillusioned prematurely, without confidence in himself, and unable even to laugh. Without a religion, without a philosophy, without elevated motivation, he aspires to the comfort of a scientific title, a privilege, a diploma.[10]

The pessimistic author frankly stated that what Brazil lacked most was Europeans to purify the blood of the nation: "What we need is new forces, originating in the strong and vigorous races which on arrival here will work by absorption to improve our race." Brazilians were well into the twentieth cen-

10. Jorge Moreal, "Americanismo," *Dom Quixote,* Ano I, No. 8 (1895), p. 3.

tury before they reevaluated their racial concepts, a reassessment which fortunately corrected most of their mistaken ideas.

Meanwhile, the end of the slave trade and the influx of European immigrants, the lower life expectancy of the blacks and the higher infant mortality rate among them were altering the complexion of the Brazilians. They tended to become whiter, the "bleaching process" to which some anthropologists refer. Table 5.5 illustrates that process, but it must be borne firmly in mind that much of the classification was done capriciously by census takers.

Table 5.5. Color Classification of the Brazilian Population, 1872, 1890, and 1940

	Population				
Year	Whites	Browns	Blacks	Yellows	Total
1872	3,854,000	4,262,000	1,996,000	——	10,112,000
1890	6,302,000	5,934,000	2,098,000	——	14,334,000
1940	26,206,000	8,760,000	6,044,000	243,000	41,253,000

SOURCE: *Contribuições para o Estudo da Demografia do Brasil* (Rio de Janeiro, 1961), p. 201.

According to the figures in the table, browns and blacks together constituted the following percentages of the population: 61.9 percent in 1872, 56 percent in 1890, and 35.9 percent in 1940. The figures, if roughly accurate, would seem to lend credence to the "bleaching" theory. A quaint concept of that process and the appreciation of it are superbly illustrated in the painting *Redemption of Ham* (the title is already very significant) by Modesto Brocos (see A Pictorial Study of Brazil, in this book). The black grandmother with hands and eyes uplifted in thanks stands at the side of her beautiful mulatto daughter who in turn is seated next to her white Portuguese husband. On her lap the mulatta bounces her white child. The implication is that the family in three generations has gone from black to white. The expression of the grandmother as well as the presence of the palm branches represent the redemption acknowledged by the old woman. The presentation may be a bit dated today, but less than a century ago it represented the feeling of most Brazilians.

Of course it is difficult as well as dangerous to speak of Brazil's large population—by 1920 Brazil was the ninth most populous country in the world—in absolute terms. The racial composition varied considerably from region to region. In the North, the Indian-Portuguese combination predominated, with a majority of the population some shade of light brown. The Northeast revealed an even wider variation caused by the amalgamation of Indian, black, and white, a characteristic of the West also. Along the coast from Pernambuco down to São Paulo the black influence was strong and the mulatto was much in evidence. The white dominated in the South. Bahia was the blackest state, Santa Catarina the whitest.

While most Brazilians solemnly accepted the European racist doctrines, a few intellectuals raised their voices in mild protest, a prelude to later, deeper questioning. Harkening back to the astute observations made by the German naturalist Karl F. P. von Martius in 1844, a few even began to speak in praise of a Brazilian "culture and race" to which the three races contributed. The literary critic Sílvio Romero preached throughout the last quarter of the nineteenth century and into the second decade of the twentieth that the African had made significant contributions to the creation of Brazilian culture. He concluded:

> The African race has had an enormous influence in Brazil, second only to that of the European. The African penetrated the confines of our most intimate life and in that way greatly molded our popular psychology. . . . The Portuguese alone could not repel the Indian nor till the soil, and therefore he had recourse to a powerful ally: the Negro from Africa. While on the one hand, the Indians proved themselves unproductive, fled, scattered into the hinterland, and died, the Africans, agile, strong, and able, arrived in ever greater numbers. They made possible the establishment of plantations and sugar mills, of towns and cities, and they penetrated the very bosom of the colonial families. The Indians, in general, were not up to the tasks and disappeared; the Negroes, allies of the white, prospered.

> Found in nearly every part of the colony, the slaves lived closely with the families as domestic servants. From that intimate

contact came a mixing of the races; the mulattoes appeared and were yet another link between the two races. The Negro worked in the fields producing the sugar, coffee, and other products known as "colonial" which Europe consumed. Just in the three factors of slavery, labor, and miscegenation, it is easy to discern the immense influence the Negroes had in the formation of the Brazilian people. Slavery, in spite of all its vices, worked as a social factor modifying our habits and customs. It enabled us to cultivate the land and to withstand in leisure the rigors of the climate. It developed as an economic force, producing our riches, and the Negro thus was a robust civilizer. The mixing of the races modified relations between the master and the slave, relaxed our customs, and produced the mulatto who constitutes the majority of our population and to a certain degree the most beautiful part of our race.[11]

Also among the first to assign the black an important historical role in the development of Brazil was Afonso Celso, a contemporary of Romero, in his blatantly nationalistic *Porque Me Ufano do Meu País* (Why I Am Proud of My Country), first published in 1901 and today in its fourteenth edition. The book was required reading in most primary schools. In sharp contrast to his other contemporary, Bonfim, Celso boldly and proudly affirmed, "Today it is a generally accepted truth that three elements contributed to the formation of the Brazilian people, the American Indian, the African Negro, and the Portuguese. . . . Any one of those elements, or any combination of them, possesses qualities of which we should be proud." Celso's book contained a chapter praising the heroic resistance of the slaves at Palmares. The author lavishly bestowed the adjectives "courageous" and "noble" on the black defenders. Brazilians at first timidly explored the idea that their unique civilization was strengthened by the contributions of the blacks. Inhibited by European racist doctrines, they slowly began to investigate those contributions. Their previous concepts changed and their doubts and misgivings disappeared. The new nationalistic temper recoiled before any concept condemning

11. Sílvio Romero, *Historia da Literatura Brasileira*, 2nd ed. (Rio de Janeiro, 1902), I, 89–90.

Brazil to an inferior status. Clearly the racist doctrines seemed to twentieth-century Brazilian intellectuals as one more European effort to subjugate their country.

The pioneer of anthropological studies of the African in Brazil was Dr. Raimundo Nina Rodrigues, a physician born in Maranhão and partially trained in the medical school at Salvador. He worked in Bahia from 1890 to 1905, and it was at that time that he made his anthropological studies. He delved into African cultures with the intention of identifying their survivals in Brazil and thus reconstituting the ethnic groups of blacks representing those cultures. He disproved the long-accepted idea that the Bantu predominated in Brazil by demonstrating the strong cultural presence of the Sudanese groups, particularly the Yoruba, in Bahia. He was the first to study the Afro-Brazilian religions. After him came a small but important group of Bahian scholars, among whom figured Braz do Amaral and Manuel Raimundo Querino, who continued research on the African contributions to Brazil.

Manuel Querino (1851–1923) maintained an active interest in labor and political affairs but increasingly devoted more of his time and energy to historical studies after the turn of the century, in particular to his research and writing on the contributions of the Africans to Brazil's growth. Those studies had a twofold purpose. On the one hand, he wanted to show his fellow blacks the vital contribution they had made to Brazil, while, on the other, he hoped to remind the white Brazilians of the debt they owed Africa and the blacks.

As Querino turned his attention to history, he hoped to rebalance what was by then the traditional emphasis on the European experience in Brazil. No black had ever given his perspective on Brazilian history before. Querino emerged as the first Brazilian—black or white—to detail, analyze, and do justice to the African contributions to Brazil. He presented his conclusions amid a climate of opinion which was at best indifferent, at worst prejudiced and even hostile.

Querino, then, brought to Brazilian historiography the perspective of the black man. Living in the Matatú Grande section of Salvador, he was immersed in, an intimate part of, the black community. He knew perfectly well the habits, aspirations, and frustrations of black Brazilians. Speaking of his source material, Querino revealed that much of his information came directly from respected black elders who spoke with him without inhibitions since they recognized in him a friend exuding understanding and sympathy. Evidence exists that besides writing about the black people, he helped to defend them. He tried to bring to the attention of municipal officials the persecution inflicted on the practitioners of the Afro-Bahian religions. The police, labeling the religions as "barbarian and pagan," frequently raided the *terreiros* where the ceremonies were held, destroying property and injuring the participants. Querino's intervention in their behalf before the local government revealed once again the unique position he held bridging different cultures and classes.

History certainly owes a heavy debt to Querino. He preserved considerable information on the art, artists, and artisans of Bahia. No one can do research on any of those subjects without consulting his works. Further, he is an excellent source for social history. His *As Artes na Bahia,* for example, includes an ample sampling of biographies of workers, artisans, and mechanics, those who qualify as "the common man." Such brief biographies are unique sketches providing an invaluable look into the lives of the humble upon whom much of the growth of Brazil rests. He also offers in his essays abundant information on popular customs, culture, and religion.

Certainly one of Querino's chief contributions to Brazilian historiography was his insistence that national history take into account its African background and the presence and influence of the blacks. Brazil, he emphasized, was the resultant fusion of the Portuguese, Indian, and African. Yet, the contributions of the Africans had gone unheralded. He sought to redress the balance in his suggestive essay "O Colono Prêto como Fator da Civilização Brasileira" (1918), now translated into English under the title *The African Contribution to Brazilian Civilization.* It abounded with insights, many of which later scholarship adopted and expanded—so much so that it is now difficult to appreciate the originality of Querino when he first suggested them. Subsequent scholars have emphasized, for example, that Africa provided the skilled and unskilled labor for Brazil. However, the essay suggested other significant contributions of the blacks on which historians have yet to dwell. For example, Querino assigned the black a principal role in the defense of Brazil and the maintenance of national unity.

At the same time, the literati looked anew at the blacks. In the late nineteenth century, the naturalist novelists gave some attention to them. Aluísio Azevedo in his *O Cortiço* (The Tenement) (1890) and Adolfo Caminha in his *O Bom Crioulo* (The Good Negro) (1895) described at length the black as a member of the urban proletariat. In some of his best novels, Lima Barreto raised his voice to protest the discrimination against the black which manifested itself in Rio de Janeiro, described it in some of its ugliest aspects, and called for justice. In his lengthy poem "Juca Mulato" (1927), Menotti del Picchia characterized the Brazilian as a mulatto, and in this work, for the first time in Brazilian poetry, a mulatto appeared as the hero. The poem received universal acclaim from the critics, both at home and abroad. The more enlightened attitudes toward the races removed embarrassments which earlier had inhibited or confused the intellectuals. Thus freed, they became increasingly proud of the nation's racial amalgamation, which they now viewed as an achievement, not a disgrace.

The more realistic appraisal of the African presence improved the blacks' position in Brazilian society. The myth has persisted that there is no racial prejudice. The facts, alas, contradict that boast. Racial prejudice still exists. Newspapers carry help-wanted advertisements which seek whites only. Until well after the mid-twentieth century both the diplomatic corps and the naval officer corps remained lily-white. After World War II, it was necessary to promulgate a law to punish overt discrimination. However, it must be emphasized that Brazil probably has less racial tension and less racial prejudice than any other multiracial society, past or present. The races mix freely in public places. Interracial marriage is fairly common.

A more formidable barrier than race may well be class.

Class membership depends on a wide variety of factors and their combination: income, family history and/or connections, education, social behavior, tastes in housing, food, and dress, as well as appearance, personality, and talent. Henry Koster noted in the early nineteenth century, "The inferiority which the mulatto feels is more that which is produced by poverty than that which his color has caused, for he will be equally respectful to a person of his own caste who may happen to be rich." The observation is equally valid in the twentieth century, as the sociologist Thales de Azevedo has affirmed in his studies. As it happens, the upper class traditionally had been and still remains mainly white, the lower class principally colored. The significant point, though, is that colored people can and do form a part, albeit a small part, of the upper class, just as whites are by no means uncommon among the humbler classes. Upward mobility exists and education promotes it. With effort, skill, and determination—as well as some luck—class barriers can be hurdled. But frankly it is a jump proportionately few people have been able to make.

Women had begun to play more varied roles in society. True, lower-class women always had worked at a variety of humble jobs and often formed a part of an economic team with their husbands and other members of the family. But now upper-class women appeared in novel surroundings and women of the middle sectors strove to change old prejudices which confined them. The literacy rates provided by the census of 1872 revealed that there were 1,012,097 literate free males and 958 literate slave males, while there were 550,981 literate free females and 445 literate slave females. In major cities, the percentage of literate women was closer to male literacy rates. Prior to World War I, few women enjoyed the right to pursue a life outside the home on an equal footing with men. Their inferior position prompted Francisca Senhorinha da Motta Diniz to speak out in 1890 in protest. She outlined a feminist program in these words:

We want our emancipation and the regeneration of our customs; we want to regain our lost rights; we want true education, which has not been granted us, so that we can educate our children; we want pure instruction so we can know our rights and use them appropriately; we want to become familiar with our family affairs so that we can administer them if ever obliged to. In short, we want to understand what we do, the why and wherefore of matters; we want to be our husbands' companions, not their slaves; we want to know how things are done outside the home. What we do not want is to continue to be deceived.[12]

Women worked but remained concentrated in relatively few occupations, especially those of the service sector, which included teachers and clerical workers as well as domestics. In 1872, a third of the teachers in Rio de Janeiro had been female, a proportion which rose to two-thirds by 1900. At that time women worked in railroad, telegraph, and mail offices. They entered the field of nursing in larger numbers.

The professions opened slowly to women. The educational reform law of 1879 gave them access to the higher institutions of learning, and within a few years some females matriculated in law and medicine, graduating in the late 1880s. Dr. Rita Lobata, who graduated from the Medical School in Bahia in 1887, was the first female physician trained in Brazil to practice medicine. Two years later a female lawyer defended a client in a courtroom for the first time. By the opening of the twentieth century, women had begun to organize—in the Feminine Republican Party, for example—to express their political views.

The Brazilians' growing understanding of themselves in the early decades of the twentieth century, coupled with their pride in the nation's prosperity and achievements, encouraged a nationalism characterized by a literary historian of the period, Júlio Barbuda, as "the emotional synthesis of the fatherland." Nationalism ceased to be that simple defensive force which had characterized it throughout the nineteenth century. In the twentieth century, it became the aggressive means of obtaining a leadership role abroad, of

12. *O Quinze de Novembro do Sexo Feminino* (Rio de Janeiro), April 6, 1890. Quoted in June E. Hahner, *Women in Latin American History: Their Lives and Views* (Los Angeles, 1976), pp. 45–46.

destroying patrimonial institutions and colonial patterns, of liberating Brazil from foreign control, and thereby of developing a modern, industrialized, indigenous society. Nationalism in its new, positive form was a powerful force described by Afonso Celso as "the incalculable dynamo of energy of our times . . . the lever which moves the world." It was bringing to Brazil a new self-confidence exemplified in Celso's cry: "We will grow, we will propser. Education and perfection will come. We are still in the dawn of our greatness. We will arrive inevitably at the brilliance and full heat of mid-day. . . . We will be the second or first power of the world." [13]

Since the Paraguayan War the military had felt itself to be the embodiment of patriotic feeling, an opinion strengthened after the overthrow of the monarchy, when it became the most important single national institution. The army officers in particular—of which there were 3,352 in 1896—felt an obligation to wield the potent moderating power as Pedro II had so wisely and ably done. From 1889 to 1894, the military openly controlled political power. In the years thereafter, the officers manipulated it more discreetly. The governments of the Old Republic deferred to the ideas and ambitions of these officers. Militarism became an increasingly important aspect of political life, and the position of the military in the republic was a paramount issue in the 1910 presidential campaign. Militarism triumphed then with the election of Marshal Hermes da Fonseca to the presidency.

Clearly there was much that was new in Brazil by 1922. Urbanization, industrialization, and modernization were trends well under way. Immigration continued to contribute to the change. Nationalism and militarism, both forces still in the process of being defined, were already powerful instruments which would significantly alter the course of Brazilian evolution.

Despite the changing aspect of Brazil, the past by no means had been eradicated. It still cast a long shadow across

13. Alfonso Celso, *Porque Me Ufano do Meu Paiz*, 7th ed. (Rio de Janeiro, n.d.), pp. 197–98.

the twentieth century. Brazil remained predominantly rural. In 1920, over 70 percent of the employed males were engaged in agriculture. A few products, among which coffee was by far the most important, dominated an economy which retained unmistakable vestiges of mercantilism. The land ownership structures were neocolonial, and the latifundia and monoculture impregnated the economy with the dependency patterns of the past. A privileged, landed oligarchy continued to rule, exercising its prerogatives under the cloak of constitutional provisions. Ignorance and paternalism neutralized the masses. In 1920, more than 64 percent of those over fifteen years of age were illiterate. Modernization as it unfolded after 1850 had not diminished dependency. Ironically it had served to strengthen foreign control. Obviously much yet remained to be changed if Brazil was to fulfill its ambition to develop.

Chapter Six

The Challenge of Change

The process of gradual but accelerating change in the twentieth century weakened the base of some archaic institutions which had long characterized Brazil. Emboldened by the growing sentiment for change, the critics of the established system intensified their attacks on monoculture, the latifundia, and the entrenched oligarchy. The leaders of a new generation announced their intention to develop the nation—spiritually and materially—in 1922. Getúlio Vargas seized power eight years later, and in the following decade and a half he implemented some of the program the dissidents had favored. The coffee interests lost their absolute control of the nation and the urban middle class and proletariat strengthened their positions. The landed class, while still powerful, had to learn to compromise and to share some of its power with those two newly potent elements. Vargas enlisted both to support his government and skillfully identified his program with the increasingly powerful force of nationalism. Waves of nationalism, the drive for development, and the effects of urbanization and industrialization combined to alter part of the social structure. Basic and well established patterns and institutions accommodated some of the change but in the long run limited the profundity of its impact and potential.

Intellectual and Political Ferment

During the 1920s, the intellectuals, always a potent force in the formation of Brazilian public opinion, articulated the challenge to established order and practice. As in the past, they did not hesitate to import from Europe ideas which suited them or their objectives. In that tradition, a small group of young and avant-garde intellectuals introduced into Brazil in the second decade of the century the latest artistic themes and expressions of the twentieth century. Returning from Europe in 1912, Oswaldo de Andrade awakened the first interest in Futurism, a radical artistic movement promoted in Europe by a group of Italians in revolt against realism. It urged a greater freedom of artistic expression to replace the hallowed dicta of the past. The idea of disregarding tradition and concentrating on the present and future fascinated the young Brazilian intellectuals. Mário de Andrade, Di Cavalcanti, Menotti del Picchia, Ronald de Carvalho, and Manuel Bandeira, among others, indicated their support of the new movement. They experimented with freer verse and literary forms. Meanwhile, in 1914, the painter Anita Malfatti had returned to São Paulo from study in Germany and presented an exhibition of her startling paintings which illustrated the German Expressionist style. Three years later she introduced cubism to the Brazilians. The sculptor Vítor Brecheret, who had studied in Italy, joined the courageous young painter to exhibit his own strong and novel works.

Reliance on European culture was regarded with mixed emotions. On the one hand, Europe provided a lively inspiration for arts, but on the other hand, overdependence on Europe disturbed the young Brazilian intellectuals, who felt they had neglected their own homeland to favor foreign modes and trends. The lure of Europe had blinded them to their own surroundings. They felt guilty that they had failed to heed the advice of Sílvio Romero, João Capistrano de

Abreu, and others to deemphasize the preference given to European values. The pulsation of an intense nationalist feeling, as evidenced by the rearmament of the army and navy, creation of the Indian Protection Service, the foundation of the *Revista do Brasil*, the organization of the League of National Defense, and the campaign in favor of obligatory military service, further stirred their consciences. They resolved to reduce their reliance on European culture and to explore their own. Futurism—itself, of course, a European import—provided the perfect formula. It freed them from all the restraints and patterns of the past. They turned their attention to the present and to their immediate surroundings. They set about to discover Brazil. To define and encourage national culture were their dual objectives, and in fulfilling them they intended to declare Brazil's cultural independence. The generation after World War I felt confident it could accomplish those tasks. With excitement and fervor, the young intellectuals abandoned their libraries and took action.

Appropriately, their activities reached a peak in 1922, during the centennial celebrations of independence. The impressive centennial exposition in Rio de Janeiro amply demonstrated the economic growth of the country in the preceding hundred years. The intellectuals in São Paulo determined to show a parallel cultural maturity and to issue a manifesto of cultural independence. The poet Menotti del Picchia phrased their goal as the "Brazilianization of Brazil." "Let us forget the marble of the Acropolis and the towers of the Gothic cathedrals," exhorted Ronald de Carvalho, "We are the sons of the hills and the forests. Stop thinking of Europe. Think of America." Impelled by such enthusiasm, a group of intellectuals in São Paulo organized the Modern Art Week, February 11–17, 1922, during which they defined and enunciated the objectives of their Modernist movement.

The activities of the Modern Art Week centered in the São Paulo Municipal Theater. Graça Aranha, a highly respected author of the previous generation and a member of the Brazilian Academy of Letters, opened the sessions with a speech proclaiming that the intellectuals were in rebellion against the stagnant state of the arts in Brazil. The younger generation spoke through Ronald de Carvalho and Menotti del Picchia. During the week, the poets Mário de Andrade, Manuel Bandeira, Guilherme de Almeida, Ribeiro Couto, and Plínio Salgado illustrated the revolutionary form and content of modern poetry by reading from their own works. Oswald de Andrade read equally novel selections from his prose. The youthful Heitor Villa-Lobos conducted his own music, based on folk themes and employing indigenous instruments. Ernani Braga contributed other compositions of a nationalistic inspiration. The precocious Guiomar Novais interpreted many of the selections, revealing a talent which soon won her international fame as a concert pianist. Modern paintings and sculpture were displayed in the foyer of the theater. In that manner, the Paulista intellectuals succeeded in introducing to a curious—at times hostile—public the latest artistic trends as well as their growing appreciation of the Brazilian environment. The intellectual excitement in São Paulo proved contagious. It spread quickly to the other major cities. Poets declaimed and writers lectured in such diverse places as Manaus, Fortaleza, Belo Horizonte, and Pôrto Alegre. New literary journals sprung up whenever the dedicated revolutionaries sowed their intellectual seeds.

True to their declared goals, the intellectuals weakened their bonds with Europe and increased their concern with national identity. A profound psychological revolution was taking place in which national values began to take precedence over foreign ones. Perhaps Graça Aranha best summarized what was happening in a speech before the citadel of literary traditionalism, the Brazilian Academy of Letters, in 1924. In it, he defined national culture as a European legacy that had been transformed by the conditions of the New World. Brazilian culture owed a debt to Europe but it was also the creation of its own environment. Such opinions harmonized with those being expressed throughout the hemisphere as the Latin Americans began their struggle to achieve their own cultural identity. Mexico, in particular, because of the profound and introspective Revolution of 1910, led the way for the Latin American community toward spiritual and cultural freedom. Brazil, after 1922, rapidly took its own place in the vanguard of that movement.

The results of the Modernist movement were quickly apparent and nowhere more so than in letters. Speaking for his fellow intellectuals, the youthful Sérgio Buarque de Holanda argued, "Brazil has to have a national literature." The best way to create such a literature in his opinion was to respect national traditions, to obtain inspiration from national sources, and to listen to the "profound voices of our race." The writers brazenly attacked the stylistic conventions inherent in their devotion to Europe, which they alleged inhibited their own inventiveness. Freedom of form, a vigorous style rich in fresh images and vernacularisms, and originality of expression characterized the new literature.

A concern with Brazilian themes accompanied the preoccupation with new styles. To better explain Brazil, the intelligentsia probed national psychology, questioned national motives, and reexamined the past. The number of folkloric studies multiplied. Lindolfo Gomes explored the folkways of Minas Gerais; João Simões Lopes published accounts of the popular culture of southern Brazil; Gustavo Barroso illuminated the folklore of the Northeast in several books. By the end of the 1920s a respectable bibliography on the subject existed. Mário de Andrade, who emerged as the dean of the scholars in the field, undertook an active campaign to acquaint his compatriots with their own folk culture and to persuade them to study that invaluable source of information and inspiration. Later he established courses in ethnography and folklore as well as a museum of folklore in São Paulo. Not surprisingly, folklore made its way into national literature, as exemplified by Mário de Andrade's novel, *Macunaíma*, published in 1928. Macunaíma, a Brazilian folk hero, has been called both the Peer Gynt and the Paul Bunyan of the tropics. He seemed to synthesize the qualities as well as the defects of the Brazilian race. Andrade delighted in employing the maximum number of regionalisms and popular expressions in order to enliven and "Brazilianize" his prose.

In Recife in 1926 at the First Brazilian Congress of Regionalism, the young sociologist Gilberto Freyre introduced into Brazilian studies and popularized a significant theme that would thereafter exercise a powerful influence on national thought. He expanded the neglected idea of von Martius and Romero that the uniqueness of Brazilian civilization was the result of the contributions of three races. In 1933, his ideas appeared in *Casa Grande e Senzala,* an immediate literary classic which later was translated into English as *The Masters and the Slaves.* The national and international acclaim given the book freed the intellectuals from many of their cultural complexes and made the African theme and the theme of miscegenation more acceptable than they had hitherto been. Miscegenation, it was at last recognized, had made Brazil a homogeneous nation, despite its gargantuan size. Freyre's cogent discussion of the creation of a unique civilization in Brazil opened vast new areas for research and study. Prior to that time, most of the works written about the blacks concerned the institution of slavery. Such was not the case after 1933, when scholars sought to emphasize the African heritage in the formation of Brazil.

In the 1930s a whole new socio-anthropological literature on the blacks appeared. Scholars such as Artur Ramos, Evaristo de Moraes, J. Bastos de Ávila, Édison Carneiro, Renato Mendonça, and Aderbal Jurema contributed to a rapidly growing bibliography. They studied the blacks as an integral element of Brazilian civilization and pointed out their contribution to national development and history. In 1935, Artur Ramos occupied the newly created chair of social psychology at the University of the Federal District. His lectures concentrated on the role of the blacks in Brazilian society. Four volumes on that subject came from his pen: *O Negro Brasileiro* (The Brazilian Negro), *O Folclore Negro do Brasil* (Negro Folklore of Brazil), *As Culturas Negras no Novo Mundo* (Negro Cultures in the New World), and *Negros Escravos* (Negro Slaves). In 1934 the first Afro-Brazilian Congress met in Recife, and two years later a second one convened in Salvador. The papers read during those sessions and the discussions which followed emphasized the revised opinion about the blacks and their newly assigned place within the Brazilian family.

Throughout Latin America during the 1920s and 1930s interest in the blacks and their contribution to the New World grew. Naturally the intellectual curiosity and activity was greatest in those areas, especially the Caribbean and Brazil, where the black populations were largest. In Cuba, the prolific intellectual Fernando Ortiz began writing about the blacks as early as 1906. Together with the prominent Nicolás Guillen, the originator of the *negrismo* school of poetry, he founded the Society for Afro-Cuban Studies in 1926 and thereafter devoted himself with increasing fervor to the study of the Afro-Cubans.

The Brazilians' new enthusiasm for the study of the blacks reached a peak during the celebrations in 1938 marking the golden anniversary of the abolition of slavery. In Belo Horizonte, the state Historical Institute and Fine Arts Society jointly sponsored an "Afro-Brazilian Studies Week," which featured an art exhibit and a series of lectures. Mário de Andrade organized for the city of São Paulo an elaborate program of speeches, dances, and music. The speeches later appeared in the *Revista do Arquivo Municipal* (Journal of the Municipal Archive). Rio de Janeiro, too, feted the occasion in a similar manner.

The literati also gave their attention to the African influences on Brazil. At the same time that Freyre was preparing his sociological study, Jorge de Lima was writing poems on black themes. Some of his works paid tribute to the moral superiority of the Negro in a manner reminiscent of the treatment earlier accorded the Indian. In his short book of poetry published in 1933, *Urucungo*, Raul Bopp treated exclusively Afro-Brazilian themes. Blacks also began to appear as the protagonists in novels—not as a curiosity, as had frequently happened in the past, but as respected members of the community. José Lins do Rego's *O Moleque Ricardo* (The Young Man Richard) and Jorge Amado's *Jubiabá*, both published in 1935, illustrated that trend.

The ferment of the 1920s also stirred the intellectuals to attempt new interpretations of their homeland. From the pen of Paulo Prado came the most penetrating analysis of Brazil in the 1920s. Pessimism dominated his *Retrato do Brasil* (Portrait of Brazil), published in 1928. His opening words, "In a radiant land live a sad people," set the tone for the study. He viewed the history of Brazil as the chaotic development of two passions, sensuality and greed. In order for Brazil to progress, according to the author, it was essential first to isolate and diagnose the weaknesses of Brazilian character and then to correct them. His pessimism contrasted sharply with the buoyant optimism of other writers, such as Afonso Celso. In fact, those two represent the extreme views Brazilians are wont to take of their own country, a duality ingrained in the Brazilian character. In the years after the publication of *Retrato do Brasil*, several other excellent analytical studies of Brazil appeared. The most significant were Sérgio Buarque de Holanda's *Raizes do Brasil* (The Roots of Brazil); Afonso Arinos de Melo Franco's *Introdução ao Estudo da Realidade Brasileira* (Introduction to the Study of Brazilian Reality) and *Conceito da Civilização Brasileira* (Understanding Brazilian Civilization); Nelson Werneck Sodré's *Formação da Sociedade Brasileira* (The Formation of Brazilian Society); and Freyre's *Brazil: An Interpretation*, which first appeared in English and later was translated into Portuguese and still later appeared in English in a revised and augmented form as *New World in the Tropics*.

It was soon apparent that beneath the excitement of cultural nationalism swirled powerful political currents. Most of the contributors to the intellectual ferment became deeply involved in politics in the 1920s and thereafter. Their political preferences varied widely from the far right to the far left. On the one hand, Plínio Salgado chose Fascism; on the other, Oswald de Andrade flirted with Communism. In common, they all shared a bitter disappointment with the effete republic and a desire to reform the political structure and to reorient the nation. By the mid-1920s, a majority of the intellectuals withheld their allegiance to the republic. The mounting discontent with the governments of the 1920s originated not from the fact that the administrations of that decade differed from their predecessors—they did not—but rather from the fact that social and economic conditions had changed, a change the political system failed to register. The intellectuals spoke out to call to the attention of the public the need for new solutions to old problems. Their persuasive arguments and their easy access to the press enabled them to mold as well as to express public opinion.

Their influential voices joined those of the single most powerful group in Brazil, the military, to express a dissatisfaction with the course the republic had taken. Few would deny the significant role of the military in the republic, but after 1894—and with the exception of the Hermes da Fonseca regime—the officers left the overt administration of the government in the hands of civilians representing the coffee elite. In turn, those governments were scrupulously careful to provide generous budgets for the army and the navy and not to sully the honor of the military. As a result, for several decades relations between the republican governments and the military hierarchy tended to be harmonious. After World War I, the tacit accord between the two ended. The change began under President Pessôa who boldly vetoed a bill to increase military pay and appointed two civilians, João Pandiá Calógeras and Raul Soares, to head the Ministries of War and Navy respectively. Since the advent of the republic, the military had been accustomed to holding those portfolios. The reaction to the unexpected appointments was immediate and negative. The navy openly, though vainly, threatened the president. The officers manifested a growing concern for their position, privileges, and honor. Offended and displeased, they drew back from the government. The situation became both more complex and dangerous in 1921, when Marshal Hermes da Fonseca returned to Brazil after an absence of six years in Europe. He provided the prestige and leadership under which various military factions could unite. In recognition of his unique role, the officers duly elected him president of the powerful Clube Militar in Rio de Janeiro, a position which lent to his pronouncements the voice of all the military. Soon he began to make ominous statements which seemed to bode no good for the civilian government. Dissatisfied with the course Pessôa pursued, Marshal Hermes observed, "The political situations change, but the Army remains." With that veiled reminder of its stability, its continuity, and its exercise of the *poder moderador*, the military warned the government of its dissatisfaction.

With exports, coffee prices, and the rate of exchange all falling as Europe recovered its prewar vitality, the Pessôa government had already experienced more than enough troubles, when, in early 1921, the question of presidential succession surfaced. In accordance with a previous agreement between the two important states of São Paulo and Minas Gerais, the young governor of Minas Gerais, Artur da Silva Bernardes, was slated to be the next president. Protest erupted from the states which had not been party to that exclusive agreement. They increasingly resented the domination of public office by those two coffee states. In disgust, they formed their own coalition, the "Republican Reaction" and nominated Nilo Peçanha for the presidency. That coalition allied Rio Grande do Sul, Rio de Janeiro, Pernambuco, and Bahia with the military. As a bitter campaign got under way it exposed deepening national divisions and frustrations.

The Republican Reaction exerted great efforts to woo the disaffected military. In October of 1921, the *Correio da Manhã*, a Rio de Janeiro daily long in opposition to the government, published a letter, allegedly written to Raul Soares and said to be in the handwriting of Bernardes, that was offensive in its remarks to the military. At once Bernardes categorized the letter as a forgery. The Clube Militar insisted it was authentic. Offended by the letter, most of the military officers followed the lead of Marshal Hermes and pledged their support to Nilo Peçanha. Events surrounding the election of the governor of Pernambuco further alienated the military from the federal government and hence from its official candidate. The opposition accused President Pessôa of putting local army units at the disposal of the gubernatorial candidate favorable to the federal government. As president of the Clube Militar, Hermes da Fonseca telegraphed the army garrison in Recife, asking it to defy the supposed orders of the federal government. The government arrested Hermes for signing the extraordinary telegram and shut down the Clube Militar for six months. The presidential elections held in March of 1922 did nothing to improve relations between the government and the military. Bernardes won, receiving 467,000 votes to the 318,000 cast for Peçanha or 56 percent of the votes. The defeated candidate and the Military Club promptly requested a recount, but the candidate favored by the military had lost. For the first time in the history of the republic, the military was alienated from the government.

In repetition of events during the last decade of the empire, alienation occurred on two levels. On the senior level were the highest-ranking officers who, although unfriendly to the government, were reluctant to take up arms to overthrow it. More than their aroused ire was needed to entice them to action. They had to be convinced that military honor, privilege, and prestige were irrevocably compromised or at stake. On the junior level the officers cared less for those vanities. Inbued with idealism, they sought a government which would reform and strengthen the nation. The apparent weakness of the republic, the pettiness and vanity of the politicians, the corruption, fraud, and inefficiency which surrounded and pervaded the government disturbed them.

The junior officers displayed little of the patience of their seniors. A small group of them resolved after the elections of 1922 to bring to an end the monopoly which the coffee interests exercised over the government and thus, perhaps, to purify it. Poorly planned and badly coordinated, a revolt broke out at the Igrejinha Fort on Copacabana Beach on July 5, 1922, under the leadership of some lieutenants stationed there, the most important of whom were Antônio Siqueira Campos and Eduardo Gomes. The cadets at the Military Academy rose to join the rebellion, but they were quickly brought to order. In the crisis, the senior officers gave their loyalty to the government and led their troops against Copacabana. The rebellious fort fired a few desultory rounds before it came under bombardment from both land and sea. Most of the rebels surrendered to the government forces, but a quixotic band of eighteen came onto the beach to fight it out, in vain, with the overpowering forces of the government. There most of them dramatically gave their lives for their vaguely defined cause.

As an isolated incident, the revolt at Copacabana appears to have little meaning or importance. In retrospect, however, it is possible to identify the heroics on the beach with a larger movement under way in Brazil in the 1920s. As part of a general protest against the eroding effectiveness of a nearly moribund republic, it assumes considerable importance. Furthermore, it initiated a series of revolts which would end with the overthrow of the republic in 1930. Its occurrence in 1922 helps to signal that year as the beginning of an active repudiation of the past, a manifestation of disappointment and frustration with the course Brazil had followed. The Copacabana revolt, coupled with the pronouncements culminating in the Modern Art Week, were notification that a new generation, representative of the increasingly well defined urban middle groups, had challenged the nation's hoary political, economic, and social institutions and sought to propel Brazil into the future. Although their plans were vague, they were adamant in their demand for change and reform.

Other manifestations favorable to change also occurred in 1922. In that year, the Roman Catholic Church expressed a new interest and concern in the plight of the proletariat. The resourceful Sebastião Leme, later to be elevated to cardinal, oversaw the foundation of Workers' Circles, whose principal purpose was to improve the temporal lot of the working class. The Circles operated cooperatives, hospitals, clinics, pharmacies, and schools for workers, activities publicly frowned upon by the more conservative elements of society.

At that time Brazilian Catholicism was undergoing a spiritual renovation. At least some of those responsible for that renewed vigor perceived Catholicism as a significant ingredient in national identity. The monthly Catholic review *Brasilea* proclaimed, "It was this religion which prepared this land to be our nation, which blessed us as free men and which is making us a cultured people." Such a statement equated religious unity with national unity.

Reflecting a desire among a small minority for radical change, the Communist Party of Brazil was founded in 1922. Three unique features for the Brazilian politics of that time characterized that party: it was national in scope and well disciplined and offered a firm and identifiable ideology.

Varied forms of protest came together in the centennial years. The intellectuals issued their proclamation of independence; the Roman Catholic Church invigorated its concern with the poor and proclaimed its indeliable imprint on Brazilian nationality; the military initiated its physical protest against the government; and the Communist party emerged to voice a radical program of change. After 1922, Brazil would never be quite the same. New forces were in motion, for the time being imperceptible in their direction and consequence.

President Bernardes proved unable to master the situation. He inherited a legacy of resentment of the domination of the coffee elite. The financial picture was "gloomy": heavy debts, budget deficits, declining exports, and the lowest rates of exchange since 1894. The political turmoil appeared equally discouraging: the Federal District and Rio de Janeiro were under a state of siege, and civil war erupted in Rio Grande do Sul. Further, Bernardes, in order to get vengeance on Nilo Peçanha, helped to create a situation in the state of Rio de Janeiro, the political base of his opponent, which required federal intervention. Nor did Bernardes display an eagerness to win the much-needed support of the military. He refused to pardon the young officers who plotted and revolted in 1922. The government tried, condemned, and sentenced them, a treatment which only increased military opposition to the president. One group which Bernardes could not afford to alienate was the coffee interests. Here he faced a dilemma. Personally he favored financial orthodoxy and thus questioned valorization. However, beholden to the coffee interests for their support, he could not neglect their appeals for guarantees that coffee prices would slip no farther on the market. He decided to turn the supervision of valorization over to São Paulo and ordered the Bank of Brazil to follow a generous policy toward the coffee planters.

Criticism cascaded over the president, who shut himself

up in Catete Palace, made few public appearances, and sternly concentrated on maintaining public order. One of the few to come to the defense of the beleaguered president was Jackson de Figueiredo, a powerful polemicist and militant Roman Catholic lay leader. In his writings, he assailed both the rising tide of nationalism and the restive young army officers. "Order above law," a phrase he coined, summarized part of his political philosophy. Indeed, the review he founded in 1921 bore the title *A Ordem*. His prescribed treatment for the protesters of his day was "Club them!" He believed that threats to Brazilian nationality came not from foreign powers, as was a conventional belief among the nationalists, but from Protestantism, Masonry, and Judaism. Also contrary to the nationalistic trends of his age, he was pro-Portuguese, appreciating and lauding those values and institutions which Portugal had transmitted to Brazil. Those opinions, forcefully stated, did little to rescue the president from unpopularity, and they serve best to represent a minority opinion expressed in the twenties by a few intellectuals.

Intensifying their demands for change, the young army officers waved the banner of revolt again on July 5, 1924, this time in São Paulo. The rebels entrusted their leadership to a retired general, Isidoro Dias Lopes, but it was the young officers, particularly Miguel Costa, Joaquim and Juárez Távora, Eduardo Gomes, Oswaldo Cordeiro de Farias, and João Alberto Lins de Barros, who provided the enthusiasm and impetus. Not all of those young advocates of revolt were in São Paulo itself at the time of the uprising. João Alberto, for example, was in Rio Grande do Sul in July carrying out a mission for the Paulista plotters. The lieutenants maintained limited but significant contacts with the local laborers—by 1924, São Paulo was the major industrial city of South America. The rebels denounced Bernardes and vaguely called for the reformation of the republic. Loyalist forces converged on the city of São Paulo from all sides. After holding the city for twenty-two days, the rebels evacuated it to move first west and then south. Meanwhile rebellion erupted briefly in Aracajú, Manaus, and Belém, and on a larger scale in Rio Grande do Sul. In November, the warship *São Paulo* mutinied in Guanabara Bay and sailed to asylum in Montevideo. Under the command of Captain Luís Carlos Prestes, rebels from Rio Grande do Sul moved northward to join the forces of Isidoro Lopes which had withdrawn from São Paulo. That unified body of rebels, which won national fame as the "Prestes Column," then began a rugged three-year odyssey (1924–1927) through the sertão. They marched northward into Maranhão before turning southwesterly and disbanding in Bolivia after a 14,000 mile trek.

Prestes, dubbed the "Knight of Hope," exerted a strong mystic appeal over his followers and many elements of the Brazilian population who admired his bold if quixotic challenge to the government. Nonetheless, his efforts to arouse the populace to take up arms against that government failed. The peasants were still too much under the powerful sway of local "coroneis" to be enlisted into the ranks of rebellion. The countryside never had been the place to foment change in Brazil. The results of the Prestes Column demonstrated that in the mid-1920s it still was not. The discontented elements centered in the cities: the column never made contact with the urban protesters and consequently never tapped that potential reservoir of support.

The federal government underplayed the significance of the rebellions and as far as possible ignored the discontent. Political maneuvering absorbed most of its energy. Coffee sales recovered from their decline of the early 1920s and in fact reached new highs. The dictum seemed true that so long as coffee sold well the government could follow whatever course it preferred. Good prices and ready sales insured the coffee interests' monopoly over the federal government.

In 1926, in accordance with a previous agreement between the two major coffee-producing states, Bernardes turned over the reins of government to the Paulista Washington Luís Pereira de Sousa, whose candidacy had not been challenged. He won 98 percent of the 700,000 votes cast. As a gesture of conciliation, the new president lifted the state of siege, an intrinsic part of the previous administration, and restored freedom of the press. Two matters dear to the hearts of the coffee planters also received his attention. First, the government encouraged road building, with the prompt initiation of two highway projects which would connect Rio de Janeiro with São Paulo and Petropolis (the first step toward Belo Horizonte). Second, the government resolved to make financial reforms. In fulfillment of time-honored goals, the budget was balanced. The government scrupulously kept public finances in order. Similar to the Conversion Office under the Pena administration, a Stabilization Office issued a new paper currency backed by gold. By the end of the Bernardes administration, the government had embarked on a new experiment in coffee marketing, leaving the administration of it in the hands of the states. The experiment continued during the Luís government. São Paulo, with its powerful Coffee Institute, directed the marketing, limiting shipments and storing the beans, when necessary, to sell when the market was favorable. Able administration of the Institute as well as optimum international conditions brought about a sharp rise in coffee prices.

The prosperity of the early years of the Washington Luís administration only thinly disguised the discontent with the republic. Of course, some discontent had existed since the beginning of the republic. First, there had been the embittered monarchists who assailed the new republic. They were joined shortly by disillusioned Republicans who voiced their disappointment with the new regime. A *"complexo de remorso"* (feeling of remorse) saddened many. Afonso Celso, a Republican who by 1893 had become a monarchist, lamented, "With remorse, I confess that I did attack, not rarely, the Emperor in the press and in parliament, attributing to him exclusive responsibility for all our ills . . . Publicly I confess my contrition." One intellectual, Alfredo de Paiva, asked bluntly in 1891, "Where are the statesmen of the Republic?" A multitude echoed that embarrassing question during the following decades. Nostalgically men looked back to the "glories of the empire." They remembered the years prior to 1889 as ones of statesmanship, order, and liberty, and contrasted them with the passions, disorders, and repressions of the republic. Some of the literati reminisced and complained in print, further developing the literature of "remorse" to which such intellectuals as Alberto Tôrres, Amaro Cavalcanti, Oliveira Viana, and Paulo Prado contributed. Their writing reflected the deepening disappointment and frustration with the republic. The reality of the republic, they emphasized, differed diametrically from the theory and principles upon which it was based. Farias Brito, a fiery partisan for the establishment of the republic, sadly reflected in later judgment of it, "All the good of which I had dreamed, I saw transformed into anarchy and disorder, perturbation and injustice." In his *Retrato do Brasil,* the patrician critic Paulo Prado deprecated the evils of the republican political system and recommended, "We have used unsuccessfully many medicines for our malady. It remains to try surgery." Many liberal democrats concurred as they surveyed the history of coffee politics, the selfish regional monopolization of power, manipulated elections, the continuation of patriarchalism and colonialism, and the consistently sterile governments. The republic had not fulfilled their hopes.

The restive young military officers, still the impatient and articulate sons of the urban middle groups, judged the republic unsatisfactory. Their dissatisfaction, then, represented the opinions of those who felt themselves marginalized politically and economically by coffee politics. Protest burst into open rebellion in 1922 and 1924 and during the Prestes march. Although their objectives were cryptic and muddled at first, the young officers gradually began to codify them. By 1926, the *tenente* (lieutenant) movement had acquired a somewhat more identifiable philosophy, even though—it must be emphasized—it never became precise. Above all else, the tenentes maintained a mystical faith that somehow a military revolution would alter the habits of the country and provide the impetus to propel it into the modern age. Reform, not democracy, was their primary concern. They wanted to retire the entrenched politicians and modernize the nation; then—and only then—they would consent to return the nation to constitutional rule. The republic they envisioned would rest on a vastly expanded political base. As it was, fewer than 5 percent of the adult population met literacy and other qualifications to become voters. Between 1894 and 1906, an average of 2.4 percent of the population voted in presidential elections; between 1910 and 1930, participation averaged 2.7 percent. Furthermore, the tenentes proposed a government that would unite all Brazilians and thereby negate the debilitating regionalisms. A powerful central government was their goal. Revealing strong "social democratic" tendencies, the tenentes proposed government recognition of trade unions and cooperatives, a minimum wage, maximum working hours, child labor legislation, agrarian reform, and nationalization of the mines. The magazine *5 de Julho*, which spoke for the Prestes Column, expressed many of the ideas of the young military revolutionaries as follows:

> Reasons: financial and economic disorder; exorbitant taxes; administrative dishonesty; lack of justice; perversion of the vote; subordination of the press; political persecution; disrespect for the autonomy of the states; lack of social legislation; reform of the constitution under the state of siege. Ideals: to assure a regime loyal to the republican constitution; to establish free primary instruction and professional and technical training throughout the country; to assure liberty of thought; to unify justice, putting it under the aegis of the Supreme Court; to unify the Treasury; to assure municipal liberty; to castigate the defrauders of the patrimony of the people; to prevent professional politicians from becoming rich at public expense; to account strictly for public funds.[1]

Clearly much of the program advocated by the *tenentes* favored the urban middle groups.

Returned to their secondary position in 1894, those middle groups increasingly resented the economic and political monopoly the large fazendeiros, particularly the coffee planters, wielded in the republic. They decried the many favors the government lavished on the planters. Burgeoning coffee harvests in the 1920s alarmed them. Between 1927 and 1929 production exceeded 21 million sacks, of which scarcely 14 million were exported. Subtracting the coffee consumed

1. Quoted in Ernest A. Duff, "Luís Carlos Prestes and the Revolution of 1924," *Luso-Brazilian Review*, 4, no. 1 (June 1967), p. 13.

in Brazil, it still meant that the public—especially the bourgeoisie—bore the financial burden of valorizing the coffee kept in storage, and, by extension, of supporting international coffee prices. The government, faithful to its coffee backers, borrowed more abroad to make valorization feasible. A foreign debt which in 1926 reached $900 million with an annual interest of $175 million shot up to $1,181 million with a service charge of $200 million in 1930. It was at that moment that the United States—whose rapid industrialization in the last half of the nineteenth century and military prowess during World War I had aroused the admiration of the middle groups—supplanted Great Britain as Brazil's major foreign investor. By 1927 North Americans owned about 35 percent of Brazil's entire federal debt. The middle groups remained spectators to all these events. In the elections of 1910 and 1922, when a possibility for change was offered, they lacked sufficient strength to seize it. Further, they failed to understand that the various military rebellions in the 1920s could have been turned to their advantage. Indicative of the weakness of the middle groups was their inability to coordinate their desires for modernization with the similar desires of the young officers.

Men professing nationalistic inclinations also counted themselves among those disgruntled with the republic. On the one hand, they harbored suspicions of the coffee oligarchy, which seemed too intimately linked with world markets and far too international in its outlook. Consequently, its interest could hardly coincide with national interests. On the other hand, the nationalists viewed with alarm the rampant regionalism which the permissive Constitution of 1891 seemed to encourage. In some state capitals, the state flag flew from every mast, while one searched in vain to locate the Brazilian colors. The militia of São Paulo employed its own French military mission to train it and stood at a strength and readiness capable of challenging the federal army. The nationalists favored a government which would subordinate both regionalism and internationalism to the well-being and advancement of the nation.

Few means of effective protest existed. Political parties—

which could have provided some alternatives—continued to be small and poorly organized. In contrast to the system fostered by the empire, there was not one national party with the minor exception after 1922 of the Communist Party. The Republican party maintained its strength in most of the important states, but the only national link between the highly individual regional organizations was through the letters, telegrams, or telephone calls of the president of the republic to the presidents of the states. The nationalists tried at various times to organize parties to reflect their views, but their organizations always remained small and local. Consequently their message seldom extended beyond the confines of half a dozen coastal cities. Their platforms contained a variety of planks, such as the transference of the capital from the coast to the interior, the nationalization of commerce, retention of profits within the country, nationalization of the press, creation of a national theater, control of rents to limit foreign control of property, establishment of agricultural credit, closer relations with the Latin American community, and a stronger federal government. The proposal to relocate the federal capital in the interior was an old dream of patriots and symbolized their aspiration to "Brazilianize" Brazil. The desires to nationalize commerce and to control rents, and, to a lesser degree, to nationalize the press, create a national theater, and keep profits within the country reflected the Brazilians' continuing resentment of the resident Portuguese and their antipathy toward the former metropolis.

From the disaffected middle groups came the rank and file as well as the leaders of the protest against the republican governments. Those groups felt most pinched and thwarted by the static political system. The masses, rural and urban, fatalistically accepted their menial position. The middle groups, through the outcries of the young military officers, the intellectuals, and the nationalists, refused to. They sought higher social distinctions and greater political power and, what is very important, they thought they saw the possibility of attaining them. As Crane Brinton cogently pointed out in *The Anatomy of Revolution*, revolutions arise from hope, not despair, from the promises of progress rather than from continuous oppression.

It took a grave political error and an international crisis to end the power monopoly exercised by the coffee oligarchy. Washington Luís made the political error by selecting as his successor another Paulista, the young and talented governor of São Paulo, Júlio Prestes. The old politicians bridled at the affront implied by the fact that one of their number had been passed over in favor of a younger candidate. The noncoffee states protested that yet another president would serve the exclusive interests of the coffee producers. All literate Brazil might have laughed when Mendes Fradique wittily noted, "The twenty states of Brazil are two: São Paulo and Minas Gerais," but that laughter rang hollow in the other eighteen states, embittered by long neglect. Of greatest significance was the friction between the two coffee allies, Minas Gerais and São Paulo, caused by the selection of Prestes. Favoring alternation in office, the Mineiros claimed that the presidency should be returned to one of them, preferably the ambitious governor, Antônio Carlos Ribeiro de Andrade. The split between São Paulo and Minas Gerais over the presidential succession offered the noncoffee states a rare opportunity to attempt to capture the presidency for themselves. Still, São Paulo might have been powerful enough to enforce its will had not a deepening world depression knocked the bottom out of the coffee market, thereby weakening its economic and psychological position. Between 1929 and 1931, the price of coffee plummeted from 22.5 to 8 cents a pound. Between 1929 and 1932, Brazil's foreign trade fell 37 percent by volume and 67 percent by value. The substantial gold reserves disappeared by the end of 1930, and the exchange rate, relatively stable between 1927 and 1930, reached a new low. The full weight of the disaster fell on São Paulo, whose warehouses groaned with unsold coffee. In 1930, 26 million sacks lay in storage, a million more than the world consumed in 1929 and twice the amount Brazil usually exported in a year. Such an economic reverse made the coffee oligarchy vulnerable to political attack at a time when disenchantment with its rule had reached a new high. The attack was mounted over the question of the presidential succession in 1930.

To combat the candidacy of Júlio Prestes, a coalition composed of the disaffected Minas Gerais, the ambitious Rio Grande do Sul, the neglected Paraíba, and by an assortment of small opposition parties, urban middle groups, young military officers, nationalists, and intellectuals took shape under the name of the Liberal Alliance. Through an agreement between the politicians of Rio Grande do Sul and Minas Gerais, the Alliance nominated the gaúcho Getúlio Vargas for president and João Pessôa of Paraíba for vice-president. Their program, announced at the end of July 1929, called for an amnesty for all participants in the 1922–1926 revolutions, new election laws, social legislation, a reorganization of the educational and judicial systems, and accelerated economic development. Those planks seemed to promise change and modernization.

During the campaign the two candidates behaved in the manner tolerated by the practices of the republic: they wheeled and dealed, double-crossed each other and their allies, contradicted themselves, and freely dispensed platitudes. In the process, Vargas made a curious pact with Washington Luís. He promised not to campaign outside of Rio Grande do Sul and to accept the results of the election in return for Luís' agreement not to support the opposition to the Liberal Alliance in Rio Grande do Sul and his promise to use his influence, along with that of Prestes, to urge Congress to seat the deputies, whoever they might be, elected from the Gaúcho state. Excitement engulfed the campaign as oratory built to a crescendo. Despite some minor disturbances, the election held on March 1, 1930, was generally peaceful. Prestes triumphed, claiming 1,100,000 of 1,900,000 votes cast. The rural oligarchy had succeeded in marshalling enough votes to more than offset those of the urban malcontents.

Disappointment over the results of the election was widespread. Vargas, however, seemed to accept them, although he perfunctorily cried fraud, a safe enough accusation which all losing candidates were expected to make. In

May, Congress refused to seat the deputies from Minas Gerais and Paraíba elected on the opposition ticket; resentment of the government candidates' victory welled up. The political situation grew tenser. It took only the crack of an assassin's pistol in Recife to set in motion a far-reaching rebellion. Personal and local matters were the principal cause of the assassination of João Pessôa on July 25, 1930, but the opposition linked the murder to the political group of Washington Luís, and the nation in general regarded it as political in motivation. The tragedy infused new energy, unity, and purpose into the Liberal Alliance and its adherents, who determinedly set about to plan the overthrow of the Washington Luís government by force.

Coordinated from three states—Rio Grande do Sul, Minas Gerais, and Paraíba—the revolt broke out on October 3. Forces from Paraíba under the command of Juarez Távora, a *tenente* from the uprisings of the 1920s, marched southward, capturing Recife and Salvador with no difficulty. Led by Pedro Aurélio de Góes Monteiro, the rebels from Rio Grande do Sul moved northward toward São Paulo. And from Minas Gerais, insurgent forces invaded the states of Espírito Santo and Rio de Janeiro. The government proved unable to halt the advances. One might have expected the coffee planters to rush to the support of the Paulista president and his hand-picked successor, but many of them, troubled by the depression and concerned by the government's reluctance to mobilize all its resources behind valorization, adopted a neutral if not hostile attitude toward the faltering government in Rio de Janeiro. Despite all the civilian support for the rebellion begun by the Liberal Alliance, its success was impossible without the support or at least the acquiescence of the military. First the tenentes active in the 1920s revolts resolutely joined the ranks of the rebels. Then unit after unit of the army spontaneously adhered to the cause. Finally the senior officers decided that the moribund republic no longer merited further support. They seized power from the president on October 24 and established a junta of three officers as an interim government. Meanwhile, the journey of the chief of the Liberal Alliance from Pôrto Alegre to Rio de Janeiro turned into a triumphal procession. Nowhere was Vargas more enthusiastically cheered than in São Paulo. Apparently to those who shouted his "vivas," he was the embodiment of hope and promise. To a considerable number, he symbolized change. He reached the capital, where the atmosphere was already festive, on October 31. Four days later, the junta handed him the sash of office. The military had played the arbiter in politics again, and the Old Republic ended as it began, with a military movement. The military coup, a political miscalculation, and a deepening world depression were the immediate causes for the demise of the republic. More basically, industrialization, urbanization, the spread of nationalism, and a growing desire for change set in motion forces with which the sterile and unimaginative Old Republic was unable to cope.

Shifting Patterns of Power

After accepting control of the nation from the military junta, Getúlio Dórtico Vargas governed for nearly a generation, first as chief of the provisional government (1930–1934), next as constitutional president elected by Congress (1934–1937), then as dictator (1937–1945), and finally as constitutional president elected by the people (1951–1954). His position in modern Brazilian history remains so dominant that even the governments of the 1960s fall under the shadow of his formidable legacy. Any man who wields such overpowering influence is bound to be controversial, and over the years Vargas has inspired paeans of praise and elicited curses of damnation.

Vargas was born in 1883 on the rich cattle estate of his family in São Borja, Rio Grande do Sul, just across the Uruguay River from Argentina. After preparatory studies in Minas Gerais, he enrolled in the military school at Rio Pardo in his natal state and, still a cadet, served in garrisons in Pôrto Alegre and Mato Grosso. He abandoned his military training to take a degree from the Faculty of Law in Pôrto Alegre in 1907. Soon thereafter he entered politics, and the formative years of his political career were spent under the tutelage and discipline of the perennial governor of Rio Grande do Sul, Antônio Augusto Borges de Medeiros, in an atmosphere of Comtian positivism. Once under way, his political rise was meteoric: federal deputy from 1924–1926, minister of finance from 1926–1928, governor of Rio Grande do Sul, 1928–1930, and chief-of-state in 1930. Short, wiry, with a winning smile, Vargas proved to be gifted with unusually keen political intuition. Above all else he was a realist, and his political decisions generally reflected that pragmatism. Often he has been termed a *caudilho* in the Spanish American tradition, but it would require exaggerated license to compare him with contemporaneous caudilhos such as Juan Vicente Gómes of Venezuela, Jorge Ubico of Guatemala, or Rafael Trujillo of the Dominican Republic. Vargas governed more or less within the Brazilian tradition. Moderation and affability tempered his administration. Absent were the pomp, terror, and inflexibility so often characteristic of Spanish American dictatorships. He seemed disposed in most cases to follow the currents of his time, to innovate, and to experiment. The prospects of change did not frighten him, but he approached change cautiously.

Surrounding Vargas and urging reforms during the early years of his administration were the *tenentes*, the radicals of the rebellion. Their initial goals were to remove the corrupt and reactionary old-line politicians from office, strengthen the central government, discipline the local oligarchies, foster nationalism, and promote economic and social change. The specifics remained vague. Those young idealists soon discoverd both the strength and conservatism of the politicians and senior army officers who thwarted their drive to initiate change. Vargas had consolidated neither a strong coalition of support nor a popular base and put forth no coherent program. He wrestled with the realities of the new situation and cast about for a power base. The tenentes applauded Vargas as he dissolved all legislative bodies from Congress down to the municipal councils, intervened in the states, removed governors, and strengthened the central government. His hesitation to move faster, however, created anxieties among the tenentes and eventually prompted them to organize themselves.

In February of 1931, they banded together to organize the *Clube 3 de Outubro*. Strongly impregnated with the ideas of Alberto Tôrres, their program advocated a strong presidency, an indirectly elected legislature composed of both sectoral and territorial congressmen, state-directed reforms to promote national development, harmony between capital and labor encouraged and facilitated by the state, land reform through differential taxation, state encouragement of agrarian and industrial development, and a wide range of social legislation which would include a labor code, a social security system, a public health system, universal education, and more equitable distribution of income. The program emphasized the predominance of the group over the individual, the union over the states, and national interests over international ones. It envisioned an authoritarian government capable of imposing reforms.

A strong surge of strength in 1931 from the politicians linked to the Old Republic turned Vargas more resolutely toward the tenentes for support. They became mutually useful allies. Vargas needed the young officers to enhance his powers; they needed the president to enact their reforms. Vargas appointed many of them as state intervenors or as advisers. In 1931, the tenentes enjoyed their maximum influence. Yet, within a year it waned and within a few years had all but disappeared. Vargas often found their determination embarrassing in his delicate political maneuvering. Further, the ranks of the *Clube* fragmented into ideological factions. Finally, the civil war in São Paulo returned the young officers to military duties and removed them from politics. While the middle class had sympathized with the tenente movement during the 1920s, its members felt the tenentes shifted to overly radical ideas in the 1930s, unpalatable with the "liberal reform" sought by the ever more cautious middle class. Nonetheless, the lower ranks of the middle class continued to back the tenentes and their ideas in the 1930s.

Those tenentes bequeathed an impressive legacy. They helped to convert a regional revolt in 1930 into a national movement; they helped keep Vargas in power during some difficult years of political maneuvering; they impressed on Vargas the need for reforms; they helped bring the urban middle class and proletariat into national politics; they strengthened the role of the state in economic and social matters; they reinforced the drive toward centralization of power; they encouraged nationalism. Even after the tenentes as a group passed from prominence, their goals continued to attract support and in many ways served as the signposts guiding Vargas. Individually the former tenentes played significant roles in the public life of the nation. Perhaps most prominent among those tenentes who held highly responsible positions during the succeeding four decades were Juarez Távora, João Alberto, Estillac Leal, Manuel Rabelo, Eduardo Gomes, Oswaldo Cordeiro de Farias, Luís Carlos Prestes, Paulo Kruger, and José Américo de Almeida.

The new regime confronted severe political and economic challenges. With declining coffee sales threatening its collapse, the economy struggled in the waves of a worldwide depression. The unstable state of the international coffee market showed once again—and all too vividly—the reflexive nature of the Brazilian economy, dependent for its well being, as it always had been, on the sale of one major raw product abroad. By 1935, Brazilian exports were only a third of what they had been in 1929, figures which reflected rather accurately the difference between coffee exports in the 1920s and those in the 1930s: in the decade before the crash of the market Brazil sold abroad 806 million pounds of coffee and in the following decade it exported only 337 million pounds. The price of coffee between 1931 and 1937 averaged only 9.8 cents per pound, as compared to 21.7 cents in 1929. At the same time, competition for the world's coffee markets increased, so that Brazil's share fell from 60 percent in 1932 to less than 50 percent in 1937, a reflection of the mounting production of coffee in the other Latin American republics and in Africa. Through an aggressive sales campaign, Brazil brought its share up to 57 percent in 1939, but at the same time, the price slipped to 7.5 cents.

Vargas' government met the economic challenge in a variety of ways. Fully cognizant of the importance of coffee to the national economy, the government did not abandon the planters during their difficult days. The National Coffee Council (after 1933, the National Department of Coffee) proved flexible in adopting various plans to relieve the plight of the planters. At once it ordered a reduction in coffee-tree planting. The number of trees had risen from 1.7 billion in 1920 to 3 billion in 1934, a figure which receded slowly to 2.5 billion in 1939 and 2.3 in 1942. In 1931, the government initiated a program of coffee burning, and before the end of the decade approximately 60 million bags of coffee were destroyed. Variations of the old valorization scheme as well as international agreements with other coffee-producing states were tried. Their success was minimal, and Brazil's coffee trade only recovered with the advent of World War II. In the meantime, the government exerted every effort to diversify the economy through industrialization and agricultural expansion. Livestock raising and cotton production showed the most significant growth in the agricultural sector. Cotton accounted for 18.6 percent of the exports in the 1935–1939 period, a marked increase over the 2.1 percent of the 1925–1929 period. Internal consumption of cotton rose as well. In São Paulo, cotton planting increased sixfold in the years 1933–1939, while at the same time coffee planting diminished. The success of the industrialization program will be treated later separately.

The crisis in the coffee market after 1929 and the government's determination to diversify the national economy rang down the curtain on the coffee civilization in Brazil. It became evident after 1930 that the dominating role of coffee over economics and politics had ended. True, coffee would continue to figure prominently in the nation's economy, but the long-term trend initiated at the time of the market crash has been to diminish the contribution of coffee and to diversify the economy. Vargas responded to the economic challenges of the thirties, and Brazil experimented with varied economic solutions.

Political challenges accompanied the economic problems. They came from the old oligarchy, dispossessed of power by the events of 1930, and the political extremists from both left and right. The coffee elite of São Paulo particularly manifested an antipathy toward the goals advocated by the nationalistic tenentes. In turn, Vargas harbored suspicions about the intentions of the richest and most powerful state, suspicions which prompted him at once to remove the governor installed by the junta in 1930, a general friendly to Júlio Prestes. To insure the loyalty of the state, Vargas dispatched General Isidoro Dias Lopes, the nominal chief of the 1924 revolt, to command the Second Military Region with headquarters in São Paulo. He sent João Alberto, a tenente from the Northeast, to serve as interventor, an appointee named by the president to replace an elected governor. The military interventor immediately earned the enmity of the Paulista establishment by decreeing a 5 percent wage raise for workers and distributing some land to veterans of the revolution. The Paulistas accused him of being a Communist and—what was probably closer to the truth—of being incompetent. The elite understood that the consequences of politics and revolution deprived them of their control of the federal government, but they bitterly resented the fact that they were not allowed to run their own rich state. If an interventor they must have, they wanted a civilian and a Paulista. At the same time, they agitated for a return to constitutional government, preferably under the lenient Constitution of 1891. Vargas was neither insensitive to their demands nor immune to their pressures. As one gesture of conciliation, he named José Maria Whitaker, a coffee banker from São Paulo, as his first minister of finance. Further, he made every possible effort to solve or ameliorate the coffee crisis. Eventually he appointed the desired civilian Paulista interventor, Pedro de Toledo, and announced elections for May of 1933 to select a constituent assembly. Instead of soothing the Paulistas, those measures appeared to them as a sign of weakness in the national government. On July 9, 1932, under the command of General Bertaldo Klinger, the Paulistas revolted.

The significance of the revolt was readily discernible in its limited geographic and popular appeal. The rebels had counted on support from Minas Gerais and Rio Grande do

Sul, but contrary to expectations those two states pledged their allegiance to Vargas, as did the rest of the union. In São Paulo, the working class, both rural and urban, refused to embrace the cause. More than anything else, the rebellion seemed to be a rearguard action by the Paulista oligarchy, who looked to the past and desired a restoration of their former privileges and power, and the government treated it as such. Federal forces headed by General Góes Monteiro converged on the bandirante capital, and after three months of seige and desultory fighting the revolt collapsed. Understanding that a prosperous and a happy São Paulo was essential for the well-being and progress of Brazil, Vargas wisely decided there would be neither punishment nor humiliation for the losers. He proceeded with the plans to constitutionalize the government.

On February 14, 1932, Vargas had promulgated an Electoral Code which lowered the voting age from twenty-one to eighteen, guaranteed the secret ballot and extended the suffrage to working women. (Earlier, in 1926, the state government of Rio Grande do Norte had given women the right to vote.) Although a liberal code in most respects, it still denied the vote to the illiterate, contrary to the practice in some other hemispheric republics. Under the provisions of the code, the representatives to the Constituent Assembly were elected, and in November of 1933, they began their deliberations. The constitution promulgated on July 16, 1934, revealed the results of their labors. The new document maintained the federal system but delegated wider powers to the executive. The sections on labor, the family, and culture expanded the social consciousness of the government. The constitution also showed a new concern with the nation's economic development. In an effort to reduce the power and influence of the rich states, fifty class representatives (delegates from labor, industry, the liberal professions, and the civil service) were admitted to the chamber of deputies along with 250 of the more traditional type of representatives of areas and populations. The president was to serve for four years and be ineligible to succeed himself. The Assembly promptly elected Vargas to that office.

As the new constitutional machinery began to function, pressures on Vargas mounted. The state elections of 1935 favored the oligarchy and politicians linked to the Old Republic, intensifying the struggle between those advocating states' rights and those favoring centralization of power. At the same time, extremist political doctrines made aggressive appeals to the populace. Always vulnerable to the penetration of foreign political ideologies, Brazil did not escape the lure of communist and fascist doctrines in the 1930s. Following its foundation in 1922, the Communist Party grew slowly, but the economic crises accelerated its activities and enhanced its attraction in the early 1930s. One faction of the party organized a popular front to combat fascism, the *Aliança Nacional Libertadora* (National Liberation Alliance), which began to take shape in 1934 but did not emerge until March 1935. With the motto "Bread, Land, and Liberty," the National Liberation Alliance (ANL) called for the cancellation of foreign debts, nationalization of foreign enterprises, full personal freedoms, a popular government, and distribution of the large estates among the rural proletariat. It remained largely an urban movement, recruiting its membership from from the middle and lower middle classes rather than from the working classes. The ANL articulated nationalistic sentiments and was the first broad open challenge to the existing system. Most supporters of the ANL did not consider themselves as Communists but passionately desired modernization and development, which they thought retarded because of foreign exploitation.

Luís Carlos Prestes, the romantic revolutionary who had led the march through the interior and then became the leader of the Brazilian Communist party, served as honorary president of the ANL In early July 1935 he issued some inflammatory calls for the defeat of the Vargas government and the establishment of a popular revolutionary government. Vargas promptly outlawed the ANL for violation of the National Security Laws. The Communists then discredited themselves by fomenting in Natal, Recife, and Rio de Janeiro three separate and bloody military uprisings between November 23 and 26, which outraged public opinion. Congress at once voted a state of seige. Federal officials arrested and jailed Communist and assorted leftist leaders. A specially created National Security Tribunal tried those implicated in the plots. From that time through 1937, the government mounted a vigorous anti-Communist campaign. Forced by Vargas to disband, the Communists ceased to be an active force for a decade. Vargas boldly used the opportunities provided by the revolts for his own advantage. He greatly strengthened his authority, increased federal powers, and silenced his critics. The military also saw its own influence increase.

By the mid-1930s, a threat from the far right also emerged. In 1932, shortly after the São Paulo revolution, the *Ação Integralista Brasileira*, the Integralist party, was formed with support of conservative elements and in frank imitation of the European fascist parties of the time. Like their European counterparts, the Integralists had their own symbol (the sigma), flag, and shirt color (green). Raising their right arm in the traditional fascist salute, they uttered the word *ananê*. Although the meaning of this Indian word is obscure, its use shows that the Indian as a nationalist symbol was far from dead. Nationalistic and somewhat mystical in its appeal, the party emphasized order, hierarchy, and obedience. "God, Country, Family" was its motto. It proposed an "integral" state under a single authoritarian head of government. The party identified the "enemies of the nation" as democrats and Communists, as well as Masons and Jews.

The young Paulista Plínio Salgado, an intellectual who had dazzled Brazil with a literary best seller, *O Estrangeiro* (The Foreigner), in 1926, emerged as the leading figure of the Integralist movement. His speeches, essays, and books resounded with nationalist phraseology. *Nosso Brasil* (Our Brazil), published in 1937, was a blindly exaggerated glorification of the fatherland. No official connection ever existed between the Integralist party, with its nationalistic doctrine, and the government, with its nationalistic programs, although some highly placed bureaucrats and army officers were integralists. Nor was there any official link between the party and the Roman Catholic Church, although many members of the Catholic hierarchy lent the party their support and prestige.

First the Communists and then the Integralists posed political threats to Vargas. Both were well-organized, disciplined, national parties which professed a rigid ideology. Never before had Brazil experienced such parties. The other parties existing in the 1930s—like their predecessors during the Old Republic—were of the traditional weak and regional stripe. While they offered little effective challenge to Vargas, they did hinder his efforts to create and enforce national unity. He believed that the political parties dissipated the nation's energies, and the politicking which intensified in 1937 as the presidential election campaign got under way confirmed him in that opinion. Three candidates presented themselves for those elections: Plínio Salgado for the Integralists; José Américo de Almeida, a former tenente from Paraíba, considered the government's candidate; and Armando de Sales Oliveira, governor of São Paulo and candidate of the Brazilian Democratic Union. The political elements which had most enjoyed power during the Old Republic endorsed the candidacy of Sales Oliveira.

Vargas disdainfully observed the campaigning for a while and then decided to terminate it and resolve the question of presidential succession himself. The immediate cause for his action was the convenient discovery of the "Cohen Plan," a crudely forged document detailing a vast Communist plan of terrorism. That fabricated threat, the general agitation caused by campaigning, and Vargas' personal desire for power motivated the coup d'état with which Brazil was confronted on November 10, 1937. By radio, Vargas explained the coup to the nation as follows:

In periods of crisis, such as the one through which we are now passing, the democracy of parties, instead of offering a certain opportunity for growth and progress within the framework necessary for human life and development, subverts the hierarchy, menaces the fatherland, and puts in danger the existence of the nation by exaggerating competition and igniting the fires of civil discord. It is necessary to note that, alarmed by the cries of the professional agitators and confronted with the complexity of political struggles, the men who do not live from such struggles but rather from the fruits of their labor abandon the parties to those professionals who live from them, and they abstain from participating in public life which would benefit from the participation of those elements of order and constructive action. Universal suffrage thus has become the instrument of the astute, the mask which thinly disguises the connivings of personal ambition and greed.[2]

On that day, he cancelled the presidential elections, dismissed Congress, and assumed all political power for himself. He announced a new constitution, drawn up for the occasion by Francisco Campos, a political philosopher whose influence extended from the early Vargas years when he served as first Minister of Education through the early years of military government of the 1960s. In fact, he authored the first Institutional Act, April 1964. The Brazilians observed some amazing constitutional hocus-pocus. The new document declared "a state of emergency" and then went on to say that so long as a state of emergency existed the constitution could not go into effect. Anyway, to have effect the constitution required the approval of a plebiscite. Vargas never mentioned the plebiscite again. Taking a puzzled look at the unpromulgated constitution, the correspondent for *The New York Times* sent off a cable to his newspaper with this rattled description: "This new Constitution sets up a somewhat Fascist State but not entirely. It is more democratic than fascism. Actually it is nationalistic."

The coup represented more than an immediate political victory for Vargas. On some levels, it signified a triumph of Vargas' long political maneuvering, the capstone of the 1930–37 period; on others, it meant the emergence of—or at least expression of—Vargas' new solutions for old problems. The president obviously had resolved the thorny problem of states' rights versus centralization in favor of the latter, incorporated the new urban elements into his political machine, and formulated, at last, his ideological commitments. Proving himself to be a master manipulator of the increasingly complex forces in Brazilian society, he had preserved na-

2. Getúlio Vargas, *A Nova Política do Brasil* (Rio de Janeiro, 1938), V, 21.

tional unity, marginalized his enemies, confronted and partially solved the tremendous problems of economic dislocation, and harnessed the power of rising nationalism. After the coup, Vargas began to rule by decree. He imposed press censorship and created a special police force to suppress any resistance to his regime. Police interrogation, torture, and imprisonment followed in due course. Possibly a hundred political prisoners were confined to the island of Fernão de Noronha, usually only for a period of months. Many others found it prudent to live abroad in self-imposed exile. In December of 1937, the new dictator disbanded all political parties. At no time did he make any effort to organize a political party of his own upon which he could rest his government. Terming his new government the *Estado Novo* (New State), he promised that it would achieve "the legitimate aspirations of the Brazilian people, political and social peace."

Reaction to the sudden coup varied. The liberals, democrats, old elite, and some politicians protested. When the Integralists understood that they too were to be excluded from power in the Estado Novo, they made a brazen attack on Guanabara Palace, the President's residence, during the night of May 10–11, 1938. Vargas, his family, and his staff repulsed the attack; loyal troops which arrived on the scene later finished the job. The Integralist attack was the only armed protest to the newly established dictatorship, and Salgado's motivations could scarcely be termed democratic. The masses, still passive to all political events in Brazil, accepted the Estado Novo. The military, nationalists, and large numbers of the middle groups welcomed it. Although the tenente movement had died out, the Estado Novo represented the regimented, nationalist renovation for which those tenentes had agitated during a decade and a half. Its accomplishments fulfilled most of the goals they had sought.

Vargas forged a careful and useful alliance with the military. The officers received good salaries and prompt promotion. Budgets were generous. The size of the military doubled from 38,000 men in 1927 to 75,000 in 1937. As one consequence of the coup, the regional army commands absorbed the state militias, a severe blow to regionalism. Most importantly, the establishment of the Estado Novo accomplished the officers' goal of creating a strongly nationalistic, military-backed, centralized government. The coup of 1937 seemed at first to place Brazil closer to the totalitarian states of Europe. The rhetoric echoed much of the phraseology current in Italy, Spain, and Portugal at the time, and the fascination with the corporative state structure momentarily strengthened the similarity. Some of the ideological motivations coincided. Certainly statements made by Vargas in the years immediately following the coup did not sound promising. He announced the demise of democracy in the twentieth century: "The decadence of liberal and individualistic democracy represents an incontrovertible fact." He proclaimed the superiority of the State over the individual: "The Estado Novo does not recognize the rights of the individual against the collective. Individuals do not have rights; they have duties. Rights belong to the collective!"

At the same time, commerce drew Brazil closer to Germany then ever before. In the decade after 1928 both the United States and Great Britain reduced their purchases of Brazilian exports, while Germany increased its purchases. Germany doubled its imports from Brazil between 1933 and 1938 to become the biggest customer for Brazilian cotton and the second largest for coffee and cacao. In 1938, Brazil shipped 34 percent of its exports to the United States, 19 percent to Germany, and 9 percent to Great Britain; it bought 25 percent of its imports from Germany, 24 percent from the United States, and 10 percent from the United Kingdom. The new importance of Germany in Brazil's international trade went a long way to explain Brazil's friendly disposition toward that increasingly belligerent European power. At any rate, as long as the United States maintained an officially neutral attitude toward the European conflict, the Brazilian leaders saw no reason why they had to take a stand, particularly if such a position would cause reverses in an already unstable economy.

Once the United States entered World War II, Brazil, in company with most of Latin America, followed suit. After the

Japanese attack on Pearl Harbor, Vargas stated, "There is no doubt about our attitude. Let us proclaim it at once: we stand solidly with the United States." On January 28, 1942, Brazil broke diplomatic and commercial relations with the Axis. In the months thereafter, German submarines repeatedly sank Brazilian ships, a campaign which reached a climax during three days in mid-August, 1942, when five Brazilian ships went down with a loss of many lives. Rio de Janeiro reacted immediately. On August 22, 1942, Brazil declared war on Germany and Italy. It was more than a paper declaration, contrary to similar declarations made by other Latin American governments. Brazil sought, within its limitations, to play a contributory role and to be a responsible ally. The government authorized the United States to establish air and naval bases in the north and northeast, strategic for the defense of the Atlantic and vital for the invasions of Africa and the subsequent campaign there. The navy patrolled the South Atlantic. A small contingent of the air force participated in the war over Italy. Finally, an expeditionary force of approximately 25,000 men arrived in Italy in late 1944 to take part in the fierce fighting there. In the military drive up the peninsula, 451 Brazilian soldiers gave their lives and another 2,000 were wounded. Their contribution to the defeat of European fascism expanded national pride, solidified Brazil's position as the leader of the Latin American community, and insured a prestigious place for Brazil in the organization of the United Nations. The war experience particularly impressed those officers who participated in the campaign, shaping their attitudes—an admiration for the United States and for technology, for example—and uniting them into a fraternity whose future influence on Brazil would be momentous. Internally the war was a mighty impetus to agricultural production and to manufacturing.

The accelerating industrialization during the Vargas years brought in its wake an urban expansion which altered many national customs. Patriarchal families abandoned their homes in the country or on the urban fringes for an apartment within the city, where frequently the larger clans dispersed into marital groupings. Multistoried apartment buildings began to appear, many in a refreshingly original style designed by an emerging school of talented Brazilian architects of whom Oscar Niemeyer is an outstanding example. They transformed the skyline of the major cities from Pôrto Alegre to Manaus. Legions of the poor migrated to the cities with the hope of taking advantage of their promise, and settled in the squalid *favelas* (slums). Pressing close to the luxurious apartment complexes, these slums offer a contrast vividly symbolic of the extremes characteristic of Brazilian society. Desperate as the situation of the urban poor was, they probably enjoyed a better diet, health, and education than their rural counterparts. In the impersonality of the city, the paternalistic relationship between the elite and the masses eroded, although it has never completely disappeared. Still, the city had no counterpart to the "colonel" who rigidly controlled hundreds, even thousands of peasants. The city offered the worker wider choices than the peasant ever had and, to make those choices, an independence which the peasant never felt possible. Foremost, of course, the city offered the worker a hope for the future of which the peasant could not even dream. Hence it was small wonder that the cities attracted ever-larger numbers of migrants. On the other hand, many of the dispossessed wandered into the city only because they had nowhere to go in the countryside. Driven from the land, they ended up in the city no better prepared to integrate into urban life than the city was to receive them.

Urban life tended to be more permissive, relaxing the traditions and habits which made a ritual out of rural life. The city dweller enjoyed greater independence and had more opportunities to improve himself as well as raise his standard of living. The merchants encouraged the desire for improvement. They introduced installment buying which put within reach of the middle groups products, even luxuries, which once had been inaccessible. Urban women enjoyed far more freedom than their rural counterparts. The granting of the vote to working women in 1932 announced their political emancipation. The presence of the daughters of the middle class in the universities became more pronounced and not a few took their places as lawyers, judges, professors, and doctors. The dynamic changes introduced by the complementary processes of industrialization and urbanization seemed at the time to threaten the oligarchical control and elitist politics characteristic of Brazil during both the Empire and the Old Republic.

Brazilian society was obviously more diverse than ever before, a diversity which provided Vargas with a new source of power. From this point onward, it is possible to abandon the use—liberally made—of the term "middle groups." Society by the 1930s and thereafter was sufficiently complex and developed to warrant the more precise use of the terms "middle class" and "proletariat." The middle class consisted of those economically independent of medium wealth and income and the salaried who depended mainly on their intellectual ability in business, industry, commerce, bureaucracy, and the professions. The ranks of the middle class expanded liberally. Factory managers, foremen, technicians, representatives, and salesmen; office workers with a host of new skills; bank managers, tellers, and accountants; university professors, and a wider diversity of businessmen joined more traditional elements of that class: the doctors, lawyers, engineers, military officers, and civil servants. In his fascinating sociological study of Itaipava, an interior city with a population of approximately 25,000 in the 1940s, Emílio Willems defined the middle class as "all the inhabitants who are more or less economically solvent, who assume in their relations with local authorities an attitude of relative freedom and criticism, who sell services or goods of relatively high social esteem, who, thanks to education, can participate in recreational activities which demand familiarity with certain rules of urban social etiquette, whose economic-professional position represents a 'political potential' highly appreciated by the parties."[3] He found that 29 percent of the city's inhabi-

3. Emílio Willems, *Uma Vila Brasileira, Tradição e Transição,* 2nd ed. (Sao Paulo, 1961), p. 44.

tants belonged to that middle class, among whom were merchants, farmers, public officials, artisans, and some highly paid employees.

The urban proletariat included all those in an inferior economic position whose income resulted primarily from manual labor. The numbers of the proletariat increased rapidly as the need for more stevedores, factory hands, and construction workers multiplied. Like the middle class, the proletariat grew not only in the large coastal cities, but ever-larger numbers of them could be found in the towns of the interior as well. Concentrated in the sensitive and restive urban areas, the proletariat and middle class wielded influence and power disproportionate to their size. Numerically they never constituted a majority; most Brazilians continued to live in the countryside. Except for the small but powerful rural oligarchy, however, they were politically inarticulate.

That Vargas understood and appreciated the importance of the urban middle class and proletariat in consolidating his power seems apparent from the first days of his administration. He intended to use them to check the traditional oligarchy. They, in turn, approved the effort Vargas made to fix the locus of power in the cities. Immediately after taking command of the government, he moved to reduce the authority of the *coroneis,* one of the foundation stones upon which the power structure of the Old Republic had rested. Many of the rural patriarchs had made the mistake of supporting President Luís in October of 1930. Vargas disarmed them and their followers—or he did so to the extent possible—and thus deprived them of much physical power. Further, he reduced the control of the coroneis over the backland municipalities by decreeing that thereafter the federal government would direct all local police forces, appoint all mayors, and supervise all municipal budgets. One historian of the Northeast, Irineu Pinheiro, concluded, "After 1930, in place of colonels of the National Guard, merchants and farmers began to dominate the municipal governments in Ceará. They were elements of the so-called liberal classes such as lawyers and doctors." The coroneis sometimes allied themselves with those new holders of power, but after 1930, in contrast with the past, they were more often than not the junior members of such an alliance.

As an early indication of his intention to broaden and strengthen his urban base of support, Vargas created in 1930 two new cabinet posts, the Ministry of Labor and the Ministry of Education. Previous governments had either neglected or persecuted labor. They often regarded unions as a source of social unrest and political disturbance. The police commonly intervened in union activities, and a law of 1927 authorized the executive to dissolve unions considered to be troublesome or obnoxious. At the time of the fall of the Old Republic, there were approximately a quarter of a million organized workers. While hostile to strikes and manifestations, Vargas, in a purely paternalistic—and some say demagogic—manner, granted to the workers more benefits than they probably could have obtained through their own organizations. The new Ministry of Labor, first headed by Vargas' close associate from Rio Grande do Sul, Lindolfo Color, served as the instrument through which the government dealt with the workers. A decree in March of 1931 authorized that ministry to organize labor into new unions under strict governmental supervision. By 1944, there were about 800 unions with a membership exceeding half a million. The government forbade strikes but did establish an elaborate set of courts and codes to protect the workers and to provide redress for their grievances. Under governmental auspices, unions could and did bargain with management. Vargas promulgated and the Ministry of Labor administered a wide variety of social legislation favoring the workers. There were retirement and pension plans, a minimum wage, a workweek limited to 48 hours, paid annual vacations, maternal benefits and child care, educational facilities, training programs and literacy campaigns, safety and health standards for work, and job security. In short, Vargas offered to the workers in less than a decade the advances and benefits which the proletariat of the industrialized nations had agitated for during the previous century. In Latin America, only the workers in Chile, Mexico, and Uruguay boasted of similar gains and privileges. In return for those broad advances, the Brazilian workers loyally, even devotedly, gave their support to Vargas. It must be emphasized, however, that those benefits accrued only to privileged workers in large industries in major cities. The majority of the workers received no benefits, although perhaps they identified with the rhetoric and entertained hopes of inclusion.

The elaborate labor courts, welfare benefits, and careful control of unions bespoke a paternalism prevalent in the Brazilian experience. Labor and the government interacted, supported, and depended upon each other. With its vision of the corporate state, the government manipulated labor into cooperating with both capital and the state to encourage industrialization. Such manipulation theoretically avoided or minimized class conflicts.

Through the Ministry of Education, Vargas reached out to the middle class, whose children predominated in the schools. Obviously, education had a crucial role to play in a developing society, particularly one in which the population was getting larger and younger. After 1930, immigration declined sharply but the population continued to grow rapidly with birth rates exceeding 3 percent per year. When Vargas assumed power in 1930, Brazil boasted of approximately 33 million inhabitants; when he lost power in 1945, it exceeded 46 million. Observing that "Education is a matter of life and death," Vargas ordered greater attention focused on the schools, which in the last analysis would shape the future of Brazilian society. Indeed, education was the portal through which Brazilians had to pass if they were to participate in a modern society which demanded increasingly greater skills and technical ability. The first minister of education, Francisco Campos, reformed the educational system in 1931 with the intention of making it more modern and efficient. Teacher training and classroom construction received new emphasis. The first university, that of Rio de Janeiro, had been created in 1920 by joining together a number of dispersed schools—law, medicine, engineering—under a central administration. In 1934, the University of São Paulo emerged from a similar unification, and four years later the University of Brazil, with its seat in Rio de Janeiro, became the third university.

Vargas also intended to use the newly centralized school system as a means to encourage the growth of national sentiment. He decreed that all instruction be given in Portuguese, a requirement aimed at accelerating the Brazilianization of European immigrants and their descendants, particularly in the South with its large concentrations of Germans, Poles, and Italians. The schools placed a greater emphasis on the teaching of Brazilian history; the new universities established for the first time chairs of national history. In short, after 1930 education sharpened national consciousness, thereby fostering a mentality favorable toward nationalism.

Technical advances facilitated Vargas' efforts to strengthen national unity and his own personal control. They permitted him to reach out to all the Brazilian people, even in the remotest hinterlands, with a speed and thoroughness none of his predecessors enjoyed. Radio broadcasting, inaugurated in the 1920s, expanded rapidly, and before the close of the 1930s a radio network spread across the entire nation. A radio became a sought-after status symbol. A Maranhense writer, Ferreira Gullar, recalled, "Around 1938, radios became accessible to the middle-class families of São Luís do Maranhão. They were displayed proudly in the center of the living room so that no visitor would fail to notice the innovation." The government regulated broadcasting and made extensive use of it to present the official point of view. Vargas himself gave occasional fireside chats. Movies, from the early days of the film industry, engrossed the Brazilians, who flocked to the ever-greater number of cinemas. The screen, through newsreels and documentaries, became an important medium to carry the government's official message. In a society in which barely a quarter of the population was literate, both the radio and the cinema were indispensable instruments of propaganda. A special agency, the Department of Press and Propaganda, promoted official propaganda as well as censored whatever the government found displeasing or imprudent to reveal, a responsibility the Department did not always exercise with subtlety. One of the government's most successful controls over the press was the tax exemption permit which it could give, withhold, or withdraw on imported newsprint, and all newsprint was imported. The prestigious *O Estado de São Paulo* proved to be a particularly recalcitrant daily and occasionally refused to adopt the government's line. A cache of weapons "discovered" by the political police in the building housing *O Estado* gave Vargas the excuse he sought to close down the paper and then take it over. A sycophantic news medium resulted which permitted Vargas to get his message across to the nation both efficiently and effectively.

The air age had dawned in Brazil. Even before independence had been declared, two Brazilians, Bartolomeu de Gusmão in his experiments and Bishop Azeredo Coutinho in his writings, had contemplated the day when man would conquer the air. In 1901, Alberto Santos Dumont—another Brazilian intrigued with the conquest of the air—flew a dirigible balloon around the Eiffel Tower, and in 1906, duplicating the more heralded feat of the Wright brothers, he flew a heavier-than-air plane. The advantage of air travel for a country as vast as Brazil, with its limited network of roads and railroads, was obvious, and the Brazilians continued to devote considerable attention to the possibilities. Commercial aviation began in 1927 with the foundation in Pôrto Alegre of the first air transport company. By 1939, 9 commercial companies were flying 81 planes over routes extending 43,000 miles. In that year, those planes carried 71,000 passengers, 223 tons of mail, and 490 tons of freight. Aware of the value of the airplane for national unification as well as its value as a means to increase his control of the nation, Vargas created the Air Ministry in 1941. Brazil soon handled three-quarters of all commercial air traffic in South America.

The surface transportation network continued to expand, of course, but not so spectacularly as the air network. By 1939, there were only 21,241 miles of railroads, 65 percent of which could be found in four states: São Paulo, Minas Gerais, Rio de Janeiro, and Rio Grande do Sul. The government, either federal or state, managed over two-thirds of the railroads. By the end of the 1930s, they were transporting 195 million passengers, 4 million animals, and 35 million tons of merchandise a year. Vargas pushed road construction, and in

1939, with obvious satisfaction, he opened the vital road between Rio de Janeiro and Salvador da Bahia. By the end of that year, there were 258,390 miles of roads—96 percent of which were dirt, most unimproved—over which approximately a quarter of a million motor vehicles passed, a third of them trucks.

The expanding transportation and communication networks welded Brazil into a tighter unity than it had ever before achieved. They facilitated the strong centralism Vargas imposed on the nation. Just as the decentralization experiments of the Regency were condemned and reversed by the Second Empire, so the laissez-faire federalism of the Old Republic came under attack by those who rebelled in 1930 and later applauded the establishment of the Estado Novo. In disapproval of previous federalism, Vargas enforced the supremacy of the government in Rio de Janeiro. He became the strongest executive Brazil had known. He exercised more power effectively over a larger area than any of his predecessors, emperors not excluded. The effective centralization of power imposed by the Estado Novo has characterized Brazil ever since.

All factors considered, Vargas seems to have exercised that omnipotence satisfactorily, although a group of unrelenting critics such as Hernane Tavares de Sá regarded the regime as the most disreputable of dictatorships and the crudest of police states. Generally Vargas seems to have listened attentively to diverse opinions; his hand grasped firmly the pulse of public sentiment. Thus oriented, he enjoyed considerable support for his programs. Certainly he understood the desire and need for reform as well as the extent to which reform could be made and accepted. Again, as had been customary in the past, reforms were handed down to the nation from above. They were not the result of popular agitation, struggle, or threat.

In introducing changes and maintaining his position, Vargas wielded new instruments of power. He recognized the potential of the middle class and proletariat and used both of them. In turn, they found Vargas to be their entrée to power. Their influence grew rapidly after 1930. The rural oligarchy, battered by the effects of the Depression, the collapse of the Old Republic, industrialization, and urbanization, lost its former political dominance. Vargas encouraged and guided that changing pattern of power. Under his aegis many groups—civilians and military, bureaucrats, technicians, professionals, and industrialists, bourgeois and proletariat—emancipated Brazil from the absolute control of the coffee interests. Vargas avoided extremes in making reforms and in altering the political balance of power. Following a recognizable Brazilian tradition, he knew how to compromise. His government acquired a decidedly populist cast, but at the same time won the support and cooperation—in some cases, even the enthusiasm—of the principal members of the business and industrial community. He tried not to antagonize the rural oligarchy. Land reform, for example, was neither an interest nor a goal of his government. He managed to offer something to both the elite and the masses. In the final analysis, he owed his long tenure to his ability to hold the support of business, labor, the military, many landowners, and the nationalists. The coordination of those seemingly diverse elements into a base of support indicated that Brazilian politics had become more complex. Two forces rapidly accelerating that complexity were industrialization and nationalism.

Nationalism and Industrialization

Industrialization and nationalism accompanied one another in twentieth-century Brazil as they did throughout much of Latin America. Industrialization was seen as a key to the future. It would unlock the door leading to development and hence to national greatness. Little wonder, then, that the nationalists pursued it. Their first efforts had been to criticize foreign merchants resident in Brazil and to demand laws to protect local industry. Modern economic nationalism found in Alberto Tôrres one of its earliest effective advocates. In a series of books published between 1909 and 1915, he bound together the concepts of development and nationalism and indicated the course nationalism would follow thereafter. In his view, any nation, in order to exercise "real sovereignty" or manifest "true nationalism," had to control its own source of wealth, its industry, and its commerce. He discussed that idea in detail in his *O Problema Nacional Brasileiro* (The National Brazilian Problem), published in 1914:

Above all else, the independence of a people is founded on their economy and their finances. . . . In order for a nation to remain independent it is imperative to preserve the vital organs of nationality: the principal sources of wealth, the industries of primary products, the instrumentalities and agents of economic circulation, transportation, and internal commerce. There must be no monopolies and no privileges. . . . A people cannot be free if they do not own sources of wealth, produce their own food, and direct their own industry and commerce.[4]

The government, Torres argued, had turned over Brazil's economic destiny to foreigners, who had sown their capital without restriction and were reaping an abundant harvest of profit at national expense. He urged the government to reconsider and to adopt a nationalist economic program. His ideas appealed to the tenentes and fitted the plans of Vargas. It was no coincidence that the second edition of *O Problema Nacional Brasileiro* appeared in 1933, just as the nationalists' campaign for economic development got under way.

In that campaign, the nationalists emphasized that only through intensive economic development with due attention to industrialization could Brazil become truly independent. They pointed to the international market crash of 1929 as conclusive proof of the vulnerability of Brazil's economy, based as it traditionally had been on one major export and the whims of foreign markets. Brazil obviously still exercised scant control over its own economic destiny. It was still an economic colony with remnants of the institutions and patterns of the past. Most offensive were the residues of the mercantilist system perpetuated by the rural oligarchy in alli-

4. Alberto Tôrres, *O Problema Nacional Brasileiro* (Rio de Janeiro, 1914), pp. 115–16, 122.

ance with foreign capitalists. Such economic backwardness and dependence could only inhibit, in their opinion, the full exercise of political independence. The nationalists clamored for diversification of the economy as a major step toward economic and hence greater political independence. Adopting the cogent arguments of economic nationalists like Roberto Simonsen that industrialization would diversify the economy, keep precious foreign exchange from being spent to import what could be produced at home, and raise national self-sufficiency, they urged the government to further stimulate manufacturing.

Those economic arguments of the nationalists did not go unanswered. Men like Eugênio Gudin spoke out to favor a continuation of the agricultural regime. They believed that Brazil lacked the resources and ability to industrialize. Such industry, they charged, always would produce at a high cost, dependent on the protection of the government. They counseled that Brazil continued to sell its agricultural products abroad—like the nativists of an earlier century they delighted in cataloging the richness of the soil—and buy whatever manufactured goods the country needed from the cheapest seller. More internationally minded, they would mesh the economy of Brazil with that of Europe and the United States. They received support from Sir Otto Niemeyer, the British economist summoned to Brazil by the government to study the economic crisis and make recommendations. His report, published in 1931, rebuked the monocultural base of the economy and recommended agricultural diversification. It ignored industrialization.

Vargas inclined toward the arguments of the economic nationalists and indicated his intention of implementing their program, while still encouraging the absolutely vital agricultural sector of the economy. From the outset, he declared himself to be a nationalist. To direct the economy and to encourage industrialization and development, Vargas introduced governmental planning and participation on a large scale into the economic life of the nation. In that way, the government assumed the principal leadership of the nationalist movement. For the first time, the intellectuals lost the control they always had monopolized. The base of support of nationalist policies at the same time broadened to include larger numbers of the military, industrialists, politicians, and the middle class. The urban proletariat for the first time began to identify with the nationalist program. After 1930, it was apparent that Brazilian nationalism, like that flourishing in most of Latin America, became increasingly characterized by resentment of foreign capital and foreign personnel, suspicion of private enterprise, a growing preference for state ownership, emphasis on industrialization, encouragement of domestic production, and a desire to create or nationalize certain key industries such as oil, steel, power, and transportation.

The growth of industrialization after 1930 resulted from more than the encouragement of a benevolent government and enthusiastic advocates. There already existed a firm industrial base upon which further industrialization could be built; the international economic crisis served to propel the cause of industrialization. After the market crash in 1929, Brazil drastically reduced its imports. They fell approximately 75 percent between 1929 and 1932, from U.S.$416.6 million to U.S.$108.1 million. Whereas exports declined as well, they did not fall nearly as far nor as fast as imports: from U.S.$445.9 million to U.S.$180.6 million. As a consequence, Brazil enjoyed favorable trade balances in the early 1930s. In addition, the government's valorization scheme maintained much of the coffee production, providing the workers with their salaries and the planters with profits. Internal demand for goods thus remained relatively normal, but the external sources of those consumer goods could no longer be easily tapped because of the government's stringent curtailment of purchases abroad. At that point, local capital, a large percentage of which came from coffee, was invested in new industries which manufactured articles formerly imported. Further, since prices on the domestic market had not fallen as much as those on the international market, it was more profitable to produce goods for home consumption than for export, a persuasive enticement to local investment. Various governmental policies, such as the prohibition of further coffee-tree planting, channeled into industry money once invested in agriculture. Industrial growth further resulted from a more efficient and intensive use of the production capacity already available. The textile industry, for example, substantially increased its output in the early 1930s without expanding its facilities. Contrary to the experience of many other countries, including the United States, Brazilian industry recovered from the Depression by 1933 and entered thereafter a period of satisfactory expansion. In 1934, the industrial production index surpassed the pre-Depression height. Vargas promulgated a host of legislation, decrees, and policies to speed it along its way. Import controls as well as depreciation of the currency discouraged purchases abroad. Import duties rose to protect new industries. In 1933, duties averaged 39 percent of the cost of goods imported. However, liberal exemptions were made for capital machinery and raw materials imported by new industries. Tax exemptions were dispensed generously. The government offered new industries direct financial assistance through long-term loans with low interest rates. Where necessary, the government supervised, operated, or owned certain industries.

Some natural resources were essential for industrialization. Fortunately, Brazil seemed to possess an abundance of them: quartz crystals, industrial diamonds, chrome ores, iron ore, manganese ores, copper, lead, zinc, and gem stones, although much of this potential had not been explored, let alone exploited. In the 1920s, the nationalists mounted a noisy campaign to protect the country's natural resources and prevent their exploitation by foreigners. Catalyst of the campaign was Percival Farquhar, an adventurous North American investor in Brazilian railroads and mines. The nationalists fumed when Farquhar obtained from the government in the early 1920s a concession for the fabulous Itabira iron-ore deposits. They protested the alienation of their country's riches. Thanks principally to the interest President Bernardes took in the case, the government eventually canceled the concession, a major victory for the nationalists. They capped their triumph with a significant amendment to the Constitution: "Mines and mineral deposits necessary for national security and the land in which they are found cannot be transferred to foreigners" (Article 72). An even stronger restriction on foreign exploitation of natural resources appeared in the Constitution of 1934: "The law will regulate the progressive nationalization of mines, mineral deposits, and waterfalls or other sources of energy, as well as of the industries considered as basic or essential to the economic and military defense of the country" (Article 119). The Constitution of 1937 included the same provision. Accordingly, Vargas placed restrictions on foreign companies to discourage or control their exploitation of the country's natural wealth. In due time, his government turned its attention to the coveted iron-ore deposits of Itabira. In 1942, it established the *Companhia Vale do Rio Doce* (Doce River Valley Company) to tap their wealth. Brazil's production of iron ore quintupled between 1939 and 1951, most of the rise taking place after 1942.

After the proclamation of the Estado Novo, economic nationalism intensified. Notification of the government's fuller participation in and direction of the economy was given in January of 1940 with the announcement of a Five Year Plan whose primary goals were to expand the railroad network, to improve and augment the state steamship service, to build up basic industry, and to create hydroelectric power. The generation of energy was crucial to any plans for industrialization. In 1940, the generation of electrical power was almost exclusively in the hands of foreign companies, a fact embarrassing to national pride. The military and the nationalists cited such foreign ownership as a threat to national security and lashed out against that monopoly of foreign capitalists.

Vargas already had initiated a search for another source of power: oil. For the Brazilians, as for most Latin Americans, petroleum became a major symbol of economic nationalism. Its discovery and exploitation were not only economically desirable but promised, in the minds of the nationalists, a brighter future for the country, and indeed its achievement of the status of a world power. Vargas organized the National Petroleum Council in 1938 to intensify the search for oil. The first discovery occurred in January of the following year just outside Salvador da Bahia. To the joy of the nation, oil gushed forth from Brazilian soil. The deposit turned out to be a modest one, but everyone expected it to be the overture to greater discoveries. Calling for the creation of a national oil industry to protect the precious new resource, the nationalists opposed any foreign search for and exploitation of petroleum. Before long it dominated their thoughts; petroleum emerged as the major issue for the nationalists. Vargas, in turn, began to appreciate the emotional importance of oil, and he too came to pay homage to it as a symbol. "Whoever hands over petroleum to foreigners threatens our own independence," he stated to the delight of the nation in general and of the nationalists in particular.

The petroleum question remained unsettled until his second administration (1951–1954), when Vargas—ever more vocal in his nationalism—resolved to bid for wider support by appealing frankly to nationalist sentiment. Honoring the symbolic significance of oil to the nationalists, he adopted the idea of establishing a national petroleum industry. In 1951, he proposed the creation of Petrobrás, a state monopoly of all activities concerned with the exploration of petroleum resources. Amid a strident nationalist campaign, the cry "O petróleo é nosso!" (The oil is ours!) echoed across the land. In response, Petrobrás was created in 1953, a major victory for the nationalists over those who argued it would be more economical and efficient to allow foreign oil companies to do the work and pay Brazil a royalty on whatever was pumped out. The question, however, was not one of economics. Emotions dominated. To the nationalists and the multitudes they stirred, national sovereignty had been at stake and had triumphed. The creation of Petrobrás was a contribution to the economic independence of Brazil. In their campaign, the nationalists had been extremely successful in convincing the masses that a national oil industry represented sovereignty, independence, power, and well-being. For the first time, they succeeded in arousing popular support for a nationalist cause. Petrobrás remains the major single permanent achievement of the nationalists. The pas-

sionate support accorded its creation recalls the dramatic nationalization of the oil industry in Bolivia in 1937 and in Mexico in 1938.

The creation of a national steel industry was another
desideratum of the nationalists. On this issue, as on the oil
question, the military joined with the nationalists. The
officers understood and preached that Brazil could only be
of military importance when it possessed its own basic industries, of which oil and steel were of primary importance. As
early as 1931, Vargas pronounced, "The biggest problem,
one might say the basic problem for our economy, is steel.
For Brazil, the steel age will mark the period of our economic
opulence." Finally, in 1940, plans were drawn up to construct
a steel mill. The National Steel Company was organized the
following year, and work on a steel plant began at once at
Volta Redonda, situated between Rio de Janeiro and São
Paulo. In 1946, the factory went into operation. By 1955,
Volta Redonda was producing 646,000 tons of steel, an annual output doubled by 1963.

Steel and oil were the showpieces of Brazilian industrialization under Vargas. In broader perspective, they reflected an impressive rate of growth for industrialization in
general. Between 1924 and 1939, industrial output grew at an
annual average cumulative rate of approximately 6 percent.
Some economists cite 1933 as the year in which the rhythm
of industrialization accelerated. In the five years thereafter,
the volume of industrial production mounted by approximately 40 percent and the value of industrial production, taking into account monetary devaluation, increased by 44 percent, making industrial production some 60 percent greater
in value than the combined output of livestock and agriculture. In the 1930s approximately three times more new industrial plants went into operation than during the preceding
decade. By 1940, capital investment in factories totaled over
700 million dollars, an impressive figure for Latin America,
but of course an almost insignificant sum compared to investments in the major industrial nations. The United States,
for example, in 1860, with only three quarters of the population of Brazil in 1940, had about a billion dollars invested in

manufacturing. The value of industrial production in the United States at the opening of World War II was approximately fifty times that of Brazil.

A modest diversification of industry occurred during the 1930s. Textiles, long a primary industry, maintained their importance but declined significantly in the total value of industrial output, while other industries, such as printing and publishing, chemical and pharmaceutical products, metals, and machinery increased to provide by 1940 a slightly more balanced industrial park. Table 6.1 compares the percentage distribution of industrial output in 1920 and 1940. In 1941, there were 44,100 plants or enterprises employing 944,000 workers. (The figures contrasted sharply with those of 1920, when there were 13,336 plants and a little over 300,000 workers.) Most of the manufacturing was done in small plants and relied heavily on hand labor. The factories, as the statistics above reveal, produced principally consumer goods, which they provided in sufficient quantity and quality so that it was no longer necessary to import them. As national industries increasingly bought more local raw products and sold their

Table 6.1. Distribution of Industrial Activity by Percentage of Total Value, 1920 and 1940

Industry Group	1920	1940
Nonmetallic minerals	4.7	5.3
Metals	4.3	7.7
Machinery	2.0	5.8
Timber	5.8	5.1
Furniture	2.0	—
Paper and allied products	1.5	1.4
Rubber products	0.2	0.7
Leather and leather products	2.4	1.7
Chemical and pharmaceutical products	6.0	10.4
Textiles	28.6	22.7
Apparel, footwear, and textile products	8.6	4.9
Food products	22.2	22.9
Beverages	5.9	4.5
Tobacco	3.9	2.2
Printing and publishing	—	3.6
Miscellaneous	1.9	1.1
Total	100.0	100.0

SOURCE: Partial reproduction of a table in Werner Baer, *Industrialization and Economic Development in Brazil* (New Haven: Richard D. Irwin, 1965), p. 17. Reprinted with the permission of the publisher.

manufactured goods in the local market, it became apparent that the economy was no longer based solely on export, as it had been for centuries. Internal sources provided four-fifths of the materials used in manufacturing. The plants depended on foreign sources for a large part of their requirements of machinery, heavy equipment, and fuel. However, by the early 1940s a trend was initiated to develop heavy industry. Almost all the manufacturing was done for the local market; few items were exported.

World War II provided an important impulse to economic growth. Brazil exported at enticing profits all its products to a warring world eager to buy anything. Manufactured goods for the first time became a noticeable export item. The export of textiles was particularly brisk, to the point where Brazil ranked as one of the world's leading textile exporters. But the industrialized nations, with their economies geared for the war, had little or nothing to sell back. As a consequence, Brazil built up sizable foreign exchange reserves, from $71 million just before the outbreak of the war to $708 million in 1945, and further expanded and diversified its industrial park. Growth occurred despite the difficulty in obtaining capital machinery, almost all of which came from Western Europe and the United States. Two economic missions from the United States, the Taub Mission in 1942 and the Cooke Mission in 1943, arrived in Brazil to advise the government on development and industrialization. The concept of the planned economy had taken hold, as the promulgation of a second five-year plan in 1943 demonstrated. (The success of the plans—or even of the implementation of them—can be questioned, but acceptance of the idea of planning was established.)

The industrialization of Brazil met some formidable obstacles. Certainly not all of the population of forty million by 1940 constituted a market. Large numbers lived outside the national economy. The minimum wages Varghas guaranteed the workers helped to expand the market, and the growing industries hired more workers who in turn became consumers. The enlightened industrialists understood that Vargas' labor policies tended in the long run to increase the size of the internal market. More concerned with producing for that internal market than in exporting raw materials or importing manufactured goods, they had reason to applaud the benefits of Vargas' social legislation. Cumulative effects caused the market to grow steadily, but it never embraced the entire population. An underdeveloped transportation network further handicapped industrialization. At some times it was impossible to get raw products to interested industries, and at others it was impossible to distribute the manufactured product throughout the nation. Inadequate transportatin underlined the difficulties caused by the geographical separation of certain interdependent natural resources. Further, Brazil lacked sufficient fuel, water power, capital, technicians, and skilled workers, handicaps which conceivably could be overcome with time and ingenuity.

Not all of Brazil entered the industrial age by any means. The southern and central-east states monopolized manufacturing, accounting for approximately five-sixths of the total value of manufactured goods. São Paulo clearly emerged as the industrial giant. With 15 percent of the country's population, it produced 43 percent of the nation's manufactured goods in 1938 (a figure which rose to 54 percent in 1943). The other industrial leaders were the Federal District, which manufactured 14 percent of the industrial goods; Minas Gerais and Rio Grande do Sul, which manufactured 11 percent each; and the state of Rio de Janeiro, which manufactured 5 percent. Those five states employed about three-fourths of all factory workers in 1940, with São Paulo alone accounting for 41 percent of that total. Obviously, in those states most subject to the economic transformation engendered by industrialization the social structure underwent the greatest change.

Important, then, as industrialization was, it affected only a part of the nation. The rest of Brazil slumbered in the past. Previous economic and social patterns remained dominant. The Vargas government made some effort to awaken the rest of the nation, but with limited success. Adopting a theme popularized by the nationalists in the 1920s, Vargas pointed to the West as the key to the realization of the nation's potential. He often spoke of his plans for the development of the hinterlands, the "March to the West." Developing that great promised land was to be "the true sense of Brazilianism." Vargas was the first chief of state to visit the interior, and he approved plans to colonize Goiás by distributing 50-acre plots to settlers. His administration also enacted programs for the arid sertão of the Northeast and the forgotten Amazon Valley. Not all his programs were carried out, but their very promulgation revealed an executive who demonstrated an interest in all of Brazil, who thought in national rather than regional terms, in sharp contrast to his Republican predecessors. Their promulgation signified a new emphasis on national integration.

Brazil remained an agricultural nation. Still, important as the soil was to the economy, only a small percentage—approximately 4 percent of the usable soil in 1945—was under cultivation. In the continental United States, in contrast, over ten times that amount of land fell under the plow. The areas of greatest use and productivity of the land were in the industrialized states: São Paulo, Minas Gerais, and Rio Grande do Sul accounted for about five-eighths of all the Brazilian farm lands. Coffee, the predominant export, still was the most important single crop, and São Paulo continued to harvest about two-thirds of it. Other important crops were cacao, tobacco, cotton, rice, sugar, fruits, wheat, corn, barley, rye, cassava, potatoes, yams, and beans, most of which fed the Brazilians, but other crops such as cacao, tobacco, and cotton also played a significant role in the export trade. Livestock raising contributed significantly to the rural economy. The largest cattle herds roamed central Brazil, which accounted for two-fifths of the cattle in the nation. The South was the second most important area with approximately a fourth of the herds. Sheep raising was concentrated in Rio Grande do Sul.

Rural Brazil retained much from the past. The prevalent way to clear the soil was still by the slash-and-burn method. The farmers seldom used fertilizer, or used it sparsely. Those two practices resulted in quickly exhausted land, badly eroded and depleted. The farmers adhered to other antiquated agrarian practices as well. Their principal instrument was the hoe, unmodified for centuries. The plow was rare, the tractor even rarer. In 1940, only a fourth of all the farms boasted of a plow, and half of those could be found in Rio Grande do Sul, a state heavily influenced by foreign immigration. About one farm in 500 owned a tractor. Latifundia predominated, although the number of large landholdings was declining gradually. The number of farms tripled from 648,000 in 1920 to 1,896,000 in 1940. The difficulties in the sugar and coffee industries, the influence of European immigrants, and subdivision through inheritance accounted for the breakdown of some large estates and the multiplication of the number of farms. Table 6.2 indicates the land-owning structure in 1940. Obviously there still existed concentrated control over the land. A total of 85.7 percent of the farm operators worked land which did not exceed 100 hectares in size. Altogether they farmed only 18.2 percent of the land under cultivation. On the opposite end of the scale, 0.3 percent of the operators owned 24.5 percent of the land. Tenants throughout Brazil cultivated about a fifth of the total land, paying rents considered to be very high.

Table 6.2. Landownership in 1940

Size of Farm in Hectares (1 hectare =2.47/acres)	Percentage of Operators with Farms of Stated Size	Percentage of Land in Farms or Estates of Stated Size
Under 1	2.1	Less than 0.1
1–4.9	19.7	0.6
5–9.9	12.6	0.9
10–19.9	16.6	2.3
20–49.9	23.9	7.2
50–99.9	10.8	7.2
100–199.9	6.5	8.8
200–499.9	4.7	13.9
500–999.9	1.6	10.9
1,000–2,499.9	1.0	14.4
2,500–4,999.9	0.3	9.3
5,000–9,999.9	0.1	7.6
10,000–99,999.9	0.1	13.3
100,000 over	Less than 0.1	3.6

SOURCE: "Sinopse de Censo Agrícola, Dados Gerais," *Recenseamento Geral do Brasil*, 1940 (Rio de Janeiro, 1948). Reprinted in T. Lynn Smith, *Brazil, People and Institutions* (Baton Rouge, Louisiana, 1954), p. 419.

Generally the rural workers suffered under harsh conditions. They received a pittance in wages, and more often than not were heavily in debt to their employer. Housing was primitive, the diet inadequate, health and sanitary conditions abysmal, and education generally nonexistent, and where existent substandard. Social mobility was rare. The many benefits conferred on the urban proletariat did not extend into the countryside. Rumors of a better life wafted through parts of rural Brazil. Often the more daring left their rustic purgatory for the promises of the city. That internal migration increased in the 1930s and continued at a rapid pace thereafter. Still, as late as 1945, nearly 75 percent of the Brazilians—the vast majority subservient, illiterate, disenfranchised, and unassimilated—lived outside the cities. The accelerating industrialization, urbanization, and modernization of the nation was bypassing them.

Chapter Seven

Reform,
Radicalization,
and Reaction

The fall of Vargas in 1945 initiated a period of democratic experiments in Brazil. Impressive economic growth encouraged by a vigorous nationalism accompanied those experiments. The pace of both industrialization and urbanization quickened. That combination of democratization, nationalism, industrialization, and urbanization created a new thrust which for a brief period seemed to propel Brazil toward development. Those who drew their power or prestige from institutions fundamentally connected with the past—latifundia, elitist education, social stratification, restricted suffrage—balked at the rapid rate of change. They hoped to retard it. Their opposition confirmed the resolution of the radicals, and at that point the customary political dialogue ended. Conservatives and reformers could have conversed with each other as they had many times in the past, but not conservatives and radicals. The radicals momentarily seemed as if they might triumph, but the conservative forces in Brazil were still powerful. On March 31, 1964, they reasserted their authority and removed the radicals from power to return Brazil to past patterns of behavior. Some see the

1945-1964 experiment with democracy as the natural consequence of gradual political maturation, while others regard it as an aberration, an unexpected hiatus between authoritarian governments.

Democratization

The Allies' march toward certain victory in Europe in 1944 marked democracy's triumph over dictatorship. Latin America felt the consequences. In the Spanish-speaking republics, one *caudillo* after another fell: in 1944, Fulgencio Batista, who had controlled Cuba since 1933, decided to step down in favor of a freely elected president; in Guatemala, in that same year, Jorge Ubico lost the power he had held since 1931 in a democratic revolution which swept him from the country; in mid-1945, President Alfonso López Pusmarejo of Colombia resigned under public pressure and President Manuel Prado of Peru, abandoning his plans to remain in office, called for elections; and in the same year General Isaías Medina of Venezuela, a hangover from the Gómez tyranny, was deposed in a revolt which pressed for democratic reforms. The Brazilians, more heavily committed to the struggle in Europe than were any of their Latin American neighbors, questioned why they should contribute to the promotion of democracy in Europe while suffering the constraints of dictatorship at home. This inconsistency annoyed them. Intellectuals and opposition politicians voiced that annoyance, as did ninety prominent Mineiros who in October of 1943 signed a manifesto which stated, "If we fight against fascism at the side of the United Nations so that liberty and democracy may be restored to all people, certainly we are not asking too much in demanding for ourselves such rights and guarantees." The students echoed that sentiment. Caught in the inconsistency of its own role, the military applied pressure on Vargas to return the nation to democratic rule. Both Generals Eurico Dutra and Góes Monteiro, long supporters of Vargas, but also representative of the pragmatic attitude of the military, agreed that the times demanded that the Estado Novo give way to democracy. Under increasing pressure by late 1944, Vargas slowly turned his attention to provisions for some sort of elections and to the restitution of democracy. Accordingly the government relaxed censorship and permitted political activity. A law appeared in Feburary of 1945 to govern voter registration and elections of the president, the governors, and the members of state and national assemblies. Vargas set December 2, 1945, as the date for presidential and congressional elections. Those were to be the first elections since 1934, and the electorate was five times larger.

Many doubted the sincerity of Vargas' intentions to restore democracy. They suspected that after enjoying fifteen years in power he really would not hand over the reins of authority. Memories of his lightning coup in 1937 had not faded. Suspicion mounted in July of 1945 when fervent followers of the wily Gaúcho began to express their *queremista* sentiment—the expression originated in the Portuguese verb *queremos,* "we want," signifying "we want Vargas." While the *queremistas* importuned, the chief of state guarded a delphic silence. His adversaries scrutinized his every move to confirm their suspicions. On October 10, he suddenly advanced the date for all state and local elections to December 2 to coincide with presidential and congressional elections. The advance meant that all those who currently held office and planned to run in the elections would have to resign their office thirty days before the election, a maneuver which would permit Vargas to appoint friends to their posts. Then, on October 25, the president goaded speculation still further by appointing his brother Benjamin, the possessor of an unsavory reputation, to the important post of chief-of-police of Rio de Janeiro. All those activities seemed to signal that Vargas was preparing something more than elections. To prevent him from staging another coup and to calm public agitation, the military themselves staged a coup and took command of the government on October 29. The military, which had assured Vargas power in 1930 and for a decade and a half thereafter, intervened in 1945 in such a way as to guarantee the initiation of the democratic process. Quietly

Vargas retired to his fazenda in Rio Grande do Sul. The officers designated José Linhares, chief justice of the Supreme Court, to head the government until after the elections. The urge to democratize Brazil was the chief force which toppled the Estado Novo and ended fifteen years of Vargas government. Vargas, however, did not agree with that conclusion. He attributed his downfall to foreign influence, particularly the influence of the foreign business community. In a speech given in Pôrto Alegre at the end of 1946, he revealed, "I was the victim of agents of international finance who intended to keep our country simply as an exporting colony for raw materials and a purchaser of industrial goods." His policies of economic nationalism, he believed, united "trusts and monopolies" against him. It was an intriguing idea well phrased within the emotional framework of economic nationalism so much in vogue during the latter years of his administration. As in years past, he scorned "old liberal capitalist democracy" and recommended his own brand of "Socialist Democracy for the workers." Apparently Vargas had changed little from his heyday, but for the moment he was out of harmony with the democratic sentiments of many Brazilians. Further, Brazil seemed to have changed; the industrialized and urbanized Brazil of the mid-forties contrasted with the coffee-dominated and rural-oriented Brazil of the late twenties.

Brazil owed at least part of that change to the guidance of Vargas. He restored unity and assigned the nation new goals. He diminished the power of the coffee interests and distributed it more broadly. He encouraged industrialization, which, in turn, fostered urban growth. The middle and working classes won political recognition for themselves. During a period of political extremism in the world, he steered a course between Communism and Integralism. The cost of those achievements came high. Political liberty and freedom of expression were part of the price paid. Yet, it would be specious to argue that Brazil under the Old Republic had enjoyed democracy. In reality, Vargas had substituted one elitist rule for another, but in the process, as an aspiring populist leader, he had broadened the base upon which the government rested. He did bequeath a certain legacy to the future growth of democracy. He trimmed the power of the coroneis, and the 1932 electoral code lowered the voting age to eighteen, conferred the right to vote on working women, guaranteed the secret ballot, and created a system of electoral courts. He introduced the civil service merit system, and after 1937 the bulk of federal appointments were made on the basis of competitive exams. While the merit system may not have worked as well as envisaged, it did establish a precedent. His impressive labor legislation improved the living conditions of the expanding number of urban workers. Bowing to political exigencies, he permitted the organization of political parties during his final year in office and even helped to create two of them.

Three important national political parties took shape in 1945, and they would influence the political life of the nation for a generation. Of equal significance, they contributed to the growing democratization of the country. The *Partido Social Democrático* (Social Democratic Party, or PSD), the largest of the three, was formed by Vargas. The main core of its strength was rural and consisted of the state machines which supported Vargas. Minas Gerais was the center of the party's strength, but it also enjoyed considerable support in Rio de Janeiro state, Pernambuco, Maranhão, Bahia, Ceará, and Goiás. Vargas also presided over the creation of the *Partido Trabalhista Brasileiro* (Brazilian Labor Party, or PTB), the smallest of the three major parties, which he regarded as his own personal machine. He had been contemplating the formation of such a party at least since 1943. It frankly and aggressively appealed to the urban worker and received most of its leadership and strength from the cities. Rio Grande do Sul and the Federal District of Rio de Janeiro formed the two strongest columns of support for that party. Finally, the *União Democrática Nacional* (National Democratic Union, or UDN) united those who opposed Vargas and his political heirs. Rejecting all that Vargas stood for, the UDN seemed to look back nostalgically to the Old Republic and included such old *políticos* as Artur Bernardes. Its orientation was conservative. Its center of strength also rested in Minas Gerais, with strong support in Bahia, the Federal District of Rio de Janeiro, Santa Catarina, Ceará, and Pernambuco. The three parties described above dominated the political scene, and only candidates from these parties reached the presidency. Together they regularly held 75 percent of the seats in the chamber of deputies. Table 7.1 illustrates their relative strength in the Chamber.

Table 7.1. Strength of the Three Principal Parties in the Chamber of Deputies, 1945–1962 (by percentage)

Party	1945	1950	1954	1960	1962
PSD	40.9	32.3	31.1	34.6	30.0
UDN	25.4	23.9	20.7	21.4	23.0
PTB	9.7	17.5	19.8	20.5	26.6

A wide variety of smaller parties also appeared. On the extreme right, the *Partido de Representação Popular* (Popular Representation Party, or PRP) continued the tradition of the Integralists. Plínio Salgado, returning to Brazil in 1945 from exile in Portugal, formed the party. He maintained it was not totalitarian, although it supported the creation of a corporative state. On the extreme left, Luís Carlos Prestes, released from prison by Vargas at the end of World War II, reorganized the *Partido Comunista Brasileiro* (Brazilian Communist Party, or PCB), which enjoyed two years of legal existence. The Communists elected one senator, Prestes, and fourteen deputies in 1945, to whom they added four more in the elections of 1947. The other minor parties—they numbered about nine by the early 1960s—were more regional in their appeal. The popular politician Adhemar de Barros formed the *Partido Social Progressista* (Social Progressive Party, or PSP) in São Paulo as the vehicle for his own political ambitions. Vague in platform, the party frankly rested on the magnetic personality of its leader. It was the dominant political force to reckon with in the key state of São Paulo. The *Partido Republicano* (Republican party, or PR) traced its roots to the Old Republic. Dominated by the landowning elite, its program was very conservative. Another minor party, the

Partido Democrática Cristão (Christian Democratic Party, or PDC), achieved some limited success. Stressing Christian, particularly Roman Catholic, social doctrine, it was one of the few ideologically oriented parties.

Concerning the political parties in general it can be concluded that platforms, programs, and policies tended to be vague. As had been true always in Brazilian politics, the personality dominated. Men took precedence over party labels. A firm sense of party loyalty failed to develop. Voters and politicians alike shifted party allegiance with bewildering rapidity. The most diverse parties often formed alliances among themselves on all political levels with little embarrassment and little regard to possible incongruities.

Imperfect as the political parties were, they did provide the machinery for selecting and putting forth candidates. And, if they did not always provide the electorate with a clear choice of issues, they did offer a choice of personalities. Democratic elections could not have been held without their participation. At least the three largest parties were national in scope. To a limited extent they reflected and expressed public opinion. Generally the parties indicated a willingness to abide by the give and take of politics. The parties— although not always their leaders—accepted the results of the elections in good grace. They paid homage to the ideals and goals of democratic government. Considering Brazil's scant experience with popular and national political parties, the organization of those parties in 1945 and their progress, often under considerable stress, in the years thereafter were satisfactory. In short, they contributed—at least superficially—to the growth of the democratic process in Brazil after 1945.

For the first elections, whose date of December 2, 1945 the coup did not alter, the UDN nominated Major General Eduardo Gomes, a former tenente, and the PSD selected General Eurico Dutra, who had been minister of war throughout the Estado Novo period. Tardily Vargas put the PTB behind Dutra. His growing coolness toward Dutra sprang from his resentment of the contact his former minister maintained with politicians and military officers who had opposed his regime. Dutra polled 55 percent of the vote, and the PSD won a majority in both houses. The election proved to be a victory for Vargas as well: he was elected senator from two states and congressman from six states and the federal district.

The congress elected at the same time also sat as a constituent assembly. Although the constitution promulgated on September 18, 1946, institutionalized the labor legislation of the Vargas era, it was in many respects a reaction to Vargas and an attempt to prevent the rise of a similar caudilho in the future. The presidency remained the key institution, but the office was sufficiently circumscribed to inhibit its holder from abusing his powers. The new constitution carefully separated the three branches of government, ensuring Congress of its independence and of its freedom from presidential control in the election of its members, and establishing an independent court system with sufficient power to review the actions of the other branches. It restored the office of vice-president. To the armed forces, it assigned the responsibility to "defend the country and guarantee the constitutional powers and law and order." Within a federal structure, the central government predominated, but restrictions were placed on it in an effort to prevent abusive intervention in the internal affairs of the states. All persons over eighteen years of age, except military enlisted men and noncommissioned officers and illiterates (a major exception in a nation with an illiteracy rate approaching 60%), enjoyed the right to vote. The Constitution of 1946, the fourth of the republic and the fifth of Brazil, seemed to be suited to the conditions of the country and to be capable of promoting democratic government.

The taciturn military career officer who entered the presidency on January 31, 1946, had supported the establishment of the Estado Novo; but later, propelled by the currents welling up within the nation in favor of democracy, he had helped to remove Vargas from office. As president, Dutra took seriously the aims of the program adopted in 1945 to encourage the growth of democracy in Brazil. In doing so, he looked askance at the activities of the local Communists.

He regarded the agitation of the PCB as a threat to the nation's nascent democracy. What annoyed him in particular was the bold declaration of Senator Luís Carlos Prestes, leader of the PCB, that in the event of war between Russia and Brazil, the Brazilian Communists would support Russia. The memories of the Communist uprising in 1935 burned too vividly in Dutra's mind for him to tolerate such talk. The electoral growth of the PCB, as evinced in the state elections of January of 1947, further disturbed him. The government reacted by outlawing the PCB on the grounds that its objectives were contrary to the goals of a democratic society, a move sanctioned by the Constitution of 1946. The Soviet press attacked Dutra. One journal sneered:

At 43 years of age, he was just a major in an army where everyone got to be a general even if there were not enough soldiers to go around. In three years he became a general. Of course in Brazil generals are not the product of battlefields but of coffee plantations. The bloody regime of Mr. Dutra is not only related to the fascism of Hitler but to all its contemporary variations: the Falange of the hangman Franco, the filthy "Estado Novo" of Salazar, and the tragicomedy dictatorship of shifty Perón! What pleasant company![1]

The Brazilian government promptly broke diplomatic relations with Moscow, and Congress expelled from its ranks those members elected on the PCB ticket. The PCB remained illegal after 1947 but by no means inactive.

Dutra presided over an essentially conservative government. The administration regarded suspiciously any opinions favorable to economic, social, or political reform, if, indeed, it did not outrightly label them Communist. As in the United States and elsewhere in the world at the time, anti-Communism became the doctrine of the status quo, and not a few of the men in positions of power had for years made a career out of being anti-Communist. They gratuitously made the charge of "Communist" against those with whom they were not in agreement, liberally applying the epithet to labor, students, and intellectuals in particular.

1. This statement appeared in the *Literary Gazette* (Moscow), October 4, 1947. Quoted in Mário Victor, *5 Anos que Abalaram o Brasil* (Rio de Janeiro, 1965), p. 421.

Dutra chose to ignore nationalism, a force he regarded with some suspicion, perhaps identifying it, or its goals, with parts of the Communist program. Although avoiding the nationalist rhetoric his predecessor had perfected, he did undertake some projects which the nationalists could only applaud: the construction of oil refineries, a tanker fleet, and port installations, the rebuilding and paving of the Rio-São Paulo highway, and the beginning of the mammoth Paulo Afonso hydroelectric project to provide the energy needed by burgeoning industrialization.

Superficially the economy seemed healthy. The price of coffee rose, and the quantity of coffee beans sold abroad reached new highs. Still, Brazil lived far beyond its means. When Dutra became president, Brazil held gold and foreign exchange reserves of nearly U.S. $800 million, a record high. The entire sum was used to buy imports, many of them luxuries, which during the war years had not been available. A spendthrift attitude prevailed and more rapidly than anyone had imagined possible the reserves were exhausted, partially, it should be noted, because Brazil paid inflated prices for the items imported.

Proof of Dutra's commitment to democracy came during the electoral campaign of 1950. Unlike his predecessors during the Old Republic, he played a minor and, as it turned out, ineffectual role in the selection of candidates and conscientiously guaranteed the honesty of the elections. Sharply in contrast to the restrictions and censorship of the Estado Novo period, freedom of expression existed, and except for its insistence on the suppression of the PCB, the government tolerated this freedom. The news media spoke out unrestrictedly, especially during the presidential campaign. The UDN once again nominated Gomes, who tarnished his luster by allying with the reactionary PRP and revealed his lack of harmony with the times by such proposals as the abandonment of the minimum wage. A colorless unknown, Cristiano Machado, weakly held aloft the banner of the PSD. The PTB and PSP offered their support to Vargas. After insuring that the military would not object, Vargas accepted the candidacy and waged a vigorous campaign on a platform of accelerated industrialization and expanded social legislation. A wide variety of supporters drawn from the ranks of the industrialists, businessmen, nationalists and the proletariat gave him 49 percent of the vote, a handsome victory over the other candidates. Thus for the first time in his long political career a popular electoral mandate opened the doors of the presidential palace to him on January 31, 1951. Vargas' running mate, João Café Filho of the PSP, with a third of the votes, won over the other candidates in a separate vice-presidential contest.

Governing under a constitution which he neither wrote nor influenced and amid a welter of political parties, many of which were hostile, challenged the former caudilho. Aged sixty-eight when he assumed office again, Vargas seemed less adept, less flexible. His own personal secretary observed that his chief showed "signs of exhaustion." The challenges in no way abated. Budgetary deficits, the rising cost of living, and inflation clouded the financial horizon. The cost of living had risen on an average of 6 percent a year from 1945 to 1950, when it jumped 11 percent, a figure repeated in 1951 and doubled in 1952. The government balanced the budget but uninhibitedly printed new currency. The volume of paper currency rose from 31 to 50 billion cruzeiros during Vargas' tenure. Vargas encountered some difficulty with the military over his labor policies. In 1951 he raised the minimum wage, the first such raise since 1943. In 1954, his minister of labor and political disciple, João Goulart, tried to double wages. The officers charged Goulart with demagogy and criticized him for using his office, its powers and finances, to enhance his own political position. A bitter "Manifesto of the Colonels" demanded his dismissal, and a cautious Vargas removed his young protégé from office—but later he enacted the wage increase and praised Goulart in the process.

Vargas faced some crucial decisions which proved extremely difficult to make for him as well as for his successors. While it was not difficult to sustain the momentum of growth, simple numerical increase, it was challenging to pursue genuine development, the utilization of Brazil's potential for the greatest good for the largest number of citizens. Basically the governments faced a series of choices which revolved around reforms of the institutional structures or encouragement of additional investments, part of which investments originated abroad. Repeatedly the presidents opted for the latter, and the forms the investments inevitably took did more to promote economic growth than to foster development. Since growth favored the privileged at the expense of the impoverished masses, the long term result of the governments' economic policies was to exacerbate social injustice. However, growth can disguise the inequities or cloak them with euphoric hope, at least for a time, creating the illusion of well-being or improvement. The governments became masters of creating economic illusions. Few steps toward development were taken and those which might have encouraged development—increased hydroelectric power and expanding road networks, for example—were used so that they contributed primarily to growth. In fairness, it must be reemphasized that under Vargas the government's commitment first to create a vast steel producing complex and later to institute an oil monopoly changed the traditional role of government. It became actively and inextricably involved in the vital economic question of planning, industrialization, modernization, and development.

President Vargas was not without his detractors, particularly within the UDN. They attacked relentlessly. In the vanguard of the attack marched the vitriolic Carlos Lacerda, editor of the *Tribuna da Imprensa,* who wielded a poisoned pen unrelentingly hostile to Vargas. Under the censorship imposed by the Estado Novo, he would have been silenced at once, but under the new democracy it seemed impossible to stop him. An attempt to do so precipitated the end of the Vargas administration, and indeed of Vargas himself.

In the early hours of the morning of August 5, 1954, Lacerda returned to his apartment in Copacabana accompanied by Air Force Major Rubens Florentino Vaz, one of a series of volunteer military body guards. As their car pulled up in front of the apartment building, shots rang out, one slightly wounding Lacerda, another killing the major. Indignant, the air force, in addition to the police, undertook an investigation to apprehend the assassin. Clues pointed to the presidential palace. Soon investigators confirmed that the chief of the president's personal guard, an intimate of Vargas, had planned the crime. The political repercussions were tremendous. First the air force, then the navy, and finally the generals demanded the resignation of Vargas. It was not constitutional principles but rather an elusive and pervasive military honor which dictated their actions. On the morning of the 24th, the president was informed that the military—for the second time—had deposed him. Upon receipt of the news he retired to his bedroom, from which a shot shattered the gloomy silence of Catete Palace. Those who rushed into his room found him dead, a bullet in his heart. A stunned nation paused. It read with bewilderment the cryptic and emotional suicide note Vargas left behind:

Once more the forces and interests against the people are newly coordinated and raised against me. . . . I follow the destiny that is imposed on me. After years of domination and looting by international economic and financial groups, I made myself chief of an unconquerable revolution. I began the work of liberation and I instituted a regime of social liberty. I had to resign. I returned to govern on the arms of the people. A subterranean campaign of international groups joined with national groups revolting against the regime of workers' guarantees. . . . I have fought month to month, day to day, hour to hour, resisting a constant aggression, unceasingly bearing it all in silence, forgetting all and renouncing myself to defend the people that now fall abandoned. I cannot give you more than my blood. . . . I offer my life in the holocaust. I chose this means to be with you always. When they humiliate you, you will feel my soul suffering at your side. When hunger beats at your door, you will feel in your chests the energy for the fight for yourselves and your children. When they humiliate you, you will feel in my grief the force for reaction. My sacrifice will maintain you united, and my name will be your battle flag. . . . I fought against the looting of Brazil. I fought against the looting of the people. I have fought bare-breasted. The hatred, infamy, and calumny did not beat down my spirit. I gave you my life. Now I offer my death. Nothing remains. Serenely I take the first step on the road to eternity and I leave life to enter history.[2]

The note highlighted the president's role as a populist and nationalist leader. His personality was many-sided, but the Vargas who wrote that farewell was the one who had served as the promoter of the rights of workers and of the creation of Petrobrás.

The unexpected crisis generated by the suicide of Vargas put the democratic experiment in Brazil to a severe test. The very military which had just deposed Vargas stepped forward to guarantee the constitutional process. Vice-President Café Filho, a marked contrast to Vargas in his conventional economic outlook and lack of nationalistic orientation, took the oath of office to complete the last seventeen months of Vargas' five-year mandate. For the first time, the declared enemies of the Estado Novo achieved power. Café Filho himself had attacked vehemently the establishment of the Estado Novo and had been exiled. By the early 1950s, he had abandoned most of his socialist ideals. In his new government, he assigned the key cabinet posts of Finance, Justice, and Foreign Affairs to stalwarts of the UDN. His administration proved to be a caretaker one, since the maneuvering for the 1955 presidential elections got under way almost at once.

The PSB and PTB, the two parties founded by Vargas, jointly put forth Juscelino Kubitschek, the highly successful governor of Minas Gerais, for the presidency and João Goulart, heir to the Vargas mantle, for the vice-presidency. They campaigned on an alluring platform promising economic progress for all. The UDN endorsed General Juarez Távora, the second former tenente to bear its standard. Acrimony characterized the campaign. Military leaders expressed their concern about the dangers of a violent electoral campaign in the midst of serious political and social crises which to them seemed threatening. They harbored suspicions about the suitability of Kubitschek for the presidency and made no ef-

2. *The New York Times,* August 25, 1954, p. 2.

fort to hide their dislike of Goulart, who had earned the enmity of the officers during his brief tenure as minister of labor. Rumors of a military coup circulated. In early October of 1955, Kubitschek and Goulart won the elections. Goulart received even more votes than the presidential victor. A month later President Café Filho, entering the hospital after a mild heart attack, turned over the duties of his office on November 8, 1955, to his legal successor, the president of the chamber of deputies, Carlos Luz, a declared adversary of Kubitschek and Goulart. Most observers believed that he would prevent his two political enemies from taking the offices to which they had just been elected. At that point, Marshal Odílio Denys and Minister of War Henrique Teixeira Lott in alliance with other officers who formed the *Movimento Militar Constitucionalista* (Constitutionalist Military Movement) staged a preventive coup on November 11, removing Acting President Luz from office to guarantee the inauguration of Kubitschek and Goulart. Congress cooperated and swore in the vice-president of the senate, Nereu Ramos, as the interim president. In due course and with no further difficulty the democratically elected Kubitschek and Goulart took office on the prescribed date, January 31, 1956. Despite tribulations and stress, the democratic process seemed to be functioning, and in this particular case the military seemingly contributed to its success.

One measure of the successful democratization was that the elections in 1945 as well as all subsequent ones held under the Constitution of 1946 were generally honest. Thus they contrasted sharply with the chicanery characteristic of elections during the Old Republic. An elaborate system of electoral courts removed the control of the elections from those in power and guaranteed the voters complete freedom at the polls and an accurate tabulation of the votes cast. Those special courts supervised the registration of parties, candidates, and voters; they also were responsible for the supervision of the balloting, the counting of ballots, and the investigation and prosecution of electoral fraud. An electoral reform in 1955 ended the custom by which each party printed and distributed its own ballots and substituted an official ballot made available through the Supreme Electoral Tribunal. The regional electoral tribunals appointed three poll-watchers at each polling place, and each party was entitled to assign one poll-watcher. The vote was secret: the voter marked the official ballot in the privacy of an enclosed booth and then dropped it in a box in the presence of the poll-watchers, who then accompanied the ballot box to the district electoral board where they oversaw the counting. The chance for fraud was minimal.

Most of the charges of fraud were made in remote rural areas where the inspection system tended to be less rigorous or, in some cases, nonexistent. In some rural areas, the coronel still held sway and he could regiment the local vote for his preferred candidate. Beholden to the coroneis, candidates so elected did not represent the voters, of course, but rather the interests of those men who had delivered the vote. Fortunately for the future of democracy in Brazil, that system was on the decline.

One means of effectively reducing the power of the coroneis and the traditional ruling families was to create new political subdivisions, principally new municipalities, often created as the result of commercial or industrial growth in a particular area. The coroneis and the traditional families often continued to control the old municipalities, but other, more progressive forces—such as a middle class, an educated working class, and a general atmosphere favorable to change and modernization—dominated in the newly created municipalities. Their number burgeoned. The increase of municipalities in Minas Gerais serves as an excellent example of this growth. That wealthy captaincy was divided into 16 municipalities during the colonial period. During the imperial period, Minas Gerais province boasted 95 *municípios*. In 1948, there were 316; in 1953, 388; in 1958, 405; and in 1963, 722. In those same years, after the promulgation of the Constitution of 1946, the number of municipalities throughout Brazil doubled. Corruption, nepotism, and poverty characterized many of the local governments, but, on the other hand, examples of good government, efficiency, and grassroots democracy could be found too.

The judicial system as it evolved under the Constitution of 1946 provided another bulwark for Brazilian democracy. Elaborate provisions of that document protected the courts' independence, an independence enjoyed to a degree unique in Latin America. The Federal Supreme Court, composed of eleven justices appointed by the president with the approval of the senate (the number of judges could be increased only at the request of the court itself), had jurisdiction to rule on the constitutionality of all legislation, federal, state, or local. The bench became increasingly bold in exercising its power of judicial review. Although the court never attained the power of its North American counterpart, it inhibited, checked, and, at times reversed arbitrary actions of the executive or legislature.

A further indication of the growth of Brazilian democracy was the steady increase in the size of the electorate. Despite the large segments of the population prohibited from voting by the constitution, the number of voters mounted steadily as the population grew and literacy rose. The percentage of the population registered to vote increased from 16 percent in 1945 to 25 percent in 1962. The number of voters increased rather steadily during that period at approximately 20 percent every four years. Two new groups, the urban proletariat and the industrial middle class, took important positions in the political spectrum. The growth of the urban electorate cut the power and influence of the rural coroneis to a fraction of what it had been during the Old Republic. The careers of both Getúlio Vargas on the national level and Adhemar de Barros on the state level amply illustrated that politicians could successfully base their support on a mass popular following rather than on the support of the elite, a trend which Lázaro Cárdenas and Juan D. Perón had already proven in Mexico and Argentina. Vargas and Adhemar appealed directly and openly to the workers, informing them of their power and advising them how to use it. As the new elements realized and exercised their power, the control of the urban elites and rural coroneis declined proportionately.

One of the major blocks to popular democracy in Brazil

was the lack of education. A faulty educational system likewise retarded modernization. Good schools were essential to prepare the Brazilians to accept technological progress as well as to participate in that progress, to encourage students to higher goals and to equip them with the means of achieving those goals. Unfortunately, about half the adult population did not even know how to sign their names. Thus they were excluded from participation in both the political and the modernization processes. Although more students were enrolled in schools than ever before, the statistics were still bleak. In 1940, there were 3¼ million students enrolled at all levels from the primary through the university level; in 1965, the total reached 11¼ million. At the same time, of course, the population had grown from 41 to 72 million. The sad result was that although the illiteracy rate was falling, the number of illiterates was growing. In 1965, of 1,000 students matriculated in primary schools, only 13 reached secondary school and only 4 completed some form of superior education. The dropout rate during the four years of primary school was exceptionally high, higher than that of Liberia or the Philippines for example. In theory, primary education was both free and compulsory, but in reality impoverished parents found it an economic hardship to send their children to school. The children were needed to contribute to the meager family income or at least to take care of their younger sisters and brothers while both parents worked. The government never provided a sufficient number of schools or the means to enforce compulsory attendance. For these reasons, a majority of the children of school age neither enrolled in school nor remained there long.

Like everything else, the educational situation varied widely from region to region. In affluent São Paulo state the budget for education equaled that of the rest of the states combined, and São Paulo city budgeted for educational purposes more than the rest of the local governments combined. Nearly 80 percent of the adult population of São Paulo state were literate in 1965. In the depressed Northeast, only 33 percent of the children of primary school age were in school, and only 6 percent of those of secondary school age attended some sort of classes. Barely 30 percent of the adults were literate.

The educational system was archaic. The classical curriculum, which educated the sons of the elite for further education in the universities, belied the desire for modernization. A rapidly developing nation with industrial pretensions required technicians of every sort, yet most of the population was excluded by lack of training from contributing to their nation's technical development. Modern educators realized the need for a structural change in the educational system. As a result, educational reforms in the early 1960s emphasized ambitious literacy campaigns to prepare the masses for technical and vocational training. A noticeable rise in enrollments for vocational training occurred, with 124,000 vocational students in 1954 increasing to 275,000 in 1962, but the numbers fell pitifully short of the need.

The number of universities increased modestly. There were more than 30 universities by the mid-1960s. But in a population well over 70 million, barely 155,000 students matriculated in them. Those that did represented the elite in every sense of the word, since only 5 percent of the university students came from proletarian families. Law remained, as it always had been, the preferred field of study of those privileged students. Of a total enrolment of 110,093 students in 1962, nearly a quarter—25,856—were in law. There were 13,325 in engineering, 13,160 in the social sciences, 10,919 in medicine, 5,548 in education, 4,274 in fine arts, 3,388 in natural scienes, 2,447 in agriculture, and 1,048 in the humanities. Extreme regional disparities in both quantity and quality of university education existed. The five states of São Paulo, Guanabara, Rio Grande do Sul, Minas Gerais, and Paraná enrolled three-quarters of the students and hired three-quarters of the professors. The universities in São Paulo and Guanabara were reputed to be the best in the nation.

All Brazilians paid at least lip service to the value of education for the future of the nation. Mário Pinto Serva wrote in his O Enigma Brasileiro (The Brazilian Enigma), "In twenty years Brazil will be literate and then it will take its position as the second or third power of the world." (Optimism has been an enduring Brazilian characteristic.) Shining through the dismal data, however, is the one reassuring statistic that the literacy rate did continue to rise slowly, thereby expanding the electorate and the base of democracy.

Developmental Nationalism

An intensifying feeling of nationalism accompanied the growth of democracy in Brazil. Both were forces which at that time seemed to challenge the past and to promise to promote change.

Resurgent nationalism displayed four major characteristics. First, it veered leftward. The Integralist party had exerted the last major effort of the right to manipulate nationalist feelings. After its suppression in 1937, the left gained control of the nationalist movement. The reliance on Marxist phraseology often exposed the movement to criticism that the Communists guided or dominated it. Such an accusation was not only false, it also oversimplifed the complexities of Brazilian nationalism and obscured efforts to understand it.

Second, nationalist leaders criticized ever more boldly foreign economic domination. They blamed enervating dependency on foreign oppression. Their campaign to oppose foreign ownership found its modern roots, as was noted, in the writings of Alberto Tôrres and in the opposition to Percival Farquhar. The nationalists termed foreign ownership "economic colonialism," which drained, impoverished, and enfeebled the underdeveloped nations to nurture the industrialized states. Despite nationalist rhetoric and agitation, the inflow of foreign investments continued at a rapid pace throughout the decade of the 1950s. By 1960 foreigners owned 69 percent of the automobile industry, 62 percent of the pharmaceutical industry, 57 percent of the auto parts industry, 38 percent of the chemical industry, 28 percent of plastics production, 22 percent of the cellulose industry, 17 percent of steel manufacturing, and 15 percent of the paper industry. They continued to repatriate handsome profits which cumulatively exceeded their investments.

Third, the nationalists concentrated their strongest attack on the United States, an obvious target since the United States was the single largest investor in Brazil. Its investment jumped from $28 million in 1914, to $577 million in 1950, to $1.5 billion in 1960—about half of the total foreign investment in Brazil. Logically any campaign undertaken against foreign investors would have to assume anti-Yankee tones. Furthermore, the nationalists thought they detected a link between their own oligarchy, the United States government, and United States investors. They all seemed to be forces partial to the status quo in Brazil and opposed to change. In several respects, then, the nationalists depicted the United States as an enemy whose influence and presence had to be challenged and defeated if nationalism was to triumph. They cultivated anti-Americanism as a convenient and certain means to arouse national feeling.

Finally, the nationalists paid ever greater attention to economic development. Defining nationalism as "the political consciousness of development," they advocated it as the single force capable of modernizing the nation. Developmental nationalism, springing from the program of the tenentes and the policies of the Estado Novo, received new emphasis when Vargas returned to power in 1951 and until the military coup of 1964. Its doctrine called for governmental control of natural resources, limitations on foreign capital, continuing industrialization, and greater commerce with all nations. It was considered to be the only way to liberate Brazil, to unchain it from the past and propel it into the future. Such a concept attracted many who did not necessarily support all of the hard-core nationalist causes.

For nearly a decade (1955–1964), the focal point of the developmental nationalist movement was the *Institutio Superior de Estudos Brasileiros* (Superior Institute of Brazilian Studies, or ISEB), established by the federal government as an autonomous agency responsible to the Ministry of Education. The Institute offered courses and conducted research on the problems of economic development. It also undertook the task of formulating the ideological doctrine for developmental nationalism. Its members agreed that a vibrant economy required national planning. They further agreed that the state would have to oversee and guide such planning and development. However, they differed as to whether a basically socialistic or capitalistic economy would best serve Brazil's interests. The disagreement eventually split the ISEB, as it divided the nationalist movement. The moderate nationalists were more tolerant of foreign investments and less enthusiastic for government ownership or control. The radical nationalists urged ownership of the principal industries and control of foreign investments. They won control of the ISEB in 1959 and imposed their ideology. Meanwhile, the officers in the Escola Superior de Guerra (Superior War College) fretted about the ideas propagated through the ISEB. They believed the orientation to be too hostile to the United States and too receptive to Marxism.

As industrialization intensified after World War II, it gradually lost some of its emergency or stopgap aspects. Brazilian leaders adopted better plans and carried them out with more resolution. They intended to alter the basic structure of the economy by reducing the nation's customary dependence on exports, encouraging import-substitution industries, and creating heavy primary industries. Companies proving they could produce an item being imported received high tariff protection, a policy which proved particularly effective in encouraging the production of consumer goods. As late as 1950, those goods still accounted for 9.7 percent of the imports, a figure which fell to 1.5 by 1961. The consumer industries concentrated on the manufacture of goods of primary necessity: food, beverages, clothing, and textiles. The factories were small. On an average, they employed sixteen workers. To the basic industries, the government gave new attention by making loans available on reasonable terms to potential entrepreneurs and by creating or helping to create some heavy industries. Volta Redonda in the 1940s and Petrobrás in the 1950s were excellent examples of those governmental efforts, as was the growing activity of the government in the development of electrical energy resources.

An unexpected impetus to industrial expansion was the rapid exhaustion of Brazil's foreign exchange reserves after

World War II. In the emergency, the government imposed import controls. Discouraging the importation of consumer items on the one hand, those controls favored the purchase of capital goods and raw materials on the other. The controls worked in such a fashion that the price of imported capital goods and raw materials remained nearly constant. At the same time, the domestic prices charged by the manufacturers of consumer products rose steadily. Good business sense prompted the purchase of capital machinery so that more goods could be manufactured internally. As that pattern was followed, a host of new industries appeared. More often than not, they became each other's customers, illustrating the self-propelling nature of industrialization once it is under way. By the time Vargas took command of the economy for the second time, the drive for industrialization was characterized by encouragement of the importation of capital goods, discouragement of the importation of items domestically manufactured, high premiums on foreign exchange, and inflation. The industrial output in 1954 doubled that of 1945. Giant industrial strides were being made despite monumental handicaps: a poorly developed transportation network, an illiterate population untrained for technical jobs, an inefficient use of the land, and insufficient national economic integration.

In pursuit of development, President Kubitschek envisioned a rise in the production of hydroelectric power, expansion of road building, rehabilitation of the railroads, encouragment to basic industries, increases in both steel production and oil refining capacity, the establishment of a vehicle industry, and accelerated agricultural production. In his campaign for the presidency, he had promised his compatriots "fifty years of progress in five," and to a large extent he fulfilled that promise. The day after his inauguration he created the National Development Council to oversee his program for economic development. A "Program of Targets" was drawn up both for the government and for private industry. In his speeches, he reiterated his belief that economic development was the key to national independence. During his administration, 1956–1961, Brazil experienced unparalleled economic growth. Industrial production grew 80 percent; steel, 100 percent; mechanical industries, 125 percent; electrical and communications industries, 380 percent; transportation equipment, 600 percent. By 1960, industry accounted for over 20 percent of the gross national product. By that time, Brazil manufactured fully half of its heavy-industry needs: machine tools, motors, transformers, mining and transportation equipment, turbines and generators, etc. Although the rates of growth for the 1947–1961 period were impressive, as Table 7.2 indicates, the rates during the Kubitschek administration were nothing short of spectacular.

Table 7.2. Average Annual Economic Growth Rates, 1947–1961

Period	Agricultural Production	Industrial Production	Gross National Product
1947–1961	4.6	9.6	6.1
1957–1961	4.8	12.7	7.0

Agricultural output increased by 52 percent during the decade of the fifties and industrial output by 140 percent, reflective of the priority given industrialization. During the 1950s Brazil's rate of economic growth was three times that of the rest of Latin America. In fact, it was one of the most impressive growth records in the Western world. Economic growth kept far ahead of rapid population increases, which averaged 3.2 percent a year, the highest rate among the heavily populated nations of the world. By 1960, 71 million people inhabited Brazil, 19 million more than a decade earlier.

Brazil achieved its economic miracle without foreign "doles." It applied for and received "hard" loans from the Export-Import Bank. Despite nationalist rhetoric, the inflow of foreign capital accelerated rapidly after 1955, attracted by the political stability, potential of the nation, and lack of restrictions. Kubitschek frankly encouraged foreign investment. The banks received their interest on the loans; the foreign capitalists, their profits. At the same time, domestic investment also reached new highs.

During the decade of the fifties, the number of industrial

plants grew by 33 percent and the labor force by 40 percent, so that in 1960 there were 110,339 industrial establishments employing 1,796,857 workers. A majority of the industries were concentrated in São Paulo and Guanabara. By 1960, São Paulo alone boasted a third of the nation's factories, half of its workers, and half of its output.

To supply the desperately needed power for industrialization, the president urged the exploitation of the nation's hydroelectric potential, estimated to be the sixth largest in the world. He authorized the construction of the gigantic Furnas hydorelectric project and the impressive Três Marias Dam on the São Francisco River. During the Kubitschek years, hydrolectric power increased from 3 to 5 million kilowatts. Table 7.3 provides a comparison of Brazil's achievement with that of the other principal producers of electric energy in the hemisphere:

Table 7.3. Comparative Electric Energy Production in Selected American Countries, 1957–1960 (in thousands of millions of Kw-Hr)

Country	1957	1958	1959	1960
United States	718.46	726.93	797.55	843.22
Canada	91.05	97.47	104.61	114.83
Brazil	16.96	19.77	21.11	23.37
Mexico	8.45	9.10	9.77	10.73
Argentina	8.80	9.39	9.55	10.37

SOURCE: United Nations, Department of Economic and Social Affairs, Statistical Office, World Energy Supplies, 1957–60, Statistical Papers, Series J, No. 5 (1962), pp. 104–6.

Whereas Brazil lagged considerably behind the United States and Canada, it far outdistanced its two closest Latin American industrial rivals, Argentina and Mexico.

Kubitschek will probably be best remembered for his most audacious scheme, which realized one of the nationalists' oldest dreams: he moved the capital from the coast to the interior. Brasília, located in the state of Goiás, became the symbol of the unification of all regions of Brazil. Kubitschek referred to it as the "capital that will unite the whole nation." In 1956, with the approval of an incredulous Congress, he created the Companhia Urbanizadora da Nova Capital (Urbanization Company of the New Capital) to take charge of building the new city. Lúcio Costa prepared a daring "airplane design" plan for the new capital, which Oscar Niemeyer matched with imaginative designs for the federal buildings: the eleven ministry buildings, the Praça of the Three Powers with its Senate and Chamber of Deputies complex, Palácio do Planalto (executive office building), and Supreme Court, the Palácio da Alvarada (presidential palace), and Itamaratí. One of his major monuments was the cathedral. Taken as a group, those magnificent and ingeniously designed buildings were a tribute to one of the foremost architects of the twentieth century, and his motifs became commonplace throughout the world as other architects adopted them. Work on Brasília began in 1957 and continued at a frantic pace, twenty-four hours a day, seven days a week. On April 21, 1960, an ebullient Kubitschek inaugurated the new capital, Brazil's third, some six hundred miles from the coast. The former Federal District of Rio de Janeiro then elected to become the union's smallest state, Guanabara. Brasília was an expensive but magnificent gesture to demonstrate that Brazil at last was going to develop its untapped hinterland, so long a promised land. The population of the new capital numbered 140,000 in 1960 and grew phenomenally in the years thereafter. The daring futuristic city with its exceptional architecture captured the admiration of the world. One early visitor, John Dos Passos, judged, "It is a city for the automotive age, for the age of jets and helicopters."

To connect Brasília with the rest of the nation, the government undertook an ambitious program to build "highways of national union." New roads radiated from Brasília to Belém, 1,400 miles to the north, to Fortaleza, 1,060 miles to the northeast, and to Belo Horizonte, 400 miles to the southeast, where that road met others leading to Rio de Janeiro, São Paulo, and the south. In total, the Kubitschek administration opened approximately 11,000 miles of new roads and highways—over a third of which were paved.

Vehicular traffic increased proportionately. The number of trucks and automobiles doubled and the number of buses tripled during the decade of the 1950s. Kubitschek autho-

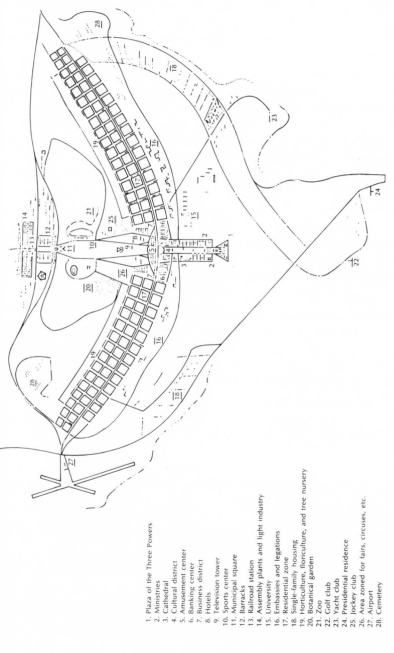

1. Plaza of the Three Powers
2. Ministries
3. Cathedral
4. Cultural district
5. Amusement center
6. Banking center
7. Business district
8. Hotels
9. Television tower
10. Sports center
11. Municipal square
12. Barracks
13. Railroad station
14. Assembly plants and light industry
15. University
16. Embassies and legations
17. Residential zone
18. Single-family housing
19. Horticulture, floriculture, and tree nursery
20. Botanical garden
21. Zoo
22. Golf club
23. Yacht club
24. Presidential residence
25. Jockey club
26. Area zoned for fairs, circuses, etc.
27. Airport
28. Cemetery

Map 5. The Plan for Brasília by Lúcio Costa.

rized and encouraged the creation of a national automotive industry, one of the major industrial achievements of his administration. Within a five-year period, that is by 1962, that new industry was turning out 200,000 units annually to make Brazil the world's seventh-largest automobile producer. By May 1967, 1.5 million cars had rolled off the assembly lines of the ten automobile manufacturers. Trucks, buses, and tractors also went into production. Brazil not only produced enough of these vehicles to satisfy its own market, but soon began to export them to its neighbors.

Kubitschek's programs bore a price tag. Being grandiose, they were also expensive. To meet part of the costs, the government simply turned on the printing presses and let the currency flow out. In 1955, there were over 60 billion cruzeiros in circulation; in 1961, approximately 200 billion. The exchange rate for the dollar fell from 70 to 210 cruzeiros. Inflation, which, despite a hopeful hesitation in 1957, had plagued the country since the end of World War II, continued to mount, spurred on by wage increases, the high rate of investment, and budget deficits on all levels—local, state, and federal. In five years, living expenses tripled. The International Monetary Fund expressed dismay over the situation and threatened to withhold loans until the government adopted more orthodox financial methods. The nationalists regarded inflation as a catalyst for industrialization; they also resented outside interference no matter how well intentioned. The president too felt that the stabilization policies urged by the IMF would retard his development plans. To the delight of the nationalists, he denounced the Fund for trying to delay the industrialization of Brazil, and in June 1959, he broke off negotiations with that international organization. Inflation spiraled upward.

The growth of Brazil after World War II was much more than material. National pride, spirit, and culture grew just as prodigiously. The world at long last began to recognize Brazilian achievements, and such recognition excited national pride. The Brazilian soccer team won the world championship in 1958, 1962, and 1970; those victories were occasions for national holidays. The Brazilians celebrated with exuber-

ant dancing in the streets. Pelé, the adored soccer ace, became a national hero and enjoyed international fame and
recognition. Brazil thrilled to other athletic victories, such as
that of tennis star Maria Bueno, who won the Wimbledon
Women's singles championship in 1960. Brazilian beauty was
also heralded abroad; there was hardly a Miss World or a
Miss Universe contest that did not include a Miss Brazil
among the finalists. The news media gave those pageants detailed coverage, and in 1963 and again in 1968, when Miss
Brazil triumphed as Miss Universe, the nation rejoiced.

Brazilian music, art, and literature also burst their national frontiers. The works of composer Heitor Villa-Lobos
received applause in concert halls around the world, and the
composer himself conducted the major symphony orchestras
of Europe and the United States until his death in 1959.
Critics heaped accolades in particular on the haunting music
of the "Bachianas Brasileiras," his pleasing combination of
Bach with Brazilian folk music. He composed more than
1,400 works. The melancholy bossa nova invaded the field of
popular music. Musicians such as João Gilberto, Antônio
Carlos Jobim, Sérgio Mendes, and Edú Lobo played before
international audiences. "The Girl from Ipanema" became a
hit song in the United States. Later, "The Band," composed
by the young Chico Buarque de Holanda, climbed to the top
of the world's hit parade.

Brazil's film industry, under the inspiration and direction
of the movement called Cinema Nôvo, began in the late
1950s to focus attention on national themes and problems.
The Cinema Nôvo films looked sharply into the two areas of
greatest poverty and injustice: the favela (urban slum) and
the sertão (the arid backlands). Carlos Diegues studied the
drama of the poor in the city in his Grande Cidade (The Big
City, 1966), emphasizing its brutalization of the rural migrant,
who, full of hope, came to the city only to be plunged into
conditions worse than those he fled. Doubtless still the masterpiece of the Cinema Nôvo is Vidas Sêcas (Barren Lives,
1963), directed by Nelson Pereira dos Santos. He brilliantly
transferred to the screen the powerful novel of the same
name. Rural poverty, dependency, and underdevelopment

were depicted with unflinching accuracy in that extraordinary document of how an impoverished family survives in the backlands. Of the many young directors at work in the Cinema Nôvo movement in the 1960s, Glauber Rocha stands out as the most productive and imaginative. He imposed a heavy symbolism on his films concerned with Brazilian reality. Possibly still the best of Rocha's growing output is *Deus e o Diablo na Terra do Sol* (*Black God, White Devil*, 1963), which introduced the viewer to the principal human types found in the sertão as well as to some of the persistent causes of the poverty characteristic of that region. The invigorated film industry reaped a rich reward in the early 1960s when Anselmo Duarte's film, *Pagador de Promessas* (*The Given Word*, 1962) received the best film award at both the Cannes and San Francisco film festivals. In 1968, the Museum of Modern Art in New York City sponsored a retrospective festival of Cinema Nôvo films.

Brazilian literature received greater international recognition as the works of Graciliano Ramos, José Lins do Rego, Érico Veríssimo, João Guimarães Rosa, Rachel de Queirós, and Jorge Amado were translated into many languages. Amado's novel, *Gabriela, Clove, and Cinnamon* became a best seller in the United States in the mid-1960s. Quite belatedly Machado de Assis received acclaim abroad as his major novels were translated. Their publication in English occurred during the 1950s and 1960s, accompanied by several critical studies.

Regionalism continued to be a dominant theme among the novelists. José Lins do Rego, Jorge de Lima, Rachel de Queirós, and José Américo de Almeida wrote about the Northeast; Jorge Amado described life in Bahia; and Érico Veríssimo covered in a triptych the history of a family in Rio Grande do Sul. Many of the novels served as penetrating social commentaries. In his pentalogy on the processing of sugar cane in Paraíba during the first third of the twentieth century, Lins do Rego realistically came to grips with the Northeast's problems of modernization. Some of the contemporary poetry likewise serves as social documentation. A significant part of the poetry of João Cabral de Melo Neto focused sharply on the problems of the Northeast and the misery of the peasants. His most important work of this genre appeared in his book *O Rio* (The River). Rapid urbanization and its attendant problems attracted the attention of some writers. Jorge Amado was one who in the course of his career turned to analyzing the problems of the city. In *Jubiabá, Suor* (Sweat), and *Capitães da Areia* (Captains of the Sand), he depicted the slums of Salvador da Bahia. José Lins do Rego portrayed the effects of progress, both good and bad, on Recife in his classic *O Moleque Ricardo* (The Young Man Richard). Many of the novels of the popular contemporary writer Fernando Sabino meticulously described life in Rio de Janeiro. His best seller, *O Encontro Marcado* (The Rendezvous), dealt with a frustrated young urban intellectual in search of the meaning of his existence. José Ferreira Condé in his *Um Ramo para Luísa* (A Bouquet for Luisa) and *Noite contra Noite* (Night Against Night) explored the life of the upper middle class in fashionable Copacabana. Two talented dramatists, Nelson Rodrigues and Dias Gomes, brutally dissected urban life in their very successful plays. In his *A Invasão* (The Invasion), Dias Gomes defended the invasion of an unfinished skyscraper by the city's poor in their search for housing.

Brazilian scholars enjoyed an increasingly favorable international reputation. As a group, they were probably accorded greater recognition than their predecessors or their contemporaries from other Latin American republics. The sociologist Gilberto Freyre, the economist Celso Furtado, the historian José Honório Rodrigues, and the literary critic Afrânio Coutinho lectured in many universities in the United States and Europe and saw their books translated into a variety of foreign languages. The list of scholars who traveled abroad to lecture or to give courses in foreign universities would be a long one, and it grew each year. Institutes of Brazilian studies were established in the United States, Japan, and a number of European nations, and chairs in Brazilian history and literature were set up at the major universities in those countries. The result of the international recognition given Brazilian achievements in the past two decades has been the shedding of former inferiority complexes and the growth of national pride. Nebulous as it might be, that pride has contributed significantly to the growth of Brazilian nationalism.

Growing Pains

The process of modernization placed heavier responsibilities on the cities, whose roles expanded and became more varied. Their primary functions were governmental, administrative, commercial, and industrial. They served as transportation hubs, and many of them became the centers of complex transportation networks. The cities provided many services, and, further, they were recreational, cultural, and educational foci. Of the various functions of the Brazilian city in the mid-twentieth century, the industrial function gave considerable impetus to urban growth. Jobs related directly or indirectly to the factories seemed to promise more social mobility. At least in the large industries salaries were comparatively high, and the workers enjoyed the benefits of the labor legislation decreed by Getúlio Vargas. Few of the untrained and/or illiterate from the countryside could compete for those jobs. However, the construction industry, based partially on the employment of the unskilled but strong, offered some hope of employment and improvement of socio-economic status to rural migrants in the city. Those migrants also performed low-skill service work. In contrast to the attraction exerted by the cities to some rural dwellers, the grinding poverty of the countryside pushed many desperate peasants into urban areas. The roads from the sertão to the city were well traveled. Approximately 60 percent of the increase in urban populations resulted from internal migration.

The rate of urban growth spurted after 1940. Urbanization became a salient characteristic of Brazilian development in the decades thereafter. During certain periods, some of the largest cities increased in population at the rate of 10 percent a year. In 1920, approximately 25 percent of the population lived in urban areas; by 1940 that proportion had reached 31 percent. From there it climbed rapidly to 36 percent in 1950; 45 percent in 1960, and 50 percent in 1970, or nearly fifty million. In the decade between 1950 and 1960, the number of cities with populations between 100,000 and 200,000 increased from 9 to 19 and those between 20,000 and 100,000 from 90 to 142. Table 7.4 indicates the growth of some of Brazil's major cities in the twentieth century and further demonstrates that the most spectacular growth occurred in the 1940–1960 period.

Table 7.4. Urban Population Growth, 1900–1960 (in thousands of inhabitants)

City	1900	1920	1940	1960
São Paulo	299	579	1,308	3,825
Rio de Janeiro	800	1,157	1,781	3,372
Recife	113	238	348	707
Belo Horizonte	13	55	211	693
Salvador	205	283	291	655
Pôrto Alegre	73	179	275	641
Fortaleza	48	78	174	514
Curitiba	49	78	142	361
Niterói	53	86	143	245
Manaus	50	75	107	175

SOURCE: Delgado de Carvalho, *Organização Social e Política Brasileira*, 2nd ed. (Rio de Janeiro, 1967), p. 51. Extracted from the *Anuário Estatístico do Brasil, 1965*.

On the other end of the scale, however, more than 2,000 of the 2,763 cities had populations of less than 5,000 inhabitants. Altogether, they accounted for a quarter of the urban population. São Paulo and Rio de Janeiro ranked as the two metropolitan giants. Yet, spectacular as their growth had been, their combined populations accounted for only about 10 percent of the nation's population. Brazil thus had no urban concentrations comparable to those in other Latin American republics. For example, Montevideo contained 50 percent of Uruguay's population, Buenos Aires 30 percent of Argentina's, Santiago 25 percent of Chile's, and Mexico City 15 percent of Mexico's. Of the four major Latin American nations, Brazil was by far the least urbanized.

Urban growth represented a swell in the ranks of the

middle class and the proletariat. Indeed, most of Brazil's middle class inhabited the cities. Estimates of their proportion in the national population during the 1960s varied from a modest 15 percent to a more liberal 40 percent. The middle class counted among its members the formulators of public opinion. It was the group most acutely aware of the restrictions imposed by the traditional oligarchy and most able to express its disapproval or resentment. The urban labor force grew at an even greater pace. The number of factory workers increased by 51 percent in the forties and by 28 percent in the fifties. Vargas and his lieutenant Goulart already had seen their political potential and had attempted to awaken them to it. The literacy rate was much higher in the cities than it was in rural areas. Hence the literacy requirement for voting increased the voting power of the urban population proportionately. Little wonder then that political power gravitated toward the city with its larger, more vocal electorate.

The urban dwellers tended to be activists or at least more so than their rural counterparts. Reading newspapers, attending the movies, watching television, listening to the radio, they were aware of change and of opportunities and they were willing to strive for them. Eagerly they busied themselves making plans for the future and executing them. They sought to control the course of their own lives rather than to rely on fate. They paid less heed to traditional values—the closely knit family unit, for example—than did the rural inhabitants. They sought the rewards modern society gave to efficiency, initiative, and responsibility. The broadly stratified urban society, which blurred the distinctions between classes, facilitated social mobility. Bored by routine and tradition, they became increasingly more individualistic. Such was true of the urban dwellers wherever they lived: the great metropolises of Rio de Janeiro and São Paulo; the smaller capitals of Manaus, Goiânia, or Florianopolis; the cities of the interior, Londrina, Corumbá, or Crato. The inhabitants of all the cities knew what was going on in the rest of the world. They cared about it and they participated in it—even if, at certain times and places, that participation was vicarious. The modernization which the cities encouraged seemed to be bringing some benefits to some inhabitants. The per capita income continued to rise. In 1960, it reached $332, which ranked Brazil seventh in the Latin American community. That per capita income was one-eighth of the United States level and one-quarter of the level of Western Europe. There were other indications of a rise in the standard of living of some of the population. While the population more or less doubled between 1930 and 1960, the number of pairs of shoes sold yearly quadrupled, the number of radios sold increased twelvefold, and the number of tubes of toothpaste increased sixfold. The urban dweller enjoyed more education, better health, and a longer life than his rural counterpart. Elegant apartment buildings, expensive specialty shops, chic society clubs, modern cinemas, trim parks, honking automobiles, together applied a veneer of glitter to urban life. Of course that tinsel often masked misery and degradation, just as it did in Lima, Calcutta, New York, or Naples. Further, one must eye per capita income statistics with the utmost suspicion. They are a contrived measurement often disguising great and growing inequities, which is emphatically true of Brazil.

For the illiterate, inexperienced, and technically untrained, jobs were hard to find, and those fortunate enough to find them earned the minimum salary. Those with the minimum wage struggled to keep the family housed and fed; those with less than the minimum wage were the scavengers of society. In the larger cities, those marginal people lived in the *hospedarias,* the flophouses providing a bed for one night, the *cabeças-de-porco,* the rooming houses in whose tiny cubicles lived entire families, and the *favelas,* the shanty towns crowded with flimsy shacks of one or two rooms. Those jerry-built hovels began to appear on the hillsides of Rio de Janeiro by the end of the nineteenth century and spread rapidly after 1930. By 1957, fully a quarter of the inhabitants of the capital lived in such slums. Life in one of the

São Paulo favelas was poignantly portrayed by one of its residents, Carolina Maria de Jesus, in a diary which by chance reached print. Its Portuguese title, *Quarto de Despejo*, was rendered *Child of the Dark* when it appeared in English in 1962. The initial entry in the diary set the tone of despair:

July 15, 1955. The birthday of my daughter Vera Eunice. I wanted to buy a pair of shoes for her, but the price of food keeps us from realizing our desires. Actually we are slaves to the cost of living. I found her a pair of shoes in the garbage, washed them, and patched them for her to wear. I didn't have one cent to buy bread.

Bitterness surfaced more than once in the pages of her unique diary. At one point, disgusted by the resignation preached by the Church, she wrote:

I thought: if Brother Luiz was married, had children, and earned the minimum wage, I would like to see if he would be so humble. He said that God blesses only those who suffer with resignation. If the Brother saw his children eating rotten food already attacked by vultures and rats, he would stop talking about resignation and rebel, because rebellion comes from bitterness.[3]

Other cities had their counterparts to those favelas. In Salvador, they were the *alagados*, miserable conglomerations of one-room hovels. There Brazil's most precious resource, its people, wasted away with bloated bellies, underdeveloped bodies, dysentery, fever, and an untold number of diseases. In his novel *Suor* (Sweat), Jorge Amado portrayed the degrading existence of the dwellers of a tenement in Salvador. Linked by a common poverty, they lived an anonymous life eking out an existence as best they could. Although no one would write of them as heroes, these people, Amado reminded his readers, "perfectly symbolized proletarian humanity."

The blight of Manaus was its curious *Cidade Flutuante* (Floating City), 2,100 small huts picturesquely built on rafts

---

3. Carolina Maria de Jesus, *Child of the Dark* (New York: 1962), pp. 19, 92. Quoted with the permission of the publisher.

crowded together on confluents of the Rio Negro. The inhabitants were, by and large, illiterate, ignorant, and ill. Manioc meal and fish composed their diet, and these were seldom available in sufficient quantity to keep hunger at bay. Sometimes families with eight or ten members inhabited huts which seemed hard pressed to serve as sleeping quarters for two persons. In addition, animals and fowl shared the quarters. Promiscuity was total. Sanitary facilities were unknown. When the rivers were at flood stage, the waters kept clean, but the rest of the year they were cesspools of disease.

Despite such dismal conditions, it was not possible to stem the tide of migration from the countryside to the cramped cities. They still represented hope, and, viewed from a distance, the glitter of their tinsel blinded the beholder. After all, rural life was no paradise for the peasant. In a frank report to the chamber of deputies in 1962, a special committee composed of representatives of all the major parties commented on the abject poverty in the countryside and the need for reform. These excerpts summed up the alarm the committee sounded:

One truth is evident: the problem of hunger in the countryside of Brazil offends human dignity, is explosive, and will lead to turmoil. The facts explain the problem. The last census, taken in 1960, showed the rural population of our nation nearing 40 million. And what is the living standard for that immense population? Unfortunately it is among the lowest in the world in its level of poverty, chronic hunger, social waste, chronic illness, illiteracy. . . . In the Northeast the average life span is 27 years. In Brazil a child dies every 42 seconds, 85 per hour, 2,040 per day. . . . Forty million Brazilians vegetate in our countryside like pariahs. Scarcely 4 percent own land.[4]

The rural institutions resisted change more than any others. They seemed inflexible in their refusal to adapt themselves to the twentieth century.

4. Quoted in I. L. Horowitz, *Revolution in Brazil: Politics and Society in a Developing Nation* (New York, 1964), p. 266. Quoted with the kind permission of E. P. Dutton & Co., Inc.

The rural workers had nothing comparable to the unions, social legislation, and labor courts which protected and aided their urban counterparts. Either as tenant farmers or menial farm hands, the majority of the workers lived at the mercy of the large landowner. Latifundia predominated. Indeed, approximately 1.6 percent of the farms covered over 50 percent of the land under cultivation. Contrasting sharply with the latifundia and their monopoly over the best lands were the minifundia, those minuscule plots of land, more often than not of marginal agricultural value, which could contribute nothing to the regional or national economy and little even to their owners. About 22 percent of the farms occupied only 0.5 percent of the land.

As in the past, the large estate, the fazenda, continued to characterize rural Brazil. Life on the fazenda still revolved around the "big house," just as it had for centuries. Within the archaic social structure, the rural worker looked to his *patrão* for protection, security, and guidance, and in return pledged labor and loyalty. Many of the fazendas were practically closed economies, confining their contacts with the outside to the sale of one cash crop, often coffee, cocoa, sugar, cotton, or tobacco. Ignorance held the peasant to his miserable existence at barely the subsistence level and debt peonage enforced his immobility. As long as the peasant owed money to his employer, he could not leave the estate for other employment. That debt was easy to acquire but nearly impossible to liquidate. Hereditary debt servitude was not uncommon. The anthropologist Claude Levi-Strauss has left this candid description of contemporary debt peonage in the interior of Brazil:

> The fazenda's sales-counter was, in effect, the only provision-store for sixty or seventy miles in any direction. The *empregados,* or employees—workers or peons—came and spent there with one hand what they had earned with the other; an entry in the books sufficed to turn them from creditors into debtors, and it was rare, in point of fact, for money actually to change hands. As most things were sold at two or three times their normal price—such was the accepted practice—it would have been quite a going con-

cern if the shop had not occupied a merely subsidiary place in the whole venture. It was heart-rending to watch the work people on a Saturday. They would arrive with their little crop of sugar-cane, press it immediately in the fazenda's *engenho* . . . evaporate the juice in a hot iron pan, and pour what remained into moulds, where it turned into tawny blocks, granular in consistency. *Rapadure,* these were called; and they would hand them in to the adjacent store. When the evening came they would re-present themselves, this time as customers, and pay a high price for the right to offer their children their own product—refurbished, by then, as the sertão's only sweetmeat.[5]

The critics of the system customarily applied the emotional adjective "feudal" to the land structure and its accompanying social institutions. They resented the power of the landowner, his interposition, as it were, between the government and the rural masses. They pointed with disgust to the difference between the modernity of the cities and the tradition of the countryside. They warned that a closed society, with no hope for evolutionary change, would breed revolution in time. Ceará symbolized the gross rural inequities and inefficiencies. In 1960, some 66 percent of the state's population resided in the countryside where a few owned most of the land. There were only 316 tractors and 1,305 plows for a labor force numbering 816,720. Food production, except for fruits, did not satisfy the needs of the inhabitants, forcing the importation of staple crops. That occurred in a region fully capable of producing food surpluses. The main reason was simple: the few who owned the land held it fallow as investment or did not work it efficiently.

Immediate reform of the rural economic and social structures, the critics advised, was essential. In the words of Minister of Agriculture Oswaldo Lima Filho in 1963: "It is urgently necessary by means of an agrarian reform, which will bring prosperity and well-being to the people, to end the feudal structure which imprisons the rural population." A statement entitled *Pacem in Terris and the Brazilian Reality*

5. Claude Levi-Strauss, *A World on the Wane* (London, 1961), pp. 146–47.

issued that same year by the Roman Catholic bishops called attention to the plight of the rural population and advocated a reform of land structures:

The majority is deprived of the exercise of many of the fundamental and natural rights which are mentioned in the encyclical Pacem in Terris: the right of existence and to a decent standard of living, the right of human liberty and dignity, the right to participate in the benefits of culture; in other words the right to live as a person in society. . . . No one can ignore the situation of millions of our brothers and sisters living in rural areas who cannot share in the development of our nation, who live in conditions of misery which are an affront to human dignity. . . . The expropriation of land in such situations is in no way contrary to the social doctrine of the Church.

That powerful call for social and economic justice reflected the growing social consciousness of the Roman Catholic Church in Brazil. The urban middle class, or at least the more enlightened elements within it, favored rural reforms, among them a redistribution of the land. For one thing, they recognized that the inefficient fazenda kept food prices high. For another, they desired to reduce further the power of the coroneis and the rural aristocracy which generally was wielded to retard modernization and to oppose the interests of the urban classes. Further, the economic development coveted by urban dwellers would be unattainable without rural reforms and a consequent improvement in agricultural support. Real economic development could not be expected if it excluded the numerically dominant rural population. The archaic latifundia represented the bleakest aspect of Brazilian agriculture.

Growing efficiency and hence productivity characterized a few farms, particularly in the South and Southeast. In the fifties, the number of tractors in use rose an impressive eightfold, from 8,000 to 63,000. Predictably, about 70 percent of those tractors were in the two states of São Paulo and Rio Grande do Sul. The advantage of the tractor is obvious, but perhaps one example will highlight its value. A tractor could farm four acres of rice land in Rio Grande do Sul in 13 hours and 25 minutes; to accomplish the same task by the customary hand labor required 54 days. Farmers, particularly those in the South and Southeast, increased their use of fertilizers. In 1958, they spread 42,000 tons of nitrogen fertilizer. Two decades before, they had used only 2,000 tons. The average use of fertilizer was a little over a pound per acre, about a third of the world average. Although its increase was far below that of industry in the fifties, agricultural growth outpaced population growth by 52 percent versus 36 percent. However, that growth reflected more an increase in export crops—still the dynamic part of the economy—rather than the subsistence crops which could have fed a malnourished population. The growth in production was due primarily to an increase in land utilization, from 40 million acres in 1948 to 65 million in 1960, rather than to an increase in productivity. Fortunately Brazil was immense, with much land unused. As late as 1961, only slightly more than 2 percent of the land was under cultivation, and of that only about half produced foodstuffs. Productivity remained low because of the system of land tenure and use, low technical and educational levels, lack of capital, poor transportation facilities, unsatisfactory marketing systems, limited scientific research, and lack of technical assistance to agriculture. Principally—and this point cannot be overemphasized—the problem lay with the land structures: they withheld land from the dispossessed, who could have been useful and efficient producers on a small scale.

Coffee in 1960 was still the dominant crop, accounting for 17 percent of the area under cultivation, 15 percent of farm income, and 50 percent of the exports. Brazil remained the world's major producer and exporter of coffee. It also ranked among the world's foremost producers of cocoa, sugar, and cotton and was one of the largest livestock raisers.

A hopeful sign of change for the countryside was the gradual, albeit slow growth of a rural middle class, which as a group seemed to avoid many of the weaknesses and disadvantages of both the latifundia and the minifundia. In 1960, there were 1,494,548 land holdings between 25 and 250 acres in size, a growth in number of 157,954 since 1920. Somewhat more impressive was the growth during those four decades of the proportion of the total agricultural area which those holdings occupied, from 8.9 to 17 percent. Not all the medium-sized farms were located in the South and Southeast by any means. Many could be found in the more tradition-bound regions as well. Whereas Minas Gerais counted 199,405 and São Paulo 139,620 such farms, Bahia contained 161,673 and Pernambuco 50,850. Agriculture definitely had progressed in the twentieth century, but its steps were measured, in comparison to the giant strides of industrial progress.

The different geographical regions further reflected the contrasts which historically have marked Brazil. In the opening chapter, five such regions were designated: the North, Northeast, Center West, East, and South. A glance at the accompanying map, titled *Regions of Brazil*, will indicate the variety among them in size, population, electorate, and income, as of 1965. Whereas the North was by far the largest region in size, it had the smallest population, electorate, and income. In diametric contrast, the South was the smallest region and yet it boasted the largest population, electorate, and income. The North was chiefly rural. It possessed only two cities of any size, Belém and Manaus. About 51 percent of the population of the South could be classified as urban and it contained such modern cities as São Paulo, Pôrto Alegre, Curitiba, Santos, Santo André, and Campinas. The South was also the most industrialized of the five regions. The state of São Paulo generated over 700,000 kilowatts of electric power. Pernambuco in the Northeast barely generated 50,000. In addition to its remarkable industrial record, the South also boasted the highest agricultural production.

Perhaps another way to view the disparities among the regions is to compare the state budgets. (These budgets for the year 1967 are given in old cruzeiros at the exchange rate of Cr$2,200 to US$1.) As was so often the case, São Paulo led the other states with a budget of Cr$3¼ trillion, while at the other end of the scale stood Acre with barely Cr$20 billion budgeted. Only five states were able to budget more than

NORTH
42% territory
4% population
3% electorate
2% national income

NORTHEAST
11% territory
21% population
18% electorate
9% national income

CENTER WEST
22% territory
4% population
4% electorate
3% national income

EAST
15% territory
34% population
35% electorate
36% national income

SOUTH
10% territory
36% population
41% electorate
50% national income

Map 6. Regions of Brazil

SOURCE: Brazil Election Factbook, No. 2, September, 1965 (Washington, D.C.: Institute for the Comparative Study of Political Systems, 1965), p. 2. Reproduced with the permission of the publisher.

half a trillion cruzeiros: three of them were in the South, São Paulo, Paraná, and Rio Grande do Sul, and the remaining two were in the East, Minas Gerais and Guanabara. The territorial giants of Amazonas and Pará operated on budgets which totaled less than Cr$100 and Cr$50 billion respectively.[6]

All statistics unmistakably pointed to the South and East as the dominant regions of Brazil. Well populated and with satisfactory transportation networks, they had urbanized, industrialized, and modernized to an extent far beyond that of the rest of Brazil. The largest numbers of well-fed and well-educated Brazilians lived in those regions. Within them were areas, as in São Paulo, where the per capita income exceeded US$1,000, giving some in those areas a standard of living comparable to that of many countries in Europe. Once again the use of the insidious "per capita" measurement hid the dismal poverty of the overwhelming majority.

The situation of the Northeast, one of the major underdeveloped areas of the hemisphere, was less fortunate. With 11 percent of the territory and 21 percent of the population, it contributed less than 10 percent of the national product. That contribution was about a third of what it was a generation earlier. Unemployment and underemployment plagued the adult male population. The peasants lived in rude clay huts with dirt floors. There was no illumination or sanitary facilities. Chances were they did not own their lands, for the dominant land pattern was one of large estates concentrated in the hands of a few owners. Their diet consisted mainly of manioc flour and black beans with occasional jerked beef. Hunger was common. Not surprisingly, life expectancy was less than 30 years. About the Zona da Mata, one of the most depressed areas of Pernambuco's backlands, Professor Nelson Chaves, director of the Nutrition Institute of the Federal University of Pernambuco, after a year's research in the town of Riberão, related, "The minimum that a man must eat in order to work is 2,600 calories. Our research into the diets of

---

6. Other statistics and disparities can be found in Luiz Fernando Mercadante, "Os Senhores Governadores," *Realidade* (March 1967), pp. 23–24.

100 workers of Ribeirão shows their daily consumption to be 1,323 calories, half of the minimum. They cannot work. They live in a state of chronic hunger, one of the most serious in the world." An article published in the *Jornal do Commércio* of Recife on June 7, 1969, reported that workers of the Salgado sugar mill and their families were in a perpetual state of hunger and that the owner dealt with complainers by firing them. In Ribeirão, the infant mortality rate was 25 times greater than that of Denmark. In the Zona da Mata, 40 percent of the children died before they reached school age. Over 95 percent of the population suffered from intestinal worms. The rate of tuberculosis was ten times greater than in more developed areas. The workers and their families probably lived worse than did the slaves in the same area a century ago.

Ignorance characterized the population in these backward areas. The illiteracy rate in the Northeast soared over 70 percent, high above the dismal national average of 50 percent. In the sugarmill settlement of Taimberé, for example, about 80 percent of the inhabitants were illiterate; only 1 percent had primary educations. In 1968, of the 600 families living there, only one sent its children to school. Statistics in other parts of the Pernambucan backlands were no better. Ponte dos Carvalhos, just 20 miles from Recife, was a decrepit eyesore with 11,000 inhabitants. Half of them were children under sixteen years of age. Of these, only 600 attended school. Over 500 prostitutes plied their profession. Intestinal worms plagued 99 percent of the population. Of 340 deaths in 1967, 226 (67 percent) were babies less than one year old. The town grew because the peasants flocked to it, attracted by its industries, medical facilities, and television. In other words, whatever its drawbacks, they found it preferable to life in and around the sugar mills. In the midst of the misery of the Northeast, the extremes between poverty and wealth stood out more noticeably. The *Diário de Pernambuco*, a newspaper published in Recife, carried in its issue of May 9, 1961, the account of a sumptuous wedding, for which Federal Deputy Ademar Carvalho de Souza, a

Northeasterner, spent Cr$20,000,000 in addition to Cr$4,000,000 for a banquet. In Recife, the minimum salary was Cr$10,000 a month. For many decades, the common explanation given for the plight of the Northeast was the droughts which periodically flagellated the sertão. The solution thought proper for the problem was hydrographic: dams and irrigation. But various hydrographic projects did little to alleviate the problem. Anyway, poverty and backwardness continued through the long periods when rainfall was sufficient, proof that something more than droughts caused the problems of the Northeast. In the fifties, economists suggested that much of the poverty resulted from low capital investment in the region. In response to that suggestion, the federal government sought to encourage investments and industrialization. Focusing his attention on the difficulties of the region, President Kubitschek created the *Superintendência do Desenvolvimento do Nordeste* (Superintendency of the Development of the Northeast, or *Sudene*) in 1959. Under the direction of Celso Furtado, Sudene prepared a comprehensive development program, which encouraged industrialization, a reorganization and intensification of agriculture, and a relocation of population surpluses.

Fortunately the economic condition of the Northeast improved after 1955. Farm income tripled, while in the rest of the country it doubled. Part of the improvement might be due to the government's programs, but certainly a large part of that increase can be attributed to the fact that the crops the Northeast was marketing were among those most in demand: sisal, beans, coconuts, tobacco, sugar, bananas, cotton, corn, and cocoa beans. The regional disparities, great as they remain, have narrowed, contrary to popular belief that they have continued to grow. Further reduction of those glaring disparities is essential to reduce the tensions which they produce. One economist, Roberto Campos, has warned that the regional disparities create and encourage a "climate of revolt." Unfortunately, as encouraging as that growth record for the Northeast was, it has not been sufficient to relieve the political and social pressures in the region. Many of the fundamental problems—unemployment, underemployment, malnutrition, and illiteracy—remain unsolved. The Center West has been the fastest-growing region in Brazil. The states of Goiás (containing the new Federal District) and Mato Grosso, together forming the Center West, offered abundant opportunities in agriculture, cattle raising, mining, and timber; income in the region has soared. In the decade of the fifties, the rural population doubled and the urban population tripled in that region. Brasília and Goiânia are two cities in the region with phenomenal growth records. Both are new capitals. Founded in 1933 to replace Goiás Velha, the old capital of Goiás, Goiânia was not officially inaugurated until 1942. It is a well-planned city with broad, tree-lined avenues, zoned, in three distinct districts in addition to spacious residential areas: one district is for government, another for commerce, and a third for industry. By 1960, the population of Goiânia exceeded 132,000.

The West attracted inhabitants from all regions of Brazil as well as foreign immigrants. It became a true melting pot, in a tradition long established for the interior. In his essay published in 1889, *Caminhos Antigos e o Povamento do Brasil* (Old Roads and the Peopling of Brazil), the historian Capistrano de Abreu pointed out the significance of the interior as the consolidator of Brazilian nationality and the unifier of the nation. In the United States four years later, Frederick Jackson Turner put forth his now celebrated thesis on the expanding frontier and its significance. The Brazilian Cassiano Ricardo echoed many of Capistrano de Abreu's observations in his two-volume study of the penetration of the interior, *Marcha para Oeste* (March to the West), published in 1942. Ricardo contrasted the feudalism of the coast with the democracy of the frontier. In the West, he concluded, "There is no preoccupation with class and position. . . . Politically, a rudimentary democracy was practiced. . . . Socially, there is no preconception about color, creed, or origin." In the past century, various Latin American intellectuals took up the theme of the interior and its influence on the formation of national character and institutions. In Argentina, first Domingo Faustino Sarmiento and later José Ingen-

ieros discussed the theme. The renowned Uruguayan essay-
ist, José Enrique Rodó, commented in his *Ariel* on the ability
of the interior to transform men. But it was the Brazilians,
quite fittingly, who dwelt at greatest length on the theme.
Euclides da Cunha took one of the most perceptive looks at
the significance of the interior in his *Os Sertões* (Rebellion in
the Backlands). Speaking of the interior as the real Brazil, he
called the backwoodsmen "the very core of our nationality,
the bedrock of our race," and their society "the vigorous
core of our national life." Vargas helped to popularize the
idea that the West held the key to the realization of the national potential. On a number of occasions, he announced
plans for a march to the hinterlands, the "March to the
West." More than anything else, the establishment of Brasília
in the middle of Goiás focused attention on the West. The
roads radiating from Brasília brought in pioneers. Now
linked more closely than ever with the rest of the nation, the
West shows every indication of maintaining its position as
the fastest growing of the five regions. The existence of a
vast interior, much of which is unexplored, most of which is
unexploited, imparts to all Brazilians a certain optimism and
faith in the future as well as a belief in the inevitability of
progress.

Great advances in communication and transportation in
the past century have done much to unify Brazil and to break
down regional barriers. A number of other factors encourage
national unity. First, there is territorial continuity. Second,
there is the common frontier with its challenge to expand
and to settle. Third, the vast majority of the people speak
Portuguese and are Roman Catholic. Fourth, the culture is
essentially European, but in a unique manner it has been
shaped and fashioned by Afro-Indian influences. Finally, permissive colonial institutions allowed a leisurely formation to
the colony, which in 1808 experienced a singular innovation:
the presence of the monarch—with all the centralization of
control and power that involved for the colony—ruling from
a seat within Brazil itself. There followed eighty-one years of
highly centralized monarchy with, until the end, few questioning or challenging the emperor's authority. These factors

help to explain (they are by no means exclusive) the unity of Brazil, noteworthy when compared to the fragmentation of the Spanish-speaking New World. Within that unity always existed—still exists—an immense variety which the regions exemplify. A theme underlying Brazilian history has been the conflict between the forces of unity and diversity, that is, between centralism and regionalism. The scales at one time or another have tipped both ways. In the long run, however, the two forces have maintained a certain balance. The essential fact is that despite stress and threat the Brazilian union remained intact. National unity and homogeneity are achievements of which Brazilians can be justifiably proud. However, so long as different levels of development characterize the regions of that union there will still be a great deal of diversity and considerable stress.

The Brazilians demonstrated their unity during the presidential election of 1960, when they elected Jânio da Silva Quadros, candidate of the UDN, to the presidency. Promising to eliminate corruption and inefficiency from government—his campaign symbol was a broom—he won 48 percent of the vote. His principal opponent, Marshal Henrique Teixeira Lott, the minister of war during the Kubitschek administration, ran on a combined PSD-PTB (Social Democratic–Labor party) ticket and received only 28 percent of the vote. The significances of Quadros' victory were many. It marked the first time the conservative, anti-Vargas UDN had captured the presidency, although it would be incorrect to identify Quadros too closely with that party. He was a maverick who campaigned on his own personal platform. The UDN, hungry for victory, recognized a winner and supported him. Quadros had no links with Vargas or those associated with him; this was another quality which endeared him to the UDN leadership. His election was a break with the Vargas legacy. Finally, his victory put a Paulista in the presidential palace for the first time since the collapse of the Old Republic. Running on the PTB ticket, João Goulart was re-elected vice-president with 36 percent of the vote.

On the whole, the new president seemed to view internal affairs rather conventionally, although he did believe in restrictions on foreign capital. In foreign affairs, however, he displayed a flair for the experimental, which, he demonstrated in his efforts to increase Brazil's independence in foreign relations. Since the era of Rio-Branco, Brazil had closely identified its international policy and behavior with that of the United States. The intensified drive to industrialize Brazil had brought the nation face-to-face with the question of the role of foreign investments in Brazil. The nationalists argued that those investments in the long run harmed Brazil and resented such investments in natural resources and primary industries. They accused the foreign investors of imperialism, and since the North Americans were the principal foreign investors, the United States bore the brunt of the attack of imperialism. The nationalists struggled to wrest their country from the suffocating embrace of the "imperialistic" United States. One method of doing so, they thought, would be to disengage Brazil from its close diplomatic alliance with Washington. Further, such a move seemed to promise a greater freedom of trade. The nationalists saw untapped markets in the socialist nations of the Eastern Bloc awaiting Brazil's products.

Public opinion indicated its desire to see Brazil play a larger role in world affairs. After all, Brazil had contributed troops to the Allied campaign in Italy and had sent men with the United Nations forces into the Middle East and the Congo. That Brazilians aspired to play an even greater role in international affairs was indicated by the titles of such books as Manuel Meira de Vasconcelos' *Brasil, Potência Militar* (Brazil, A Military Power) and Pimentel Gomes' *O Brasil entre as Cinco Maiores Potências ao Fim deste Século* (Brazil among the Five Major Powers by the End of the Century). The popular press often predicted the rise of Brazil to a world power status, an ambition which had motivated Ruy Barbosa at The Hague, as well as Brazil's behavior in both the League of Nations and the United Nations. In reassessing their international interests and strengths, the Brazilians became more aware of their country's advantageous geopolitical position. The giant of South America, it comprised half of the continent's territory and population and bordered on all but two of the nations of that continent. With an extensive coastline, it dominated the South Atlantic and was strategically located vis-à-vis Africa. Its racial amalgamation gave it a unique position in the world community.

The foreign policy which Quadros formulated with the assistance of his minister of foreign relations, the able Afonso Arinos de Melo Franco, pursued the basic goals of encouraging economic development and of displaying greater diplomatic independence. To carry out that new foreign policy, Quadros thought it necessary to remove Brazil as far as possible from the "cold war" battlefield. Rigid adherence to the Western bloc and subservience to the leadership of the United States had seemed—at least to Quadros and the nationalists supporting his foreign policy—to have inhibited Brazil's scope of action. Quadros affirmed that the doctrines of neither the West nor the East served the nation's best interests. Brazil wanted to develop; one way to develop was to trade; and trade knew no ideology. He wanted to preserve traditional markets, but he hoped to find new ones as well. Quadros sent a trade mission to China and initiated the steps to reestablish diplomatic relations with Moscow and other Eastern countries. Trade was obviously only one of the reasons for this recognition. The desire to exert independence of action was a compelling motive too. Augmented prestige through increased diplomatic representation both abroad and at home cannot be overlooked as a motive either.

Disengagement from the "cold war" not only brought Brazil closer to the East but it also put Brazil in closer contact with the neutralist countries of Africa and Asia. Those nations shared the view that development should take precedence over alliances which encouraged the bipolarization of the world into two armed camps. Brazil had much in common with those underdeveloped countries. United in their common desire for development, they could demand—so their reasoning went—a fair price from the industrial nations for their raw products. United, they also could regulate foreign capital investment more to their own advantage. At the same time, Brazil also envisioned for itself an excellent opportunity for leadership among the underdeveloped nations. In particular, Quadros saw an opportunity to exert Brazilian leadership among the newly emergent African states. Geography and history provided a convincing rationale for this hope. The Brazilian subcontinent juts out into the South Atlantic, providing the closest point of physical contact between the Western Hemisphere and Africa. Furthermore, during the three centuries in which the slave trade flourished between the two areas, Africa supplied a large percentage of Brazil's population. As a consequence, African blood flows in the veins of a majority of Brazilians. In every sense, the African presence is very much a part of contemporary Brazil. Anyone who reads Gilberfto Freyre's study *The Masters and the Slaves* will understand fully the African contributions to the new tropical civilization. Based on these considerations, Quadros found in Africa a new dimension for Brazilian foreign policy. He wanted Brazil to serve as a link between the newly independent Africa and the rest of the world. Accordingly, he recognized the new states, exchanged ambassadors with them, dispatched trade missions, offered fellowships to African students, established an Afro-Asian Institute, and denounced Portuguese colonial policies in Africa.

Brazil made its independence felt in the Western Hemisphere through its treatment of Cuba. As a presidential candidate, Quadros had made a leisurely visit to the island at a time when the United States was putting pressure on the Latin American governments to break relations with the government of Fidel Castro. Later, as president, he welcomed to Brasília Ernesto "Che" Guevara, whom he decorated with the nation's highest honor, the Order of the Southern Cross. Seemingly Quadros was maneuvering to play the role of mediator between Havana and Washington.

Acceptance of the new foreign policy was by no means unanimous. Many asked whether Brazil's best interests could be served by closer association with Yugoslavia, Egypt, and India. The critics argued that Brazil needed greater capital investments and despaired of seeing any forthcoming from either the Eastern or the neutralist countries. They agreed that new markets were desirable but pointed out with irrefutable statistics that most of the nations of the Southern Hemisphere exported the same or similar raw products. The fact was that as the world's economy was structured in the mid-twentieth century, the underdeveloped countries were more competitors than potential customers of Brazil. One of the fiercest critics of the policy was Carlos Lacerda, no longer the fiery editor but now the querulous governor of Guanabara. The first break between the president and the governor came on April 16, 1961, over the U.S.-sponsored invasion of Cuba. Quadros denounced it; Lacerda defended it. The relations between the two men deteriorated thereafter.

The new president experienced other difficulties as well. His efforts to halt inflation proved to be unpopular, and Quadros himself began to doubt the wisdom and desirability of his measures. His campaign against corruption elicited screams of protest from Congress, where the PSD and PTB held a majority. Congress charged the president and his UDN backers with seeking political revenge against those who had held power. Quadros soon regarded Congress as the major impediment to his reforms. In fact, to the new president's way of thinking, the very political structure of the nation prevented good and effective goverrnment.

The Constitution of 1946 seemed to institutionalize a basic conflict detrimental to good government. On the one hand, the presidents were elected by popular vote. Since the majority of the literate citizenry lived in the urban, industrialized East and South, those two regions in effect elected the presidents. In fact, in the four presidential elections after World War II, 1945, 1950, 1955, and 1960, the four states of Rio Grande do Sul, São Paulo, Minas Gerais, and Guanabara cast between 50 and 60 percent of the votes. Their vote was thus decisive in electing the president. On the other hand, Congress was elected by a restricted vote in which rural power dominated. Each state had an equal number of senators—three. The four heavily industrialized, urbanized, and populated states could raise but a weak voice in the senate in comparison to the eighteen rural and largely underdeveloped states, where in most cases the coroneis and landed aristocracy still wielded considerable influence. Hence the traditional rural oligarchy dominated the senate. In the chamber of deputies, the situation was somewhat similar. Representation there was proportionate to the population of each state. However, only literates could vote. It is easy to see that the vote of a literate citizen in a state with a high percentage of illiteracy, Sergipe for example, outweighed that of his counterpart in a state with a low degree of illiteracy, Guanabara for example. Since the traditional rural oligarchy exerted more control in the states with high illiteracy rates, it meant that they exercised a power in the chamber of deputies disproportionate to their numbers. Obviously illiteracy and the requirement that voters be literate were props supporting the traditional rural oligarchy and perpetuating their influence and power. While the urban voters could elect the president, rural interests could control Congress. This created two centers of power, by their very nature antagonistic to one another. Such certainly was the case after 1950. Great tensions developed between the two opposing branches of government, which often brought the government to a standstill. A popularly elected president, under these conditions, could suggest reforms which appealed to wide segments of the people, only to have their enactment stalled or refused by the rural oligarchy or their representatives. This situation created mounting frustrations.

Quadros in particular confronted a recalcitrant Congress. As he began to organize his program in the months after his inauguration, he encountered increasing obstinacy and hostility from that body. The president proved to be an impatient man. He had expected his federal experience to mirror his experience during the years in which he governed São Paulo and dominated the state legislature; instead he met delay and frustration. Understanding the constitutional basis for the conflict between the executive and the legislature, he thought in terms of a basic constitutional reform to rectify the situation. But just at that moment, August 19, 1961, he stepped on the toe of his foremost critic, Lacerda, by awarding the Order of the Southern Cross to Che Guevara. Lacerda, a rabid enemy of Castro, howled in protest. On August 23, he appeared on television in São Paulo to denounce a coup d'état which, he claimed, Quadros planned in order to dismiss Congress and decree some basic reforms. The following day, the governor spoke on television in Rio de Janeiro to repeat his charge. The next afternoon, August 25, 1961, President Quadros suddenly resigned and left Brasília.

The president's abrupt departure after less than seven months in office met disbelief and astonishment from the people. His cryptic letter of resignation, a strange echo of Vargas' suicide note, spoke of those "forces"—"foreign" and "terrible"—that opposed and hindered him. "I wanted Brazil for the Brazilians," he wrote, perhaps proving that his conversion to the nationalist cause had been complete.

The reasons for the precipitate resignation are still not clear. Interpretations vary and conflict. The following interpretation is based upon Quadros' own explanation of his resignation. In São Paulo, as he paused on his way into voluntary exile, Quadros reflected on the situation in Brazil and concluded that right then Brazil needed three things: authority, hard work, and courageous and rapid decisions. The political structure of the nation, in his opinion, was not viable. The lack of cooperation between Congress and the president prohibited progress. Quadros resigned purposefully, to create a crisis. He believed that the nation would not accept Vice-President João Goulart. He was convinced that the military would not. He fully expected the senior military officers to block Goulart, whom they suspected to be demogogic, populist, and dangerous and whom they had opposed on previous occasions. Vaguely he envisioned the military establishing an authoritarian regime under which he would be returned to the presidency with greater powers, or, if he was not, he expected that another president would receive the powers to enable him to govern effectively. On only one point did Quadros figure correctly: his resignation plunged the nation into a crisis. However, the resolution of that crisis did not follow his script.

The Promise or Threat of Reform

Dismay characterized the popular reaction to the president's resignation. In their disappointment over his abuse of his mandate, the majority of the citizenry turned away from Quadros. In the midst of the resignation crisis, opinion firmly advocated the constitutional solution: the elevation of Vice-President Goulart to the presidency. That respect for the legal solution reflected the success of the democratization process during the previous decade and a half. At that moment, Goulart was far away in China on a trade mission. In his absence, the legal formality called for the president of the chamber of deputies to assume the role of interim president, and Pascoal Ranieri Mazzilli stepped into that office. Simultaneously the military cabinet officers led by Minister of War Odílio Denys voiced their opposition to Goulart and indicated their refusal to honor his constitutional elevation. Denys well represented those senior military officers who viewed politics since 1945 in terms of a titanic struggle between communism and democracy. In Denys' own words during the constitutional crisis: "The situation obliges us to choose between democracy and Communism, and the armed forces have already decided: they will carry on to the end in the defense of our democratic traditions." Obviously Denys and those of similar opinions judged Goulart as part of the Communist thrust to alter Brazil and a threat to their brand of democracy. The military's dislike of Goulart extended back into the second administration of Vargas, when Goulart as minister of labor settled a maritime strike in favor of the stevedores, encouraged unions with radical tendencies, and proposed a 100 percent increase of minimum wages. His activities, both as labor minister and as chief of the PTB, hinted that he had learned much about using labor as a political base of support from his mentor Vargas as well as from Juan D. Perón, when the latter governed Argentina (1946–1955). The military hierarchy, as well as their allies among the conservative political elements, regarded such politics as pure demagogy, to be avoided if at all possible. Instant and vociferous popular reaction countered that attempted military intervention in the democratic process. Men who held no brief for Goulart rushed to defend the constitution. The news media and many congressmen proved to be strong bulwarks of the democratic process, and they seemed to reflect public opinion accurately. The crisis divided the military. Lott, in retirement, supported Goulart's elevation and appealed to his former comrades-in-arms to observe the order of succession provided by the constitution. For a moment, civil war threatened. Fortunately cooler heads prevailed. In a time-honored Brazilian custom the two sides compromised. The military agreed to permit the investiture of Goulart; Congress agreed to amend the constitution to change the presidential system to a parliamentary one and thus diminish some of the new president's power. In the new government, a Council of Ministers named by the president would be drawn from and responsible to the legislature. That council would share executive powers with the president. As a result of that compromise, voted by congress on September 2, 1961, Goulart, who had entered Brazil at Pôrto Alegre the previous day, took office officially on the seventh. He acquiesced in the compromise as the only way to get the presidency, but the dilution of the powers of that office clearly disappointed him. From the start, the new president was determined to end the parliamentary system as quickly as possible. Nor did all the public accept the amendment. The Brazilian Socialist party and the National Student Union, to mention two groups, promptly denounced it as unconstitutional. The crisis awoke genuine sympathy for Goulart, who emerged from the whole affair as a true democrat abused by military arbitrariness. He thus began his administration with far wider support than he had ever enjoyed in his career. Entering office modestly and treading carefully for the next few months, the new president thereby won, at least temporarily, the acceptance of the moderates and even of some conservatives. But after a period of grace, he alienated many of those supporters with his nationalistic and radical programs.

In foreign affairs, Goulart seemed content to follow the path cut by his predecessor. His scholarly foreign minister, San Tiago Dantas, spoke often of the nation's "independent foreign policy" which "corresponded to the permanent interests and aspirations of our nationality." As the Goulart government interpreted them, those interests and aspirations prompted the withdrawal of Brazil from the political-military blocs. The new government courted Cuba. Goulart welcomed a Chinese trade mission to Rio de Janeiro and reestablished relations with most of the eastern European states. Diplomatic missions were dispatched also to such diverse countries as Algeria and Ceylon. If Rio-Branco had once weakened Brazil's ties with Europe in favor of a closer friendship with the United States, the nationalists of the mid-twentieth century were ready to deemphasize those connections in favor of a new alliance between the underdeveloped nations of Latin America, Africa, and Asia.

In domestic affairs, Goulart lacked the firm and clear commitments which characterized foreign affairs. Opportunism rather than conviction often seemed to guide him. Perfecting his nationalist rhetoric, he leaned ever more heavily on the nationalists for support. Since their programs assumed a more radical ring in the sixties than previously, Goulart became associated with the drive for far-reaching changes. The nationalists, in turn, regarded him as unreliable—they questioned his commitment—but still an effective ally. After all, he did say the right things: he condemned foreign economic imperialism, encouraged economic development, and promised to carry out basic reforms. In truth, he supported and enacted two measures long advocated by the nationalists.

After years of frustrated efforts, a new national agency, *Electrobrás*, was finally created in 1961 to coordinate a system of state and private electric power plants. Its objective was to undertake studies, projects, construction and operation of generating plants and transmission lines, and distribution of electric energy. The government undertook vast new hydroelectric projects in an attempt to meet the insatiable demand for more electric energy. Electrobrás gave the government authority over a power resource vital to the future development of the country, a resource the nationalists were loath to see in the hands of foreigners.

The second measure enacted at the urging of the nationalists limited the profits that foreign companies could withdraw from Brazil. Foreign investment was high: more than 70 percent of the capital was invested in the 34 largest private companies and more than 30 percent invested in the 650 corporations with capital of a million dollars or more. It had grown in the decade of the fifties. The nationalists charged that foreign investors received higher profits from their Brazilian investments than they did from similar investments in the United States or Europe. The statistics are confusing, but the charge probably was valid. One North American economist, Eric Baklanoff, concluded that during the period 1947–1953, when there was a profit remittance law, the inflow of venture capital averaged only $15 million a year, while profit remittances averaged $47 million. In the period 1954–1961, when there were no restrictions, venture capital inflow reached $91 million a year, while profit remittances were $33 million, a sharp decline but still a healthy return. Official governmental figures for the period 1947–1960 recorded an alarming capital outflow. The inflow for the period amounted to $1,814 million in new investments and loans; at the same time, an outflow of $2,459 million in profits and interest and $1,022 in payment for "services" totaled $3,481 million. Such figures as these last ones excited and annoyed Brazilians, who saw their nation in the same role as the "mulch cow" which once had fattened Portugal. The nationalist case against foreign profiteering had wide popular appeal. It offered a simple and understandable explanation for low wages, high prices, and poverty, all of which could conveniently be blamed on foreign exploitation. Goulart relied heavily on the foreign-profits issue to win popular support.

On September 3, 1962, the president signed a law limiting profit remittances. According to the provisions of the law, all foreign capital was to be registered with the Brazilian government and, in effect, no profit remittances in excess of 10 percent of invested capital were permitted. The most immediate result of the law was a drastic drop in foreign investments, from $91 million in 1961 to only $18 million in 1962. The nationalists rejoiced at the promulgation of the law, a major victory for their cause. In their opinion, nationalism clearly was in ascendancy in Brazil. How could it be otherwise when one president after another enacted policies from the nationalist program and spoke in increasingly nationalistic tones? Those presidents thus lent their power and prestige to the nationalist movement, and, on certain key issues, they even provided a welcome leadership for the otherwise heterogeneous nationalist group, which by this time included large segments of the intellectuals, politicians, students, urban proletariat, and middle class, as well as certain elements among the military and the industrialists.

Heady rhetoric could not disguise for President Goulart some serious economic problems. He committed himself to development and had as precedent the exhilarating record of Kubitschek. At the same time, he and Brazil faced a serious inflation. The purchasing power of the cruzeiro plummeted, accelerating a tendency under way since the Dutra administration. In 1961, it fell 30 percent, in 1962, 50 percent, and in 1963, 80 percent. The cost of living exceeded the rising minimum wage, and the two spiraled upward with numbing regularity. Budget deficits became habitual. To meet expenses, the government printed mountains of cruzeiros. The international value of the cruzeiro, never strong, collapsed. In 1961, it took Cr$390 to buy US$1; in 1962, it took Cr$795; in 1963, Cr$1,235; and in 1964, Cr$1,820. The economists who had the president's ear convinced him that inflation encouraged development. Their policies certainly persuaded Brazilians to withdraw their depreciating cruzeiros from the banks in order to spend or invest them. Real estate and industry were popular investments—as were bank accounts in the United States and Switzerland. The rapid advance of prices over wages enticed investors in production who hoped to reap a rich harvest of profits. The economists further convinced the president that a major cause for inflation was scarcity of goods. According to their analysis, as soon as there were enough factories to sufficiently supply demands for goods, or enough houses and apartments to meet the requirements of a growing population, prices would fall and the inflation would taper off. These convincing arguments explained and justified the inflation. Goulart accepted them and eventually abandoned any serious effort to control the situation. He thus disregarded the concern of large numbers of the population over the galloping inflation. His failure to bridle it alienated the moderates, whose support in 1961 switched to opposition by 1963.

Although still capable of wielding considerable power, the president protested that the parliamentary system minimized the ability of his government to handle Brazil's problems. To contain the inflation, which frightened the conservatives and moderates, and to enact basic reforms, so desirable to the working classes, Goulart insisted that full presidential powers be restored to him. Confident of a growing popular desire to end the governmental lethargy—not to say outright confusion—he agitated to place before the electorate a choice between presidential and parliamentary government. Backing him were the labor unions, well coordinated by the powerful *Comando Geral do Trabalho* (General Labor Command, or CGT, created in 1962, and by late that year known as the General Strike Command). That central labor organization operated without legal status but with the support and approval of Goulart. Many critics accused it of being run or at least dominated by the Communists. Goulart had a long history of good relations with labor, and as president he received from labor what proved to be his strongest and most consistent support. The urban workers were well organized (thanks in part to Goulart's past efforts), increasingly vocal, and sufficiently literate to possess the vote. Correctly used, labor could be a potent weapon for any politician, and Goulart was not hesitant to make use of it. The highly political and pro-Goulart CGT called for strikes to propel the drive for a return to presidential government. The labor unrest added to the chaos disturbing the nation, and contributed to the argument that a stronger government was needed. Popular support swung behind Goulart and demanded a plebiscite to resolve the question. Even members of the UDN read the handwriting on the wall and favored giving their bête noire of the PTB his full presidential powers. Governor José de Magalhães Pinto of Minas Gerais counseled, "The uncertainties, the difficulties, and the anxieties which the dilution of authority has brought us in the past fourteen months indicate a need to return to the presidential system." Congress set the date for a plebiscite. On January 6, 1963, more than twelve million voters went to the polls to voice their opinion. By a 5 to 1 majority they restored to Goulart those full presidential powers contained in the Constitution of 1946. On January 23, 1963, Brazil officially returned to the presidential system. The people quite understandably then expected effective government and an end to the crises which had plagued the nation for a year and a half.

Goulart still had to deal with a recalcitrant Congress, no more cooperative than it had been with his predecessor. The legislature flatly refused to back the reforms the president suggested. Goulart spoke out in favor of a land reform which would expropriate large estates, pay the former owners with bonds, and redistribute the land. Such a reform would entail a major restructuring of Brazil's archaic rural structures, a change, if effective, of revolutionary proportions. In March of 1963, he submitted an agrarian reform bill to Congress. It required a constitutional amendment to enact it, that is, a two-thirds approval from congress. The legislature defeated the proposed reform in early October. The president's efforts at tax reform, anathema to the middle classes and elites who did not bear their proportionate share of the tax burdens, met no greater success. The dialogue between those favoring reform and those protecting the status quo fell to silence. On the one hand, Goulart watched his support from the moderates dissipate, and on the other, he witnessed rivals wooing labor. His articulate brother-in-law, Governor Leonel Brizola of Rio Grande do Sul, emerged as a major political rival. Brizola had expropriated a local subsidiary of ITT in January of 1962, to the undisguised joy of the nationalists and working class. To preserve his leadership over labor,

Goulart became increasingly more radical. The conservatives and moderates watched with foreboding as the government swung farther to the left. The middle class, whose members for some time had encouraged and spoken for nationalism, watched with apprehension as Goulart roused the urban masses. He promised them fundamental changes; he exploited their latent nationalistic sentiments. The spectre of a proletarian revolution frightened the middle class for the first time.

In February of 1964, Goulart presented a "package plan," the basic reforms demanded by his government of Congress. They called for fundamental economic and political changes which would benefit the lower classes. The elites and middle classes perceived them as restrictions, potential and actual, of their privileged positions. The plan sought the vote for illiterates, eligibility of noncommissioned officers and enlisted men to participate in politics, legalization of the Communist Party, tax reforms, periodic wage adjustments, state monopolies over coffee and ore exports, revision of all mining concessions, and immediate expropriation of all but small properties along highways, railways, and water projects as a means of initiating agrarian reform. Such expropriation might seem a curious way to begin the much needed land reform, but it was the simplest way since the government enjoyed some residual powers over lands adjacent to means of public transportation.

The concern of the moderates and conservatives mounted as radicalism manifested itself in the countryside, that bulwark of elitist privilege. The rural land and labor structures had served and would serve to deflect any meaningful change and to minimize the impact of urbanization, industrialization, and modernization. Accustomed to urban agitation, the rural oligarchy—and for that matter the urban elites and middle class as well—panicked at the sight of peasant unrest, no matter how slight. In the miserable Northeast, the lawyer Francisco Julião had been organizing the peasants since 1955 into groups known as Peasant Leagues. From modest initial desires that their members receive a decent burial, the peasants turned to demands for an agrarian reform to restructure the rural economic system. The Leagues represented the peasants in land-tenancy courts. It politicized the peasants, making them aware of the possibility of mitigating their misery. Still, the Leagues operated in a limited area and never reached the largest portion of the dispossessed. At the same time, other groups advocated rural changes. Some courageous and vocal clerics of the Roman Catholic Church also called for rural reforms. But the Peasant Leagues attracted national and international attention, partly because it was difficult to deny the injustices of the impoverished Northweast but mainly because of the political potential embodied in the Leagues. To a hemispheric elite reacting with fear to the Cuban Revolution directed by Fidel Castro, the exhortations of Julião awoke real fears. In October 1960, Julião identified the enemy of the peasants and suggested revolution as a means to change the system: "Your cruel enemy, the large estate, will die as it died in China . . . and in Cuba, where the great Fidel Castro handed a rifle to each peasant and said, 'Democracy is the government that arms the people.' " On other occasions, Julião boldly called for strikes:

It is already time, peasant, that you should learn to utilize unity against your cruel enemy which is the latifundia. Follow the lesson of the worker, of the student. What does the worker do to overcome the employer? What does the student do to defend liberties? He relies on the strike as his weapon. The strike is the unity of all. It has the strength of the river's current and the roar of the waterfall. The worker stops the factory and gains a better salary. The student closes the university and goes into the streets to proclaim liberty and peace and to agitate for a national oil industry and free education. Use the strike as your weapon![7]

Goulart lent his support to demands for rural change. Both the president and Julião attended a Peasant Congress in Belo Horizonte in November 1961, whose slogan was "We Want Land by Law or by Force." Goulart called for a far-reaching

7. Translated in Horowitz, *Revolution in Brazil*, pp. 40–41. Quoted with the permission of the publisher.

land reform at the congress. In March of 1963, the president promulgated a "Statute of the Rural Worker," whose aim was to provide for the rural laborer what Vargas had achieved for the urban. The threats and rhetoric of reform alienated the increasingly frightened rural oligarchy. They manifested a particular hatred of Julião, who to peasant and landlord alike symbolized the potential for pervasive changes. The landowners vilified the Leagues, labeling them Communist. Their tactic was an old one, even then: better to confuse the public with labels than to recognize legitimate needs for change.

Although distressed by the course of events, neither the middle class nor the elites nor a combination of them seemed able to slow the radical momentum. Frustrated, the civilian political opponents to Goulart turned to the military to persuade the armed forces to act, a recourse they had used in other historical circumstances. In Brazilian history, military involvement in politics had occurred when cohesion among relevant political elites was low. As in the past, the elites provided the military with a legitimacy to intervene. The press mounted a campaign to involve the military in politics, to exercise its "moderating power." The leading newspapers reminded the military of its "duty."

Goulart facilitated the alliance between the military and his civilian opponents by alienating the officer class, a group always suspicious if not outrightly hostile to the PTB chief. A decision of the Supreme Court that sergeants could not hold seats in the legislature sparked a spontaneous rebellion of six hundred enlisted men in Brasília on September 12, 1963. The senior officers quickly put down the rebellion, but only after the enlisted men had paralyzed the government, holding Congress and several high administrators prisoner. The incident revealed two significant factors. First, the enlisted men had allied themselves with the radical left. The CGT and the National Student Union, among others, defended their action. Second, Goulart refused to commit himself, neither condemning nor condoning the rebellion, an ominous sign to most of the officers. It seemed to indicate that the president's sympathies had swung to the radical left. The officers waited for a confirmation of that suspicion.

It was confirmed by Goulart during an emotional political rally directed by the CGT in Rio de Janeiro on March 13, 1964, to initiate the drive for "basic reforms." About 150,000 people, a majority from the working class, gathered to cheer the president on that fateful Friday. Expectation and excitement ran high. The charismatic orator Leonel Brizola, then an extremely popular federal deputy from Guanabara, spoke first. He reminded his audience that the president represented the people and that he was prevented from enacting his reforms by a reactionary Congress, representative of the oligarchy. "Congress will give nothing to the people because it does not represent the aspirations of the people," he shouted. The alternative to a hostile Congress, he suggested, was to take matters directly to the people so that they could act. He called on the president to organize a strictly populist and nationalist government. With the crowd thus brought to a highly emotional pitch, Goulart came to the microphone and in his speech further identified his government with the people. As a climax, he signed there in public a decree initiating a modest land reform expropriating lands within ten kilometers of federal highways, railways, and water projects and another nationalizing all oil refineries. Two days later, in a message addressed to Congress, the president again challenged that body: "I have chosen to fight the privileged and to take the initiative for basic reforms." He had in mind two such reforms: a redivision of the land and the extension of the vote to illiterates and enlisted men, two powerful blows against the oligarchy. Apparently he no longer intended to compromise with the moderates and conservatives. Conciliation seemed out of the question. Carried forward by the support and enthusiasm of the left, the only political base he had, Goulart sought to radicalize the nation.

His opponents reacted. They organized rallies, and none surpassed the mammoth "March of the Family with God for Liberty" in São Paulo on March 19, 1964. Largely organized by upper and middle class women with the backing of the Roman Catholic Church as well as the conservative and moderate political parties, the march of several hundred thousand signaled the determination of significant social groups to stem the tide of projected reform. Like the newspaper editorials of the day, those demonstrators helped persuade the military officers to take political action, particularly as they witnessed a growing insubordination within the enlisted ranks.

Within the armed services, many of the politically inclined enlisted men approved the course the president took. The Sailors and Marines Association decided to call a special meeting to pledge their support to Goulart, an act the minister of the navy forbade. Admiral Sílvio Mota categorized the Association as subversive. Nonetheless, on March 25, over 2,000 sailors and marines met. To shouts of approval from the youthful gathering, the president of the Association denied the accusation of subversion and added, "The ones in this country who are trying to subvert order are those allied with the dark forces which caused one president to commit suicide, another to resign, and which tried to prevent Jango [Goulart] from taking office, and who now try to prevent basic reforms." The minister of the navy dispatched troops to arrest the participants in the meeting. At that point, Goulart intervened to grant an amnesty to the marines and sailors. The enlisted men rejoiced. Later, Goulart indicated his intention of investigating the conduct of certain admirals whom he accused of precipitating the mutiny. The officers sullenly interpreted the president's action as an endorsement of insubordination. In their eyes, military discipline had broken down. The morale of the officers slumped. Their honor had been besmirched.

Reserved for the officers was yet a stronger rebuff. On the 30th, the president addressed an assembly of the Military Police Sergeants Association in Rio de Janeiro, and his words were carried by television to the nation. He appealed emotionally to the sergeants for their support and charged the officers—those who had tried to prevent his legal accession to the presidency in 1961—with lack of discipline.

In the broadest sense, the mounting crisis of late March reflected the more fundamental tensions generated by development—or lack of it. Neither Quadros nor Goulart had provided the dynamic and positive leadership which had characterized the Kubitschek administration. Economic growth had slowed, a circumstance guaranteed to provoke crises because it forced the government to make difficult decisions. Usually governments opted to encourage greater foreign investments to stimulate the economy. This time, however, Goulart had frightened away the capitalists with the profit remission law. He was left with the alternative of implementing some basic reforms, a decision certain to arouse the ire of the small but potent privileged classes. Growing fiscal instability, hyperinflation, and the default on international debts further frightened the upper and middle classes. Predictably the public complained of the upwardly spiraling cost of living. Political uncertainty caused by frequent labor strikes and pronouncements, rumors of a presidential coup, and demogogic appeals and threats further agitated the nation.

The military watched solicitously from the wings, but until the night of March 30 hesitated to stride onto the political stage. Goulart's attack on the military hierarchy during his televised speech that night excited an immediate and unified response from the officers. They yielded to the exhortations of the "linha dura" (hard line) group within the military to intervene in and control the political process. Accusing the president and his government of Communism, the military moved to overthrow Goulart. As one apologist of the coup, Juracy Magalhães, explained it, "The Brazilian Revolution was born out of the indomitable will of the people not to allow themselves to become dominated by Communism or by the corruption which was undermining our National life." On March 31, army units marched on Rio de Janeiro from Minas Gerais. The forces ordered from Rio de Janeiro to oppose them joined them instead. The key Second Army in São Paulo adhered to the rebellion on April 1.

Surprised by the swiftness and the extent of the revolt, Goulart flew from Rio de Janeiro to Brasília and thence to Pôrto Alegre in the hope of stirring up support for himself. Few stepped forward to defend the president. A small number of labor leaders, politicians, and intellectuals called the people to rush to the barricades. Silence answered that call. With no appreciable support, Goulart quietly slipped out of Brazil into exile in Montevideo on April 4. As a president, he had revealed many serious defects, but he had actively favored reform throughout his political career and in no way had limited the democratic process during his administration.

The Brazilian military received approval in their planning and execution of the coup from the United States government and the large U.S. military mission in Brazil. So committed was the U.S. government that it dispatched warships to Brazil at the end of March in case they were needed. A U.S. naval unit with an aircraft carrier, a helicopter carrier, six destroyers, and oil tankers was ordered to take positions off the Brazilian coast near Santos. The top secret orders to the naval commander were: "Purpose of Carrier Task Force Group is to establish U.S. presence in the area when so directed and to be prepared to carry out tasks as may be assigned. . . ."

Washington considered Goulart to be far too radical, unfriendly to foreign businesses and investment, and a potential danger to hemispheric security. Revolution in Cuba was more than enough challenge for Washington. The fear of similar events overtaking the South American giant consternated U.S. officials, who once again confused the need, desire, and thrust for change with Communism. The United States had stopped most aid and cut off sources of loans for Brazil in an effort to deepen the economic woes of the Goulart government. The Central Intelligence Agency had financed a major covert political campaign to deny Goulart control of congress in the 1962 elections. In mid-March of 1964, Assistant Secretary of State for Inter-American Affairs Thomas Mann announced that the U.S. government would not oppose the establishment of military governments in Latin America, a clear signal to the Brazilian military leaders that they could expect prompt approval from Washington if they toppled the Goulart government. How prompt that approval would be amazed even the generals. Within four hours of taking power, even before they had formed a government, and while President João Goulart was still in Brazil, the officers who executed the coup d'etat received a telegram from President Lyndon B. Johnson congratulating them on their maneuver. U.S. Ambassador to Brazil Lincoln Gordon then judged the military takeover "the single most decisive victory for freedom in the mid-twentieth century." If any further approval from Washington was needed, it came in the form of generous aid and loans which virtually inundated the new military government. Clearly involved in the military overthrow of the constitutional and democratic government of Brazil, the U.S. government became intimately associated with the military dictatorship which followed.

Chapter Eight

Military
Patterns

The experiment with democracy gave way to military dictatorship. A succession of generals with technocratic advisers prescribed capital accumulation at the expense of workers' salaries, greater investments, rapid industrialization, and unquestioned obedience. The governments never hesitated to resort to violence to achieve their goals. A period of impressive economic growth, 1969–1974, disguised the brutality with momentary euphoria, but by the mid-1970s it was apparent that while solving none of Brazil's old problems the military governments had created new ones.

The Military in Power

Having pushed Goulart from the presidential saddle, the military seized the reins of political power. For purposes of constitutional decorum, President of the Chamber of Deputies Ranieri Mazzilli once again served as acting president, the sixth time in his career he had occupied that office, but it proved to be a purely honorific position. This time the three military ministers, headed by Marshal Artur da Costa e Silva and collectively bearing the title of "Supreme Revolutionary

Command," exercised power. The Command reflected the dissatisfaction many officers felt about the course democracy had taken in Brazil during the previous two decades. To those officers, democracy seemed to permit and even encourage corruption, subversion, chaos, and demagogy. Twice they had removed Vargas from the presidential palace, only to see the voters return him or his heirs. Such an electorate, concluded the military in disgust, could not possibly understand its own best interests and certainly not those of the nation.

The voice of the "tenentes," now aging generals and marshals, spoke out again. Juarez Távora seemingly echoed the sentiments of many of his military contemporaries when he expressed a reluctance on the part of the armed forces to turn the government over to civilians. They were not reliable; in the past they had betrayed the military. Távora affirmed, "In 1930 we exercised restraint by not taking direct control of the government. We planned to put civilians in the government and influence them. It was an illusion. They soon pushed us aside and proved incapable of doing any of the things we had planned." Other officers shared that complaint, indicating that the military would not suffer a repetition of the politicians' perfidy this time.

In the twentieth century prior to 1964, the officers had intervened in politics with increasing frequency to change the chief executive, in 1930, 1945, 1954, 1955, and 1961, thus exercising a function comparable—in the military mind—to the *poder moderador*. They had changed the presidents much as the emperor had arbitrarily alternated the Liberals and Conservatives in power during the Second Empire. The key military figure in promoting or coordinating the military coups was the chief of staff. This officer was likely to be much more attuned to and representative of the sentiments and opinions of the officer class than was the minister of war, an officer appointed by the president because of his loyalty. The officers who plotted were, in the vast majority, men from areas outside the traditional triangle of economic and political power, that is, São Paulo, Minas Gerais, and Rio de Janeiro. Quite often they came from Rio Grande do Sul and the Northeast. In that respect, they represented a widely felt frustration over the narrow base of political power in Brazil. The military plots originated in other frustrations as well. Officers have been notably unsuccessful in winning presidential elections in contemporary Brazil. In 1945, two military candidates ran for the three major parties, so logically one had to win, and General Dutra did. However, in 1950, Vargas defeated General Eduardo Gomes at the polls; in 1955, Kubitschek triumphed over General Juarez Távora; and in 1960, Quadros overwhelmed Marshal Henrique Lott. Apparently officers did not appeal to the electorate. Hence the ballot box did not seem likely to serve as the portal through which the military could enter into political power.

It is difficult to establish a pattern for the military interventions. At times, they favored the growth of democracy; 1955 serves as an excellent example. Yet at other times they threatened constitutional development; 1961 represents that aspect of the interventions. A volatile emotionalism often seemed to be prompting the interventions. The concept of "military honor" which emerged so menacingly in the last decade of the Empire continued to influence the decisions of the officers; their attachment to that concept cannot be described as a force buttressing democracy. The overthrow of Vargas in 1954 illustrated their emotionalism in action, indeed, in control. The military considered neither the constitution nor public well-being. Certainly the preservation and encouragement of democracy were far from the officers' minds. Had the military shown political maturity and confidence in the constitutional process, they would have awaited the presidential elections, only a few months away, and the change those elections could have brought about democratically. But the urge to vindicate that illusive honor took precedence, as it did on other occasions.

The military seldom acted alone. A discernible pattern reaching back to 1889 showed that the armed forces were called into action by civilian groups, often the middle class which was closely linked to the officer class. In fact the military sometimes served as the surrogate for the frustrated middle class when it felt helpless or threatened in the political process. It had cultivated the habit of relying on the armed forces for short-run solutions to political problems. Those solutions consisted principally of forestalling any social, economic, or political reforms of consequence. The middle class seemed to resort to those patterns in calling forth the military to overthrow Goulart, but the military threw aside the traditional script on that occasion.

In 1964, the military radically altered its behavioral pattern. The soldiers did not retire to the barracks after the coup. The Supreme Military Command resolved this time not to return the government to the civilians at once. Influenced by the teachings of the Superior War College (Escola Superior de Guerra), the commanding officers espoused a common ideology. They believed that the military fostered national unity and that the best way to insure national security was to encourage economic development through a highly centralized government. (Their subsequent actions, however, revealed a greater concern with economic growth than with development.) They were determined after 1964 to involve the military more intimately in national life. The Command indicated the direction the new government would take when it issued, on April 9, 1964, the First Institutional Act, drawn up by none other than Francisco Campos, intellectual mentor of the Estado Novo and author of the Constitution of 1937. The Ato Institucional significantly modified the Constitution of 1946. Basically, the Act enlarged the powers of the president at the expense of the judiciary and the legislature. It called for the immediate election of a president who could propose constitutional amendments which Congress had to consider within 30 days and which needed only a majority vote for their passage; he could also propose expenditure bills which Congress could not increase, declare a state of siege, and deprive citizens of their rights for a period of ten years.

The military officers in control of the government selected General Humberto de Alencar Castelo Branco for the presidency and the subservient congress complied with their votes. Son of a military family of the Northeast, he had served in the army since 1918 and had seen action in Italy with the Brazilian Expeditionary Force during World War II. Like many of his contemporary fellow officers, he had received advanced military instruction at the Superior War College. The officers were confident that Castelo Branco would deal firmly with the Brazilian Communists, whom they blamed for the chaos, corruption, and subversion in the nation. Congressmen, for their part, thought of the laconic general as a highly cultured officer and a defender of the democratic process. There was no difficulty, then, in electing him president on April 11. For the vice-presidency, Congress chose José Maria Alkmim, a PSD congressman from Minas Gerais.

The government of Castelo Branco, primarily one of military officers and technocrats, pursued two primary goals: to put the nation's finances back in order and to combat the spread of Communism, both internally and externally. Association of any desire for reform with Communism characterized the mentality of those responsible for the coup, and, in fact, was a common association convenient for the Brazilian elites to make. It became immediately evident that the new president represented the wing of the "linha dura," whose main concern was to eradicate Communism anywhere it could be found. The opposite wing, while no less implacable toward Communism, placed its emphasis on a very fundamental nationalism, more reminiscent of the Integralist variety than of the nationalism which had held sway from 1951 until April of 1964. Castelo Branco's definition of Communism was very broad and tended to include most movements or persons to the left of his own position. He showed a strong suspicion of the nationalists who had dominated the previous governments. In his thinking, they were associated with if not equated to the Communists. Their economic policies, he feared, would stifle private initiative and open the door to socialism and thus to Communism. The nationalists' foreign policy, with its emphasis on the Third World and its friendship toward the Eastern bloc particularly annoyed him. He viewed the international scene as a struggle between East and West in which there could be no neutral position. Acknowledging the United States as the unquestionable leader of the "free world," he vowed to follow the international leadership of Washington. Brazil at once broke diplomatic relations with Cuba and began voting against the seating of the People's Republic of China in the United Nations. The government expressed its solidarity with the United States intervention in Viet Nam. Brazilian troops participated in the intervention in the Dominican Republic in 1965, a decision defended by one officer in the following words: "The Armed Forces brilliantly stopped Communism from taking over Brazil. Another brilliant example is their participation in the Dominican Republic in the operation initiated by the American marines, where they also stopped Communism from taking over that country."[1] The military government actively supported the controversial Inter-American Peace Force, and the minister of foreign relations even visited most of the South American capitals to urge the support of that force, a mission which proved to be a notable failure.

Internally the government's hand fell heavily on the leftists and nationalists, although whim and caprice often dictated the definition of those two vague terms. Fifty-five Congressmen were expelled from the legislature and lost their political rights, thereby increasing the conservative proportion of Congress. Castelo Branco removed the governors of Amazonas, Pará, Pernambuco, Sergipe, Acre, Rio de Janeiro, and Goiás. Former presidents Kubitschek, Quadros, and Goulart were deprived of their political rights for ten years. Approximately 4,500 federal employees lost their jobs. The military ranks were purged and several hundred officers either went into retirement or were dismissed. The hastily created Military Courts of Inquiry summoned more than 9,000 persons to answer charges of corruption or subversion. The Superior Institute of Brazilian Studies was closed, the National Student Union disbanded, labor unions purged, and the Peasant Leagues outlawed. A book-burning mentality predominated—not only figuratively but literally. In Rio

---

1. Quoted in Mário Afonso Carneiro, "Opinião Militar," *Cadernos Brasileiros*, no. 38 (November–December, 1966), p. 25.

Grande do Sul, the commander of the Third Army, General Justino Alves Bastos, ordered burned all the books which he branded as subversive. His capricious list of dangerous literature contained, it is reported, Stendhal's *The Red and the Black.*

At the same time, Castelo Branco struggled to put an end to corruption in government, of which there had been a considerable amount, and to stem the tide of inflation. The latter task proved to be both difficult and unpopular. Inflation did not abate following the coup of March 31. The cost-of-living index for 1964 continued to rise, taking a record-breaking 86.6 percent jump, a six-point increase over the previous year. Wages failed to keep pace with prices. In 1965, the wage earners lost 14 percent of their purchasing power; in 1966, 22 percent. After the coup and until December 31, 1964, the government emitted an unprecedented amount of currency: Cr$1,340,000,000,000. The cruzeiro sank even lower in international value. If business and industry had expected an immediate miracle from the military coup, they were disappointed. Both exports and production fell. Business interests complained that the government kept too tight a rein on the economy and accused the administration of showing preference to foreign capital. Indeed, both foreign capital and foreign control of Brazilian firms increased in the years after Goulart's fall. Foreign investment by 1968 reached $3.5 billion, approximately 8 percent of Brazil's total capital stock. The United States, with about $1.22 billion, remained the single largest investor, followed by France, Britain, Switzerland, and Germany. Further reflecting its distance from the nationalists, the government sold the Fábrica Nacional de Motores, the only Brazilian company manufacturing vehicles, to Alfa-Romeo of Italy and Loide, the national coastal shipping company; it reversed a previous prohibition of foreign exploitation of iron-ore deposits.

During the first two years after the coup, the economy stagnated as the government turned its attention from encouraging development to fighting inflation. Throughout his tenure, Castelo Branco rigidly maintained a severe fiscal policy. Beginning in 1965, he restricted the new issues of bank notes so that the increase in the volume of paper money totaled 46.4 percent in 1965, 30.6 percent in 1966, and 26.9 percent in 1967. He slowed down the rise in the cost of living to 45.4 percent in 1965, 41.1 percent in 1966, and 24.5 percent in 1967. By the end of his administration, the economy showed some signs of recovery from the lethargy into which his fiscal measures had plunged it. Economic growth advanced from an overall rate of 4 percent in 1966 to 5 percent in 1967, an improvement but still below the rapid growth rates of the fifties and early sixties. The year 1967 ended with a trade balance of $200 million in Brazil's favor. Coffee maintained its customary primacy, accounting for 44 percent of Brazil's exports. Manufactured goods, everything from ships to television sets, were the second most important export item.

The government's monetary policies did not appeal to a majority of the population, which remembered the dramatic development projects of the past and the previous record of wage increases. Complaining of the official austerity, many questioned the government's priorities, which favored foreigners over Brazilians, businessmen over workers, and sound finance over development. In their thinking, the budgets had not been drawn up in the best interests of a nation eager to develop rapidly. The allocations, however, did reveal at least one new priority. In the last civilian budget, that of 1963, some 7 percent went to the military, while 19 percent was set aside for education. For the first full-year's budget drawn up by the Castelo Branco government, that of 1965, the military received 11 percent, while the amount allotted for education was cut to 9 percent. The military establishment was small, only about 250,000 men under arms in a population numbering 80 million, but the cost to maintain that establishment was disproportionately high. That cost rose spectacularly. Using a 1967 constant price base, the amount spent on the military went from $386 million in 1962, to $756 in 1967, to $1,102 in 1971, at which time Brazil was spending nearly 50 percent of the total arms expenditures of the six Latin American nations with the largest military budgets. At the same time, Brazil received from the United States the most military assistance of any nation in the hemisphere. Under the stern eye of Castelo Branco, the budget was balanced, the currency was stronger, the inflation was more under control, but there were still legions of unemployed, illiterate, hungry, and ill Brazilians who did not even have the solace of reform rhetoric, much less actual reforms. The government proudly labeled itself "revolutionary" but it failed to undertake any basic structural reforms which would directly affect the masses. There was no land reform, although the omnipotent military government could have promulgated such a reform overnight if it had so desired.

Dissatisfaction with the military regime appeared quickly and grew rapidly. The workers complained that prices rose while their wages remained frozen. In late 1968, Minister of Labor Jarbas Passarinho conservatively estimated that the workers' real wages had fallen between 15 and 30 percent in the past four years. The intellectuals lamented the loss of their liberties. Democrats despaired as the government grew more authoritarian. Young Brazilians began to express their dissatisfaction through the medium of music. They abandoned the melancholic *bossa nova* for protest songs based on ethnic and folk music. The lyrics called for a return to freedom and decried the hunger, misery, and social injustice in the country. One of the most popular themes was the plight of the impoverished Northeast. A hit song of 1965, "Carcará," lamented the poverty and hunger of the Northeast that forced the poor to abandon their homes. To standing-room-only audiences, the students of São Paulo's Catholic University presented the musical drama *Vida e Morte de Severino* (Life and Death of Severino), a poem of João Cabral de Melo Neto set to music by Chico Buarque de Holanda. The drama told of the peasant Severino who wandered through the arid backlands of the Northeast observing unhappiness, misery, and death. At one point, during the burial scene of a peasant, the chorus sang: "This land where you lie is just the right size—not too long, not too wide. Here is your share of the latifundium." Blared forth from the ubiquitous transistor radios, protest music provided a most effective form of communication in a land where half the population was illiterate.

Dissatisfaction existed within the military itself, which was by no means unified in its political orientation. On one level, the decision of the senior officers to hold the reins of political power divided the military, many of whom did not favor the extreme ideas of the "linha dura." Following a long tradition in the services, many officers held that the military should play at most a restricted role, which did not include the actual governing of the nation. They advocated returning the military to its traditional and historic role as the *poder moderador*. General Estévão Leitão de Carvalho forcefully argued that idea in his book *Dever Militar e Política Partidária* (Military Duty and Partisan Politics). Further dividing the military was the issue of nationalism. The nationalistic officers of moderate or liberal tendencies favored intense economic development directed by the state, basic structural reforms, an independent foreign policy, and restriction on foreign influence, including capital, in Brazil. The right-wing nationalists of the "linha dura" took a chauvinistic stance. But Castelo Branco and the officers who surrounded him maintained their suspicions of nationalism. They preferred fiscal stability to economic development, foreswore an independent foreign policy to align Brazil closely with the United States, shied away from basic reforms, and welcomed foreign investment and influence in Brazil.

Elections scheduled for 1965 offered Brazilians the opportunity to express their dissatisfaction. In the March mayoral elections of São Paulo, the candidate endorsed by Jânio Quadros won, to the obvious chagrin of the military government. The crucial test of confidence, however, was the gubernatorial election held in October in 11 states. The candidates favored by the government lost in 9 of those states, including the key states of Minas Gerais and Guanabara.

Disappointed with what it considered an ingrate electorate, the government reacted swiftly. On October 27, 1965, Castelo Branco promulgated the Second Institutional Act, which further strengthened the powers of the president in matters of legislation, state of siege, and intervention in the states; dissolved all political parties; instituted indirect elections for the president and vice-president; conferred on the government the power to cancel the political rights of those considered to be security risks to the state; increased the number of judges on the Supreme Court from 11 to 16; exempted certain actions of the government from judicial review; and authorized military courts to try individuals accused of subverting the state. A Third Institutional Act, promulgated on February 5, 1966, ended the popular elections of governors and vice-governors of the states and of mayors of the state capitals. Thereafter, the state legislatures selected the chief executives of the states, and the governors appointed the mayors of the capital cities. Those two Institutional Acts administered the *coup de grâce* to the democratic experiment in Brazil.

The government replaced the political parties with two official parties: the *Aliança Renovadora Nacional* (the National Renovating Alliance, called *Arena*), the official government party, and the *Movimento Democrático Brasileiro* (the Brazilian Democratic Movement, or MDB), an official opposition party. One wag noted that the difference between the two parties was that the first answered the government with a "Yes, Sir!" while the second just answered "Yes." In 1972, the leader of the MDB, Oscar Pedroso Horta, labeled both officially sponsored political parties a farce since they were artificially created, tightly controlled, and devoid of "the slightest possibility of discussion."

The purge of Congress accompanied by the substitution of official parties for the disbanded ones made of the legislature a rubber stamp. The packing of the Supreme Court did the same thing to the judiciary. Censorship and the threat to cancel political rights were weapons the government wielded to reduce criticism and opposition. The Constitution of 1967, which centralized the power of the nation in the hands of the president, did little to diminish authoritarianism.

Marshal Castelo Branco reaffirmed his intention to relinquish office in March of 1967, as he had promised he would. The achievements of his three-year administration contrasted sharply with the previous evolution of contemporary Brazil. The rate of industrialization slowed, the experiment in democracy ended, military rule replaced traditional civilian rule. While the inflation was checked, so was economic development; and while a political drift to the left was halted, so was the thrust toward basic reforms. A few Communists and their sympathizers had been removed from power, but at the same time so had many able democrats and nationalists. Where once the positive policy of development had dominated government councils, the negative and sterile policy of anti-Communism held sway. The mercurial Carlos Lacerda, who participated in the March coup but later turned against the military government, warned, "For fear of Communism, the country accepted a policy which, if it continues, will lead Brazil directly to Communism because it leaves the people no other democratic alternative."

The military government of Castelo Branco set patterns of political and economic behavior which succeeding general-presidents would follow. Those governments imposed a high degree of centralization of all powers in the hands of the chief executive. State and local governments as well as the federal legislature and judiciary witnessed the steady erosion of their responsibilities and authority. The goal was to depoliticize the nation and in doing so every form of liberty and freedom was repressed, at times brutally. Economically those governments concentrated on efforts to reduce and control inflation, but those efforts have fallen far short of success. The military governments pursued whatever policies might promise economic growth, regardless of whether it might mean neglect of agriculture or denationalization of industry. Faced with an old dilemma, those military governments opted to open the doors to foreign investment as a "safe" means of encouraging growth rather than to undertake basic reforms which might not only stimulate growth but foster development. Reform and development suggested change, a prospect the military and their allies judged as negatively as they did Communism.

Castelo Branco picked as his successor Marshal Artur da Costa e Silva and arranged for Congress to elect him as president and Deputy Pedro Aleixo as vice-president. The new president took office on March 15, 1967, for a four-year term, and began to govern under Brazil's sixth constitution. He conveyed the impression of being more affable than his predecessor, and that appearance of humanness, in contrast with the aloof demeanor of Castelo Branco, gave the people hope of a relaxation of national tensions. He certainly showed a concern for public opinion which his predecessor never had. Questions of a balanced budget, sound financial practices, and "purification" of the body politic concerned him less. He seemed more inclined to support industrialization, economic growth, and an independent foreign policy. The nationalists, momentarily repressed and demoralized by the March coup, gathered their strength again to encourage developmental nationalism. They criticized the government's conservative economic policies, as the favorable attitude toward foreign capitalists exemplified by the repeal of the profit remittance law and the concession of new mining privileges to foreigners. The new president listened attentively to the pleas of the national business community, which, jealous of the privileges bestowed on foreigners under Castelo Branco, had been resorting to some of the traditional nationalist arguments against foreign capital. In due course he announced that his government was "restudying" the agreement signed by Castelo Branco with the United States to guarantee American investments in Brazil. His government enacted regulations to prohibit investment by foreign capitalists in the new petrochemical industry. He and his foreign minister spoke of an external policy in which Brazil would be aligned only with Brazil. He reversed the position of his predecessor with regard to the Inter-American Peace Force. Announcing that Brazil had definitely abandoned the idea of a hemispheric police force, he reasserted Brazil's traditional respect for the principle of nonintervention in the affairs of other nations. Whether out of political conviction or simply because he was of a more easygoing nature, Costa e Silva permitted a wider latitude of action in Brazilian political life. The influence and power of that wing of the "linha dura" obsessed with anti-Communism seemed to decrease. The sudden death of Castelo Branco in an air accident in July 1967 doubtless gave Costa e Silva greater freedom and maneuverability than he might otherwise have enjoyed.

Both the left and right pressured the government of Costa e Silva, and both sides resorted to terrorist tactics. The far right advocated undisguised dictatorship. The far left called for a socialist revolution. Between the two extremes a genuine desire for a return to civilian, democratic government increased. As that desire went unfulfilled, frustration mounted. Student riots against the government erupted across the nation. The young demonstrators advocated a variety of basic reforms as well as the restitution of lost freedoms. In the words of one of the officers of the Student Federation of the University of Brasília, "The government must do away with the old structures. We demand reforms. We demand them now. Talk is nothing. We want action." Under the banner of the Brazilian Mothers' Union, the matrons of Rio de Janeiro and São Paulo allied to protest the government's harsh treatment of the students and to proclaim the right to assemble and to speak freely. Many of the leading intellectuals added their voices, where and when censorship permitted, to the cries of dissatisfaction. Some Church leaders likewise spoke out. Unofficially led by Monseigneur Helder Câmara, the archbishop of Olinda and Recife, the clerics reproved the military government and advocated a wide range of social, economic, and political reforms. Curiously, this mounting criticism and unrest took place while the economic situation of the country improved. Inflation was under control, prices remained relatively steady, and production rose.

Ineffectual and indecisive, Costa e Silva lost support on all sides. The anti-Communist wing of the "linha dura" felt that his leniency encouraged the left. Yet, on the other hand, the students, intellectuals, and nationalists pleaded in vain for basic reforms. To the extent censorship permitted, the press criticized the government. Finally, despite heavy controls, the other two branches of the government, whose members were practically all handpicked by the executive, made a sudden and surprising demonstration of independence. The Supreme Court granted a writ of habeas corpus for three leftist student leaders who had languished in jail for over two months. Congress emulated that display of independence on December 12, 1968, with the rejection by a vote of 216 to 141 of a request from the government to lift the immunity of Deputy Márcio Moreira Alves so that he could be tried on charges of abusing his position. Alves had been a vehement critic of the military. A year earlier he had published a book exposing military brutality toward political prisoners. To protest the storming of the Brasília University campus some months before, he had spoken in the chamber of deputies to urge his countrymen to boycott the Independence Day parades as a sign of their disapproval of the campus invasion. The senior officers considered that the outspoken deputy had besmirched military honor and they sought to punish him. Congress, usually compliant, showed an unusual degree of independence when it refused to surrender Alves to the wrath of the military.

The growing unrest, capped by the defiance of the government first by the Supreme Court and then by Congress, united many officers behind the anti-Communist wing of the "linha dura." The far-right officers seized command of the situation and demanded that Costa e Silva crack down at once. In what amounted to a coup d'état on December 13, 1968, Costa e Silva promulgated the Fifth Institutional Act, which conferred on the president dictatorial powers in "defense of the necessary interests of the nation." The act disbanded Congress, closed down the state legislatures, suspended the constitution, imposed censorship, cancelled the political rights of many, waived writs of habeas corpus. During a wave of arrests, the military police took into custody Juscelino Kubitschek, Carlos Lacerda, and a host of newspapermen, among others.

The outward forms of the military authoritarian government contained a contradiction. The executive exercised absolute powers at the expense of the legislature and judiciary. Still, the democratic charade included the presence of those two traditional branches even though reduced to ceremonial functions or totally beholden to the executive. Any attempt at independent action, and it happened on very rare occasions such as in December of 1968, was severely punished. As a result of the rigid censorship, none of the news media could report those December events. When the newspapers appeared following the coup they contained a queer assortment of information which brilliantly reflected the indomitable Brazilian sense of humor. The staid *Correio da Manhã* bore the glaring headline, "Rich Cat Dies of Heart Attack in Chicago." The *Journal do Brasil* carried prominently a wry weather report, "Weather black. Temperature suffocating. The air is unbreathable. The country is being swept by a strong wind." Censorship extended to the international press media. Foreign correspondents had to submit all their cables for governmental approval before sending them.

The government explained its own coup by saying that subversives were trying to overthrow the regime, a frequently used and much abused rationalization which could surprise no one. Costa e Silva seemed almost embarrassed and apologetic when he announced to the nation:

The promulgation of Institutional Act Number 5 after 24 hours of intense discussion and meditation did not seem to the President of the Republic as the best solution but as the only solution. Intensified to high levels of drama which had the possibility of humiliating, belittling, and provoking the Armed Forces, the crisis of insignificant dimension was headed for an unfortunate outcome whose consequence made it imperative for the Chief of State to act in order to save the nation the pain and agony of fratricidal struggle.[2]

He informed his listeners that the coup had saved them from both corruption and subversion. It was apparent that he had been reduced to functioning as a compliant mouthpiece for the anti-Communist wing of the "linha dura." Further evidence of the triumph of the "linha dura" was the resignation in January 1969 of Minister of the Interior Afonso Augusto de Albuquerque Lima, who was known to favor agrarian reforms and social welfare legislation. The militaristic, anti-Communist hard-liners did not look with sympathy on such goals.

2. *Boletim Especial*, no. 1 (January 2, 1969), Brazilian Embassy, Washington, D.C., p. 1.

Apparently what the government mistook for subversion was a genuine desire among all classes of the population for a return to democracy. At that very time, a song entitled "Walking," by a young composer, Geraldo Vandré, gained unprecedented popularity throughout the nation. Sung in the streets of the city or in the lanes of the country, the lyrics not only protested against unpopular military government but challenged it:

There are soldiers who are armed but not loved
Mostly lost with their weapons in their hands.
In the barracks they learn the old lesson
Of dying for the country and living for nothing.

There is hunger on the great plantations
And desperation walking through the streets.
But still the people take the flower as their strongest weapon
In the belief that flowers can overcome the cannon.

General Luís de França Oliveira, in charge of public security in Rio de Janeiro, classified the lyrics as "subversive" and cautioned that the song was "a musical cadence of the Mao Tse-tung type that can easily serve as the anthem for student street demonstrations." But the song, like the protests and demonstrations which preceded it, only indicated once again the estrangement of the government from the people.

While most Brazilians adopted a policy of passive resistance to the government, a tiny band of urban guerrillas intensified their activities in the major cities to oppose the military regime. They robbed banks to finance their campaign of terrorism and struck at police or military armories to obtain weapons. They made international headlines on September 4, 1969, by kidnaping the United States ambassador to Brazil, Charles Burke Elbrick. In return for his life, they made two demands to which the government quickly agreed. First, the radio and TV stations had to read and the newspapers had to print an antigovernment manifesto written by the urban guerrillas. Second, the government had to free fifteen political prisoners and fly them to sanctuary in Mexico. When those demands were met, the abductors freed Ambassador Elbrick on September 7.

In the meantime, an unforeseen event once again rocked the nation's political equilibrium. On August 30, 1969, President Costa e Silva suffered a cerebral hemorrhage which left him partially paralyzed on his right side and unable to speak. The three military ministers, General Aurélio de Lyra Tavaros, Admiral Augusto Rademaker, and Air Marshal Márcio de Souza e Mello, seized power at once and thus brushed aside the civilian vice-president, Pedro Aleixo, who, according to the constitution should have assumed the presidency in such an emergency. The triumvirate announced it would "remain faithful to the ideals of the 1964 revolution." Marshal Souza e Mello and Admiral Rademaker represented the conservative wing of the military. Almost at once the crisis of the abduction of the U.S. ambassador confronted them, and they saw themselves outwitted by the imaginative guerrillas. The junta reacted by restoring the death penalty— outlawed for three-quarters of a century—for acts of violence and subversion.

When Costa e Silva failed to recover from his stroke, the junta deliberated to pick a new president for Brazil. Their search initiated a debate within the armed services between the conservatives, who concerned themselves with continuing the search for subversion and Communists, and the reformists, who evinced more interest in economic and social reform. On October 7, the trio named to that office General Emílio Garrastazú Médici, an officer identified with the policies of Costa e Silva. Admiral Rademaker was selected as vice-president. Revived for the occasion, *Arena*, the official pro-government party, endorsed the two officers. The junta then called a purged Congress back into session on October 22, and it dutifully voiced its approval of what the military had already done. A native of Rio Grande do Sul, where he owned large estates, General Médici was a career military officer. He had served as military attaché in Washington in 1964–1966 and was known for his friendly attitude toward the United States. Under Costa e Silva, he headed the National Intelligence Service (the secret police) before taking command of the Third Army. Inaugurated in the presence of Congress on October 30, 1969, Médici was to serve a full term of office, another victory for the "linha dura," which wanted the new president to have a full term of his own rather than merely serve out the unfinished term of Costa e Silva.

October 30 also witnessed the promulgation of a new constitution, the one drawn up by Costa e Silva and his civilian vice-president and changed only slightly by the military junta. It concentrated power in the hands of a president chosen indirectly by an electoral college made up of Congress and delegates from state legislatures. It further weakened Congress by significantly reducing the immunity of congressmen. The constitution no longer protected them against charges of libel or slander, and they were liable to prosecution on matters deemed "vital to national security," a catch-all category which put them at the mercy of the military. One theoretically hopeful aspect of this constitution was the facility with which it could be amended: a vote of two-thirds of Congress could change it.

President Médici presided over some years of phenomenal economic growth, rates averaging around 10 percent per year. To many observers, that heady boom seemed to announce that finally Brazil had reached the "economic take-off." A host of third world nations looked to Brazil as a kind of economic model. Only a few observers bothered to investigate the effect of that boom on the majority of the Brazilians and their preliminary conclusions showed that no "trickle down" had taken place. At the same time, the government's sobering record of torture and abuse of political prisoners received growing international attention and condemnation. The repressive apparatus detracted from the economic euphoria. The government resented any criticism. For example, students arrested during demonstrations in early 1972 were promptly and routinely branded as subversives by the police. Yet, the students largely had limited their action to appeals for more schools, pointing out that the government regularly spent more money on military hardware than on the nation's education.

In consultation with top military officials, Médici selected his successor, another general, Ernesto Geisel, a selection which the compliant congress seconded in January 1974. Born in Rio Grande do Sul, he had helped to found the Superior War College, served as president of Petrobrás, and had enjoyed close contacts with previous military governments. Taking office on March 15, President Geisel promised the nation a *distensão*, a gradual relaxation of authoritarian rule and a restoration of civilian constitutional government. One logical consequence of the implementation of distensão was the questioning, even challenge of executive absolutism. The inconsistency of Geisel's application of distensão resulted from the executive's unwillingness to accept the policy's inevitable consequences: a strengthening of the legislature and judiciary, rising criticism of the governments, proposals for genuine change, and, of course, the inevitable diminution of executive power. While there were periods in which a greater measure of freedom was tolerated, Geisel demonstrated that on occasion he could crack down when executive fiat was challenged. In April of 1977, he closed congress for two weeks when the MDB delegation refused to pass a government-sponsored judicial reform bill, but that was really an excuse for the government to rule by decree. Geisel then issued his so-called "April Package," measures to weaken congress still further and to guarantee that the government, through its official party, Arena, would dominate any future elections. Still, during his term of office, Geisel did ease censorship and restrain the military's repressive apparatus, including the use of torture. The government confronted escalating economic problems: a declining growth rate, a rising rate of inflation, the high cost of imported oil, and a national debt reaching nearly $40 billion.

During the Geisel administration, opposition to military government mounted, some of it emanating from unexpected sources. The Roman Catholic Church, through the leadership of men like Dom Helder Câmara and Cardinal Ernest Arns, Archbishop of São Paulo, raised its voice against social injustice and demanded economic opportunities for the masses and freedom for all. Labor showed a renewed independence. In May of 1978, a strike in São Paulo involving some 50,000 workers was the first in a decade. Those workers sought higher wages and the government responded with adjustments. The students, too, became vocal again. In 1977, they organized a number of important demonstrations. More surprisingly, the business community began to voice criticism. In November of 1977, some 2,000 businessmen gathered in Rio de Janeiro called for democratic liberties, and in July of the following year a document signed by eight wealthy industrialists advocated a more just socio-economic system. The document stated that full democracy was the only way to insure economic development. Businessmen, particularly middle-level capitalists, suffered since 1964 from the competition of the powerful multinational corporations and blamed the government for allowing those giant firms to dominate them. Finally, within the ranks of the military, reform sentiment was growing, and it became increasingly difficult for the governing generals to disguise the cracks in the facade of unity they had wanted to project.

Unlike his military predecessors, Geisel did not consult his colleagues to select a consensus candidate to replace himself in the presidency. Arbitrarily he selected General João Baptista Figueiredo, a relatively unknown figure who formerly had directed the National Intelligence Service. A reduction of political repression permitted a mild opposition, the National Front for Redemocratization (FNR), to nominate a presidential candidate, General Euler Bentes Monteiro. The FNR denounced the violations of human and civil rights, opposed the government's economic policies, supported the strike movements of students and workers, and decried the arbitrary powers of the president. It drew wide public support. Clearly its success revealed a political crisis: the rupture of the former consensus of the bourgeoisie and armed forces. The failure of the military dictatorship to solve any basic problems was increasingly apparent to even the supporters of the general-presidents. The government needed all of its considerable force to win the elections even though it managed the electoral machinery. While the Electoral College gave Figueiredo 335 votes, it cast 266 for Bentes Monteiro.

Assuming the presidency on March 15, 1979, for six

years, President Figueiredo expressed a hope to preside over the political transition from dictatorship to democracy. He announced, "I intend to turn this country into a democracy. . . . I hold out my hand in conciliation." Action followed. Within four months he proposed an amnesty for all those who since 1961 had been accused of political crimes, had their political rights suspended, and had been punished as a result of the various arbitrary institutional acts. Congress promptly approved that major act of justice to ease both past political bitterness and the transition to the liberal, though controlled, democracy the military promised. Whether the return to bourgeois government would be accompanied by any basic reforms of Brazil's iniquitous institutions remained speculative, not to say dubious.

Strengthening the Past

Reviewing the sweep of events in twentieth-century Brazil, one cannot fail to note some remarkable transformations. Brazil became both an industrialized and urbanized nation. After the 1960s, for the first time, more Brazilians lived in cities than in the countryside. In 1980, fully 70 percent of the population was urban. The transportation infrastructure expanded impressively; after mid-century the road and air networks in particular reached out to embrace previously isolated corners of the vast nation. New groups played increasingly influential roles, notably the military, organized labor, the urban middle class, students, industrialists, and businessmen. The social structure became increasingly diverse and complex.

Yet, it is not those transformations which are the most striking feature of this century. Rather, the truly amazing characteristic of Brazil is how little it has changed despite those new and seemingly significant features. On a very fundamental level Brazil followed well delineated and deeply rooted patterns, an impressive tribute to continuity. The few still govern the many and enjoy most of the benefits from society. The latifundia, as strong as ever, grows in size, and the number of large estates increases as the huge interior opens to exploitation. There the landowners continue to dispossess the remaining Indians of what is left to them in the once trackless Amazon. For those Indians the sixteenth century is being reenacted. The export sector remains the most dynamic and dominant part of the economy. Production for export still takes precedence over internal needs. Witness the rush to grow and to market soybeans at the expense of producing basic goods for the Brazilians. Soybean production leaped from 350,000 tons a year in the mid-1960s to 12,200,000 tons in 1977. The government encouraged the production since it complemented the drive to augment exports. Meanwhile, black beans, a dietary staple for most Brazilians, became scarce with the inevitable rise in price. The price jumped 100 percent in 1973 alone. Dependency, a major characteristic of the past, still prevails, still shapes the economy and politics of Brazil. It assumed a new form in conformity with new times: industrial dependency.

The tragedy of Brazil has been its inability to achieve its enormous potential. Foreigners seem to have profited more from Brazil's riches than the Brazilians have. Still excluded from participation in the political and economic life of the nation are the majority of the citizenry. They still do not share in that subcontinent's limitless wealth and potential, although they certainly bear the burden of production. There has been no change in the restrictive and unjust institutions. Such a failure of change precludes real development. Growth continues, but, as nearly five centuries of sporadic growth have demonstrated, growth does little to improve Brazil and even less to help the impoverished majority.

The historical argument has been made that approximately from the mid-1930s to the mid-1960s some feeble and somewhat ineffectual efforts were made to get development underway. Whatever the attempts, they were reversed by a decade and a half of military rule. The military as the surrogate of the elites, middle class, and foreign interests stand guilty of returning Brazil to patterns of the past, to colonial inequities which have characterized Brazil for nearly half a millenium. The military appropriated an exciting word, "revolution," and applied it to their coup d'état of 1964, but words do not a revolution make. The coup was rather a reaffirmation of the past, a strengthening of a pattern which bestowed privilege on a small frightened upper class and a very nervous middle class, a pattern which prevented the majority from gaining access to power and enacting reforms. To term the strengthening of the past a "revolution" revealed either cynicism or ignorance of the meaning of the word. Even the economic growth the military boasted so loudly of has been elusive and ever less evident; of economic development there has been little. The argument can be made that a decade and a half of military rule worsened the living conditions of the majority and tightened the bonds of dependency.

To consider Brazil under military rule as a model for development, as many did, revealed another semantic confusion. Brazil during some years recorded a remarkable growth, a quantitative increase, without a realization of the nation's vast potential for improvement of the well-being of the majority. Perhaps the distinction between growth and development can be made clearer by examining the behavior of the huge, 100 percent foreign-owned, Brazilian vehicular industry. In 1973, Brazil ranked ninth among the world's auto producers, manufacturing that year approximately 850,000 units. The trend was toward luxury cars, weighty steel fortresses in which the middle class sat perspiring but apparently happy in the clogged streets of Brazil's cities. They created urban traffic nightmares while at the same time Brazil suffered a shortage of sturdy pick-up trucks for the rough back roads and large trucks to transport crops and goods. That same year Brazil had to hire Argentine trucks to help transport part of its harvest, particularly soybeans in the center-south, a testimony to the misdirection of the vehicular industry's goals—goals, by the way, set by foreign owners of the automobile industry—an indication of growth but hardly of development. The numerical increase of automobiles added no qualitative improvement to the lives of the majority. In fact, the pollution caused by industry—to say nothing of the cars—and the misuse of resources in addition to the substantial capital flow abroad in the form of profits, dividends, patent fees, etc., affected all Brazilians adversely. Economic growth concentrated in the consumer industries to cater to the demands of the privileged classes.

Likewise, growth centered on a relatively small geographical area, the Southeast, which contained less than one-fifth of the national territory although about one-third of the population. It also contained a disproportionately large share of the middle and upper classes. Some figures from 1973 suggest why the Southeast grew. FIAMNE, a financial enterprise connected with the National Bank of Economic Development, spent 13 percent of its resources in the Northeast, 1.5 percent in the entire North, but a massive 68 percent in the Southeast with 47 percent going to São Paulo alone. The *Caixa Econômica* invested 9.3 percent in the Northeast, 1.2 percent in the North, but 64.5 percent in the Southeast with 35.4 percent reserved for São Paulo. The Council for Economic Development distributed a paltry 3 percent of its funds in the Northeast, while spending most of the rest in the Southeast. Again São Paulo reaped the lion's share with an impressive 77.1 percent. Absorbing most of the capital and investments, the dynamic Southeast imposed in turn a kind of "internal colonialism" over the rest of the nation.

Like so many of the Latin Americans, the Brazilian generals and their civilian technocrats believed in the panacea of industrialization as the certain solution to most national problems, even though planners had become increasingly skeptical of the "magic solutions" attributed to it, particularly that variety based on consumer items. And Brazilian industrialization focused largely on the production of consumer goods. Scant evidence exists to suggest that industrialization remedied any of the traditional economic disparities. In fact, to the contrary, some economists concluded that industrialization increased initial disparities and further unbalanced the economy. The rapid Brazilian industrialization proceeded without a commensurate increase in the purchasing power of the population. Perhaps the basic problem was that industrialization hardly involved the major-

ity. The capital-intensive industries hired relatively few workers. Unemployment and underemployment continued to be
a major problem. Unemployment by 1978 was officially estimated to be 20 percent, a figure some disputed as too optimistic. Further, the industries concentrated on the production of goods the majority could not afford. Thus, it led to a
new form of dependency: the necessity of exporting the
manufactured goods in order to operate the factories and to
maintain prosperity. At the same time Brazilian industry became more vulnerable to transnationals than ever before.
They dominated some key sectors of the economy and provided stiff competition for the Brazilian entrepreneurs,
frequently driving them into bankruptcy. By 1971, transna-
tional corporations accounted for 70 percent of total net
profits in five major sectors of the economy: rubber, automobiles, machinery, household appliances, and mining.
Further, profit remittances abroad outdistanced investments.
The ten largest foreign companies in Brazil invested $98.8
million but remitted $774.5 million abroad between 1965 and
1975. As one specific example during that decade, Anderson
Clayton, the huge international agrobusiness firm, invested
$1.6 million in Brazil but took out $16.8 million in profits and
dividends. *Business Week* advised its readers that the South
American giant offered what was probably the highest rate of
profits in the world. Brazil, in reality, provided capital for the
capitalist world rather than absorbed it.

Choking pollution was another price Brazilians paid for
industrialization. In 1975, the Itau Cement Plant owned by
Portland poured 108 tons of fine dust every day over the
town of Contagem, Minas Gerais, while in Salvador, the Ti-
biras factory daily pumped 500 cubic meters of residues containing sulphuric acid into the bay. Those residues killed the
fish near the shore and polluted the city's drinking water. A
new law exempted any plant from being shut down for pol-
luting if its production was "of high priority for national development and security," a convenient loophole for almost
all industries. Lack of enforcement of pollution controls
helped to lure foreign investors to Brazil.

Pollution was only one aspect of the danger to the Brazilian environment threatened by ill-conceived plans to promote quick growth. The danger seemed most acute in the Amazon where accelerating road building and more intensive use of the land for agriculture and lumbering were upsetting the delicate ecology. Roberto Burle Marx, Brazil's most internationally respected landscape architect, warned, "Immense areas are being destroyed for pasturage and colonization schemes. These areas are being transformed into deserts because there is no precise knowledge of what to plant and what is best for the soil." At the mid-1970s pace of deforestation, the Amazon rain forest, as we have known it, would disappear before the end of the century. In a thoughtful essay, *Time* magazine (May 22, 1978); pointed out how deforestation spelled disaster for a 300-square-mile region in the state of Espírito Santo, where the rain forest was felled for agriculture. Rivers once navigated by 5,000-ton ships became choked by sand bars. The dry hard soil resembled baked clay. Some 204 species of birds and 450 varieties of plants once native to the region disappeared and skin cancer disfigured the human beings who lived there. Wanton destruction of nature created havoc in the region, and fear existed that the same disregard for ecology in the Amazon foretold similar disasters in that vast center of South America.

While industrialization grew rapidly under the military, it embodied many weaknesses: a concentration on goods for the wealthy and middle class, a dependency on foreign investment, technology, and markets, a denationalization of Brazilian-owned industry, a low rate of labor absorption since it was capital intensive, ecological threats and pollution, and regressive income distribution. The accelerating industrialization process marked a shift from the traditional agro-extractive primary production, but it by no means served as an index either of real internal development or of reduced dependency.

The military governments neglected agriculture. That sector of the economy grew at rates averaging around 2.5 percent a year, somewhat less than the population growth, which fluctuated between 2.5 and 3 percent. Land concentration continued to characterize rural Brazil. As of late 1978, the concentration of land ownership in the hands of a few landowners was one of the highest in the world. Less than 2 percent of the landowners held half of the rural property. More graphically stated, 126 latifundia of more than 100,000 hectares each totaled more area than one million of the small farms. Table 8.1 indicates that more and more people depend on fewer and fewer farm workers to feed them, and there is a serious question of whether or not that declining number has the wherewithall or efficiency to fulfill its responsibility. Although Brazil ranked as the world's fifth largest exporter of agricultural products in 1978, nearly 60 percent of the population suffered from an insufficient diet. Any effort to reform the land structures through division and distribution of land came to a halt in the 1970s. In fact, the governments of the 1970s believed large estates should replace the small farms on the principle that size increased efficiency, a conclusion without factual basis. One Minister of Agriculture stated, "The solutions adopted for industry will also be good for agriculture." Such an idea did not bode well for the rural working class. The grossly inefficient and highly export-oriented agricultural system insured high food prices, forcing Brazilians to spend a disproportionate share of their income on food. They had little left over to buy the consumer items produced by a more efficient industrial sector. The Brazilian situation offered a thoughtful study of the problems raised by imposing industrialization on antiquated agrarian structures. The emphasis on the agrarian export sector, the increasing participation of multinationals in the exploitation of the countryside, and the further marginalization of the rural poor prompted another Minister of Agriculture,

Table 8.1. Brazil's Economically Active Population, 1950–1976 (in millions)

	Agricultural Workers	All Workers	Percent of Agricultural Workers in Working Population
1950	10.2	17.7	60
1960	12.3	22.7	54
1970	13.1	29.5	44
1976	14.6	40.2	36

Luís F. Cirne Lima, to resign in 1973 in protest against those trends. He complained that the exporters were "likely to be foreign" and the nation's prosperity "less and less Brazilian."

The economic record of the military governments was one of a rising GNP, particularly during the years 1969–1974, when growth rates averaged an impressive 10 percent a year. Pursuit of an ever higher GNP is never a search for social objectives but a blind chase of numbers which can be expanded to infinity without much social value resulting. Brazil, in fact, provided a perfect example of a rising GNP without much development or resultant social benefits. The Brazilian GNP recorded to a depressing degree the increasing affluence of the few, the overproduction of consumer luxuries, the growth of export agriculture at the expense of subsistence agriculture, and the handsome sums paid to foreign investors and creditors in the form of royalties, patent fees, interest rates, and profits.

The generals and their apologists spoke glowingly of an economic "miracle," an assessment based almost entirely on the high growth rates of the 1969–74 period. The more sober might question what was miraculous about the rich getting richer. While the *Wall Street Journal* waxed eloquently on its front page of April 11, 1972, about the economic "miracle," it had enough perception to follow that eulogy on April 21 with a more realistic front-page article headlined, "While Brazil Booms, Big Areas Stay Poor, Millions Barely Subsist." The essay noted, "The boom has had practically no impact at all on well over half the country's 95 million citizens. In fact, millions are actually poorer now than they were five years ago. . . . Most of the tangible results of this growth accrue to the affluent few." To its credit, the *Wall Street Journal* looked behind the government's glittering growth figures to discover that for most Brazilians the miracle was meaningless. As the *Los Angeles Times* pointed out in an editorial on July 21, 1974, "Despite Brazil's impressive growth rate, the gap between the rich and the poor is wider than ever." Indeed, Brazilian governmental officials already had reached a similar conclusion. When questioned about the state of the economy in 1972, President Médici candidly responded,

"The economy is going well, the people not so well." That same year Finance Minister Antônio Delfim Neto, the principal architect of the "miracle," agreed that the rich had become richer but rationalized that such a condition was normal in a "rapidly developing" nation. Carried to its conclusion, the minister's logic indicated then that what distinguished a "rapidly developing" nation from a more slowly growing one was the speed with which the rich became richer.

Grim statistics emerged to substantiate the growing iniquities. None of them revealed any benefits for the majority. As early as 1972, the U.S. economist Albert Fishlow observed, "Even now the real minimum wage, despite all intervening wage supplements, is not far different from what it was in the mid-1950s. Two decades of growth have gone for naught for the poorest segment of the population." Of the total gain in Brazillian income during the 1964–74 period, which included those years of greatest growth, the richest 10 percent of the population absorbed 75 percent, while the poorest 50 percent garnered less than 10 percent. Table 8.2 illustrates the declining share of the national income not only of the poorest 50 percent but also of the following 30 percent between 1960 and 1976. In other words, fully 80 percent of the population suffered an income decline. Compounding that iniquity was a regressive tax system which put the heaviest burden on the working class.

That class in the 1970s found it had to work harder just to maintain its precarious standard of living. A worker's real monthly wage in 1963 was worth 780 cruzeiros, compared with its 1975 level of 533. To purchase a monthly subsistence ration (meat, milk, beans, flour, potatoes, tomatoes, coffee,

Table 8.2. Share of National Income among Income Groups

Economically Active Population	Percentage of Participation in Income		
	1960	1970	1976
Poorest 50%	17.72	14.91	11.8
Following 30%	27.92	22.85	21.2
Following 15%	26.67	27.38	28.
Richest 5%	27.69	34.86	39.

Table 8.3. The Deterioration of the Minimum Wage

Year	Nominal Minimum Wage in Cruzeiros	Sum Required to Maintain the Purchasing Power of the 1959 Minimum Wage
1964	42.00	53.00
1968	129.00	254.00
1972	268.00	587.00
1974	376.80	1,162.25
1978	1,500.00	3,520.00

SOURCE: Comercio Exterior de México, 25, no. 3 (March 1979), p. 104.

sugar, bananas, and cooking oil), a worker in 1965 put in 87 hours and 20 minutes; in 1976, the same worker labored 182 hours and 11 minutes to purchase the same quantity of the same items. Food prices rose much faster than the official inflation rate, as indicated by this headline of the *Journal do Brasil* (May 14, 1976): "Food Prices Climbed 300 Percent in Rio in One Year." Table 8.3 further illustrates the decline of the purchasing power of the minimum wage. For the working masses, military governments meant a reduction in both their purchasing power (real wages) and the absence of state services.

Social maladjustments further pinched the poor. Sums spent on housing and education benefited the middle class more than the masses. The rate of infant mortality leaped upward. In 1961, 61 babies out of every 1,000 live births died in the privileged and progressive state of São Paulo; in 1975, the number of such deaths reached 95 per 1,000. Likewise, life expectancy shortened. The Brazilian Center of Demographic Studies reported a decline in life expectancy in the nation's industrial centers from 64.7 years in 1960 to 63.9 in 1970. The poor died young in Brazil so that the wealthy might live well and long. Life expectancy for the poor in the Northeast and the rich in the Southeast differed by twenty years. Nutritional standards were low even in the supposedly more affluent areas. A report dated 1973 on the "developed" city of São Paulo revealed that some 60 percent of the population did not get enough vitamins A, B, and C and had barely enough daily caloric intake to keep working. Little wonder then that people fell victim to plagues like that of meningococcal meningitis, which afflicted the greatest cities of the Southeast in the early 1970s. The government placed announcements in the leading newspapers of Rio de Janeiro and São Paulo advising the population that if they wanted to avoid catching meningitis they should eat more protein and avoid crowded places. Such advice could provide little comfort to the impoverished millions of slum dwellers in those populous cities. A link obviously existed between declining purchasing power of the workers' wages, the collapse of public services in the burgeoning cities, and the low governmental health expenditures and the increasing incidence of disease.

By the mid-1970s, the euphoria dissipated, the economic "miracle" was recognized for what it was: a short period of extraordinary growth which had benefited only a favored few at the expense not only of a majority of the Brazilians but in terms of ecological disaster and foreign exploitation at the expense of the entire nation. As the growth rate slowed to about 4.5 percent in 1977, blame was put on several important causes related to Brazil's dependency: the rising price of imported oil and declining prices for Brazilian raw materials on the world markets. A deteriorating trade balance troubled Brazil. Foreign debts rose spectacularly, exceeding $50 billion in 1980 and requiring as much as half of foreign earnings just to service. Certainly those increased expenditures and reduced incomes adversely affected the Brazilian economy, but the real causes for the economic problems lay in the lack of internal reforms which might lessen the blows constantly dealt by overdependency, a problem which historically bedeviled Brazil. As throughout the past, Brazil remained excessively vulnerable to world economic fluctuations. The English periodical Latin America (June 21, 1977;) concluded, "One fact which is not disputed by either the admirers or the critics of Brazilian economic management is that the country has become an integral part of the world trading community, more dependent or interdependent than it was before 1964." Whatever its record of material growth—and most agree it was exceedingly impressive—the economic '''miracle'' left an overwhelming negative legacy in the forms of increasing monopolistic tendencies, denationalization of the economy, mounting foreign debt, and a deepening dependency on foreign investments, expansion of foreign markets, and increasing exports. The inflation which had so preoccupied the military presidents persisted and in 1976, after a decline, climbed back to about 43 percent. Estimates for 1979 placed the figure at about 75 percent. The military and the technocrats had failed to control inflation. Ironically the rates by the mid-1970s surpassed those under the populist presidents Vargas and Kubitschek. A political record of brutality, repression, dictatorship, and violence accompanied the "miracle."

From the long range view, the military governments had frustrated the attempts to reform basic institutional structures, attempts which the populist governments of Vargas and Goulart—and to a lesser extent of Kubitschek—had made, however ineffectually. In so doing, the military strengthened those iniquitous institutions whose roots burrow deep in the colonial past. Under the military, Brazil offered a study in middle-class and elite reaction to the possibility of change. They benefited from growth but feared development which inevitably would necessitate structural and institutional changes. Brazilian history has amply demonstrated that those privileged groups do not welcome fundamental change and that they have been capable of employing apparently limitless violence to stem it. Feeling threatened by such changes, they demonstrated in 1964 and thereafter that it was possible to ally with the military to entrench themselves in power and enrich themselves at an increasing cost to the majority.

The foremost of Brazil's popular song composers, Chico Buarque de Holanda, had written a song in the early 1970s whose seemingly innocuous lyrics, "In spite of you, tomorrow will be another day," incurred the wrath of the military whose censors forbade the singing of it. That incident seemed to symbolize the military government's preference for yesterday—a partiality toward the conservative, oligarchical, and paternalistic patterns of the past—rather than their willingness to meet the challenge of change which tomorrow must inevitably bring. Changeless in an age seeking change, the military outlook counters the widespread desire for development characteristic of a majority of the Brazilian people. The people remain impoverished in a land of relative abundance, an enigma which challenges the future.

Appendices

Chiefs of State of Brazil

Name	From	To
FIRST EMPIRE		
Pedro I, Emperor of Brazil	9/7/1822	4/7/1831
SECOND EMPIRE		
José Joaquim Carneiro de Campos, Marquês de Caravelas Nicolau Pereira de Campos Verguerio General Francisco Lima e Silva	4/7/1831	6/17/1831
José da Costa Carvalho, Marquês de Monte Alegre João Braúlio Muniz Francisco Lima e Silva	6/17/1831	10/12/1835
Padre Diogo Antônio Feijó	10/12/1835	9/19/1937
Pedro de Araújo Lima, Marquês de Olinda	9/19/1837	7/23/1840
Pedro II, Emperor of Brazil	7/23/1840	11/15/1889
REPUBLIC OF BRAZIL		
Marechal Deodoro da Fonseca	11/15/1889	11/23/1891
Marechal Floriano Peixoto	11/23/1891	11/15/1894
Prudente José de Morais	11/15/1894	11/15/1898
Manuel Ferraz Campos Sales	11/15/1898	11/15/1902
Francisco de Paula Rodrigues Alves	11/15/1902	11/15/1906
Afonso Augusto Moreira Pena	11/15/1906	6/14/1909
Nilo Peçanha	6/14/1909	11/15/1910

Name	From	To
REPUBLIC OF BRAZIL (cont.)		
Marechal Hermes da Fonseca	11/15/1910	11/15/1914
Venceslau Brás Pereira Gomes	11/15/1914	11/15/1918
Delfim Moreira	11/15/1918	6/?/1919
Epitácio Pessôa	6/?/1919	11/15/1922
Artur da Silva Bernardes	11/15/1922	11/15/1926
Washington Luís Pereira de Sousa	11/15/1926	10/24/1930
Getúlio Vargas	11/3/1930	1/29/1945
José Linhares	10/29/1945	1/31/1946
Marechal Eurico Gaspar Dutra	1/31/1946	1/31/1951
Getúlio Vargas	1/31/1951	8/24/1954
João Café Filho	8/24/1954	11/8/1955
Carlos Luz	11/8/1955	11/11/1955
Nereu Ramos	11/11/1955	1/31/1956
Juscelino Kubitschek	1/31/1956	1/31/1961
Jânio da Silva Quadros	1/31/1961	8/25/1961
João Goulart	9/7/1961	3/31/1964
Ranieri Mazzili	4/2/1964	4/15/1964
Humberto Castelo Branco	4/15/1964	3/15/1967
Artur da Costa e Silva	3/15/1967	8/30/1969
Aurélio de Lyra Tavaros ⎫ Mácio de Souza e Mello ⎬ Augusto Rademaker ⎭	8/30/1969	10/7/1969
Emílio Garrastazú Medici	10/7/1969	3/15/1974
Ernesto Geisel	3/15/1974	3/15/1979
João Baptista Figueirdo	3/15/1979	

A Chronology of Significant Dates
in Brazilian History

COLONY

1494   Treaty of Tordesillas divided the world between Spain and Portugal.

1500   Pedro Alvares Cabral discovered Brazil.

1502   King Manuel licensed Lisbon merchants to export brazil-wood from the New World.

1530   Expedition of Martim Afonso de Sousa to colonize.

1532   Founding of São Vicente and Piratininga.
First sugar mills built.

1534–1536 King granted Brazil to twelve donees.

1538   First known shipment of slaves arrived from Africa.

1540–1542 Francisco de Orellana explored the Amazon.

1549   Centralized government instituted under Tomé de Sousa in Bahia. First Jesuits arrived.

1551   Creation of the bishopric of Brazil.

1555   The French established a colony in Guanabara Bay.

1565   Foundation of Rio de Janeiro.

1567   Mem de Sá expelled the French and occupied Guanabara Bay.

1580   The union of the Iberian crowns.

1599   Natal, Rio Grande do Norte founded.

1604   The India Council established to oversee the administration of the Portuguese empire. In 1642, the name is changed to Overseas Council.

(COLONY)

1612–1616 French invasions of the North.

1614–1616 Portuguese captured the North and expelled the French.

1616 Belém founded.

1621 Creation of the state of Maranhão.

1624–1625 The Dutch captured Salvador da Bahia.

1630 The Dutch seized Recife and began their conquest of the northeast.

1637–1639 Pedro Teixeira explored the Amazon and founded Tabatinga.

1640 Portugal declared its independence from Spain.

1654 Treaty of Taborda and the Dutch withdrawal from Brazil.

1680 Colônia do Sacremento founded to insure Portuguese access to the River Plate.

1695 Gold discovered in Minas Gerais.

1697 Luso-Brazilians destroyed Palmares, one of the largest fortified settlements of runaway black slaves.

1708–1709 War with the Emboabas pitted the Paulistas against those outsiders entering the interior to prospect for gold.

1709 The creation of the captaincies of São Paulo and Minas de Ouro.

1710–1711 War of the Mascates, clash between planter class of Olinda and merchant class of Recife, in which the latter emerged victorious.

1720 The governors-general of Brazil henceforth known as viceroys. Brief revolt in Minas Gerais against the governor.

1724 Foundation of the Brazilian Academy of the Forgotten, first of the European-type academies of the Enlightenment.

1727 Introduction of coffee into Brazil.

1750 Treaty of Madrid marked the abandonment of the Treaty of Tordesillas and the adoption of uti possidetis to settle boundaries.

Pombal began to rule in Portugal.

1759 Pombal expelled the Jesuits from the empire.

1761 Treaty of El Pardo annulled the Treaty of Madrid.

1763 The capital transferred from Salvador da Bahia to Rio de Janeiro.

1772 Extinction of the state of Maranhão.

1777 Treaty of San Ildefonso redrew the Portuguese-Spanish

(COLONY)

frontiers in South America, and confirmed Spain's possession of the Banda Oriental and Portugal's possession of the Amazon basin. Pombal dismissed.

1789 The *Inconfidência Mineira,* a conspiracy to establish a republic, exposed.

1792 Tiradentes, a leader in the Inconfidência, executed.

1798 The outbreak of the Bahian conspiracy, the "Revolt of the Tailors."

1808 The Braganzas arrived in Rio de Janeiro.

João VI opened the ports to world trade and lifted the restrictions on manufacturing.

The first printing press established.

1810 Treaties signed with Great Britain giving that nation commercial dominance over Brazil.

KINGDOM

1815 Brazil raised to the status of a kingdom.

1816 Luso-Brazilian troops occupied Uruguay. French artistic mission arrived in Rio.

1817 The republican revolution in Pernambuco failed.

Princess Leopoldina of Austria, future empress of Brazil, arrived in Rio de Janeiro.

1818 Land grants to Swiss and German settlers.

1819 At Bahia, first steamship put into operation.

1820 First organized colony of non-Portuguese immigrants established at Nova Friburgo, after their arrival in 1819.

1821 Uruguay annexed as the Cisplatine Province.

João VI returned to Lisbon.

EMPIRE

1822 Prince Pedro declared Brazil's independence and received the title of emperor.

1824 Pedro promulgated the first constitution.

The United States recognized Brazil.

1825 Great Britain and Portugal recognized Brazil.

War broke out between Argentina and Brazil over Uruguay.

1827 By treaty Great Britain consolidated its commercial predominance over Brazil.

Establishment of law schools at Olinda and São Paulo.

1828 Argentina and Brazil agreed to the creation of Uruguay

(EMPIRE)

as an independent nation, thus ending the war between the two Platine rivals.

1831   Pedro I abdicated. A three-man regency assumed control.

1834   Additional Act to the 1824 Constitution instituted federalism and a one-man regency.

1835   Outbreak of the Farroupilha Revolt in Rio Grande do Sul.

1840   Interpretive Law ended the experiment with federalism. Proclamation of the majority ended the regency. Pedro II ascended the throne.

1843   The first steamboat navigated the Amazon.

1844   Anglo-Brazilian Treaty of 1827 expired and was not renewed. Alves Branco Tariff raised duties.

1845   Caxias put down the Farroupilha Revolt.

1850   The Queiróz Law abolished the slave trade.

1851   The first regular steamship line to Europe inaugurated.

1852   Mauá founded the Amazon Steam Navigation Company. Brazil intervened in Argentina to help overthrow Rosas.

1854   Beginning of the railroad era.

1857   Publication of José de Alencar's novel *O Guaraní*.

1865   Argentina, Brazil, and Uruguay allied against Paraguay.

1867   Opening of the Amazon to international traffic.

1870   The Triple Alliance defeated Paraguay. The Republican party issued its manifesto.

1871   The Law of the Free Womb freed all children born to slave mothers.

1873   The number of Italian immigrants arriving began to surpass the number of Portuguese.

1874   Transatlantic cable went into service.

1873–1875 Conflict of Church and State over the privileges of regalism.

1885   The Saraiva-Cotegipe Law freed all slaves at the age of sixty.

1888   The Golden Law abolished slavery, without compensation for slaveholders.

1889   The emperor dethroned by the army and the republic established.

REPUBLIC

1890	Church and State separated.
1891	A new constitution promulgated.
1893	A naval revolt threatened the republic.
1894	The first civilian president took office.
1895	The Missions Territory award favorably settled Brazil's frontier with Argentina.
1897	Destruction of Canudos and the death of the religious mystic, Antônio Conselheiro.
1900	Amapá boundary dispute with French Guiana settled favorably for Brazil.
1902	Publication of *Rebellion in the Backlands* and *Canaan*.
1903	Treaty of Petropolis ceded Acre to Brazil.
1906	The Convention of Taubaté instituted valorization of coffee.
	The Third Pan-American Conference met in Rio de Janeiro.
1907	At Second Hague Peace Conference, Brazil participated in its first worldwide conference.
1910	Indian Protection Service established.
1917	Brazil declared war on Germany, and joined the Allied powers.
1920	Creation of the first university to replace scattered faculties.
1922	Modern Art Week initiated a new phase of introspection in national culture.
	Copacabana revolt; *tenente* movement began.
1924–1927	March of the Prestes Column through the backlands.
1930	Rebellion which brought Getúlio Vargas to power.
1932	Rebellion of São Paulo and civil war.
1937	Establishment of the *Estado Novo*.
1942	Brazil declared war on the Axis powers.
1944	An expeditionary force sent to Europe.
1945	The military deposed Vargas.
1946	A new constitution promulgated.
1950	Vargas reelected president.
1954	Vargas committed suicide.
1960	The capital moved inland to Brasília.
1961	The election and resignation of Jânio Quadros.
	The establishment of a parliamentary system.
1963	Parliamentary system extinguished by national plebiscite.

(REPUBLIC)

1964 The military deposed João Goulart. A purged Congress elected Humberto Castelo Branco president. First Institutional Act.

1965 The legal guidelines for political parties renovated by the Second Institutional Act.

1967 A new constitution promulgated. General Artur da Costa e Silva inaugurated president.

1968 A military coup gave Costa e Silva dictatorial power. Fifth Institutional Act.

1969 U.S. Ambassador to Brazil Charles Burke Elbrick kidnapped, freed after government acceded to urban guerrillas' demands.

President Costa e Silva incapacitated by stroke. Military junta took power, bypassing civilian vice-president. Death penalty restored for acts of violence and subversion.

General Médici named as president by military junta, new constitution promulgated.

1974 General Ernesto Geisel named president.

Economic growth falters and decline begins.

1978 Agitation mounts for return to civilian and democratic government.

1979 General João Baptista Figueiredo named president. Political amnesty promulgated.

A Glossary of Portuguese Words
Used in the Text

Aldeia: a village. It frequently refers to the Indian settlements administered by the religious orders in the colonial period.

Amerindian: an American Indian.

Bandeira: an armed expedition in the colonial period that penetrated the interior to explore, to capture Indian slaves, or to search for gold. The dispatch of these expeditions from the coastal settlements and particularly from São Paulo was a chief characteristic of colonial activity from 1650 to 1750.

Branco: a white person, phenotypically Caucasoid.

Bolas: a kind of missile weapon consisting of balls of stone attached to the end of a thong or rope, used by Gauchos for hurling at and entangling an animal.

Caatinga: the stunted spare forest found in the drought areas of northeastern Brazil.

Caboclo: either an Indian who has been Europeanized, or a Brazilian of Caucasian and Indian parentage.

Candomblé: a Brazilian folk religion of predominantly African influence.

Cangaceiro: a bandit or outlaw of the *sertão.*

Capitão-mor (plural, *capitães-mor*): a military rank formerly given to commanders of the local militia.

Carioca: native of or pertaining to the city of Rio de Janeiro.

Casa grande: the large plantation house, residence of the rural aristocracy.

Caudilho: a strong leader, often referring to a party or government chief who exercises complete authority over his subordinates.

Colégio: a three-year preparatory course of secondary school; the second phase of a seven-year high school education.

Conto: a unit of money equal to one thousand cruzeiros, written thus: Cr$1.000.00. Prior to 1942, it equaled one thousand *mil-reis.*

Coronel (plural, *coroneis*): a civilian political boss of a municipality. The system of political control founded on the political bosses came to be known as *coronelismo.*

Correição: an official inquiry into the conduct of a public employee.

Côrtes: Portuguese parliament.

Cruzeiro: the Brazilian monetary unit which replaced the mil-reis on November 1, 1942.

Degredados: criminals exiled to serve out their sentence. Frequently the term refers to those minor Portuguese criminals sent to Brazil in the sixteenth century as their punishment.

Devassa: an inspection or inquiry into the conduct of a public official.

Distensão: a term used after 1974 to signify gradual relaxation of authoritarian rule and a restoration of civilian constitutional government.

Emboada: a pejorative term used by a native of an area to refer to an outsider. In eighteenth-century Minas Gerais, the local inhabitants used this term for the adventurers who came from Portugal or the coast in search of gold and diamonds.

Encilhamento: from the verb meaning "to saddle," this is the term used to designate a period of frantic financial speculation during the early 1890s.

Entrada: a penetration by a band of explorers from the coast into the hinterlands.

Favelas: city slums, a term used most frequently in Rio de Janeiro.

Fazenda: a plantation, ranch, or farm.

Fazendeiro: the owner of a *fazenda;* a planter, farmer, or rancher on a large scale.

Gaúcho: a native of Rio Grande do Sul, but literally a cowboy of the southern plains.

Homens bons: literally the "good men," those who belonged to the upper echelon of Brazilian colonial society. Their prestige, power, and position permitted them to vote for members of the town council.

Inconfidência: a conspiracy among the Brazilians for independence. Often it is used to refer to the *Inconfidência Mineira,* the plot in Minas Gerais in 1789 to declare Brazil's independence from Portugal.

Irmandades: a lay religious order or brotherhood.

Lasso: a rope or long thong of leather with a running noose, used for catching horses or cattle.

Lavrador: a small landholder.

League: any of various units of distance from about 2.4 to 4.6 statute miles.

Linha dura: meaning "hard line," it refers to a small group of right-wing military officers who believe the military must rule to "purify" the nation.

Macumba: a Brazilian folk religion of predominantly African influence.

Mameluco: the offspring of Caucasian and Indian parents.

Maranhense: an inhabitant of Maranhão.

Mascate: literally, "peddler of wares"; the term was used, sometimes pejoratively, in the eighteenth century to refer to the incipient merchant class.

Massapê: a fertile, clayey soil very suitable for sugar-cane growing found in northeastern Brazil.

Mazombo: a Brazilian born in the New World of Caucasian, European parents.

Mestizo or *Mestiço:* a person of mixed parentage. If the person has mixed European-Indian lineage he is a *caboclo;* if he has European-African parents he is a *mulatto.*

Mineiro: an inhabitant of the state of Minas Gerais.

Mulatto: a person of mixed Caucasian and Negroid parentage.

Município: an administrative division including a town and its surroundings. It corresponds roughly to a county.

Ouvidor-mor: the office of chief justice in the governments of colonial Brazil.

Pardo: a brown person, a general catch-all color designation.

Paulista: an inhabitant of or referring to the state of São Paulo.

Poder moderador: the fourth branch of government provided by the Constitution of 1824. It empowered the emperor to oversee the three traditional branches and to balance them. After the fall of the monarchy, the military took upon itself the extralegal responsibility to exercise that power.

Prêto: a black person with physical characteristics of the African Negro.

Procuradores dos mestros: representatives of tradesmen found on a few of the city councils in colonial Brazil.

Provedor-mor: the office of treasurer in the governments of colonial Brazil.

Quilombo: a colony of runaway slaves; such colonies existed in the Brazilian interior until 1888, when slavery was abolished.

Rancho: a rude hut where herdsmen or travelers may find rest or shelter.

Reinol (plural, *reinóis*): a Portuguese born in the Old World who resided temporarily or permanently in Brazil during the colonial period. The term can be contrasted with *mazombo.*

Relação: a high court in Portugal or in colonial Brazil.

Residência: a formal inquiry into the conduct of a public official at the end of his term of office.

Riograndense: an inhabitant of or referring to the state of Rio Grande do Sul.

Senado da Câmara: the municipal government, in particular the town council.

Senhor de engenho: the owner of a sugar mill and often by extension a plantation owner.

Senhor de terras: the large landowner.

Senzala: plantation slave quarters.

Seringueiro: a rubber gatherer.

Sertanejo: one who lives in the *sertão,* a frontiersman.

Sertanista: a person who knows the *sertão* well. Often in the North sertanistas employed that knowledge for purposes of trade and commerce.

Sertão: the interior, backlands, or hinterlands of Brazil. The term refers particularly to the hinterland region of northeastern Brazil.

Sesmaria: a land grant in Portugal and colonial Brazil.

Tenente: an army lieutenant.

Tenentismo: a reform movement among junior army officers which began in the early 1920s and played a significant role in bringing Vargas to power.

Tropas de resgate: men who hunted and captured Indians in the interior to use or sell as salves.

Tropeiro: a driver of pack animals. Often he was a wandering merchant carrying his goods throughout Brazil on muleback.

Vaqueiro: a cowboy; this term is used most frequently in the Northeast.

Visitação: an official inquiry into the conduct of a public employee.

Xango: a Brazilian folk religion of predominantly African influence.

Suggestions for

Additional Reading

This brief bibliographical essay will introduce those who want to read further in Brazilian history to other books in English. There exists, of course, a rich bibliography of books in Portuguese as well as a vast array of essays and articles in various languages. The last paragraph of this essay will suggest some guides to the periodical and Portuguese-language historical literature.

There are three general introductions to Brazil: *Brazil: The Land and the People* (New York, 1968) by Rollie E. Poppino, *An Introduction to Brazil*, 2nd ed. (New York, 1971) by Charles Wagley, and *Brazil: From Colony to World Power* (New York, 1973) by Donald E. Worcester. The first emphasizes the social and economic evolution of Brazil. The second is a perceptive socio-anthropological interpretation of the country. One of Professor Wagley's principal aims is to show why a nation as diversified as Brazil remains unified. The third offers a political and chronological sweep through the Brazilian past. A personal and informal approach, with considerable attention to geography, was taken by William L. Shurz in his *Brazil: The Infinite Country* (New York, 1961).

Of extreme importance are the interpretations the Brazilians have made of themselves. *New World in the Tropics* (New York, 1959) by Gilberto Freyre offers a series of introspective essays, as does *The Gilberto Freyre Reader* (New York, 1974). José Honório Rodrigues presents a challenging and nationalistic view in his *The*

Brazilians: Their Character and Aspirations (Austin, 1967). Manuel de Oliveira Lima makes a unique contribution in his *The Evolution of Brazil Compared with that of Spanish and Anglo-Saxon America*, 2nd ed. (New York, 1966), interpreting Brazil by comparing and contrasting its evolution with that of Spanish American republics and the United States. Another comparative study of the United States and Brazil was undertaken by Vianna Moog, *Bandeirantes and Pioneers* (New York, 1964). Disturbed by the unequal growth of the two huge nations, Vianna Moog sets out to answer the question of why the younger United States has outstripped the older Brazil. Motives for settlement, the psychological background of the settlers, and geography contribute to a partial explanation of the differences. More than half of the book studies Brazilian and American national character. The only history of Brazil translated into English is João Pandiá Calógeras' *A History of Brazil*, 2nd ed. (New York, 1963). He emphasizes primarily the colonial period and secondarily the Empire, saying very little about the twentieth century.

To follow the course of Brazilian history through its documents, official and unofficial, from 1494 to 1964 is the object of *A Documentary History of Brazil* (New York, 1966), edited by E. Bradford Burns. Richard Graham has gathered twenty-four informative selections from the works of several international scholars, but principally Brazilians, to present varying views of some major issues and problems in *A Century of Brazilian History Since 1865* (New York, 1969). The lengthy, fact-laden *U.S. Army Handbook for Brazil* (Washington, 1964) encompasses a wealth of information on the widest variety of topics. It concentrates, however, on contemporary Brazil.

There are in English a number of period histories which taken together provide a full perspective of Brazilian history. In *The Colonial Background of Modern Brazil*, the eminent economic historian Caio Prado describes, analyzes, and interprets Brazil's colonial past. Bailey W. Diffie covers the same era with excellent interpretation and style in his *Latin-American Civilization: The Colonial Period*, 2nd ed. (New York, 1967). A series of specialized essays which give depth and flavor to the long colonial past appears in Dauril Alden (ed.), *Colonial Roots of Modern Brazil* (Berkeley and Los Angeles, 1973). Alexander Marchant covers the early years of discovery, settlement, and confrontation between Europeans and Indians in *From Barter to Slavery: The Economic Relations of Portuguese and Indians in the Settlement of Brazil, 1500–1580*, 2nd ed. (Gloucester, Mass., 1966). John Hemmings deals admirably with

Portuguese-Indian relations over a longer period of time in *Red Gold: The Conquest of the Brazilian Indians, 1500–1760* (Cambridge, Mass., 1977). C. R. Boxer has contributed much of consistently high quality to an understanding of the colonial past. *Salvador de Sá and the Struggle for Brazil and Angola, 1602–1686* (London, 1952) depicts seventeenth-century Brazil as the principal theater of action for one of the most remarkable Portuguese figures of the century. *The Dutch in Brazil, 1624–1654* (Oxford, 1957) treats in detail the foremost threat to Portugal's empire in America. *The Golden Age of Brazil, 1695–1750* (Berkeley and Los Angeles, 1962) discussed the colony during its heady gold-rush days. Finally, *Some Literary Sources for the History of Brazil in the Eighteenth Century* (Oxford, 1967) provides valuable historiographical and intellectual insights into the last colonial century of Brazil. Stuart B. Schwartz offers a fascinating study of the social backgrounds of judges and their activities and interactions within the Portuguese colonial bureaucracy in *Sovereignty and Society in Colonial Brazil: the High Court of Bahia and Its Judges, 1609–1751* (Berkeley and Los Angeles, 1973). Dauril Alden takes a close look at military, economic, and political affairs in eighteenth-century Brazil in *Royal Government in Colonial Brazil with Special Reference to the Administration of the Marquis of Lavradio, Viceroy, 1769–1779* (Berkeley and Los Angeles, 1968). In *Fidalgos and Philanthropists, the Santa Casa da Misericórdia of Bahia, 1550–1775* (Berkeley and Los Angeles, 1969), A.J.R. Russell-Wood reveals how economic power shifted from a rural, patriarchal, religious, and conservative sugar plantation aristocracy to an urban, secular, and speculative mercantile class. A study of the adventurous explorers of the hinterlands of Brazil as well as a number of important documents from the period of their greatest activity can be found in Richard M. Morse's *The Bandeirantes: The Historical Role of the Brazilian Pathfinders* (New York, 1965). The expansion into and settlement of Rio Grande do Sul is the theme of Moysés Vellinho, *Brazil South: Its Conquest and Settlement* (New York, 1968). Probably still the most widely known interpretation of the colonial period—the fusion and contributions of three races to create a unique Brazilian civilization—appears in Gilberto Freyre's *The Masters and the Slaves,* first published in English in 1946 and slightly abridged in a paperback edition in 1964.

The period of transition from a colony to an independent empire receives excellent coverage in two fine books. In his *Conflicts and Conspiracies: Brazil and Portugal, 1750–1808* (Cambridge, England, 1973), Kenneth R. Maxwell studies the shifting relationship between the mother country and its major colony. A.J.R. Russell-Wood has edited a most useful collection of essays on the causes of and transition to independence, *From Colony to Nation: Essays on the Independence of Brazil* (Baltimore, 1975).

A short, incisive history of the imperial period, *Empire in Brazil* (Cambridge, Mass., 1958) by C. H. Haring, concentrates on political affairs. Bertita Harding provides a more personal approach in her popular biography of the Braganzas in Brazil, *Amazon Throne* (Indianapolis, 1941). The two emperors have been the subjects of individual biographies. Sérgio Correa da Costa brings Pedro I to life in *Every Inch a King* (New York, 1953). *Dom Pedro the Magnanimous* (Chapel Hill, 1937) by M. W. Williams does the same for the second emperor, who has been the subject of a more recent biographical study by Harry Bernstein, *Dom Pedro II* (New York, 1973).

The controversial process of modernization moved ahead during the Second Empire and has attracted the attention of a number of scholars. A conventional discussion of the slippery concept of modernization appears in Joseph A. Kahl, *The Measurement of Modernism: A Study of Values in Brazil and Mexico* (Austin, 1968). Gilberto Freyre traces the decline of the sugar patriarchate, the rise to power of the coffee bourgeoisie, and urban growth in his interpretive *The Mansions and the Shanties* (New York, 1963). Richard Graham carefully documents the influence of Great Britain on a changing Brazil in *Britain and the Onset of Modernization in Brazil, 1850–1914* (Cambridge, England, 1968). Further English influence over the course of events as well as the English economic dominance over nineteenth-century Brazil are ably discussed by Alan K. Manchester in *British Preeminence in Brazil: Its Rise and Decline* (Chapel Hill, 1933). The biography, *Viscount Mauá and the Empire of Brazil* (Berkeley and Los Angeles, 1965) by Anyda Marchant, relates the activities of the most important figure in the economic growth of Brazil during the nineteenth century. Stanley J. Stein has written authoritatively on two important aspects of the economy: *The Brazilian Cotton Manufacture: Textile Enterprise in an Underdeveloped Area, 1850–1950* (Cambridge, Mass., 1957) and *Vassouras, a Brazilian Coffee Country, 1850–1900* (Cambridge, Mass., 1957). The latter is a classic study of the plantation economy. Peter L. Eisenberg treats a special aspect of the complex modernization process in *The Sugar Industry in Pernambuco: Modernization without Change, 1840–1910* (Berkeley and Los Angeles, 1974). Two crises beset that industry: sugar beet competition and the abolition of slavery. Some modernization attempted to meet the crises; the effort seemed to preserve many traditional socio-economic structures as well as cause a deterioration of the quality of life of the majority. Warren Dean details the history of a São Paulo município, *Rio Claro: A Brazilian Plantation System, 1820–1920* (Stanford, 1976), which demonstrates the effects of the rapid incorporation of land into the export economy. The rural poor did protest their deteriorating lot as evidenced in some of the essays published in Ronald H. Chilcote (ed.), *Protest and Resistance in Angola and Brazil* (Berkeley and Los Angeles, 1972).

Increasingly more has been written on the subject of the emancipation of the black slaves. The long process is well covered in three books: Leslie Bethell, *The Abolition of the Brazilian Slave Trade: Britain, Brazil, and the Slave Trade Question, 1807–1869* (Cambridge, England; 1970); Robert Conrad, *The Destruction of Brazilian Slavery, 1850–1888* (Berkeley and Los Angeles, 1973); and Robert Brent Toplin, *The Abolition of Slavery in Brazil* (New York, 1972). The 1883 classic abolitionist statement by Joaquim Nabuco has been translated into English, *Abolitionism: The Brazilian Antislavery Struggle* (Urbana, 1977).

Three books explore the two events in which the military played a key role in the last half of the nineteenth century. For a background to the war with Paraguay, a struggle which shook the empire, Pelham H. Box's solid study, *The Origins of the Paraguayan War* (Urbana, 1929) is recommended. Charles J. Kolinski studies that war from the Paraguayan perspective in his readable *Independence or Death!* (Gainesville, 1965). Charles Willis Simons stresses the role of the military in the overthrow of the Second Empire in his *Marshal Deodoro and the Fall of Dom Pedro II* (Durham, 1966).

Many of the bevy of foreign travelers to Brazil in the nineteenth century left engaging accounts of what they saw. That rich literature provides a valuable perspective on Brazil. One useful guide to the travel books is by Bernard Naylor, *Accounts of Nineteenth-Century South America: An Annotated Checklist of Works by British and United States Observers* (London, 1969). Some of the most informative and well-written accounts are: Henry Koster, *Travels in Brazil* (London, 1816); John Luccock, *Notes on Rio de Janeiro and the Southern Parts of Brazil Taken During a Residence of Ten Years in That Country from 1808 to 1818* (London, 1820); Maria Graham, *Journal of a Voyage to Brazil and Residence There During Part of the Years 1821, 1822, 1823* (London, 1824); R. Walsh, *Notices of Brazil in 1828 and 1829* (Boston, 1831); Daniel P. Kidder,

Sketches of Residence and Travels in Brazil (London, 1845); James C. Fletcher and Daniel P. Kidder, *Brazil and the Brazilians* (Philadelphia, 1857); and Herbert H. Smith, *Brazil, the Amazons and the Coast* (London, 1880).

For the republican period, the standard history is *A History of the Republic, 1889–1964* (Stanford, 1966) by José Maria Bello. Rollie E. Poppino brought it up to date. The emphasis is on the years 1889–1930, but an unfortunate style and organization make this insightful book difficult both to read and to digest. Gilberto Freyre synthesizes the early years well in *Order and Progress: Brazil from Monarchy to Republic* (New York, 1970). In *Brazil: A Political Analysis* (Boulder, Colo., 1978), Peter Flynn gives a political overview from 1889 to 1977.

The political aspects of the Old Republic are treated in a variety of monographs. June E. Hahner provides insight into the early years in her *Civilian-Military Relations in Brazil, 1889–1898* (Columbia, S.C., 1969). Four excellent works provide splendid perspectives of the regional politics, which were, after all, the dynamic of the period: Joseph L. Love, *Rio Grande do Sul and Brazilian Regionalism: 1882–1930* (Stanford, 1971); John D. Wirth, *Minas Gerais in the Brazilian Federation 1889–1937* (Stanford, 1977); and Robert M. Levine, *Pernambuco in the Brazilian Federation, 1889–1937* (Stanford, 1978); and Eul-Soo Pang, *Bahia in the First Republic: Coronelism and Oligarchies, 1889–1934* (Gainesville, 1979). Growing discontent with the Old Republic provides the backdrop for John W. F. Dulles, *Anarchists and Communists in Brazil: 1900–1935* (Austin, 1973) and Neill Macaulay, *The Prestes Column: Revolution in Brazil* (New York, 1974). The first treats labor unrest and the second dissatisfaction among young military officers. The clash between the interior and the coast attracted the attention of Euclides da Cunha. He produced a classic of Brazilian literature when he published *Os Sertões* in 1902, an account of the siege of the followers of the mystic Antônio Conselheiro at Canudos. Samuel Putnam translated it brilliantly into English as *Rebellion in the Backlands* (Chicago, 1944). Ralph Della Cava has written an outstanding study of similar phenomena in the backlands. His *Miracle at Joaseiro* (New York, 1970) looks at Padre Cícero and places him within the context of the Old Republic, the Northeast, and messianic movements.

Coffee was the real ruler of the Old Republic. Thomas H. Holloway studies the dominance of coffee and the consequences in his *The Brazilian Valorization of 1906: Regional Politics and Economic Dependence* (Madison, 1975).

The diplomatic maneuvering and triumphs of the early decades of the Old Republic are recounted in E. Bradford Burns, *The Unwritten Alliance: Rio-Branco and Brazilian-American Relations* (New York, 1966). Richard Collier surveys the new importance of the Amazon region in *The River that God Forgot: The Story of the Amazon Rubber Boom* (London, 1966). In his *The Industrialization of São Paulo* (Austin, 1969), Warren Dean shows, among other things, how coffee income gave impetus to industrialization. Billy Jaynes Chandler explores the importance of families, the process of political control through manipulation, and police control in a backland region of Ceará in *The Feitosas and the Sertão do Inhamuns: the History of a Family and a Community in Northeast Brazil, 1700–1930* (Gainesville, 1972). A unique and needed insight into Brazilian science comes from the pen of Nancy Stepan, *Beginnings of Brazilian Science: Oswaldo Cruz, Medical Research and Policy, 1890–1920* (New York, 1976). Elizabeth Bishop has translated and edited *The Diary of "Helena Morley"* (New York, 1977), the diary kept by a young girl in a provincial town of Minas Gerais, 1893–1895.

An able political history of the years from the rise to power of Getúlio Vargas to the overthrow of João Goulart can be found in Thomas E. Skidmore, *Politics in Brazil, 1930–1964* (New York, 1967). In *The Brazilian Revolution of 1930 and the Aftermath* (New Brunswick, N.J., 1967), Jordan M. Young focuses attention on the demise of the Old Republic and the beginning of the Vargas period. John W. F. Dulles has written a lengthy biography of the Gaúcho politician entitled *Vargas of Brazil* (Austin, 1967). The illustrations are magnificent. Another political biography *Getúlio Vargas of Brazil, 1883–1954: Sphinx of the Pampas* (London, 1974) comes from Richard Bourne. It provides considerable information on the social and military background of the period. Robert M. Levine delves into what he considers to be the pivotal period in *The Vargas Regime: The Critical Years, 1934–1938* (New York, 1970), while John D. Wirth examines trade, steel, and petroleum in *The Politics of Brazilian Development, 1930–1954* (Stanford, 1970). For the diplomatic history of those years, there exist two informative monographs: Stanley E. Hilton, *Brazil and the Great Powers, 1930–1939: The Politics of Trade Rivalry* (Austin, 1975); Frank D. McCann, Jr., *The Brazilian-American Alliance, 1937–1945* (Princeton, 1973). A study of the major role played by a dynamic state in national politics is Carlos E. Cortés's *Gaúcho Politics in Brazil: The Politics of Rio Grande do Sul, 1930–1964* (Albuquerque, 1974). Banditry, a significant theme in Brazilian history, receives its only book-length treatment in English by Billy Jaynes Chandler, *The Bandit King: Lampião of Brazil* (College Station, Texas, 1978).

Historians have treated the period from 1945 to 1964 in two ways: the first years often fall into studies of Vargas, while the later years serve as a prelude to the 1964 military coup. There has been little treatment of it as a cohesive political period. Surprisingly there is no full-length or exclusive study of Juscelino Kubitschek. John W. F. Dulles provides a most useful and detailed chronology of events in his *Unrest in Brazil: Political-Military Crises, 1955–1964* (Austin, 1970), a virtual encyclopedia for those years and most helpful as a reference and resource tool. For the Goulart years, Irving L. Horowitz paints, with the help of many fully translated documents, an arresting picture in *Revolution in Brazil* (New York, 1964).

Questions of economic growth and development came to the fore after 1930 and account for the increasing number of economic studies. A valuable survey is Celso Furtado's *The Economic Growth of Brazil: A Survey from Colonial to Modern Times* (Berkeley and Los Angeles, 1963). John Dickenson provides a general overview in *Brazil: An Industrial Geography* (Boulder, Colo., 1978). Werner Baer concentrates on industrialization after World War II in *Industrialization and Economic Development of Brazil* (New Haven, 1965). Interested in the same period but from a different point of view is Robert T. Daland, who examines the nature and effectiveness of national planning in *Brazilian Planning: Development Politics and Administration* (Chapel Hill, 1967). Developmental nationalism is one of the key themes in E. Bradford Burns, *Nationalism in Brazil: A Historical Survey* (New York, 1968). Donald Edmund Rady provides a history of the principal steel complex from it construction in the early 1940s until the early 1960s, *Volta Redonda: A Steel Mill Comes to a Brazilian Coffee Plantation. Industrial Entrepreneurship in a Developing Economy* (Albuquerque, 1973). Werner Baer also offers a study of that vital industry, *The Development of the Brazilian Steel Industry* (Nashville, 1969). Luella Dambaugh describes the continuing westward march of coffee in a short monograph, *The Coffee Frontier in Brazil* (Gainesville, 1959).

Events surrounding and following the military coup d'état on March 31, 1964, have attracted considerable attention. The Brazilian

sociologist Octávio Ianni attempts to explain the economic and po-
litical causes of the coup in *Crisis in Brazil* (New York, 1970). John
W. F. Dulles has written a lengthy biography of the first military
president, *Castello Branco: The Making of a President* (Austin,
1978). *The Political System of Brazil: Emergence of a "Modernizing"
Authoritarian Regime, 1964–1970* (New York, 1971) by Ronald M.
Schneider investigates the programs of presidents Goulart, Castelo
Branco, and Costa e Silva. Under the editorship of Riordan Roett,
Brazil in the Sixties (Nashville, 1972) includes a wide variety of
thoughtful essays on politics, economics, society, and literature.
Despite the late seventies imprint date of Jean Claude Garcia-
Zamor (ed.), *Politics and Administration in Brazil* (Washington,
D.C., 1978), most of the essays by U.S. and Brazilian scholars date
from the sixties. They serve as an introduction to Brazilian politics
and administration. The editor, by the way, has included his own
informative essay on the social mobility of blacks. A meaty but difficult collection of essays analyzing Brazil after the coup will be
found in Alfred Stephan (ed.), *Authoritarian Brazil: Origins, Policies, and Future* (New Haven, 1973). For an optimistic assessment
of nearly a decade of military rule, consult Georges-André Fiechter,
Brazil since 1964: Modernization under a Military Regime (New
York, 1975). Another appraisal of the military governments emerges
from *Brazil: Politics in a Patrimonial Society* (New York, 1978) by
Riordan Roett. Ronald H. Chilcote looks at the history of a significant political force in his *The Brazilian Communist Party: Conflict
and Integration, 1922–1972* (New York, 1974). The military's relationship with labor constitutes one theme in Kenneth Paul Erick-
son's *The Brazilian Corporative State and Working Class Politics*
(Berkeley and Los Angeles, 1977).

Several Brazilians opposed to the military regimes have written
strong denunciations translated into English: João Quartim, *Dictatorship and Armed Struggle in Brazil* (New York, 1971); Miguel Ar-
raes, *Brazil: The People and the Power* (Baltimore, 1972); and
Márcio Moreira Alves, *A Grain of Mustard Seed: The Awakening of
the Brazilian Revolution* (Garden City, 1973). The theoretician of
the urban guerrilla movement in the 1960s, Carlos Marighela, ex-
pounds his ideas in *For the Liberation of Brazil* (Baltimore, 1971).
The role of the United States in the events in Brazil receives a critical examination by Jan Knippers Black, *United States Penetration of
Brazil* (Philadelphia, 1977). Ronald M. Schneider gives us insight
into the military's world view in *Brazil: Foreign Relations of a Future
World Power* (Boulder, Colo., 1977).

Not surprisingly the military has been the subject of several monographic studies. Alfred C. Stepan III analyzes the behavior of the military during the Goulart government as well during the 1964–1968 period in *The Military in Politics: Changing Patterns in Brazil* (Princeton, 1971). Luigi R. Einaudi and Alfred C. Stepan III make a thoughtful comparison and contrast between the Brazilian and Peruvian military governments whose goals seem similar but whose means have differed, *Latin American Institutional Development: Changing Military Perspectives in Peru and Brazil* (Santa Monica, Calif., 1971).

Since the military's record and reputation rest heavily on the nation's economic performance, there has been considerable emphasis on studying the economic well-being of Brazil since 1964—or the lack of it. Howard S. Ellis has edited a series of twelve essays, *The Economy of Brazil* (Berkeley and Los Angeles, 1969), on industrialization, the steel industry, agriculture, inflation, capital markets, imports, economic planning and policy making, and agriculture, covering the time span from the end of World War II through the Castelo Branco government. These essays become a bit technical for the general reader. A particularly optimistic view emerges from Stefan H. Robock's *Brazil: A Study in Development Progress* (Lexington, Mass., 1975). The government's policies concerning land reform and exports are the subjects of Marta Cehelsky, *Land Reform in Brazil: The Management of Social Change* (Boulder, Colo., 1979) and José Augusto Arantes Savasini, *Export Promotion: the Case of Brazil* (New York, 1978). Martin T. Katzman reviews the policies for controlling frontier settlement, regional integration, and urbanization in *Cities and Frontiers in Brazil: Regional Dimensions of Economic Development* (Cambridge, Mass., 1977). The critical question of oil is the concern of *Oil and Politics in Modern Brazil* (Toronto, 1976) by Peter Seaborn Smith. Essays in *Man in the Amazon* (Gainesville, 1974), edited by Charles Wagley, range in an exemplary interdisciplinary fashion over the past, present, and future of that huge region. Dennis J. Mahar provides detail and overview for the complex problems of the still relatively unknown Amazon in *Frontier Development Policy in Brazil: A Study of the Amazon Experience* (New York, 1979). The ecological impact of economic growth in the Amazon seems to predict disaster for the sensitively balanced region, and its effects on the Indian population can only be termed genocide: these are the conclusions of Shelton H. Davis in his *Victims of the Miracle: Development and the Indians of Brazil* (Cambridge, England, 1977). Lucien

Bodard corroborates those conclusions in *Green Hell: Massacre of the Brazilian Indians* (New York, 1971). A final look at the interior before its sacrifice to growth appears in the pages of *Mato Grosso: Last Virgin Land* (New York, 1971) by Anthony Smith.

Indeed, the government's growth policies affect adversely the majority of the population. In his geographical analysis, *The Changing Face of Northeast Brazil* (New York, 1974), Kempton E. Webb emphasizes the lack of development in the huge Northeast. From the series of books listed below the reader readily understands the burdens borne by most Brazilians so that a few can prosper under the highly restrictive institutional structures: Josué de Castro, *Death in the Northeast: Poverty and Revolution in the Northeast of Brazil* (New York, 1969); Paul Gallet, *Freedom to Starve* (Baltimore, 1972); Robert W. Shirley, *The End of a Tradition: Culture Change and Development in the Munícipio of Cunha, São Paulo, Brazil* (New York, 1971); Allen W. Johnson, *Sharecroppers of the Sertão: Economics and Dependence on a Brazilian Plantation* (Stanford, 1971); and Shepard Forman, *The Brazilian Peasantry* (New York, 1975). Anthony Hall carefully points out in *Drought and Irrigation in Northeast Brazil* (New York, 1979) that irrigation has not solved the problem of poverty which originates from socio-economic institutions rather than the climate.

Three books deal with differing aspects of Brazil's international relations: Wayne A. Selcher, *Brazil's Multilateral Relations: Between First and Third Worlds* (Boulder, Colo., 1978); Michael A. Morris, *International Politics and the Sea: The Case of Brazil* (Boulder, Colo., 1979); and Riordan Roett (ed.), *Brazil in the Seventies* (Washington, D. C., 1976), four essays on international aspects of Brazil's recent development.

The changing role of the Roman Catholic Church in the 1960s is the subject of three books: José de Broucker, *Dom Helder Camara: The Violence of a Peacemaker* (Maryknoll, N. Y., 1970); Charles Antoine, *Church and Power in Brazil* (Maryknoll, N. Y., 1973); and Thomas C. Bruneau, *The Political Transformation of the Brazilian Catholic Church* (London, 1974). A much needed introduction to popular religions is provided by Seth and Ruth Leacock in their *Spirit of the Deep: Drums, Mediums, and Trance in a Brazilian City. A Study of an Afro-Brazilian Cult* (Garden City, 1972). Their research centered on Belém. Finally a work by one of the pioneers of the study of the Afro-Brazilian religions, the perceptive Roger Bastide, has been rendered into English: *The African Religions of Brazil: Toward a Sociology of the Interpretation of Civili-*

zations (Baltimore, 1979). A still very useful introduction to Afro-Brazilian religions—and one which is a delight to read—is Ruth Landes's *The City of Women* (New York, 1947), a vivid portrayal of Salvador da Bahia.

Urbanization is only beginning to receive attention in Brazilian history. One of the first to emphasize it, Richard M. Morse has discussed the phenomenal growth of Brazil's largest city, São Paulo, in his *From Community to Metropolis* (Gainesville, 1958). *Manchester and São Paulo: Problems of Rapid Urban Growth* (Stanford, 1978), edited by John D. Wirth and Robert L. Jones, studies the *bandeirante* capital in the twentieth century and provides some insights into the consequences of rapid urbanization and industrialization. Two other fascinating cities merited the attention of Norma Evenson in her *Two Brazilian Capitals: Architecture and Urbanism in Rio de Janeiro and Brasília* (New Haven, 1973). David G. Epstein uses Brasília for a study in urban anthropology, *Brasília: Plan and Reality. A Study of Planned and Spontaneous Urban Settlement* (Berkeley and Los Angeles, 1973). Challenging widely held ideas, Janice E. Perlman concludes that the slum dwellers of Rio de Janeiro, poor, exploited, and frustrated, are integrated into national society and profess most of the values of the bourgeoisie in her *The Myth of Marginality: Urban Politics and Poverty in Rio de Janeiro* (Berkeley and Los Angeles, 1976). A dramatic voice from the slums of São Paulo rings loud and clear in Carolina Maria de Jesus, *Child of the Dark* (New York, 1962).

The intriguing racial evolution and structure of Brazilian society have attracted considerable attention. Dorothy B. Porter prepared an indispensable guide, *Afro-Braziliana: A Working Bibliography* (Boston, 1978). C. R. Boxer discusses the racial policies—in theory and in practice—of the Portuguese under the title *Race Relations in the Portuguese Colonial Empire, 1415–1825* (Oxford, 1963). Mathias C. Kieman concentrates on Luso-Amerindian relations in *The Indian Policy of Portugal in the Amazon Region, 1614–1693* (Washington, 1954). The relations between Africa and Brazil and between white and black concern José Honório Rodrigues in *Brazil and Africa* (Berkeley and Los Angeles, 1965). It is an informative study which reveals the interdependence of Angola and Brazil. Donald Pierson wrote a pioneer study of racial relations in Brazil, *Negroes in Brazil: A Study of Race Contact at Bahia* (Chicago, 1942), which, in many ways, is still considered a model. More recent works have been *Amazon Town: A Study of Man in the Tropics* (New York, 1964) by Charles Wagley; *Race and Class in*

Rural Brazil (Paris, 1952) edited by Professor Wagley; *Social Change in Brazil* (Gainesville, 1962) by Thales de Azevedo; and *The Negro in Brazilian Society* (New York, 1969) by Florestan Fernandes. Carl N. Degler's fascinating, lively, and provocative *Neither Black Nor White: Slavery and Race Relations in Brazil and the United States* (New York, 1971) tries to explain historically the difference in slave systems and contemporary racial patterns between Brazil and the United States. Much of the author's argument hinges on his "mulatto escape hatch" theory. The attitudes of intellectuals toward racial questions make an intriguing study, well handled by Thomas E. Skidmore in *Black into White: Race and Nationality in Brazilian Thought* (New York, 1974). For a black Brazilian's view of the past in 1916, see Manuel R. Querino, *The African Contribution to Brazilian Civilization* (Tempe, Ariz., 1978). Those volumes by Gilberto Freyre already mentioned all treat the subject of racial relations in detail. T. Lynn Smith offers considerable information about the populations of Brazil in *Brazil: People and Institutions* (Baton Rouge, 1954). For an insight into how the literati treated the subject of the blacks there is Raymond S. Sayers' important *The Negro in Brazilian Literature* (New York, 1956). David Miller Driver does the same thing for the Amerindian in *The Indian in Brazilian Literature* (New York, 1942). An introduction to the Japanese in Brazil is provided by Teiti Suzuki, *The Japanese Immigrant in Brazil* (Tokyo, 1969).

For an introduction to Brazil's intellectual history, there are two weighty works in English: *Brazilian Culture* (New York, 1950) by Fernando de Azevedo and *A History of Ideas in Brazil* (Berkeley and Los Angeles, 1964) by João Cruz Costa. The history of education, particularly in the twentieth century, concerns Robert J. Havighurst and J. Roberto Moreira in their *Society and Education in Brazil* (Pittsburgh, 1965). Fay Haussman and Jerry Haar provide a quick reference guide to Brazil's educational system since 1964 in *Education in Brazil* (Hamden, Conn., 1978). The major work by Brazil's internationally renowned philosopher of education, Paulo Freire, is available in an English translation: *Pedagogy of the Oppressed* (New York, 1970). In it, the author reflects on the ways in which "dialogical pedagogy," in which the teacher and the learner concentrate on problems of reality affecting the learner, can be used to support reform and change.

The background as well as some aspects of the seminal Modern Art Week are treated by John Nist in his *The Modernist Movement in Brazil* (Austin, 1967). The musical aspect of the fusion of culture and nationalism receives the attention of Vasco Mariz, *Villa-Lobos: Life and Work* (Washington, 1970). Two studies are dedicated to Brazil's internationally acclaimed architect: Stamo Papadaki, *Oscar Niemeyer* (New York, 1960) and another by the Library of Contemporary Architects, *Oscar Niemeyer* (New York, 1971). A handsome publication of the Ministry of Foreign Relations traces the history of art in Brazil: *Brazilian Art* (São Paulo, 1976). It is richly illustrated. Another concentrates on the art movements from the events of 1922 onward: P. M. Bardi, *Profile of the New Brazilian Art* (Rio de Janeiro, 1970). Selden Rodman makes a unique contribution with his *Genius in the Backlands: Popular Artists of Brazil* (Old Greenwich, Conn., 1977).

Literature of course provides a keen insight into the history and thought of a country. Afrânio Coutinho outlines the growth of "Brazilianism" in the literature of his country in *An Introduction to Literature in Brazil* (New York, 1969). An older and very personable guide to Brazilian literature is Samuel Putnam's entertaining *Marvelous Journey: Four Centuries of Brazilian Literature* (New York, 1948). For the more recent literature, there is Wilson Martins, *The Modernist Idea: A Critical Survey of Brazilian Writing in the Twentieth Century* (New York, 1970). Two helpful guides to Brazilian literature translated into English are: Claude L. Hulet, *Latin American Prose in English Translation: A Bibliography* (Washington, 1965?) and Juan R. and Patricia M. Freudenthal, *Index to Anthologies of Latin American Literature in English Translations* (Boston, 1977).

Rio de Janeiro in the early nineteenth century furnished the background for the picaresque *Memoirs of a Militia Sergeant* (Washington, 1959) by Manuel Antônio de Almeida. A less romantic look at the capital at the end of that century is available in Aluísio Tancredo Azevedo's *A Brazilian Tenement* (New York, 1926). In *Canaan* (Boston, 1920), Graça Aranha verbosely dissects Brazilian society and examines it through the eyes of both foreign immigrants and natives. *Plantation Boy* (New York, 1966) by José Lins do Rego depicts the waning patriarchism of the moribund sugar plantations of the Northeast during the early decades of the twentieth century. Rachel de Queiroz movingly depicts life for a female in a provincial city during the early decades of the twentieth century in *The Three Marias* (Austin, 1963), while Graciliano Ramos has written a grim document on peasant life in the arid Northeast, *Barren Lives* (Austin, 1965).

J. M. Machado de Assis remains as Brazil's greatest and most penetrating novelist. Helen Caldwell, besides being a major and sensitive translator of his works, provides both a biography and literary study of him in *Machado de Assis: The Brazilian Master and His Novels* (Berkeley and Los Angeles, 1970). His principal novels, some of his minor novels, and a representative number of his short stories have been translated into English. In 1952, 1953, and 1954, *Epitaph of a Small Winner, Dom Casmurro,* and *Philosopher or Dog* appeared. *Esau and Jocob* (Berkeleyn and Los Angeles, 1965) is a literary interpretation of history, a novel set in Rio de Janeiro during the last days of the empire and the first days of the republic. The last of his five major novels to appear in English is *Counselor Ayres' Memorial* (Berkeley and Los Angeles, 1972). Leading contemporary novelists such as Jorge Amado, Érico Veríssimo, and João Guimarães Rosa now have editions available in English.

Perspectives on Brazilian History (New York, 1967) edited by E. Bradford Burns, is an introduction to Brazilian historiography. In it, six Brazilian historians, João Capistrano de Abreu, José Honório Rodrigues, Sérgio Buarque de Holanda, Pedro Moacyr Campos, Caio Prado Junior, and Oiliam José, comment in a variety of translated essays on the problems and progress of writing the history of their country. In addition, the book includes the perceptive essay of K.F.P. von Martius on "How the History of Brazil Should Be Written." The *Hispanic American Historical Review* has published several very useful historiographical essays which will guide interested persons to historical literature. "The Historiography of Brazil, 1808–1889" (May 1960; pp. 234–78) by Stanley J. Stein is a lucid analysis of contemporary historical treatment of imperial Brazil. Thomas E. Skidmore carries that study to 1964 in "The Historiography of Brazil, 1889–1964," Part I (November 1975; pp. 716–48) and Part II (February 1976; pp. 81–109).

For those who might wish to go on and read more deeply in Brazilian history there are two outstanding—although now dated—bibliographical guides to the abundant material available: Rubens Borba de Moraes and William Barrien, *Manual Bibliográfico de Estudos Brasileiros* (Rio de Janeiro, 1949) and Rubens Borba de Moraes, *Bibliographia Brasiliana,* 2 vols. (Amsterdam, 1958). Of considerable help and more up to date are Nelson Werneck Sodré's *O Que Se Deve Ler para Conhecer o Brasil,* 3rd ed. (Rio de Janeiro, 1967) and Américo Jacobina Lacombe, *Introdução ao Estudo da História do Brasil* (São Paulo, 1974). The most useful current guide is the *Handbook of Latin American Studies* published annually since 1935. It locates and annotates periodical literature and books in many languages on all topics related to Brazil. Also extremely useful are the sections on Brazil in Charles C. Griffin (ed.), *Latin America: A Guide to the Historical Literature* (Austin, 1971). Three scholarly journals contain much of the latest research being done on Brazilian history in the United States: *The Americas,* the *Hispanic American Historical Review,* and the *Luso-Brazilian Review.* The venerable (since 1839) *Revista do Instituto Histórico e Geográfico Brasileiro* contains some of the historical work being done in Brazil. The newer *Revista de História* (São Paulo) reflects research by scholars connected with departments of history in Brazilian universities.

Index